The Economics of Chocolate

The Economics of Chocolate

Edited by
Mara P. Squicciarini and Johan Swinnen

OXFORD
UNIVERSITY PRESS

Great Clarendon Street, Oxford, OX2 6DP,
United Kingdom

Oxford University Press is a department of the University of Oxford.
It furthers the University's objective of excellence in research, scholarship,
and education by publishing worldwide. Oxford is a registered trade mark of
Oxford University Press in the UK and in certain other countries

Published in the United States of America by Oxford University Press
198 Madison Avenue, New York, NY 10016, United States of America

British Library Cataloguing in Publication Data
Data available

Library of Congress Control Number: 2015944569

ISBN 978–0–19–872644–9

Acknowledgements

To some extent, working and living in Belgium means the idea of producing a book on the economics of chocolate comes naturally. However, our work was also inspired by the rapidly growing field of the economics of wine, another luxury product, and the economics of beer, another Belgian specialty with sometimes surprisingly similar economic characteristics as chocolate.

A precursor to the book was a conference on the economics of chocolate for which economists and other social scientists from all over the world gathered in Leuven and Brussels in September 2012. The combination of listening to chocolate economics and tasting specialties was inspiring. The conference provided inputs and raw material for this book. Several of the chapters in this book are based on presentations at the conference. These chapters are complemented by contributions from experienced researchers in this field, drawing upon their earlier work on the economics and history of chocolate, and new research which was inspired by our project.

The chapters in this book demonstrate that 'the economics of chocolate' covers a vast set of issues. The various contributions cover history and economic development, demand and supply, trade and investment, geography and scale economies, psychology and politics, technology and innovation, health and nutrition, quantity and quality, industrial organization and competition, taxation and regulation, and so on. This not only makes the chocolate market an interesting sector to study in itself but also yields important general economic insights.

Many people contributed to the process of what ultimately resulted in this book. First and foremost, Di Mo—then in Leuven and now at Stanford (and always somewhere in China doing experiments)—played a crucial role in developing the idea of the conference and the book, and it was only her total dedication to the field experiments with poor children in the rural areas of China (and Stanford Rural Education Action Program's (REAP's) insistence on total commitment) which prevented her from co-editing this volume. But she still managed to co-author two excellent chapters.

The members of the local organization committee of the conference (Paola Corsinovi, Giulia Meloni, Astrid Sneyers, and Anneleen Vandeplas) did a wonderful job in helping to plan and organize the conference and the social events surrounding it. Also, the members of the international scientific committee were enthusiastic supporters of the conference and the follow-up work.

Oxford University Press responded enthusiastically to the proposal to publish this book and it has been a pleasure working with them in this process. Elfriede

Acknowledgements

Lecossois provided much appreciated and excellent assistance in the editorial process.

The Research Council of the University of Leuven (Methusalem Project) and the Flemish Scientific Research Foundation (FWO) provided financial support for the research for several of the book chapters. Stanford University's Centre for Food Security and the Environment provided a great place to test ideas and to hide from emails and phones to concentrate on writing and editing. Finally, thanks to the *Piazza* guys for the wonderful music and service during our editorial meetings.

Mara P. Squicciarini
Johan Swinnen

Leuven, 30 April 2015.

Contents

Contents

List of Figures

List of Figures

List of Tables

List of Tables

Notes on Contributors

Filip Abraham is Professor of International Economics at University of Leuven (KU Leuven) and Professor at the Vlerick Business School. He teaches courses on international economics and international business. His research is mainly focused on the impact of international trade on the performance of countries and the strategies of countries.

Heike C. Alberts has a PhD in Geography from the University of Minnesota. She is an Associate Professor of Geography at the University of Wisconsin Oshkosh. Her research focuses on international migration and urban development, but she also has a long-standing interest in chocolate. Together with Julie L. Cidell she published articles about chocolate quality in Europe and North America in *Geoforum* and *Geography*. She also published an article about how to teach human geography with chocolate examples in the *Journal of Geography*.

Catherine Araujo Bonjean holds a PhD in Economics. She is a permanent CNRS (Centre National de la Recherche Scientifique) researcher and works at Centre d'Etudes et de Recherches sur le Développement International (CERDI), a research centre in development economics at the University of Auvergne (UdA) in Clermont-Ferrand (France). Her main fields of research are: commodity markets, agricultural and food policies, household behaviour and family economics. She has published numerous papers in international academic journals, and has worked as an expert on agricultural trade and development in West Africa for international organizations such as the World Bank and the Food and Agriculture Organization (FAO).

Stephanie Barrientos is Professor of Global Development in the School of Environment, Education and Development at the University of Manchester. She has published extensively on gender, trade and labour standards, corporate social responsibility, and ethical trade. She coordinated research for Cadbury's *Mapping Sustainable Cocoa Production* in Ghana and India, which informed the formation of the Cadbury Cocoa Partnership, and subsequently the Mondelēz Cocoa Life programme, as well as Cadbury's move towards Fairtrade in 2009. She currently holds a Leverhulme Major Fellowship (2013–16), allowing her to research a book on work, gender, and global value chains (GVCs).

Jean-François Brun is Associate Professor of Economics at CERDI—UdA, France. He is the co-director of a Master's degree on Public Finance in Developing Economies at the School of Economics (UdA). His research focuses on public finance in developing economies and on prices of raw materials. He has published numerous papers in international academic journals and is a consultant for international organizations such as the International Monetary Fund (IMF), World Bank, European Commission, and the African Development Bank (AfDB).

Sabrina Bruyneel holds a Master's degree in Psychology (2003) and a PhD in Applied Economics (2006) from the University of Leuven. She is Assistant Professor of Marketing and Chair of the Behavioral Engineering Research Group at the University of Leuven. She studies consumer decision-making at the intersection of psychology and economics. Her primary research focus is on self-control and dynamic processes underlying self-control issues.

Saule Burkitbayeva is a PhD student at LICOS (University of Leuven). She holds a Master's degree in Agricultural Economics from University of Saskatchewan, Canada, and previously worked for the United Nations Development Programme (UNDP) and the Ministry of Agriculture in Kazakhstan.

Julie Cidell is an Associate Professor of Geography and Geographic Information Science (GIS) at the University of Illinois at Urbana–Champaign. Her main research areas are urban sustainability and transportation/mobilities, but she retains a keen interest in the geographies of food, including chocolate and the production of sweets in North America

William G. Clarence-Smith is Professor of the Economic History of Asia and Africa at the School of Oriental and African Studies (SOAS), University of London. He has written *Cocoa and Chocolate, 1765–1914* (2000), and edited *Cocoa Pioneer Fronts since 1800: The Role of Smallholders, Planters and Merchants* (1996). With Steven Topik, he also edited *The Global Coffee Economy in Africa, Asia and Latin America, 1500–1989* (2003). He also works on the history of diasporas, slavery, sexuality, transport, and livestock. He is chief editor of the *Journal of Global History*.

Koen Deconinck is an Affiliated Researcher at LICOS (University of Leuven). He holds a PhD in Economics from the University of Leuven, and was previously an Agricultural Policy Analyst at the Organisation for Economic Co-operation and Development (OECD). His research has been published in leading international journals. He is co-author of the book *Quality Standards, Value Chains, and International Development* (forthcoming).

Siegfried Dewitte obtained his PhD in Psychology (University of Leuven) in 2000. He is a Professor of Marketing and researcher at the behavioural engineering research group at University of Leuven. He studies consumer self-control and cultural evolution. He blends theories and methods from marketing, psychology, evolutionary biology, and economics with a grain of philosophy.

Niels Fold is Professor in Development Geography at the University of Copenhagen. His research addresses the relationship between economic–geographic globalization processes and local responses, primarily examined through the analytical lens of GVCs. He is particularly interested in settlement development and rural–urban relations in rural areas characterized by mono-production. He has worked on cocoa sector restructuring in Ghana on and off for the last 15 years.

Ingrid Fromm is a Research Associate in International Agriculture at the Bern University of Applied Sciences, School of Agricultural, Forest and Food Sciences in Zollikofen, Switzerland. She holds a PhD in Development Economics from the University of Leipzig, Germany, a Master's degree in Small Business Promotion and Training from the University of Leipzig, and a Bachelor's degree in Agriculture (Ing. Agr.) from Zamorano University in Honduras. Her area of expertise is value chain research, particularly the cocoa and coffee industries in Latin America and Africa.

Maria Garrone is a PhD candidate in Economics at LICOS, University of Leuven. Prior to working at LICOS, she worked as economic consultant in Brussels, specializing in European Union (EU) agri-food policy and economic analysis. She holds an MSc in Development Economics from SOAS, University of London. Her research focuses on agricultural and food economics.

Christopher L. Gilbert is Adjunct Professor at the School of Advanced International Studies (SAIS) Bologna Center, Johns Hopkins University. He has degrees from Oxford and the

London School of Economics and Political Science (LSE). His previous university positions were at the University of Trento (Italy), the Free University (Amsterdam), London (both Queen Mary and Birkbeck), and Oxford and Bristol universities. He has consulted extensively for international organizations on commodity futures markets, agricultural, energy and metals markets, food security issues, and financial econometrics.

Monika Hartmann is Professor in Agricultural and Food Market Research at the Institute for Food and Resource Economics, University of Bonn, Germany. Prior to this, she was professor at the University of Halle, Germany, and at the Leibniz Institute of Agricultural Development in Central and Eastern Europe (IAMO) (Halle, Germany). From 2008 to 2011 Monika was president of the European Association of Agricultural Economics (EAAE). Currently she is chairman of the International Advisory Board at the Wageningen School of Social Sciences, vice-chair of the International Center for Food Chain and Network Research (FoodNetCenter) at the University of Bonn, as well as a co-editor of *Agribusiness: An International Journal*.

Emma Janssen is a PhD researcher at LICOS. Before joining LICOS, she worked as an intern for The Young Foundation in London and as a research assistant for both the Overseas Development Institute (ODI) and for the Association of ASIA Scholars. Emma holds an MSc in Development Studies from SOAS and an MSc in Economics from University of Leuven. As part of her PhD, she is studying the value chains in the dairy sector of Punjab, India. Her research interests include agricultural economics as well as environmental and food security issues.

Nina Langen is Assistant Professor at the Department of Agricultural and Food Market Research at the Institute for Food and Resource Economics (ILR), University of Bonn, Germany. She has a PhD from the University of Bonn. Her expertise is analysing determinants of consumer (ethical and food waste) behaviour and purchase decision-making. Dr Langen is founding member of the German Speaking Network for the Prevention of Food Waste and member of the FoodNetCenter at the University of Bonn.

Anna Laven is a senior advisor at the Royal Tropical Institute (KIT), the Netherlands. She works in the field of sustainable economic development and gender, and on gender mainstreaming of the World Cocoa Foundation's Cocoa Livelihood Programme. Anna obtained her PhD in Social Sciences at the University of Amsterdam (UvA). Her research focuses on governance processes and opportunities for small-scale cocoa farmers in the Ghana value chain.

Fan Li is a PhD student studying Economics at LICOS, University of Leuven. His main research interests focus on promoting the development of rural education in China, in cooperation with Rural Education Action Program (co-founded by Stanford and the Chinese Academy of Sciences), the Centre for China Agricultural Policy (CCAP), and the Centre for Experimental Economics in Education (CEEE) in China.

Giulia Meloni is a PhD candidate at LICOS, University of Leuven. She holds a Master's degree in Advanced Economics from the University of Leuven and a Bachelor's degree in Economics from Libera Università Internazionale degli Studi Sociali 'Guido Carli' (LUISS University), Rome. She was previously a consultant at the European Commission and the United Nations. She has published on political economy, European agriculture, institutional reform, and wine history.

Di Mo is a postdoctoral fellow at Stanford University and University of Leuven. She is also a researcher at REAP in the Freeman Spogli Institute (FSI) at Stanford University. She received her BA from Zhejiang University, and MA and PhD from University of Leuven. Her research focuses on rural education and health in China, and on the food market in China, including chocolate products.

Stefania Moramarco is a PhD researcher in Nursing Science and Public Health at University of Rome Tor Vergata. She holds a Bachelor's degree in Dietetic from Università Cattolica del Sacro Cuore and a Master's in Human Nutrition Sciences from Tor Vergata University. She worked as a nutritional counsellor for the Italian Cancer League (LILT), focusing on the prevention on health diseases with a nutritional approach, and as a nutritionist in community-based therapeutic programmes in Zambia.

Sander Muilerman is a social scientist based in Ghana, employed by the International Institute of Tropical Agriculture (IITA), performing qualitative and mixed method research within cocoa-based farming systems in Cameroon, Côte d'Ivoire, Ghana, and Nigeria. Sander has an MA degree in Cultural Anthropology and Development Sociology from Leiden University and received an additional Bachelor's degree in Marketing and Management. He is currently pursuing a PhD at Wageningen University and the African Studies Centre in Leiden.

Jeff Neilson is a Senior Lecturer in Economic Geography at the University of Sydney, with research interests in rural development across Southeast Asia. He is particularly interested in how processes of rural change are being affected by new modes of engagement with GVCs. Jeff has undertaken field research on the Indonesian cocoa industry since 2004, and he collaborates with the Indonesian Coffee and Cocoa Research Institute, the Indonesian Cocoa Sustainability Partnership, and Hasanuddin University.

Loreto Nemi is a dietitian and nutritionist working for a private medical centre promoting nutrition rehabilitation. He organizes courses on nutrition education for schools and private associations. He holds a Bachelor's degree in Dietetic from Università Cattolica del Sacro Cuore and a Master's in Human Nutrition Sciences from University of Rome Tor Vergata. He currently runs a blog about diet and wellness, relating nutritional sciences to practical solutions for healthy living.

Hannah Pieters is a PhD researcher at LICOS. She holds an MSc in Research in Economics from the University of Leuven. As part of her PhD, she is involved in an international research project on food and nutrition security (FoodSecure). Her research focuses on agricultural value chain analysis, the political economy of food price volatility, and food security and poverty issues.

Eline Poelmans is Assistant Professor in International Economics at the Faculty of Economics and Business (Campus Brussels) of the University of Leuven. She obtained Master's degrees in Economics, in History, and in International Relations, and she holds a PhD, all from the University of Leuven. She specializes in economic history, the economics of food, and international economics.

Olivia Riera is a senior researcher and lecturer at LICOS. Previously she worked on microfinance projects in New Delhi (India) and Cape Verde, on extensive data collection in India (Karnataka) and Ethiopia, and as research analyst at the World Bank (Brussels office). She has a PhD from the University of Leuven and an MSc in Advanced Economics from the University of Louvain-la-Neuve. Her research interests include microfinance and labour market outcomes, biofuels, food security and poverty, and agricultural market performance.

Scott Rozelle holds the Helen Farnsworth Senior Professorship at Stanford University and is Senior Fellow and Professor in the Food Security and Environment Program at the Shorenstein Asia-Pacific Center, FSI for International Studies. He holds a PhD from Cornell University. Dr Rozelle's research focuses on agricultural policy, rural resources, and poverty, education, and health in China. Dr Rozelle is the co-director of REAP.

Zuzanna Studnicka is a postdoctoral researcher in international trade at the University of Leuven. She has a PhD in Economics from the University of Leuven, an Advanced Studies Certificate from the Kiel Institute for the World Economy, and a Master's degree in International and Development Economics from the Paris 1 Panthéon-Sorbonne University. Her research interests are international trade and development economics.

Seneshaw Tamru is currently working on his PhD in Development Economics and Food Security at the Centre for Institutions and Economic Performance (LICOS) at the University of Leuven. Before he joined LICOS in September 2013, he worked at the International Food Policy Research Institute (IFPRI) and at the Ethiopian Development Research Institute (EDRI). His research focuses on agricultural production, consumption behaviour, marketing, price analyses, and value chain analysis in Ethiopia. He has published several articles in peer-reviewed journals.

Giel Ton graduated as an agricultural economist at Wageningen University, the Netherlands. He worked with local farmers' associations in Nicaragua and for the national coordinating platform of economic farmer organizations in Bolivia. Since 2006, he has worked as a senior researcher at LEI Wageningen UR. He is involved in a diversity of research projects, focusing on innovation grants, contract farming, collective marketing arrangements, certification programmes, and agricultural value chains.

Jan Van Hove is an international trade economist at the University of Leuven and a Visiting Professor at the Université Libre de Bruxelles. He teaches courses on European integration and international economics. His research is mainly focused on empirical aspects of trade phenomena. Currently he is the chair of the International Network for Economic Research (INFER) and director for economic research at the Leuven Centre for Irish Studies.

Jana Vandoren works for the European Investment Bank on agricultural projects and rural development worldwide. She has a Master's degree in Agricultural Economics and Food Policy from the University of Leuven. Previously, she undertook an internship in FAO and worked as representative of the Belgian government in policy discussions with FAO, the World Food Programme (WFP), and the International Fund for Agricultural Development (IFAD).

Sietze Vellema is a University Lecturer at the Knowledge, Technology and Innovation Group at Wageningen University, the Netherlands. His research focuses on partnerships, certification, and institutional arrangements in value chains, both globally and locally organized. He contributes to methodological debates about integrative research and impact evaluation.

Pieter Vlaeminck is a doctoral researcher at the Division of Bioeconomics, Department of Earth and Environmental Sciences at the University of Leuven. He has a Master's degree in Economics and a Master-After-Master's degree in Financial Economics, both from the University of Leuven. His research focuses on the ex-ante assessments of different policy instruments on consumer behaviour.

Liesbet Vranken is Assistant Professor at the Division of Bioeconomics, Department of Earth and Environmental Sciences at the University of Leuven. She has a Master's degree in Agricultural Sciences and a PhD in Economics, both from the University of Leuven. Her research focuses on sustainable food consumption and production, sustainable use of natural resources (particularly land resources), and the behaviour of food consumers.

Linxiu Zhang is a Professor and deputy director at CCAP, Chinese Academy of Sciences (CAS). She is a co-director of REAP. She obtained her PhD from Reading University. She has published numerous papers and policy-relevant studies on rural development in China, particularly on poverty alleviation, labour market development, public investments, and the economics of rural education and health care.

Editors

Mara P. Squicciarini is a Senior Economist at the LICOS-Centre for Institutions and Economic Performance at the University of Leuven and a Visiting Scholar at the Department of Economics at Northwestern University. She holds a PhD from the University of Leuven and has also been visiting researcher at Stanford University and at the Anderson School of Business at UCLA. Her research has appeared in journals such as *Science, Nature,* and *The Quarterly Journal of Economics* and has been profiled in media outlets such as *The Economist, The Globe and Mail,* and *Freakonomics.*

Johan Swinnen is Professor of Economics and Director of the LICOS- Centre for Institutions and Economic Performance at the University of Leuven; a Visiting Scholar at the Centre for Food Security and the Environment at Stanford University; and President of the International Association of Agricultural Economists and of The Beeronomics Society. He has published widely on global food security, political economy, institutional reform, trade, global value chains, and product standards. His books include *Quality Standards, Value Chains and International Development* (Cambridge University Press, 2015), *Political Power and Economic Policy* (Cambridge University Press, 2011), *The Economics of Beer* (Oxford University Press, 2011), and *From Marx and Mao to the Market* (Oxford Univ Press, 2006).

From Cocoa to Chocolate: Process, Products, and Agents

Process	Process Description	Products	Agents
Harvesting	During the harvest seasons, cocoa pods are collected and opened up to expose the beans.	**Cocoa pods**: the leathery oval pod (fruit) of the cocoa tree. A typical pod contains between 20 and 50 beans.	Farmers
Cleaning, fermenting and drying	Once the beans have been removed from the pods, they are cleaned (to remove all extraneous material) and fermented for 3–7 days. Then, the beans are dried (usually in the sun) packed into sacks and sold to intermediaries or delivered to the grinder's plant.	**Cocoa beans**: seed of the cocoa tree, contained in the cocoa pods.	
Roasting and alkalization	The beans are roasted. Depending on the preferences, this can happen with the shell intact, or without the shell (roasting only the nib). Nibs are alkalized usually with potassium or sodium carbonate to develop the flavor and colour.	**Nibs**: Inside of the cocoa bean. A winnowing machine is used to remove the shells from the beans to leave just the cocoa nibs. This can happen before or after the roasting process.	Cocoa processors
Grinding	The nibs are ground into a paste, called cocoa liquor. The temperature and degree of grinding varies according to the type of nib used and the product required.	**Cocoa liquor (or cocoa mass)**: the fluid mass produced by grinding the cocoa nibs.	
Pressing	The cocoa liquor is pressed to divide the liquor into cocoa butter and cocoa cakes. The cocoa cake can be sold as such or pulverized into cocoa powder.	**Cocoa butter**: fat extracted by pressing the cocoa liquor **Cocoa cakes (or cocoa solids)**: solid mass (no-fat cocoa material) extracted by pressing the cocoa liquor **Cocoa powder**: powder obtained by pulverizing the cocoa cakes	
Mixing	Cocoa liquor is mixed with cocoa butter, sugar and (for	**Couverture**: Intermediate chocolate product, produced	Chocolate

(continued)

From Cocoa to Chocolate: Process, Products, and Agents

Continued

Process	Process Description	Products	Agents
	milk chocolate) powdered milk. The proportions of the different ingredients depend on the type of chocolate being made.	after the mixing and conching process used to make final chocolate products	manufacturers (Couverture)
Conching	The mixture is then placed into conches to knead it and smooth it. The conching affects the flavor and texture of the chocolate. The resulting liquid mixture is called couverture. The couverture is sold in liquid form or in blocks after cooling		
Chocolate (and confectionary) production	Chocolate manufacturers, dairies, or bakers buy the couverture to make the final chocolate products: chocolate bars, bonbons, truffles, confectionaries etc.	**Final chocolate products:** chocolate bars, truffles, bonbons, confectionaries, etc.	Chocolate manufacturers (and food industry)

Source: Worldcocoafoundation.org (last accessed 6 September 2015) and Chapter 17.

1

The Economics of Chocolate

Introduction and Overview

Mara P. Squicciarini and Johan Swinnen

The title of this book is *The Economics of Chocolate*, but we should start by pointing out that this book is about more than economics in the narrow sense of the word. The book addresses many issues that are of interest to economists and most chapters use economic concepts and frameworks to analyse developments in the production, trade, and consumption of chocolate. However, many of the contributions in this volume cover fields such as geography, history, political science, psychology, nutrition, and so on. In fact, several of the contributors would not identify themselves as economists.

That said, the economic aspects of the cocoa–chocolate value chain is the major theme running through the book (and the publishers at Oxford University Press thought the chosen title was by far the best among the alternatives that we suggested). We hope that the book makes a contribution in a rapidly changing field. While there is quite a lot of literature on economic aspects of cocoa production, markets, and trade, there is less on chocolate markets and consumption, and how they are related. In addition, much is changing in this field, as new consumer standards are being imposed with major implications for cocoa farmers. The value chains have undergone tremendous changes in recent years. We hope that this book can contribute by addressing some of the emerging issues as well as by presenting them within a global and historical perspective.

The book is organized in five parts, and we briefly summarize here key insights from the various sections and chapters.

History

Cocoa and chocolate have a long history in (what is now) Central America but a relatively short history in the rest of the world. For thousands of years, tribes and empires in Central America produced cocoa and consumed drinks based on it. It was only when the Spanish arrived in those regions in the fifteenth and sixteenth centuries that the rest of the world learned about it. Initially, cocoa production remained in the original production regions. With the local population decimated by war and imported diseases, slave labour was brought in from Africa. As the popularity of chocolate grew in Europe and North America, production spread to other parts of Latin America, and to Asia and Africa, to satisfy increasing demand. Interestingly, cocoa only arrived in West Africa in the late nineteenth century. But by the 1960s West Africa dominated global cocoa production. These changes are documented by Eline Poelmans and Johan Swinnen in Chapter 2.

At the same time as cocoa production spread to Asia and Africa, consumption increased rapidly in Europe and North America. The Industrial Revolution raised incomes of the poor, while its scientific innovations turned chocolate from a drink for the wealthy to a food of energy for the masses. In addition, the temperance movement supported chocolate as a substitute for alcoholic beverages. As a result of these forces, demand grew rapidly at the end of the nineteenth and in the early twentieth century: The 'Great Chocolate Boom' as Clarence-Smith (Chapter 3) refers to it.

While chocolate is now a popular food in Western countries—and its consumption is sharply increasing in several emerging markets—over the centuries different countries specialized in the production of different types of chocolate. European countries, for instance, established a tradition of high-quality chocolate production. Among them, Switzerland and Belgium represent two interesting examples.

Switzerland can boast an old and prestigious tradition of chocolate manufacturing. In Chapter 4 Ingrid Fromm analyses the history and developments of the Swiss chocolate industry, starting from a tradition of small craftsmen. The industry survived periods of crises and consolidated in the late nineteenth and early twentieth century. The chapter discusses how small-scale businesses are now facing strong competition from large multinationals but are able to remain well established in their market niche, with consumers appreciating artisanal production and willing to pay higher prices for it. The chapter ends by explaining how the Swiss chocolate industry has responded to concerns for 'socially responsible consumption', and analyses the different transparency and corporate social responsibility (CSR) activities that the main Swiss companies are implementing.

'Belgian chocolates' are now world famous. Pralines and truffles and other chocolate delicacies originate from Belgium, but this small country also hosts one of the largest multinationals in cocoa processing and production of intermediate chocolate products. As Maria Garrone and her colleagues explain in Chapter 5, these are relatively recent developments. It was only after 1960 that Belgium became a major chocolate exporter. Since then, its 'Belgian chocolates' have conquered the world. However, at the same time the world has taken over many Belgian chocolate companies. Most are now owned by international holdings—and a sizeable amount of 'Belgian chocolate' is produced elsewhere. This, and growing counterfeiting with increasing demand, has induced attempts to protect and regulate the 'Belgian chocolate' label.

Consumption

Whether considered a healthy food or a sinful indulgence, a pleasurable break or a gift, a socially responsible product or a quality purchase, chocolate consumption is a fascinating and controversial issue. What is important for consumers when choosing a chocolate product? How much are consumers willing to pay for quality chocolate? What are the nutritional, psychological, and health effects of chocolate? And how has the perception (and reality) of chocolate consumption from the perspective of health and nutrition changed over time? These are some of the questions addressed in Part 2.

One of the intriguing questions related to chocolate is what 'quality' exactly means. In Chapter 6, Heike C. Albert and Julie Cidell explain that while, for many foods (from fresh produce, such as fish and vegetables, to more refined foods, such as coffee and wine), the concept of 'quality' is strongly related to the location where the basic ingredients are grown, the quality of chocolate is associated mostly by the final stages of its complicated supply chain. One factor is that the high number of smallholders producing cocoa beans (that leads to large variations in bean variety, growing conditions, harvesting methods, fermentation procedure, and storage and transport conditions), as well as the presence of over 600 aromatic compounds in chocolate, make the manufacturing process (rather than the origin of cocoa) crucial in the determination of quality.

Another factor, they argue, is that chocolate quality is not only materially but also socially constructed. 'Quality' can be defined in different ways and therefore mean different things to different people, so that what is preferred by one consumer can be considered low quality by another. Comparing chocolate consumption patterns and understanding of quality in North America and in Europe, the authors also show that consumers' preferences are largely dependent on the manufacturing innovations and techniques implemented in their own country and therefore on the kind of chocolate they are most familiar with—this includes the smoothness of Swiss chocolate from long conching, the milkiness of British chocolate, and the preference of American consumers for chocolate that Europeans consider inferior.

For much of history, chocolate (or cocoa drinks more general) was praised for its positive effects on health and nutrition. In recent years chocolate has been more associated with negative health issues such as obesity. In Chapter 7, Stefania Moramarco and Loreto Nemi systematically review the health, nutritional, as well as psychological and aphrodisiac effects of chocolate, distinguishing between types of chocolate and quantities consumed. While chocolate is found to reduce the risk of cardiovascular diseases, delay the development of chronic disease, cancer, and other age-related problems, its health impact is closely linked to the composition of the chocolate product and to the quantity consumed. In general, consuming darker, lower-fat, and lower-sugar varieties, as well as avoiding overconsumption and including it in a balanced diet, is more likely to lead to positive health effects.

In this perspective, chocolate consumption is now often considered a 'vice', a food consumed on impulse, often implying a self-control problem. This was not a problem when people were poor and hungry, but is more so nowadays when obesity is on the rise and systematic overconsumption of chocolate may bring about health problems. In Chapter 8, Sabrina Bruyneel and Siegfried Dewitte explore behavioural techniques which support consumers in moderating their chocolate consumption. They show that various cues in the decision environment can threaten consumer self-control by favouring short-term over long-term considerations about food consumption—for example, consumers may prefer a piece of chocolate cake (a relative vice) over a fruit salad (a relative virtue). The chapter presents a behavioural engineering approach to help consumers deal with situational influences, and change behaviour in a sustainable way: first, nudging can be applied in support of food choice-making. However, as the effect of nudges typically fades once they disappear from the decision environment, the authors also explore mechanisms that can extend the behavioural effects of nudges, and show how consumers could be supported to resist the lure of chocolate and make a 'healthy choice'.

Advertising and branding are important aspects of chocolate consumption. An interesting question is to what extent consumers might be affected by brand information. In Chapter 9, Di Mo and colleagues show that the preferences of Chinese consumers change when they are informed about the brand. More specifically, looking at four different brands, Chinese consumers have higher preferences for imported chocolate brands than for the domestic or foreign brands produced in China.

In recent years, consumers are becoming increasingly concerned about the ethical characteristics of the products they buy. Given the origin of cocoa beans—produced by smallholders in developing countries—the preference for a socially responsible product is very relevant in the case of chocolate. However, these general concerns are not always translated into actual consumers' behaviour when it comes to spending money. Based on a survey and choice experiment, Pieter Vlaeminck and his colleagues show, in Chapter 10, that consumers are willing to pay a price premium for chocolate with a fair trade (FT) label—especially when cocoa is produced under good labour conditions and when these conditions are frequently controlled. The authors also suggest that current labels do not adequately incorporate consumers' values towards FT practices, thereby limiting their effectiveness in current food markets. Linking the FT label closer with people's preferences and communicating clearly what the label stands for could, therefore, provide opportunities to expand the FT market.

Governance and Industrial Organization

Part 3 deals with the complex structure of the global cocoa–chocolate value chain. Geography, and more specifically its (until recently) extreme 'South-to-North' orientation, plays a crucial role in the structure of trade and the governance of the value chain. It also influences the regulations and standards that are being implemented.

Cocoa production is dominated by smallholders in many countries where cocoa is grown. However, the grinding and manufacturing processes are highly concentrated amongst a small number of large multinational firms. There are many issues to consider. How are the roles and responsibilities of the public and private sector changing? To what extent are consumers' concerns for cocoa smallholders and preferences for 'socially responsible' consumption driving these changes? How have policy reforms and public regulations affected the value chains, and why and when have they been introduced?

In Chapter 11, Niels Fold and Jeff Neilson explain how the cocoa–chocolate value chain has experienced significant transformations in institutions and governance over the past years. Focusing on West Africa and Indonesia, they analyse new hybrid forms of public–private governance that are emerging in the world's cocoa chains. They show that these new regulatory systems are reinforced by consumer awareness around labour conditions in African smallholder production, and increasingly shaped both by a corporate discourse of 'sustainability' and by the need to sustain supplies of cheap cocoa in the face of predicted growth in global chocolate consumption. Finally, the chapter reflects on the impact of these new forms of regulation on the livelihoods of the world's cocoa smallholders.

Similarly, in Chapter 12, Stephanie Barrientos examines the changing profile of the cocoa–chocolate sector over recent decades in relation to producers, the cocoa–chocolate value chain, and consumers. Focusing on the role of Cadbury's Cocoa Partnership in developing community-level initiatives for cocoa farmers, the chapter shows how consumers' concerns and civil society campaigns around poor socio-economic conditions of producers (such as child labour) have affected companies' strategies and responses. These involved: (a) sustainability initiatives with different civil society and governments and (b) certification initiatives including Fairtrade, Rainforest Alliance, and UTZ. In concluding, the author reflects on whether more structural shifts are needed, both within value chains, but also through a wider rethinking of development strategies in a global commercial context.

In this context of evolving interactions between companies, non-governmental organizations (NGOs), and governments, Sietze Vellema and colleagues (Chapter 13) adopt a comparative framework to investigate how policy reforms in producing countries and supply chain governance interact and govern the cocoa sector. Looking at two major West African producing countries (Ghana and Côte d'Ivoire) and at one Latin American country (Ecuador), they show how the transition from a system with strong state involvement in price setting and international trade to a system where transactions are more market based (and the subsequent increased 'instability') has been mediated by important arrangements between private chain partners and the state. Moreover, the authors suggest that policies targeting sustainability may be more effective when connected to existing governance structures (rather than when an entirely new organizational architecture is adopted), and that a transparent public–private configuration can facilitate coordination around the cocoa supply chain.

Being involved in the ethical production of chocolate is a necessary but not a sufficient condition for companies to differentiate themselves in the chocolate market. The provision of adequate information to stakeholders and employees is essential to reap the full benefits of their CSR activities and to affect stakeholders' loyalty to the company and perception of the firm. In Chapter 14, Nina Langen and Monika Hartmann categorize the ways companies communicate to signal their CSR involvement with respect to addressees (different stakeholders), the character of communication (controllability, credibility, and visibility), and third party involvement. Focusing on Germany (the second biggest importer of cocoa and a country where consumers are generally concerned about CSR-related issues), the authors analyse whether and how companies use labels and websites in their CSR communication strategies, show the substantial gap that exists between communication on chocolate sold in conventional retail stores compared to organic stores, and investigate the relation between prices and CSR labels.

In the final chapter of Part 3, Giulia Meloni and Johan Swinnen review the types of regulations that have been introduced by governments in the cocoa–chocolate chain and markets through history and in different countries. Both in Europe in the sixteenth through the nineteenth century, and in Africa in the post-colonial period, governments introduced trade taxes to extract revenue from cocoa production and trade. From 1850 onwards, new quality and safety regulations were introduced to protect consumers against fraudulent practices by chocolate manufacturers—and sometimes to protect chocolate companies against foreign competition. The authors explain how differences in official definitions of chocolate among European countries created problems with the integration of chocolate markets in the EU. They conclude by discussing recent initiatives for new public regulations and private standards.

Markets and Prices

Many factors, including demand shifts, policy reforms, and changes in regulations and governance structures of the cocoa–chocolate supply chain influence prices, trade, and local and global markets. Part 4 analyses these issues.

Extending back to 1850, Christopher L. Gilbert constructs a unique data series on cocoa prices and models cocoa price dynamics in Chapter 16. The long productive life of cocoa trees (more than 40 years) and the specifics of cocoa consumption lead to cycles of cocoa prices of approximately 25 years. The author shows that while year-to-year price volatility is due to harvest shocks (as the standard view in economics suggests), long-term price movements depend on changes in the taste for chocolate and other cocoa products. Key concerns of the cocoa industry are whether cocoa production will manage to keep pace with the growing demand for chocolate and whether the current prices are sufficient to ensure sustainable production. The chapter presents some forecasts and suggests a significant rise in the cocoa price by the end of the current decade (that is, 2020).

Another crucial aspect for understanding this complex market is to look at how power relationships in the chain affect the prices received by various agents, including the cocoa farmers. In Chapter 17, Catherine Araujo Bonjean and Jean-François Brun evaluate prices at different stages of the cocoa–chocolate chain: from the African cocoa growers to the French consumers of chocolate tablets. They relate these to the recent changes in the structure and in the power relationships within the chocolate industry. The authors argue that in Côte d'Ivoire, the main cocoa-producing country, at the beginning of the 2000s, the liberalization process benefited mostly cocoa processors rather than cocoa farmers.

Another aspect of the international market is international trade of chocolate products. In Chapter 18, using data on Belgian chocolate exporting firms from 1998 till 2010, Filip Abraham and colleagues show how the international competitiveness of Belgian chocolate exporters is affected by the quality of chocolates as well as by competition faced in foreign markets. Belgian chocolate exports are rather diversified, both in terms of the markets they serve and the (chocolate and non-chocolate) products they export. They argue that chocolate export relations, as an example of high-quality, culture-related goods, are relatively long-lasting. Moreover, export survival is positively affected by the exporting firm's size, its geographical differentiation, and its chocolate export variety.

New Chocolate Markets

One of the main concerns for the future of the cocoa–chocolate sector is whether cocoa production will manage to keep pace with the growing demand for chocolate. In Chapter 2, Eline Poelmans and Johan Swinnen document what they call a second global boom in cocoa and chocolate after 1990. This boom is being driven by growing demand coming from emerging markets, such as Russia, China, India, and Africa. What is driving this increase in demand? When did it start and what do we expect for the future?

In Chapter 19, Fan Li and Di Mo discuss the driving factors and the main dynamics of chocolate consumption growth in China. Thanks to the unprecedented growth of the past decades, China became a major chocolate market—even though per capita consumption is still quite low. As income continues to rise, and urbanization and globalization continue to transform the country, China's chocolate market is expected to grow further in the future. Nevertheless, the authors point out that major challenges still have to be faced. Both domestic and foreign producers have to confront the problems of an underdeveloped supply chain, including major food safety issues (that became a key concern after the 2008 milk scandal), an inefficient transportation system, inadequate cooling facilities and equipment, and a fragmented retailing sector.

A second major growth market is Russia. In Chapter 20, Saule Burkitbayeva and Koen Deconinck analyse the emergence and the dynamics of the Russian chocolate market, starting from the mid-nineteenth century—when chocolate first arrived in the country. The chapter documents the strong growth experienced during the Soviet period (1922 to 1991) and explains the impact of the collapse of the Soviet Union on domestic consumption and the shift towards imported Western confectionary. The authors show how domestic production recovered in the mid-1990s, and document the fact that the Russian chocolate market has grown strongly ever since. Given the relatively low level of consumption per capita, the Russian market seems to be promising both in terms of upward potential and of switching to more expensive chocolates. Finally, the chapter gives insights on the 'chocolate war' between Russia and Ukraine in 2013 that has significant connections with the political crisis between the two countries.

The country with—by far—the highest recent growth rates in chocolate consumption is India. With its more than 1 billion consumers and high growth, India presents a huge potential market. In Chapter 21, Emma Janssen and Olivia Riera take us through the history of chocolate in India, which starts with the British company Cadbury trying to promote chocolate consumption during British colonial times. They then analyse the determinants of the recent boom of the chocolate industry (such as India's sweet taste, rising incomes, etc.). The most successful companies have adapted to the specificities of the India market (addressing specific consumer tastes and preferences) and have also developed new production technologies to make chocolate more resilient to India's heat. Several challenges remain such as the inadequate infrastructure and logistical services. However, the untapped market potential, especially in rural areas, and an increasing preference for premium chocolates, are key factors with regard to a promising future of chocolate production and consumption in India.

The final chapter is about growing chocolate consumption in the region where most of cocoa are produced now but where traditionally very little consumption took place: Africa. Seneshaw Tamru and Johan Swinnen document how Africa is increasingly participating in other parts of the cocoa–chocolate value chain. Cocoa grinding inside Africa is increasing rapidly, as is chocolate consumption. The strong economic growth over the past 15 years, coupled with growing urbanization and the spread of modern retail companies, is turning Africa from a source of raw materials into a consumer growth market.

Part I
History

2

A Brief Economic History of Chocolate

Eline Poelmans and Johan Swinnen

Introduction

In 1573, the Swedish botanist Carl Von Linné (known as Linnaeus) gave a scientific name to the cocoa plant in his famous book *Species Plantarum*. He called it *Theobroma* or 'food of the gods' in Latin (Katz 2003). While cocoa production and the consumption of derived products had existed for millennia, its existence was largely unknown outside Central America until the Spanish arrived in the early sixteenth century.

In the following centuries the production of cocoa and the manufacturing and consumption of chocolate were totally transformed. Cocoa production spread around the world. Today, Africa is the main producing region. Consumption patterns changed dramatically. The Spaniards added sugar to make chocolate sweeter, later fat was pressed out of the cocoa to make the chocolate more digestible, then milk was added to create 'milk chocolate', solid bars were created, and so on.

The first global boom in the cocoa–chocolate sector occurred in the late nineteenth and early twentieth century, driven by growing incomes, new products, falling prices, and changing consumer preferences in Europe and North America. The second global boom started around 1990, with major growth in emerging markets.

With the growth in demand, trade and global value chains developed. While many chocolate companies started as small family enterprises, several have evolved into multinational organizations. Liberalization in commodity markets, the need for quality control, and scale economies have led to increased integration and concentration in global value chains.

In this chapter we document these changes through history. Our overview draws importantly on some excellent and more detailed studies of cocoa and chocolate in specific historical periods and regions, such as Clarence-Smith (2000), Coe and Coe (1996), Dreiss and Greenhill (2008), Heijbroek and Konijn (1995), Rosenblum (2005), Ruf and Siswoputrano (1995), and Szogyi (1997). Some topics and will be discussed in more detail in the chapters by Heike Alberts and Julie Cidell;

Stefanie Barrientos; Niels Fold and Jeff Neilson and Christopher Gilbert (see Chapters 6, 11, 12, and 16).

The chapter is organized as follows. The next section provides an overview of the origins and use of the cocoa bean from the ancient Central American civilizations to the end of the fifteenth century. We then discuss the Spanish discovery of cocoa and the spread of chocolate consumption in Europe and the growth of trade and globalization of cocoa production from the sixteenth to the nineteenth centuries. Scientific discoveries and innovations in the nineteenth century and the first chocolate boom between 1880 and 1940 are discussed next. The final sections analyse cocoa production and trade in the twentieth century, and the second global chocolate boom since the mid-1990s.

Liquor of the Gods and Money Growing on Trees: Cocoa in the Ancient Central American Civilizations (3000 BC–AD1500)

Most likely, it was the first civilization of the Americas, the *Olmec*, living some three millennia ago in the humid lowlands of (what is now) the Mexican Gulf Coast, who first domesticated the cocoa plant (MacLeod 2000). The first reconstructed linguistic mentioning of anything resembling the cocoa tree of today is by the Olmec and dates back to 1000 BC. The Olmec civilization dwindled around 400 BC, but cocoa production and consumption grew in importance in later American civilizations (McNeil 2006). The ancestors of the Classic Maya, living around 1000 BC in the lowlands of today's Guatemala, were primitive farmers. However, based on the discovery of rather sophisticated hydraulic systems, Kaplan (2008) argues that they were producing cocoa in some sites, like Izapa and Chocolá.

Cocoa became very important under the *Maya* empire (AD 250–900). The Mayas gained an intimate knowledge of cocoa cultivation and established the first actual cocoa plantations. Cocoa played several roles in their society. It was used both as the basic ingredient of a drink for human consumption and in religious rituals as an offering to the gods (often in association with human blood). The third important function of cocoa (beans) was as a commodity for exchange (i.e. money) in trade relations. Money literally 'grew on trees' (Rosenblum 2005).[1]

From the tenth century onwards, the Maya empire was partially replaced by that of the *Toltecs*, but they were in constant war with rival tribes. Control over the richest cocoa-producing lands played an important role in the wars. For example, tribes based in Yucatan (today's south-eastern Mexico) fought to get access to cocoa production sites or to cocoa via trade, because it was difficult to grow cocoa trees in Yucatan itself due to natural constraints (scanty rainfall, few rivers and little rich alluvial soils for cocoa plantations). Fighting concentrated in

---

[1] The importance and value of the cocoa bean as medium of exchange is reflected in archaeological findings of fake cocoa beans, counterfeited with simple clay (Dreiss and Greenhill 2008).

Soconusco (the plains along the coast, in today's Chiapas region in Mexico), where the highest-quality cocoa was produced (Gasco 2006).

During the fourteenth century, the *Aztecs* conquered a large part of Central America and became the dominant power. The Aztecs used both trade and war to access cocoa. They conquered Soconusco, the region with the best cocoa beans, and they established trade relationships with the Maya traders in the highlands and lowlands to the east of the empire (e.g. those in Yucatan and Tabasco) (Katz 2003).

As the civilizations before them, the Aztecs used the cocoa beans to make drinks, for religious ceremonies, as a currency, as a medicine, and as an aphrodisiac (Wilson 1999).[2] The Aztecs produced several chocolate beverages, made by extracting the crushed and dried seeds of the cocoa tree, with the addition of herbs, sweeteners, and flavours (Boudewijn and Lang 1959). The liquid brew was poured from one vessel into another from a height, in order to produce a good head on the brew, and, as the Maya before them, they called it *cacao* (Bond 2011).

However, not everybody was allowed to consume the cocoa brews. Only the emperor and his elite and warriors were so favoured. Warriors were paid with cocoa beans and it was a regular part of their military rations, as the Aztecs realized cocoa had a large nutritious value, necessary for good soldiers.[3] The priests used cocoa in religious rituals but were not allowed to drink cocoa brews as they had to live a life of austerity and penance (McNeil 2006).[4]

The Spanish Discovery of Cocoa

According to the official account of Columbus' trip to Guanaja (today one of the islands of Honduras) in 1502, the Spaniards encountered a canoe with some 'strange people' carrying 'some kind of almonds' that seemed very valuable to them (Smith 2004). During their conquest of the region in the early sixteenth century, the Spaniards realized that the cocoa bean was indeed a very valuable fruit, as it was used as currency in the local economy.

As a beverage, however, they disliked the bitter brew. The aversion of the Spanish conquerors for the brew changed when they started to add other flavours (such as vanilla and cinnamon) and especially sweeteners, such as cane sugar, to reduce the bitterness. The Spaniards also started to drink the brew hot. To obtain

[2] For instance, one rabbit cost about ten cocoa beans and a slave about one hundred.

[3] Cocoa brews were also popular among the elite because the alternative drink for them was octli (the native wine), an alcoholic drink. However, there were strong puritanical rules in their life with heavy restrictions on the use and consumption of luxury goods. Drunkenness was not looked upon favourably by the Aztecs and was even punishable by death. For this reason, cocoa brews were a very popular alternative to the alcoholic octli drank and seen as a more desirable beverage, especially for warriors and the nobility. That said, it should be noted that it was already known to the Aztecs that if they fermented the cocoa mix, it could also become alcoholic (Wilson 1999).

[4] The cocoa bean was worshipped by the Aztecs because the god of air, Quetzalcoatl, was said to have left the 'quachahuatl' tree to the human beings after he had been driven out of the Garden of Eden (Wilson 1999).

the foam on top of the beverage, they no longer poured the brew from one vessel to another, but beat the hot drink with a so-called *molinillo*, a large, wooden swizzle-stick (Clarence-Smith 2000).

Another innovation, which had important implications for trade, was the production of tablets of ground cocoa to which water and sugar could be added to make the cocoa beverage. This procedure was already known by the Aztecs, but the Spaniards extended it on a larger scale. Dry tablets of cocoa were much easier to transport to the Old World and to trade throughout Europe. According to some sources, Spanish Catholic missions also fabricated a kind of solid 'cocoa sweets' at that time, that is, long before the inventions of the nineteenth century that would turn cocoa into an eatable product (cf. the section 'Scientific Discoveries and Innovations in the Nineteenth Century') (Coe and Coe 1996).

During this period the name chocolate also appeared. Cortés simply named the beverage *cacao*, using the local name. However, by the end of the sixteenth century, the Spanish referred to the cocoa brews with another name: *chocolatl* and later—under European influence—*chocolate*.[5] The use of the cocoa bean also changed partially. As the native cultures before, the cocoa bean was used by the Spanish as a currency in the conquered regions and as the basis for the cocoa beverage. They also used cocoa as a medicine and a sexual stimulant (Dreiss and Greenhill 2008).[6] However, unlike the native people, the Spanish did not use the bean in religious ceremonies.

The Spanish tried to control the production and trade of the beans. Initially they refrained from getting involved in the production itself, possibly because of the demands of working in a tropical climate or because they lacked the specific knowledge for cocoa production. Instead, they imposed taxes on production. Later on, they set up cocoa plantations and taxed both production and trade (MacLeod 2000).

[5] Several reasons have been given for this change in naming. Two of them seem the most plausible. The first explanation is that the name comes from a combination of a Maya word *chocol* (hot) and an Aztec world *atl* (water). This way, the Spanish conquerors referred to the new beverage that was hot and sweetened with sugar. The second explanation is that it comes from the Aztecs who referred to the cold, bitter, and water-based cocoa drink as *cacahuatl*, literally cocoa water. However, in Spain the word caca means faeces, and because of the embarrassing meaning of the first syllable, the original word *caca-huatl* was transferred into the European linguistic setting, and adjusted to *chocolatl*. For more detailed information on the history of the words 'Cacao' and 'Chocolatl', we refer to Kaufman and Justeson (2006).

[6] Until the first half of the 19th century, when modern medicine started to flourish, the basis of the European medical practice went back to the humoral theory of disease and nutrition of the Classical Greeks Hippocrates (460–377 BC) and Galen (AD 130–210), who were convinced that the body contained four 'humours': blood, phlegm, yellow bile, and black bile, which would, in a right proportion and mixture, result in good health, and in a bad proportion or mixture, in disease. Humours, diseases, and the medicines to cure these diseases, could be hot or cold and moist or dry. A cold disease had to be cured by a hot drug (or food) and vice versa. The medical knowledge of the Spanish was still based on this humoral theory. Philip II of Spain sent his Royal Physician Francisco Hernandez to the New World in 1570 to study the healing properties of the newly discovered plants. Hernandez concluded that since the cocoa seed was cold and humid in nature, brews made of it 'are good in hot weather, and to cure fevers'. Another type of cocoa brew was good to 'excite the venereal appetite' (Dreiss and Greenhill 2008: 141).

Trade and the Spread of Chocolate Consumption in Europe (1500–1800)

Cocoa and chocolate were introduced in Spain during the early sixteenth century, but it was not until the late sixteenth century that trade seriously took off. The hot and sweetened drink gained popularity and became a common drink for the nobility during the first half of the seventeenth century. The cocoa concoctions were commended as medicine to cure illnesses, but soon became liked for their taste, their 'filling nature', and their stimulation (Wilson 1999; Clarence-Smith 2000).[7]

From Spain, chocolate spread to the rest of Europe, a continent divided by religious conflicts. It first spread to other Catholic regions, especially among religious networks and the aristocracies of (what is now) Italy and France.[8] Internationally, religious networks of convents, monasteries, and priests that linked the different countries within Europe as well as the Old and the New World contributed to the spread of chocolate. The Society of Jesus (the Jesuits) played an important role. This religious congregation—founded in 1534 and considered as the Pope's troops in the Catholic Counter-Reformation—were politically strong in Europe and in the New World. The Jesuits were known as avid chocolate drinkers and would become important cocoa traders (Coe and Coe 1996).

An important issue was the Catholic Church's rule on whether or not the drinking of chocolate conflicted with the ecclesiastical fast periods, that is, the hours between midnight and the Holy Communion and the forty days of Lent before Easter. Was it a drink that would nourish the body, or did it only quench the thirst? More than two and a half centuries of discussion would be devoted to this question. Several arguments were mentioned: Could it be compared with the use of wine during Lent? Was there a difference regarding the substance and thickness—and thus the nourishing content—of the brew, and so on? The Jesuits (and, with them, most Popes), realizing the importance of the brew for their treasury, argued that one was allowed to drink chocolate during Lent. Despite long debates, the issue was never officially settled, but it became common practice in the Catholic Church to consider cocoa and wine as drinks which could be taken during the religious fast (see Chapter 15, this volume).

The 1496 Treaty of Tordesillas between Spain and Portugal divided the New World into two parts, according to an imaginary north–south line. Spain got the

---

[7] The Spanish used the production method developed in the Americas: after processing the cocoa beans into a cake, brick, or roll, the compressed cocoa was put into hot water in a chocolate pot. A hole in the middle of the pot was for the handle of the *molinillo*, used to beat the liquid and make it foam. This method became universal throughout Europe, although the French invented the *chocolatière*, a metal pot with a fixed, straight wooden handle at right angles to the spout, used to stir and beat the heavy chocolate liquid into a palatable drink.

[8] During the first part of Louis XIV's (1638–1715) reign, he served chocolate regularly to the many noblemen residing in his palace in Versailles. However, after the death of his first wife, the Spanish Maria Teresa, and his marriage to the puritanical Madame de Maintenon, life in his court became more frugal.

territories to the west of this line, Portugal the territories to the east. Very soon, the Spanish Crown established a trade monopoly in its overseas territories (Rosenblum 2005). All imported goods in its New World territories had to be imported from Spain, and all gold and silver, and many agricultural products—including cocoa— produced in these regions had to be exported to Spain, through the Spanish port of Cadiz. Moreover, the traders themselves had to be Spanish.

However, the Spanish monopoly on cocoa trade did not last. When Dutch and English pirates realized the value of the cocoa bean, they captured part of the Spanish trade. Moreover, from the moment the Dutch had established a naval base in Curaçao in the 1620s, Dutch merchants started to trade with Venezuela, shipping goods—including cocoa beans—to Amsterdam. While the Spanish tried to prevent this 'illegal' trade with Dutch and English traders, trade grew, and by the end of the seventeenth century Amsterdam had become the main cocoa market of Europe (MacLeod 2000).

Only in the mid-seventeenth century did chocolate arrive in England, but so did coffee and tea. In contrast to the situation in continental Europe, where chocolate was consumed mostly by the aristocracy, in England it was available to all who could afford it. People could drink chocolate, as well as coffee and tea, in the so-called *coffee-houses* of the seventeenth century (Wilson 1999).

After spreading in Europe, chocolate was introduced in other regions as well, such as in the North American colonies by the end of the seventeenth century.[9] In some regions of the world, chocolate never really got accepted by consumers, such as in the coffee-loving Near East and in India, Southeast Asia, and the Far East (except for the Philippines, which had been conquered by the Spaniards in 1543) (Clarence-Smith 2000).

The popularity of chocolate differed between regions, religions, and social classes in Europe. Schivelbusch (1992) argues that chocolate consumption was 'southern, catholic and aristocratic'; coffee consumption was 'northern, protestant and middle class'; and alcohol was the beverage for the proletariat. However, these differences changed over time. The eighteenth century was an age of extreme political, economic, religious, and cultural changes that affected chocolate consumption. The ideas of the *Enlightenment* and the *French Revolution* (1789–99), and the *Napoleonic reign* (1804–15), reduced the power of the Catholic Church and the aristocracy in France and in other European nations.[10] The adherents of the Enlightenment preferred coffee or tea over chocolate, even in Spain. However, in

[9] Cocoa beans were first traded to Spanish possessions in what is today Louisiana, Florida, California, and the Southwest USA (Smith 2004). The popularity of the chocolate beverage also increased in Mesoamerica, due to the creolization (i.e. mix of Spanish and local people and cultures) in the mid-16th century and under influence of the Jesuits. Chocolate was no longer the prerogative of the rich people—as was still the case in continental Europe—but became a drink for the masses, including the religious clergy (Coe and Coe 1996).

[10] In Italy—still consisting of several independent states until its unification in 1870—the popularity of chocolate differed from region to region. In Rome and the Vatican, the clergy and aristocrats drank large amounts of chocolate. Naples, under the Bourbons, was heavily influenced by the Spanish Crown and consumed lots of chocolate as well. In Venice, more open to the ideas of the Enlightenment, coffee was more popular than chocolate (Coe and Coe 1996).

other parts of Europe, the success of chocolate grew. For example, Quaker families played a very important role in the development of the chocolate industries in the nineteenth and twentieth centuries (see the section 'Scientific Discoveries and Innovations in the Nineteenth Century').

Trade and Globalization of Cocoa Production (1500–1800)

The increase in consumption of chocolate in the Old and New World increased the demand for cocoa beans and raised cocoa prices. This induced attempts to increase cocoa bean production in the original regions and in new regions. A key problem in the original production regions was the supply of labour. The Spanish tried to increase the intensity of cultivation by forcing native producers to intensify planting and harvesting, and by enslaving the local population for work on new plantations (MacLeod 2000). However, the combination of mistreatment by the conquerors and the epidemic diseases brought by them, caused the native population to collapse. It is estimated that, by the end of the seventeenth century, only 10 per cent of the original population survived.

The Spanish first tried to solve the labour supply problem in the cocoa plantations by bringing in Maya natives from further away, and later by importing slaves from Africa. African slaves were imported through the *triangular trade system*, a network of trade which operated from the late sixteenth to the early nineteenth century between Europe, Africa, and the Americas. Slaves, cash crops, and manufactured goods were traded between Europe, West Africa, and the (Caribbean and American) colonies. European goods (e.g. textiles, rum, guns) were used to acquire resources and products from Africa. Products such as gold, timber, and rubber were exported back to Europe. African slaves were transported over the Middle Passage (the sea lane west from Africa to America) to the New World to work on the plantations there. The cash crops (e.g. sugar, tobacco, cocoa, cotton) that were produced with their labour were then transported to Europe (Bulliet et al. 2001).

The position of the Catholic Church vis-à-vis slave labour was ambiguous. Triggered by reports of enslavement in the New World, in 1537 the Pope published a bull prohibiting the enslavement of the native population. However, the 1537 bull only prohibited the enslavement of the native population of Latin America. There was no restriction on the use of slave labour from African countries. Moreover, some kind of 'forced labour' by the local population was still possible if the Spaniards Christianized the natives in return (McNeil 2006).

With increasing demand-and-supply problems in the original cocoa-producing regions, the prices for cocoa beans remained high. This induced the spread of cocoa production to other regions. Initially this was mainly in Latin America, in regions which today are part of Ecuador, Venezuela, and Brazil (MacLeod 2000). In Ecuador, cocoa plantations were established near the coast and African slaves were imported to work on them. The produced cocoa was of low quality and thus rather cheap. It was destined for the Guatemalan and Mexican markets and sold at a low price. Ecuadorian cocoa was referred to as '*cocoa of the poor*'. Venezuela produced cocoa of a higher quality which was destined mostly for Europe in the seventeenth and eighteenth centuries. Also, the plantations in (present-day) Venezuela first used local workers and later African slaves.

In Brazil, the Jesuits had discovered regions in the Amazon where wild cocoa trees were growing. They used the native population to collect cocoa beans in the jungle. The trade in cocoa beans was lucrative for the Jesuits because religious orders were free of paying trade taxes. However, the profitable businesses did not last. Production and trade were interrupted when the local workers were decimated by smallpox and measles in the 1740s and 1750s. Cocoa trade by the Jesuits came to a complete stop in the following years because of growing opposition to the group within the Catholic Church. In 1767, the Jesuit order was expelled from Brazil and Portugal by King José I of Portugal.[11]

The Portuguese government then established a cocoa state monopoly in Brazil, which controlled production and trade. African slaves were used as workers on the cocoa plantations. However, by the end of the nineteenth century, when slavery was abolished in Brazil and epidemics had killed many native and African workers, the cocoa plantations in the Amazon region had disappeared. Cocoa would still be produced in Brazil afterwards, but only in the coastal regions (Coe and Coe 1996).

The production of cocoa also spread to the West Indies (the Spanish colonies in the Caribbean) and surrounding islands, but faced great difficulties (MacLeod 2000). As elsewhere, the native inhabitants of the West Indies were decimated by the brutality of the Spanish conquistadores and by imported diseases. In addition, the islands in the Caribbean were under continuous attack by Dutch and English pirates. Later, the islands were conquered: Jamaica and Trinidad by the English and Martinique and Guadeloupe by the French. England and France then introduced cocoa production in Jamaica, Martinique, and Guadeloupe in the late seventeenth and early eighteenth centuries. African slaves were imported for the cocoa plantations. The produced cocoa beans were mostly intended for the home markets in Europe.

The cultivation of cocoa beans also spread to Asia. By the end of the sixteenth century, the Dutch had already planted the first cocoa seeds in Ceylon (Sri Lanka) and later in the East Indies (Java and Sumatra). Cocoa beans were introduced in the Philippines by the Spaniards around 1670.

Only in the nineteenth century did cocoa production start in Africa. The first cultivation in Africa occurred in the 1820s, when the Portuguese introduced the cocoa seed in São Tomé and Principe. Then the cocoa cultivation spread to Equatorial Guinea (1850s) and Nigeria (1870s). Only at the end of the nineteenth century did cocoa finally reach the Gold Coast (Ghana) (1879) and Ivory Coast (1905); the latter went on to become the largest cocoa producer in the world (Rosenblum 2005).

---

[11] Also Charles III of Spain wanted to break the power of the Church in his territories. He expelled the Jesuits from Spain and its colonies, and, in 1773, the Jesuit Society was abolished by Pope Clement XIV.

Scientific Discoveries and Innovations in the Nineteenth Century

The *Industrial Revolution* (1750–1850) and discoveries in the nineteenth century transformed chocolate production and consumption.[12] Several inventions revolutionized the manufacturing of chocolate by transforming chocolate from a liquid into a solid form. The most important scientific discoveries of this period took place in the Netherlands, England, Switzerland, and in the USA.

Two inventions of the Dutchman Coenraad Van Houten between 1815 and 1828 transformed the chocolate industry (Rosenblum 2005). He was looking for an alternative to boiling of cocoa and skimming off the fats, and for extracting the cocoa butter from the cocoa beans. First, he invented the *cocoa press*, a hydraulic press to press out—and thus remove—most of the fat (the 'butter') of the cocoa mass. This way the cocoa mass could be divided into cocoa powder (i.e. a cake that could be pulverized) and cocoa butter. The butter was used to make a new product: plain eatable chocolate. In a second invention—known as the *'Dutching process'*—the cocoa cake was treated with alkaline salts in order to cause the product to mix well with water. The resulting chocolate drink was darker in colour, milder in taste, and easier to digest than previously. This paved the way for a consumption boom in chocolate. The cocoa powder could be used for all kinds of applications, including chocolate drinks for children, while the remaining fat could be used in chocolate bars and candies.

Several of the first chocolate companies were founded by Quakers, known for their pacifist and teetotal beliefs; they considered chocolate a good alternative to alcoholic drinks (Beckett 2008). In England, two Quaker families, the Frys and the Cadburys played a very important role. In 1787 Joseph Fry became a chocolate manufacturer in Bristol. After his death, his son and grandson established the first factory to produce an eatable pure chocolate product. They made use of Watt's steam engine to produce chocolate. In 1847, Fry's great-grandson invented a way to mix cocoa powder, sugar, and melted cocoa butter (instead of water) to produce a paste that could be cast into a mould to make chocolate bars. Around that time, another Quaker, John Cadbury, opened a shop in Birmingham where he sold coffee, tea, and chocolate in its liquid form. However, after the purchase of a model of Van Houten's machine in 1866, he started to make his own cocoa powder. Soon Cadbury and Fry started competing and transformed the entire English chocolate industry (see Chapter 15, this volume).

Not just in England, but around the world, the 1840s are seen as the beginning of commercial cocoa and chocolate production. Very quickly, the new eatable cocoa product became popular. As a result, the price of cocoa butter increased, resulting in a division of the type of chocolate product that people could afford to buy: drinkable chocolate from cocoa powder became the chocolate for the masses, and eatable, solid chocolate from cocoa butter became the chocolate for the rich. However, soon, even more products could be purchased. Cocoa powder was also

---

[12] See Chapter 3, this volume, for more details on this period.

used as a flavouring ingredient for a diverse variety of products, such as biscuits, cakes, and even ice creams. The Cadbury family in England became known for the boxed chocolates they sold, the 'ideal present to give to a woman'.

Switzerland was also home to important innovations in chocolate production in the nineteenth century (see also Chapter 4, this volume). The first Suisse chocolate manufacturers (François Cailler and Philippe Suchard, who opened their doors respectively in 1819 and 1826) made their chocolate products with machines of their own invention. The *mélangeur* (mixing machine) of Suchard became especially important in the further development of the chocolate-producing process. Two other Suisse chocolate entrepreneurs (Henri Nestlé and Daniel Peter) made crucial breakthroughs (one in 1867 by Nestlé and one in 1879 by Peter), which allowed the invention and production of *milk chocolate* (Alberts and Cidell 2006). Rodolphe Lindt invented the *conching procedure* in 1879, to make solid chocolate more smooth, better tasting, and less gritty. His *fondant chocolate* would become very popular (Katz 2003). Lastly, Jean Tobler invented the *tempering method*, which destroyed the crystal structure of the cocoa butter so that it would become smooth instead of crystallizing out and becoming blotchy and granular in chocolate confections.

Due to all these inventions, chocolate manufacturing became possible on a larger scale. In the USA, Milton Hershey, a Mennonite from Pennsylvania, had established an actual 'chocolate town' in 1905 (called 'Hershey') with a factory, schools, a department store, a park, churches, and so on. In this town everything was centred around the production of chocolate, which was organized following Henry Ford's mass production model, to produce large amounts (Smith 2004). As was the case in Ford's auto industry, Hershey had totally mechanized his chocolate company, with machines and conveyor belts, into a true assembly-line operation. He used milk from his own dairy farms and sugar from his own factory in Cuba (and he built Cuban railways to get the sugar to the ports to ship it to Pennsylvania).[13]

Around the same time, a series of inventions by Belgian chocolate manufacturers improved both the quality and marketing (e.g. the invention of the 'pralines') and the development of 'chocolate couverture' by the Callebaut company, which lowered the cost of producing and transporting intermediate chocolate products for use in various end products (see Chapter 5, this volume).

The First Chocolate Boom, 1880–1940

These innovations transformed chocolate production and marketing. By the beginning of the twentieth century, the three processes of modern chocolate manufacturing that result in three different products: *cocoa powder*, *dark chocolate*, and *milk chocolate*, were in place.

The inventions made chocolate production possible on a larger scale and led to an increased quality and stability of eating chocolate and product diversification

---

[13] For more detailed information on Hershey's 'chocolate town', we refer to chapter 5: 'The Bittersweetest Town on Earth', in Rosenblum (2005).

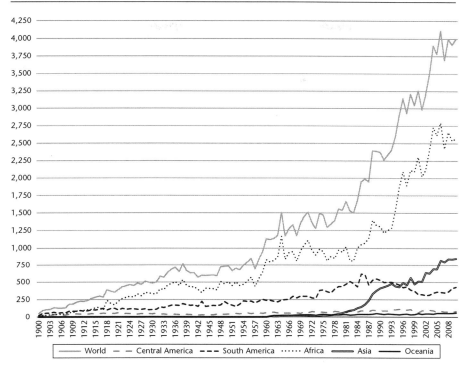

Figure 2.1 World production of cocoa beans (1900–2010), by region in 1000 metric tons
Source: Mitchell (2007a, 2007b, and 2007c) and FAOSTAT (2013a).[1]

[1] For the Asian region no data was available in Mitchell's historical statistics. Therefore, Mitchell's historical statistics were combined with data from FAOSTAT, available from 1961 onwards.

(milk chocolates, chocolates with improved taste and colour, the fabrication of more digestible powders, easier to mix with liquids, etc.). The impact of the inventions was reinforced by falling transport costs and reduced import taxes on cocoa beans after 1860, lowering the price of chocolate, as well as urbanization, increasing purchasing power, and advertising.

All these factors contributed to what Clarence-Smith (2000) calls the 'great chocolate boom' in both chocolate production and consumption, especially in Europe and North America, during the period 1880–1914.[14] It is estimated that, around 1870, about 50 million people drank chocolate, compared to 500 million drinking tea and 200 million drinking coffee. Between 1870 and 1900, the world imports of cocoa beans grew nine times, compared to an increase with only about half for coffee and a doubling for tea. However, as Figure 2.1 shows, the cocoa— and hence chocolate—boom did not end in 1914. In fact, it continued until 1940.

[14] In other regions, like South and Central America, Asia, and Africa, the increase in chocolate consumption was much less apparent. The Western boom was not replicated in these regions (Clarence-Smith 2000).

By 1940, cocoa production was more than ten times higher than in 1900 (from 53,000 tons to 632,000 tons), while consumption had already increased dramatically since 1870.

A crucial factor in the growth of chocolate consumption was the impact of the Industrial Revolution on the incomes of the poor and, in particular, industrial workers. It induced a massive increase of chocolate consumption among the working class.

In summary, the combination of new, easily accessible, chocolate consumer products, falling production and transport costs, and a growing mass of consumers with higher incomes, who were increasingly concentrated in urban areas, contributed to a dramatic increase in chocolate consumption. In addition, chocolate consumption was propagated by public bodies as a nutritious food item because it was considered to be healthier than coffee or tea (Clarence-Smith 2000).

Cocoa Production in the Twentieth Century

The production of cocoa beans increased dramatically in the twentieth century. In 1900 the total world cocoa production was 53,000 tons, by 1950 it was 736,000 tons, and by 2010 4.2 million tons (Figure 2.1). However, the growth was not continuous throughout the twentieth century. There were three periods of strong growth: the 1900–40 period, the 1965–75 period, and the 1990–2008 period. The growth of the first period was driven by growing consumption in Europe and North America (see section 'The First Chocolate Boom, 1880–1940'). The 1965–75 growth was associated with strong increases in cocoa prices (see Figure 2.2). The growth of the last period was driven by consumption growth in emerging countries, especially in Asia (see the section 'The Second Chocolate Boom').

The origin of the cocoa beans production changed dramatically as well. As we explained in the section 'Liquor of the Gods and Money Growing on Trees', cocoa production originated in South and Central America, and spread, from the seventeenth and eighteenth centuries onwards, to other regions. In the late nineteenth and early twentieth centuries, cocoa cultivation had spread to the main countries in Africa. In 1900, cocoa production was spread roughly equally between Africa (37 per cent) and Latin America (63 per cent, of which 36 per cent was in South America and 27 per cent in Central America) (Table 2.1). The principal cocoa-producing countries at that time were Ecuador (36 per cent) and Brazil (34 per cent) in South America, São Tomé, and Principe (32 per cent) in Africa, and Trinidad and Tobago (26 per cent) in Central America (Table 2.2).[15] But soon Africa became the world's leading cocoa producer. Ghana, Nigeria, and the Ivory Coast especially became major cocoa-producing centres. By the 1930s, 68 per cent of total production was already in (West) Africa, against 31 per cent in Latin America.

[15] See Poelmans and Swinnen (2015) for more details.

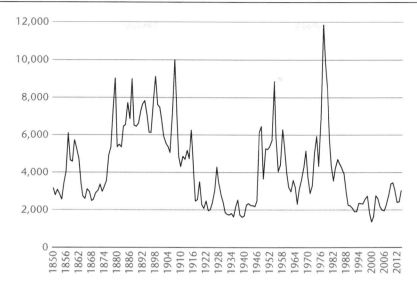

Figure 2.2 Historical real cocoa prices, 1850–2013, in $ per ton (2013 values)
Source: See Chapter 16, this volume.

Table 2.1 Regional production of cocoa beans (1900–2010), in % of world production

	Latin America	Africa	Asia	Oceania
1900	63	37	/	/
1910	60	40	/	/
1920	51	49	/	/
1930	31	68	/	/
1940	33	68	/	/
1950	32	68	1	0
1960	27	72	1	0
1970	24	68	1	2
1980	30	56	4	2
1990	25	52	16	2
2000	12	68	15	2
2010	12	61	20	2

Note: Latin America = South America and Central America (including the Caribbean).
Source: Mitchell (2007a, 2007b, and 2007c); FAOSTAT (2013a); and Boudewijn (1959).

This remained relatively constant until the 1970s. From the 1980s onwards, Asia became an important producer of cocoa beans, especially Indonesia. By 2010, Asia already accounted for 20 per cent of world production. At the same time, the share of Latin America reduced to 12 per cent (2 per cent for South America and 10 per cent for Central America respectively). Despite the growth in Asia, the largest part of the cocoa is still produced in Africa (61 per cent in 2010 and 66 per cent in

Table 2.2 The largest cocoa-producing countries, 1900–2012, in tons and in % of world's total production

Country	1900 (1901)		1960		2012	
	Tons	%	Tons	%	Tons	%
Ivory Coast	0 (0)	0 (0)	94,000	8	1,559,441	34
Indonesia	0 (0)	0 (0)	1000	0	712,200	15
Ghana	1,000 (2,400)	2 (3)	439,000	39	700,020	15
Nigeria	0,200 (0,300)	0 (0)	189,000	17	400,000	9
Cameroon	0,500 (0,700)	1 (1)	74,000	7	272,000	6
Brazil	0 (18,000)	0 (19)	163,000	14	248,524	5
Ecuador	19,000 (23,000)	36 (24)	44,000	4	224,163	5
Dominican Republic	0 (7,000)	0 (7)	40,000	4	54,279	1
Colombia	0 (3,000)	0 (3)	14,000	1	44,241	1
Mexico	0 (1,000)	0 (1)	17,000	2	27,000	1
Trinidad and Tobago	14,000 (12,000)	27 (13)	6000	1	2000	0
São Tomé and Principe	17,000 (17,000)	32 (18)	9000	1	2000	0
Malaysia	0 (0)	0 (0)	1000	0	18,000	0
World	52,700 (94,400)	100 (100)	1,131,000	100	4,608,121	100

Source: FAOSTAT (2013a).

2012). Seven countries (the Ivory Coast, Indonesia, Ghana, Nigeria, Cameroon, Brazil, and Ecuador) together accounted for 89 per cent of the world cocoa production. in 2012, with the Ivory Coast alone responsible for 34 per cent of the world's crop. Ghana and Indonesia come second, each with 15 per cent (see Table 2.2).

In Indonesia, total production of cocoa has increased enormously since the 1960s. Output has grown from zero to about 712,200 tons in 2012 due to a combination of policy reforms and improved economic incentives.[16] The country overtook Malaysia in 1993 to become the largest producer in Asia. Malaysian production dropped by more than two-thirds between 1986 and 2000 because

[16] There were strong economic incentives that encouraged production in Indonesia. First, as in West Africa, markets were liberalized; second, there was no taxation on cocoa; and third, there were frequent currency devaluations that made cocoa exports more competitive internationally. Furthermore, the government also promoted several secondary business opportunities linked to cocoa production such as: distribution, shipping, grinding, and packaging opportunities, and the Indonesian smallholders were very efficient farmers who used new, superior farming techniques to help boost productivity and reach higher yields on their farms throughout the 1990s (Ruf and Siswoputranto 1995 and 2007). Moreover labour costs were lower than in Malaysia, which meant Indonesian cocoa farmers could produce cocoa at low prices throughout the 1990s. Lastly, before the Asian crisis in 1998, farmers enjoyed subsidies, but after the crisis most subsidies were stopped. However, around the same period there was also an outbreak of diseases affecting the Indonesian cocoa crop and forcing production to reallocate in some regions (Heijbroek and Konijn 1995). In this respect, and as Indonesia's productivity per hectare was deteriorating compared to other countries, the government decided to start a five-year revitalization plan in 2009 to boost cocoa production. This plan should increase the yields on the smallholders' farms in the future through intensification and rehabilitation activities (Taylor 2013).

many producers found it advantageous to switch from cocoa to oil palm plantations (Clay 2004).[17]

The main Latin American producers also saw their share decline strongly. Brazil and Ecuador both had around 35 per cent of the world market in 1900. As of 2012, this has fallen to 5 per cent each. Brazil still had a share of 14 per cent in 1960 and remained one of the world leading producers of cocoa beans during the 1980s (with a share of 20 per cent).[18] However, Brazilian cocoa production collapsed in the late 1980s due to an outbreak of Witches' Broom, a fungus.

Trade in Cocoa Beans and Intermediate Products

Since the Spanish discovery of cocoa in Central America there has been a strong geographical and economic divide between the centres of production and consumption. Production of raw material (cocoa) was in poor countries in Latin America, Asia, and (now) especially Africa. Consumption of the final products (chocolates and confectionary) was mostly located in the rich countries of Europe and North America. In fact, although many farmers in Africa depend on cocoa for their livelihood, and the largest cocoa-producing countries are situated in Africa, most of these farmers have never tasted a final chocolate product and chocolate demand in many African-producing countries was very low until recently (see Chapter 22) (Hütz-Adams and Fountain 2012). For instance, in 2012, 56 per cent of all traded cocoa came from just Ivory Coast and Ghana, yet chocolate consumption in these countries only represented 0.6 per cent of the world market.

This, of course, implies that trade plays an important role in the cocoa–chocolate value chain, and that cocoa-producing countries are major exporters and consuming countries major importers of cocoa products. Initially, trade was mostly in the form of raw material (cocoa beans). The cocoa-processing industry, where cocoa beans are processed into intermediate products and industrial chocolate—a raw material for the food industry—was mainly located in the developed world, near the major centres of cocoa consumption. Table 2.3 compares the grindings by region.[19] Between 1975 and 1995, Europe and North America accounted for more than 60 per cent of total world grindings (i.e. more than 60 per cent of all cocoa beans were exported and processed into intermediate and final products in the developed world). Europe accounted for around 50 per cent and the USA for around 12 per cent. Less than 40 per cent of total world grindings took place in the cocoa-bean-producing countries (i.e. less than 40 per cent was processed locally prior to export). However, since 1995, the cocoa-producing countries' share of processing cocoa beans has grown significantly and trade is increasing in

---

[17] In many other Asian countries several agricultural economies were also damaged due to the devastations caused by wars, such as that in Vietnam (Ruf 2007).

[18] The lowest share in the decade of the 1980s was the year 1980 (17%) and the highest share the year 1986 (22%) (FAOSTAT 2013a).

[19] Grindings is the industry's term for processing cocoa beans into intermediate products, such as cocoa butter, paste, and powder/cake.

Table 2.3 Grindings by region as percentage of world total (1975–2010)

	1975	1985	1995	2005	2010
Total Europe	48.9	49.9	50.7	41.8	41.7
Western Europe	37.1	38.6	44.0	37.8 (EU)	38.0 (EU)
Eastern Europe	11.8	11.3	6.7	4.0% (rest of Europe)	3.7% (rest of Europe)
North America	12.2	11.7	12.7	12.3	10.2
Total Latin America, Africa, and Asia and Oceania	38.9	38.4	36.6	45.9	48.1
Latin America	/	/	/	12.7	11.8
Africa	/	/	/	13.9	17.5
Asia	/	/	/	19.3	18.8
Oceania	/	/	/	0.02	0.02

1995: data for 1994

North America: mainly the USA; Latin America: Central America, South America, and the Caribbean.

Source: Calculated with data from Heijbroek and Konijn (1995: 37–40); ICCO (2010: 40–41); and ICCO (2012: 1).

intermediate products (ECOWAS 2007). As Table 2.3 shows, by 2010, the combined share of Europe and the USA had fallen to around 50 per cent and most of the growth was in Africa.

Both in 1975 and in 2010, three countries (the Netherlands, Germany, and the USA) had a combined market share of more than 30 per cent of total grindings (30.8 per cent in 1975 and 35.1 per cent 2010). The Netherlands is the world's leading cocoa-processing country (Table 2.4). However, the share of the world grindings by cocoa-bean-producing countries—in particular the Ivory Coast, Malaysia, Ghana, Brazil, and Indonesia—is almost half now.[20] All these countries now have between 5 per cent and 10 per cent of the world's grindings, and their share is increasing (Kox 2000). The reason for their increasing interest in grinding activities lies in the division of the value added in the chocolate production chain. According to estimates by the International Cocoa Organization (ICCO), only 3.3 per cent of consumer spending on finished chocolate products goes to the cocoa farmers, that is, the cocoa-producing countries. A total of 96.7 per cent goes to all the other parties involved: especially chocolate processing (22 per cent, including the cocoa processors and the fabrication of chocolate products) and wholesale and retail (26 per cent) (ICCO 2010). In order to gain a part of the value added, cocoa-bean-producing countries have started to produce intermediary products themselves, instead of just exporting the cocoa beans. As we will explain in the section 'Restructuring of the Cocoa–Chocolate Value Chain in Recent Years', this process was stimulated by liberalizations of the cocoa sector in Africa in the 1980s, and takeovers of local cocoa companies and investments by multinational companies in the 1990s and 2000s.

All this is reflected in Table 2.5, which shows, for 1961 and 2011, how exports and imports of cocoa beans and cocoa products differ by regions. Africa and Latin

[20] Grindings carried out by countries where production of cocoa beans take place are called origin grindings.

Table 2.4 The largest cocoa grinding countries in 1975 and 2010 (shares in % of world's total grindings)

	1975	2010
Netherlands	8.3	13.7
Germany	10.3	11.2
United States	12.2	10.2
Ivory Coast	2.5	9.2
Malaysia	0.5	7.6
Brazil	6	6.1
Ghana	n/a	5.9
Indonesia	n/a	5.7
Rest of World	n/a	30.4

Note: For the year 1975, there was no data available for the share of Ghana and Indonesia in total world grindings. As the exact data for 2010 for Malaysia were missing, we have used the data of 2009.

Source: Calculated with data from Heijbroek (1995) and ICCO (2007, 2010, 2012).

Table 2.5 Net exports of cocoa beans and intermediate cocoa products, 1961 and 2011 (in million US$)

1961	Cocoa Beans	Cocoa Butter	Cocoa Paste	Cocoa Powder and Cake	All Cocoa Products
	Net Exports	Net Exports	Net Exports	Net Exports	Net Exports
Africa	375.35	2.96	0.00	2.01	380.32
Asia	−10.11	−6.20	−0.16	−1.26	−17.73
Europe	−301.76	−5.55	−1.66	15.80	−293.17
North America	−163.50	−13.21	−8.00	−10.43	−195.14
Latin America	79.62	19.17	−0.26	0.17	98.70
Oceania	−3.34	−3.13	−0.03	−0.31	−6.81

2011	Cocoa Beans	Cocoa Butter	Cocoa Paste	Cocoa Powder and Cake	All Cocoa Products
	Net Exports	Net Exports	Net Exports	Net Exports	Net Exports
Africa	6728.72	455.19	550.25	72.30	7806.46
Asia	−1460.38	708.85	−59.91	317.76	−493.68
Europe	−5735.75	−724.98	−739.62	331.45	−6868.90
North America	−1657.60	−461.30	−84.90	−767.97	−2971.77
Latin America	566.49	126.66	25.09	−102.28	615.96
Oceania	192.85	−81.61	−45.89	−125.62	−60.27

Note: Net exports = the value of the region's exports minus the value of its imports.
Source: FAOSTAT (2013b).

America were net exporters of cocoa beans and Europe and North America were net importers of cocoa beans, both in 1961 and 2011. With regard to the intermediate products (cocoa butter, paste, powder, and cake), the trade picture reflects changes in regional processing. For instance, while Europe was a net importer of cocoa butter and paste, it was a net exporter of cocoa powder and cake, both in 1961 and 2011.

North America was a net importer in all intermediate products, both in 1961 and 2011. The data clearly show the strong growth of the intermediates from Africa and Asia in recent years. Asia became a large net exporter of cocoa butter and cocoa powder and cake. Africa became a large net exporter of all derivatives.

Interestingly, as in the nineteenth century, these liberalizations of cocoa trade also preceded a major growth in global cocoa trade and chocolate consumption (see sections Restructuring of the Cocoa-Chocolate Value Chain in Recent Years' and 'The Second Chocolate Boom').

Restructuring of the Cocoa–Chocolate Value Chain in Recent Years

The cocoa–chocolate value chain of the twenty-first century is characterized by a fragmented supply structure, strong concentration in the intermediate industry, and a mixed set of final producers. Not surprisingly, parts of the supply chain have undergone important changes over time—both horizontally and vertically.

Key factors in these changes have been the Industrial Revolution and several innovations which created scale economies in the twentieth century, the liberalization of the African cocoa marketing systems in the 1980s and 1990s, and globalization, growth, and changing consumer preferences in the chocolate consumer markets.

Cocoa Production and Trade

Today, over 90 per cent of the world's cocoa is grown on about five million small farms, averaging between one and five hectares. Production in West Africa and Southeast Asia is mainly on these small farms.[21] Larger farms and plantations are found in Brazil, Ecuador, and Malaysia (UNCTAD/WTO 2001).

Cocoa farmers often sell their beans to small traders who sell to wholesalers, who in turn resell the beans to exporters or, increasingly, local cocoa grinding companies (Musselli 2008). The nature of the cocoa marketing system has changed dramatically over the past two decades.

Cocoa was a major source of government revenue for several developing countries after their independence. State regulation of cocoa production, marketing, and exports was therefore very strong in the 1960s and 1970s. State-controlled bodies coordinated all aspects of the internal and external cocoa marketing chain by setting producer prices, buyer margins, and export taxes (Abbott and Wilcox 2004). Domestic trade and exports were controlled by state monopolies. The surplus revenues of

---

[21] In these regions, the sector is characterized by very poor conditions. Cocoa is heavily dependent on natural resources as well as low-cost labour (Doussou 2009). Severe cases of child labour, child slavery, low income for cocoa farmers, forest exploitation, and other factors are issues that the industry struggles with daily. These issues are attracting more and more attention in the media and abolishing these problems will remain a challenge in the future (Cappelle 2008; Doussou 2009).

these marketing boards were directed to a stabilization fund, which would cover potential losses if world market prices moved in an adverse direction (Fold 2001). Their official objectives were to achieve price stabilization (i.e. protect farmers from volatile world prices), assuring cocoa quality and providing services for farmers (Gilbert 2009). However, the taxes imposed on the cocoa exports were a very important source of government income (Abbott and Wilcox 2004). For example, in Ghana the implicit taxation on cocoa farmers increased from 20 per cent in 1960 to more than 80 per cent around 1980 (see Chapter 15, this volume).

In many African countries, a wave of market liberalizations in the 1980s and 1990s changed the market structure of cocoa production. The liberalization process was driven by a number of factors. The state-controlled bodies were suffering from low world market prices and increased competition in the 1980s. Indonesia and Malaysia were two rising world producers with free market conditions that were increasing production successfully. Historically low commodity prices resulted in a struggle by the controlling and regulatory institutions in many African countries to maintain producer prices that were viable, and many stabilization agencies headed towards insolvency (ECOWAS 2007; Gilbert 2009). In addition, the International Monetary Fund (IMF) and the World Bank supported the liberalization process and insisted on reducing the producer taxation by removing the expensive and extractive state operations from the cocoa marketing chain as part of structural adjustment programmes.

The liberalizations of these systems occurred in 1986 for Nigeria, between 1991 and 1994 for Cameroon, and between 1998 and 2002 for the Ivory Coast, while partial liberalization in Ghana took place in the 1980s and 1990s (see Chapter 13, this volume).

After the reforms, cocoa farmers generally received higher shares of the world prices than before liberalization (Gilbert 2009). For example, in Ghana, government taxation of cocoa farmers fell from more than 80 per cent in the early 1980s to around 30 per cent in the 1990s (see Chapter 15, this volume).

After the liberalization processes of the 1980s and 1990s, (para)statal companies have been privatized or liquidated, and trade is now mostly by private companies. The liberalization of the cocoa sector in Africa has also resulted in increased concentration in the export sector. During the first years of the market liberalization, several local, private companies entered the cocoa industry as buyers or traders, and a number of large private exporters emerged in the export markets (Fold 2000; Musselli 2008). However, soon foreign companies took over (a share of) the local cocoa export companies, either directly or through agents. Some of the local traders have managed to remain independent, but most are now subsidiaries of multinational companies or in joint ventures with multinationals (see Chapter 11, this volume). For instance, in 2011, and in West and Central Africa, only 37 per cent of all cocoa beans was still purchased (and exported) by African companies, of which one company—Public Buying Company (PBC)—had 11 per cent.[22] Five foreign

---

[22] Most of these African companies sell their beans on to the five foreign leading companies (George 2012).

Table 2.6 The largest cocoa trading companies in 2011 (in % of West and Central Africa's total cocoa trade)

Company	Share (in %)
Cargill	14
Archer Daniels Midland (ADM)	11
Olam	8
Barry Callebaut	7
Armajaro	7
Cemoi	4
Noble	4
Touton	3
Ecom	3
Novel	2
Public Buying Company (PBC)	11
Other African companies	26

Source: George (2012: 9).

companies now dominated the cocoa export market: Cargill, Archer Daniels Midland (ADM), Olam, Barry Callebaut, and Armajaro, with a joint share of 47 per cent (see Table 2.6).

Cocoa Grinding and Processing

The concentration that has taken place over time in the cocoa trade and in the grinding sector are closely linked to each other, as most traders also have active operations as cocoa grinders. Cocoa grinders have strengthened their position in the market through vertical integration into chocolate processing, which, as a result, has also become more concentrated. Grinders have started liquid chocolate production activities and are increasingly supplying chocolate manufacturers. In the process, many corporate deals have taken place in the cocoa-processing and chocolate-processing industry. Many of the leading grinding companies are also important cocoa trading companies. For instance, in 1990 there were over forty grinders in Europe, but by 2000 this number had decreased to only nine (Musselli 2008). In 2008, about two-thirds of all grindings worldwide was carried out by just ten firms (see Table 2.7).

While vertical integration has taken place at the trading-grinding-processing part of the cocoa–chocolate value chain, the opposite has occurred at the downstream side of the value chain. The chocolate manufacturing industry has outsourced certain manufacturing activities, such as the production of cocoa liquor, cocoa butter, or liquid chocolate (couverture chocolate). Due to the outsourcing of cocoa processing by some large chocolate manufacturers, some trading, grinding, and industrial-processing companies, such as Cargill and Barry Callebaut, successfully reinforced their position in the processing market,[23] as they took

---

[23] For instance, Nestlé has subcontracted its cocoa processing to grinding companies such as Cargill, Petra Foods, and ADM.

Table 2.7 The largest cocoa grinders in 2008 (in % of world's total cocoa grindings)

Company	Share (in %)
Archer Daniels Midland (ADM)	14
Cargill	14
Barry Callebaut	13
Blommer	6
Petra Foods	5
Cadbury	3
Nestlé	3
Ferrero	2
Cémoi	2
Kraft Foods	2
Other grinders	36

Source: Musselli (2008: 23).

over processing activities from the chocolate manufacturers (Cappelle 2008; Weiligmann et al. 2009).

The changes are well illustrated by the three largest deals: those by *Cargill*, *ADM*, and *Barry Callebaut*, companies which are in the top four of the largest trading and grinding companies (see Tables 2.6 and 2.7).

Cargill, the multinational cocoa processor and trader, became a leading cocoa processor and supplier in the sector as of 1987 when it acquired General Cocoa Company Holland B.V. and Gerkens Cocoa products. After the takeover, the company was active in cocoa trade, the manufacturing of semi-finished products, and the manufacturing of couverture chocolate, both in cocoa-producing and chocolate-consuming countries. Later on, in 2005, the company expanded its cocoa activities by buying facilities in Vietnam and by acquiring the German industrial chocolate facility, Schierstedter Schokoladenfabrik GmbH & Co. KG. In 2008, Cargill invested over 100 million US$ for establishment of a new processing plant in Ghana. Today Cargill is even involved in the consumer market (Musselli 2008; Cargill 2011).

ADM entered the cocoa business in 1997 and has grown impressively since. In 2009, ADM expanded its global cocoa practices significantly through the acquisition of Schokinag-Schokolade-Industrie Herrmann GmbH & Co., a leading producer of cocoa intermediates. ADM is active in producing and consuming countries and is involved in the trade of cocoa as well as the production and trade of semi-finished products and the manufacturing of couverture chocolate. It also became more involved in the consumer market over time (Musselli 2008; Weiligmann et al. 2009; ADM 2014).

The 1996 merger of Callebaut, which produced couverture chocolate, and Barry, which had complementary activities in cocoa sourcing and processing firms, created the vertically integrated Barry Callebaut group. The firm also became involved in the production of consumer chocolate (Musselli 2008). In 2012, Barry Callebaut acquired the cocoa business from Petra Foods, then the world's number six in cocoa grinding (Table 2.7). Both companies are complimentary in terms of business, products, and geography (Barry Callebaut 2013).

These three companies are now among the largest firms both in cocoa trade, grinding, and processing, that is, in the entire 'middle segment' of the value chain. ADM, Cargill, and Barry Callebaut had, in 2008, a joint share of 41 per cent of world grindings (see Table 2.7). The same three companies were also amongst the largest cocoa traders and together accounted for one-third (33 per cent) of the world's cocoa trade (see Table 2.6). Moreover, as these firms have been investing considerably in capacity expansion and new factories in the recent past, ICCO (2010) expects that their share will continue to expand in the future.

Chocolate Manufacturing

Today, the chocolate manufacturers can be divided into three broad types of manufacturers, based on size and business interests: first, the global confectioners; second, the producers of industrial chocolate (who moved into consumer markets); and third, the smaller artisanal chocolatiers and the gourmet chocolate processors (Musselli 2008).

First, the 'global confectioners' are a small group of large multinational firms that manufacture branded consumer goods and are active around the globe. Between the 1970s and 1990s more than 200 takeovers took place globally among the manufacturing companies, leading to only 17 firms that had a combined market share of about 50 per cent of the global chocolate market by 2001 (Dand 1999; Fold 2001). The top four companies had a joint market share of 26 per cent in 2001, which increased to 39 per cent by 2004, and to 49 per cent by 2013. The top four chocolate manufacturers in 2013 were Mondelēz International Inc. (with 14.7 per cent); Mars Inc. (with 14.1 per cent); Nestlé SA (with 12.2 per cent); and Ferrero Group (with 7.7 per cent) (Table 2.8). The largest company, Mondelēz International Inc., was formed in 2009 by the merger of Cadbury and Kraft Foods Inc., which combined two leading chocolate confectioners in the market.

The second group we have already discussed: the large merchants of industrial chocolate, which are also active in upstream segments, such as cocoa processing and industrial chocolate manufacturing. Some are also present in the consumer section

Table 2.8 The largest chocolate manufacturers in 2013 (company shares in % of world's total production)

Company	Share (in %)
Mondelēz International Inc. (USA)	14.7
Mars Inc. (USA)	14.1
Nestlé SA (Switzerland)	12.2
Ferrero Group (Italy)	7.7
Hershey Food Corp (USA)	6.6
Private Label (USA)	4.6
Chocoladefabriken Lindt & Sprüngli AG (Switzerland)	3.7
Obiedinenye Konditery UK (Russia)	1.9
Other	34.5

Source: Euromonitor International (2013b).

of the market. An example is Barry Callebaut, which acquired companies in the consumer segment to establish itself in the consumer market (Musselli 2008). Some became involved in (final) consumer markets because chocolate manufacturing companies are increasingly outsourcing certain manufacturing activities, to cut costs or to focus more on specific brands (ICCO 2007). To gain a global market position in a specific field for their brands requires increasing budgets for marketing and branding and for product development and innovation.[24] Companies do this by outsourcing specific production activities to cut other costs (Weiligmann et al. 2009). Manufacturers not only subcontract grindings or the production of liquid chocolate to processors, but even the manufacturing of the final chocolate products. An example of the outsourcing of final products is Nestlé, which handed over Lion Bar production to Barry Callebaut (Franchise Help 2014).

The last group are the artisanal chocolatiers and gourmet chocolate processors, many of which are small and medium-sized confectionery companies. There is little data available about this group. Garrone, Pieters, and Swinnen (see Chapter 5, this volume) report that, in Belgium, more than 90 per cent of the chocolate companies are small scale: Fromm also argues that small artisanal producers remain important in the Swiss chocolate market (see Chapter 4, this volume).

The Second Chocolate Boom

Figure 2.1 clearly shows that cocoa production has increased exponentially since 1990. This growth in cocoa production follows a rapidly growing demand in consumer markets and the reduction of cocoa taxation in developing countries, in particular Africa (see section 'Restructuring of the Cocoa–Chocolate Value Chain in Recent Years'). Table 2.9 illustrates how chocolate consumption has increased rapidly since 2000 (there is no representative consumer data before).[25]

---

[24] The major chocolate manufacturers invest, on average, 20 per cent of their total budgets on marketing and branding. In 2009 the annual marketing budget of the six largest companies amounted to about US$86 million (Weiligmann et al. 2009).

[25] Cocoa and chocolate consumption is more difficult to measure than cocoa production because 'consumption' can refer to various intermediate or final products along the value chain, and chocolate is used in various final consumption products. For example, major cocoa grinding countries re-export much of their production of cocoa liquor, butter, cake, and powder. Another indicator that is often used to measure cocoa consumption at a country level is 'apparent domestic cocoa consumption', which is the amount of cocoa beans used for the confectionery of the final chocolate goods (food, cosmetics, etc.) that are actually consumed in a country or region (ICCO 2012) (see Poelmans and Swinnen 2015).

In Tables 2.9–2.13 we use data on 'chocolate confectionary' as data on 'all chocolate manufacturing'—i.e. according to Caobisco 'chocolate confectionary' (on average 80 to 90% of the total) and 'other chocolate products' (10 to 20% of the total) are not available for all regions over a longer time frame. Caobisco defines 'chocolate confectionary' as: unfilled chocolate; filled tablets and bars; bonbons, pralines, and other chocolate confectionery; sugar confectionery containing cocoa; and white chocolate; and 'other chocolate products' as a.o. spreads containing cocoa and sweetened cocoa powder (preparations), ready for retail use (Caobisco 2013). Euromonitor further divides the 'chocolate confectionary products' by product type: countlines; tablets; bagged straightlines; boxed assortments; seasonal chocolate; chocolate with toys; alfajores; and other chocolate products (Euromonitor International 2013a).

Table 2.9 Chocolate confectionary retail consumption (in million tons and million US$), between 2000 and 2013

Year	Volume (in million tons)	Value (in million US$)
2000	5.60	51,314.5
2005	6.30	71,057.8
2010	6.77	94,515.8
2013	7.15	109,991.5

Source: Euromonitor International (2013a).

The retail volume has increased from 5.6 million tons in 2000 to 7.15 million tons in 2013. The retail value more than doubled (from 51 billion $ to 110 billion $) over the same period.

The growth in consumer markets has been particularly strong in emerging and (rapidly growing) developing countries. The growth in chocolate retail value was especially strong in Eastern Europe (+ 316 per cent), the Middle East and Africa (+ 239 per cent), Latin America (+ 228 per cent), Australasia (+ 219 per cent), and Asia Pacific (+ 113 per cent) (see Table 2.10).

In 2013, more than half of all chocolate confectionary retail was still based in Europe, both in volume and value (which was the same share as 15 years earlier (Table 2.10)). However, the share stayed constant because the growth in the emerging countries of Eastern Europe exactly offset the falling share of Western Europe. Overall, in Europe, confectionary retail volume increased by 29 per cent, but there was much stronger growth in Eastern Europe (+ 79 per cent) than in Western Europe (+ 10 per cent). North America's share in the world volume fell from 31 per cent in 2000 to 22 per cent in 2013, and in value from 25 per cent of total value in 2000 to 18 per cent in 2013 (Table 2.10). The USA had a negative growth in volume between 2010 and 2013 (-11 per cent). Over the past decade, it seems that the North American market has become close to saturation (Green 2013). The share of the other regions (i.e. the developing and emerging markets) increased significantly: Asia Pacific's share went from 8 per cent to 12 per cent, Latin America's share from 6 per cent to 9 per cent, and the Middle East and Africa's share from 3 per cent to 5 per cent.

The largest increase in volume occurred in the Middle East and Africa, where the chocolate confectionary retail volume has more than doubled since 2000 (+ 104 per cent). The growth in volume between 2000 and 2013 was also strong in Asia Pacific and Latin America, where the chocolate retail volume increased by 87 per cent and 82 per cent respectively.

At the country level, the USA maintained the largest chocolate confectionary market in 2013 (with a share of 16 per cent of total world confectionary retail value), followed by Russia (10 per cent), UK (9 per cent), Germany (7 per cent), and Brazil (6 per cent) (Table 2.11).

Table 2.10 Chocolate confectionary retail consumption by region (in 1000 tons and million US$) and their respective shares of total volume/value in 2000 and 2013

Geographies	2000				2013				Growth in volume between 2000 and 2013 (in %)	Growth in value between 2000 and 2013 (in %)
	Volume (in 1000 tons)	Share (in %)	Value (in million US$)	Share (in %)	Volume (in 1000 tons)	Share (in %)	Value (in million US$)	Share (in %)		
World	5,598	100	51,314.50	100	7,147	100	109,991.30	100	+28	+114
Total Europe	2,799	50	25,942.00	51	3,622	50	56,344.70	52	+29	+117
Western Europe	2,030	36	21,545.10	42	2,242	31	38,057.40	35	+10	+77
Eastern Europe	769	14	4,396.90	9	1,380	19	18,287.30	17	+79	+316
North America	1,727	31	13,005.00	25	1,542	22	20,184.80	18	−11	+55
Latin America	360	6	3,688.10	7	654	9	12,098.20	11	+82	+228
Asia Pacific	461	8	6,231.90	12	861	12	13,262.10	12	+87	+113
Australasia	87	2	997.90	2	133	2	3,180.20	3	+53	+219
Middle East and Africa	164	3	1,449.60	3	335	5	4,921.30	4	+104	+239

Note: North America: mainly the USA; Latin America: Central America, South America, and the Caribbean; Asia Pacific: especially Japan and some of the emerging economies.

Source: Euromonitor International (2013a).

Table 2.11 The largest chocolate confectionary countries' retail consumption (in 1000 tons and million US$) and their respective shares of total volume/value in 2000 and 2013

Countries	2000				2013				Growth in Volume between 2000 and 2013	Growth in Value between 2000 and 2013
	Volume (in 1000 tons)	Share (in %)	Value (in million US$)	Share (in %)	Volume (in 1000 tons)	Share (in %)	Value (in million US$)	Share (in %)		
World	5,596	100	51,314.50	100	7,146	100	109,991.50	100	28	114
USA	1,631	29.1	11,912.10	23.2	1,423.7	19.9	17,443.50	15.9	–13	46
Germany	712	12.7	5,294.20	10.3	645.6	9	7,665.50	7	–9	45
Russia	403	7.2	2,077.70	4	740.9	10.4	10,577.00	9.6	84	409
UK	382	6.8	6,040.90	11.8	480.5	6.7	9,453.20	8.6	26	56
France	251	4.5	2,841.50	5.5	264	3.7	5,558.60	5.1	5	96
Japan	160	2.9	3,258.00	6.3	136.3	1.9	3,625.70	3.3	–15	11
Brazil	151	2.7	1,254.70	2.4	314	4.4	6,603.70	6	108	426
Italy	132	2.4	1,619.50	3.2	144.3	2	3,094.40	2.8	9	91
Canada	96	1.7	1,093.00	2.1	118.4	1.7	2,741.40	2.5	24	151
Poland	84	1.5	595.2	1.2	166.4	2.3	1,982.20	1.8	98	233
Ukraine	82	1.5	386.6	0.8	211	3	2,324.40	2.1	157	501
Australia	79	1.4	882.9	1.7	119.5	1.7	2,733.70	2.5	51	210
Switzerland	69	1.2	973.2	1.9	71.8	1	1,902.80	1.7	4	96
Spain	65	1.2	545.3	1.1	90.7	1.3	1,259.30	1.1	39	131
Argentina	63	1.1	669.9	1.3	113.4	1.6	1,735.80	1.6	79	159
China	62	1.1	453.3	0.9	192.5	2.7	2,415.10	2.2	210	433
Mexico	54	1	781.9	1.5	92	1.3	1,438.70	1.3	72	84
Turkey	49	0.9	415.9	0.8	124.9	1.7	1,449.70	1.3	153	249
Norway	27	0.5	420.3	0.8	36.8	0.5	1,066.20	1	38	154
India	24.3	0.4	192.8	0.4	129.2	1.8	1,477.70	1.3	432	666
Other	1,020	18.2	9,605.60	18.7	1,530	21.4	23,442.90	21.3	50	144

Source: Euromonitor International (2013a).

Table 2.12 Chocolate confectionary consumption in kg/capita by region

Regions	2000	2013	Growth between 2000 and 2013 (in %)
	Volume (in kg/capita)	Volume (in kg/capita)	
World	0.9	1.0	+11
Western Europe	4.5	4.6	+2
Eastern Europe	2.3	4.2	+83
North America	5.5	4.4	−20
Latin America	0.7	1.1	+57
Asia Pacific	0.1	0.2	+100
Australasia	3.8	4.8	+26
Middle East and Africa	0.2	0.3	+50

Source: Euromonitor International (2013a).

However, the rich countries are not only losing market share, their consumption is actually declining in volume. For example, the retail volume declined in Japan (−15 per cent), the USA (−13 per cent), and Germany (−9 per cent). In contrast, emerging countries such as Brazil, Russia, India, and China (BRIC) saw rapid growth and increasing share in total retail. The growth in chocolate retail was especially strong in India (+ 432 per cent in volume and + 666 per cent in value); China (+ 210 per cent in volume and + 433 per cent in value); Brazil (+ 108 per cent in volume and + 426 per cent in value); and Russia (+ 84 per cent in volume and + 409 per cent in value).

The main reason for the strong growth in the BRIC countries and also in the Middle East and Africa is strong economic growth, rising incomes, and a youthful population—as is discussed and analysed in greater detail in Chapters 19, 21 and 22 in Part 5 of this book.

These figures clearly show that a convergence is occurring, with chocolate consumption stagnating in richer countries and consumption growing fast in poorer countries. However, at this point, the consumption levels are still far apart (except for the growing countries in Eastern Europe).

In 2013, Western Europe, Australasia, and North America had similar chocolate consumption levels in kilogram per capita, with 4.6, 4.8, and 4.4 kg/capita respectively (Table 2.12). Germany is the country with the highest chocolate consumption per capita in 2010 (11.6 kg/capita), followed by the USA (10.5 kg/capita), the UK (9.7 kg/capita), Norway (9.4 kg/capita), and Denmark (8.5 kg/capita) (Table 2.13 and Figure 2.3). Consumption is much lower in the southern European countries like Spain (3.6 kg/capita) or Portugal (2.7 kg/capita).

Eastern Europe has doubled its per capita consumption level, from about 2.3 kg per capita in 2000 to 4.2 kg per capita in 2013, but the other growing regions are still far behind. Despite strong growth, in China and India, chocolate consumption per capita was still much lower, at 1.0 kg/capita and 0.7 kg/capita respectively in 2010.

Table 2.13 Chocolate confectionary consumption in kg/capita in some selected countries

	2000	2010	Growth in Volume between 2000 and 2013 (in %)
	Volume (in kg/capita)	Volume (in kg/capita)	
Germany	9.97	11.56	16
Switzerland	10.75	10.51	−2
UK	9.41	9.72	3
Norway	8.13	9.44	16
Denmark	8.22	8.49	3
Austria	7.37	8.16	11
Finland	6.02	7.26	21
Sweden	7.61	6.37	−16
France	6.97	6.34	−9
Estonia	n/a	6.21	/
Belgium	8.05	6.1	−24
Lithuania	n/a	5.4	/
USA	5.32	5.29	−1
Australia	5.79	4.51	−22
Italy	3.62	3.74	3
Poland	n/a	3.61	/
Spain	3.93	3.6	−8
Greece	2.83	3.51	24
Hungary	n/a	3.33	/
Brazil	1.84	2.93	59
Portugal	2.81	2.72	−3
Japan	2.18	2.09	−4
Bulgaria	n/a	1.26	/
Netherlands	4.79	n/a	/
China	n/a	1.0	/
India	n/a	0.7	/

Note: Data provided includes consumption of white chocolate.
Source: ICCO (2010, 2012) and Caobisco (2013).

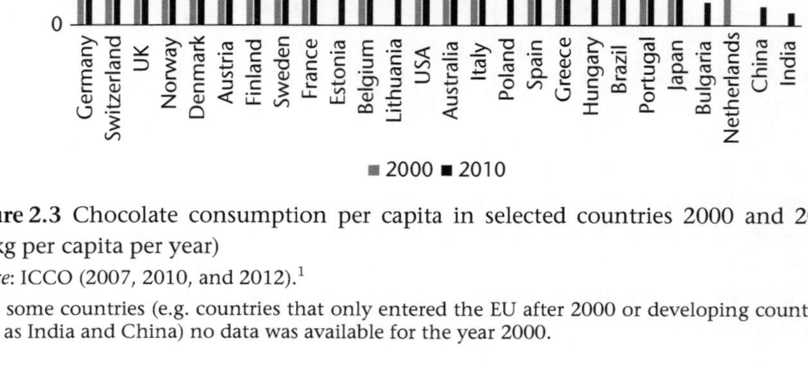

Figure 2.3 Chocolate consumption per capita in selected countries 2000 and 2010 (in kg per capita per year)

Source: ICCO (2007, 2010, and 2012).[1]

[1] For some countries (e.g. countries that only entered the EU after 2000 or developing countries, such as India and China) no data was available for the year 2000.

Conclusion

This chapter has documented major changes in the cocoa–chocolate industry and value chain through history.

The cocoa plant originated around 3000 BC. It was a drink and a monetary medium of exchange in South and Central America under the Olmec, the Mayas, and Aztecs (3000 BC–AD 1500). After the Spanish discovery of the New World, the cultivation of cocoa beans and the consumption and production of drinkable chocolate spread over the world during the early modern times (1500–1800). In the Age of Enlightenment (eighteenth century) the popularity of the cocoa drink declined as it became linked to the clergy and elite, in contrast with other drinks of that time: coffee and tea. However, globalization and scientific discoveries from the sixteenth through to the nineteenth century transformed the cocoa and chocolate industry. Scientific discoveries and the Industrial Revolution in the nineteenth and twentieth centuries led to eatable chocolate, made production possible on a larger scale and at lower cost, and raised incomes such that chocolate became also available for the common people. The twentieth century was characterized by a large increase in cocoa and chocolate production and consumption, and shifts in consumption patterns. Growth in the early twentieth century was concentrated mostly in North America and Western Europe, as a result of rapid income growth in these regions. The recent growth in consumption (in the 2000s) has been particularly strong in emerging and (rapidly growing) developing countries.

Today, most cocoa beans are produced in three regions: Africa, Asia, and South America, with seven countries (the Ivory Coast, Indonesia, Ghana, Nigeria, Cameroon, Brazil, and Ecuador) that accounted together for 90 per cent of the world cocoa production. In past centuries, most cocoa beans were exported and processed into intermediate products in the developed world. However, by now almost half of all grindings is done in the cocoa-producing countries, which are gaining a larger part of the value of the finished product.

One of the key features of the cocoa chain is the growing domination of a few multinationals in trading, processing, and manufacturing activities. The production of finished chocolate products takes mostly place in the developed world and is done in a relatively few large companies and many small chocolatiers. In 2013, the largest four manufacturers—Mondelēz International Inc., Mars Inc., Nestlé SA, and Ferrero Group—had a joint share of around 50 per cent of total world chocolate production.

There are many important issues for the future. One is the question of whether the rapid growth of chocolate consumption in emerging markets will lead to a global shortage of cocoa—and rising prices—an issue addressed by Christopher L. Gilbert (Chapter 16, this volume), and in Chapters 19–22 on emerging markets in Part 5 of the book. Another global development is the spread of various standards on production of cocoa. Over time, non-governmental organizations (NGOs) launched initiatives such as Fairtrade and UTZ, but large commercial players are now also increasingly introducing such standards. These standards apply to various aspects of the cocoa production, including (child) labour use and environmental sustainability criteria. These issues are addressed in Chapters 11, 12, and 14. Yet another important trend is the switch in consumer attitudes regarding the health impacts of chocolate. While, for much of history, chocolate (and cocoa drinks more generally) were considered a healthy food and a source of nutrition, in recent years growing chocolate consumption has become associated with health concerns—issues addressed in Chapters 7 and 8. Finally, an interesting observation is that, through history, chocolate has also played a role which was not directly related to consumption. In the ancient American empires cocoa beans were used as currency. Later on, chocolate played an important role as presents and gifts—and some chocolates have been explicitly developed and designed for this.

References

Abbott, P. and M. Wilcox. 2004. *Market Power and Structural Adjustment: The Case of West African Cocoa Market Liberalization.* Department of Agricultural Economics. Available at: <http://ageconsearch.umn.edu/bitstream/20084/1/sp04wi05.pdf> (accessed 1 June 2015).

ADM (Archer Daniels Midland). 2014. *Our Company: History.* Available at: <http://www.adm.com/en-US/company/history/Pages/2000-present.aspx> (accessed 19 March 2014).

Alberts, H. C. and J. L. Cidell. 2006. 'Chocolate Consumption, Manufacturing and Quality in Western Europe and the United States'. *Geography* 91 (3): 218–26.

Barry Callebaut. 2013. *Barry Callebaut: Annual Report 2012/2013.* Zurich. Available at: http://annual-report-2012-13.barry-callebaut.com/ (accessed 3 September 2015).

Beckett, S. 2008. *The Science of Chocolate*, 2nd edn. Cambridge: The Royal Society of Chemistry.

Bond, T. J. 2011. *Teas, Cocoa and Coffee: Plant Secondary Metabolites and Health: The Origins of Tea, Coffee and Cocoa as Beverages.* London: Wiley-Blackwell.

Boudewijn, C. and A. Lang. 1959. *The Manuring of Coffee, Cocoa, Tea and Tobacco.* Geneva: Centre d'étude de l'azote.

Bulliet, R. W., Crossley, P. K., Headrick, D. R., Hirsch, S. W., and Johnson, L. L. eds.). 2001. *The Earth and its People: A Global History*, 2nd edn. Boston: Houghton Mifflin Company.

Caobisco. 2013. *Caobisco Statistical Bulletin 2013.* Caobisco Statistics Network. Available at: <http://caobisco.eu/> (accessed 28 June 2015).

Cappelle, J. 2008. *Towards a Sustainable Cocoa Chain: Power and Possibilities within the Cocoa and Chocolate Sector.* IPIS vzw Research Centre. Available at: <http://www.icco.org/sites/www.roundtablecocoa.org/comment_documents/77_Towards%20a%20Sustainable%20Cocoa%20Chain%20Report_ENGLISH.pdf> (accessed September 2015).

Cargill. 2011. *Cargill Timeline: 1865–Present.* Cargill Incorporated. Available at: <https://www.cargill.com/wcm/groups/public/@ccom/documents/document/doc-cargill-history-timeline.pdf> (accessed 13 July 2015).

Clarence-Smith, W. G. 2000. *Cocoa and Chocolate 1765–1914.* London and New York: Routledge.

Clay, J. 2004. *World Agriculture and the Environment: A Commodity-by-Commodity Guide to Impacts and Practices.* Washington, DC: Island Press.

Coe, S. D. and M. D. Coe. 1996. *The True History of Chocolate.* London: Thames & Hudson Ltd.

Dand, R. 1999. *The International Cocoa Trade*, 2nd edn. Cambridge: Woodhead.

Doussou, T. 2009. 'Cocoa and Coffee Value Chains in West and Central Africa: Constraints and Options for Revenue-Raising Diversification', AAACP Paper Series: No. 3. Food and Agriculture Organization of the United Nations. Available at: <http://www.fao.org/fil eadmin/templates/est/AAACP/westafrica/FAO_AAACP_Paper_Series_No_3_1_.pdf> (accessed 12 June 2015).

Dreiss, M. L. and S. E. Greenhill. 2008. *Chocolate: Pathway to the Gods: The Sacred Realm of Chocolate in Mesoamerica*. Tucson: The University of Arizona Press.

ECOWAS (Economic Community of West Africa States–SWAC/OECD). 2007. *Atlas on Regional Integration in West Africa: Cocoa*. Available at: <http://www.oecd.org/swac/publica tions/39596493.pdf> (accessed 15 April 2015).

Euromonitor International. 2013a. *Market Sizes*. Passport Statistics. Available at: <http://www.portal.euromonitor.com> (accessed 3 March 2015).

Euromonitor International. 2013b. *Company Shares*. Passport Statistics. Available at: <http://www.portal.euromonitor.com> (accessed 4 December 2014).

FAOSTAT (Food and Agriculture Organization of the United Nations Statistics Division). 2013a. *Production Statistics: Crops*. Available at: <http://faostat3.fao.org/browse/Q/QC/E> (accessed 30 June 2015).

FAOSTAT (Food and Agriculture Organ ization of the United Nations Statistics Division). 2013b. *Trade Statistics: Crops and Livestock Products*. Available at: <http://faostat3.fao.org/ browse/Q/QC/E> (accessed 30 June 2015).

Fold, N. 2000. 'A Matter of Good Ta ste? Quality and the Construction of Standards for Chocolate Products in the European Union'. *Cahiers d'Economie et Sociologie Rurales* 55–6: 91–110.

Fold, N. 2001. 'Restructuring of the European Chocolate Industry and Its Impact on Cocoa Production in West Africa'. *Journal of Economic Geography* 1 (4): 405–20. Available at: <http://joeg.oxfordjournals.org/> (accessed 7 December 2014).

Franchise Help. 2014. *Chocolate Industry Analysis 2014: Cost and Trends*. Available at: <https://www.franchisehelp.com/industry-reports/chocolate-industry-report/> (accessed 20 August 2014).

Gasco, J. 2006. 'Soconusco Cacao Farmers Past and Present: Continuity and Change in an Ancient Way of Life'. In *Chocolate in Mesoamerica: A Cultural History of Cacao*, ed. C. L. McNeil, pp. 322–40. Gainesville: University Press of Florida.

George, E. 2012. *Structure and Competition in West Africa's Cocoa Trade*. Ecobank. Available at: <http://www.ecobank.com/upload/2013100804104885683757w49rm2gK.pdf> (accessed 19 May 2015).

Gilbert, C. L. 2009. 'Cocoa Market Liberalization in Retrospect'. *Review of Business and Economics* 54: 294–312. Available at: <http://www.econ.kuleuven.be/rebel//jaargangen/ 2001-2010/2009/2009- 3/RBE%202009-3%20-%20Cocoa%20Market%20Liberalization% 20in%20Retrospect.pdf> (accessed 3 September 2015).

Green, A. 2013. *Healthy Chocolate in 2013*. Available at: <http://adampaulgreen.com/ wp-content/uploads/2011/06/Chocolate-White-Paper-2013-HIRES.pdf> (accessed 12 April 2015).

Heijbroek, A. M. A. and R. J. Konijn. 1995. *The Cocoa and Chocolate Market*. Utrecht: Food and Agricultural Research, Rabobank Nederland, Marketing Services.

Hütz-Adams, F. and Fountain, A. C. 2012. *Cocoa Barometer 2012*. Available at: <http://www.cocoabarometer.org/Download_files/Cocoa%20Barometer%20Full%202012.pdf> (accessed 12 June 2015).

ICCO (International Cocoa Organization). 2010. *The World Cocoa Economy: Past and Present*. 30 July. Available at: <http://www.icco.org/about-us/international-cocoa-agreements/cat_view/ 30-related-documents/45-statistics-other-statistics.html> (accessed 3 September 2015).

ICCO (International Cocoa Organization). 2012. *Quarterly Bulletin of Cocoa Statistics* 38 (2).

ICCO Market Committee (International Cocoa Organization). 2007. *Cocoa Resources in Consuming Countries. (Report NO. MC/10/6)*. London. Available at: http://s3.amazonaws.com/zanran_storage/www.icco.org/ContentPages/16291656.pdf (accessed 2 July 2015).

Kaplan, J. 2008. 'Hydraulics, Cacao, and Complex Developments at Preclassic Chocolá, Guatemala: Evidence and Implications'. *Latin American Antiquity* 19 (4): 399–413.

Katz, S. H. (ed.). 2003. *Encyclopedia of Food and Culture*, vol. 1: *Acceptance to Food Politics*. New York: Thomson Gale Group.

Kaufman, T. and J. Justeson. 2006. 'The History of the Word for "Cacao" and Related Terms in Ancient Meso-America'. In *Chocolate in Mesoamerica: A Cultural History of Cacao*, ed. C. L. McNeil, pp. 117–39. Gainesville: University Press of Florida.

Kox, H. 2000. *The Market for Cocoa Powder*, background paper for Modelling and Forecasting the Market for Cocoa and Chocolate, prepared for Ministry of Foreign Affairs, the Netherlands. Amsterdam: Economic and Social Institute.

MacLeod, M. 2000. 'Cacao'. In *The Cambridge World History of Food*, vol. 1, ed. K. F. Kiple and K. C. Ornelas, pp. 635–40. Cambridge: Cambridge University Press.

McNeil, C. 2006. 'Introduction: The Biology, Antiquity, and Modern Uses of the Chocolate Tree'. In *Chocolate in Mesoamerica: A Cultural History of Cacao*, ed. C. L. McNeil, pp. 1–30. Gainesville: University Press of Florida.

Mitchell, B. R. 2007a. *International Historical Statistics: Africa, Asia and Oceania, 1750–2005*, 6th edn. Basingstoke: Palgrave Macmillan.

Mitchell, B. R. 2007b. *International Historical Statistics: Europe 1750–2005*, 6th edn. Basingstoke: Palgrave Macmillan.

Mitchell, B. R. 2007c. *International Historical Statistics: The Americas, 1750–2005*, 6th edn. Basingstoke: Palgrave Macmillan.

Musselli, I. 2008. *Cocoa Study: Industry Structures and Competition*. (UNCTAD/DITC/COM/2008/1). United Nations Conference on Trade and Development. Available at: <http://unctad.org/en/docs/ditccom20081_en.pdf> (accessed 19 February 2015).

Poelmans, E. and J. Swinnen. 2015. 'Cocoa and Chocolate: "Liquor of the Gods?"' LICOS Working Paper.

Rosenblum, M. 2005. *Chocolate: A Bittersweet Saga of Dark and Light*. New York: North Point Press.

Ruf, F. 2007. *Background Note: The Cocoa Sector*. Overseas Development Institute. French Agricultural Research Center for International Development. Available at: <http://www.odi.org.uk/sites/odi.org.uk/files/odi-assets/publications-opinion-files/586.pdf> (accessed 13 July 2015).

Ruf, F. and P. S. Siswoputranto (eds.). 1995. *Cocoa Cycles: The Economics of Cocoa Supply*. Cambridge: Woodhead Publishing Ltd.

Schivelbusch, W. 1992. *Tastes of Paradise*. New York: Pantheon.

Smith, A. F. (ed.). 2004. *The Oxford Encyclopedia of Food and Drink in America*, vol. 1. Oxford: Oxford University Press.

Szogyi, A. (ed.). 1997. *Chocolate: Food of the Gods*. Westport, CT: Greenwood Press.

Taylor, M. 2013. *Indonesia's 2013 Cocoa Exports to Drop 14 Percent y/y: Industry Body*. Reuters. Available at: <http://www.reuters.com/article/2013/11/04/indonesiacocoa-association-idUSL3N0IP0IZ20131104> (accessed 2 July 2015).

Weiligmann, B., S. Panhuysen, M. van Reenen, and G. Zwart. 2009. *Cacaobarometer 2009*. Tropical Commodity Coalition. Available at: <http://www.cocoabarometer.org/> (accessed 3 September 2015).

Wilson, K. C. 1999. *Coffee, Cocoa and Tea*. Cambridge: CABI Publishing.

3

Chocolate Consumption from the Sixteenth Century to the Great Chocolate Boom

William G. Clarence-Smith

Introduction

A psychoactive alkaloid, theobromine, makes chocolate mildly stimulating and slightly addictive.[1] This brings chocolate into competition with similar beverages, governed by complex social rituals. Theobromine has a less violent effect on the nervous system and is possibly less addictive than alkaloids in rival products. Coffee and tea both depend on caffeine for their impact, as do *maté* and *guaraná*, grown in South America. Stimulating alkaloids are also found in products that are smoked, such as nicotine in tobacco, or chewed, such as caffeine in kola nuts and cocaine in cocoa leaves (Macmillan 1925; Coe 1996; Grieve 1984).

There is a long tradition of distinguishing between stimulants, on the one hand, and drugs and alcohol on the other. However, this distinction is fraught with difficulties, reflecting social attitudes as much as scientific evidence (Sherratt 1995). Cocaine is a prohibited alkaloid today, whereas Sigmund Freud regarded it as a useful stimulant. Similarly, opium was widely consumed in East and Southeast Asia as a stimulant, to combat physical fatigue and hunger (Newman 1995). The distinction between 'good stimulants' and 'bad drugs' was nevertheless of vital historical importance, as temperance campaigners championed the former and attacked the latter.

Many products could replace the 'demon drink', but beverages made with boiled liquids enjoyed a great hygienic advantage over cold drinks. It was not until the advent of chlorination, pasteurization, and industrial production methods in the late nineteenth century that rivalry became more intense. Alkaloids extracted from coca leaves and kola nuts were added to industrially produced soft drinks from

[1] This chapter is a reprint of 'The Consumption of Chocolate', in William G. Clarence-Smith, *Cocoa and Chocolate 1765–1914*, ©2000, Routledge Publications. Reproduced by permission of Taylor & Francis Books UK.

the 1870s, most famously in Coca-Cola, launched in Atlanta in 1886 as a temperance drink and a 'brain tonic', albeit losing cocaine from its formula in 1906 (Burnett 1999).

Unlike most hot beverages available before 1914, chocolate had great nutritional value. Its high fat content, together with some protein, bridged the gap that often existed between stimulants and food. Drinking chocolate thus acquired a particular association with cold climates and seasons, even though the beverage originated in tropical Mesoamerica and was sometimes taken cold. At the same time, excessive fat in chocolate posed problems of solubility and digestibility, not overcome till cocoa butter was regularly and effectively pressed out of the bean in the late nineteenth century.

A little chocolate was eaten as a snack throughout its history, but eating chocolate only developed a truly significant market at the end of the nineteenth century. This helped chocolate consumption to grow faster than that of tea, coffee, and other established competitors. The invention of milk chocolate brought about a convergence of interests with the dairy industry, and the incorporation of chocolate into sweets, biscuits, and cakes strengthened links with sugar and wheat. However, as late as 1914, chocolate was probably still consumed more as a drink than as food.

The unique taste of chocolate is its final, and most elusive, characteristic. Although partial substitutes have been found for cocoa butter, no product has ever been discovered to match the subtle taste of cocoa powder. The roasted pods of the Mediterranean carob tree, probably eaten since antiquity as 'Saint John's bread', come closest. However, the use of carob as an alternative to chocolate is quite recent, the result of concerns about fat and alkaloids in chocolate (http: 'Carob').

Apart from its physical properties, chocolate was vulnerable to changing social perceptions. Entering the industrial age as a prestigious luxury for Western aristocrats and an article of daily necessity for Amerindians, chocolate was often rejected as decadent in the West and uncivilized in Latin America. The image of chocolate reached its nadir in the first half of the nineteenth century, when it was typecast as a superannuated and indigestible beverage. A generation later, chocolate was rescued by temperance campaigners, technical change, and advertising magic. Pressing out cocoa butter made chocolate drinks a wholesome alternative to alcohol, chocolate bars became a weekly treat in proletarian households, and attractively wrapped chocolate confectionery became an esteemed gift.

The Spread of Chocolate and Its Competitors

Spanish expansion in the sixteenth century widened chocolate consumption, both socially and geographically. When the Spaniards arrived in Mesoamerica, cocoa beans were a currency and chocolate was drunk cold or hot, unsweetened, and mixed with strong spices, including chilli. Sumptuary and ritual restrictions dictated when it could be taken, and by whom. The Spaniards swept away these restrictions, and diffused a novel beverage, sweetened with cane sugar and flavoured with vanilla or cinnamon. In this form, the drink had its greatest success around the Caribbean Basin, and across the Pacific in the distant Philippines (Harwich 1992; Coe 1996). Chocolate made less progress south of the equator, where it tended to remain confined to Spaniards and wealthy Creoles. However, chocolate was banned by the Jesuits in the River Plate area in 1677, together with similar substances, indicating that it must have been a temptation to some (Garavaglia 1983). Rich and poor drank chocolate in Quito, the capital of modern Ecuador, but the Amerindians of the Andes hardly touched it (Arosemena 1991).

Chocolate's main competitors in the New World were plants related to the common holly and containing caffeine. The Spanish conquest transformed an Amerindian infusion made from the parched and broken leaves of maté (*Ilex paraguariensis*) into an item of mass consumption. Mainly collected from forests in eastern Paraguay and neighbouring parts of Brazil, maté was domesticated by the Jesuits. It was exported on a large scale to southern ranching zones, Chile, the mines of Peru, and the Quito highlands. In contrast, little maté was consumed in the heartlands of Brazil, the viceroyalty of New Spain, or Europe (Linhares 1969; Garavaglia 1983). A related plant, *guayusa* (*Ilex guayusa*), grew in the Amazonian forests of modern Ecuador (http: 'Maté'; Garavaglia 1983: 46). *Yaupon* (*Ilex cassine* or *vomitoria*) was another relative. Growing from Florida to North Carolina, it was prized by both Amerindians and immigrants (Simmonds 1888; Emerson 1908; Scott 1964).

Two further pre-Columbian legacies blocked the advance of chocolate in the New World. The indigenous peoples of the high Andes, as far north as Santa Marta in modern Colombia, preferred to chew the leaves of the coca bush (*Erythroxylon coca*). Debilitating addiction was a danger, for cocaine was a stronger alkaloid than caffeine (Simmonds 1888; Eder 1913; Garavaglia 1983). Much consumed in northern and central Brazil was *guaraná* (*Paullinia cupana* or *sorbilis*), a bitter seed with a high caffeine content, from a woody climbing plant cultivated on the middle Amazon. The seeds were dried, roasted, powdered, made into a dough, and then dried again into hard cylinders, to be grated and mixed with water (Simmonds 1888; Macmillan 1925).

From the range of stimulants discovered in the New World, Europe embraced only chocolate and tobacco. Indeed, such was the success of chocolate in Catholic Europe that it became part of Baroque civilization (Coe 1996). Nowhere was this truer than in Spain, where even servants regularly drank it by the early eighteenth century, and their masters indulged in it, hot or cold, from morning till night. France and regions under Habsburg rule took to chocolate, but Portugal's consumption remained low (Stols 1996). The Portuguese had developed a taste for tea from their early contacts with China, which they passed on to their British allies when Charles II married a Portuguese princess (Walvin 1997). Competition from coffee and tea was generally stiff in Protestant northern Europe, although chocolate was accepted by Protestant preachers as one way to combat alcohol (Bizière 1979; Harwich 1992; Schivelbusch 1992). North Europeans drank chocolate more regularly in their Caribbean colonies, where cocoa beans were cheaper and more readily available (Coe 1996; Walvin 1997).

With the exception of the Philippines, chocolate failed to make significant inroads beyond Europe. An Ottoman Turkish official in the late seventeenth century pronounced it to be disgusting. In Monsoon Asia, chocolate was chiefly consumed by Catholic missionaries (Coe 1996). Chinese scholars accepted it into their pharmacopoeia as an aphrodisiac, but made no great use of it (Pelletier 1861). Alternative beverages barred the way. Tea reigned supreme in the Confucian world of East Asia, and was taken to Russia early in the seventeenth century (Scott 1964). Tea was also favoured in Central Asia, Persia, and North Africa, but coffee dominated the central lands of Islam from the sixteenth century, spreading to South and Southeast Asia (Haarer 1956). More anciently established in the lands of Islam was *salep* (*sahleb*), a 'nervine restorative', and, like chocolate, a 'fattener' (*EB* 1929). Originating in Persia, salep was made from the roasted and pounded roots of wild orchids. It was popular from the Balkans to northern India, and had some adepts in the West (Simmonds 1888; Anon. 1890; Grieve 1984).

Masticatories containing stimulants were another barrier to the spread of chocolate in the tropics. Southeast Asians and many South Asians chewed a mixture of areca nuts (*Areca catechu*), betel leaf (*Piper betle*), and ground lime, which released a cocktail of alkaloids (Reid 1988). Related to betel was *Piper methysticum*, the root of which was chewed and fermented to make *kava*, the 'national drink' of the South Pacific. The fresh *qat* leaf (*Catha edulis*) was favoured in South Arabia and adjoining parts of East Africa (Macmillan 1925; Grieve 1984). Kola nuts, mainly *Cola nitida* and *Cola acuminata*, were chewed throughout much of tropical Africa. They contained caffeine and a little theobromine, and were nutritious (Bauer 1963; Lovejoy 1995).

The Passing of the Baroque Age, 1760s to 1790s

Although chocolate consumption continued to increase in the second half of the eighteenth century, the threat to Baroque civilization undermined the commodity's future. Chocolate was associated with the idle clergy and nobility of Catholic and absolutist regimes. A popular motif for painters was the breakfast scene, in which a noble woman, often in bed and revealing much of her ample flesh, languidly took her morning chocolate in the company of a priest and assorted menfolk (Schivelbusch 1992). The persecution of the Jesuits, starting in Portugal in 1759 and culminating in the dissolution of the order in 1773, was an early blow to chocolate consumption, and an omen of worse to come (Coe 1996).

Tea and coffee were serious rivals, perceived as incarnating the values of the rising bourgeoisie (Bizière 1979; Schivelbusch 1992). Coffee-houses spawned newspapers, clubs, and radical ideas, although chocolate was often served in these establishments (Schneider 1998). Tea and coffee represented sobriety, serious purpose, trustworthiness and respectability, contrasting with the feckless excesses of the aristocracy. Moreover, Baroque cuisine was slowly falling out of favour, as strong flavours and smells became unfashionable, whereas lightness and moderation were all the rage (Burnett 1999). Chocolate stood accused of being more expensive than its competitors, more time-consuming to prepare, and too oily (Walvin 1997).

Spain remained by far and away the most significant Western market for chocolate, albeit seduced by rival beverages. To lack chocolate was said to be the same as being short of bread in France, and some chocolate was eaten with almonds or hazelnuts (Schneider 1998). People of the middling sort commonly partook of a thick chocolate beverage at breakfast, dipping little cakes into it. The habit reached down to the 'common people', in whom it was seen by some as a 'regrettable extravagance', although most workers broke their fast with alcohol. At the same time, radicals condemned chocolate as part of the absolutist lifestyle, and some people began to take coffee and tea, to appear more European. Coffee- houses patronized by men emerged in major towns, although they also served chocolate (Kany 1932).

Italy was the land where 'the precious chocolate ... was the basis of everybody's breakfast and the evening *rinfreschi*' (Vaussard 1962: 194). Italian cooks showed considerable inventiveness, even adding chocolate to pasta and meat dishes. The Roman Church was among the best customers, and it was rumoured that Pope Clement XIV died after imbibing poisoned chocolate in 1774. Spanish influence was strong in southern Italy, a bastion of the chocolate habit. In the north, some Venetian artists drank coffee for its radical chic and cheapness (Coe 1996). However, Casanova praised chocolate's qualities, as did other Venetian intellectuals of the time (Bernard 1996; Schneider 1998).

It is not clear how much French social and ideological divisions affected chocolate consumption. It was said of Paris in 1768 that 'the great sometimes partake of it, old people often, but the common people never' (Bernard 1996: 85–6). The magistrates of Bayonne declared in 1763 that chocolate had long formed part of the 'daily food' of the town, but this ancient Basque centre of chocolate manufacture, much influenced by Spain, was not typical (Léon 1893). The *philosophes* defiantly drank coffee in the *salons* where they propagated subversive ideas, even though Voltaire preferred to drink chocolate for breakfast. Conversely, Queen Marie-Antoinette was as fond of coffee as of chocolate for her breakfast. The Marquis de Sade, an icon of aristocratic decadence, was a true 'chocoholic', who pestered his wife from prison to obtain supplies of the 'food of the gods'. A French peculiarity was an early taste for eating chocolate in biscuits, marzipan, desserts, ices, and sweets. Even the gritty mass used to prepare drinking chocolate was sometimes eaten by people in a hurry (Coe 1996).

In the Austrian possessions, Catholic and culturally close to Spain, chocolate spread beyond the aristocracy. In Austria and Hungary, beer and wine vanished from the breakfast tables of the bourgeoisie from the mid-eighteenth century, giving way to chocolate and coffee. However, coffee was the senior partner in 'civilizing' the middle class, and it alone was mentioned in connection with artisans (Sandgruber 1986). Chocolate was slowly losing ground to coffee in the southern Low Countries (Belgium), but the urban poor drank what was called 'little coffee' in 1776, made from roasted cocoa shells boiled with milk, sugar, and cinnamon (Libert 1996; Swaelen 1996).

North Germans and Dutch were the greatest European coffee drinkers, including poor people in town and country, but a number of German poets and writers loved chocolate, notably Schiller and Goethe, and there was quite a market for chocolate in the Netherlands. It is not clear why only imports of coffee and tea were banned in 1768 by Frederick the Great, when he sought to improve Prussia's balance of payments (Slijper 1927; Schneider 1998). Frederick assiduously propagated the virtues of the roasted and ground root of locally grown chicory (*Cichorium intybus*), as a partial or total substitute for coffee, and Prussia boasted the first factory to powder the root in 1770 (Schivelbusch 1992; Barr 1998). Chicory had been eaten since antiquity, but its use as a coffee substitute was pioneered in the Netherlands around 1750. Its main disadvantage was that it contained no stimulating alkaloid (Smith 1996: 208; Burnett 1999: 84; Grieve 1984).

The reduction of British tea duties in 1784 led to a surge of imports from China, possibly contraband entering legal channels, making tea an item of mass consumption among labourers in southern Britain by the 1790s (Barr 1998; Burnett 1999). The growing popularity of tea led to a 'sharp decline in the sale of coffee, cocoa and chocolate', ruining coffee and chocolate houses (Drummond and Wilbraham 1939: 244). However, upper-class men continued to partake of chocolate inside and outside the home, even if coffee was more esteemed by the 1790s (Burnett 1999). At the other end of the spectrum, the Royal Navy issued slabs of chocolate to seamen in the Caribbean from 1780, spreading an appreciation of the hot chocolate beverage among the poor (Wagner 1987).

Despite the rarity of places of public consumption in British North America, drinking chocolate was available and was consumed by the well-to-do. Boston pharmacists advertised the availability of chocolate as early as 1712, and some leading figures breakfasted regularly on it towards the end of the century (Scott 1964; Coe 1996). Colonial Virginians made chocolate in the manner of northern Europe, with boiling milk rather than water, although they might add egg yolks in the Spanish fashion. Competing beverages were coffee, green tea, black tea, and salep, the latter drunk 'in china cups as chocolate' (Fitchett 1906: 64).

Chocolate stood to benefit from the independence of the USA, as tea became a symbol of the iniquities of colonial taxation and regulation. The Boston Tea Party of 1773, the launching pad for the American Revolution, was prolonged by a boycott of tea (Scott 1964; Barr 1998). John Adams, the second president, declared his enthusiasm for chocolate while on a visit to Spain in 1799 (Coe 1996). Thomas Jefferson, the third president, hoped that nourishing chocolate would become the preferred beverage of the USA (Young 1994). In practice, however, independence allowed free access to supplies of tea and coffee, which poured into the USA in ever increasing quantities. In the great New England port of Salem, coffee was the usual breakfast drink, although hot chocolate or tea were consumed with a light supper (Phillips 1947).

Standard accounts of chocolate in this period underestimate the scale of consumption in Latin America, where chocolate was an item of basic consumption (Humboldt 1811). This was especially true of Mexico, where the poor and slaves drank it (Arcila Farías 1950; León Borja and Szászdi Nagy 1964). Valets, cobblers, muleteers, and coachmen took chocolate at least twice a day, sometimes four times or more, and every household possessed a stone to grind cocoa in 1775. Indigenous peoples sometimes consumed their chocolate cold, whereas Creoles and Mestizos preferred it hot (Stols 1996). In the dry northwest, missionaries 'ordered large quantities of it annually' (Deeds 1995: 90). Spanish traders breakfasted on it every morning (Brading 1971). A famous Mexican dish for festive occasions was *mole poblano*, turkey or chicken in a chocolate and chili sauce, allegedly invented in a colonial convent (Lambert Ortiz 1968).

Chocolate in Central America had long been 'a basic food staple, drunk in huge, if not incredible quantities by Indians, and enjoyed by the poorer Creoles' (MacLeod 1973: 242). It remained king in Guatemala, drunk at breakfast and after meals, and incorporated into nine different beverages (Rubio Sánchez 1958). In Costa Rica in 1785, 'the poor people nourish themselves with chocolate, which they drink at any time', mixed with unrefined sugar. The Bishop of Honduras opined in 1791 that 'even the poorest person drinks cacao twice a day, and many drink it three or four times a day', resulting in imports from other provinces (Fernández Molina 1992: 425). Chocolate was among the basic rations issued to labourers on an estate in León in 1773, as was carefully entered in the accounts (Romero Vargas 1976).

The continuing use of cocoa beans as currency boosted demand in Central America. Repeated attempts to demonetize cocoa in Nicaragua foundered on the scarcity of silver coins and Amerindian preferences (Newson 1987). Guatemala's Maya traders used beans for their commercial operations in 1763 (Solórzano 1963). The exchange rate between cocoa beans and silver was thus officially confirmed in Costa Rica in 1778 (Saenz Maroto 1970).

The threat from coffee was no more than a cloud on the horizon for Mesoamerica. Jesuits arranged a public drinking of the new beverage in Guatemala City in 1743, but it was slow to catch on (King 1974). In 1778, the Mexican authorities warned that people might turn to coffee were imports of cheap Guayaquil cocoa beans to be restricted, but this was a ploy to put pressure on Madrid not to place high import duties on imports from Guayaquil, or even ban imports entirely. (Arcila Farías 1950). Nevertheless, Tabasco was sending coffee as well as cocoa to Veracruz by 1784, and great hopes were pinned on the crop in 1794 (Florescano and Gil Sánchez 1976; Ruiz Abreu 1989).

The threat from coffee was greater in the Spanish and French Antilles. Chocolate was the usual breakfast beverage in eighteenth-century Havana (Arcila Farias 1950). The same was true of Puerto Rico, even among the poor (Gil-Bermejo 1970). In Santiago de Cuba, guests who called after the siesta in 1800 were offered chocolate, served with fancy breads and fruit preserves (Wright 1910). The sparse population of Santo Domingo consumed a great deal of locally grown chocolate, although they also grew coffee for themselves by the 1780s (Sevilla Soler 1980). The first coffee house opened in Cuba in 1722, and the island's limited coffee output was supplemented with imports from Puerto Rico in the 1790s (Pérez de la Riva 1944). The people of the French islands were reported to drink a particularly delicious chocolate, even though Saint-Domingue was the most dynamic coffee producer in the world (Coe 1996).

The northern marches of South America were addicted to chocolate. Venezuela was estimated to retain about a quarter of its large harvest for local needs (Humboldt 1941). Prosperity in the gold mines of the Nuevo Reino (Colombia) resulted in a tenfold increase in imports of beans between 1740 and 1805, brought by ship and mule (Patiño 1963; Twinam 1982). The populations of the central highlands and coast consumed much chocolate, made from local beans (McFarlane 1993). The usual breakfast and night-time drink in Cartagena was chocolate (Walker 1822). The wealthy in Bogotá drank chocolate three times a day, brought from Cúcuta and Neiva by mule. Furthermore, chocolate was an 'essential part of the diet of the poor' of the city, who eked out their meagre purchases by adding maize or wheat. After salt, cocoa was the most important article of internal commerce (Brungardt 1974: 91).

Chocolate made some progress in the viceroyalties of Peru and the River Plate, especially the former, as political reforms stimulated an influx of Spaniards (León Borja and Szászdi Nagy 1964). One Lima official recorded in his diary that he drank chocolate morning and night in 1790 (Descola 1968). Chocolate came to be seen by Creoles as European and progressive, although this reputation was shared with coffee and tea, and Buenos Aires distributed Guayaquil cocoa in the River Plate region (Garavaglia 1983). However, Jesuit fathers of the Mojos missions, keen to sell their cocoa, complained in the 1760s that 'the very Spaniards of Peru, even though they dispose of an abundance of cocoa, prefer maté' (Eder 1985: 151). In 1775, Lima households rarely owned grinding stones to make chocolate (Stols 1996).

Competition came from both old and new products. Coffee arrived in Peru some time after 1760, coming from Guayaquil, where production for local consumption reached a mere four tons in 1788. The first coffee house in Lima appeared in 1771, and there were half a dozen 20 years later. However, the novel drink was narrowly restricted to the male urban elite (*MP*). Maté imported from Paraguay was still the usual hot beverage taken at home by speakers of Spanish in Peru and Quito (Parrón Salas 1995; *MP*). Exports of Paraguayan maté reached a peak in the late eighteenth century, and some Brazilian maté began to find its way to Spanish colonies (Garavaglia 1983). As for Amerindians in the Andes, they stuck to chewing coca leaves (*MP*).

In Brazil, the wealthy drank tea from China, copying the Portuguese practice, and the maté habit only caught on in the far south (Linhares 1969). Coffee houses in Salvador were supplied with locally grown coffee by the 1810s (Spix and Martius 1976). In the great forests of the north, Amerindians sucked the sweet pulp around bitter unfermented cocoa beans, which they then spat out, while missionaries helped to diffuse *guaraná* (Humboldt 1852; Patiño 1963).

Chocolate was well established in the Philippines. By 1810, 'the use of chocolate [was] greatly extended among the natives of easy circumstances' (Comyn 1969: 12). In the independent Islamic state of Sulu, sultan and nobles breakfasted on chocolate in gilded tumblers, in which they dipped macaroons obtained from Manila. Indeed, chocolate had become 'the common beverage of all classes' in Sulu, probably due to the large number of Christian Filipinos taken as slaves (Moor

1968: 44). Elsewhere in Asia, Catholics remained the main consumers of chocolate, such as missionaries and Portuguese traders in Thailand (Coe 1996). In 1778, cocoa was found in Malaya, growing in the garden of a Portuguese widow in Dutch Malacca (Burkill 1966).

The Impact of Revolution and War, 1790s–1820s

Political associations and geographical factors may have done a disservice to chocolate, as the old order collapsed. To the extent that it was identified in the minds of revolutionaries with the decadence and immorality of the nobility and clergy, chocolate seemed destined to be consigned to the dustbin of history (Collet 1996). That said, such an issue must have paled into insignificance as the tide of revolution and war submerged Europe. Cocoa also lacked an Asian 'back door' into Europe, unlike tea and coffee. At the end of the eighteenth century, there was a sudden surge in Russia's overland imports of tea from China, much of which was taken on to German markets (Blanchard 1989; Gardella 1994). Similarly, Yemeni and Ethiopian coffee could travel overland, although production was too small to take up much of the slack in Europe (Thurber 1881).

The main beneficiaries from chocolate's discomfiture were probably local substances, protected by naval blockades and punitive taxation (Brillat-Savarin n.d.). Thus, the use of chicory spread from Germany to France (Burnett 1999). Salep, now made from wild English orchid roots rather than imported from the Levant, took the fancy of the labouring population of London. Drunk with milk and sugar, it was not unlike the chocolate of the time. Charles Lamb declared it to be an ideal breakfast for chimney sweeps, taken with a slice of bread and butter (Barr 1998; Grieve 1984). A bewildering variety of products was tried in Austria, ranging from roast barley and other cereals, through to acorns, beech masts, figs, and blue lupin beans (Sandgruber 1986). However, none of these substitutes contained the alkaloids that consumers craved, with the possible exception of the latter.

Disruptions in supplies of cocoa beans in Latin America varied, but only Cuba and Puerto Rico were really vulnerable to naval blockade. In the self-sufficient Nuevo Reino, war had no discernible effect at all (Brungardt 1974). There may have been some increase in the consumption of coffee, available locally, and the loosening of the Iberian mercantilist straitjacket facilitated imports of tea, albeit at great expense. In eastern Venezuela, chocolate was drunk first thing in the morning and last thing at night in the 1810s, but coffee was already being taken after dinner. During 'collations' offered by the Caracas elite, chocolate, coffee, tea, and Spanish wines were served (Walker 1822).

As chocolate was a local drink, consumed by the poor, revolutionaries in Spanish colonies do not appear to have condemned it. Incomes were probably not seriously affected in most countries until the closing years of the independence struggle. In Mexico, chocolate was 'held in high estimation', and there was no sign of a quest for alternatives (Bullock 1824: 285). There were eight cafes in Lima in 1815, but also a guild of chocolate makers (Anna 1979). Tea, easily accessible, was the beverage of choice of Chinese traders and artisans in the Philippines. There was also a sudden spurt in coffee cultivation from the 1790s, spearheaded by missionaries, but this was probably a response to high coffee prices after the Haitian Revolution (Mallat 1983).

The Slump of the 1820s to the 1840s

Hampered by economic recession and a deeply unfashionable image, chocolate faced one of its most difficult periods after the defeat of Napoleon and the independence of continental Latin America. Incomes plummeted in Spain and in newly independent countries, which were thrown into turmoil for decades. Substitutes adopted during the war years kept some of the market, albeit more because of economic recession than out of choice, as indicated by the frustrated aspirations of consumers in Austria-Hungary (Sandgruber 1986).

Mesoamerica, the most important New World market, was devastated by independence. Mexican income per head fell from around $73 in 1800 to $56 in 1845, in 1950 US dollars. The collapse of the mining industry reduced demand for foodstuffs, roads were not repaired, and swarms of bandits infested the countryside (Haber 1989). Even though excellent chocolate was found in the most remote locations, Mexico's consumption fell sharply in the 1820s (Ward 1828; Bologne 1996). This did not reflect any marked changes in taste. People in Yucatán in the 1830s liked to partake four times a day of a traditional gruel, made of roast maize, cocoa, sugar, and water (Waldeck 1838). Coffee was available in rural stores in Chiapas in the late 1830s, but chocolate was still the normal breakfast drink across southern Mexico and Central America, consumed after siesta and in the evening (Stephens 1993).

Income was again the problem in the northern marches of South America. Venezuelan chocolate consumption slumped to some 750 tons of cocoa beans a year between 1830 and 1860, under half Humboldt's estimate for 1797 (Middleton 1871; Humboldt 1941). A decline in gold mining hit Colombia, although cocoa-producing provinces were still the best markets for Bogotá merchants distributing imported goods in the late 1830s (Schneider 1981). Coffee was little in demand (Mollien 1824; Gosselman 1962). Indeed, coffee houses were almost unknown around 1850 in Colombia, although the upper classes copied the French habit of taking coffee and the English one of taking tea (McGreevey 1971; Fuentes 1992).

The Andean countries to the south of Colombia were in a state of flux, as Chinese tea began to push maté aside (http: 'Maté'). Tea had become the standard breakfast drink in Guayaquil in 1832, 'even among the descendants of Spaniards', whereas locally grown coffee and cocoa were spurned (Terry 1834: 66). That said, chocolate was widely consumed in Quito in 1833, and was allegedly one of the three passions in women's lives in 1847, while maté and *guayusa* were still very popular (Toscano 1960). Similarly, people of modest means in the old viceroyalty of Peru drank more chocolate after independence, as a full-fat beverage, taken with milk and sugar (Romero 1961; Garavaglia 1983). Incomes also revived early in Peru, due to the guano boom from 1840 (Mathew 1981).

Cuba under Spanish rule did not suffer from recession, but coffee became the 'national drink', allegedly 'replacing classic Spanish-style chocolate' (Pérez de la Riva 1944: 175, 177). Cubans were certainly precocious coffee drinkers, consuming about 6000 tons by the middle of the century (Sagra 1963). However, coffee houses served both coffee and chocolate, and the numerous immigrant Spaniards preferred chocolate prepared at home. Coffee was perceived as a beverage of 'carters, gamblers and people of ill repute', and the authorities cracked down on coffee-houses as centres of subversion (Pérez de la Riva 1944: 178). Cubans who breakfasted on chocolate tended to be wealthier than those who chose coffee, although chocolate was consumed by all levels of Cuban society, including slaves (Mangin 1860; Marrero 1972–89).

The vast empire of Brazil escaped economic recession, but remained indifferent to chocolate and coffee, despite a surge in exports of both. Maté was available everywhere in the country, and in its traditional form was the favourite beverage from Paraná to the south. Well-roasted maté was a poor person's substitute for tea in Rio de Janeiro and the centre of the country. The persistence of the Portuguese attachment to China tea was demonstrated by attempts to grow it in São Paulo and Rio de Janeiro, and by the fact that production did not match consumption (Kidder 1845; Linhares 1969; Spix and Martius 1976). *Guaraná*, grown in the middle Amazon and consumed as a cold sweetened beverage, was of much greater importance. It was popular in the mines of Mato Grosso and Goiás, other parts of Brazil, and Amazonian regions of Peru and Venezuela (Spruce 1908).

Chocolate kept a particularly strong position in the Philippines, experiencing an economic boom under continued Spanish rule. Mallat said of the immigrant Spaniard, 'hardly has he opened his eyes, when he asks for his *chicara de chocolate* from the Indio or Negrito serving him'. He took chocolate again after his evening stroll, although tea was a possible substitute. Lower down the social scale, 'the natives take cocoa once or twice a day, in the same way that the Chinese take tea, dipping in it pieces of sugar cane in place of plain sugar' (Mallat 1983: 86, 345). Beyond the areas under Spanish control, chocolate remained 'the general drink of natives, which rich and poor take every day' in the Sulu sultanate (Anon 1849: 110).

There are scattered references to chocolate consumption elsewhere in Asia and Africa. Wealthy Makasarese in southern Sulawesi offered chocolate to European guests in the 1820s, made with beans imported from Manila (Olivier 1834–37). In Penang, the main consumers in 1841 were Catholic missionaries (Buckley 1965). One Dutch planter in Java drank an exquisite chocolate, made with his own beans (Hogendorp 1830). However, coffee was the usual beverage of Javanese peasants in the 1820s (Elson 1994). Salep retained its popularity in the Middle East and India, and was found, together with coffee, in Yemeni entrepots in the 1820s (Milburn 1825; Simmonds 1888). A little cocoa was grown for local use in Sierra Leone, indicating that freed slaves brought New World habits to Africa (Peterson 1969).

Schivelbusch, like so many others, errs when he declares that old-fashioned chocolate 'vanished with the ancien régime', to be replaced from 1828 by defatted beverages and chocolate bars (Schivelbusch 1992: 92–3). In reality, Catholic aristocrats and clerics were reinstated from 1815 to 1848. Moreover, the patenting of Van Houten's famous cocoa butter press in 1828 had no immediate consequences, not even in the Netherlands (Schrover 1991). Unsweetened bars of full-fat Zeeland chocolate were boiled up with milk or water in the Netherlands until 'far into the nineteenth century' (Slijper 1927: 140). The mixing of a little dried chocolate mass with hot milk remained typical of northern Europe as a whole, while the poor in Ireland and the Low Countries made do with cheap cocoa shells. Southern Europeans dissolved larger amounts of chocolate mass in hot or cold water, sometimes adding egg yolks for a richer feast (Mangin 1860; Pelletier 1861). The persistence of traditional beverages, frequently mixed with various starchy substances to absorb the fat, partly accounted for the high premium paid for Caracas Criollo, with its good flavour and low-fat content (Hewett 1862).

Chocolate suffered from an unfashionable image. The Dutch, in their earthy way, declared it a drink fit only for teetotallers and middle-class ladies suffering from constipation (Schrover 1991). Balzac vaunted the virile virtues of coffee, airily denouncing chocolate for contributing to the fall of Spain, by encouraging sensuality, laziness, and greed. For Musset and Flaubert, chocolate was the breakfast drink of the idle rich (Bernard 1996; Bologne 1996). Dickens reflected another old stereotype, portraying a corrupt Catholic cleric as a chocolate drinker (Coe 1996). However, such pejorative views were not universal. Goethe made 'a cult of chocolate and avoided coffee' until his death in 1832 (Schivelbusch 1992: 92). Moreover, chocolate retained a reputation as a remedy for many maladies, even though its alleged aphrodisiac properties were widely discounted (Barreta 1841).

While France still imported less cocoa than Spain, Brillat-Savarin asserted in 1825 that 'chocolate has become quite normal in France, and everybody has taken it into their heads to prepare it'. He described chocolate desserts and confectionery in loving detail, while noting that chocolate was still mainly a breakfast drink, and that coffee was spreading (Brillat-Savarin n.d.: I, 119). Balzac's novels suggest that the French bourgeoisie had taken up drinking chocolate from the aristocracy, and gave chocolate confectionery to their children (Bologne 1996).

British imports for consumption progressed, but at a lower level than those of France. The Royal Navy replaced breakfast gruel with an ounce of chocolate in 1824, halved the rum ration a year later, and consumed 179 tons of cocoa in 1830 (Knapp 1923; Wagner 1987; Barr 1998). However, chocolate was still prepared in pharmacies and drunk largely for health reasons. Advertisements stressed its medicinal properties, and Quaker manufacturers promoted it as an alternative to alcohol (Williams 1931; Vernon 1958). The temperance movement now advocated complete abstinence from all alcohol, not just spirits, but coffee was the main beneficiary. Coffee spread to the working class and consumption per head rose nearly to that of tea by 1840. It was frequently mixed with cheap chicory, imported from Belgium or produced in England. Moreover, salep remained popular (Barr 1998; Burnett 1999).

Iberian contrasts deepened. Spain remained the largest European market for chocolate, as imports recovered in spite of economic and political travails

(Prados de la Escosura 1982). In contrast, the value of Portugal's small cocoa imports trailed far behind those of tea and coffee in the 1840s (*MGCP*). Portuguese settlers in Príncipe in 1836, surrounded by coffee and cocoa trees on their estates, preferred to purchase tea at exorbitant prices from the few foreign ships that called (Omboni 1846).

Modest Recovery, 1850s to 1870s

Although economic conditions improved from around 1850, the performance of drinking chocolate continued to lag behind that of its two main rivals. By about 1880, it was estimated that 500 million people drank tea around the world, compared to 200 million for coffee and only 50 million for chocolate. Green tea was dominant in the Confucian world of East Asia, and in the Islamic lands of Central Asia and North Africa. Black tea ruled the roost in Britain and many British colonies, notably India. Russians drank cheap brick tea mixed with melted butter, which looked like chocolate. The domain of coffee lay in the USA, much of continental Europe, the Near East, and the Malay world. The only countries where chocolate clearly prevailed were Spain, Mexico, Colombia, and the Philippines (Johnston 1865; Simmonds 1888).

Although mainly a coffee drinking nation, France overtook Spain as the world's largest cocoa importer. Rejecting both the heavy traditional southern beverage and the low-fat variety gaining ground in northern Europe, the French stuck to a little full-fat chocolate mass dissolved in hot milk. They were also unusual in the extent to which they ate chocolate, both assortments, small centres enrobed in chocolate, and plain dark chocolate with bread, a favourite with children at tea time (Debay 1864; Fonssagrives 1875–76; Lami 1885). That said, only around a million people, or 3 per cent of the population, regularly consumed chocolate in 1867, despite growing sales to people of more modest means (Cerfberr de Medelsheim 1867). Coffee's greater stimulating effect was highly prized, Michelet writing in 1863 that coffee was 'the sober drink, the mighty nourishment of the brain' (Schivelbusch 1992: 35). Coffee imports accounted for 79 million francs in 1866, compared to 12 million for cocoa (Larousse).

Britain's take-off came towards the end of the 1860s, stimulated by rising living standards, the temperance movement, and the pressing out of cocoa butter to make a more digestible drink. Consumption was further helped by revulsion against harmful substances in food, culminating in the Adulteration of Food Acts of 1872 and 1875. Advertising campaigns now stressed the purity and nutritional qualities of defatted chocolate powders (Williams 1931; Othick 1976; Fitzgerald 1995). The large Italian community in London further 'served to extend the sale and popularize the beverage' (Simmonds 1888: 211). Declining sales of coffee may have been a factor, although this was mainly to the advantage of tea (Bannister 1890).

Cocoa imports for consumption grew fast from a small base in the USA, possibly linked to the arrival of immigrants from south-western Europe. The temperance movement also developed strongly from 1841, despite some reverses (Barr 1998; Cook and Waller 1998). In any event, the value of chocolate output doubled between 1849 and 1869, although this paled into insignificance beside the phenomenal growth of coffee (Thurber 1881; Chiriboga 1980).

Spaniards remained faithful, poor, and conservative chocolate consumers, sticking to the full-fat beverage of earlier times (Pelletier 1861). The country had the highest consumption of chocolate per head of any country in Europe. It was even said that denying a prisoner his chocolate was one of the worst punishments in the country's gaols (Simmonds 1888). In contrast, coffee was marginal. Of the European nations, only tea-drinking and impoverished Russia consumed less coffee per head than Spain in 1879 (Thurber 1881).

Mexican incomes per head continued to fall until the end of the 1870s, due to domestic and foreign conflicts (Haber 1989; Bulmer-Thomas 1994). However, the Mexican passion for drinking chocolate was undimmed. Regularly offered to strangers as a mark of hospitality, it was found in the most humble and remote rural inns (Mangin 1860). Henri de Saussure was offered chocolate wherever he went in 1854–56. He noted that there was often nothing else for sale in country stores, and joked that revolutions in Mexico lasted as long as stocks of chocolate (Stols 1996). Consumption of coffee was estimated at only 500 tons of beans in 1888. Some Amerindians cultivated it for their own use, however, suggesting that coffee was spreading to those seen as most culturally attached to chocolate (United States 1888).

Central America, fast becoming dependent on coffee exports, was drinking larger amounts of coffee than before (Thurber 1881; United States 1888; Rubio Sánchez 1958). However, higher incomes may simultaneously have promoted chocolate consumption. Some Nicaraguan families had taken to drinking coffee at breakfast and after the evening meal, but still preferred chocolate with their midday meal, and last thing at night. Furthermore, cocoa beans continued to be widely used as currency for small transactions (Scherzer 1857).

Coffee was even more clearly ahead in the larger Antilles, but chocolate retained a clientele. The 1862 Cuban census listed 111 cafes and only 9 chocolate shops in Havana, and 11 cafes to 4 chocolate shops in Santiago, the second city, although chocolate beverages were routinely served in cafes (Pezuela 1863–66). Cuban 'rich people, or simply those comfortably off, partake of chocolate every day, and at almost any hour'. The wealthy preferred imports from Venezuela, leaving the local variety to poor people and slaves (Mangin 1860: 37). That said, Cuba imported nearly 4000 tons of coffee from Puerto Rico in 1877 (Thurber 1881). Puerto Rico itself continued to consume some cocoa, despite drinking much coffee (United States 1888). Haiti retained around 500 tons of its cocoa crop every year for its own needs, compared to around 7000 tons of coffee (Thurber 1881; Rouzier 1892–93). Drinking chocolate of a traditional kind was 'in general use' in the Dominican Republic in 1871, where coffee consumption may have been lower than elsewhere (Rodríguez Demorizi 1960).

Colombia was unusual in sticking to chocolate, whereas coffee was clearly in the lead in Venezuela, with some 9000 tons consumed in 1888 (United States 1888). Such was the level of demand in Colombia that traders found it more remunerative to sell cocoa beans in Antioquia and Bogotá than to ship them abroad in the 1870s (Schenck 1953). Colombians liked to partake of chocolate first thing in the morning and last thing at night, especially in cold mountain climates. Balls of an ounce of dried chocolate mass were boiled with water and whipped to a foam. Usually incorporating sugar, such balls were common items of retail trade, even eaten with dry bread by the poor (Holton 1967). To the north of Bogotá, in 1877–78, chocolate was 'the favourite drink of the natives, which even coffee cannot displace' (GCR 1879). For all that, coffee was increasing in popularity in Colombian towns in the 1870s (Beyer 1947).

The Andean lands to the south consumed little coffee, and it was China tea that was blamed for the collapse of maté imports (Thurber 1881; United States 1888; Linhares 1969). Chinese traders were reputedly making fortunes in Lima by selling tea, although Guayaquil chocolate and coffee were also on sale in Quito (Orton 1876). Chocolate was proclaimed to be one of the three 'articles of the first necessity and of daily consumption' near Cuzco around 1870, possibly a regional peculiarity (Marcoy 1875: 331).

The situation in the Amazon-Orinoco Basin was complicated by the relation between chocolate and *guaraná*. Cultivated especially downstream from the confluence with the Madeira River, *guaraná* was drunk as far as southern Venezuela and eastern Bolivia. It was said that 'the natives, particularly up the southern tributaries, are passionately fond of *guaraná*'. However, some chocolate was also made and drunk by Amazonian peoples (Orton 1876: 524–5). Moreover, it was common to add ground cocoa to the dried cylinders of *guaraná*, or to mix chocolate and *guaraná* to make a 'more exciting' beverage (Larousse). This was probably the origin of the confusing appellation 'Brazilian cocoa', sometimes given to *guaraná*. As for the fiercely independent people of eastern Ecuador, they drank *guayusa* rather than *guaraná* (Spruce 1908).

The inflow of European immigrants led to new patterns of chocolate consumption further south, highly influenced by France, and with Buenos Aires taking the lead in 'civilizing' Latin American taste (Rocchi 1997). However, maté remained the people's choice from Paraná to southern Chile (Linhares 1969). Moreover, Brazil was drinking much more of its coffee, retaining some 60,000 tons for internal consumption by the 1870s (Thurber 1881; Simmonds 1888).

The Philippines shared with Mexico and Colombia the distinction of remaining mainly a chocolate drinking country. The Spanish and Filipino elite drank sweetened chocolate, made with water, as other nations partook of coffee or tea. Poorer Filipinos mixed their chocolate with roasted rice, or incorporated roasted *pili* nuts (*Canarium commune*) (Jagor 1875). Monasteries and convents were particularly famous for their excellent chocolate (Loney 1964). As the economy boomed, strong demand drove up cocoa prices in Manila (González Fernández 1875; Clarence-Smith 1998). Chocolate also remained 'the national beverage in Sulu' in the 1870s, including lands claimed by the sultan in north-eastern Borneo (Burbidge 1989: 221). However, there were signs that coffee consumption was increasing in the archipelago, and the ever more numerous Chinese population propagated tea (González Fernández 1875; Sancianco y Goson 1881).

The rest of Asia probably consumed even less chocolate than before. To be sure, Europeans and Burgers (people of mixed race) consumed part of the cocoa crop of the Moluccas (Clarence-Smith 1998). However, 'natives' in the Moluccas grew coffee for their own use in 1870, and the government auctioned some 3000 tons of coffee in Java for local consumption in the same year (ANRI 1870a, 1870b).

The Great Chocolate Boom, the 1880s to 1914

The explosive growth of a mass market for chocolate from the 1880s transformed the world cocoa economy more radically than at any other time in history. The consumption of chocolate increased more rapidly than that of either coffee or tea in the West, and prices held up better (Othick 1976). World imports of cocoa beans grew ninefold between 1870 and 1897, whereas those of tea doubled, and those of coffee rose only by about half (Crawford de Roberts 1980). Progress was especially marked in north-western Europe and North America. Consumption of cocoa per head rose by a factor of nearly six in Britain between 1870 and 1910, while that of tea did not even double, and that of coffee actually fell by half (Othick 1976). Germans in 1907 accounted for more than five times the cocoa imports of 1886, although they still consumed six times more coffee than cocoa (*Gordian*). A similar pattern of rapid rise from a low base characterized the USA between 1898 and 1908, though coffee imports were worth $73 million in 1905–06, compared with $15 million for tea and only $9 million for cocoa (*Gordian*; *SYB* 1907).

The success of chocolate was partly based on product diversification. While remaining primarily a beverage prior to 1914, sales expanded as lighter and more digestible powders came onto the market, alkalized to improve taste, colour, and ease of mixing with liquids. At the same time, Swiss technical breakthroughs in the 1870s revolutionized the quality of eating chocolate and created milk chocolate (Fincke 1936; Othick 1976). Urbanization, falling transport costs, and increasing purchasing power created new opportunities. Chocolate, a classic 'impulse buy', was at the forefront of new techniques of advertising (Fraser 1981; Fitzgerald 1995). One drawback of eating chocolate, however, was marked seasonal peaks in sales, at Easter and Christmas (Schrover 1991). Moreover, Proust considered it too vulgar to serve at tea time (Bologne 1996).

The spread of chocolate consumption to the industrial working class was a crucial development (Othick 1976). A survey in 1891 showed no trace of chocolate in the spending patterns of Belgian workers, but in 1910 it had become an established part of expenditure. A Belgian male labourer needed to work 60 hours to buy a half kilo bar of chocolate in 1893, but only just over an hour in 1913 (Scholliers 1996). Consumption had penetrated to 'the lowest classes' in Germany by the 1900s. Shortly before 1914, it was even feared that a rise in the price of the weekly chocolate bar would provoke revolutionary violence on the streets (BAAP 1906, 1908).

Concerned at levels of alcohol abuse in expanding industrial towns, the apostles of temperance enjoyed considerable success from the 1870s, notably in Britain,

Germany, and the USA (Fraser 1981; Roberts 1984; Cook and Waller 1998). Chocolate, considered more wholesome than coffee or tea, benefited particularly from falling alcohol consumption, leading advertisers to emphasize its nutritional qualities (Norero 1910; Knapp 1920; Othick 1976). 'British workman cocoa houses' were even built (Diaper 1988). In Germany, chocolate was considered the best drink for labourers, as it had more protein and fat than coffee or tea, and a less negative effect on the nervous system and the heart (BAAP 1906).

Public bodies vigorously propagated chocolate. German troops were regularly issued with it from the 1880s, helping to democratize consumption (Stollwerck 1907; Klopstock 1937). The USA supplied tons of chocolate to its troops in the brief war with Spain in 1898, and the British did likewise during the Boer War of 1899–1902 (Leonard 1973). Even the Prussian Railway Administration encouraged workers to turn to hot chocolate (BAAP 1906). Britain's Royal Navy also did its bit, although it was peculiar in remaining doggedly attached to full-fat drinking chocolate of the traditional Latin American type (Knapp 1923).

The Western boom was not replicated in the rest of the world. An expanding Latin American middle class frowned upon beverages associated with 'primitive' Amerindians. Eager to copy European cultural models, they switched to coffee and tea (Fuentes 1992: 279). That said, more peaceful conditions and rising incomes stimulated consumption. 'Civilized' forms of drinking and eating chocolate also made some headway, especially in the temperate southern cone of South America, even though refrigeration was in its infancy.

Mesoamerican chocolate consumption benefited from a rough doubling of incomes per head in Mexico between 1877 and 1910 (Haber 1989). Cocoa butter was not pressed out from little cakes and balls, which were sold everywhere in Mexico as a convenience food. Rich and poor alike broke their fast with this traditional product, which became more a porridge than a beverage through the addition of pre-soaked maize, sugar, and milk (Hart 1911). The Tabascan poor made their chocolate with water rather than milk, which was reserved for sick children (Arias et al. 1987). Guatemalans added cinnamon to their chocolate, which was churned or beaten into a froth before drinking, and contrasted with the poor quality of locally brewed coffee (Brigham 1887). Nicaraguans were fond of *tiste*, cold water with ground cocoa, maize flour, and sugar, and sometimes cinnamon (Rouma 1948–49; Preuss 1987). In Soconusco, many rituals of the Mame Maya people continued to revolve around cocoa (Medina Hernández 1993). In addition, cocoa beans were still used for small monetary transactions in Guatemala and Nicaragua (Brigham 1887; Dunkerley 1988).

Colombia was the New World country most faithful to chocolate (Arosemena 1991). 'Cacao is one of the most important articles of production in Colombia. It is in daily use in every household, rich and poor, in every district of the country, to quite as great an extent as tea is in England' (PP 1888). There was hardly a family, rich or poor, that did not drink hot chocolate at least once a day in 1909. Three cups were often taken, especially in the mountains and Cauca, and chocolate was as important to Colombians as beer to Bavarians (*Gordian*). The millions of trees in the Cauca valley were entirely for local consumption in the early 1910s, and

Antioqueños were paying up to twice European prices (Patiño 1963). Servants insisted on receiving part of their wages in the form of a daily chocolate ration (*Gordian*). Nevertheless, competition from coffee was growing in 1909, and coffee figured alongside chocolate as one of the eight key items of internal trade in 1913 (Eder 1913; Beyer 1947).

Despite the undoubted progress of coffee in Venezuela, people continued to drink much chocolate. Cocoa butter was not pressed out, and the beverage seemed indigestible and unpalatable to Europeans (Preuss 1987). In the 1930s, Amerindians still drank *chorote cerrero*, an unsweetened chocolate beverage, while Mestizos drank their *chorote* with sugar and cinnamon, sometimes adding aniseed or pepper (Rouma 1948–49).

The non-Hispanic Caribbean community predominantly consumed coffee or tea, but chocolate had not disappeared. Landowners in the Cap-Haïtien region consumed cocoa from their estates in the traditional manner, crushed into a paste, mixed with syrup, and served on banana leaves (Aubin 1910). Old-fashioned *chocolate criollo* was also popular in the neighbouring Dominican Republic (Thomasset 1891; Deschamps 1907). Surinam consumed some 50 tons of cocoa in 1914, not bad for a country with only 90,000 inhabitants (Benjamins and Snelleman 1914–17). British Guiana's beans were almost entirely consumed on the spot, and local demand was reported to be 'steady' (Maclaren 1924). Tea was preferred by the better-off in Jamaica, however, and this may have been true elsewhere in the British Caribbean (United States 1888).

Cubans manufactured and consumed much chocolate, but it may have been in the form of confectionery, as coffee was so dominant as a beverage (*EUIEA*). In families and in eating houses of the 1900s, coffee with milk was usually taken first thing in the morning, and thick black coffee was drunk at frequent intervals during the day. Indeed, 'coffee in the coffee cup' became a standard promise of politicians (Wright 1910). While upper- and middle-class Cubans started their day with coffee, the poor downed a glass of rum (Clark 1899).

Unusually for this period, Peruvian chocolate consumption may have increased. Upwards of 2000 tons a year of cocoa beans were retained for consumption in 1905–06, much more than in the colonial period, when the figures also included Bolivia (Bonilla 1975–76; Contreras 1990). Moreover, the country had a particularly dynamic local chocolate industry (Rippy 1946). That said, coffee made inroads into Peru's chocolate market (Romero 1961; Bonilla 1975–76). Indeed, Marcoy was offered a cup of coffee after dinner on a cocoa estate in the Cuzco area (Marcoy 1875).

Chocolate consumption declined in Ecuador, and possibly in Bolivia. Ecuadorian consumption per head was allegedly one of the lowest in Latin America (Arosemena 1991). Cocoa beans retained for consumption averaged only 65 tons a year in 1905–08, about a tenth of the late colonial figure (Guislain and Vincart 1911; Laviana Cuetos 1987). Despite the continuing loyalty of some Bolivian consumers to 'mission chocolate', coffee had become Bolivia's usual highland breakfast beverage by the 1900s. Coffee was offered to visitors in the tropical lowlands, where people also made much use of *guaraná* from Brazil (Walle 1925).

Grated and added to cold water, *guaraná* was an 'excellent tonic', with a taste 'rather like maté' (Fawcett 1953: 71).

Brazilian consumption of chocolate remained low, although 'cacao soup' was a delicacy in the Amazon, served on the feast of Saint John and similar occasions. Coffee was king for everyday purposes in the Amazon, small strong demi-tasses being taken continuously throughout the day (Lange 1914). Nevertheless, the dominance of coffee in Brazil should not be exaggerated, *as guaraná* was grown more widely than ever (*EB* 1911; Fawcett 1953) . It was even called 'the most popular non-intoxicating beverage in Brazil' (Emerson 1908: II, 378). How much cocoa was added to *guaraná* remains a mystery, but the practice was still reported in the 1920s (*EB* 1929). Maté producers did not dare attack the country's coffee barons, but they fulminated against tea, 'entrenched in our customs' (Linhares 1969: 224).

Despite the passion for maté in the southern cone of South America, chocolate retained a niche. New European kinds of chocolate suited the cosmopolitan and wealthy coastal regions, and there was even demand for the old-fashioned variety, imported from Bolivia, in the northern provinces of Argentina (Malaurie and Gazzano 1888). This was not an insignificant market, as Argentina was at this time one of the richest countries in the world (Topik and Wells 1998).

The chocolate habit in the Philippines was only slowly undermined by coffee after the USA takeover in 1898. Early in the American period, it was noted that 'chocolate and not coffee . . . is the common morning drink among the better class of Filipinos' (Atkinson 1905: 176). Furthermore, 'in every household of any pre-tensions the afternoon caller is invited to " *merendar con chocolate*", which corresponds to the English "5 o'clock tea"' (Foreman 1906: 302). By 1920, coffee had become an alternative morning drink, although chocolate remained the usual afternoon beverage (Miller 1920).

Even though there was no breakthrough for chocolate elsewhere in colonial Africa and Asia, the often repeated dictum that Africa produced cocoa but consumed no chocolate is not entirely accurate. The Duala interpreter of the Germans drank chocolate in Cameroon in 1884, a habit probably acquired from his Baptist mentors (Wirz 1972). As Uganda's cocoa before 1914 was 'consumed locally', a small market of this kind existed more widely (Great Britain 1920). Catholic missionaries grew cocoa for their own use in south-western India, and sold some to local Europeans (Watt 1889–96). Station buffets along the Javanese rail network in the 1890s stocked chocolate, and chocolate desserts were popular with Westerners, even if coffee was the preferred drink (Scidmore 1984).

A little chocolate was imported into the lands of the eastern Mediterranean by the turn of the century, largely for a European clientele (*Gordian*). Jewish families were fond of chocolate cakes, made with almonds for Passover, but the habit did not spread to the Muslim population (Claudia Roden, email 24 June 1999). Salep was sold as a warming drink by the street vendors of Istanbul in the cold winter months, and Greeks took it, sweetened with honey, as an early morning beverage (Grieve 1984).

Conclusion

Economic historians are notoriously suspicious of cultural explanations. They breathe a sigh of relief when the popularity of a commodity can be explained by something quantifiable, especially comparative fiscal burdens (Smith 1996). Technical changes in methods of production are another reassuring standby (Othick 1976). While there can be no doubt that both industrialization and taxation played a part in the consumption of chocolate, it is surely dangerous to reduce such a complex phenomenon to solidly material and satisfyingly calculable causes.

Debate still rages over whether chocolate is physiologically addictive, and, if so, whether theobromine is the cause, or other mood-enhancing substances. It may also be that a psychological dependence turns people into 'chocoholics'. In any event, it is clear that chocolate has long been seen as having an effect on the mind, and more research is needed on changing perceptions of this impact. Addiction, or at least a quest for stimulation, must have affected the elasticity of demand for chocolate, however difficult it may be to quantify this for the period before 1914.

Closely related are the ways in which chocolate was perceived in different cultures, and how they changed over time. The obsessions of upper-class Westerners have long been pored over, and social historians have begun to explore the changing tastes of the emerging industrial proletariat. However, we know much less about poor people in the tropics. Chocolate held the greatest wealth of ritual significance for Mesoamerican Amerindians, and yet it is surprisingly hard to trace how this changed in the liberal era, and how coffee found a place for itself beside chocolate in the diet of these societies.

References

Archival documents

ANRI (Arsip Nasional Republik Indonesia, Jakarta, Indonesia)
- 1870a: Residency Archives, 52, 60, Report for the outer possessions.
- 1870b: Residency Archives, 52, 1659, Java cultivation report.
BAAP (Bundesarchiv, Abteilung Potsdam, Germany) [Transferred to Berlin, Lichterfelde].
- 1906: Reichskolonialamt, 8003, 'Kakao und die deutschen Kolonien'.
- 1908: Reichskolonialamt, 8003, Redaktion des Gordians, 29 January.
GCR (German Consular Reports, Bucaramanga, Colombia—supplied courtesy of T. Fischer).
- 1879: Report for 1879.

Series and encyclopaedias

EB: *Encyclopaedia Britannica*. London and Chicago.
EUIEA: *Enciclopedia universal ilustrada Europeo-Americana*. Barcelona: Espasa.
Gordian: *Der Gordian, Zeitschrift für die Kakao- Schokoladen- und Zuckerwarenindustrie*. Hamburg: Der Gordian.
Larousse: *Grand dictionnaire universel du XIXe siècle*. Paris: Librairie Larousse et Boyer.

MGCP: *Mappas geraes do commercio de Portugal com as suas possessões ultramarinas e as nações estrangeiras*. Lisbon: Direcção Geral das Alfândegas [title varied].
MP: *Mercurio peruano*. Lima: Biblioteca Nacional del Perú [facsimile reprint].
PP: *Parliamentary papers* (House of Commons Sessional Papers). London.
SYB: *Statesman's Year-Book*. London: Macmillan.

Internet sources

'Carob': <http://ds.dial.pipex.com/town/place/vu87/carob.shtml>.
'Maté': 'Maté (Ilex paraguariensis)', by G. C. Giberti
<http://www.hort.purdue.edu/newcrop/1492/mate.html>.

Published items and theses

Anna, T. E. 1979. *The Fall of the Royal Government in Peru*. Lincoln: University of Nebraska Press.
Anon. 1849. 'Laboean, Serawak, de Noord-Oostkust van Borneo en de Sultan van Soeloe'. *Tijdschrift voor Nederlandsch Indië*: pp. 66–83, 97–111, 237–42.
Anon. 1890. *Universal-Lexicon der Kochkunst*. Leipzig: J. J. Weber.
Arcila Farías, E. 1950. *Comercio entre Venezuela y México en los siglos XVII y XVIII*. Mexico City: El Colégio de México.
Arias, M. E., A. Lau, and X. Sepúlveda. 1987. *Tabasco: una historia compartida*. Villahermosa: Instituto Móra.
Arosemena, G. 1991. *El fruto de los dioses: el cacao en Ecuador, desde la colonia hasta el ocaso de su industria, 1600–1983*. Guayaquil: Editorial Graba.
Atkinson, F. W. 1905. *The Philippine Islands*. Boston: Ginn & Co.
Aubin, E. 1910. *En Haïti: planteurs d'autrefois, nègres d'aujourd'hui*. Paris: Armand Colin.
Bannister, R. 1890. 'Sugar, Coffee, Tea and Cocoa, their Origin, Preparation and Uses; Lecture IV'. *Journal of the Society of Arts* 7: 1038–52.
Barr, A. 1998. *Drink: A Social History*. London: Pimlico.
Barreta, C. J. 1841. *Manuel complet, théorique et pratique, du chocolatier*. Paris: Mathias.
Bauer, P. T. 1963. *West African Trade: A Study of Competition, Oligopoly and Monopoly in a Changing Economy*. London: Routledge & Kegan Paul.
Benjamins, H., and J. F. Snelleman (eds.). 1914–17. 'Cacao'. In *Encyclopaedie van Nederlandsch West-Indië*, pp. 185–94. The Hague and Leiden: M. Nijhoff and E. J. Brill.
Bernard, B. 1996. 'Est-il moral de boire du chocolat?'. In *Chocolat, de la boisson élitaire au bâton populaire*, ed. E. Collet, pp. 83–90. Brussels: CGER.
Beyer, R. C. 1947. 'The Colombian Coffee Industry: Origins and Major Trends, 1740–1940'. PhD thesis, University of Minnesota.
Bizière, J.-M. 1979. 'Hot Beverages and the Enterprising Spirit in Eighteenth-Century Europe'. *Journal of Psychohistory* 7 (2): 135–45.
Blanchard, I. 1989. *Russia's Age of Silver, Precious Metal Production and Economic Growth in the Eighteenth Century*. London: Routledge.
Bologne, J.-C. 1996. 'Le chocolat et la littérature française et européenne des XIXe et XXe siècles'. In *Chocolat, de la boisson élitaire au bâton populaire*, ed. E. Collet, pp. 223–36. Brussels: CGER.
Bonilla, H. (ed.). 1975–76. *Gran Bretaña y el Perú: informes de los cónsules británicos*. Lima: Instituto de Estudios Peruanos.

63

Brading, D. A. 1971. *Miners and Merchants in Bourbon Mexico, 1763–1810*. Cambridge: Cambridge University Press.

Brigham, W. T. 1887. *Guatemala, the Land of the Quetzal*. New York: Charles Scribner's Sons.

Brillat-Savarin, J. A. n.d. *La physiologie du goût*, vol. 1. Paris: Henri Piazza.

Brungardt, M. P. 1974. 'Tithe Production and Patterns of Economic Change in Central Colombia, 1764–1833'. PhD thesis, University of Texas at Austin.

Buckley, C. B. 1965. *An Anecdotal History of Singapore in Old Times*. Kuala Lumpur: University of Malaya Press.

Bullock, W. 1824. *Six Months Residence and Travel in Mexico*. London: John Murray.

Bulmer-Thomas, V. 1994. *The Economic History of Latin America since Independence*. Cambridge: Cambridge University Press.

Burbidge, F. W. 1989. *The Gardens of the Sun, a Naturalist's Journal of Borneo and the Sulu Archipelago*. Singapore: Oxford University Press.

Burkill, I. H. 1966. *A Dictionary of the Economic Products of the Malay Peninsula*. Kuala Lumpur: Ministry of Agriculture and Co-operatives.

Burnett, J. 1999. *Liquid Pleasures, a Social History of Drinks in Modern Britain*. London: Routledge.

Cerfberr de Medelsheim. A. 1867. *Le cacao et le chocolat, considérés aux points de vue hygiénique, agricole et commercial*. Paris: Société des Livres Utiles.

Chiriboga, M. 1980. *Jornaleros y gran propietarios en 135 años de exportación cacaotera, 1790–1925*. Quito: Consejo Provincial de Pichincha.

Clarence-Smith, W. G. 1998. 'The Rise and Fall of Maluku Cocoa Production in the Nineteenth Century: Lessons for the Present'. In *Old World Places, New World Problems: Exploring Resource Management Issues in Eastern Indonesia*, ed. S. Pannell and F. von Benda-Beckmann, pp. 113–42. Canberra: Centre for Resource and Environmental Studies.

Clark, W. J. 1899. *Commercial Cuba: A Book for the Businessman*. London: Chapman & Hall.

Coe, S. D. and M. D. Coe. 1996. *The True History of Chocolate*. London: Thames & Hudson.

Collet, E. (ed.). 1996. *Chocolat, de la boisson élitaire au bâton populaire*. Brussels: CGER.

Comyn, T. de. 1969. *State of the Philippines in 1810*. Manila: Filipiniana Book Guild.

Contreras, C. 1990. *El sector exportador de una economía colonial: la costa del Ecuador, 1760–1830*. Quito: Colección Tesis Historia.

Cook C. and D. Waller. 1998. *The Longman Handbook of Modern American History, 1763–1996*. Harlow: Addison Wesley Longman.

Crawford de Roberts, L. 1980. *El Ecuador en la época cacaotera: respuestas locales al auge y colapso en el ciclo monoexportador*. Quito: Editorial Universitaria.

Debay, A. 1864. *Les influences du chocolat, du thé et du café sur l'économie humaine*. Paris: E. Dentu.

Deeds, S. M. 1995. 'Indigenous Responses to Mission Settlement in Nueva Vizcaya'. In *The New Latin American Mission History*, ed. E. Langer and R. H. Jackson. Lincoln: University of Nebraska Press.

Deschamps, E. 1907. *La República Dominicana: directorio y guía general*. Santiago de los Caballeros: J. Cunill.

Descola, J. 1968. *Daily Life in Colonial Peru, 1710–1820*. London: Allen & Unwin.

Diaper, S. 1988. 'J. S. Fry and Sons, Growth and Decline in the Chocolate Industry, 1753–1918'. In *Studies in the Business History of Bristol*, ed. C. Harvey and J. Press, pp. 33–54. Bristol: Bristol Academic Press.

Drummond, J. C. and A. Wilbraham. 1939. *The Englishman's Food: A History of Five Centuries of the English Diet*. London: Jonathan Cape.

Dunkerley, J. 1988. *Power in the Isthmus: A Political History of Modern Central America*. London: Verso.

Eder, F. J. 1985. *Breve descripción de las reducciones Mojos, c. 1772*. Cochabamba: Historia Boliviana.

Eder, P. J. 1913. *Colombia*. London: Fisher Unwin.

Elson, R. 1994. *Village Java under the Cultivation System, 1830–1870*. Sydney: Allen & Unwin.

Emerson, E. R. 1908. *Beverages Past and Present: An Historical Sketch of their Production, together with a Study of the Customs Connected with their Use*. New York: G. P. Putnam's Sons.

Fawcett, P. H. 1953. *Exploration Fawcett*. London: Hutchinson.

Fernández Molina, J. A. 1992. 'Colouring the world in Blue: The Indigo Boom and the Central American Market, 1750–1810'. PhD thesis, University of Texas at Austin.

Fincke, H. 1936. *Handbuch der Kakaoerzeugnisse*. Berlin: Julius Springer.

Fitchett, L. S. 1906. *Beverages and Sauces of Colonial Virginia, 1607–1907*. New York: Neale Publishing Co.

Fitzgerald, R. 1995. *Rowntree and the Marketing Revolution, 1862–1969*. Cambridge: Cambridge University Press.

Florescano, E. and I. Gil Sánchez (eds.). 1976. *Descripciones económicas regionales de Nueva España, provincias del centro, sudeste y sur, 1766–1827*. Mexico City: INAH.

Fonssagrives. 1875–76. 'Cacao', and 'Chocolat'. In *Dictionnaire encyclopédique des sciences médicales*, vol. XI, pp. 359–64, 724–36. Paris: G. Masson & P. Asselin.

Foreman, J. 1906. *The Philippine Islands*. Shanghai: Kelly & Walsh.

Fraser, W. H. 1981. *The Coming of the Mass Market, 1850–1914*. London: Macmillan.

Fuentes, C. 1992. *The Buried Mirror: Reflections on Spain and the New World*. London: Houghton Mifflin.

Garavaglia. J. C. 1983. *Mercado interno y economía colonial*. Mexico City: Grijalbo.

Gardella, R. 1994. *Harvesting Mountains, Fujian and the China Tea Trade, 1757–1937*. Berkeley: University of California Press.

Gil-Bermejo García, J. 1970. *Panorama histórico de la agricultura en Puerto Rico*. Seville: Escuela de Estudios Hispano-Americanos.

González Fernández, R. 1875. *Manual del viajero en Filipinas*. Manila: Tip. de Santo Tomás.

Gosselman, C. A. 1962. *Informes sobre los estados sudamericanos en los años de 1837 y 1838*. Stockholm: Ibero-Amerikanska Biblioteket och Institutet.

Great Britain. 1920. *A Handbook of the Uganda Protectorate*. London: Admiralty, Naval Intelligence Division.

Grieve, M. 1984. *A Modern Herbal*. Harmondsworth: Penguin (1st edn 1931).

Guislain, L. and L. Vincart. 1911. 'La culture du cacaoyer au Vénézuéla et à l'Equateur'. *L'Agronomie Tropicale* 3 (4): 65–73.

Haarer, A. E. 1956. *Modern Coffee Production*. London: L. Hill.

Haber, S. H. 1989. *Industry and Underdevelopment, the Industrialization of Mexico, 1890–1940*. Stanford: Stanford University Press.

Hart, J. H. 1911. *Cacao, a Manual on the Cultivation and Curing of Cacao*. London: Duckworth & Co.

Harwich, N. 1992. *Histoire du chocolat*. Paris: Éditions Desjonquères.

Harwich Vallenilla, N. 1996. 'The Eastern Venezuela Pioneer Front, 1830s–1930s: The Role of the Corsican Trade Network'. In *Cocoa Pioneer Fronts since 1800, the Role of Smallholders, Planters and Merchants*, ed. W. G. Clarence-Smith, pp. 23–44. London: Macmillan.

Hewett, C. 1862. *Chocolate and Cocoa: Its Growth and Culture, Manufacture, and Modes of Preparation for the Table*. London: Simpkin, Marshall & Co.

Hogendorp, C. S. W. de. 1830. *Coup d'oeil sur l'île de Java et les autres possessions néerlandaises dans l'archipel des Indes*. Brussels: C. J. de Mat.

Holton, I. F. 1967. *New Granada: Twenty Months in the Andes*, abridged edn. Carbondale: Southern Illinois University Press.

Humboldt, A. von. 1811. *Essai politique sur le royaume de la Nouvelle Espagne*. Paris: F. Schoell.

Humboldt, A. von. 1852. *Personal Narrative of Travels to the Equinoctial Regions of America during the Years 1799 to 1804*. London: George Routledge & Sons.

Humboldt, A. von. 1941. *Viaje a las regiones equinocciales del nuevo continente*. Caracas: Ministerio de Educación.

Jagor, F. 1875. *Travels in the Philippines*. London: Chapman & Hall.

Johnston, J. 1865. *The Chemistry of Common Life*. London: W. Blackwood.

Kany, C. E. 1932. *Life and Manners in Madrid, 1750–1800*. Berkeley: University of California Press.

Kidder, D. P. 1845. *Sketches of Residence and Travel in Brazil*. London: Wiley & Putnam.

King, A. R. 1974. *Coban and the Verapaz: History and Cultural Process in Northern Guatemala*. New Orleans: Tulane University.

Klopstock, F. 1937. *Kakao: Wandlungen in der Erzeugung und der Verwendung des Kakaos nach dem Weltkrieg*. Leipzig: Bibliographisches Institut.

Knapp, A. W. 1920. *Cocoa and Chocolate, their History from Plantation to Consumer*. London: Chapman & Hall.

Knapp, A. W. 1923. *The Cocoa and Chocolate Industry, the Tree, the Bean, the Beverage*. London: Pitman.

Lambert Ortiz, E. 1968. *The Complete Book of Mexican Cooking*. New York: Bantam Books.

Lami, E. A. 1885. *Dictionnaire encyclopédique et biographique de l'industrie et des arts industriels*, vols 2 and 3. Paris: no publisher.

Lange, A. 1914. *The Lower Amazon*. New York: G. P. Putnam's Sons.

Laviana Cuetos, M. L. 1987. *Guayaquil en el siglo XVIII: recursos naturales y desarollo económico*. Seville: Escuela de Estudios Hispano-Americanos.

Léon, H. 1893. *Histoire des Juifs de Bayonne*. Paris: A. Durlacher.

León Borja, D. and A. Szászdi Nagy. 1964. 'El comercio del cacao de Guayaquil'. *Revista de Historia de América* 57–8: 1–50.

Leonard, P. G. 1973. 'A Drincke called Chocolate'. *Mankind Magazine* 4 (3): 44–51.

Libert, M. 1996. 'La consommation du chocolat dans les Pays-Bas Autrichiens'. In *Chocolat, de la boisson élitaire au bâton populaire*, ed. E. Collet, pp. 75–80. Brussels: CGER.

Linhares, T. 1969. *Historia econômica do mate*. Rio de Janeiro: Livraria José Olympio.

Loney, N. 1964. *A Britisher in the Philippines*. Manila: National Library.

Lovejoy, P. 1995. 'Kola Nuts, the "Coffee" of the Central Sudan'. In *Consuming Habits: Drugs in History and Anthropology*, ed. J. Goodman, P. Lovejoy, and A. Sherratt, pp. 103–25. London: Routledge.

McFarlane, A. 1993. *Colombia before Independence: Economy, Society and Politics under Bourbon Rule*. Cambridge: Cambridge University Press.

McGreevey, W. P. 1971. *An Economic History of Colombia, 1845–1930*. Cambridge: Cambridge University Press.

Maclaren, W. A. 1924. *Rubber, Tea and Cacao, with Special Sections on Coffee, Spices and Tobacco*. London: Benn.

MacLeod, M. 1973. *Spanish Central America: A Socioeconomic History, 1520–1720*. Berkeley: University of California Press.

MacMillan, H. F. 1925. *Tropical Gardening and Planting, with Special Reference to Ceylon*. Colombo: Times of Ceylon.

Malaurie, A. and J. M. Gazzano. 1888. *La industria argentina y la exposición del Paraná*. Buenos Aires: J. M. Gazzano e Cía.

Mallat, J. 1983. *The Philippines: History, Geography, Customs, Agriculture, Industry and Commerce of the Spanish Colonies in Oceania*. Manila: National Historical Institute.

Mangin, A. 1860. *Le cacao et le chocolat, considérés aux points de vue botanique, chimique, physiologique, agricole, commercial, industriel et économique*. Paris: Guillaumin et Cie.

Marcoy, P. 1875. *Travels in South America: From the Pacific Ocean to the Atlantic Ocean*. London: Blackie & Son.

Marrero, L. 1972–89. *Cuba: economía y sociedad*. Madrid: Playor.

Mathew, W. M. 1981. *The House of Gibbs and the Peruvian Guano Monopoly*. London: Royal Historical Society.

Medina Hernández, A. 1993. 'Los Mames'. In *La población indígena de Chiapas*, ed. Víctor M. Esponda Jimeno, pp. 399–482. Tuxtla Guttiérez: Gobierno del Estado de Chiapas.

Middleton. 1871. 'Report by Mr. Consul-General Middleton upon the Production of Cocoa and Coffee in Venezuela'. *Parliamentary Papers 1871*, House of Commons, LXV, *c.* 343.

Milburn, W. 1825. *Oriental Commerce*. London: Kingsbury, Parbury & Allen.

Miller, H. H. 1920. *Economic Conditions in the Philippines*. Boston: Ginn & Co.

Mollien, G. T. 1824. *Travels in the Republic of Colombia in the Years 1822 and 1823*. London: C. Knight.

Moor, J. H. (ed.) 1968. *Notices of the Indian Archipelago and Adjacent Countries*. London: Cass.

Newman, R. 1995. 'Opium Smoking in Late Imperial China: A Reconsideration'. *Modern Asian Studies* 29 (4): 765–94.

Newson, L. A. 1987. *Indian Survival in Colonial Nicaragua*. Norman: University of Oklahoma Press.

Norero, A. 1910. *El cacao y su cultivo: ensayo sobre la agricultura del Ecuador*. Madrid: Librería General de Victoriano Suárez.

Olivier, J. 1834–37. *Reizen in den Molukschen archipel naar Makassar en z., in het gevolg van den Gouverneur-Generaal van Nederlandsch-Indië*. Amsterdam: G. J. A. Beijerinck.

Omboni, T. 1846. *Viaggi nell'Africa occidentale*. Milan: Civelli.

Orton, J. 1876. *The Andes and the Amazon*. New York: Harper & Bros.

Othick, J. 1976. 'The Cocoa and Chocolate Industry in the Nineteenth Century'. In *The Making of the Modern British Diet*, ed. D. Oddy and D. Miller, pp. 77–90. London: Croom Helm.

Parrón Salas, C. 1995. *De las reformas borbónicas a la República: el Consulado y el comercio marítimo de Lima, 1778–1821*. San Javier (Murcia): Academia General del Aire.

Patiño, V. M. 1963. *Plantas cultivadas y animales domesticos en America Equinoccial, Tomo I, frutales*. Cali: Imprenta Departamental.

Pelletier, E. and A. 1861. *Le thé et le chocolat dans l'alimentation publique*. Paris: Compagnie Française des Chocolats et des Thés.

Pérez de la Riva, F. 1944. *El café, historia de su cultivo y explotación en Cuba*. Havana: J. Montero.

Peterson, J. 1969. *Province of Freedom: A History of Sierra Leone, 1787–1870*. London: Faber and Faber.

Pezuela, J. de la. 1863–66. *Diccionario geográfico, estadístico, histórico de la isla de Cuba*. Madrid: Mellado.

Phillips, J. D. 1947. *Salem and the Indies*. Boston: Houghton Mifflin Co.

Prados de la Escosura, L. 1982. 'Comercio exterior y cambio económico en España, 1792–1849'. In *La economia española al final del antiguo régimen, III, comercio y colonias*, ed. Josep Fontana, pp. 173–249. Madrid: Alianza.

Preuss, P. 1987. *Cocoa, Its Cultivation and Preparation*. Brussels: International Office of Cocoa and Chocolate.

Reid, A. 1988. *Southeast Asia in the Age of Commerce, 1450–1680*, vol. 1: *The Lands Below the Winds*. New Haven: Yale University Press.

Rippy, J. F. 1946. 'The Dawn of Manufacturing in Peru'. *Pacific Historical Review* 15 (2): 147–57.

Roberts, J. S. 1984. *Drink, Temperance and the Working Class in Nineteenth-Century Germany*. Boston: Allen & Unwin.

Rocchi, F. 1997. 'Building a Nation, Building a Market: Industrial Growth and the Domestic Economy in Turn-of-the-Century Argentina'. PhD diss., University of California, Santa Barbara.

Rodríguez Demorizi, E. (ed.) 1960. *Informe de la comisión de investigación de los E. U. A. en Santo Domingo en 1871*. Ciudad Trujillo: Editora Montalvo.

Romero, E. 1961. *Geografía económica del Perú*. Lima: Universidad Nacional Mayor de San Marcos.

Romero Vargas, G. J. 1976. 'Les structures sociales du Nicaragua au XVIIIème siècle'. PhD thesis, Université de Paris-IV.

Rouma, G. 1948–49. *L'Amérique latine*. Brussels: La Renaissance du Livre.

Rouzier, S. 1892–93. *Dictionnaire géographique et administratif universel d'Haïti*. Paris: C. Blot.

Rubio Sánchez, M. 1958. 'El cacao'. *Anales de la Sociedad de Geografía e Historia de Guatemala* 31: 81–129.

Ruiz Abreu, C. 1989. *Comercio y milicias de Tabasco en la colonia*. Villahermosa: Gobierno del Estado de Tabasco.

Saenz Maroto, A. 1970. *Historia agrícola de Costa Rica*. [San José]: Universidad de Costa Rica.

Sagra, R. de la. 1963. *Cuba 1860, selección de artículos sobre agricultura cubana*. Havana: Edit. Nacional de Cuba.

Sancianco y Goson, G. 1881. *El progreso de Filipinas*. Madrid: Va. de J. M. Pérez.

Sandgruber, R. 1986. *Bittersüsse Genüsse: Kulturgeschichte der Genussmittel*. Vienna: H. Böhlaus.

Schenck, F. von. 1953. *Viajes por Antioquia en el año de 1880*. Bogotá: Banco de la República.

Scherzer, C. 1857. *Travels in the Free States of Central America: Nicaragua, Honduras and San Salvador*. London: Longman, Brown, Green, Longmans & Roberts.

Schivelbusch, W. 1992. *Tastes of Paradise, a Social History of Spices, Stimulants and Intoxicants*. New York: Pantheon Books.

Schneider, J. 1981. *Frankreich und die Unabhängigkeit Spanisch-Amerikas: zum französischen Handel mit den entstehenden Nationalstaaten, 1810–1850*. Stuttgart: Klett-Cotta.

Schneider, J. 1998. 'Die neuen Getränke: Schokolade, Kaffee und Tee, 16. –18. Jahrhundert'. In *Prodotti e tecniche d'oltremare nelle economie europee, secc., XIII–XVIII*, ed. S. Cavaciocchi, pp. 541–90. Florence: F. Datini.

Scholliers, P. 1996. 'De la boisson élitaire à la barre populaire: la production et la consommation du chocolat en Belgique aux XIXe et XXe siècles'. In *Chocolat, de la boisson élitaire au bâton populaire*, ed. E. Collet, pp. 161–84. Brussels: CGER.

Schrover, M. 1991. *Het vette, het zoete en het wederzijdse profijt: arbeidsverhoudingen in de margarine-industrie en in de cacao- en chocolade-industrie in Nederland, 1870–1960*. Hilversum: Verloren.

Scidmore, E. R. 1984. *Java, the Garden of the East*. Singapore: Oxford University Press.

Scott, J. M. 1964. *The Tea Story*. London: Heinemann.

Sevilla Soler, M. R. 1980. *Santo Domingo, tierra de frontera, 1750–1800*. Seville: Escuela de Estudios Hispano-Americanos.

Sherratt, A. 1995. 'Introduction, Peculiar Substances'. In *Consuming Habits, Drugs in History and Anthropology*, ed. J. Goodman, P. Lovejoy, and A. Sherratt, pp. 1–10. London: Routledge.

Simmonds, P. L. 1888. *The Popular Beverages of Various Countries*. London: J. G. Smith.

Slijper, H. J. 1927. *Technologie en warenkennis, tweede deel, organische producten en eenige ook voor Ned.-Indië belangrijke cultures*. Purmerend: J. Muusses.

Smith, S. D. 1996. 'Accounting for Taste: British Coffee Consumption in Historical Perspective'. *Journal of Interdisciplinary History* 27 (2): 183–214.

Solórzano, V. 1963. *Evolución económica de Guatemala*. Guatemala City: J. de Pineda Ibarra.

Spix, J. B. and C. F. P. von Martius. 1976. *Viagem pelo Brasil, 1817–1820*. Rio de Janeiro: Melhoramentos.

Spruce, R. 1908. *Notes of a Botanist on the Amazon and Andes*. London: Macmillan.

Stephens, J. L. 1993. *Incidents of Travel in Central America, Chiapas and Yucatán*, abridged edn. Washington: Smithsonian Institution Press.

Stollwerck, W. 1907. *Der Kakao und die Schokoladenindustrie, eine wirtschafts-statistische Untersuchung*. Jena: Fischer.

Stols, E. 1996. 'Le cacao: le sang voluptueux du nouveau monde'. In *Chocolat, de la boisson élitaire au bâton populaire*, ed. E. Collet, pp. 37–56. Brussels: CGER.

Swaelen, L. 1996. 'La Flandre et le chocolat'. In *Chocolat, de la boisson élitaire au bâton populaire*, ed. E. Collet, pp. 57–74. Brussels: CGER.

Terry, A. R. 1834. *Travels in the Equatorial Regions of South America in 1832*. Hartford: Cooke & Co.

Thomasset, H. 1891. 'Agricultura, industria y obras públicas: informe dirijido al Sr. Ministro de Fomento y Obras Públicas'. *Gaceta Oficial de Santo Domingo* 857, 24 January.

Thurber, F. B. 1881. *Coffee, from Plantation to Cup, a Brief History of Coffee Production and Consumption*. New York: American Grocer Publishing Association.

Topik, S. and A. Wells (eds.). 1998. *The Second Conquest of Latin America, Coffee, Henequen and Oil during the Export Boom, 1850–1930*. Austin: University of Texas Press.

Toscano, H. (ed.). 1960. *El Ecuador visto por los extranjeros: viajeros de los siglos XVIII y XIX*. Puebla: J. M. Cajica Jr.

Twinam, A. 1982. *Miners, Merchants and Farmers in Colonial Colombia*. Austin: University of Texas Press.

United States. 1888. *Cultivation of, and Trade in, Coffee, in Central and South America*, Washington, 50th Congress, House of Representatives, 1st session, Consular Reports on Commerce etc., no. 98.

Vaussard, M. 1962. *Daily Life in Eighteenth-Century Italy*. London: Allen & Unwin.

Vernon, A. 1958. *A Quaker Business Man, the Life of Joseph Rowntree, 1836–1925*. London: Allen & Unwin.

Wagner, G. 1987. *The Chocolate Conscience*. London: Chatto & Windus.

Waldeck, F. de. 1838. *Voyage pittoresque et archéologique dans la province d'Yucatan, Amérique centrale, pendant les années 1834 et 1836*. Paris: Bellizard Dufour.

Walker, A. 1822. *Colombia, being a Geographical, Statistical, Agricultural, Commercial and Political Account of that Country*. London: Baldwin, Cradock & Joy.

Walle, P. 1925. *Bolivia, Its People and Its Resources, Its Railways, Mines and Rubber-Forests*. London: Fisher Unwin.

Walvin, J. 1997. *Fruits of Empire: Exotic Produce and British Taste, 1660–1800*. Basingstoke: Macmillan.

Ward, H. J. 1828. *Mexico in 1827*. London: Henry Colburn.

Watt, G. 1889–96. *A Dictionary of the Economic Products of India*. London: Department of Revenue and Agriculture.

Williams, I. A. 1931. *The Firm of Cadbury, 1831–1931*. London: Constable.

Wirz, A. 1972. *Vom Sklavenhandel zum Kolonialen Handel: Wirtschaftsräume und Wirtschaftsformen in Kamerun vor 1914*. Zürich: Atlantis.

Wright, I. A. 1910. *Cuba*. New York: Macmillan.

Young, A. M. 1994. *The Chocolate Tree, a Natural History of Cocoa*. Washington: Smithsonian Institute Press.

4

From Small Chocolatiers to Multinationals to Sustainable Sourcing

A Historical Review of the Swiss Chocolate Industry

Ingrid Fromm

Introduction

The food industry is currently focusing on increasing transparency along the entire chain, from production to consumption. Consumers are demanding that the food they put on their tables is sustainably produced, sourced, and consumed. Having information about the origin of products will, in the future, become the norm rather than the exception. Transparency in the food chain has many dimensions and although consumers might be motivated to buy products that are sustainably produced, these decisions can potentially have a positive impact for farmers—be it within national boundaries or abroad—as well as for the environment. One example is represented by the chocolate industry. Chocolate is produced and consumed across multiple boarders. Having a transparent chain is a tremendous challenge. Cocoa beans come mostly from developing countries, where small-scale farmers are responsible for most of the global production. However, it is big players who dominate this industry and they are also the ones who are transforming it.

Switzerland has long been known as a leader in chocolate production. Swiss chocolates are recognized around the world as high-quality products and the demand for them is growing. The Swiss chocolate industry reported an increase in sales of almost 4 per cent in 2013. Switzerland exports over 60 per cent of the chocolate it produces. The foreign sales of Swiss chocolate remained strong, with an increase of 5.6 per cent. Although the main export market for Swiss chocolate is the European Union (EU), Switzerland exports chocolate to 150 countries. According to the latest report by Chocosuisse (2014), Germany was the largest market for Swiss chocolate (24.7 per cent share of exports), followed by the UK (12.8 per cent), France (8 per cent), and Canada (6.3 per cent). In 2013, an increase in export sales was seen outside the EU, particularly in China, the Russian Federation, Saudi

Arabia, Turkey, and the United Arab Emirates. In terms of global sales, two Swiss companies are among the top ten global confectionery companies manufacturing chocolate: Nestlé, which reported sales of close to US$12 billion and Lindt & Sprüngli, with sales of US$3 billion in 2013. These companies, global players in the industry themselves, are competing in an industry which is expected to expand in the next decade. As the chocolate market in Asia, and particularly in China, starts acquiring a taste for chocolate, there is prospect of growth.

However, the expansion of the chocolate industry already has great challenges ahead, despite the prospect of growth. On the supply side, while the industry needs to expand, the cocoa sector is frail, afflicted by poor agronomic practices (such as poor soil management and the use (often no use) of farm inputs) and by the high incidence of pest and diseases. Particularly in West Africa, the ageing plantations and lack of access to improved planting materials (i.e. hybrids) pose a great risk for farmers who already struggle to make an income from cocoa farming. A basic infrastructure in the farm, which would allow farmers to properly dry and ferment the cocoa beans and maintain the bean quality is often lacking. Furthermore, reaching markets can be a daunting challenge for farmers, especially when the only access is through difficult roads in remote areas.

Cocoa production takes place mostly in small farms in developing countries and more than half of the world production of cocoa comes from two countries: Ivory Coast and Ghana (KPMG 2012). The incidence of poverty in the cocoa sector worldwide is high. The market information systems often do not favour the farmer. Farm-gate prices are low in comparison to the world market prices, impeding farmers from reaching a break-even point. The prospects of growth in the sector barely reach the farmers, who are as vulnerable as ever at the other end of the chain. In many countries they have little access to credit. If they do not belong to some form of farmers' association or cooperative, the chances of accessing credit are low. Moreover, climate change, problems associated with monoculture and lack of diversification, eroded soils, deforestation, and water stress also contribute to putting the already vulnerable cocoa farmers at risk. For the sector to grow sustainably, much change is needed. The good news is that the big industry players are increasingly working towards improving the cocoa sector and making all the operations, from the farm all the way to the consumer, more sustainable. This chapter will present the historical development of the Swiss industry from the nineteenth century up to recent years, and it will examine how the Swiss chocolate industry is reacting to the new challenges and what initiatives it is taking in order to make chocolate production more sustainable throughout the entire chain.

The Nineteenth Century: The Roots of the Chocolate Industry in Switzerland

Cocoa can trace its origins to the Mesoamerican region. Historians have found traces of cocoa consumption in the Ulúa valley in Honduras and traced cocoa consumption as far back as 1150 BC (Joyce and Henderson 2010). Cocoa was of great importance in Toltec, Mayan, and Aztec cultures. For the Mayas, the cocoa bean was of great value and was also used as a form of currency. Cocoa was consumed as a thick and bitter beverage, known as *xocolatl*, made from ground cocoa beans mixed with water, black pepper, vanilla, and spices. When the Spanish conquistadors arrived in the sixteenth century, they took interest in this exotic drink and brought it to Spain where it became popular in the Spanish court. Because sugar was rare and expensive at the time, it was first sweetened with honey. The bitterness of chocolate did not suit the taste buds of Europeans, but once it was sweetened it gained popularity (Bensen 2008). The European aristocracy quickly developed a taste for chocolate, which was at this time consumed mainly as a beverage. In Paris, chocolate was regarded as a drink of the aristocracy and it was almost exclusively consumed by the privileged class until the invention in 1828 of the Van Houten press, a hydraulic machine which enabled the pulverization of the cocoa 'cake' into cocoa powder. To improve this powder's ability to mix with liquid, Van Houten treated it with alkaline salts, which reduces the bitterness of the cocoa. This process is known as 'Dutching'. This invention revolutionized chocolate production and the era of mass production of chocolate began.

By the eighteenth century, Italy already had made its mark in the chocolate industry by becoming the first centre of confectionary. Many pioneers in the industry travelled to Italy to learn the art of chocolate-making (Wey 2006). The Swiss François-Louis Cailler was one of these industrial pioneers who first developed an interest in chocolate production at a local fair in Italy. He subsequently spent four years in Turin learning the art of chocolate-making. In 1819 he returned to Switzerland, where he set up the first Swiss chocolate factory in Corsier, near Vevey. Cailler is the oldest Swiss chocolate brand and still exists today.

A few years later, in 1825, Philippe Suchard opened a *confiserie* in Neuchâtel, and a year later set up a chocolate factory nearby. By the 1880s Suchard employed over 200 people and was the largest Swiss chocolate producer. Charles-Amédée Kohler, a wholesale grocer in Lausanne trading ready-made chocolate, opened a factory in 1830, and created nut chocolate—an important contribution for the Swiss chocolate industry. Moreover, the Kohler family also trained several famous apprentices, including Rudolf Lindt (in 1872–75) and Robert Frey (in 1880–83), who would become major players in the chocolate industry themselves, creating some of the most recognizable and successful Swiss chocolate brands.

Another important innovator of the chocolate industry is Daniel Peter. Son-in-law of François-Louis Cailler, he established the famous firm Peter-Cailler et Compagnie in 1867, and he was the first one to combine milk with chocolate, in 1875 (Chocosuisse 2001). Perhaps thanks to his proximity to Henri Nestlé, this young food producer had the idea of combining powdered milk to chocolate. He had tried for many years to add milk to chocolate, but mildew always formed. By removing the water content in the milk, this problem was solved.

In the early years of the Swiss chocolate industry, proximity between the chocolate pioneers played an important role in the success and innovation of the industry. For instance, if Daniel Peter had not been in contact with Henri Nestlé in Vevey, the invention of milk chocolate using condensed milk (a method developed by Nestlé), would have not been possible. Similarly Kohler, by training innovators such as Lindt and Frey—who would later move on to establish their own brands—made a great contribution to the industry.

The Swiss chocolate industry was initially located in the area around Lake Geneva in the western part of Switzerland. By the 1870s, chocolate factories were founded in Zurich and Bern. In 1845, Rudolf Sprüngli-Ammann first started producing chocolate in Zurich, and in 1874 Johann Georg Munz established a chocolate factory in Flawil, close to St Gallen. Aquilino Maestrani, who originally opened his chocolate factory in Lucerne in 1852, relocated to St Gallen seven years later.

Towards the last quarter of the nineteenth century, Rodolphe Lindt, a young apprentice trained at Amédée Kohler & Fils in Lausanne, established in Bern a firm producing arguably the most famous Swiss chocolate brand to this day. He succeeded in improving quality of chocolate by developing a conching machine. His ingenuity resulted in the addition of cocoa butter to the chocolate mass. This is now a standard procedure in chocolate production, but back in his day, it was not done. Lindt sought to improve the quality with a machine that is, in essence, a surface scraping mixer and agitator which evenly distributes cocoa butter within the mass. The texture is smoother and the aroma improves after three days of uninterrupted mixing. The result was a chocolate liquid that could easily be poured in moulds, rather than the tough mass that had to be knocked and pressed into moulds. Thus, by creating the first 'chocolate fondant' or melting chocolate, Lindt greatly contributed to the improvement of quality in the chocolate industry.

By 1899, Lindt was unable to meet demand, so he sold his company to Rudolph Sprüngli. He kept working in the factory in Bern until his retirement in 1905. This same year, Theodor Tobler founded the Fabrique de Chocolat de Berne, Tobler & Cie. Jean Tobler, his father, opened a Confiserie Spéciale in 1868, where he sold, among other products, chocolates produced by Rudolphe Lindt. Son Theodor, true to his entrepreneurial spirit, always had plans for growth and expansion. Just eight years later he introduced a very well-known Swiss chocolate: Toblerone, the triangular milk chocolate bar with honey and nougat.

The Twentieth Century: From Small-Scale Chocolate Producers to Multinationals

The turn of the twentieth century brought about many changes in the Swiss chocolate industry, as it went through periods of crisis but also through years of sustained growth. It was during the twentieth century that Switzerland gained its international reputation as one of the best chocolate producers in the world. The consolidation of Lindt and Sprüngli marked the beginning of an era of industrial consolidation and growth. Shortly afterwards, in 1904, Peter and Kohler merged under the name Peter et Kohler Chocolats Suisses S.A. The company had a contract to produce a sweet milk chocolate for Nestlé. By 1911, they merged with Cailler to form Peter, Cailler, Kohler Chocolats Suisses S.A. In 1929 they were taken over by Nestlé and Anglo-Swiss Condensed Milk Co., becoming the largest food company and chocolate producer in Switzerland. Nestlé, already an international company by then, had focused on the production of infant food and milk.

According to Chocosuisse (2001), in 1905 Switzerland produced 13,000 tons of chocolate. By 1918 the production was 40,000 tons. Switzerland, with a population of roughly 3.5 million at the turn of the twentieth century, was barely able to consume all the chocolate it produced, and these chocolate firms had to adopt an internationalization strategy in order to sell their output. What originated as small chocolatiers in Switzerland soon took the challenge and expanded beyond the Swiss boarders. For example, in 1915 Lindt & Sprüngli exported around three quarters of its chocolate production to about twenty countries around the world.

The two world wars and the economic crises in the 1920s and 1930s brought many challenges to the Swiss chocolate industry, which had to deal with an almost complete loss of international markets. In 1937, for example, the total exports shrank to CHF 1.9 million, down from CHF 106 million in 1919. In order to survive, companies in neutral Switzerland had to be completely reorganized. The Second World War resulted in tough import restrictions on sugar and cocoa, posing further risks for the industry. Tough economic times, rationing of raw materials, and protectionism truly tested the resilience of the Swiss chocolate industry, but it was exactly during these hardships that caused it to become more innovative. A clear example of the innovative spirit of the Swiss chocolate industry is Camille Bloch. After a few years of apprenticeship at Chocolat Tobler AG in Bern, Camille Bloch founded Chocolats et Bonbons fins Camille Bloch in 1929 in Bern. In 1935 the firm moved to Courtelary in the Bernese Jura. Because of the shortage of cocoa and sugar and the blocked transport routes for raw materials, in 1942 Camille Bloch came up with the idea of processing ground hazelnuts from Turkey into a paste and adding whole hazelnuts. By spreading this paste in flat moulds and covering them on both sides with a thin layer of chocolate which would then be cut them into rectangular 50 gram bars, cocoa was economized. Ragusa chocolate, a Swiss favourite, was born.

The development of local demand also came hand in hand with the economic crisis that the industry experienced until the end of the Second World War. At the beginning of the twentieth century chocolate was rather a luxury good enjoyed by the privileged. However, between 1940 and 1950, the annual per capita chocolate consumption in Switzerland rose from 3.5 kg to 6.2 kg. In 1960, Switzerland consumed 6.9 kg and, by 1970, 9 kg a year. The rapid automation of the industry and the increased economic growth of the country made it possible for most citizens to be able to consume chocolate. By the mid-twentieth century, it was no longer a good exclusively enjoyed by the privileged class.

The rapid consolidation and industrial growth of chocolate production in Switzerland meant that chocolate could be widely consumed by the entire population. However, all the structural changes in the industry also had an effect on small-scale, artisanal production. Chocolate production for mass consumption and export markets by the end of the twentieth century was in the hands of big multinational or large local retailers. To this day, they maintain a central role in the governance of the cocoa and chocolate chain. Small-scale production has been somewhat limited to local *chocolatiers* in larger towns and cities in Switzerland. Their market segment is a small and specific, catering to consumers willing to buy artisanal or handmade products rather than mass-produced chocolates. The price for handmade chocolate in a smaller *chocolatier* or *confiserie* is normally higher than for the mass-produced chocolate. It is interesting to note that, despite the fact these small-scale businesses face strong competition from large multinationals, they are well established in their market niche. Their success has much to do with the consumers, who value artisanal production and are willing to pay a higher price for it.

The Twenty-First Century: Sustainable Sourcing

The Swiss chocolate industry has reported an increase in sales over the last few years, although the latest report states that last year closed with lower sales than in previous years. Export sales have grown in the EU, traditionally the main market for Swiss chocolate. However, markets such as China, the Russian Federation, Saudi Arabia, Turkey, and the United Arab Emirates provide an opportunity for further sales growth. It is expected that these markets will expand and demand more Swiss chocolate in the near future. When compared to the main industry players worldwide, two Swiss companies still maintain their position in the top ten global confectionery companies (Table 4.1): Nestlé, which reported sales of close to US$12 billion, and Lindt & Sprüngli, with sales of US$3 billion in 2013 (Chocosuisse 2014).

Consumers in Europe, and especially in Switzerland, are increasingly demanding more information on the products they buy, thus motivating corporations to find alternative ways to fulfil these demands. In response to the changing market

Table 4.1 Top ten global confectionery companies

Company	Country	Net Sales 2013 (US$ millions)
Mars Inc.	USA	17,640
Mondelēz International Inc.	USA	14,862
Nestlé SA	Switzerland	11,760
Meiji Holdings Co Ltd.	Japan	11,742*
Ferrero Group	Italy	10,900
Hershey Foods Corp	USA	7,043
Arcor (Argentina)	Argentina	3,700
Chocoladefabriken Lindt & Sprüngli AG	Switzerland	3,149
Ezaki Glico Co. Ltd.	Japan	3,018*
Yildiz Holding	Turkey	2,500

* This includes production of non-confectionery items.
Source: ICCO (2014).

trends and consumer concerns, chocolate manufacturers in Switzerland are engaging in projects and partnerships to improve the transparency of the cocoa chain. They are responding to this drive for sustainable sourcing through different initiatives, which range from certifications and labelling to producing 'carbon neutral' chocolate.

In the latest *State of Sustainability Initiatives Review* (IISD 2014), the compliance of cocoa production with global sustainability standards was examined. According to this report, in 2012, 22 per cent (an estimated 899,000 metric tons) of the world's cocoa was produced in compliance with a global sustainability standard. The sustainability standards commonly used in the sector include Organic, Fairtrade, UTZ Certified, and Rainforest Alliance. The premiums at the first point of sale (typically farmers and/or cooperatives) for standard compliant cocoa ranged from 5 per cent to 18 per cent or more in recent years. The highest premiums were observed for organic cocoa and the lowest premiums were for UTZ cocoa (IISD 2014).

One of the drivers for cocoa production to become more sustainable has been the increasing scrutiny since the end of the 1990s on child labour. By 2002, the International Cocoa Initiative (ICI) was established 'as a result of a groundswell of opinion urging the chocolate industry to ensure child and forced labor were not used in the production of their products' (ICI 2014). The ICI Secretariat is located in Geneva, Switzerland, but offices in Abidjan, Ivory Coast, and Accra, Ghana, have been opened to implement different projects.

Similarly, the World Cocoa Foundation, established in 2000, is an international membership organization representing more than 100 companies, which account for 80 per cent of the global corporate market. They are committed to creating a sustainable cocoa economy by taking into account farmers' needs, promoting agricultural and environmental stewardship, and strengthening development in cocoa-growing communities (WCF 2014). The creation of these organizations has brought about major changes in the industry, as member companies officially manifested their commitments to source cocoa sustainably. The drive for sustainable sourcing in the case of the cocoa value chain started as an industry effort in order to respond to major issues affecting cocoa production. Although much work needs to be done, steps towards sustainability have been taken by the industry leaders (CAOBISCO 2012).

Transparency Initiatives in the Swiss Chocolate Industry

The Swiss chocolate industry is comprised by big multinationals (such as Nestlé and Lindt & Sprüngli), but also by numerous retailers, both large and small. In most towns in Switzerland it is common to find *chocolatiers* and artisans offering consumers a wide range of chocolates, truffles, pralines, and seasonal chocolate creations. Other corporations, such as Barry Callebaut, produce diverse chocolate products for manufacturers and artisans. All of these companies respond in one way or another to different consumer demands. For many, buying from local artisans is important to help small-scale businesses. These consumers also appreciate the craftsmanship of handmade chocolate truffles or pralines. Locally, retailers offer a wide variety of products at all price ranges. For Swiss chocolate consumed internally, retailers such as Migros and Coop play an important role in responding to consumers' concerns. Migros and Coop are the largest retailers in Switzerland and both companies produce chocolate through subsidiary companies. These companies all have specific work areas and programmes they have implemented in order to increase transparency in their operations and produce in a more sustainable way.

Transparency Assessment of the Industry

An analysis of the Swiss chocolate industry, conducted in 2013,[1] reveals how the sector is moving towards more transparency and corporate social responsibility (CSR). The study focused on the initiatives that the various companies are taking in different aspects of sustainable production, how these initiatives were benefiting stakeholders in the chain, and, finally, how these actions were reported in the companies' CSR statements. To be able to understand the practices implemented by the industry, four companies were studied in detail. The specific initiatives related to transparency and sustainability will be compared and discussed.

Out of the 18 companies which belong to Chocosuisse, the main association representing chocolate producers, 16 were contacted by telephone or email to request an interview to collect data for this study. Leading chocolate producers in Switzerland, like Chocolats Halba and Frey were interviewed face to face and via email. Other companies like Nestle, Lindt & Sprüngli, Chocolates Bernrain, and Camille Bloch responded to the interview request by referring to their companies' specialized web pages for CSR, transparency activities, or specialized programmes such as the Nestle Cocoa Plan. Finally, some companies were not willing to be a part of the research or did not respond at all. The information collected was complemented by data from the companies' websites, annual reports, and CSR statements.

A comparative analysis of the industry as a whole was conducted. Using dichotomous variables based on a scale of 0–1, where 0 equals no activities on a specific issue and 1 equals the presence of activities, a comparison between the companies was established. In the case of transparency issues, aspects such as the recognition of companies of issues such as child labour, social issues, ethical sourcing, safety, and quality were examined. If companies reported they were working on these issues, the score assigned was 1. The absence of these sorts of activities was given a score of 0. For the other variables such as sustainability, the scoring was done in the same way. For the certification variable, four different certifications were taken into account: Fair Trade, UTZ Certified, Rainforest Alliance, and Organic. The same comparative analysis was conducted and a score was assigned. The other variables

[1] Master's thesis conducted at the Bern University of Applied Sciences, School of Agricultural, Forest and Food Sciences HAFL. Submitted by M. Milojevic in 2013.

studied were child labour (if companies are working to eradicate this or not), CSR strategy (if companies have a clear and defined CSR strategy) and transparency and CSR reporting (whether or not they clearly report their commitment to the issues they undertake and work towards). A final score (not weighed) was assigned in order to have an idea of which companies are at the forefront and which are still lagging behind in the issues mentioned (see Table 4.2).

The results of this investigation show that larger companies (Chocolats Halba, Frey, Nestlé, Lindt & Sprüngli) are more likely to be involved in transparency and CSR activities than smaller and medium-sized enterprises (SMEs). One possible explanation could be a lack of knowledge and of a clear understanding of transparency and CSR. It could also be an issue of big corporations such as Nestlé coming 'under fire' from the consumer side for issues such as child labour more than smaller chocolatiers. Another explanation can be the lack of money to invest in transparency activities, especially in an uncertain economic scenario where SMEs are more prone to be affected than large corporations.

Why are bigger companies better positioned to be 'more transparent' than SMEs? In the case of Barry Callebaut, which, according to the results of the investigation, ranks among the top companies in transparency practices, they have clearly addressed, in their CSR statements, their work regarding child labour, sustainability, the environment, and safety standards. The company has released statements where it explicitly mentions its commitment to sustainability, encompassing sustainable production in the field, in sourcing, and in manufacturing. Barry Callebaut has taken a leading role among the industry by organizing events such as CHOCOVISION, a conference which brings together key stakeholders in the cocoa and chocolate industry from around the world. Top executives representing the large chocolate manufacturers attend, as well as influential politicians and key representatives of non-governmental organizations (NGOs).

To have a better understanding of the transparency initiatives undertaken by the chocolate industry in Switzerland, let us examine four companies. Two of them are big retailers (Nestlé and Lindt) and two of them are subsidiaries of the biggest retailers in Switzerland (Coop and Migros). The main reason these companies were selected was the fact that they represent the chocolate industry as a whole. Nestlé and Lindt are two of the oldest and most established manufacturers in Switzerland. On the other hand, Coop and Migros, as the largest Swiss retailers, also play a major role in the industry. Although they sell a wide variety of chocolates from several different brands (particularly in the case of Coop), they also have subsidiary companies producing chocolate under their own brand names. In the case of Coop, the subsidiary company is Chocolats Halba; in the case of Migros it is Frey AG.

The Nestlé Cocoa Plan

Nestlé, in its 2013 'Nestlé in Society' report states that: 'Responsible sourcing is an investment in our future and the future of the farmers and producers on whom we depend. It calls for continuous improvement that goes far beyond a simple exchange of goods and money, placing shared responsibility on all parties in the

Table 4.2 Comparison of the Swiss chocolate industry

Company	Transparency Initiatives	Sustainability	Certification				Child Labour	CSR Strategy	Transparency and CSR Reporting	Score
			Fairtrade Yes = 1 No = 0	UTZ Certified Yes = 1 No = 0	Rainforest Alliance Yes = 1 No = 0	Organic Yes = 1 No = 0				
Barry Callebaut Schweiz AG	Child labour, food safety and quality, social issues, environment 1	Environment protection, social programmes, energy management 1	1	1	1	0	Programmes for child labour prevention 1	CSR strategies, main fields covered 1	Information on website and in printed form 1	8
Mondelēz Schweiz GmbH	Child labour, improvement of farmers' social and environmental conditions, cocoa sourcing 1	Sustainability programme Cocoa Life programme, environment 1	1	0	1	1	Statement of Principles on child and forced labour 1	Sustainability, environment, health 1	Information on web page 1	8
Chocolats Halba AG	Child labour, reforestation, ethical sourcing, quality and safety 1	Environment and climate, reforestation, cocoa production, 1	1	0	0	1	Better Chocolate, Awareness and Reforestation programme 1	Sustainability, employees, ethical sourcing, environment protection 1	Detailed information on company website 1	7
Frey AG	Quality, child labour, sourcing of cocoa 1	Environment and climate, social conditions of farmers, cocoa production 1	1	1	0	0	Collaboration with UTZ Certified 1	Sustainability, quality, environment, employees, social conditions 1	Some information on sustainability 1	7
Nestlé SA	Child labour, quality and safety, sourcing of cocoa 1	Environment and climate, social conditions of farmers, cocoa production 1	1	1	0	0	Nestle Cocoa Plan 1	Safety and health, sustainability, employees, ethical sourcing, environment protection 1	Reports on website and in printed form 1	7

Company										Score
Chocolat Stella AG	No activities 0	Environment activity, CO$_2$ reduction, water efficiency, farmer training 1	1	1	0	1	No activities 0	Only towards sustainability 1	Some information on website 1	6
Lindt & Sprüngli AG	Sourcing of cocoa, quality and food safety 1	Sustainability programme, environment protection 1	1	0	0	0	Startrust collaboration 1	Education of farmers, health and safety, environment 1	Information on website and in printed form 1	6
Chocolat Bernrain AG	No activities 0	Environment activity, CO$_2$ reduction, water efficiency, farmer training 1	1	1	0	1	No activities 0	Only towards sustainability 1	Some information on website 1	5
Maestrani AG	No activities 0	Environment protection, ecological efficiency, IFS standard 1	1	0	0	1	No clear activities 0	Only towards sustainability and environment 1	Some information on website, full sustainability report in 2013 1	5
Camille Bloch SA	Sourcing of cocoa, socially responsible cultivation 1	Ecologically and socially responsible cultivation 1	0	0	0	0	No clear activities 0	Quality, social responsibility in Ghana 1	Some information on website 1	4
Felchlin AG	Sourcing of cocoa, high and fair prices 1	Sustainability programmes 1	0	0	0	0	No clear activities 0	Sustainability, sourcing 1	Information on company website 1	4
Gysi AG	Quality and safety of products 1	No activities 0	1	0	0	1	No clear activities 0	No clear activities 0	No reporting 0	3
Läderach AG	Quality and safety of products 1	No activities 0	0	0	0	0	No clear activities 0	Employees, quality and safety 1	No reporting 0	2
Favarger SA	Product quality and safety 1	No activities 0	0	0	0	0	No clear activities 0	No clear activities 0	No reporting 0	1
Villars SA	No information 0	No information 0	1	1	0	0	No information 0	No activities 0	no communication 0	1
Chocolat Alprose SA	No activities 0	No activities 0	0	0	0	0	No activities 0	No activities reported 0	No reporting 0	0

Source: Adapted from Milojevic (2013).

supply chain to address social and environmental issues that can affect supply, livelihoods and sustainability' (Nestlé 2013b). In fact, Nestlé has been an industry leader in sustainability and in making its operations more sustainable, both in the chocolate sector and other products. In 2002 Nestlé, Unilever, and Danone created the Sustainable Agriculture Initiative (SAI) Platform with the aim to facilitate sharing of knowledge and initiatives to support the development and implementation of sustainable agriculture practices involving the different stakeholders of the food chain. The SAI Platform has over fifty members. According to SAI Platform (SAI 2014), it is the only global food industry initiative for sustainable agriculture which develops knowledge on sustainable agriculture. It developed, among other instruments, the principles and practices for sustainable water management at farm level, recommendations for Sustainability Performance Assessment (SPA), and the Executives Training on Sustainable Sourcing. Specifically through the Nestlé Cocoa Plan, the most relevant sustainability issues in the cocoa sector are addressed.

The Nestlé Cocoa Plan was officially launched in 2009. Currently, the Cocoa Plan is active in the countries with the world's largest cocoa origins, Ivory Coast, Ghana, and Indonesia, but also in the countries with the world's largest fine cocoa origins, Ecuador and Venezuela. Nestlé intends to invest CHF 110 million in cocoa, creating shared value initiatives over the next decade, almost twice as much as was spent over the past 15 years (Nestlé 2013b).

According to Nestlé (2013b), it uses an estimated 10 per cent of the total world cocoa production. In 2013, Nestlé purchased over 62,000 tons of cocoa—14.5 per cent of the total—through the Cocoa Plan, a 34 per cent increase over 2012 (2014 target: 80,000 tons). The specific aims of the Nestlé Cocoa Plan are (Nestlé 2013c):

- For farmers to choose cocoa farming, rather than enter it by default.
- For cocoa farmers to improve their lives and those of their families.
- For local communities to be empowered and thrive through the cocoa economy.

The Cocoa Plan has three main action pillars:

- Enabling farmers to run profitable farms.
- Improving social conditions.
- Sourcing good quality, sustainable cocoa.

The Lindt & Sprüngli Promise

One of the most recognized Swiss chocolate brands is Lindt. Lindt & Sprüngli was founded in 1845 and, in over 160 years of its existence, it has become a brand found in more than 100 countries worldwide. It is one of the leaders in the market for premium-quality chocolate. Its origins were simple—in their small pastry shop in Zurich, confectioner David Sprüngli-Schwarz and his 29-year-old son Rudolf Sprüngli-Ammann decided to make chocolate in solid bars. One of the great contributions of Lindt to the industry has been the creation of the first truly melting chocolate. With sales of over US$3 billion in 2013 (ICCO 2014), Lindt & Sprüngli has become one of the leading chocolate brands worldwide.

Lindt & Sprüngli is engaged in continuously improving sustainability in most aspects of their operations. In order to live up to the company's commitment to be sustainable along the entire supply chain, the 'Lindt Promise' was launched as their official pledge. It is a set of commitments and policies related to their sustainable actions along the chain. There are three sustainability aspects which are taken into close consideration: sustainably sourced, sustainably produced, and sustainably consumed. Under their sustainably sourced pledge, for example, Lindt & Sprüngli guarantees the sustainable, long-term supply of essential resources. They are committed to establishing the traceability of all their raw materials and building partnerships with all their suppliers, ensuring an equivalent treatment. The Lindt & Sprüngli Supplier Code of Conduct sets out the requirements expected of the suppliers and vendors regarding compliance with laws and regulations, corruption and bribery, social and working conditions, child labour, and the outside environment (Lindt & Sprüngli 2014).

Ghana is the only country in West Africa where Lindt & Sprüngli sources cocoa beans. Thus, they started in 2008 a pilot project called Ghana Traceable, together Cocobod, the Ghanaian Cocoa Board, and an NGO named Source Trust. The aim of the project is to trace the origin of the cocoa beans to the communities, allowing for quality control all the way back to the source and ensuring the best quality of the raw material. Quality checks to monitor fermentation, moisture, and size of beans take place at the collection points. Lindt & Sprüngli works directly with the local licensed buying company which buys the beans, in which they also have shares. Complete transparency and traceability is therefore guaranteed for each and every bag of cocoa beans purchased. On the other hand, Source Trust, a British NGO, works to promote traceability in farming practices. It collects traceability premiums for the Cocobod Armajaro Traceable Foundation (CAFT) and distributes them between CAFT members. The aim is of this partnership is to improve the livelihoods of farmers. Furthermore, over US$7 million has been invested in regional infrastructure. Warehouses have been built and traceability documents improved. Although these types of improvements are necessary to make sure the cocoa beans are traceable to the communities where they originate, other investments in the communities have been made (such as the construction of wells for clean and safe water supply, of new schools where students could also study mathematics, natural and agricultural sciences, and the provision of mosquito nets (close to 40,000 delivered) to prevent malaria).

With the funds received from the premiums, Village Resource Centres (VRC) have been set up near schools. These are structures, usually prefabricated, which are equipped with computers and internet access. In the daytime, schoolchildren can visit them as a regular part of their education. In the evenings and weekends, VRCs are open for farmers, who can use them to access the Internet or complete training modules on cocoa production, which helps them have a better understanding of sustainable production practices.

Migros and Chocolat Frey AG

Migros, Switzerland's largest retail company and employer, is also one of the forty largest retailers in the world. Founded in 1925 in Zurich as a private enterprise by Gottlieb Duttweiler, it evolved in its early years from a private company to a cooperative with about 2 million members (Migros 2014). Migros initially sold only a few basic products at low prices—coffee, rice, sugar, noodles, oil, and soap, from lorries that went from one village or hamlet to another. Then the intermediaries were cut and Migros started creating its own lines of products such as meat, milk, and chocolate. Today, the concept of having its own assortment of goods is still valid. Over 90 per cent of the goods sold are produced by Migros subsidiaries.

Chocolat Frey AG is one of these subsidiaries, and is owned entirely by Migros Group. They manufacture chocolate and chewing gum and have a market share of 36.8 per cent, thus making them the main manufacturer of chocolate for the Swiss market. Frey has a foreign market share of 10.9 per cent (Frey 2014). Because of issues such as degradation of forests in West Africa, child labour, and poor productivity in the cocoa sector, the Migros Group started to focus on improving sustainability along the cocoa value chain. By working together with Max Havelaar and UTZ Certified, the entire assortment of chocolate sold at Migros (over 500 products) was sold with a certification. Sustainable development is a main concern for Chocolat Frey AG, and the company has the goal of achieving the best possible solution by considering economic, social, and ecological criteria, focusing on three areas: procurement, transport, and production.

Coop and Chocolats Halba

Coop is a cooperative and the second largest retailer in Switzerland after Migros. In 2001, Coop merged with 11 cooperative federations which had been its main suppliers for over 100 years. According to Bio Suisse, the Swiss organic producers' association, Coop accounts for half of all the organic food sold in Switzerland. Coop has three primary brands with a sustainability selling proposition: Coop Oecoplan (various daily life products), Coop Naturaline (textile products), and Coop Naturaplan (food) are brands focusing on lowering environmental impacts and optimizing social outcomes in the supply chain. However, the company also sells a considerable amount of products bearing the Max Havelaar Fairtrade label. Chocolats Halba, a division of Coop, produces chocolate and chocolate specialty products for retailers (mainly Coop) and the industry. They produce over 12,000 tons of chocolate per year. The company was founded in 1933, but was merged with the Coop Group in 1972.

Chocolats Halba has been addressing sustainability issues for a long time and the company has developed one of the most comprehensive approaches to incorporating sustainability in most aspects of production, starting from the farmers. It has also launched its 'Better Chocolate' initiative, which generates added value all along the value chain: for customers, consumers, cocoa farmers, the environment and climate, and for Chocolats Halba itself. The company's sustainability work is taken into account in these areas (Chocolats Halba 2014): purchasing, origin, climate neutrality, packaging, and employees.

Chocolats Halba has demonstrated its commitment to sustainability through a pilot project in Honduras, where, together Helvetas Swiss Intercooperation, a private NGO, and a local farmers' cooperative, they have joined forces to create a new and sustainable supply chain. This led to Chocolats Halba and Helvetas joining forces to construct a completely new and sustainable supply chain. Through this project, a direct link between cocoa farmers in Honduras and the Swiss company was established. Chocolats Halba has trained farmers in improved, organic farming practices, and fermenting and drying procedures. Farmers have received financial assistance and training to plant high-value hardwood trees with the cocoa. In turn, Chocolats Halba buys their entire production to produce organic chocolate, Fairtrade and organic labelled, which is also labelled as Honduran cocoa. In fact, the packaging holds information on the farmers who have produced the cocoa. Chocolats Halba prides itself in having established a supply chain where the cocoa can be traced back to the farm where it came from (Chocolats Halba 2014).

Conclusion

Although Switzerland's chocolate industry is cemented on tradition, craftsmanship, and quality, it has been resilient and flexible enough to weather several storms. Market forces drove the industry to consolidate in the late nineteenth century and early twentieth century. It was a survival strategy in the wake of wars, financial crisis, and other external shocks taking place in Europe at the time. Yet the chocolate industry survived these crises and thrived. It is the most unlikely of success stories: a small alpine country, itself fragmented with regard to language and religion, and isolated from its bigger and stronger neighbours, and an industry that relies exclusively on the import of its very basic raw material. Even in the war years, with shortages and irregular flow of raw materials, Switzerland relied on innovativeness to survive. In more recent times, consumer concerns regarding issues such as child labour in cocoa production has challenged the industry, which, once again, has responded.

Food chains are rapidly evolving and serious moves towards making food production, logistics, processing, and consumption more transparent and sustainable are taking place in the Swiss chocolate industry. The complex network of farmers, cooperatives, intermediaries, traders, exporters, buyers, processors, manufacturers, retailers, consumers, and related service providers makes achieving transparency a real challenge. For a chocolate bar to be produced, hundreds of people across multiple national borders have been involved. Yet consumers are increasingly aware of the importance of being able to trace their products back to the farm, whether for their own consumer safety or to make sure that the cocoa beans are being produced in a sustainable and fair way. The demand for information about the origin of cocoa beans will only continue to increase in the next few years.

The chocolate industry in Switzerland is clearly taking the necessary steps to increase transparency. Only a decade or so ago, these very same actors were coming under serious scrutiny because of a lack of transparency in their operations. Consumers cringed at the thought of child labour in cocoa plantations, while large corporations kept buying beans without taking serious measures to improve the living conditions in cocoa-producing countries. 'Business as usual' was no longer an option and the Swiss chocolate industry, together with local partners, NGOs, governments, cooperatives, academics, and international bodies, worked to address these issues. Although there is still much to be accomplished, the first steps in the right direction have been taken.

Sustainability is, however, an issue that requires concerted action to be achieved. In the face of the great challenges in the cocoa sector in most producing countries, the sector is as vulnerable as it has ever been. The market prices for chocolate remain stable and demand is increasing—certainly good news for the chocolate industry, even though the increase in market prices barely reaches small-scale farmers. Even with all the certification schemes out there nowadays, the farmers' situation has improved only marginally. If they do not belong to some form of farmers' association or cooperative, the chance of becoming a certified farmer is low. Problems associated with monoculture and lack of diversification, eroded soils, deforestation, and water stress all affect yields. If farmers are unable to access new hybrids, their yields will continue to remain low while their plantations get older. Sustainable production methods need to be promoted along with certification efforts. Each one of the initiatives presented addresses one or several issues related to sustainability. Whether it's by building a VRC in Ghana to give farmers better training or by promoting the use of mahogany in agroforestry systems in Honduras, all of these initiatives are favourably contributing to increased sustainability in the cocoa value chain. However, given the prospects of increased demand in the future, one thing remains certain—a lot more work needs to be done.

References

Bensen, A. 2008. 'A Brief History of Chocolate'. *Smithsonian Magazine*, 1 March. Available at: <http://www.smithsonianmag.com/arts-culture/a-brief-history-of-chocolate-21860917/>.

CAOBISCO (Association of Chocolate, Biscuit and Confectionery Industries of the European Union). 2012. *2012 Annual Report of the Chocolate, Biscuits and Confectionary of Europe*. Available at: <http://caobisco.eu/public/images/page/caobisco-25062013115711-caobisco_annual_report_2012.pdf>.

Chocolats Halba. 2014. *Chocolats Halba Sustainability*. Available at: <http://chocolatshalba.ch/en/sustainability.html>.

Chocosuisse. 2001. *Chocology: The Swiss Chocolate Industry Past and Present*. Berne: Vögeli AG.

Chocosuisse. 2014. 'The Swiss Chocolate Industry in 2013'. Press release. Available at: <http://www.chocosuisse.ch/web/chocosuisse/en/documentation/press_release.html>.

Frey. 2014. *About Frey: Facts and Figures*. Available at: <http://www.chocolatfrey.com/about-frey-w/facts-and-figures/>.

ICCO (International Cocoa Association). 2014. *The Chocolate Industry: Who are the Main Manufacturers of Chocolate in the World?* Available at: <http://www.icco.org/about-cocoa/chocolate-industry.html>.

ICI (International Cocoa Initiative). 2014. *International Cocoa Initiative, History and Mission.* Available at: < http://www.cocoainitiative.org/en/about-us/about-us >.

IISD (International Institute for Sustainable Development). 2014. *The State of Sustainability Initiatives Review 2014: Standards and the Green Economy.* Available at: <http://www.iisd.org/pdf/2014/ssi_2014.pdf>.

Joyce, R. A. and J. S. Henderson. 2010. 'Forming Mesoamerican Taste: Cacao Consumption in Formative Period Contexts'. In *Pre-Columbian Foodways Interdisciplinary Approaches to Food, Culture, and Markets in Ancient Mesoamerica*, ed. J. E. Staller and M. Carrasco, pp. 157–73. New York: Springer Science and Business Media.

KPMG. 2012. *Cocoa Certification: Study on the Costs, Advantages and Disadvantages of Cocoa Certification*, commissioned by the International Cocoa Organization (ICCO). The Netherlands: KPMG Advisory N.V.

Lindt & Sprüngli. 2014. *Lindt & Sprüngli Corporate and Social Responsibility.* Available at: <http://www.lindt.com/swf/eng/company/corporate-sustainability/>.

Migros. 2014. *Migros: Geschichte.* Available at: <http://www.migros.ch/de/ueber-die-migros/geschichte/geschichte-slider.html>.

Milojevic, M. 2013. 'Evaluation of Transparency Practices in the Swiss Chocolate Industry'. Master's thesis, Bern University of Applied Sciences.

Nestlé. 2013b. 'Nestlé in Society: Creating Shared Value and Meeting our Commitments 2013'. Annual Report. Vevey, Switzerland.

SAI (Sustainable Agriculture Initiative). 2014. *Sustainable Agriculture Initiative Platform.* Available at: <http://www.saiplatform.org/>.

WCF (World Cocoa Foundation). 2014. *World Cocoa Foundation: Our Approach.* Available at: <http://worldcocoafoundation.org/our-work/our-approach/>.

Wey, A. 2006. 'How Swiss Chocolate Conquered the World'. *Swiss Review* 6: 8–10.

5

From Pralines to Multinationals

The Economic History of Belgian Chocolates

*Maria Garrone, Hannah Pieters, and Johan Swinnen**

Introduction

Today 'Belgian chocolates' are famous all over the world.[1] Belgium is associated with high-quality chocolate products such as pralines and truffles, with brand names such as Godiva, Neuhaus, and Leonidas recognized globally. The Belgian successes in the chocolate business go beyond the final consumer market. Those with more knowledge of the sector know that the Barry Callebaut company has grown to become a dominant player on the intermediate chocolate products market.

However, the global success and reputation of Belgian chocolate is a relatively recent phenomenon.[2] In 1847, at the eve of the first 'great chocolate boom', the jury in charge of awarding prizes for innovative and successful industries at the Exhibition of Belgian Industry in Brussels, decided not to give an award to emerging chocolate companies, believing that chocolate had no future in Belgium: 'Chocolate manufacturing (...), it is one of those industries that do not present a particular advantage for the country, given that few workers are required and the raw materials come partly from abroad'(Mercier 2008: 92).

* The authors would like to thank Rudi Cabergs and his colleagues at the FOD Economie who helped with the collection of the data and Guy Gallet and Laurent Gerbaud who offered their time, support and expertise that greatly assisted the research, although the interpretations and conclusions of this chapter may not necessarily represent their views.

[1] This is supported by the findings of an online survey by the Belgian Brewers Association in 2012, which asked 1,230 non-Belgians 'what comes to their mind when thinking about Belgium?': 52% of respondents spontaneously stated chocolate. The respondents were from neighbouring countries, such as the Netherlands, Germany, and France, as well as other European countries including the UK, Denmark, Italy, and Spain, and non-European countries including the USA, Russia, and Japan (WHY5 Research 2012).

[2] It was most likely during the Spanish occupation of the territory which is now Belgium that chocolate was first brought into this region. The first evidence of chocolate in the country was reported in 1635 by the abbot of Baudeloo in Ghent (Mercier 2008).

While exports grew significantly between 1900 and 1930, Belgium was still importing more chocolate than it exported for much of this period. It is only since the 1960s that Belgian exports have dominated imports. However, the rise has been rapid. Since 1980, exports of 'Belgian chocolates' have grown exponentially and conquered the world.

In this brief historical overview, we will document the growth of the chocolate sector in Belgium and relate its success to a combination of various elements and diverse growth strategies.

The sector's growth has also led to challenges for Belgian chocolate. In fact, the concept of 'Belgian chocolate' is under siege, as several of the most successful companies are no longer owned by Belgian families or companies but by international investors instead. Another challenge is that the strong demand has led others to imitate 'Belgian chocolates'. These challenges have induced attempts to protect 'true' Belgian chocolate.

The chapter is structured as follows. The next sections, 'The Growth of Chocolate Consumption and Lagging Production in the Nineteenth Century' and 'Increased Competitiveness of Belgian Chocolate in the Early Twentieth Century', provide an overview of the initial challenges faced by Belgian chocolate manufacturers to benefit from the rapidly growing chocolate demand in Europe in the nineteenth century, and examine some of the main factors that have driven the competitiveness of the Belgian chocolate industry. Afterwards we focus on the growth and globalization process of the Belgian chocolate industry since the second half of the twentieth century, and discuss the international dimension of Belgian firms operating in the chocolate industry. We then outline the historical development of the business growth of four of the largest Belgian companies. The next to last section 'Defining and Protecting "Belgian Chocolate"' discusses key issues related to the definition of and quality standards for 'Belgian chocolate'. The final section concludes.

The Growth of Chocolate Consumption and Lagging Production in the Nineteenth Century

Across Europe, chocolate demand grew rapidly at the end of the nineteenth century (Clarence-Smith 2000), but production in Belgium did not follow. The production of chocolate in Belgium was still characterized by craftsmanship and small-scale production. The average size of chocolate companies was just three employees (Scholliers 1996). Although some chocolate manufacturers started investing in steam engines in the 1860s, the industrialization of the Belgian chocolate sector remained very limited.

The increased domestic demand for chocolate products was mostly absorbed by imports. From the 1850s onwards, chocolate imports grew rapidly while exports were negligible. There was an exponential increase in imports in the 1870s and 1880s (see Figure 5.1a).

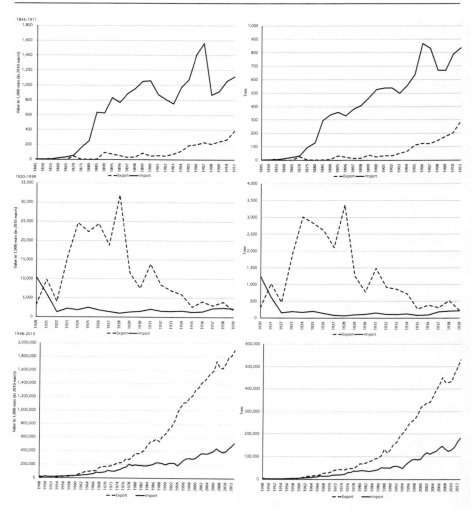

Figure 5.1 Imports and exports of chocolate in volumes and values

Source: FOD Economie (1845–1911, 1920–39, 1955–92); National Bank of Belgium (2014b).

Notes:

[1] The real values were calculated by deflating the values according to the historical database of Mitchell (1998) for the years 1845 to 1954. For the years after 1954, the deflator provided by the OECD (2014) was used.

[2] The data on exports and imports of Belgian chocolate were collected from the yearly statistics of foreign trade. Each year corresponds to the year of publication. In other words, we have used the books which have been published in the following years: 1845, 1850, 1855, 1860, 1870, 1875, 1880, 1885, 1890, 1895, 1896, 1897, 1898, 1899, 1900, 1901, 1902, 1903, 1904, 1905, 1906, 1907, 1908, 1909, 1910, 1911, 1920, 1921, 1922, 1923, 1924, 1925, 1926, 1927, 1928, 1930, 1931, 1932, 1933, 1934, 1935, 1936, 1937, 1938, 1939, 1955, 1956, 1957, 1958, 1959, 1960, 1961, 1962, 1963, 1964, 1965, 1966, 1967, 1968, 1969, 1970, 1971, 1972, 1973, 1974, 1975, 1976, 1977, 1978, 1979, 1980, 1981, 1982, 1983, 1984, 1985, 1986, 1987, 1988, 1989, 1990, 1991, 1992. The data of the National Bank of Belgium was used for the years 1993 to 2013.

[3] Chocolate is defined as chocolate used for consumption. It excludes export and imports of cocoa beans, cocoa paste, cocoa butter, fat and oil, and cocoa powder.

Belgian chocolate producers lobbied the government to constrain the increased competition by foreign companies. In an attempt to contain the increasing import flows, in 1885 the Belgian government increased the import tax on chocolate from 30 to 45 Belgian francs per 100 kilogram of chocolate (Scholliers 1996).[3] Yet the government's interventions had little effect: chocolate imports continued to grow. By the end of the nineteenth century, chocolate imports in Belgium were estimated at around 467 tons, while chocolate exports were around 39 tons (see Figure 5.1a).

Increased Competitiveness of Belgian Chocolate in the Early Twentieth Century

In the decade before the First World War and during the interbellum, things changed: imports stabilized and exports increased significantly. A combination of several factors turned the tide for the Belgian chocolate producers.

First, taxes on the two main ingredients for chocolate production were reduced. The abolishment of import taxes on cocoa in 1898 as well as the halving of the consumption tax on sugar in 1903 resulted in a significant reduction of production costs for manufacturers (Scholliers 1996).

Second, Belgian chocolate manufacturers invested in new technologies and grew in size, thereby capturing economies of scale. The average number of workers per chocolate company increased from 3 employees in the 1850s to 18.6 in 1896, and to 30.4 in 1910 (Scholliers 1996).

Third, innovations enabled Belgian manufacturers to compete with imports and gain new export markets. One crucial product innovation was the creation, by Jean Neuhaus in 1912, of the 'praline', a hard chocolate shell with a softer filling (see also section 'Four Historical Cases of "Belgian Chocolate"'). Another important development was the introduction of the Belgian chocolate bar 'batton' by Kwatta in 1920. Reducing the size of chocolate bars to 30g and 45g and making them into tablet shape further contributed to making chocolate an affordable snack (Callebaut 2014).

Another important innovation was the discovery of a method to produce, store, and transport 'couverture chocolate'—an intermediary product in the cocoa–chocolate value chain—in liquid form. This new technique eliminated the refrigeration and reheating phases of the chocolate production, thereby reducing overall production costs (Mercier 2008). The innovation was made in 1925 by Octaaf Callebaut, the founding father of the Callebaut chocolate factory. As documented in section 'Growth and Globalization after the Second World War', the chocolate couverture would become a leading product of the Belgian chocolate sector from 1970 onwards.

This groundbreaking production innovation by Callebaut had two main implications for the growth of the Belgian chocolate sector in following decades. On the one hand, thanks to the use of innovative technologies, Callebaut was able to grow and concentrate the supply of gourmet chocolate couverture at competitive prices.

---

[3] This is equivalent to an increase from 0.74 to 1.12 euros per 100 kilogram of chocolate.

On the other hand, it allowed Belgian chocolate makers to focus on their core business, such as the production of pralines, while procuring couverture directly from Callebaut rather than producing it in-house.

Innovations were not limited to production, but also occurred in marketing. In 1915 Neuhaus introduced the 'ballotin', a carton praline box, to protect pralines from being damaged and to enhance the 'gift' aspect of the buying of chocolate. In 1935, Basilio, the predecessor of Leonidas, inaugurated its first window shop, with the so-called 'guillotine-window' from where they could sell directly to passers-by who could witness the production process on display. This is still a distinctive feature of Leonidas shops today (Leonidas 2014).

All these factors improved the competitiveness of 'Belgian chocolate' on the domestic market and its export opportunities. As production costs fell and Belgian companies became more competitive, the price of exported chocolate decreased significantly. Belgian chocolate exports increased from 25 tons in 1900 to 290 tons in 1911. During the interbellum, exports, for the first time, became larger than chocolate imports both in terms of volume and value (see Figure 5.1b). As imports fell to low levels, exports grew strongly until the 1920s, reaching a record level of 3,372 tons in 1928. The neighbouring countries were the most important export destinations: exports to Germany, France, and the Netherlands accounted for around 70 per cent of total exports (FOD Economie 1925). However, the export sector collapsed in the 1930s due to the Great Depression. At the end of the 1930s, export levels had fallen back to the level of 1920.

Growth and Globalization after the Second World War

At the end of the Second World War, chocolate consumption grew rapidly in Europe. Chocolate was no longer a luxury product, but rather a food item of mass consumption. As Figure 5.2 illustrates, over the following 60 years, real gross domestic product (GDP) per capita increased fourfold, while the real price of chocolate declined. As chocolate became cheaper and incomes grew, the working class in Belgium and in Europe included chocolate bars in their regular diet (Mercier 2008; Callebaut 2014).

Belgian chocolate producers responded to this increased demand. The Belgian chocolate sector boom started with the 1958 World Expo in Brussels. A major campaign was launched by both the government and the industry to boost Belgian chocolate worldwide. In particular, it appeared that companies such as Côte d'Or were very active in promoting their chocolate products. Côte d'Or developed a brand new product, 'Dessert 58', for the Expo. The story goes that as soon as you left Brussels' Midi Train Station for the Expo, you could smell a chocolate aroma coming from the Côte d'Or factory, which was opposite the station.

Further mechanization and scaling-up of the production process improved productivity in the sector. The number of workers in the chocolate factories remained consistent between 1965 and 1990, with, respectively, 6,557 workers

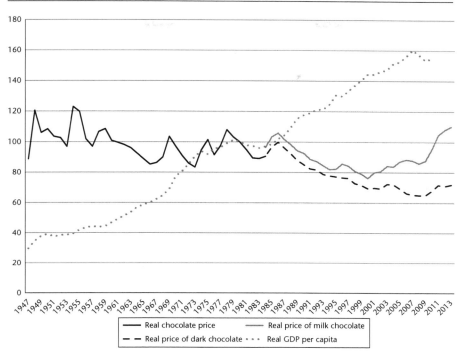

Figure 5.2 Index of real chocolate price and real GDP per capita in Belgium (1980 = 100), 1947–2013

Source: National Bank of Belgium (2014a).

Note: The authors received the original data from the National Bank of Belgium after direct correspondence.

in 1965 and 6,224 workers in 1990. As a result, the average production per worker increased greatly, from 11.1 to 44.2 tons per worker (FOD Economie 1965, 1990).

Production grew tremendously from the 1960s onwards. In 1965, Belgium produced 70,650 tons of chocolate, by 1990 268,068 tons, and by 2013 production had increased to 545,200 tons, most of which was exported (see Figure 5.3).[4]

The competitive strength of the Belgian chocolate industry became also apparent in trade (see Figure 5.1c). Since the 1960s, exports exceeded imports, and grew rapidly in the next few decades.[5] Growth has been particularly strong in 1980s, 1990s, and 2000s. The average annual growth rates of export values was 6.1 per cent in the 1980s and 7.2 per cent in the 1990s. Annual growth rates then slowed down in the 2000s, due to the economic crisis, to a rate of 2.5 per cent per year

---

[4] It should be noted that the data of 2013 are an underestimation of the real production figures as the EUROSTAT data does not include the production data in categories with a low number of producers due to confidentiality (Williams 2008).

[5] For more information on the recent developments in the Belgian chocolate export sector see Chapter 18, this volume.

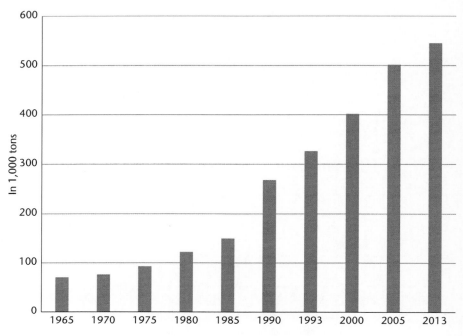

Figure 5.3 Production of Belgian chocolate in volume (1965–2013)

Source: FOD Economie (1965–93); FOD Economie (2000–2007)—covering 2000–05; Eurostat—Industrial Statistics (2015).

Notes:

[1] The data on production of Belgian chocolate were collected from the yearly statistics of production. Each year corresponds to the year of publication. In other words, we have used the books which have been published in the following years: 1965, 1966, 1967, 1968, 1969, 1970, 1971, 1972, 1973, 1974, 1975, 1976, 1977, 1978, 1979, 1980, 1981, 1982, 1983, 1984, 1985, 1986, 1987, 1988, 1989, 1990, 1991, 1992, 1993.

[2] The data were collected from the yearly statistics on industrial production of the PRODCOM industry. Each year corresponds to the year of publication. In other words, we have used the books which have been published in the following years: 2000, 2001, 2002, 2003, 2004, 2005, 2006, 2007.

[3] The data in 2013 were calculated based on the EUROSTAT data (2015). Total production is calculated by summing up the production categories from 1082130 to 1082290. This calculation is an underestimation of the real production figures as the EUROSTAT data does not include the production data in categories with low number of producers due to confidentiality (Williams 2008).

(see Table 5.1). By 2013, the last year of data, Belgium was exporting more than 500,000 tons of chocolate worth more than 500 million euros.[6]

The European Union (EU) is still the main market for Belgian chocolate, but its share has been declining in the past two decades. At present, it accounts for 77 per cent of total Belgian chocolate export values, while the share of exports to the EU member states in 1993 accounted for 89 per cent of the total export value. Total

---

[6] Expressed in 2010 euros.

Table 5.1 Average annual growth rates of export volumes and values (1950–2013)

Period	1950–59	1960–69	1970–79	1980–89	1990–99	2000–09	2010–13
Volume	2.9%	19.8%	7.5%	5.8%	9.2%	3.3%	6.9%
Value	0.8%	18.3%	6.9%	6.1%	7.2%	2.5%	3.8%

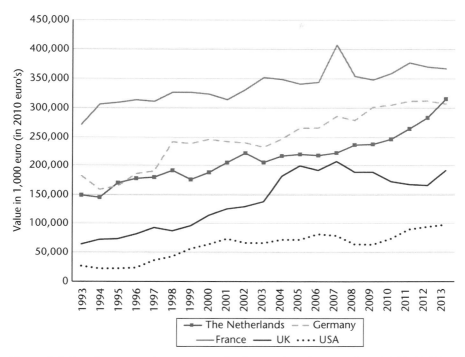

Figure 5.4 Top five export destinations of Belgium chocolate in values (1993–2013)

Source: National Bank of Belgium (2014b).

Notes:

[1] Chocolate is here defined as chocolate used for consumption. It excludes export and imports of cocoa beans, cocoa paste, cocoa butter, fat and oil, and cocoa powder.

[2] The authors received the original data from the National Bank of Belgium after direct correspondence.

volume of exports to EU members increased from 173,345 to 437,368 tons (respectively 804 million to 1.4 billion in 2010 euros) between 1993 and 2013. The top five export destinations for Belgian chocolate in 2013 were the Netherlands, Germany, France, the UK, and the USA (see Figure 5.4). While exports to France have been relatively stable over time, exports to the Netherlands have increased by 111 per cent, and to Germany by 69 per cent, over the past 20 years. Exports to the UK and USA in 2013 were over three times higher than in 1993.

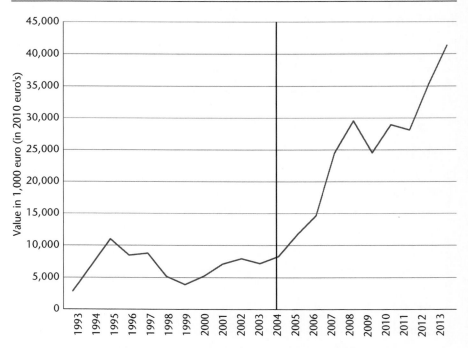

Figure 5.5 Exports to the EU new member states entering in 2004 in values

Source: National Bank of Belgium (2014b).

Notes:

[1] Aggregation of exports to Slovenia, Cyprus, Malta, Estonia, Latvia, Slovakia, Hungary, Poland, Lithuania.

[2] Chocolate is here defined as chocolate used for consumption. It excludes export and imports of cocoa beans, cocoa paste, cocoa butter, fat and oil, and cocoa powder.

The accession of new EU member states has further stimulated exports to the EU market. Figure 5.5 shows that exports to the countries that joined the EU in 2004— Cyprus, Estonia, Hungary, Lithuania, Latvia, Malta, Poland, Slovenia, Slovakia, and the Czech Republic—dramatically increased after 2004.

The share of exports to non-EU countries has increased in the past two decades, rising from 11 per cent to 23 per cent from 1993 to 2013 (see Figure 5.6), and non-EU exports are now over four times as high as they were twenty years ago. The USA, Japan, and Canada are the main importing countries outside the EU. In recent years, China, Malaysia, Turkey, Brazil, Thailand, and Mexico have become important new trade destinations for Belgian chocolate.

Chocolate Products

A key driver of the considerable growth of the sector since the 1960s has been couverture chocolate (Figure 5.7). Broken down by product category, data on chocolate production volumes reveal that the share of filled and unfilled chocolate

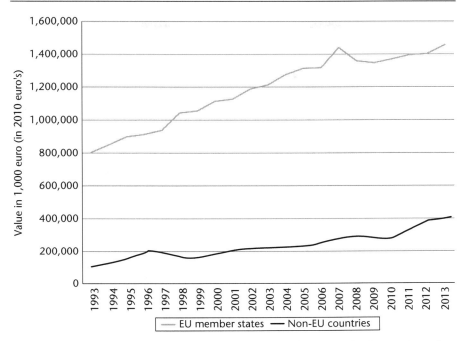

Figure 5.6 Exports to European countries and countries outside Europe in values (1993–2013)

Source: National Bank of Belgium (2014b).

Note: Chocolate is here defined as chocolate used for consumption. It excludes export and imports of cocoa beans, cocoa paste, cocoa butter, fat and oil, and cocoa powder.

in total production decreased substantially between 1970 and 2013.[7] Couverture chocolate, on the other hand, became the leading product of the Belgian chocolate sector. The share of couverture chocolate increased from 27 to 70 per cent between 1970 and 2013. The share of bonbons and pralines remained more stable over time, fluctuating between 14 and 20 per cent.

Most of the production of couverture in Belgium is used for the production of final consumption goods which are sold in both the domestic and export market. Only one third of the couverture chocolate produced in Belgium is exported. Couverture is still the largest export product when we analyse the export shares by product category in total export volume (Figure 5.8). But pralines and bonbons are the leading product of the Belgian export market in terms of value. In 2013, the share of pralines and bonbons accounted for 45 per cent of the total export value. Unfilled chocolate was the second largest export product, with a share of 21 per cent in total value. Couverture chocolate had only a share of 19 per cent in total

---

[7] For a technical definition of these categories see note at Figure 5.7. Generally speaking, unfilled chocolate refers to chocolate bars and tablets, milk or plain, with or without added fruits, cereals, and nuts, while filled chocolate refers to bars and tablets (CAOBISCO 2013).

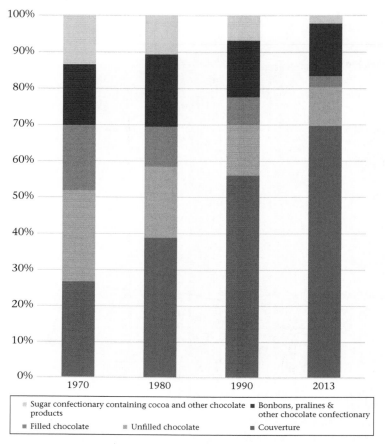

Figure 5.7 Production of Belgian chocolate by product category in percentage of total production volumes (1970–2013)

Source: FOD Economie (1970–1993); FOD Economie (1997–2007)—covering 2000–05; Eurostat—Industrial Statistics (2015).

Notes:

[1] Chocolate is here defined as chocolate used for consumption. It excludes export and imports of cocoa beans, cocoa paste, cocoa butter, fat and oil, and cocoa powder.

[2] The data on production of Belgian chocolate were collected from the yearly statistics of production. Each year corresponds to the year of publication. In other words, we have used the books which have been published in the following years: 1965, 1966, 1967, 1968, 1969, 1970, 1971, 1972, 1973, 1974, 1975, 1976, 1977, 1978, 1979, 1980, 1981, 1982, 1983, 1984, 1985, 1986, 1987, 1988, 1989, 1990, 1991, 1992, 1993.

[3] The data were collected from the yearly statistics on industrial production of the PRODCOM industry. Each year corresponds to the year of publication. In other words, we have used the books which have been published in the following years: 2000, 2001, 2002, 2003, 2004, 2005, 2006, 2007.

[4] For the years in 1970, 1980, and 1990, the categorization is obtained by summing the following categories found in the Maandelijkse Industriële Statistieken provided by the FOD Economie: 'Dekchocolade' for 'Couverture'; 'Volle chocolade (zonder melk)' and 'Volle melkchocolade' for 'Unfilled chocolate'; 'Gevulde chocolade (repen en tabletten)' for 'Filled chocolate'; 'Volle chocolade bonbons' and 'Suikergoed met cacao: chocolade bonbons' for 'Bonbons, pralines and other chocolate confectionary'; and 'Ander suikergoed met cacao' for 'Sugar confectionary containing cocoa and other chocolate products'. For 2013, the categorization was based on grouping the following PRODCOM codes provided by the EUROSTAT database: 10822130–10822190 for 'Couverture'; 10822235, 10822239, and 10822255 for 'Unfilled chocolate'; 10822233 for 'Filled chocolate'; 10822243 to 10822253 for 'Bonbons, pralines and other chocolate confectionary'; and 10822260 to 10822290 for 'Sugar confectionary containing cocoa and other chocolate products'.

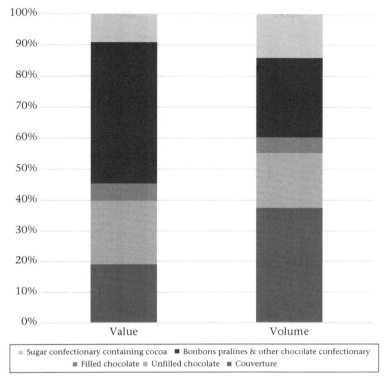

Figure 5.8 Export of Belgian chocolate by product category in percentage of total export values and volumes in 2013

Source: National Bank of Belgium (2014b)—export data in 2013.

export value in 2013. Filled chocolate, and other sugar confectionary containing cocoa, had shares of, respectively, 10 and 5 per cent.

From Crafts to Multinationals

The growth in the chocolate sector is also reflected in changes in the industry structure. Since the mid-1960s, several family-owned enterprises and artisan producers have evolved into or have been taken over by large chocolate manufacturers, some of which are now major global players present at most stages of the chocolate production chain—from the production of intermediate products, such as chocolate couverture, to final consumer goods, such as pralines and chocolate bars.

Table 5.2 provides a non-exhaustive overview of some of the key larger chocolate companies with Belgian origins in 2013. With more than a thousand workers, Puratos (Belcolade) is the largest Belgian chocolate company in terms of employees, followed by Barry Callebaut Belgium NV (850), Leonidas (385), and

Table 5.2 Overview of key large chocolate companies of Belgian origin

Company	Foundation Year	Headquarters	Ownership History	Country Destination	Turnover 2013 MLN Euro	Employment 2013	NBO Company Share of Chocolate Confectionary %, 2013
Côte d'Or (Mondelez Belgium)	1883	Mechelen	• Founded by Charles Neuhaus • Purchased by the Swiss company Jacobs Suchard in 1987 • Purchased by the American multinational company, Kraft General Foods in 1990, which was renamed Mondelez International in 2012	Over 50 countries	402.2	155	34.6
Neuhaus	1857	Brussels (Vlezenbeek)	• Founded by Jean Nehaus • In 1974 the Belgian company Beukelaer acquired Neuhaus Group. • In 1997 Neuhaus was introduced on the stock exchange • In 2006 Compagnie du Bois Sauvage purchased all the company shares	Over 1,000 sales outlets in more than 50 countries	66.0	320	1.7
Callebaut (Barry Callebaut Belgium NV)	1850	Zurich (Lubbeek)	• Brewery and milling company founded by Eugène Callebaut in 1850 • In 1996 Callebaut merged with French chocolate maker Cacao Barry to form the Barry Callebaut Group, which has its corporate headquarters in Zurich, Switzerland	35 countries (as Barry Callebaut Group)	18.994	846	2.9
Leonidas (Confiserie Leonidas)	1913	Brussels (Anderlecht)	• Founded in 1913 by Greek-Cypriot American confectioner Leonidas Kestekides in Ghent	1,250 shops in around 50 countries	72.9	384	4.4

Company	Founded	Location	History	Destination			
Godiva (Godiva NV)	1926	Brussels (Koekelberg)	• ...since the 1970s, the company has been on the Belgian Stock Exchange, even though the family still played a role in its administration[1] • Founded in Brussels by Pierre Draps Senior in 1926 • In 1967 it was purchased by the American company Campbell Soup • In 2008, Godiva was acquired by the Turkish company Yıldız Holding	80 countries	74.9	307	2
Galler (Galler chocolatiers)	1930	Liège (Vaux-sous-Chèvremont)	• Founded in 1976 by Jean Galler • In 2006 Galler increased its financial base by 3 million euros to permit its expansion in London, Lebanon, and Qatar. Control of the company remains with the Galler family (52% shareholding), but now expands to include 33% holding by two members of the Qatari royal family, Al-Thani, and 15% by the company executives[2]	10 countries	17.5	97	1.7
Guylian (Chocolaterie Guylian)	1960	Sint-Niklaas	• Founded by Guy Foubert in 1960 • In 2008, Lotte Confectionery from South Korea bought the company for $164 million[3]	Over 100 countries	79.8	215	0.9
Puratos (Belcolade)	1988	Brussels (Groot-Bijgaarden)	• In 1988, Puratos, a Belgian international group specializing in bakery, pastry, and chocolate, launched a new brand, Belcolade	Puratos products, including Belcolade sold in over 100 countries	396.9	1,069	

Source: Data on turnover and employment are from the company guide developed by De Tijd and Graydon (2013)'. Data on NBO company share of chocolate confectionary are from Euromonitor International (2014). Information on ownership history and country destination is from company's websites, if not otherwise specified.

Notes:

[1] Information retrieved from Rosenblum (2006).

[2] Lamfalussy (2006).

[3] Yeon-hee and Ju-min (2008).

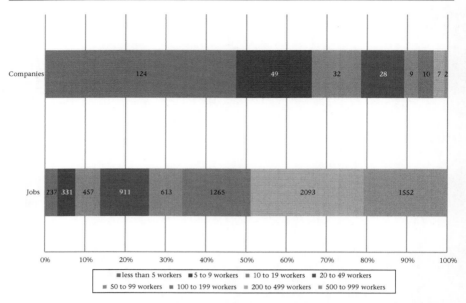

Figure 5.9 Distribution of companies and jobs by size for the chocolate industry Q1 2014

Source: Data received from Choprabisco based on Belgian National Office Social Security (RSZ 2014).

Note: The authors received the original data from Choprabisco after direct correspondence.

Neuhaus (320). Both Barry Callebaut and Puratos are mostly industrial producers while Leonidas and Neuhaus produce final consumption chocolate goods. In terms of revenue, Barry Callebaut Belgium NV is ranked first, with an annual turnover of approximately 1.9 billion euros, with second-ranked Mondelēz Belgium and third-ranked Puratos (Belcolade) a long way behind (both around 400 million euros).

Before discussing some of these companies in more detail, it should be noted that many Belgian chocolatiers are still small scale. Data for 2014 show that,[8] out of a total of 261 Belgium chocolate companies, 173 companies are micro enterprises (with less than 10 employees), 70 per cent of which employ less than 5 workers. Together with small-sized companies (between 10 and 50 employees), they account for more than 90 per cent of the total number of Belgian chocolate companies (see Figure 5.9).[9] Most of these micro and small chocolate enterprises

[8] These statistical data refer to the 10.82 category, which also includes sugar confectionary. They refer to number of companies with at least one employee, so self-employed producers are not included.

[9] This categorization of companies follows a European Commission definition of small and medium-sized enterprises (SMEs): micro = less than 10; small = 10 to 49; medium-sized = 50 to 249; large = more than 250 employee (EU recommendation 2003/261).

tend to position themselves in the upper premium segment and target niche markets of the chocolate sector.

Four Historical Cases of 'Belgian Chocolate'

We use four case studies to illustrate the historical development of the business growth of four key Belgian chocolate companies which, in different ways and for different reasons, have played a distinctive role in the Belgian chocolate industry at home and worldwide.

Neuhaus: Inventor of the Praline

In 1857, Jean Neuhaus immigrates from Neuchatel in Switzerland to Brussels and opens a pharmacy-confectioners shop in Galerie de la Reine in the centre of the city.[10] There, he sells his medicines covered in chocolate to make them more appetizing to customers. The business becomes such a huge success that, in 1885, he sets up the Neuhaus–Perrin Confectionery and Chocolate factory.

In 1912, his grandson, Jean Neuhaus Jr, produces the first filled chocolate that he names 'praline', a new product that will become an essential feature of 'the Belgian chocolate'. Louise Agostini, his wife, designs the 'ballotin' (praline box), an invention that prevents pralines from being damaged. The design of ballotin is registered on 16 August 1915 and it becomes the most used chocolate box by all Belgian chocolate manufacturers (Neuhaus 2015).

Neuhaus also took the lead in introducing franchising in the late 1940s. The company requests employers or partners responsible for sales of Neuhaus products to do a six-month internship at the Neuhaus shop in Galerie de la Reine in Brussels. Shops and boutiques selling Neuhaus products must have a distinctive look and decor (Mercier 2008).

In the 1970s, Neuhaus starts exporting overseas and expanding sales of Neuhaus pralines in the USA, Canada, Colombia, and Japan (Mercier 2008). At the end of the 1990s, the company is introduced on the stock exchange, and, in 2006, the Belgian holding group Compagnie du Bois Sauvage acquires all the shares of the company. Today, Neuhaus is one of the few 'Belgian chocolate' makers that are still fully Belgian-owned. It mostly manufactures in Belgium, while exporting its products and running its own shops in around fifty countries worldwide (Bois Sauvage 2014).

---

[10] This section is based on Neuhaus (2015), Bois Sauvage (2014), and Mercier (2008).

Côte d'Or: Merged into a Multinational Company

Charles Neuhaus founds the Côte d'Or factory in 1870 in Schaarbeek, Belgium.[11,12] In 1889 the Bieswal family buys the Neuhaus chocolate factory, and merges in 1906 with the Michiels family company to create Alimenta S.A. The new company develops the 'Côte d'Or' chocolate with its famous elephant trademark and expands: the number of workers increases from around 100 before the First World War to 350 in the 1930s. In 1931, the Côte d'Or trademark is registered in the USA. At the Brussels World Fair in 1935 the company presents the 'Cream tablets', 'Mignonettes', 'Bouchées', and 'Chokotoffs'—products that are still very popular today (Olivier 1997).

During the Second World War, the company decides to temporarily replace Côte d'Or with a lower-quality chocolate brand 'Congobar', because it cannot guarantee the delivery of high-quality chocolate. After the war, the company stops the production of 'Congobar', reintroduces its classic products, and launches several new Côte d'Or products (Côte d'Or 2014).

In the 1960s and the 1970s, the company continues to expand abroad, with new operations in France, the Netherlands, Switzerland, the UK, and Japan (Olivier 1997). In 1982, the company is launched on the stock exchange, and in 1987 the Swiss Suchard company acquires 66 per cent of the Côte d'Or shares. In the 1990s, Suchard is taken over by the US firm Philip Morris, which is in turn integrated into Kraft General Foods (KGF) International. In 1993, KGF Europe and Jacobs Suchard are merged to form Kraft Jacob Suchard, a unit of KGF International. In 1995, Kraft General Foods changes its name to Kraft Foods and, in 2012, following a split in the group, two separate companies are established: Mondelēz International, one of the world's largest multinational companies in the snack sector, and Kraft Foods Group, the North American grocery products company. Côte d'Or becomes part of Mondelēz International (Mondelēz 2014). While now part of a global multinational, Côte d'Or still retains significant chocolate production activities in Belgium. In 2013, Mondelēz Belgium S.A. was ranked number one in chocolate confectionery in Belgium, accounting for 35 per cent of Belgian chocolate retail value. With a 21 per cent value share, Côte d'Or is currently the company's greatest asset (Euromonitor International 2014).

(Barry) Callebaut: A Dominant Player in the Global Chocolate Supply Chain

In 1850, Eugène Callebaut founds a brewery and milling company in Wieze, Belgium. Sixty-one years later, in 1911, Octaaf Callebaut, his grandson, turns one of the company divisions towards chocolate production.[13]

---

[11] This section is based on Oliver (2007), Euromonitor International (2014), Côte d'Or (2014) and Mondelēz (2014).

[12] Remarkably, Charles Neuhaus appears not to be related to the inventor of the pralines, Jean Neuhaus. The name Côte d'Or refers to the country of origin of the cocoa beans: 'Gold Coast', now Ghana.

[13] This section is based on Barry Callebaut (2013, 2014), Callebaut (2014), and Cohen and Covell (2005).

In 1925 Octaaf invents a mechanism for the storage and transport of 'couverture chocolate' in liquid form. This dramatically reduces production and transport costs and thus facilitates the use of chocolate in other foodstuffs, such as cereals, bread, biscuits, and so on. The company reorients its business and specializes in supplying chocolate makers, bakeries, and confectionaries with high-quality couverture chocolate. The production of the couverture chocolate becomes the Callebaut company's core business. While initially focusing on supplying to Belgian chocolate makers, after the Second World War the company expands its business in both Europe and North America (Callebaut 2014).

The 1980s mark the end of the family control of the Callebaut business. In 1981, the company is bought by Interfood, a subsidiary of the Swiss chocolate manufacturer Tobler-Suchard. In 1983, Interfood merges with Klaus J. Jacobs to form Jacobs Suchard, resulting in one of the world's leading chocolate companies (Cohen and Covell 2005). In 1990, Philip Morris acquires the sweet division of Jacob Suchard, while Klaus Jacobs, through his company KL Jacobs AG, keeps the industrial chocolate divisions of Jacobs Suchard, holding 100 per cent control of Callebaut operations (Cohen and Covell 2005). In 1996, Jacobs also acquires the French company Cacao Barry and creates the Barry Callebaut Group.[14] With the merger, the Barry Callebaut Group becomes a leading player in the global cocoa–chocolate supply chain, with activities worldwide. The group has cocoa and chocolate factories in 35 countries. In 2013, Barry Callebaut acquires Petra Foods, a cocoa ingredients business based in Singapore. This increases the company's cocoa grinding capacities by 60 per cent, making it the world's top cocoa processor. The enlarged company has around 50 production facilities worldwide, sells its products in over 100 countries, and employs around 8,500 people. Although Europe still represents the company's largest market, accounting for 43 per cent of total sales volume, recent growth of sales is strongest in the Asian-Pacific region (Barry Callebaut 2014).

The company is present in all stages of the supply chain, from sourcing and processing cocoa beans to couverture and final chocolate production, such as chocolate fillings, decorations, and compounds. It supplies both to large multinational and industrial customers and to small gourmet customers, such as artisanal chocolatiers, bakers, and pastry chefs.[15]

Godiva: Luxury Chocolates around the World

Godiva's history dates back to 1926,[16] when chocolate maker Pierre Draps Senior creates his chocolate pralines in a small atelier of his home in Brussels. His

---

[14] As of 2013 Jacobs Holding AG is the group's ultimate parent with a share of 50.11% of the shares issued (Barry Callebaut 2013).

[15] The Barry Callebaut group is divided into three main business units: cocoa products (such as cocoa butter, cocoa powder, and cocoa liquor), food manufacturers' products, and gourmet products. The latter are produced and supplied by the Callebaut unit in Belgium and the Cocoa Barry unit in France, which still operate separately under the umbrella of the Barry Callebaut Group (Barry Callebaut 2013).

[16] This section is based on Godiva (2015a, 2015b, 2015c), e-Business W@tch (2006), Grant (2004).

chocolate business quickly becomes a family affair. His four children are involved in the production, packaging, and delivery of the family chocolates. These chocolates are initially sold in department stores in Brussels. Later the family opens a Godiva shop in Brussels (Godiva 2015a, 2015b).

Since the beginning, the Draps family wants to position the Godiva brand in the luxury segment of the chocolate market. This is done through the development of distinctive products with elegant packaging, such as the 'Fabiola' brand, created in 1958 to celebrate the engagement of Queen Fabiola to King Baudouin I of Belgium (Grant 2004).

Godiva is the first Belgian chocolate company to open a Belgian chocolate shop outside Belgium, launching a Godiva shop in Paris in 1958. Other shops are soon opened in the UK, Germany, and Italy. Godiva expands to the USA, in Philadelphia, in 1966. And to the Asian market, firstly Japan in 1972, followed by Hong Kong in 1998, and Taiwan and Singapore in the early 2000s. The first store in China opened in 2009. Today, the Godiva brand is present in over 80 countries and the company owns and runs more than 450 boutiques and shops worldwide (Godiva 2015a, 2015c).

For the first 40 years, until 1966, the Godiva company is owned exclusively by the Draps family. In 1967, Pepperidge Farm acquires a two-thirds stake and, later, Campbell Soup Company completes the purchase of the remainder of the Godiva company and sets up a US production facility in Reading, Pennsylvania (Grant 2004). The Pennsylvania plant supplies the whole North American market while the Belgian manufacturing facilities supply the markets in Europe, the Middle East, and Asia (e-Business W@tch 2006). The US plant produces approximately the same amount of chocolate for the North American market as the Belgian plant does for the rest of the world (Godiva 2015b). In 2008, the Campbell Soup Company sells its Godiva Chocolatier unit to the Turkish company Yildiz Holding.

During its 80 years of operation, the Godiva has conducted an effective marketing strategy and brand image advertising, which have made the company one of the world's leaders of the luxury segment of the chocolate sector. For example, in the late 1970s in the USA, customers at a Godiva 'boutique' (as the company name its shops) are treated like buyers at a fine jewellery store. Products include model kits of Porsche, Rolls Royce, and Mercedes automobiles, which can be 'glued' together by melting included extra pieces of chocolate. In 1995, a survey carried out via Godiva's website reveals that the typical customer is a woman earning an average salary of $60,000 per year (Grant 2004).

Key Elements in the Growth and Global Expansion of 'Belgian Chocolates'

Just as companies' innovations in both products and marketing have played a crucial role in making the history of Belgian chocolate, so too have the entrepreneurship skills and effective management strategies of many of the artisan firms that later became large chocolate Belgian manufacturers.

These cases illustrate several characteristics of the global expansion of 'Belgian chocolates'. First, the exports were associated with a global expansion of chocolate retailing by many Belgian companies. This was especially the case for luxury chocolate, such as pralines. The first Godiva shop outside Belgium was inaugurated in Paris in 1958. Similarly, Leonidas opened its first European store in Lille, France, in 1969, and in 1978 Neuhaus' pralines were launched overseas in the USA, Canada, and Japan. At present, the large companies selling luxury Belgian chocolates own and operate shops in many—some more than 100—countries around the world (see Table 5.2).[17]

Second, a very different international strategy was followed by the companies producing intermediate chocolate products, especially the Callebaut company, which produces mostly chocolate couverture. They have achieved a dominant position in the global cocoa/chocolate industry. Since the merger of Callebaut with the French company Cocoa Barry, Barry Callebaut has dominated the entire supply chocolate chain, producing its industrial couverture chocolates for the whole food industry, from food manufacturers to artisans and professional users of chocolate such as chocolatiers, pastry chefs, or bakers, as well as producing products for vending machines. Over the last years, Barry Callebaut has continued its expansion, moving to emerging markets. The recent acquisition of the Singapore-based company Petra Foods, has expanded the production capacity of the company as well as giving them a strong position in the Asian markets (see section 'Four Historical Cases of "Belgian Chocolate"').

From an analysis of the sector, it can be seen that these two strategies have been mutually reinforcing. As mentioned, many Belgian chocolate makers can focus on their core business, such as the production of pralines, while procuring couverture directly from a Belgian intermediate chocolate producer, such as Callebaut and Puratos, rather than producing it in-house.

Finally, as the Belgian chocolate industry has evolved, so have its ownership and management structures. The successful global business of several Belgian chocolate companies—such as Godiva, Guylian, and Côte d'Or—have led to their introduction on stock markets. Although most of these companies are still manufacturing in Belgium, foreign multinational corporations have taken over their businesses (see Table 5.2). Côte d'Or was bought by the US Kraft General Foods in 1990 and become part of Mondelēz International in 2012. In 1967 Godiva was acquired by the Campbell and in 2008 sold to Turkish company Yıldız Holding. Guylian was purchased by Lotte Confectionery from South Korea. As mentioned, Callebaut merged with French chocolate maker Cacao Barry to form the Barry Callebaut Group, with a majority of the shares owned by Jacob Suchard, and its corporate headquarters in Switzerland.

---

[17] In the 1930s, some Belgian companies had already achieved their international dimension; the brand Côte d'Or was, for example, registered in the USA in 1931.

Defining and Protecting 'Belgian Chocolate'

The worldwide success of the Belgian chocolate industry has led to a series of challenges which are threatening the notion of 'Belgian chocolate' per se. Frequent attempts by copycats to imitate 'Belgian chocolates' and benefit from the increasing global demand for it have led the Belgian chocolate sector to define and seek protection for 'Belgian chocolate'. Yet the internationalization of some of the most successful Belgian companies, which have undergone an extensive ownership transformation through mergers and acquisitions with global investors and, in some cases, delocalization (partially or entirely) of their production process outside Belgium, makes the definition, qualification, and protection of 'Belgian chocolate' more challenging. Surging global demand for Belgian chocolate, mainly driven by emerging markets in Asia, has led to an expansion of fraudulently labelled 'Belgian chocolate' products, as imitators seek to benefit from the rising demand. However, this is nothing new. Attempts to define Belgian chocolate are almost as old as the industry itself. As early as 1894, a Belgian royal decree limited the circulation of chocolate imitations that replaced cocoa with poor-quality fats.[18] Article 2 of this decree established that it was 'illegal to sell, have in possession or expose for sale, or to transmit any product whatever, under the designation "chocolate", that is not manufactured exclusively from shelled cocoa, and that in a minimum proportion of 35 per cent, and ordinary sugar, with or without admixture of spices' (for further detail see Chapter 15, this volume).[19]

The definition of Belgian chocolate became a particularly sensitive issue during the 30-year 'chocolate war' in the EU (see Cidell and Alberts 2006; Chapter 15, this volume). The so-called chocolate war refers to a dispute on what could be called 'chocolate'. It began in 1973, between new member states the UK, Ireland, and Denmark, and older member states Belgium, France, Italy, Spain, and Germany. Belgium, together with France, Italy, and Spain refused to allow products to be called 'chocolate' if they contained cocoa butter substitutes. The war was ended by the EU 'Chocolate Directive' adopted in 2003,[20] which allowed up to 5 per cent of cocoa butter in chocolate to be replaced. The 2003 Chocolate Directive was seen by most Belgian manufacturers—who explicitly indicate that their chocolate products contain 100 per cent cocoa butter and no vegetable fats—as a potential threat of reduced quality standards for chocolate.

In 2000, before the EU Directive was adopted, the Belgian Federal Government tried to address the concerns of the Belgian chocolate industry by creating the chocolate collective trademark 'AMBAO' (with AMBAO meaning 'chocolate' in

---

[18] Arrêté royal du 18 novembre 1894 relatif au commerce du cacao et du chocolat. *Moniteur Belge du 3–7 Décembre 1894.*

[19] Author's own translation of Article 2 of Arrêté royal 1894: 'Il est défendu de vendre, d'exposer en vente, de détenir ou de transporter pour la vente sous la simple dénomination de chocolat, aucun produit qui ne serait pas exclusivement composé de cacao décortiqué, dans la proportion de 35 p. c. au moins, et de sucre ordinaire (saccharose), avec ou sans addition d'aromates' (Moniteur Belge 1894).

[20] Directive 2000/36/EC of the European Parliament and the Council of 23 June 2000 reading on cocoa and chocolate products intended for human consumption.

Swahili). The AMBAO trademark stipulated quality and manufacturing criteria. The criteria included that 'Belgian chocolate' products contain 100 per cent cocoa butter. To produce 'AMBAO chocolate', any company, whether Belgian or foreign, had to register and pay a licence fee to obtain the AMBAO trademark. However, the initiative failed, with only a few companies registering for AMBAO. Over the past decade, no company has applied for or used an AMBAO logo.

There are several reasons for the initiative's lack of success. Belgian chocolate manufacturers were not willing to pay for the trademark, which was mostly perceived as a certification and administrative cost only, rather than an investment to help protect the quality of their products. The AMBAO logo design did not have any reference to Belgium, making it very difficult for consumers to associate AMBAO with Belgian chocolate quality and, more generally, understand its meaning. Moreover, as any manufacturer, Belgian or otherwise, could register for the AMBAO trademark, Belgian companies did not see it as an effective tool to distinguish high-quality Belgian chocolate from other products (LCM International 2006). Some Belgian companies, producing high-quality niche chocolate products, were even worried about harm to their reputation if they applied it.

The Belgian Chocolate Code

In 2007, the chocolate companies themselves took the initiative. The Belgian national association of chocolate manufacturers (Choprabisco) approved the 'Belgian Chocolate Code' in order to implement EU Directive 2000/13, a 2000 EU Directive,[21] which established specific rules concerning the labelling and advertising of foodstuffs, to prevent consumers from being misled.

The Code is a private standard, with no legal weight, signed by chocolate manufacturer members. It sets out specific criteria for 'Belgian chocolate' products such as bars and pralines. The criteria include that the complete process of mixing, refining, and conching is done in Belgium. Foreign manufacturers that use Belgian chocolate as an ingredient can only refer to it, indicating 'Made with chocolate from Belgium/Belgian chocolate'. For instance, Choprabisco explained to the press in 2013 that some foreign companies procure the chocolate couverture from the Belgian factory of large manufactures such as Barry Callebaut. 'That shouldn't count as Belgian chocolate. What you should be saying is: "Made with Belgian chocolate"' (Blenkinsop 2013).[22]

Exceptions are given to products for which an historical heritage link with Belgium is proven. In this case, the references 'Belgian flavour', 'Belgian tradition', 'Belgian recipe', and 'Belgian style' are permitted, but they can only be indicated on the back of the packaging and should not lead the average consumer to believe the product is of Belgian origin (Choprabisco 2007).[23]

---

[21] Directive 2000/13/EC of the European Parliament and of the Council on the approximation of the laws of the member states relating to the labelling, presentation, and advertising of foodstuffs.

[22] Blenkinsop (2013).   [23] Choprabisco (2007).

In an attempt to counter both misleading and fraudulent practices, the Belgian Chocolate Code also provides guidelines for Belgian manufacturers on how to deal with and react to misleading labelling practices of foreign companies, including, if appropriate, pursuing legal action. Since the Code's entry into force, several cases of misleading practices have been exposed, including in Hungary, Turkey, Australia, and China. Choprabisco reported that in 2014 at least five letters were sent to foreign chocolate manufacturers to demand modifications to their labelling, which, it is believed, mislead consumers by using text or illustrations referring to Belgium.

Since the adoption of the Belgian Chocolate Code, 55 Belgian manufacturers have signed up and 70 new members are in the process of joining.[24] Together, these businesses represent 85–90 per cent of the total volume of the country's chocolate production. However, not all companies support the initiative. The Code is particularly problematic for companies with historical links to Belgium but which also have a very strong production presence outside the country. They feel penalized by the Code, which emphasizes strongly the Belgian location of the production process. For example, as a large part of its production is now localized in the USA, Godiva seems to find that the criteria laid down in the Belgian Chocolate Code, which narrows the labelling of 'Belgian chocolate' to chocolate produced in Belgium only, are very restrictive. They were reported as saying in March 2013 that: 'these Godiva chocolates [coming from the US operations] are still essentially Belgian, in the same way that one might think of a BMW made in South Carolina as still essentially a German car' and that 'It would be very limiting if only chocolate produced in Belgium could be considered' (Blenkinsop 2013).[25]

GI Protection for Belgian Chocolate?

In January 2013, the EU updated its rules on the protection of quality agricultural and food products, through Regulation 1151/2012 on the so-called 'geographical indication' (GI) regime.[26] Broadly speaking, this new EU legislative framework for protecting agri-food products other than wine and spirits introduced two main changes, which could potentially have some important implications for Belgian chocolate.

First, the 2012 Regulation included widening the eligibility scope for food products, such as chocolate—allowing all 'chocolate and derived products' to apply for a 'PDO' (Protected Designation of Origin) or 'PGI' (Protected Geographical

---

[24] Choprabisco is made up of 170 members, ranging from the small-sized enterprise to the multinationals company. The 70 new members are all artisanal small-sized companies.

[25] Blenkinsop (2013).

[26] As explained clearly in Chapter 15, this volume: 'Agricultural products and foodstuffs are divided into "products with a Geographical Indication" and "products without a Geographical Indication". Within the first category, there are two subcategories: "Protected Designation of Origin" (PDO) and "Protected Geographical Indication" (PGI), with PDO as the highest quality level as all the stages of production take place in the same defined geographical area.' For a PGI, only one of the production stages must be in the defined area.

Indication) label.[27] Previously, 'chocolate and other food preparations containing cocoa' could only apply for the lesser 'TSG' (Traditional Specialty Guaranteed) label (Council Regulation (EEC) No 2082/92).[28] However, as the PDO label requires all the production steps (production, processing, and preparation) to take place within a given geographical area,[29] this cannot be applied to Belgian chocolate, which is instead eligible for PGI or TSG status.[30]

Second, Regulation 1151/2012 also introduced other changes to the GI rules. Article 5 (2c) states that GI is a term that identifies a product originating from a specific place, region, or country, whereas before it was only a place or region. It is therefore now possible for countries to apply for a PGI, meaning that in principle a group of Belgian chocolate producers or processors could apply for a PGI designation for 'Belgian chocolate' coming from all parts of Belgium.

This could be a potential opportunity for the Belgian chocolate industry to apply for an EU GI label (i.e. PGI) such as those in place for other processed products like wine and ham. This is reflected in the statement of the export manager of one of the top Belgian chocolate companies: 'We want Belgium to be thought of as the chocolate version of the Champagne region among sparkling wines' (Blenkinsop 2013).[31]

If Belgian chocolate was to be granted PGI status, this could have important trade implications for Belgian chocolate manufacturing. If it had PGI status, Belgian chocolate protection could be discussed at trade negotiations between the EU and third countries. This could potentially be a mechanism to protect 'Belgian chocolate' from misleading and fraudulent commercial practices inside and outside the EU. The current EU trade policy includes pro-active efforts to ensure recognition of its GI products (European Commission 2015). This was evident in the bilateral trade deal with Canada agreed in October 2013,[32] in which Canada committed to recognizing nearly 150 EU GI products (both PDO and PGIs). The European Commission has made clear its hopes for a similar deal on GIs in a potential EU–US 'Transatlantic Trade and Investment Partnership' (TTIP) currently being negotiated.[33]

However, it could be a long time before a potential EU PGI is applied to Belgian chocolate. The GI application process is a complex one for a sector as large as that

[27] Regulation (EU) 1551/2012 of the European Parliament and of the Council of 21 November 2012 on quality schemes for agricultural products and foodstuffs.

[28] The Traditional Specialty Guaranteed (TSG) is the lowest 'quality' label scheme where protection can be granted to products without a link to the origin (a geographical area) (see Chapter 15, this volume, for more details). Council Regulation (EEC) No. 2082/92 of 14 July 1992 on certificates of specific character for agricultural products and foodstuffs.

[29] The exception to this rule only applies to certain raw materials (live animals, meat, and milk), which can come from an area different from the defined geographical area, with the final product nonetheless still eligible for a PDO (Regulation (EU) No 1151/2012).

[30] Cocoa beans are all imported from third countries and therefore they are not produced in the same geographical area where they are processed, i.e. Belgium.

[31] Blenkinsop (2013).

[32] The EU–Canada 'Comprehensive Economic and Trade Agreement' (CETA), was agreed in October 2013 but is not yet fully ratified.

[33] Speech by EU Commissioner for Trade Cecilia Malmström on 18 November 2014, available at <http://europa.eu/rapid/press-release_SPEECH-14-1921_en.htm>.

of chocolate. The National Association of Belgian chocolate manufacturers and the Belgian authorities, both at federal and regional level, have just started the process of assessing and studying what is needed to obtain GI status.

Conclusions

This chapter has provided an historical overview of the remarkable evolution of the Belgian chocolate industry, which has led 'Belgian chocolates' to be well known and appreciated all over the world. But it has also shown that it is only in recent decades that the Belgian chocolate sector has achieved its tremendous success. Throughout the nineteenth century, Belgian chocolate manufacturers struggled to benefit from the rapidly growing chocolate demand in Europe. Until the 1960s, the performance of Belgium as chocolate exporter was mixed.

This chapter has also identified the specific elements and factors that contributed to Belgian chocolate producers being able to compete globally in the early twentieth century: a favourable import regime combined with investment in new technologies and new product and marketing innovations.

Once chocolate became a food item of mass consumption after the Second World War, Belgian producers were finally able to respond to the dramatic increase in European demand. From the 1960s onwards, production boomed, mechanization and scaling-up of the production process improved productivity in the sector, and exports grew rapidly. In the 1990s, the average annual growth rate was some 9 per cent per year. Although the European market is still the main export destination for Belgian chocolate, the share of exports to non-EU countries increased from 10 per cent to 17 per cent from 1993 to 2013.

Three main elements seem to characterize the global growth of 'Belgian chocolates'. First, the international expansion of chocolate retailing by many Belgian companies, some of which now have shops in over a hundred countries. Second, some Belgian suppliers have achieved a dominant position in the global cocoa/chocolate industry. And third, there has been a strategic restructuring of the ownership and management of many Belgian chocolate companies. This multinationalization of 'Belgian companies' is reflected in the historical development of the business growth of the four big companies, Neuhaus, Côte d'Or, Barry Callebaut, and Godiva, we studied. These companies have, in different ways and for different reasons, played a distinctive role in the Belgian chocolate industry at home and worldwide: Neuhaus made its name globally with the invention of pralines; Côte d'Or (Mondelēz) has enjoyed a tremendous expansion internationally and domestically—and is now ranked number one in chocolate confectionery in Belgium; Callebaut, the inventor of couverture chocolate, merged with Barry to create the Barry Callebaut Group, a dominant player in the global chocolate supply chain with production houses worldwide; and Godiva has expanded its market and production globally and positioned itself as one of the world's leaders in the super-premium chocolate category.

Several attempts have been made by the Belgian Federal Government, as well as by the industry, to define and protect 'Belgian chocolate'. The AMBAO trademark has not been adopted by most manufacturers, while an initiative by the country's private industry association—the 'Belgian Chocolate Code'—is still in place today, as a tool for defining Belgian chocolate in order to tackle misleading and fraudulent practices. Following the introduction of EU Regulation 1151/2012 on protected GIs in 2012, the Belgian chocolate industry could potentially apply for GI protection status, such as that applied to other processed products, including wine.

However, these discussions and commercial conflicts on the use of the term 'Belgian chocolate' itself signal the dramatic success of this product around the globe. And recent export data suggest that the global growth is far from finished.

References

Barry Callebaut. 2013. 'Annual Report 2012/13'. *Barry Callebaut AG.* <http://annual-report-2012-13.barry-callebaut.com/assets/pdf/Barry_Callebaut_Annual_Report_2012-2013.pdf> (accessed 28 January 2015).

Barry Callebaut. 2014. 'Half-Year Results 2013/14'. *Media Conference 3 April 2014.* Available at: <https://www.barry-callebaut.com/sites/default/files/publications/half_year_results_2013_14_final_media_without_speaker_notes.pdf> (accessed 15 February 2015).

Blenkinsop, P. 2013. 'Belgian Chocolate Makers Seek Protection from Copycats'. *Reuters,* 27 March. Available at: <http://www.reuters.com/article/2013/03/27/us-belgium-chocolate-idUSBRE92Q05M20130327> (accessed 15 January 2015).

Bois Sauvage. 2014. *Neuhaus.* Available at: <http://www.bois-sauvage.be/actien/BSACTINAVSTRA4.htm> (accessed 15 March 2015).

Callebaut. 2014. *Histoire du chocolate.* Available at: <http://www.callebaut.com/frfr/chocophilia/histoire-du-chocolat>.

CAOBISCO. 2013. 'Caobisco Statistical Bulletin'. *Caobisco.* Available at: <http://www.mah.se/PageFiles/55093/caobisco-statistical%20bulletin%202013.pdf>.

Choprabisco. 2007. *Belgian Chocolate Code.* Available at: <http://www.choprabisco.be/engels/documents/BelgianChocolateCodeEN030507DEF.pdf> (accessed 16 February 2015).

Cidell J. L and H. C. Alberts. 2006. 'Constructing Quality: The Multinational Histories of Chocolate'. *Geoforum* 37: 999–1007.

Clarence-Smith, W. 2000 Cocoa and Chocolate 1765-1914. Routledge, London.

Cohen, M. and J. Covell. 2005. *Barry Callebaut AG.* International Directory of Company Histories. Available at: <http://www.encyclopedia.com/topic/Barry_Callebaut_AG.aspx> (accessed 12 December 2014).

Côte d'Or. 2014. *Notre Histoire.* Available at: <https://www.cotedor.be/home/histoire-de-la-marque> (accessed 17 March 2015).

e-Business W@tch. 2006. *Case Study: ICT in Support of CRM at Godiva Chocolatier Europe.* DG Enterprise & Industry European Commission. Available at: <http://ec.europa.eu/enterprise/archives/e-business-watch/studies/case_studies/documents/Case%20Studies%202006/CS_SR01_Food_5-Godiva.pdf> (accessed 18 February 2015).

Euromonitor International. 2014. *Chocolate Confectionery in Belgium.* Retrieved from Euromonitor Passport GMID database.

European Commission. 2015. *Geographical-Indications.* Available at: <http://ec.europa.eu/trade/policy/accessing-markets/intellectual-property/geographical-indications/>.

Eurostat. 2015. *Industrial Statistics.* Available at: <http://ec.europa.eu/eurostat/data/data base> (accessed 28 February 2015).

FOD Economie. 1845–1993. *Statistieken over de Buitenlandse handel.* Nationaal Instituut voor de Statistiek Brussels.

FOD Economie. 1965. *Jaarlijkse Productiestatistieken.* Nationaal Instituut voor Statistiek, Brussels.

FOD Economie. 1965–1993. *Maandelijkse Industriële Statistieken.* Nationaal Instituut voor de Statistiek, Brussels.

FOD Economie. 1990. *Jaarlijkse Productiestatistieken.* Nationaal Instituut voor Statistiek, Brussels.

FOD Economie. 2000–2007. *Industriële Productie: PRODCOM sectoren.* National Instituut voor de Statistiek, Brussels.

Godiva. 2015a. *Our History.* Available at: <http://www.godiva.com/experience-godiva/ourStory.html>.

Godiva. 2015b. *History of Godiva.* Available at: <http://www.godiva.com/careersgodivahistory/careersGodivaHistory.htm> (accessed 14 February 2015).

Godiva. 2015c. *Godiva.* Available at: <http://www.godivachocolates.eu/en/godiva-the-story> (accessed 24 June 2014).

Grant. 2004. *International Directory of Company Histories,* vol. 64. Pennsylvania State University: St. James Press.

Lamfalussy, C. 2006. 'Percée arabe du chocolat Galler'. *La Libre,* 21 December. Available at: <http://www.lalibre.be/economie/actualite/percee-arabe-du-chocolat-galler-51b89139e4b0de6db9aef2c2> (accessed 17 April 2015).

Leonidas. 2014. *Leonidas, History from a Belgian Chocolatier.* Available at: <http://www.leonidas.com/be_en/about/history> (accessed 28 May 2015).

LMC International. 2006. The Impact of Directive 2000/36/EC on the Economies of those Countries Producing Cocoa and Vegetable Fats other than Cocoa Butter. *Main Report prepared for the European Commission-DG Agriculture and Rural Development.*

Mercier, J. 2008. *The Temptation of Chocolate.* Brussels: Lannoo.

Mitchell, B. R. 1998. *International Historical Statistics, Europe 1750–1993.* London: Macmillan; New York: Stockton.

Mondelēz. 2014. *Our Corporate Timeline.* Available at: <http://www.mondelezinternational.com/about-us/our-corporate-timelines> (accessed 28 March 2015).

National Bank of Belgium. 2014a. Price data on chocolate from 1947 to 2013. Brussels.

National Bank of Belgium. 2014b. Export data and import data by category and destination from 1993–2013.

Neuhaus. 2015. *Our Belgian Chocolate Heritage.* Available at: <http://www.neuhaus-online-store.com/en/heritage.htm?or=6274264124&cu=euro> (accessed 17 March 2015).

OECD (Organisation for Economic Co-operation and Development). 2014. *CPI Index.* Available at; <http://stats.oecd.org/Index.aspx?querytype=view&queryname=221> (accessed 22 March 2015).

Oliver, E. 1997. 'Collection Chocolate: Nos Marques, Nos Images Nos Appetits . . .'. *Journal du Collectionneur* 62, 9–17.

Rosenblum, M. 2006. *Chocolate: A Bittersweet Saga of Dark and Light.* New York: North Point Press.

RSZ (Belgian National Office Social Security). 2014. *Verdeling werkgevers en arbeidsplaatsen naar grootteklasse voor de chocoladesector Q1 2014.*

Scholliers, P. 1996. *Van drank voor de elite naar een reep voor iedereen. Chocolade van drank voor edelman tot reep voor alleman 15de -20ste eeuw.* Brussels: ASLK galerij.

De Tijd, and Graydon. 2013. Company guide. http://www.tijd.be/ (Accessed 15 November 2014).

WHY5Research. 2012. Survey for Belgian Brewers Association with Regards the Creation of a Belgian Beer Experience Centre at the Stock Exchange.

Williams, B. 2008. 'Europroms. Prodcom Data'. Eurostat. Latest version 03/09/2008.

Yeon-hee K. and P. Ju-min. 2008. 'UPDATE 1-S.Korea Lotte buys Belgium's Guylian for $164 mln', ed. Jonathan Hopfner. *Reuters*, 23 June. Available at: <http://uk.reuters.com/article/2008/06/23/guylian-lotte-idUKSEO22252520080623> (accessed 17 January 2015).

Part II
Consumption

6

Chocolate Consumption, Manufacturing, and Quality in Europe and North America

Heike C. Alberts and Julie Cidell

In this chapter, we compare chocolate consumption patterns and understandings of quality in North America and Europe. Although many factors go into determining why consumers in one country or region prefer certain foods to others, the quality of that food is certainly a key factor. What this chapter shows, however, is that 'quality' can be defined in different ways and therefore means different things to different people, so that what is preferred by one consumer can be considered low quality by another. Here we outline different patterns of consumption and then explore the role of the manufacturing process, ingredients, and scientific tests in determining quality and therefore consumption differences.

While recent academic research on food has focused on how quality is defined and valued (e.g. Ilbery and Kneafsey 2000; Morris and Young 2000; Mansfield 2003; Cidell and Alberts 2006), most of that work has focused on foods that are processed only lightly, or not all, such as fresh produce, coffee, wine, and fish. For coffee and wine, for example, quality is strongly tied to the location in which they are grown and produced, with the French concept of *terroir* encapsulating the value that the land imparts to the products grown there. Chocolate, however, is a highly processed food product, and it is rarely consumed in the same regions of the world where its raw materials originate. The complicated global commodity chain that stretches between producer and consumer makes it nearly impossible to tie a chocolate bar to its geographical origin for all but the most exclusive products. At the same time, the presence of over 600 aromatic compounds in chocolate means that flavour depends on not only the ingredients, but also on how they are processed (Afoakwa et al. 2008). Quality therefore becomes tied to the final stages of the commodity chain, including production methods and marketing.

Furthermore, chocolate is a special food in that it is often imbued with social or cultural meanings above and beyond its nutritional value. Chocolate is given as a gift more than any other food and is almost expected in certain holiday settings. While the health value of dark chocolate continues to be studied for its antioxidant properties as well as the potential value of the stimulant theobromine (e.g. Jacobsen 2003), the value of a piece of chocolate as a pick-me-up or as an affordable luxury is well established. Even the manufacture of chocolate has cultural meaning, with *chocolatiers* in France and Spain rising up against the proposed inclusion of vegetable fats in chocolate under European Union (EU) guidelines, on the grounds that it would tarnish their traditions. Nationalist sentiment when it comes to chocolate can be as strong as that regarding wine or cheese, particularly when the product and the quality of life it embodies is threatened from outside. The quality of the production process can also include safeguarding the livelihoods of those who are part of the global commodity chain, including the farmers who harvest cocoa beans. All of these factors make determining what counts as quality chocolate a complex undertaking. We begin to unravel this complicated picture by outlining the basic differences in consumption patterns between North America and Europe. This includes the level of consumption, but also the form in which chocolate is consumed.

Chocolate Consumption

Western Europe and North America are the main chocolate-consuming regions globally, accounting for 32 per cent and 20 per cent of the global market share of chocolate respectively (KPMG 2012), but consumption patterns vary significantly between both sides of the Atlantic. Per capita consumption is significantly higher in Western Europe. Currently, the British consume by far the most chocolate per capita—11kg (24 pounds) per person per year. The reported numbers for the Irish and Swiss are at about 9.6 and 9.5kg, respectively, but it is often argued that Swiss consumption may actually be less as so much chocolate in Switzerland is bought by tourists. Austria and Germany are also among the top five chocolate-consuming nations, at about 7.5 kg per person. Consumption in the Scandinavian countries, Belgium, and the Netherlands exceeds 5kg per person. In the USA about 4.6kg of chocolate are consumed per person per year, and 3.5kg in Canada (<http://www.barry-callebaut.com>).

In addition to amounts, how chocolate is consumed also varies between the two main chocolate regions. For example, while Europeans predominantly eat chocolate bars (Khodorowsky and Robert 2001) as well as pralines (individually shaped chocolates), many Americans consume much of their chocolate in the form of chocolate chips (e.g. in cookies) or as chocolate cake (Albright 1997). Americans also eat more chocolate than Europeans in the form of candy bars, many containing peanuts or peanut butter (Albright 1997), neither of which enjoys much popularity in Western Europe. Americans have been reported to be resistant to change in regard to candy bars, so most 'new' bars are actually variations of traditional flavours, and many popular candy bars were invented several decades ago and have changed only minimally (Pottker 1995; Brenner 2000). More generally, people tend to favour the tastes they grew up with, so that many Americans continue to prefer Hershey's products (Brenner 2000).

Generally speaking, Americans' attitude towards chocolate is also different to Europeans': American chocolate is often either marketed as healthy or as the exact opposite, a sinful indulgence (Albright 1997). Europeans, by contrast, are more likely to consider chocolate as a real food that can be part of a balanced diet; it is therefore consumed more frequently (Pottker 1995). Jacobsen (2003) argues that chocolate is indeed a food rather than a treat. For example, it contains protein, fibre, zinc, iron, copper, and magnesium, all of which are important nutrients or help the body with processing foods. The obvious problem with chocolate is its high sugar content, but even milk chocolate contains less sugar than many other popular snack foods and soft drinks (Jacobsen 2003). The belief that chocolate is a food may also explain why European chocolate producers and consumers place more emphasis on quality (Coe and Coe 1996).

Beyond attitudes and consumption volume, there are some material differences in chocolate between the two regions, starting with the recipes and production process. American mass- market chocolates, on average, have a significantly lower cocoa content than European chocolates, so European chocolates tend to have a stronger and richer chocolate taste. By contrast, the sugar content tends to be higher in American chocolates, partly because sugar is cheaper than cocoa (Pottker 1995; Coe and Coe 1996; Khodorowsky and Robert 2001). At the same time, while European chocolates are conched (rolled) for extended periods of time, many American chocolates are not conched at all or are conched for much shorter times, leaving them grittier. We will discuss this issue in greater depth in the section 'Chocolate Manufacturing'.

Second, on average, European chocolate manufacturers offer a much wider variety of different chocolate bars than their American counterparts (Pottker 1995). For example, at the time of writing, the Ritter Sport company, based in Germany, offered 18 different varieties on its US website (<http://ritter-sport.us/#/en_US/treadmill>). However, the German website (<http://www.ritter-sport.de/#/de_DE/treadmill>) listed 24 standard varieties as well as a series of organic chocolates, seasonal chocolates (e.g. yogurt varieties in summer, chocolates with spices for Christmas), and specialty chocolates such as cookies and cream, macadamia nuts, and à la crema catalana. By comparison, Hershey's website (<http://www.hersheys.com>) at the time of writing listed only eight different chocolate bars. While Hershey also offers seasonal products in autumn, winter, and spring, the different flavours appear in the fillings of their Kisses, rather than their chocolate bars as with the European products mentioned above.

The Italian-based company Ferrero also offers a wide range of products, but, contrary to Ritter Sport, is not focused on different varieties of chocolate bars but on a wide range of different chocolate products. Currently Ferrero offers confections such as Raffaello, Rocher, and Giotto for adult consumers, and a wide variety of products including milk chocolate and milk cream for children (e.g. Kinder chocolate, Kinder Bueno, Kinder Country, and Kinder Happy Hippo) (<http://www.ferrero.de>). Ferrero also produces wafer bars such as Duplo and Hanuta, a strawberry-cream-filled chocolate called Yogurette, as well as its popular Nutella spread. Compared with Ritter Sport, Ferrero more specifically targets its products at certain population groups (e.g. the Kinder line at children), a different approach to offering variety within products.

Swiss-based Lindt, similar to Ritter Sport, offers a wide range of different chocolate bars but targets the premium market. While Lindt produces a number of different white and milk chocolates, a large percentage of its offerings are dark chocolates with different levels of cocoa content (e.g. 70, 85, and 90 per cent), strawberry, cranberry, or blackcurrant filling; sea salt or chilli; and specialties such as crème brûlée and tiramisu (<http://www.lindtusa.com>). Recently Lindt also launched a new series of chocolates called Hello, aimed specifically at introducing the younger generation to the premium market (Nienburg 2013). While Hello was first launched in Germany (where it is produced), the flavours are specifically targeted at US customers: strawberry cheesecake, cookies and cream, and caramel brownie. As Whiteman (2014) describes, Lindt is 'on a mission to cultivate chocolate connoisseurs among the American public and bring the kind of chocolate experiences Europeans have enjoyed for years to the U.S.' While premium chocolates have a market share of about 30 per cent in Europe, the US share was only about 2 per cent until Lindt began to aggressively target the US market. To this end, Lindt opened over a hundred specialty stores and massively expanded its New Hampshire manufacturing plant.

In the USA, among the larger manufacturers, only Ghirardelli (<http://www.ghirardelli.com/store>) offers a wide range of different premium chocolate bars such as dark chocolate with hazelnuts, sea salt, or cherry, bars filled with toffee, caramel, or raspberry cream, and a variety of other flavours. However, as Jacobsen (2003) argued, the USA is now experiencing a chocolate revolution, as Americans increasingly turn towards darker chocolates and pay more attention to health benefits. Because of concerns with obesity and health more generally, a niche market of healthier chocolates is now developing in the country. For example, in 2011 Nestlé USA launched a lower calorie chocolate line called Skinny Cow, followed one year later by Hershey's Simple Pleasures, which has significantly less fat than regular chocolate. Some of these healthier chocolates are gluten-free or sugar-free, and some have additives that are advertised as bringing health benefits (Fox News 2013). 'Health' chocolates such as these are virtually unknown in Europe.

Another aspect of the chocolate revolution in the USA is that American consumers are expanding their consumption beyond traditional mass-market chocolate such as Hershey's (Albright 1997). This not only explains why there are now more premium chocolates produced in the USA and more dark varieties offered, but also why more European chocolates are available. A decade or two ago, European chocolates were largely limited to specialty food stores and import stores, but now brands such as Milka, Ritter Sport, and Lindt are available in many grocery stores, department stores such as Target and Walmart, and drugstores such as Walgreens and CVS. The selections in most stores are more limited than in Europe (e.g. just two to four kinds of Ritter Sport rather than the dozen or more available even in smaller European grocery stores), but they have increased over the last decade or so. A manager of the Germany-based discount store Aldi in

Oshkosh (Wisconsin) confirmed that European chocolates, in this case mass-market chocolates produced in Germany, 'are flying off the shelves', and that especially around Christmas, when the chocolate selection is vastly expanded, 'we can hardly stock the shelves fast enough as people buy so much German chocolate'.

In summary, there are significant differences in consumption patterns, but the US is currently experiencing a chocolate revolution which may lead to a convergence of the two regions over time in terms of quality and types of chocolate offered. The question remains how those differences came to be; as the section 'Chocolate Manufacturing' shows, the history of manufacturing provides some clues.

Chocolate Manufacturing

The desired quality of chocolate depends in part on the form in which it is consumed. Chocolate was initially brought from Central America to Spain as a drink. The Spanish innovation was to introduce sugar to the drink, in step with their growing sugar production on Caribbean plantations (Presilla 2009). The preparation of drinking chocolate in Spain continued much as it had in Central America: grinding the beans on a warm stone slab or *metate* into a paste with a combination of flavourings such as cinnamon, chilli, vanilla, or almonds, and then shaping the paste into tablets or balls for storage. When it was time to consume the chocolate, the paste was blended with water or milk and frothed by pouring it between two cups or stirring it with a handheld device called a *molinillo* (Coe and Coe 1996; Presilla 2009). The labour and expensive ingredients required to produce a cup of chocolate made it an upper-class drink, beginning the association of chocolate with luxury or indulgence. At that time, quality referred as much to the additives as to the cocoa—signifying the wealth of the chocolate drinker who could afford exotic spices—and was reflected in the manner in which it was presented, such as being poured from a silver pitcher into a specially made porcelain cup (Presilla 2009).

The Industrial Revolution, however, changed the production process and thus the consumption mode of chocolate. In 1847, the production of solid chocolate began in Great Britain, spurred by the Dutchman Van Houten's hydraulic press that enabled the separation of cocoa butter from cocoa solids. This made it possible to add cocoa butter into the mix, instead of water, to produce a solid chocolate bar with a creamy texture (Coe and Coe 1996). The mass production (and subsequent price drop) of chocolate in solid and powdered form meant it was no longer an elite food. Chocolate consumption, which had changed little over several centuries, now increased dramatically. The transformation of chocolate from a drink to a solid food also meant a geographical shift: chocolate consumption in Southern European countries, where most of the early history of chocolate in Europe had taken place, started to fall behind that of Northern and Central Europe (Coe and Coe 1996).

Further innovations came in the form of changes in the manufacturing process rather than the form in which chocolate was consumed. For example, the British introduced milk to solid chocolate, although it was initially difficult to keep the milk chocolate from spoiling. In 1867 the Swiss chemist Nestlé discovered how to make powdered milk through an evaporation process, thus solving the problem (Coe and Coe 1996). Both Britain and Switzerland eventually became known for their milk chocolate. In 1879, conching was invented in Switzerland. Conching refers to a process where heavy granite rollers break down the sugar and cocoa particles. This process not only makes the chocolate smoother, but also increases the intensity of the chocolate taste (Coe and Coe 1996; Brenner 2000; Torres-Moreno et al. 2012). The Swiss require chocolate, by law, to be conched for 72 hours, contributing to Switzerland's reputation (and Swiss consumers' preference) for smooth and aromatic chocolate.

Other innovations had less to do with the process of making chocolate *qua* chocolate, but chocolate as a luxury food or gift. The practice of displaying small chocolate bonbons or pralines in elaborately decorated boxes was developed by the Belgian company Neuhaus (Rosenblum 2005). While Belgian chocolate is considered among the finest in the world, a great deal of that reputation has to do with the presentation rather than the contents: 'In Brussels or Bruges, shops with an artisan air seem to dominate every square and street corner. But most sell industrial chocolate under old family names' (Rosenblum 2005: 21). Similarly, the perception of French *chocolatiers* as individual artisans preserving craft traditions that are hundreds of years old has been actively constructed by producers to appeal to French nationalism in the face of EU pressures for harmonization: 'French chocolates had a distinct market niche based on their mode of production—family and craft—and ceremonial purchase appeal, not exclusively on taste' (Terrio 2000: 36). The French have also sought to attach the concept of *terroir* to chocolate through varietal or single origin bars, as they have so successfully done for wines and cheeses.

The desire of French *chocolatiers* to position themselves as traditional, artisanal craftspeople stands in sharp contrast, of course, to most US chocolate manufacturers. Two large manufacturers—Hershey and Mars—dominate the market, not so much with their chocolate bars but with candy bars and other chocolate products (Rosenblum 2005), such as M&Ms, Snickers bars, baking chips, and Hershey's Kisses. The contribution of North American chocolate makers is not to the manufacturing process, but to strategies to capture market share. The battle between Hershey and Mars has been well reported, along with the extraordinary levels of secrecy involved (Rosenblum 2005). Ironically, the character of Hershey's chocolate is due to this same tendency for secrecy within the industry. Milton Hershey could not gain access to Swiss chocolate makers to learn their recipes or methods, so he figured them out for himself as best he could. As Rosenblum notes, 'he came up with his own trial-and-error formula for milk chocolate, which left a strong note of sour. His conching process, shorter than most, produced a peculiar grainy texture. He was generous with sugar but tightfisted with cacao' (Rosenblum 2005: 99). Nevertheless, he made a reliable product and put it in as many hands as possible, perhaps most notably through ration bars distributed to US soldiers during the Second World War. The widespread consumption of this chocolate within the USA has tempered the palate to the point where most Americans prefer Hershey's or Mars chocolate to products with a higher cocoa content.

In summary, by tracing chocolate quality through the manufacturing process, we find that national preferences often map quite closely the history of manufacturing in that country: chocolate in Spain is often for drinking and/or flavoured with nuts and spices; Swiss chocolate is milky and smooth; the Dutch are known for their cocoa powder more than their bars of chocolate; the French and Belgians concentrate on the mode of production and the presentation of their product; and American manufacturers define success by sales rather than quality. Of course, there are variations within each country in both producers and consumers. However, as a highly processed food where there are significant difficulties in tracing ingredients back to their physical origins, unlike the grapes in a bottle of wine, defining quality chocolate has to be based on where and how the ingredients are processed (Cidell and Alberts 2006). It is also important to remember that 'manufacturing' does not consist solely of the physical production within the factory or workshop of the cocoa-based foodstuff, but the discursive production, too: the marketing and packaging of that foodstuff is said to have a certain high quality by virtue of the way or the place in which it was made. Increasingly, that production includes a discussion of where and how the ingredients were sourced, as the section 'Ingredients' shows.

Ingredients

Food scholars have shown the wide variety of ways in which food quality can be defined, including not only taste or physical properties, but where the ingredients were sourced and/or the conditions under which the product was manufactured. Increasingly important is the traceability of food, being able to determine where it came from and what has been done to it along the way. Organic, local, and fair trade foods all have different definitions of what constitutes quality food, some of which are only tangentially related to flavour (Parrott et al. 2002; Mansfield 2003; Renard 2003). Knowing how the food was produced, including both human and environmental conditions, has become a key component in how many consumers make their food choices.

For a processed food such as chocolate, the question of quality revolves around not only the character of the ingredients and how they are combined in the production process, as explained in the section 'Chocolate Manufacturing', but what the ingredients are in the first place (Cidell and Alberts 2006). Chocolate basically has three ingredients: cocoa, fat, and sugar. Milk chocolate reduces the cocoa contribution in order to add milk, and other ingredients such as fruits, nuts, spices, candies, and so on, can be included as well. This section will discuss each of the three fundamental ingredients in turn, considering how they contribute to the final product.

The fundamental ingredient in chocolate is cocoa. The cocoa bean comes from a tree called *Theobroma cacao* ('food of the gods'). This tree is restricted to the tropics because of its need for warm temperatures, high moisture, and specialist pollinators. Chocolate is thus, ironically, a food that is rarely consumed in the same locale as its raw ingredients are produced. Cocoa pods are harvested and cut open by hand, releasing thirty to forty bitter-tasting beans surrounded by a sweet, juicy pulp. The beans are fermented to develop the typical chocolate taste by reducing astringency and bitterness and increasing acidity and the cocoa aroma (Young 2007; Saltini et al. 2013). After one to ten days of fermentation, the beans are dried for transport, occasionally with additional storage time planned to reduce acidity (Coe and Coe 1996; Info-Zentrum Schokolade 2009; Lima et al. 2011; Saltini et al. 2013).

Cocoa beans fall into one of three or four types. Forastero is by far the dominant one, accounting for 95 per cent of supply (Lima et al. 2011). Criollo beans were the first to be cultivated, and despite being considered higher quality, they are less popular because they have relatively low yield and pest resistance. Trinitario is the third type, a hybrid of the previous two, and, along with Criollo, is found in higher-quality chocolate. A fourth bean, the Nacional variety of Ecuador, is sometimes separated out as being different to Forastero (Afoakwa et al. 2008; Saltini et al. 2013). Each variety of beans has its own flavour profile, although even the same variety can produce different results depending on where and how it is grown. For example, 'aromatic, floral, spicy, raisin, molasses, and winy' are some of the terms used to describe cocoa originating in Ecuador, Sri Lanka, Venezuela, Grenada, and Trinidad, respectively (Afoakwa et al. 2008: 843). The largest producers of cocoa are Côte d'Ivoire with about 40 per cent of the world's total, followed by Ghana, Indonesia, Nigeria, Cameroon, Brazil, and Ecuador (WCF 2012). Across these countries, 90 to 95 per cent of production is done on smallholdings of around three hectares, with little standardization in production methods (Lima et al. 2011; Saltini et al. 2013). This makes it extremely difficult to trace the origin of cocoa back to where it was grown, as seventy different farmers' beans can mix in a single shipment, and on average, seven to ten actors are involved between farmer and manufacturer (Saltini et al. 2013). Furthermore, as with most fruits, cocoa pods do not all ripen at the same rate, but the labour-intensive process means that multiple rounds of harvesting are not feasible. Unripe, ripe, and overripe pods can therefore end up being harvested together (Lima et al. 2011). The fermentation process creates further differentiation, such as changing the chemical composition of the resulting cocoa butter, but this process is not nearly as standardized as in other processed foods such as cheese or wine (Saltini et al. 2013).

Despite these multiple sources of variation in bean quality, chocolate manufacturers need to produce a consistent product (Rusconi and Conti 2010). Some of the differences in bean quality can be overcome by adjusting roasting and conching times, but this depends on knowing the beans' origins in some detail, which is not possible for mass-market chocolate (Torres-Moreno et al. 2012). The usual solution is to use widely sourced blends of beans in hopes of evening out the various characteristics, which further removes the chocolate bar from its source. Historically, therefore, the sourcing of beans has not been fundamental to the marketing of chocolate, with the manufacturing location being more important (i.e. Swiss or Belgian chocolate, not Ghanaian or Ecuadorian beans) (Cidell and Alberts 2006). Some producers have argued that rather than just overcoming differences in bean quality, blending beans from different regions produces a better overall taste as the characteristics of one balance those of another.

However, in recent years specialty chocolate manufacturers have begun to produce single-origin or varietal chocolates, attempting to attach the same sense of *terroir* to chocolate as already exists for wine and coffee (Barham 2003; Greenwood and Walker 2005). This identification of quality with location, or more importantly, with the ability to trace the cocoa back to a single location, is relatively new within the chocolate industry (Greweling 2009). Some major European manufacturers such as Lindt have not been successful at selling varietal chocolate, while others such as Michel Cluizel and Valrhona have been able to produce and sell single-origin chocolate bars with greater success, claiming their boutique nature attracts a different kind of customer (Greenwood and Walker 2005). Within North America varietal chocolate has also been limited to small manufacturers. In both regions, the attachment of cocoa quality to place may have caught on, but only at the higher ends of the market. Additionally, as more and more manufacturers seek to take advantage of health claims related to dark chocolate, traceability begins to become more important, as the amount of polyphenols (the source of antioxidants) in a chocolate bar depend upon the original type of bean as well as how it is processed (Rusconi and Conti 2010).

In contrast to tracing varietal or single-origin cocoa back to a single plantation, it may sound odd to suggest that the nature of something as mundane as vegetable fat should matter to the quality of a luxury food like chocolate. In fact, it was the driving factor in the so-called Chocolate Wars of the late twentieth century. Recall that Van Houten invented the hydraulic press that made it possible to press the butter (or fat) from the cocoa bean to produce cocoa powder (Burleigh 2002) and that the leftover cocoa butter is used to make solid chocolate bars (Coe and Coe 1996). However, cocoa butter is not the only type of vegetable fat that can be used in chocolate manufacturing. UK chocolate manufacturers have always substituted palm oil, coconut oil, or another CBE (cocoa butter equivalent) in the chocolate-making process for reasons of cost and/or to impart a different texture. One of the many conditions under which the UK joined the EU in 1973 was that chocolate could be made with fats other than cocoa butter, which was forbidden in the rest of the EU (Andrews 1997). However, the original members of the EU subsequently declared that chocolate with CBEs could not be sold under the label of 'chocolate' within their borders. The result was the 'Two Chocolates Policy', which endured as a temporary measure for nearly 25 years (McNeil 2000). The final decree by the European Parliament came in 2000, when they ruled that chocolate made with up to 5 per cent CBEs could be sold as chocolate if it was labelled as 'family milk chocolate' (Cidell and Alberts 2006).

By law in both the USA and Canada, chocolate can only be made with cocoa butter. If a CBE is used, it must be labelled as 'chocolate flavored candy' or 'made with chocolate'. However, in 2007, the Chocolate Manufacturers' Association in the USA petitioned the Food and Drug Administration (FDA) to allow the use of vegetable fats in addition to cocoa butter (Bridges 2007). Public opinion in the form of comments to the FDA was overwhelmingly against the proposed change, and American chocolate retained its purity in regard to the use of fats.

While the type of fat that goes into a chocolate bar is clearly a matter of contention, the amount necessary is determined by the desired physical properties of the resulting mix. That leaves the other two elements of cocoa and sugar to be traded off against each other. According to high-end chocolate makers, the less sugar and more cocoa a chocolate bar has, the higher quality it is (Fabricant 1998). While consumer preference tests show that going higher than 50 to 60 per cent cocoa solids is undesirable for most consumers (Januszewska and Viaene 2001), *chocolatiers* produce bars with up to 90 per cent solids and consider those to be the best. Cocoa is more expensive than sugar, and therefore a higher percentage of cocoa results in a more expensive product, so chocolate manufacturers have an interest in increasing sugar if they value cost over quality. Sugar, of course, is granular, and if it is not pulverized in the chocolate manufacturing process through conching, also results in a grittier bar. To the extent that quality is determined by the texture of the chocolate as well as its flavour, this can be a distinguishing characteristic as well.

Another issue aside from the nature and relative amounts of the ingredients has to do with the conditions under which they are produced. Slave labour has produced cocoa since the seventeenth century (Walker 2007), and concern over the labour conditions under which cocoa is grown goes back over 150 years (Off 2006). Part of ensuring a low price for beans over the years has been paying workers, including children, minimally or keeping them under abusive conditions. As the largest producer of cocoa, Côte d'Ivoirean producers are known to keep child workers under *de facto* if not *de jure* slave conditions, including luring children from Mali with promises of work and then not allowing them to leave once they discover how bad the conditions are (Robbins 2010). While chocolate-consuming countries have attempted to reach an accord with chocolate manufacturers to certify all their chocolate is produced without slave labour, this has not been successful on the ground (Off 2006). The same difficulty, as outlined, with identifying the source of beans grown by smallholders makes it all but impossible for large manufacturers to verify that their cocoa is slave-free (Robbins 2010).

Instead, fair trade standards incorporate these conditions into their voluntary labelling. These standards include setting a minimum price for cocoa so that producers are less vulnerable to significant swings in the market (FI 2011) and requiring a guarantee that no forced labour of any kind is being used, including child labour. Major manufacturers using fair trade practices for at least some of their products include Barry Callebaut, Cargill, and Nestlé, along with many smaller labels. While fair trade represents a tiny fraction of cocoa sales (0.5 per cent, according to the International Cocoa and Chocolate Organization), equal to that of organic cocoa, that percentage is growing. Besides the ethical considerations involved, manufacturers might want to move in this direction for one key reason: consumers place a higher value on ethically sourced chocolate, and not only in monetary terms. A German study found that consumers gave a higher tasting score to chocolate they were told was Fair Trade certified, even those who did not express a belief ahead of time that there was a taste difference (Lotz et al. 2013). The source of ingredients can therefore matter to perceptions of quality, not only in terms of where they come from, but how they are produced.

Testing for Quality

As these discussions of manufacturing and ingredient sourcing show, representations and image can influence consumers to a great extent. At the same time, there are other qualities that can be measured and quantified in a more scientific setting. For example, in Germany Stiftung Warentest (Foundation Product Testing) carries out independent testing of different kinds of products. Many products proudly display a top rating from this organization on their packaging and in commercials, and it is widely believed that its ratings have a significant influence on consumer behaviour. In 2007, Stiftung Warentest conducted separate tests of milk and dark chocolate bars widely available in Germany (Stiftung Warentest 2007a, 2007b). The actual testing was broken down into five categories: sensory experience (45 per cent of overall score), contaminants (20 per cent), microbial quality (10 per cent), packaging (10 per cent), and labelling (15 per cent).

A panel of trained food testers judged the chocolates in the category 'sensory experience'. They tested and described flavour, aroma, consistency, and so on. Chocolates that were sandy or grainy, had a slightly sour taste, or were particularly fatty or oily were marked down. Chemical tests were used to determine contaminants (e.g. cadmium, nickel) and microbial quality (e.g. salmonella, e-coli). The suitability of the packaging was evaluated and the labelling was checked for conforming to food-related regulations, but also for claims made, correctness of ingredient lists, and allergy warnings. Overall, 11 of the 20 milk chocolates tested were judged to be good (among them well-known brand names such as Milka, Ritter Sport, and Lindt), 6 satisfactory, 1 acceptable, and 2 poor. Probably surprising for consumers, the top-rated milk chocolates include both relatively expensive chocolates (e.g. Lindt at 1.95 euros per 100g) and chocolates sold in discount grocery stores such as Lidl and Netto for as little as 0.35 euros per 100g. Clearly cost is not automatically an indicator of quality for milk chocolates.

Similar results were reported for the 25 tested dark chocolates, where once again the chocolates sold at discount grocery stores scored highly. As the quality of cocoa beans plays a larger role in dark chocolates, many of the chocolates tested have information about the cocoa on their packaging, ranging from general statements such as 'premium cacao' to very precise descriptions such as 'arriba cacao from the Los Rios Province of Ecuador' or 'pure premium cocoa from selected plantations close to the city of Quevedo in Ecuador', confirming that origin of the cocoa is an important factor in marketing dark chocolates.

In 2013 Stiftung Warentest followed up with a test of chocolates containing nuts (Stiftung Warentest 2013). In this test, criticisms of the lower-ranked chocolates included trace amounts of mineral oil, weak cocoa aroma, bitter nuts, and delayed melting. The overall results of this test were somewhat different from the previous two—some of the chocolates sold at discount grocery stores once again received high marks, but the highest rankings went to premium brands Lindt, Feodora, and Hachez, which cost two or three times as much as the cheaper chocolates.

Several important conclusions can be drawn from these tests. First, professional testers use a wide variety of different criteria, ranging from sensory experience to microbial purity, but also include criteria such as packaging and labelling, going beyond testing the quality of the food itself. Second, cost and quality do not necessarily correlate. Chocolates sold in discount grocery stores performed very well, and among milk and dark chocolate received better marks than more expensive brands, many of which customers believed to be of particularly good quality. Third, while these tests were standardized as much as possible, some tests involved panels of human testers. The weighting of factors could also influence the overall results, meaning that 'scientific' tests have their own subjectivities.

The importance of weighting factors became clear in a contentious case. In the nut chocolate test, Ritter Sport, which had received high rankings for its milk and dark chocolates, was chastised for saying on its labels that it uses natural aromas, while the chemical analysis found piperonal, described by Stiftung Warentest as a synthetic aroma. The Ritter Sport nut chocolate received an overall 'unacceptable' rating, even though the supposedly synthetic aroma was the only point of criticism. Ritter Sport felt that it did not deserve the poor ranking and the possible loss of revenue that would come from losing the trust of consumers. The company went to trial, arguing that the aroma used in its nut chocolate was made from plants and therefore not synthetic. The court ruled in favour of Ritter Sport in January 2014, arguing that Ritter Sport did not mislead its customers as piperonal can be produced naturally or synthetically (Spiegel 2014) and declared that the testing was unfair. In September 2014 Stiftung Warentest also lost the final appeal. The ruling stated that the Stiftung could not prove that the piperonal was indeed made synthetically (Gassmann 2014). This was the first time in its 50-year history that Stiftung Warentest lost a legal challenge to its testing.

While this controversy erupted over one minor ingredient, it raises wider questions about how to define and control food quality. For example, when the quality of a food is examined, who has the right to determine which criteria should be used, how they should be measured, and how they should be weighted? Which approach or information is most meaningful for the consumer? For instance, does the consumer care whether the aroma is natural or synthetic as long as it is not harmful and the product tastes good? As the Ritter Sport versus Stiftung Warentest case has shown, food quality testing is highly complex and cannot be completely objective, and is further complicated by matters of individual preference.

Conclusions

Existing research on food quality and its role in consumer choice has expanded from considering the physical properties of the food in question to other factors such as food origin, processing practices, and social and political factors. Most of this work, however, has looked at foods consisting of a single ingredient or undergoing minimal processing: wine, cheese, fresh produce, and so on. In the case of chocolate, as this chapter has shown, there are many reasons why it is difficult to base an assessment of quality, and therefore consumer preference, on the origin of the ingredients alone. The fact that cocoa is produced by a large number of smallholders results in variations in bean variety, growing conditions, harvesting methods, fermentation length and procedure, storage and transport conditions, and the roasting process. Major chocolate manufacturers attempt to overcome this variety by blending beans from different locations in order to ensure a consistent product. Therefore, quality becomes a factor of the chocolate manufacturing process rather than the cocoa origin.

As we have shown, today's process of manufacturing chocolate was based on innovations that occurred in several different countries; not surprisingly, the preference of consumers in each country for a specific type of chocolate is largely based on which innovation that country can lay claim to and therefore what kind of chocolate consumers are most familiar with (see also Cidell and Alberts 2006). This includes the smoothness of Swiss chocolate from long conching, the milkiness of British chocolate, and the preference of American consumers for chocolate that Europeans consider inferior. It is therefore not surprising that differences not only exist between countries and regions with regard to the level and mode of consumption of chocolate, but also in regard to what constitutes quality chocolate. Attempts to determine quality on a more 'scientific' basis can also run into problems because of the inevitable choices that have to be made with regard to elements evaluated, testing procedures, and weighting of factors. Our findings therefore reinforce the notion that food quality is both socially and materially constructed, which offers a wide array of possibilities for large and small-scale manufacturers seeking to differentiate themselves in the market.

References

Afoakwa, E., A. Paterson, M. Fowler, and A. Ryan. 2008. 'Flavor Formation and Character in Cocoa and Chocolate: A Critical Review'. *Critical Reviews in Food Science and Nutrition* 48: pp. 840–57.

Albright, B. 1997. 'Trends in Chocolate'. In *Chocolate. Food of the Gods*, edited by A. Szogyi, pp. 137–44. Westport, CT: Greenwood Press.

Andrews, E. 1997. 'Great Chocolate War Reveals Dark Side of Europe'. *New York Times*, 24 October.

Barham, E. 2003. 'Translating *Terroir*: The Global Challenge of French AOC Labeling'. *Journal of Rural Studies* 19: pp. 127–38.

Brenner, J. G. 2000. *The Emperors of Chocolate*. New York: Broadway Books.

Bridges, A. 2007. 'In the United States, a Bittersweet Battle over the Future of Chocolate'. *New York Times*, 7 August.

Burleigh, R. 2002. *Chocolate: Riches from the Rainforest*. New York: Harry N. Abrams, in association with The Field Museum Chicago.

Cidell, J. and H. Alberts. 2006. 'Constructing Quality: The Multinational Histories of Chocolate'. *Geoforum* 37: pp. 999–1007.

Coe, S. D. and M. D. Coe. 1996. *The True History of Chocolate*. London: Thames & Hudson.

Fabricant, F. 1998. 'The Intense Pleasures of Dark Chocolate'. *New York Times*, 16 December, F1.

FI (FairTrade International). 2011. 'Standards for Small Producer Organizations'. <http://www.fairtrade.net/small-producer-standards.html>, accessed 20 March 2014.

Fox News. 2013. 'Demand for Healthier Chocolate on Rise in US'. June. <http://www.foxnews.com/health/2013/06/04/demand-for-healthier-chocolates-on-rise-in-us/>, accessed 1 March 2014.

Gassmann, M. 2014. 'Quadratisch, Praktisch und nicht mehr Mangelhaft'. *Die Welt*, 10 September.

Greenwood, H. and K. Walker. 2005. 'Hot for Chocolate'. *The Age*, 22 February. <http://www.theage.com.au/news/Epicure/Hot-for-chocolate/2005/02/21/1108834695972.html>, accessed 27 March 2014.

Greweling, P. 2009. *Chocolates and Confections: At Home with the Culinary Institute of America*. New York: Houghton Mifflin Harcourt.

Ilbery, B. and M. Kneafsey. 2000. 'Producer Constructions of Quality in Regional Speciality Food Production: A Case Study from Southwest England'. *Journal of Rural Studies* 16: pp. 217–30.

Info-Zentrum Schokolade. 2009. 'Schokoladenseiten. Über die Natur eines Genusses'. <http://www.infozentrum-schoko.de>, accessed 10 March 2014.

Jacobsen, R. 2003. *Chocolate Unwrapped: The Surprising Health Benefits of America's Favorite Passion*. Montpelier, VT: Invisible Cities Press.

Januszewska, R. and J. Viaene. 2001. 'Acceptance of Chocolate by Preference Cluster Mapping across Belgium and Poland'. *Journal of Euromarketing* 11 (1): pp. 61–86.

Khodorowsky, K. and H. Robert. 2001. *The Little Book of Chocolate*, translated by B. Mellor. Luçon: Flammarion.

KPMG. 2012. 'The Chocolate of Tomorrow: What Today's Market Can Tell Us About the Future'. <https://www.kpmg.com/CH/en/Library/Articles-Publications/Documents/Sectors/pub-20120613-chocolate-of-tomorrow-en.pdf>, accessed 1 March 2014.

Lima, L., M. Almeida, M. Nout, and M. Zwietering. 2011. '*Theobroma Cacao* L., "The Food of the Gods": Quality Determinants of Commercial Cocoa Beans, with Particular Reference to the Impact of Fermentation'. *Critical Reviews in Food Science and Nutrition* 51: pp. 731–61.

Lotz, S., F. Christandl, and D. Fetchenhauer. 2013. 'What is Fair is Good: Evidence of Consumers' Taste for Fairness'. *Food Quality and Preference* 30 (2): pp. 139–44.

McNeil, D. 2000. 'Britain's Sweet Victory: Europe accepts Candy'. *New York Times*, 16 March, A4.

Mansfield, B. 2003. 'Fish, Factory Trawlers, and Imitation Crab: The Nature of Quality in the Seafood Industry'. *Journal of Rural Studies* 19: pp. 9–21.

Morris, C. and C. Young. 2000. ' "Seed to Shelf", "Teat to Table", "Barley to Beer" and "Womb to Tomb": Discourses of Food Quality and Quality Assurance Schemes in the UK'. *Journal of Rural Studies* 16: pp. 103–15.

Nienburg, O. 2013. 'Lindt says Hello to New Brand to Tap Millennials'. *Confectionary News*, June. <http://www.confectionerynews.com/Manufacturers/Lindt-says-Hello-to-new-brand-to-tap-Millennials>, accessed 1 March 2014.

Off, C. 2006. *Bitter Chocolate: The Dark Side of the World's Most Seductive Sweet.* New York and London: The New Press.

Parrott, N., N. Wilson, and J. Murdoch. 2002. 'Spatializing Quality: Regional Protection and the Alternative Geography of Food'. *European Urban and Regional Studies* 9: pp. 241–61.

Pottker, J. 1995. *Crisis in Candyland: Melting the Chocolate Shell of the Mars Family Empire.* Bethesda, MD: National Press Books.

Presilla, M. 2009. *The New Taste of Chocolate: A Cultural and Natural History of Cacao with Recipes.* Berkeley, CA: Ten Speed Press.

Renard, M. 2003. 'Fair Trade: Quality, Market, and Conventions'. *Journal of Rural Studies* 19 (1): pp. 97–6.

Robbins, J. 2010. 'Is There Slavery in Your Chocolate?' <http://johnrobbins.info/blog/is-there-slavery-in-your-chocolate>, accessed 1 March 2014.

Rosenblum, M. 2005. *Chocolate: A Bittersweet Saga of Dark and Light.* New York: North Point Press.

Rusconi, M. and A. Conti. 2010. '*Theobroma Cacao* L, the Food of the Gods: A Scientific Approach beyond Myths and Claims'. *Pharmacological Research* 61: pp. 5–13.

Saltini, R., R. Akkerman, and S. Frosch. 2013. 'Optimizing Chocolate Production through Traceability: A Review of the Influence of Farming Practices on Cocoa Bean Quality'. *Food Control* 29: pp. 167–87.

Spiegel. 2014. 'Schokoladenstreit: Ritter Sport siegt gegen Stiftung Warentest'. <http://www.spiegel.de/wirtschaft/service/aromen-streit-ritter-sport-gewinnt-gegen-stiftung-warentest-a-943171.html>, accessed 22 February 2014.

Stiftung Warentest. 2007a. 'Ran an die Tafel. Milchschokolade'. *Test* 11/2007: pp. 23–8.

Stiftung Warentest. 2007b. 'Dunkler Genuss. Bitterschokolade'. *Test* 12/2007: pp. 16–22.

Stiftung Warentest. 2013. 'Zum Reinbeissen. Nussschokolade'. *Test* 12/2013: pp. 20–7.

Terrio, S. 2000. *Crafting the Culture and History of French Chocolate.* Berkeley, CA: UC Press.

Torres-Moreno, M., A. Tarrega, E. Costell, and C. Blanch. 2012. 'Dark Chocolate Acceptability: Influence of Cocoa Origin and Processing Conditions'. *Journal of the Science of Food and Agriculture* 92: pp. 404–11.

Walker, T. 2007. 'Slave Labor and Chocolate in Brazil: The Culture of Cacao Plantations in Amazonia and Bahia (17th–19th Centuries)'. *Food and Foodways* 15 (1–2): pp. 75–106.

WCF (World Cocoa Foundation). 2012. 'Cocoa Market Update'. <http://worldcocoafoundation.org/wp-content/uploads/Cocoa-Market-Update-as-of-3.20.2012.pdf>, accessed 22 February 2014.

Whiteman, P. 2014. 'Lindt & Sprüngli: Chocolate Connoisseurs'. *Industry Today* <http://industrytoday.com/article_view.asp?ArticleID=FDQ_125>, accessed 1 March 2014.

Young, A. M. 2007. *The Chocolate Tree: A Natural History of Cacao.* Gainesville, FL: University Press of Florida.

7

Nutritional and Health Effects of Chocolate

Stefania Moramarco and Loreto Nemi

Introduction

Chocolate is a highly processed food whose flavour and aroma depend on more than 500 substances, contained in a fully grown cocoa bean (Albright 1997).

For centuries cocoa products, obtained by processing cocoa beans, have had a long tradition of medicinal and ritual use, originating among the Olmec, Mayan, and Aztec civilizations, and then progressively spreading all over the world. The appreciation and popularity of the final product, chocolate, has fluctuated over the centuries, generating both myths and real knowledge, changing its status from 'food of the gods' to 'a high source of sugars and fats', and reaching more recently a undisputed prestige for its benefits to human health. This historical background of controversial hedonistic and nutritional properties has largely contributed to making chocolate a fascinating and interesting food. The recent scientific approach based on research and clinical expertise has allowed the investigation of, and thereby the support or destruction of, the oldest myths, cultural beliefs, and practical evidences.

In this chapter, we first review the medical use of chocolate through a centuries-long history, from its origins in Central and Latin America to its more recent development. Then, when exploring the current clinical literature on chocolate's health, nutritional, psychological, and aphrodisiac effects, we use a very specific definition of chocolate: we focus on 'unadulterated' chocolate, that is, dark chocolate with at least 70 per cent cocoa solids, distinguishing it from confectionaries, candies, snacks, and all types of surrogate products. Based on the studies analysed, we find that 'unadulterated' chocolate might be a *functional food* (meaning that, beyond basic nutrition, it contains biologically active components which have potentially positive-enhancing health effects) that can be fully integrated into a balanced diet.

The Medical Use of Cocoa and Chocolate in History

The scientific name *Theobroma cacao* was given to the cocoa tree by the Swedish botanist Carl Linnaeus in 1753. The term *Theobroma* means 'food of the gods'—from the Greek: *broma* (food) and *Theo* (God)—while the term *chocolate* is derived from the Nahuatl (Aztec) word *xocolatl*, and means 'bitter water'—from *xococ* (bitter) and *atl* (water). In fact, for Mesoamerican civilizations, cocoa had divine origins: it played a mystic role, and was widely used during sacrificial rituals and religious ceremonies.

The earliest documented use of cocoa occurred around 1100 BC, by the Olmec, who were also the first to discover the chocolate-making process, mainly using chocolate as a beverage for the elite. According to Aztec beliefs, cocoa pods symbolized life and fertility and had several nourishing, fortifying, and aphrodisiac qualities. Eating the fruit of the cocoa tree gave them wisdom and power, and a cocoa liquid concoction was considered a health-promoting elixir (Lippi 2009). Mexicans saw cocoa as a valuable and prestigious food, reserved for the nobility. They also believed that it was an intoxicating food and therefore unsuitable for women and children. For this reason it was only consumed by adult males, more specifically, by priests, the highest government officials, military officers, distinguished warriors, and occasionally by sacrificial victims for ritual purposes (Coe and Coe 1996; Dillinger et al. 2000). After the discovery of America, Columbus was the first European to experience cocoa. The beans were highly prized and used as a source of currency to buy items and slaves (Beckett 2008). However, Columbus was unaware of the use of cocoa as food (Coe and Coe 1996; Henderson et al. 2007). When the Spanish introduced cocoa in Europe after the conquest of Mexico, it was kneaded and mixed with other ingredients to better suit the European palate: cocoa products were extracted and chocolate was made. Since the sixteenth century, more than a hundred culinary and medicinal uses for cocoa and chocolate have been described in many manuscripts and publications and, starting from the seventeenth century, the medical use of chocolate entered the academic debate, becoming the subject of some degree theses at the Medical Faculty of Paris. During this period, the literature described several uses of these products as a remedy/treatment for specific diseases. For example, the Badianus Manuscript of 1552 reports that cocoa flowers were used to reduce fatigue, especially in men who worked in government administration. In the Florentine Codex, dated 1590, cocoa was mentioned as part of prescriptions to reduce fever, shortness of breath, childhood diarrhoea, and heart weakness.[1] In 1741, the naturalist Linnaeus examined in his monograph the medicinal uses of chocolate, confirming a tradition already existing in the Pre-Columbian culture: cocoa was very nourishing, an excellent aphrodisiac, and it cured many illnesses, such as wasting or thinness due to lung and muscle diseases, hypochondria, and haemorrhoids. The dual role of chocolate, as a medicine and a food, entered the pharmacopeia literature as well. In 1834 the Dispensatory of the United States reported that chocolate was

---

[1] Childhood diarrhoea was treated with a prescription that used five cocoa beans.

nutritive and digestible, and often was served as a drink in the morning, being an excellent substitute for coffee (Bloom 1998; Dillinger et al. 2000; Lippi 2009, 2012; Wilson and Hurst 2012).

During the Industrial Revolution, with the development of mass production and the increasing incomes of the poor, the role of chocolate changed: from a divine food and an elite beverage it became accessible to a much larger segment of society. This is also when the idea of chocolate as a healthy food began to strongly feed the market (Richardson 2003). Chocolate was proposed as an energy food rich in nutrients, and manufacturers started to sell chocolate-based foodstuffs for breakfast, designed particularly for children. Since then, it has become one of the most popular foods, consumed by men and women, rich and poor, children and adults. Moreover, chocolate and cocoa products also appear to be some of the most ubiquitous added ingredients—not only to ice cream, cake, and cereals, but also body creams, lotions, and so forth.

So what is chocolate really? Is it a confectionary, a candy, just a food, or can it also be a functional food?

Definition and Nutritional Composition

Chocolate vs Candy or Confectionery

When defining chocolate it is important to distinguish it from confectionary (or candy), thus avoiding transforming a 'pure' food into a 'junk' food.

Confectionary is a term which generally refers to all the snacks and surrogate products, which may contain only a very small percentage of chocolate (e.g. chocolate-coated snack) and/or where cocoa butter has been replaced by cheaper vegetable oils, mixed with other ingredients and additives. These final products not only taste different but are very rich in fats, sugars, and calories, and might have a negative impact on health. Clinical observations show that a craving for this type of products—including foods such as chocolate drinks and chocolate snacks—is associated with obesity and represents a common obstacle to successful weight reduction (Drewnowski et al. 1992). Moreover, regular consumption of such products certainly contributes to a weight gain (Davey 2004), and to a higher incidence of type 2 diabetes, obesity, and cardiovascular diseases (Gross et al. 2004; Jenkins et al. 2004).

Therefore, while the negative effects of candies are well known in literature, these do not have to be confused with the effects of 'unadulterated' chocolate, that is, chocolate containing at least 70 per cent of cocoa solids.

When evaluating the nutritional and health impact of chocolate, three issues are very relevant: the type, the quality, and the quantity consumed, which all translate into different compositions in terms of nutrients and bioactive compounds.

Type of Chocolate

Chocolate is the main final product of the cocoa beans, from which cocoa butter and cocoa solids are extracted. Cocoa butter is the fatty component of chocolate and the substance that gives the characteristic melting sensation in the mouth; cocoa solids are a mixture of many substances left after the extraction of cocoa butter, and they are rich in minerals and polyphenols. The unique composition of fatty acids and anti-oxidants (especially polyphenols) determines the natural stability of cocoa against oxidation, thereby diminishing the need to add preservatives to the final product.

We can identify three main categories of chocolate: dark, milk, and white chocolate (from which many other combinations have been made). Dark chocolate has the highest proportion of cocoa solids (50–80 per cent), and the lowest amount of sugar—that makes it more bitter than the other two types. Milk chocolate has at least 25 per cent of cocoa solids and it additionally contains milk powder or condensed milk—that makes it sweeter. Finally, white chocolate does not contain any cocoa solids, but it has at least 20 per cent of cocoa butter together with milk or milk products (European Parliament and Council 2000). These proportions vary significantly worldwide, depending on the legislation in the different countries. For example, in most European countries milk chocolate must contain at least 30 per cent cocoa solids, while in the US it can contain as little as 10 per cent cocoa solids. For dark chocolate, the standard of cocoa solids is 43 per cent for European chocolate and 35 per cent for US chocolate (Khodorowsky and Robert 2001).

Table 7.1 shows the general composition of macronutrients contained in the main types of chocolate.

Among the micronutrients, appreciable levels of minerals, vitamins, and anti-oxidants are present. Contributions to daily requirements are provided by magnesium, iron, zinc, phosphorus, and liposoluble vitamins. Recent studies found that chocolate is also a major source of dietary copper (Joo and Betts 1996) and a good source of anti-oxidants, in particular of polyphenols—including flavonoids such as epicatechin, catechin, and procyanidins (Gu et al. 2006). Polyphenols protect human cells from oxidative stress damage, the mechanism which plays an important role in several human pathologies and chronic inflammation processes, such as cardiovascular diseases, metabolic syndrome, and cancer. Rusconi and Conti (2010) show that the amount of polyphenols in chocolate depends upon the variety of cocoa beans, as well as on how it has been processed. Effectively, although the polyphenol content of the non-fat fraction of raw cocoa is high (12–18 per cent of dry weight), it is hard to preserve the beneficial components in the final products.

Table 7.1 Energy and macronutrients of the main types of chocolate

Food Components	Energy	Protein	Carbohydrates	Fat
Contained per 100g/unit	(Kcal)	(g)	(g)	(g)
White chocolate	529	8	58.3	30.9
Milk chocolate (cocoa 20–30%)	565	8.9	50.8	37.6
Dark chocolate (cocoa 70%)	561	8.2	29.8	45.4

Source: Food Composition Database for Epidemiological Studies in Italy (BDA), European Institute of Oncology, 1998 (<http://www.ieo.it>).

All the conventional industrial chocolate-manufacturing steps (such as roasting, drying, and fermentation) have a huge impact on the final level of polyphenols, and can progressively decrease it by more than 80 per cent.

The high variability in cocoa processing and the different methodologies used in the measurement of the polyphenol content of chocolate make it difficult to establish a standard quantification. Chocolate products currently on the market show high variability in their polyphenol content but their amount is not mentioned on the labels. As a result it is very difficult to generalize a health claim deriving from cocoa polyphenols (Rusconi and Conti 2010). Generally speaking, the highest amount of polyphenols can be found in dark chocolate, and, more specifically, in dark chocolate with a high content of cocoa solids, 70 per cent or more (Bernaert et al. 2012). Some studies have reported that the total amount of polyphenols in dark chocolate is about 500mg/100g (Taubert et al. 2003; Grassi et al. 2005a). The polyphenol quantity in milk chocolate is lower because of the lower amount of cocoa solids compared to dark chocolate (Wollgast and Anklam 2000). Moreover, the action of polyphenols in milk chocolate is markedly reduced due to the milk proteins that bind polyphenols and decrease their absorption, therefore limiting their positive health effects. The same is true when dark chocolate is consumed together with milk. Serafini and colleagues (2003) conducted a crossover study on 12 volunteers who consumed the same amount of anti-oxidants in three different conditions, that is, in dark chocolate, in dark chocolate while they were drinking milk, and in milk chocolate. After one hour, plasma levels of anti-oxidants were measured, and it was found that they had significantly increased only after the consumption of dark chocolate alone. Furthermore, Afoakwa and colleagues (2008) argue that white chocolate differs from milk and dark since it does not contain cocoa solids, and therefore polyphenols.

These observations suggest that, to have health benefits from the consumption of chocolate, it is advisable to choose dark chocolate with 70 per cent or more cocoa solids.

Quality of Chocolate

The quality of chocolate can be defined in different ways, and thus mean different things to different people. However, when focusing on the health impacts, the quality of a chocolate is determined by the quality of its ingredients, the proportions in which they are mixed, and the methods of processing (Afoakwa et al. 2008).

To define a high-quality chocolate, a few basic ingredients have to be considered: cocoa solids, cocoa butter, sugar, and milk powder. In recent years, cocoa solids contained in the final product have become the most important standard and *chocolatiers* claim that the higher their percentage, the 'better' the chocolate (Fabricant 1998). This, in turn, implies a lower amount of sugar and milk, and thus a stronger and more bitter flavour. In 2000 the European Union (EU) promulgated a law which allowed the replacement of up to 5 per cent of the cocoa butter with approved vegetable fats, as long as this was declared on the food label. While the use of these other fats increases the shelf life of chocolate and reduces the cost, many continental European manufacturers affirm that high-quality chocolate can contain only cocoa butter (Fold 2000; Terrio 2000; Schoko-ladenmuseum 2005). It is important to emphasize the role of adequate labelling to help customers in the choice of a good-quality chocolate. Generally speaking, it is better to select a chocolate product clearly mentioning on the label the percentage of cocoa solids, with reduced amounts of added sugars and extra fats.

Quantity of Chocolate

Although an 'exact' quantity of chocolate has not been yet defined, we will now review various studies on the role of chocolate consumption on human health and try to define which dose can optimize its beneficial effects.[2] In the Zutphen Elderly Study, a habitual chocolate consumption of 10g of dark chocolate per day (corresponding to 4.2g of cocoa) was associated with lower systolic blood pressure, compared to no or very low cocoa intake (Buijsse et al. 2006).

Taubert and colleagues (2007a) demonstrated that a supplementation for 18 weeks with low doses (6.3g daily) of dark chocolate in adults with hypertension can reduce blood pressure and induce vasodilatation, without changes in body weight or plasma levels of lipids and glucose.

To evaluate the anti-inflammatory properties of dark chocolate intake, the Moli-sani Project performed a cohort study, selecting a random sample of 4849 subjects aged 35 years or more. Two subpopulations were extracted based on their consumption of dark chocolate: a test group of 824 (17 per cent) subjects who had regularly eaten dark chocolate, and a control group of 1317 (27.2 per cent) subjects who had not eaten any type of chocolate during the past year. The study found that regular consumption of small doses of dark chocolate might have anti-inflammatory properties on the body (reducing serum C-reactive protein concentration in the blood). The research also showed that the effect of dark chocolate was present up to the intake of 6.7g daily, corresponding to 20g every three days, and tended to disappear at higher doses (Di Giuseppe et al. 2008).

Another study showed that an average consumption of 10g/day of chocolate induced positive effects on cognitive performance, with maximum benefit depending on the variety of chocolate consumed (flavonoids-rich type) (Nurk et al. 2009), while Almoosawi and colleagues (2012) found that 20g per day of dark chocolate improved cardiovascular risk factors in healthy, overweight, and obese subjects.

The prospective epidemiologic study Atherosclerosis Risk in Communities (ARIC) has shown that a moderate amount of chocolate (28g per week) also reduced the risk of diabetes in an inversely proportional way to the frequency of chocolate intake (Greenberg 2015).

As we can see, although an unique beneficially effective dose of dark chocolate has not yet been identified, all these studies, as well as many others in the literature,

---

[2] In the next section, 'Health Benefits and Specific Medicinal Purposes', we will focus on the different effects separately.

suggest that small amounts of dark chocolate (5–10g daily or a mean of 30g weekly), even when irregularly consumed, can positively enhance human health.

Health Benefits and Specific Medicinal Purposes

Till a few years ago, most dieticians and nutritionists tended to recommend their patients eliminate from their diet all chocolate and chocolate products regardless of the type.

This was mainly due to the fact that chocolate was merely considered an high-energy food, a pleasurable and caloric snack, and it was also often confused with its surrogates—which had plenty of saturated fats and sugars. In many cases this approach seemed to be founded more on moral than on scientific grounds (Rossner 1997), posing the question as to whether chocolate consumption had negative metabolic effects.

Those beliefs generated a 'topos' in medical and non-medical literature, in which chocolate was associated with obesity, diabetes, high blood pressure, and an increase in plasmatic lipids, and therefore should not be included in a 'healthy' diet (Wilson 2012).

As we report in the subsection 'Impact on Obesity and Body Mass Index (BMI)', more recently several publications have argued whether chocolate may or may not have the mentioned adverse effects, especially when included in a balanced diet. We review some epidemiological and clinical studies exploring the complex interplay of specific types of chocolate and health, focusing on the benefits associated with the consumption of high-quality chocolate, such as the prevention of certain diseases and the improvement of specific medical conditions, as well as its impact on mood and human behaviour.

Reduction of Cardiovascular Risk

Cardiovascular diseases (CVD) are a group of disorders of the heart and blood vessels that may lead to heart attack and stroke. There are multiple factors associated with the development of CVD, including elevated blood lipids, high blood pressure, and obesity.

Several studies support the hypothesis that regular consumption of polyphenol-rich chocolate can reduce cardiovascular diseases (Ding et al. 2006; Engler and Engler 2006; Corti et al. 2009; Buijsse et al. 2010; Latif 2013). Interestingly, particular epidemiological evidence for the beneficial effects of chocolate on CVD has come from the Kuna Indians of Panama. This population was characterized by a low prevalence of cardiovascular diseases, attributable also to the intake of at least three 10oz servings of homemade cocoa beverages per day.[3] However, this trait was lost after migration to urban areas and subsequent changes in diet, such as the

---

[3] The Kuna cocoa sources (home-grown and Columbian cocoa powder) were shown to be high in certain flavonoids, especially the flavanols and procyanidins.

consumption of a lower amount of cocoa, especially if commercially processed (McCullough et al. 2006).[4]

Some possible mechanisms by which chocolate consumption may be involved in the reduction of cardiovascular risk are described in what follows.

BLOOD PRESSURE LOWERING EFFECT

If hypertension is one of the key risk factors for cardiovascular diseases, conversely the lowering of high blood pressure is associated with a reduction in cardiovascular morbidity and mortality.

Evidence from recent studies points to a unique conclusion, that is, that a regular intake of cocoa/dark chocolate significantly lowers blood pressure by promoting blood vessel dilatation (Taubert, Roesen, and Schömig 2007; Taubert et al. 2007; Desch et al. 2010; Ried et al. 2010).

The main effect that cocoa has on vasodilatation has been attributed to the polyphenols activity on nitric oxide (NO), a molecule directly involved in modulating blood pressure and vascular tone. The physiological production of this vascular-relaxing factor protects the vessel wall by antagonizing the initial pathological steps of atherosclerosis and thrombosis; however, NO can be inactivated by oxygen-free radicals. Polyphenols of cocoa enhance the bioactivity of NO and reduce its inactivation by oxygen-free radicals (Fisher et al. 2003; Vlachopoulos et al. 2005). Moreover, chocolate contains moderate concentrations of potassium, which is known to stimulate the excretion of sodium, therefore contributing to the maintenance of a healthy blood pressure.

Buijsse and colleagues (2006) conducted a large-scale longitudinal study in a cohort study of elderly men (aged 65–84 years) in the Netherlands. They found that, over the subsequent 15 years, a regular intake of cocoa was negatively associated with blood pressure and with cardiovascular mortality. Regarding the type of chocolate, the lowering of blood pressure was especially related to the consumption of dark chocolate, because of its high polyphenol content.

A study conducted on 21 healthy adult men aged between 25 and 30, treated for 28 days with dark chocolate (polyphenols-rich) and white chocolate (undetectable polyphenols value) confirms these results. The participants in the study were allocated to eat 75g/day, divided into three doses of 25g at three different times of the day (4, 6, and 8 p.m.), of dark chocolate or white chocolate, over four weeks. A decrease in blood pressure was observed in the dark chocolate group only (Rusconi et al. 2012).

Consumption of dark chocolate bars for 15 days has been reported by Grassi and colleagues (2005a) to reduce systolic blood pressure in healthy subjects as well as in young (Grassi et al. 2005b) hypertensive patients. Taubert and colleagues (2003) found the same in elderly hypertensive patients. Furthermore, other data indicate that a single dose of polyphenol-rich cocoa is not sufficient to get any anti-oxidant

---

[4] Postharvest handling, and manufacturing practises can lead to significant reduction or total elimination of flavanols that may have been present in freshly harvested food crops.

effect, but that five to seven days are required to reach a steady response (Fisher et al. 2003; Hollenberg and Norman 2006).

ANTI-ATHEROSCLEROTIC EFFECT

Atherosclerosis is a chronic disease related to the endothelial dysfunction characterized by the build-up of plaques on artery walls (such as fats, cholesterol, and other substances), which restrict blood flow and increases the risk of blood vessel occlusion. Atherosclerosis is the major cause of morbidity and mortality from CVD; it leads to serious problems, including heart attacks and strokes.

Oxidative stress plays a crucial role in endothelial dysfunction, promoting the initiation and progression of atherosclerosis. Low-density lipoprotein (LDL) oxidation is an early event in atherosclerosis because oxidized LDL is a potent inducer of inflammatory molecules, promoting the formation of the plaques (atheroma) on the wall of the arteries (atherogenesis). Through the years, the potential benefits of cocoa/chocolate consumption have progressively been demonstrated. We hereby report several studies focusing on the different mechanisms through which chocolate can prevent the formation of atheroma. The main potential benefits of cocoa include anti-oxidant and anti-inflammatory effects, which in turn improve endothelial function. The first human clinical study showing an inverse relationship between cocoa intake and LDL oxidation was performed by Kondo and colleagues in 1996. Due to its richness in polyphenols, dark chocolate in particular can promote anti-oxidant activities on plasma lipids, thereby delaying the onset and/or progression of atherosclerosis (Mursu et al. 2004).

Wan and colleagues (2001) argue that a daily consumption of 16g of dark chocolate and 22g of cocoa powder inhibits the development of atherosclerosis by 38 per cent. Moreover, the concentration of high-density lipoprotein (HDL) cholesterol was 4 per cent higher compared with a control average American diet.

In a study conducted on 15 women, aged 20–40 years, eating dark chocolate (70 per cent cocoa solids) for seven days, Di Renzo and colleagues (2013) demonstrated that a regular consumption of dark chocolate could be useful in maintaining a good atherogenic profile. Subjects were instructed to eat 100g of chocolate daily, distributed into two servings, 50g as a morning snack and 50g as an afternoon snack or after dinner. After chocolate consumption, a significant increase in the HDL cholesterol level and a significant decrease of total cholesterol/HDL cholesterol ratio were observed. In addition, a reduction in abdomen circumference was noted.

Another important feature of atherosclerotic lesions is platelet dysfunction. Cocoa has been shown to have aspirin-like effects on platelet function (Pearson et al. 2002), with a dual effect on platelets: it decreases platelet aggregation (Martin et al. 2009) and reduces platelet adhesion (Hermann et al. 2006).

The protecting vascular effect of dark chocolate polyphenols can also be helpful for smokers, because the products of tobacco combustion damage the arterial endothelium, promoting atherogenesis. Hermann and colleagues (2006) report that dark chocolate—with more than 70 per cent cocoa—has improved vasodilatation by 80 per cent in young healthy smokers, starting from two hours after chocolate ingestion and lasting for up to 8 hours.

IMPROVEMENT OF PLASMA LIPID PATTERN

The cocoa butter of dark chocolate contains approximately 33 per cent oleic acid, which has a positive effect on lipid levels (American Dietetic Association 2000), and 33 per cent stearic acid, which may not have any effect on lipid levels (Kris-Etherton and Yu 1997).

Baba and colleagues (2007) argue that a regular intake of cocoa increases the 'good' HDL cholesterol, reduces triglycerides, and decreases the 'bad' LDL cholesterol, positively modulating the plasma lipid profile and improving values of the markers of cardiovascular disease.

The concentration of HDL cholesterol rose in healthy humans ingesting 75g per day of dark chocolate for three weeks (Mursu et al. 2004). This study found that the increase in HDL cholesterol was 11 per cent after the consumption of dark chocolate only, and 14 per cent after the consumption of dark chocolate enriched with cocoa polyphenols, whereas no effect was observed after the consumption of white chocolate.

Milk chocolate may also have a positive effect. It was demonstrated that, when a milk chocolate bar (46g daily) was substituted for a high-carbohydrate snack in healthy young men, it has no effect on plasma total and LDL cholesterol while HDL cholesterol concentration increased and plasma triglycerides fell significantly (Kris-Etherton et al. 1994).

Antidiabetic Effect

In a healthy person, body tissues respond to the hormone insulin (insulin sensitivity), allowing glucose utilization from cells. Type 2 diabetes occurs when, after a series of events, receptors on the body cells fail to respond normally to the action of insulin (insulin resistance), leading to high blood glucose (hyperglycemia), with a subsequent increase in circulating insulin levels (hyperinsulinemia). Oxidative stress is one of the factors contributing to reducing the insulin activity/sensitivity and to increasing the insulin resistance. Foods that are rich in polyphenols are able to contrast oxidative stress: the consumption of dark chocolate (polyphenols-rich and moreover low in sugars) can consequently reduce the risk factors for type 2 diabetes. Grassi and colleagues (2005a) observed a reduction in insulin resistance and an increase in insulin sensitivity after the ingestion of 100g of dark chocolate in healthy subjects, and hypertensive (Grassi et al. 2005b) and diabetic patients (Grassi et al. 2013). Conversely, the same positive results were not found after the ingestion of white chocolate, which contains mainly sugar and cocoa butter.

A recent epidemiological study on the association between long-term chocolate consumption and risk of diabetes has been conducted in a US cohort study of 7802 participants. The consumption of a moderate amount of chocolate (1oz of chocolate less than monthly) showed a reduction in the risk of diabetes, and the risk decreased as the frequency of chocolate intake increased to up to two to six servings per week (Greenberg 2015).

Favourable Effect on the Parameters of Metabolic Syndrome

Metabolic syndrome is a chronic disorder defined by the co-presence of three out of five medical conditions: insulin resistance, low HDL cholesterol, high serum triglycerides, raised blood pressure, and central abdominal obesity. In patients with metabolic syndrome the risk for cardiovascular diseases and other health problems is greater than in any patient presenting one factor alone. Although the exact mechanism of these complex pathways is still under investigation, chronic inflammation has been identified as the basis for the development and progression of metabolic syndrome.

The positive effects of polyphenol-rich dark chocolate on various parameters of metabolic syndrome have been recognized in a study on female overweight and obese subjects. Volunteers were divided in two groups. One group consumed 20g of polyphenol-rich dark chocolate per day for four weeks and the other group consumed a dark chocolate with negligible polyphenol content. The study provided evidence of the metabolic benefits of consuming polyphenol-rich dark chocolate, especially on biomarkers of glucose metabolism and cardiovascular risk factors (Almoosawi et al. 2012).

Moreover, it has recently been concluded that daily consumption of dark chocolate for ten years in a population with metabolic syndrome was effective in the prevention of cardiovascular events (Zomer et al. 2012), thanks to the efficacy of polyphenols in contrasting the chronic inflammatory mechanisms which are at the basis of metabolic syndrome (Gu and Lambert 2013).

Impact on Obesity and Body Mass Index (BMI)

The word chocolate has usually been associated with energy and calories. To give an example, during the Civil War in the US chocolate was a vital part of the soldiers' rations, since it was able to offer maximum nourishment with minimum bulk. It was used, in emergency conditions, to substitute an entire meal, because the caloric content of a ration could sustain a soldier for a day. Despite some popular beliefs, energy and calories derived from chocolate consumption do not always translate into weight gain and there is still disagreement in the literature on whether chocolate plays a role in gaining weight or combating obesity. Recent research has evaluated the possibility that chocolate may help people to remain slim. Golomb and colleagues (2012) found that people (average age of 57 years) who used to frequently eat chocolate (five times a week) and exercise regularly (an average of 3.6 times a week) had a lower body mass index (BMI) than those who eat chocolate less often. Moreover, regular chocolate eaters weighed less than others, even though they consumed a higher amount of total calories and saturated fats.

It is only recently that dark chocolate has been recognized as a functional food in the management of obesity through several mechanisms, such as decreasing fat absorption and synthesis, modulating carbohydrate metabolism, and stimulating satiety (Matsui et al. 2005). Some studies highlight that, due to its small contribution to total calorie intake, the right dose of dark chocolate does not have harmful effects on anthropometric variables such as BMI and waist circumference (Di Giuseppe et al. 2008). An observational study on 1458 European adolescents (ages 12.5–17.5 years) participating in HELENA-CSS (Healthy Lifestyle in Europe by Nutrition in Adolescence Cross-Sectional Study) found that a higher chocolate consumption is associated with lower total and central fatness, determined through BMI and waist circumference (Cuenca-García et al. 2014).

On the other hand, a recently published prospective epidemiological analysis found that chocolate habits were associated with long-term weight gain, in a dose-response manner. In a cohort study of 15,732 participants at the first visit and 12,830 at the second visit, three categories of chocolate eaters were identified based on the frequency of consumption of a 28g serving: <1/month, 1–4/month, and ≥1/week. During the six-year study period, the greatest weight gain was seen in participants with the highest frequency of chocolate intake: compared with participants who ate a chocolate serving less than once monthly, those who ate chocolate 1–4 times a month and at least weekly experienced an increase in BMI of 0.26 and 0.39 respectively. The main limitation of this finding is that it does not distinguish between types of chocolate (white, milk, dark), and thus it is not possible to test whether dark chocolate yields smaller prospective BMI increases than milk or white chocolate (Greenberg and Buijsse 2013).

Satiety Response, and Appetite Reduction

Research conducted in the Netherlands on young healthy women explored the relationship between appetite and levels of gastrointestinal hormones involved in the regulation of appetite, after smelling and eating chocolate. Results showed that both smelling and eating 30g chocolate induced appetite suppression and were inversely correlated with levels of ghrelin, a hormone which stimulates appetite (Massolt et al. 2010).

Among the various categories, dark chocolate has a more intense cocoa flavour than the milk type: this stronger sensory signal may lead to a stronger sensory satiety response (Weijzen et al. 2008). Dark chocolate is able to satisfy 'a sweet tooth' for longer than milk chocolate. After the consumption of dark chocolate, people feel more satiated, less hungry, and have lower ratings of prospective food consumption than after having milk chocolate. Moreover, ratings of the desire to eat something sweet, fatty, or savoury, as well as energy intake at the following *ad libitum* meal, seem to all be lower after the consumption of dark chocolate (Sørensen and Astrup 2011).

Improvement of Cognitive Function

A Norwegian study found that regular chocolate consumers performed better in cognitive tests and had a significantly reduced risk for poor test performance.

A maximum beneficial effect on cognitive performance might be gained at a mean intake of chocolate of 10g/day but the real effect of polyphenols in chocolate may be even stronger, depending on the type of chocolate consumed (however, this was not specified in the study). Moreover, in elderly patients with mild impairment, a reduction in the risk of dementia and improved cognitive function has been associated with a regular intake of chocolate, as well as of other foods rich in polyphenols (Nurk et al. 2009).

In their study on healthy volunteers, Walters and colleagues (2012) showed the acute positive effects of a bar (100g) of dark chocolate or milk chocolate on cerebrovascular activity through the improvement of cerebral blood flow.

Anti-Tumour Effect

Oxidative stress is one of the risk factors in the promotion and development of various types of cancer. Due to their high concentration of anti-oxidant bioactive compounds, the effect of cocoa and dark chocolate consumption in inhibiting the growth of cancerous cells has been investigated (Carnesecchi et al. 2002). Examining the anti-carcinogenic properties of cocoa, using several human cancer-cell lines, Romanczyk and colleagues (1997) indicate that dark chocolate consumption exerts an anti-carcinogenic activity, but data from a small number of observational epidemiologic studies offers weak support for a reduction in cancer-related mortality. Further large-scale studies are needed to assess and confirm the potential role of dark chocolate in the prevention and/or treatment of cancer (Maskarinec 2009).

Other Effects on Human Health

A double-blind study in 30 healthy subjects reports a positive action of cocoa on skin health. The patients were randomly divided into two groups, one consuming a 20g per day of high-flavanol-level chocolate, and one consuming a conventional dark chocolate in the same amount. Results of the study confirmed that a regular consumption of rich-in-polyphenols chocolate confers significant photoprotection and can be effective at protecting human skin from harmful UV effects (Williams et al. 2009).

Chocolate was found to coat the teeth, thereby preventing tooth decay from chocolate's high sugar content. Tannins in cocoa were found to promote healthy teeth as they inhibited the formation of dental plaque (Matsumoto et al. 2004).

The anti-oxidant capacity of cocoa products may act locally in the gastrointestinal tract, causing benefits for the intestine and the whole organism and improving quality of life (Jenny et al. 2009). Furthermore, chocolate supplementation before physical exercise results in a rapid recovery of post-exercise physiological and metabolic changes induced by exercise (Chen et al. 1996).

Psychological Effects

Impact on Mood and Craving

It is indisputable that chocolate consumption gives instant pleasure and comfort, especially during episodes of 'emotional eating', which involves searching for food (generally in large amounts) even if not physiologically hungry in order to get relief from a negative mood or bad feelings (e.g. stressful life situations, anxiety, depression).

The pleasure experienced in eating chocolate can be, first of all, due to neurophysiological components. Chocolate is high in branch-chain amino acids, and especially in tryptophan, which increases the blood level of serotonin, the neurotransmitter which produces calming and pleasurable feelings. The increase in plasma serotonin concentration has been observed especially in white chocolate-eating people, probably because of the higher content of carbohydrates in this type of chocolate rather than dark chocolate. Moreover, the presence of magnesium improves the body's ability to adapt to stress.

But the pleasure experienced in eating chocolate cannot be justified solely by neurophysiological components. Chocolate can be desired because it provides a unique sensory experience. It has a hedonistic appeal to most people, based on sight, preparation, memories of past chocolate experiences, texture, and taste. Therefore, we should not underestimate the idea that chocolate consumption assumes a positive value because it is primarily linked to memories of childhood, maternal instinct, affection, moments of celebration, and emotional contexts, such as festive situations and family gatherings. In fact, there is a reciprocal relationship between mood and food: food can influence the mood of an individual and, conversely, specific emotional states can lead to the choice of a particular food. So it is no wonder if, on some occasions, we consider 'chocolate cheaper than therapy, with the appointment not necessary' (Molinari and Callus 2012).

Parker and colleagues (2006) indicate that chocolate is one of the most craved foods. The experience of 'craving' can be defined as an intense desire for a particular item. Chocolate craving was reported also by Wurtman and Wurtman (1989) to have an interesting impact on brain neurotransmitters, with antidepressant benefits, and has been used as a form of self-medication in atypical depression and in seasonal affective disorder.

Nearly three thousand individuals who had experienced clinical depression were interviewed about food cravings when depressed. Of the whole sample, 45 per cent reported craving chocolate when depressed, especially among females, with the following related explanations: its pleasure-enhancing role; its capacity to improve depression and to decrease irritation and anxiety; its unique taste; its 'feeling in the mouth'; its texture; its smell; and finally its colour (Parker and Crawford 2007). A specific association between cravings for sweets in general and, more specifically, for chocolate products during the menstrual period has been found. Women eat more and seem to have very strong cravings for chocolate just prior to and during their menstrual cycle, when feelings of tension or depression occur. This is when progesterone levels are low and pre-menstrual symptoms tend to appear as well. It has been demonstrated that there is a physiological and hormonal basis for this kind of craving (i.e. a pre-menstrual desire for chocolate) (Tomelleri and Grunewald 1987). Chocolate may provide an antidepressant effect during this critical period and also when women enter menopause, when, in fact, they often develop a sudden strong craving for chocolate.

Rozin and colleagues (1991) believed that chocolate contains pharmacologically active substances responsible for the craving. However, it is still not clear whether the secret of the 'chocolate craving' can be only attributed to a pharmacological effect or whether sensory properties are more important with regard to the psychological aspects of this food. It is still unknown whether these substances are present in sufficient amounts to play a major role in chocolate consumption or to cause physiological addiction. Smit (2011) thought that some publications have only fed myths about chocolate craving.

Weingarten and Elston (1991) reported that, while the craving for carbohydrates can be satisfied from any fatty or sweet food, including chocolate, the majority of the chocolate cravers cannot replace chocolate with any other food in times of strong desire. This is why it is very important not to deprive someone completely of chocolate if he/she desires it. Doing it could lead to the opposite effect: the subject, not having the opportunity to eat chocolate at will, will overconsume it as soon as it becomes available (Polivy et al. 2005). This confirms the fact that chocolate is a unique food which inspires unusually strong desires in people.

It is therefore important to distinguish the phenomena of 'pure' chocolate craving from the one of 'general' carbohydrate craving in the context of emotional eating. It is probable that each phenomenon is driven by different motivations and so produces different outcomes.

A neologism referring to a perceived physical or psychological addiction to chocolate and/or its chemical composition has been devised: 'chocoholic' combining the word 'chocolate' with the word 'alcoholic' (Wilson and Hurst 2012). Chocoholics tend to be female rather than male because they are more susceptible to the effects of the two compounds phenylethylamine and serotonin, which can be mildly addictive (Salonia et al. 2006).

However, since depriving one of chocolate fails to produce scientifically relevant withdrawal symptoms, chocolate is not technically classed as a physically addictive substance.

Aphrodisiac Properties

The aphrodisiac role of chocolate was well known within the Mayan and Aztec cultures; these peoples believed that it invigorated men and made women less inhibited. Rumours abounded on how the Aztec emperor Montezuma drank 50 goblets of chocolate concoction each day (Ross 2007) before having sexual intercourse with his numerous wives. Various chocolate substances have been investigated, trying to document the various mechanisms at the base of this theory. First of all, since eating chocolate gives an instant energy boost it can increase sexual stamina. Chocolate has been claimed to contain several potentially psychoactive chemicals noted to temporarily raise blood pressure and heart rate, heightening sensations and blood-glucose levels. It also contains a large number of psycho-active compounds that, acting on the human brain and body, create feelings of euphoria, happiness, even sexual arousal or other psychological effects. For example, chocolate contains small amounts of the amino acid tyramine, which can powerfully induce the release of adrenaline, with the consequent heightening of arousal, anxiety, and failure to sleep.

Moreover, chocolate is rich in theobromine (an alkaloid stimulant that acts on the body in ways similar to caffeine) and other compounds similar to the cannabinoids, that act on the central nervous system, producing euphoric, aphrodisiac, and stimulating effects (Di Tomaso et al. 1996). It also contains phenylethylamine, a molecule released during intimacy, when people are infatu-ated or fall in love, and it further promotes the release of serotonin into the human system, producing some aphrodisiac and mood-lifting effects. Chemical content apart, scientists continue to debate whether chocolate should be classified as an aphrodisiac. Although it contains substances that increase passion and feelings of happiness and well-being, there is still not univocal evidence that chocolate is indeed an aphrodisiac (Afoakwa 2008). Bianchi-Demicheli and colleagues (2013) highlight the need of conducting randomized studies to confirm all these hypotheses.

Negative Effects of Chocolate Consumption

Over the years, numerous academic books and popular articles have split the reputation of chocolate. As discussed, recent studies have demolished elements of its previous negative reputation, especially regarding the rise of obesity and gaining body weight, while some other health risks linked to chocolate consump-tion can be still found in literature. However, few adverse effects of chocolate consumption have been reported compared with the many studies on its benefits on human health (Latif 2013). Medical problems attributed to chocolate consump-tion include pruritus, rashes, rhinorrhea, and asthma (Ghosh 1977; Fries 1978; Wilson 1985), as well as childhood hyperactivity (Kaplan et al. 1989) and various allergic reactions, though evidence for this last is generally weak (Fries 1978). A few studies have also documented allergic reactions to chocolate in children (Steinman and Potter 1994; Businco et al. 2002).

Chocolate also is rich in a variety of vasoactive amines that can cross the blood–brain barrier and affect the cerebral blood flow, eventually triggering headaches and migraines (Nehlig 2004). Moreover, Friedman (1980) does not recommend chocolate for patients with irritable bowel symptoms, while Murphy and Castel (1988) discourage its consumption in patients with reflux esophagitis because one of its constituents, the theobromine, is able to relax the oesophageal sphincter muscle, allowing stomach acidic contents to enter into oesophagus.

Comment

Cocoa products and chocolate have always had a privileged position in history, due to their mystical uses and their medicinal effects on human health. Some ancient traditions and myths on the beneficial effects of chocolate have recently been supported by medical and scientific studies, thus restoring the traditional belief of chocolate as 'the food of gods' (as Linnaeus defined the bountiful plant *Theobroma cacao*). Following a period in which chocolate was blamed as being just a candy, nowadays chocolate can be considered not merely a source of sugar and fats but a melting pot of micronutrients and anti-oxidants, elevating its status to functional food (Latif 2013). Because of its potential nutritional and health properties, chocolate has actually attracted the attention of many researchers as well as the general consuming public. However, given chocolate's interesting and complex nutritional composition, scientists continue to investigate in order to unlock all of its secrets.

Over the past decades, many human studies involving the use of cocoa and chocolate have been carried out, and have provided important insights into the positive effects of chocolate on human health, that is, several studies have reported benefits in reducing the risk of cardiovascular diseases, and delaying the development of cancer, chronic, and other age-related diseases, as well as positive impacts on mood and human behaviour. The link between chocolate and health has also recently generated significant interest for the nutraceutical (nutritional + pharmaceutical) industry, thanks to the most recent findings of biomedical technologies focusing on food analysis.

However, because the health potential of chocolate is closely linked to the composition of the end product, the choice of a high-quality chocolate is imperative in order to obtain the desired health benefits. This is why it is necessary to clarify the meaning of the word 'chocolate', and thus to distinguish a 'divine food' from a 'junk food'. In this chapter, we refer exclusively to unadulterated, high-quality chocolate, while all types of confectionary and surrogated products (containing a small amount of chocolate) are excluded by this definition. When choosing a chocolate bar we should read the labels, and prefer darker, lower-fat, and lower-sugar varieties, selecting in particular the products that clearly state the percentage of cocoa solids. In addition, recognizing that 'the dose makes the poison' (Paracelsus), chocolate must be consumed in the right amount, used and not abused, and thus included in a balanced diet.

Although the composition, as well as the manufacturing, packaging, and labelling, of chocolate products are all regulated by legislation, there is still not a proper consideration of the real potential for health effects, for example by establishing the minimum concentration of polyphenols in cocoa products and different types of chocolate (Rusconi and Conti 2010).

We recognize that further investigations and research have still to be conducted in order to guarantee the choice of the highest-quality chocolate for the consumers.

Chocolate is more than a sweet or a beverage and more than the sum of its interesting nutrients and phytochemicals. It is a complex food, with an important role within the history of civilizations.

References

Afoakwa, E. 2008. 'Cocoa and chocolate consumption: Are there aphrodisiac and other benefits for human health?' *South African Journal of Clinical Nutrition* 21 (3): pp. 107–13.

Afoakwa, E., A. Paterson, M. Fowler, and A. Ryan. 2008. 'Flavor formation and character in cocoa and chocolate: a critical review'. *Critical Reviews in Food Science and Nutrition* 48 (9): pp. 840–57.

Albright, B. 1997. 'Trends in Chocolate'. In *Chocolate: Food of the Gods*, ed. A. Szogyi, pp. 137–44. Westport, CT: Greenwood Press.

Almoosawi, S., C. Tsang, L. M. Ostertag, L. Fyfe, and E. A. Al-Dujaili. 2012. 'Differential effect of polyphenol-rich dark chocolate on biomarkers of glucose metabolism and cardiovascular risk factors in healthy, overweight and obese subjects: a randomized clinical trial'. *Food Functional* 3 (10): pp. 1035–43.

American Dietetic Association. 2000. *Chocolate: Facts and Fiction*. Nutrition fact sheet. Chicago: American Dietetic Association Foundation.

Baba, S., N. Osakabe, Y. Kato, M. Natsume, A. Yasuda, T. Kido, K., Fukuda, Y. Muto, and K. Kondo. 2007. 'Continuous intake of polyphenolic compounds containing cocoa powder reduces LDL oxidative susceptibility and has beneficial effects on plasma HDL-cholesterol concentrations in humans'. *American Journal of Clinical Nutrition* 85 (3): pp. 709–17.

Beckett, S. T. 2008. *The Science of Chocolate*. 2nd edn. London: Royal Society of Chemistry.

Bernaert, H., I. Blondeel, L. Allegaert, and T. Lohmueller. 2012. 'Industrial Treatment of Cocoa in Chocolate Production: Health Implications'. In *Chocolate and Health*, ed. R. Paoletti, A. Poli, A. Conti, and F. Visioli, pp. 17–31. Milan: Springer.

Bianchi-Demicheli F., L. Sekoranja, and A. Pechère-Bertschi. 2013. 'Sexuality, heart and chocolate'. *Revue Medicale Suisse* 9 (378): pp. 624, 626–9.

Bloom, C. 1998. *All about Chocolate: The Ultimate Resource for the World's Favorite Food*. New York: Macmillan.

Buijsse, B., E. J. Feskens, F. J. Kok, and D. Kromhout. 2006. 'Cocoa intake, blood pressure, and cardiovascular mortality: the Zutphen Elderly Study'. *Archives of Internal Medicine* 166 (4): pp. 411–17.

Buijsse, B., C. Weikert, D. Drogan, M. Bergmann, and H. Boeing. 2010. 'Chocolate consumption in relation to blood pressure and risk of cardiovascular disease in German adults'. *European Heart Journal* 31 (13): pp. 1616–23.

Businco, L., P. Falconieri, B. Bellioni-Businco, and S. L. Bahna. 2002. 'Severe food-induced vasculitis in two children'. *Pediatric Allergy Immunology* 13 (1): pp. 68–71.

Carnesecchi, S., Y. Schneider, S. A. Lazarus, D. Coehlo, F. Gossé, and F. Raul. 2002. 'Flavanols and procyanidins of cocoa and chocolate inhibit growth and polyamine biosynthesis of human colonic cancer cells'. *Cancer Letters* 175 (2): pp. 147–55.

Chen, J. D., H. Ai, J. D. Shi, Y. Z. Wu, and Z. M. Chen. 1996. 'The effect of a chocolate bar supplementation on moderate exercise recovery of recreational runners'. *Biomedical and Environmental Science* 9 (2–3): pp. 247–55.

Coe, S. D. and M. D. Coe. 1996. *The True History of Chocolate*. London: Thames & Hudson.

Corti, R., A. J. Flammer, N. K. Hollenberg, and T. F. Lüscher. 2009. 'Cocoa and cardiovascular health'. *Circulation* 119 (10): pp. 1433–41.

Cuenca-García, M., J. R. Ruiz, F. B. Ortega, and M. J. Castillo. 2014. 'Association between chocolate consumption and fatness in European adolescents'. *Nutrition* 30 (2): pp. 236–9.

Davey, R. C. 2004. 'The obesity epidemic: too much food for thought?' *British Journal of Sports Medicine* 38 (3): pp. 360–3.

Desch, S., D. Kobler, M. Sonnabend, V. Adams, M. Sareban, I. Eitel, M. Blüher, G. Schuler, and H. Thiele. 2010. 'Low vs. higher-dose dark chocolate and blood pressure in cardiovascular - high-risk patients'. *American Journal of Hypertension* 23 (6): pp. 694−700.

Di Giuseppe, R., A. Di Castelnuovo, F. Centritto, F. Zito, A. De Curtis, S. Costanzo, B. Vohnout, S. Sieri, V. Krog, M. B. Donati, G. De Gaetano, and L. Iacoviello. 2008. 'Regular consumption of dark chocolate is associated with low serum concentrations of C-reactive protein in a healthy Italian population'. *Journal of Nutrition* 138 (10): pp. 1939−45.

Di Renzo, L., M. Rizzo, F. Sarlo, C. Colica, L. Iacopino, E. Domino, and A. De Lorenzo. 2013. 'Effects of dark chocolate in a population of normal weight obese women: a pilot study'. *European Review for Medical and Pharmacological Sciences* 17 (16): pp. 2257−66.

Di Tomaso, E., M. Beltramo, and D. Piomelli. 1996. 'Brain cannabinoids in chocolate'. *Nature* 382 (6593): pp. 677−8.

Dillinger, T. L., P. Barriga, S. Escarcega, M. Jimenez, D. Salazar Lowe, and L. E. Grivetti. 2000. 'Food of the gods: Cure for humanity? A cultural history of the medicinal and ritual use of chocolate'. *Journal of Nutrition* 130 (8): pp. 2057–72.

Ding, E. L., S. M. Hutfless, X. Ding, and S. Girotra. 2006. 'Chocolate and prevention of cardiovascular disease: a systematic review'. *Nutrition & Metabolism* 3 (2). doi: 10.1186/ 1743-7075-3-2.

Drewnowski, A., C. Kurth, J. Holden-Wiltse, and J. Saari. 1992. 'Food preferences in human obesity: carbohydrates versus fats'. *Appetite* 18 (3): pp. 207−21.

Engler, M. B. and M. M. Engler. 2006. 'The emerging role of flavonoid-rich cocoa and chocolate in cardiovascular health and disease: a systematic review'. *Nutrition Reviews* 64 (3): pp. 109–18.

European Parliament and Council. 2000. Directive 2000/36/EC Relating to Cocoa and Chocolate Products Intended for Human Consumption, 23 June. OJ 2000; L197 (August):19–25.

Fabricant, F. 1998. 'The intense pleasures of dark chocolate'. *New York Times*, 16 December; http://www.nytimes.com/1998/12/16/dining/the-intense-pleasures-of-dark-chocolate.html (accessed 6th July 2015).

Fisher, N. D., D. L. Naomi, M. Gerhard-Herman, and N. K. Hollenberg . 2003. 'Flavanol-rich cocoa induces nitric-oxide-dependent vasodilation in healthy humans'. *Journal of Hypertension* 21 (12): pp. 2281–6.

Fold, N. 2000. 'A matter of good taste? Quality and the construction of standards for chocolate products in the European Union'. *Cahiers d'Economie et Sociologie Rurale* 55−6: pp. 91−110.

Friedman, G. 1980. 'Nutritional therapy of irritable bowel syndrome'. *Gastroenterology Clinics of North America* 18 (3): pp. 513−24.

Fries, J. H. 1978. 'Chocolate: a review of published reports of allergic and other deleterious effects, real or presumed'. *Annals of Allergy, Asthma & Immunology* 41 (4): pp. 195−207.

Ghosh, J. S. 1977. 'Allergic reactions to chocolate'. *American Journal of Clinical Nutrition* 30: pp. 834−5.

Golomb, B. A., S. Koperski, and H. L. White. 2012. 'Association between more frequent chocolate consumption and lower body mass index'. *Archives of Internal Medicine* 172 (6): pp. 519−21.

Grassi, D., G. Desideri, and C. Ferri. 2013. 'Protective effects of dark chocolate on endothelial function and diabetes'. *Current Opinion in Clinical Nutrition and Metabolic Care* 16 (6): pp. 662−8.

Grassi, D., C. Lippi, S. Necozione, G. Desideri, and C. Ferri. 2005a. 'Short-term administration of dark chocolate is followed by a significant increase in insulin sensitivity and a decrease in blood pressure in healthy persons'. *American Journal of Clinical Nutrition* 81 (3): pp. 611–14.

Grassi, D., S. Necozione, C. Lippi, G. Croce, L. Valeri, P. Pasqualetti, G. Desideri, J. B. Blumberg, and C. Ferri. 2005b. 'Cocoa reduces blood pressure and insulin resistance and improves endothelium-dependent vasodilation in hypertensives'. *Hypertension* 46 (2): pp. 398–405.

Greenberg, J. A. 2015. 'Chocolate intake and diabetes risk'. *Clinical Nutrition* 34 (1): pp. 129–33.

Greenberg, J. A. and B. Buijsse. 2013. 'Habitual chocolate consumption may increase body weight in a dose-response manner'. *PloS one* 8 (8). doi: 10.1371/journal.pone.0070271.

Gross, L. S., L. Li, E. S. Ford, and S. Liu. 2004. 'Increased consumption of refined carbohydrates and the epidemic of type 2 diabetes in the United States: an ecologic assessment'. *American Journal of Clinical Nutrition* 79 (5): pp. 774–9.

Gu, L., S. E. House, X. Wu, B. Ou, and R. L. Prior. 2006. 'Procyanidin and catechin contents and antioxidant capacity of cocoa and chocolate products'. *Journal of Agricultural and Food Chemistry* 54 (11): pp. 4057–61.

Gu, Y. and J. D. Lambert. 2013. 'Modulation of metabolic syndrome-related inflammation by cocoa'. *Molecular Nutrition and Food Research* 57 (6): pp. 948–61.

Henderson, J. S., R. A. Joyce, and G. R. Hall. 2007. 'Chemical and archeological evidence for the earliest cacao beverages'. *Proceedings of the National Academy of Sciences USA* 104 (48): pp. 18937–40.

Hermann, F., L. E. Spieker, F. Ruschitzka, I. Sudano, M. Hermann, C. Binggeli, T. F. Lüscher, W. Riesen, G. Noll, and R. Corti. 2006. 'Dark chocolate improves endothelial and platelet function'. *Heart* 92 (1): pp. 119–20.

Hollenberg, N. K. and M. D. Norman. 2006. 'Vascular action of cocoa flavanols in humans: the roots of the story'. *Journal of Cardiovascular Pharmacology* 47: S99–102.

Jenkins, D. J., C. W. Kendall, A. Marchie, and L. S. Augustin. 2004. 'Too much sugar, too much carbohydrate, or just too much? *American Journal of Clinical Nutrition* 79 (5): pp. 711–12.

Jenny, M., E. Santer, A. Klein, M. Ledochowski, H. Schennach, F. Ueberall, and D. Fuchs. 2009. 'Cacao extracts suppress tryptophan degradation of mitogen-stimulated peripheral blood mononuclear cells'. *Journal of Ethnopharmacology* 122 (2): pp. 261–7.

Joo, S. J. and N. M. Betts. 1996. 'Copper intakes and consumption patterns in chocolate foods as sources of copper for individuals in the 1987–88 nationwide food consumption survey'. *Nutrition Research* 16: pp. 41–52.

Kaplan, B. J., R. D. McNicol, R. A. Conte, and H. K. Moghadam. 1989. 'Dietary replacement in preschoolaged hyperactive boys'. *Pediatrics* 83 (1): pp. 7–17.

Khodorowsky, K. and Robert, H. 2001. *The Little Book of Chocolate*. Luçon: Flammarion.

Kondo, K., R. Hirano, A. Matsumoto, O. Igaraschi, and H. Itakura. 1996. 'Inhibition of LDL oxidation by cocoa'. *Lancet* 348 (9040): p. 1514.

Kris-Etherton, P. M. and S. Yu. 1997. 'Individual fatty acid effects on plasma lipids and lipoproteins: human studies'. *American Journal of Clinical Nutrition* 65 (5): pp. 1628S–44S.

Kris-Etherton, P. M., J. A. Derr, V. A. Mustad, F. H. Seligson, and T. A. Pearson. 1994. 'Effects of milk chocolate bar per day substituted for a high-carbohydrate snack in young men on an NCEP/AHA Step 1 Diet'. *American Journal of Clinical Nutrition* 60 (6): pp. 1037S–42S.

Latif, R. 2013. 'Chocolate/cocoa and human health: a review'. *Netherlands Journal of Medicine* 71 (2): pp. 63–8.

Lippi, D. 2009. 'Chocolate and medicine: Dangerous liaisons?' *Nutrition* 25 (11–12): pp. 1100–3.

Lippi, D. 2012. 'History of the Medical Use of Chocolate'. In *Chocolate in Health and Nutrition*, edited by R. Watson, V. R. Preedy, and S. Zibadi. New York: Humana Press: pp. 11–21.

McCullough, M. L., K. Chevaux, L. Jackson, M. Preston, G. Martinez, H. H. Schmitz, C. Coletti, H. Campos, and N. K. Hollenberg. 2006. 'Hypertension, the Kuna, and the epidemiology of flavanols'. *Journal of Cardiovascular Pharmacology* 47 (2): pp. S103–9.

Martin, F. P. J., S. Rezzi, E. Pere-Trepat, B. Kamlage, S. Collino, E. Leibold, J. Kastler, D. Rein, L. B. Fay, and S. Kochhar. 2009. 'Metabolic effects of dark chocolate consumption on energy, gut microbiota, and stress-related metabolism in free-living subjects'. *Journal of Proteome Research* 8 (12): pp. 5568–79.

Maskarinec, G. 2009. 'Cancer protective properties of cocoa: a review of the epidemiologic evidence'. *Nutrition and Cancer* 61 (5): pp. 573–9.

Massolt, E. T., P. M. Van Haard, J. F. Rehfeld, E. F. Posthuma, E. Van der Veer, and D. H. Schweitzer. 2010. 'Appetite suppression through smelling of dark chocolate correlates with changes in ghrelin in young women'. *Regulatory Peptides* 161 (1–3): pp. 81–6.

Matsui, N., R. Ito, E. Nishimura, M. Yoshikawa, M. Kato, M. Kamei, H. Shibata, I. Matsumoto, K. Abe, and S. Hashizume. 2005. 'Ingested cocoa can prevent high fat diet induced obesity by regulating the expression of genes for fatty acid metabolism'. *Nutrition* 21 (5): pp. 594–601.

Matsumoto, M., M. Tsuji, J. Okuda, H. Sasaki, K. Nakano, K. Osawa, S. Shimura, and T. Ooshima. 2004. 'Inhibitory effects of cacao bean husk extract on plaque formation in vitro and in vivo'. *European Journal of Oral Sciences* 112 (3): pp. 249–52.

Molinari, E. and E. Callus. 2012. 'Psychological Drivers of Chocolate Consumption'. In *Chocolate and Health*, ed. R. Paoletti, A. Poli, A. Conti, and F. Visioli, pp. 137–46. Milan: Springer.

Murphy, D. W. and D. O. Castel. 1988. 'Chocolate and heartburn: evidence of increased esophageal acid exposure after chocolate ingestion'. *American Journal of Gastroenterology* 83 (6): pp. 633–6.

Mursu, J., S. Voutilainen, T. Nurmi, T. H. Rissanen, J. K. Virtanen, J. Kaikkonen, K. Nyyssönen, and J. T. Salonen. 2004. 'Dark chocolate consumption increases HDL cholesterol concentration and chocolate fatty acids may inhibit lipid peroxidation in healthy humans'. *Free Radical Biology and Medicine* 37 (9): pp. 1351–9.

Nehlig, A. 2004. *Coffee, Tea, Chocolate, and the Brain*. Boca Raton, FL: CRC Press.

Nurk, E., H. Refsum, C. A. Drevon, S. Tell Grethe, H. A. Nygaard, K. Engedal, and A. D. Smith. 2009. 'Intake of flavonoid-rich wine, tea, and chocolate by elderly men and women is associated with better cognitive test performance'. *Journal of Nutrition* 139 (1): pp. 120–7.

Parker, G. and J. Crawford. 2007. 'Chocolate craving when depressed: a personality marker'. *British Journal of Psychiatry* 191: pp. 351–2.

Parker, G., I. Parker, and H. Brotchie. 2006. 'Mood state effects of chocolate'. *Journal of Affective Disorders* 92 (2–3): pp. 149–59.

Pearson, D. A., T. G. Paglieroni, D. Rein, T. Wun, D. D. Schramm, J. F. Wang, R. R. Holt R. Gosselin, H. H. Schmitz, and C. L. Keen. 2002. 'The effects of flavanol-rich cocoa and aspirin on ex vivo platelet function'. *Thrombosis Research* 106 (4–5): pp. 191–7.

Polivy, J., J. Coleman, and C. P. Herman. 2005. 'The effect of deprivation on food cravings and eating behavior in restrained and unrestrained eaters'. *International Journal of Eating Disorders* 38 (4): pp. 301–9.

Richardson, T. 2003. *Sweets: A History of Candy*. New York: Bloomsbury.

Ried, K., T. Sullivan, P. Fakler, O. R. Frank, and N. P. Stocks. 2010. 'Does chocolate reduce blood pressure? A metaanalysis'. *BMC Medicine* 8: p. 39.

Romanczyk, L. J., J. F. Hammerstone, M. M. Buck, L. S. Post, G. G. Cipolla, C. A. McClelland, J. A. Mundt, H. H. Schmitz 1997. 'Cocoa extract compounds and methods for making and using the same'. Patent Cooperation Treaty (PCT) WO 97/36497, Mars incorporated, USA.

Ross, S. M. 2007. 'Chocolate: be bad, to feel good'. *Holistic nursing practice, 21*(1): pp. 50–1.

Rossner, S. 1997. 'Chocolate: Divine food, fattening junk or nutritious supplementation?' *European Journal of Clinical Nutrition* 51 (6): pp. 341–5.

Rozin, P., E. Levine, and C. Stoess. 1991. 'Chocolate craving and liking'. *Appetite* 17 (3): pp. 199–212.

Rusconi, M. and A. Conti. 2010. 'Theobroma cacao L., the food of the gods: a scientific approach beyond myths and claims'. *Pharmacological Research* 61 (1): pp. 5–13.

Rusconi, M., M. G. Rossi, T. Moccetti, and A. Conti. 2012. 'Acute Vascular Effects of Chocolate in Healthy Human Volunteers'. In *Chocolate and Health*, ed. R. Paoletti, A. Poli, A. Conti, and F. Visioli, pp. 87–102. Milan: Springer.

Salonia, A., F. Fabbri, G. Zanni, M. Scavini, G. V. Fantini, A. Briganti, R. Naspro, F. Parazzini, E. Gori, P. Rigatti, and F. Montorsi. 2006. 'Chocolate and women's sexual health: an intriguing correlation'. *Journal of Sexual Medicine* 3 (3): pp. 476–82.

Schokoladenmuseum. 2005. <http://www.schokoladenmuseum.de/archiv.htm> accessed May 2005.

Serafini, M., R. Bugianesi, G. Maiani, S. Valtuena, S. De Santis, and A. Crozier. 2003. 'Plasma antioxidants from chocolate'. *Nature* 424 (6952): p. 1013.

Smit, H. J. 2011. 'Theobromine and the pharmacology of cocoa'. *Handbook of Experimental Pharmacology* 200: pp. 201–34.

Sørensen, L. B. and A. Astrup. 2011. 'Eating dark and milk chocolate: a randomized crossover study of effects on appetite and energy intake'. *Nutrition and Diabetes* 1 e 21. doi:10.1038/nutd.2011.17.

Steinman, H. A. and P. C. Potter. 1994. 'The precipitation of symptoms by common foods in children with atopic dermatitis'. *Allergy and Asthma Proceedings* 15 (4): pp. 203–10.

Taubert, D., Roesen, R., and Schömig, E. 2007. 'Effect of cocoa and tea intake on blood pressure: a meta-analysis'. *Archives of Internal Medicine* 167 (7): pp. 626–34.

Taubert, D., R. Berkels, R. Roesen, and W. Klaus. 2003. 'Chocolate and blood pressure in elderly individuals with isolated systolic hypertension'. *Journal of the American Medical Association* 290 (8): pp. 1029–30.

Taubert, D., R. Roesen, C. Lehmann, N. Jung, and E. Schömig. 2007. 'Effects of low habitual cocoa intake on blood pressure and bioactive nitric oxide'. *Journal of the American Medical Association* 298 (1): pp. 49–60.

Terrio, S. J. 2000. *Crafting the Culture and History of French Chocolate.* Berkeley: University of California Press.

Tomelleri, M. S. and K. K. Grunewald. 1987. 'Menstrual cycle and food cravings in young college women'. *Journal of American Dietetic Association* 87 (3): pp. 311–15.

Vlachopoulos, C., K. Aznaouridis, N. Alexopoulos, E. Economou, I. Andreadou, and C. Stefanadis. 2005. 'Effect of dark chocolate on arterial function in healthy individuals'. *American Journal of Hypertension* 18 (6): pp. 785–91.

Walters, M. R., C. Williamson, K. Lunn, and A. Munteanu. 2012. 'Acute effect of chocolate ingestion on the cerebral vasculature'. <http://www.neurology.org/content/early/2012/08/29/WNL.0b013e31826aacfa/reply>.

Wan, Y., J. A. Vinson, T. D. Etherton, J. Proch, L. A. Sheryl, and P. M. Kris-Etherton. 2001. 'Effects of cocoa powder and dark chocolate on LDL oxidative susceptibility and prostaglandin concentrations in humans'. *American Journal of Clinical Nutrition* 74 (5): pp. 596–602.

Weijzen, P. L. G., E. H. Zandstra, C. Alfieri, and C. De Graaf. 2008. 'Effects of complexity and intensity on sensory specific satiety and food acceptance after repeated consumption'. *Food Quality and Preference* 19: pp. 349–59.

Weingarten, H. P. and D. Elston. 1991. 'Food cravings in a college population'. *Appetite* 17 (3): pp. 167–75.

Williams, S., S. Tamburic, and C. Lally. 2009. 'Eating chocolate can significantly protect the skin from UV light'. *Journal of Cosmetic Dermatology* 8 (3): pp. 169–73.

Wilson, N. M. 1985. 'Food related asthma: a difference between two ethnic groups'. *Archives of Diseases in Childhood* 61 (1): pp. 861–5.

Wilson, P. K. 2012. 'Chocolate as Medicine: A Changing Framework of Evidence throughout History'. In *Chocolate and Health*, ed. R. Paoletti, A. Poli, A. Conti, and F. Visioli, pp. 1–16. Milan: Springer.

Wilson, P. K. and J. W. Hurst. 2012. *Chocolate as Medicine: A Quest over the Centuries*. Cambridge: Royal Society of Chemistry.

Wollgast, J. and E. Anklam. 2000. 'Polyphenols in chocolate: Is there a contribution to human health?' *Food Research International* 33 (6): pp. 449–59.

Wurtman, R. J. and J. J. Wurtman. 1989. 'Carbohydrates and depression'. *Scientific American* 260: pp. 68–75.

Zomer, E., A. Owen, D. J. Magliano, D. Liew, and C. M. Reid. 2012. 'The effectiveness and cost effectiveness of dark chocolate consumption as prevention therapy in people at high risk of cardiovascular disease: best case scenario analysis using a Markov model'. *British Medical Journal* 344: e3657.

8

Health Nudges

How Behavioural Engineering Can Reduce Chocolate Consumption

Sabrina Bruyneel and Siegfried Dewitte

Chocolate is typically regarded as an enticing food by a vast proportion of consumers. This is not without costs, as chocolate also is known to be relatively unhealthy (i.e., it contains high amounts of fat and sugar). In fact, literature on consumer self-control often uses chocolate as the prototypical example of a so-called 'vice', a good that is likely to be consumed on impulse and therefore may impose a self-control problem (Wertenbroch 1998; Wansink and Chandon 2014). For example, ignoring long-term health consequences, consumers may prefer a piece of chocolate cake (a relative vice) over a fruit salad (a relative virtue), because they prefer the taste of chocolate. Ignoring short-term taste differences however, the same consumers may prefer the fruit salad over the chocolate pie when they consider the long-term health consequences of a fatty diet. Such preference orders can give rise to dynamically inconsistent choices by consumers whose trade-offs between short-term and long-term consequences of consumption depend on a variety of factors, some of which we will discuss in more detail in this chapter.

The fact that consumers may be tempted to overconsume vices like chocolate, without doubt contributes to the obesity epidemic the Western world struggles with these days. According to the World Health Organization (WHO), worldwide obesity has nearly doubled since 1980. In 2008, over 1.4 billion adult consumers were overweight, of which over 500 million were obese. In 2012, over 40 million children under the age of 5 were overweight or obese. This upsurge in obesity puts a lot of pressure on health-care systems worldwide, given that common health consequences of obesity are diseases that are expensive to treat, like cardiovascular diseases, diabetes, or some cancers. As this example clearly shows, welfare of consumers and societies worldwide could be greatly improved if consumers succeeded in making more competent decisions, or decisions in which there is a healthy balance between short-term and long-term considerations. Consumers should be able to enjoy a good piece of chocolate cake once in a while, yet they should not systematically overconsume and put their health at risk.

The aim of the present chapter is to propose a set of strategies designed to change human behaviour in a sustainable way, and to apply them to food decision-making. Specifically, we want to explore strategies aimed at stimulating enduring healthy food choices in consumers. Food decision-making is rather complex, and has proven relatively resistant to change. Policymakers typically pursue two major avenues for changing behaviour and increasing consumer welfare: (1) they want to provide more and more objective information such that consumers can make better-informed and hence better decisions (e.g., clearly indicate the number of calories on food packaging); and (2) they want to provide more options such that the likelihood increases that consumers can select the option that supports their welfare best (e.g., also provide low-fat alternatives). Although policy campaigns based on these premises are often successful in increasing awareness (e.g., consumers know that eating fatty food is bad for them), they are often less successful in changing behaviour (e.g., obesity is on the rise), let alone in triggering enduring behavioural change.

In the 'Nudges' section, we will present nudging as a novel and cost-effective behavioural technique that can be applied in support of healthy food choice-making. Nudges are defined as subtle rearrangements in the decision environment that support consumers in adopting welfare-enhancing behaviours, like choosing healthy food options (Thaler and Sunstein 2008). Nudges support autonomous decision-making and require little effort from consumers. However, nudges typically also have the disadvantage that their effect fades once they disappear from the decision environment (i.e., their influence is short-lived). Therefore, in the 'Behavioural Consolidation' section, we also elaborate on the potential of nudges to influence autonomous motivation to pick healthy food options in the long run (after the nudge has been removed), and eventually lead to stable changes in behaviour (i.e., we put forward the idea that the influence of nudges could be longer lived than is typically assumed). Before going into these issues, however, we will present some empirical evidence for consumers' vulnerability to the lure of chocolate, which stresses the need for behavioural techniques to overcome this temptation.

Consumer Vulnerability

Dual-process theories put forward the idea that behaviour results from two distinct but interacting systems: a slow, deliberate, and rational system on the one hand, and a fast, impulsive, and affective system on the other hand (e.g., Thaler and Shefrin 1981). Whereas the former system has received most attention traditionally, research has increasingly focused on the latter in recent years, and evidence for it has accumulated. Various choices including food choices are quick, intuitive, automatic, and/or cued by environmental stimuli (based on habit, affect, or impulse). Deliberation about the long-term consequences of choices or actions is often lacking (Kahneman 2011). An imbalance between both systems puts consumers at risk of making suboptimal decisions.

Situations in which consumers tend to give in to the lure of chocolate arise rather easily. For instance, research has shown that mundane events, like brief shopping trips to the supermarket, can drain consumers' cognitive resources to the extent that they become rather impulsive towards the end of their shopping trip, and susceptible to salient affective product features. Specifically, in one lab study (Bruyneel et al. 2006), participants were asked to visit a simulated store and select products, relying on an incentive-compatible procedure. Participants were randomly assigned to one of two conditions: a choice or a no-choice condition. Participants in both conditions received a shopping list. In the choice condition, the shopping list consisted of product category names. For each of these product categories, participants had to decide which out of two options to select. In the no-choice condition, the shopping list contained the names of products instead of product categories, hence participants did not make active product decisions. To increase comparability between the two conditions, no-choice participants were yoked to the choice participants with respect to the product choices, meaning that product choices were identical across conditions. The major difference was that the no-choice condition involved no active choice-making regarding the products on the shopping list. Only for the last product category, which represented the dependent measure, did participants in the no-choice condition (like participants in the choice condition) make a decision between two product options. This product category was chocolates, and one type of chocolate (Santa Claus-shaped chocolates) was more attractive (following the results of a pretest) but more expensive than the other type of chocolate (elf-shaped chocolates). Functionality of both types of chocolates (e.g., size, weight, taste) was identical. Prices for both chocolates were selected such that the price difference between the options was larger than the price difference participants would probably expect (i.e., a price difference based on the results of a pretest). Participants in the choice condition were relatively more influenced by attractiveness than price in comparison with participants in the no-choice condition (i.e., the former selected the more attractive but expensive chocolate type more often). This study shows that consumers become relatively impulsive after a series of active product choices (compared with after a series of compliances with purchase instructions), suggesting that active choice-making is the process through which cognitive resources get drained and that impulsivity is increased during shopping.

Another example of a factor frequently encountered in advertising and retail contexts that has been shown to stimulate impulsive purchase behaviour is exposure to sexually laden cues. In one lab study (Festjens et al. 2014), participants were asked to rate a piece of clothing that typically has a sexual connotation (i.e., a pair of boxer shorts for female participants, and a bra for male participants), and that was either placed in front of them ready to be touched (i.e., tactile sex cue condition) or placed behind a barrier of Plexiglas (i.e., visual sex cue condition). Participants in the control condition were asked to rate a (gender neutral) T-shirt that was put in from of them ready to be touched. Next, all participants were asked to indicate the amount of money they would be willing to pay for rewarding products like a box of chocolates and a bottle of wine. Both men and women's willingness to pay for chocolates and wine was increased after they had touched sexually laden pieces of clothing compared with after they had touched a neutral T-shirt. In addition, men's willingness to pay was also increased after they had merely seen (and not touched) a bra. This was not the case for women, who needed to touch the sexually laden piece of clothing (and not merely see it) before their economic decisions were altered. These findings clearly show that both genders are vulnerable to the influence of sexually laden cues, and become more impulsive if they encounter such cues in their decision environment. Hence, exposure to sexually laden cues is another factor influencing the equilibrium between short-term and long-term considerations.

In a study that was recently conducted in our lab (Stamos et al. 2015), we attempted to obtain more insight into the influence of a dual-processing system on the economic rationality of consumers, using a direct measure of economic rationality. Relying on the theory of revealed preferences, a task was developed to investigate rationality of choices based on the deliberative system on the one hand, and the affective system on the other (cf. Thaler and Shefrin 1981), as well as the overall rationality level across both systems. This was done by capturing budget loss resulting from choice behaviours relying on either one of the systems. Specifically, we created a choice task to assess consumers' revealed preferences. The task included several sequential choice problems, with each choice problem consisting of four products: two vice, relatively tasty but not so healthy (chocolate bar and Dorito chips), products and two virtue, relatively healthy but not so tasty (baby carrots and raisins), products. The prices of the products differed for every choice problem. Participants were asked to indicate the quantities they wanted from each product given the different price regimes and their budget (10 tokens, which they were asked to spend entirely). Participants completed this task twice, once in a hungry (affective) state, and once in a satiated (deliberative) state. In the hungry state, participants were instructed to not eat for at least four hours prior to the study. In the satiated state, participants were instructed to eat a full meal within an hour prior to the study. A visceral state like hunger is known to have a direct hedonic impact and influence the relative desirability of different goods and actions (Loewenstein 1996). Specifically, visceral influences have been associated with more affective and less deliberate behaviours. Hence, we expected the visceral state hunger to trigger more affective system behaviours and less deliberate system behaviours relative to the satiated state. The fact that participants engaged in the choice task twice allowed us to not only assess rationality within one state, but also to assess rationality across the states. The order of the tasks was counterbalanced and separated by one week. As expected, participants selected more vice products when in a hungry state than when in a satiated state, which again shows that decision makers are easily influenced by a variety of factors (in this case hunger) when making trade-offs between the short-term and long-term consequences of consumption. Results further showed that rationality levels (as measured through budget loss) of deliberative and affective system evaluations were high and comparable, but that the overall rationality level across both types of evaluations was significantly lower. It thus seems that a discrepancy between deliberative system and affective system evaluations is responsible for a loss of utility in consumers' economic decisions, rather than a specific type of evaluation (deliberative versus affective, as is more typically assumed) itself.

In the rest of the chapter, we will focus on behavioural engineering techniques that can help consumers strike a balance between the short-term and long-term consequences of consumption, and hence engage in more competent decision-making. We will first look at the idea of nudging, and then explore the possibility of triggering enduring behavioural change in consumers.

Nudges

As argued, a lot of decisions relating to eating behaviour are made without much conscious deliberation. This implies that consumers tend to rely on salient cues in the decision environment that trigger 'easy' responses (Wansink 2004). For instance, whereas consumers may not have an explicit intention to choose the chocolate pie over the fruit salad, they may end up doing so when the chocolate pie is within reach and the fruit salad is not. Given the observation that food decisions are often made relatively mindlessly and that environmental cues can therefore play a large part in steering these decisions, we explore the possibility that nudging is a potentially powerful technique to trigger behavioural change.

Nudging builds on insights derived from psychology and behavioural economics, suggesting that a lot of behavioural decisions result from quick-and-easy (heuristic) rather than elaborate processing, which helps explain the limited success of standard health-promotion strategies that rely on the rationality of the decision maker. Nudges should be understood as simple changes in the decision environment that make the (in this context) healthy food choice the easy, automatic, or default one (Thaler and Sunstein 2008). Nudges sidestep undue intervention and preserve consumers' autonomy (Hausman and Welch 2010). For instance, putting the fruit salad rather than the chocolate pie within reach nudges consumers towards selecting the fruit salad, though they still have the option to go for the chocolate pie if they really want to.

There is empirical evidence for the impact of distance to food on food consumption. In one recent paper, it was shown that making chocolates less accessible by increasing the distance to them decreased the probability of consumption and also the number of chocolates consumed (Maas et al. 2012). Specifically, participants were randomly assigned to one of three experimental conditions in which a bowl of chocolates was placed in close proximity (distance of 20 cm), within reach (distance of 70 cm), or relatively far away such that participants needed to get up and walk over to the chocolates in order to take some (distance of 140 cm). In all three conditions, the chocolates were clearly visible to participants. After participants had been exposed to the chocolates for five minutes while engaging in unrelated tasks, their chocolate intake was measured. Probability of consumption and the number of chocolates consumed decreased significantly when the distance to the chocolates increased from 20 to 70 cm. An additional increase in distance from 70 to 140 cm did not decrease the probability of consumption or the number of chocolates consumed further, however. These findings suggest that the exact position of tempting foods in decision environments has an impact on food choices, and thus may be used as a nudge to trigger change in food choices.

In one recent study conducted in our lab (Joye and Bruyneel 2015), we sought to exploit the finding that men more easily process the global level of visual stimuli, whereas women more easily process the local level of visual stimuli they encounter in their decision environment, and apply it as a nudge to influence food choices. For instance, in Navon tasks—in which participants are exposed to pictures of larger letters composed of smaller letters, and are asked to either identify the large or the small letters—men typically identify the larger letter quicker, whereas women typically identify the smaller letter quicker. Such findings have been explained by gender differences in brain lateralization (e.g., Roalf et al. 2006). Given that easy processing of visual stimuli presentations boosts desirability and liking (e.g., Lee and Labroo 2004), we expected men to display a greater liking for food items arranged in a global manner, and women to display a greater liking for food items arranged in a local manner. We also used a Navon task to manipulate global versus local presentation, but we used large letters made up of small pictures of chocolate letters instead of regular print letters, as is usually done in Navon studies. Participants were randomly assigned to one of two conditions. In the global condition, they were presented with global Ts and global Hs which consisted of small Ls or Fs. In the local condition, we presented participants with global Ls and global Fs which consisted of small Ts or Hs. All participants were instructed to identify as quickly as possible whether the letter presented was a T or H. As such, they had to repeatedly focus on either the global (global condition) or the local letter (local condition), allowing them to adopt a global or local visual perspective, respectively. In the second phase of the study, participants rated the pictures of the chocolate letters that were used in the Navon task, and indicated how attractive they found the chocolate, and how much they wanted to eat it at that moment. We observed that female participants were quicker to identify the local letters than the global letters, whereas male participants were directionally quicker to identify the global letters than the local letters, which is in agreement with earlier research providing evidence for gender differences in preferential visual focus. Interestingly, ease of processing accordingly influenced liking for the chocolate presented. That is, female participants indicated liking the chocolate more in the local versus global condition, whereas male participants' liking for the chocolate letters was directionally higher in the global rather than the local condition. These preliminary findings suggest that the way in which food is presented (i.e., whether it requires global versus local processing) can be used as a nudge to influence food choice and consumption. Specifically, decision makers will be more eager to select food that is presented in such a way that it is easy to process, or conversely, will be less eager to select food that is presented in such a way that it is difficult to process.

In the section 'Behavioural Consolidation', we will explore mechanisms underlying enduring behavioural change in consumers.

Behavioural Consolidation

In the section 'Nudges', we discussed how the environment can be designed in such a way that the lure of chocolate can be weakened, which leads to less impulsive behaviour. Although nudges can be very effective they have an important weakness: they entirely rely on the situation. If, for some reason, the decision maker is no longer in the well-crafted decision situation or the situation cannot be controlled sufficiently effectively, the nudges lose their power. Schools could, for instance, design their food distribution system based on the principle of nudges. They could offer healthy alternatives, put the vending machine with chocolate in a remote section of the school, or set up a system that requires the young consumers to use a token to buy chocolate or sweets, which sets an additional hurdle to consume vice products. But then again, as soon as the adolescents leave the school, chocolate and other unhealthy snacks are up for grabs. In this section, we explore a more sustainable technique: behavioural consolidation.

The basic and crucial assumption underlying behavioural consolidation builds on the insight that preferences, although relatively stable across time, are malleable to some extent. There is plenty of evidence that taste preferences, most relevant to our discussion of chocolate consumption, change in the short as well as the long run (Kemps et al. 2014). The short-run fluctuations, although not trivial as determinants of real life chocolate consumption, are well known (e.g., nudging consumers to avoid chocolate by putting if further away, see Maas et al. 2012). We focus on more stable preference changes here. Research in our lab (Geyskens et al. 2008) brought female young adult respondents in a situation in which chocolate was present (in the form of Quality Street© sweets), and the respondents were invited to engage in a product knowledge test. They received a sheet of paper showing different types of Quality Street sweets (Quality Street sweets come in different flavours) and flavour descriptions, and were asked to connect the wrappings of the sweets to the flavours. The sweets were presented physically on the side to help them see the wrappings better. As eating the sweets during this task would make the test useless, this task subtly nudged them towards not eating the sweets. Indeed, throughout the studies, no one took any of the sweets during the product knowledge test. Subsequently, respondents engaged in a different study, which was a taste test with the purpose of rating a new type of chocolate (a new type of M&Ms©) on several product characteristics. This task required them to sample the chocolate but did not specify how much they had to eat to provide a valid assessment. The researchers measured how much respondents spontaneously ate. This treatment (pre-exposure without consumption) was compared to: (1) a group that did not see the real chocolate sweets (but only the pictures of the sweets) during the product knowledge test and (2) a group that was not exposed to chocolate sweets at all but got a similar knowledge task during the first phase of the study. The researchers found that those in the pre-exposure/no-consumption treatment condition consumed less during the taste test than the other two groups. Further studies with the same treatment but with other measurements suggested that respondents in the exposure/no-consumption treatment condition relied on strategies to deal with the tempting situation: they seemingly liked the chocolate less, which presumably was their way of resisting the presented sweets and being able to focus on the task at hand. This happened only in the pre-exposure/no-consumption condition and not in the two control conditions. As the respondents had been randomly assigned to the conditions, this difference is most likely due to the differential treatment. These findings suggest that consumers may change their preference for chocolate as a strategy to deal with the challenge of not eating the chocolate. These results hold promise for designing more durable treatments.

In the wake of this initial set of studies, several studies have been undertaken to investigate the scope and the nature of this effect. Understanding what underlies it sets the stage for applying the effect in real life contexts. One line of efforts has focused on children. Tasks were designed that would be more involving for children. In one study, children of 7 to 9 years old had to solve word puzzles. One group got letter sweets to do so, whereas the other group received cardboard letters. The children who had made word puzzles with letter sweets in the first phase sampled fewer chocolate sweets (Smarties©) in the subsequent taste test than children who had made the word puzzles with cardboard letters (Grubliauskiene and Dewitte 2014). Subsequent studies with flower drawings that had to be constructed either with Lego© or similarly shaped and coloured gummy bear sweets confirmed these findings: the children who had been pre-exposed to the bear sweets in a context that discouraged eating sweets in the first phase, subsequently ate less (Grubliauskiene and Dewitte 2015). These studies suggest that the behavioural consolidation technique may also work for children, which suggests a broad scope and a relatively unsophisticated underlying process, as children of this age are still developing their cognitive build-up and have been demonstrated to be poor self-regulators (Mischel and Baker 1975).

Many studies about eating behaviour and overconsumption have looked at female populations only. This choice is typically pragmatically motivated because women tend to be more homogeneous in their reactions to food stimuli and treatments, which makes them a more convenient population to study. In the domain of clinical psychology this restriction also makes sense as the incidence of many eating disorders (e.g., bulimia nervosa) is substantially higher among women than among men. In addition, researchers in the health domain share the assumption that (young) women are more concerned about the role food plays in their attractiveness and health. However, the economic costs of overeating are not smaller for men than for women. As the assumed process (changing preferences) underlying the temptation pre-exposure effect discussed does not rely on gender-specific factors, this research programme has avoided the common practice of investigating female populations only. The results were remarkable. Studies relying on men as well as on women as respondents have never shown any reliable difference between both genders in the strength of the effect. For instance, a replication of the initial Geyskens and colleagues (2008) study described showed that men as well as women reduced their spontaneous sampling of chocolate cookies in the context of a taste test when they had been pre-exposed to Quality Street sweets in the context of a product knowledge test (Grubliauskiene and Dewitte 2015). With children, the findings have been mixed: using various para-digms, the studies produced effects among boys only (Grubliauskiene and Dewitte 2014), among girls only (de Boer et al. 2015), or for both genders (Grubliauskiene and Dewitte 2015). All reported studies show the effect for at least one gender. This suggests that ill-understood situational details that act differently for boys and girls may suppress the effect. It is also noteworthy that the effect was flawlessly repli-cated in a sample of (predominantly black) South African students (both men and women) from poor neighbourhoods (Duh et al. 2015), attesting to the robustness of the effect.

Although managers and policymakers are primarily interested in the question *if* and *for whom* an effect works, rather than *how or why* it works, we argue that the question as to how something works can be of high relevance for practitioners. Compare the two following scenarios: the pre-exposure effect described may rely on the distractive nature of the task that respondents engage in during the pre-exposure phase (such as making the word puzzles). The distraction could reduce the lure of the chocolate during the pre-exposure phase. This reduction could then subsequently be consolidated and be revealed later on, even if the distraction is removed. Alternatively, the effect could also require that respondents experience a struggle between wanting to act on impulse and doing the task correctly, which are mutually exclusive. In this scenario the task does not distract the consumer from the temptation but instead induces a behavioural conflict. This subtle and seem-ingly irrelevant psychological difference has profound implications for the imple-mentation of the effect. The former mechanism (distraction) would urge us to make the distracting task as distracting as possible during the phase in which consumers are exposed to chocolates, whereas the latter mechanism (conflict) would, on the contrary, imply that a task that is very distracting would merely serve as a nudge to not consume and hence reduce the respondent's need to deal with the situation (thus hindering behavioural consolidation). A study in our lab (de Boer et al. 2015), conducted in a primary school, set out to distinguish these mechanisms and give respondents (8-year-old children) the choice to eat their sweets immediately, or wait and have it tripled for later consumption. There was no distraction in this setting as respondents could freely choose to consume or to postpone (and triple their profit) while the sweets were right in front of them during three tempting minutes. Interestingly, those who had been put in front of the sweets in the first phase (without consuming it) consumed less chocolate sweets in the subsequent taste test than those who had faced the same conflict with an equally attractive but non-edible toy: marbles. This finding suggests that it is not the distraction that produces the effect but, on the contrary, the conflict that respondents face. Consistent with the interpretation that the effect relies on a conflict, a follow-up study showed that the effect became even stronger when respondents were asked to imagine how the chocolate would taste and feel like in their mouths, rather than when they were asked to imagine that the sweets were toys. Such instructions had been shown before to make the lure more difficult to resist, however (Mischel and Baker 1975). Those who had been asked to focus on the taste of the chocolate during the pre-exposure phase, with the same prospect that waiting would triple their profit, were found to salivate less when given the offer to consume chocolate later on. Salivating is considered to be an index of consumption motivation (Wooley and Wooley 1973).

We acknowledge that this combination of treatments is hard to translate outside the lab into a conveniently applicable nudge. However, thinking in terms of underlying processes allows us to distil the essence of the pre-exposure effect: why does asking respondents to think about chocolate as toys, which *does* reduce immediate consumption, not yield behavioural consolidation? We suggest that focusing on the non-consumption features of the sweets removes the need to actively deal with the lure. Interestingly, some popular practices that are used to control other people's consumption choices may share this essence. Specifically, prohibiting people to consume chocolate, a practice that parents and teachers rely on frequently, may effectively remove the need to resist chocolate in the pre-exposure phase, and thus limit the chances of increasing children's competence when it comes to resisting the lure of chocolate. Indeed, a study in our lab replicated the original Geyskens and colleagues' (2008) study but added a group of respondents who were told explicitly not to eat the sweets in the pre-exposure phase (Grubliauskiene and Dewitte 2015). Against the background that respondents do not eat anyway during the pre-exposure phase as the task invites them not to, this instruction basically added nothing to the situation. Subsequent consumption in the taste test again diminished after pre-exposure, but when we explicitly told participants not to eat during the product knowledge test, the pre-exposure effect disappeared (i.e., they consumed as much chocolate in the second phase of the study as respondents who had received no treatment at all). Apparently, telling respondents not to eat removed the need to solve the behavioural conflict. This set of studies adds an important insight that has broad implications for the behavioural engineering approach: the respondent has to experience the lure of temptation for the beneficial effects to consolidate.

One of the main aims of this research programme was to show that the effect of pre-exposure to chocolate temptations would lead to relatively stable behavioural changes as a result of relatively stable preference shifts. However, this claim relies on the very notion that preferences are malleable. We needed to make sure that the observed changes in food choices and consumption would last. In the set of lab studies described (Grubliauskiene and Dewitte 2015) we inserted a delay of 15 minutes between the pre-exposure phase and the behavioural measurement. Fifteen minutes is limited from a practical point of view but it is an important step in establishing the longevity of the behavioural change, as most transient effects of situational cues (such as nudges or framing effects; Kahneman and Tversky 1979) typically fade in seconds or minutes. The studies showed that the effects remained intact after a 15-minute delay. In a follow-up study with children (de Boer et al.

2015) we increased the delay to 24 hours. Children who had been exposed to sweets repeatedly without consuming it (as they were betting on a higher profit) ate less chocolate 24 hours later than children who had followed the same procedure but without the lure of sweets. These studies are consistent with the idea that the pre-exposure treatment has lasting effects on consumer preferences, which subsequently makes them more competent in dealing with the lure of chocolate.

Conclusion

The observation that chocolate not only provides immediate utility but also contributes to the rise of obesity and, in its wake, a host of preventable diseases, was the initial motivation for our investigations. We illustrated consumer vulnerability to situational cues and asked ourselves: (1) how the economic environment could be (re)designed to help curb chocolate overconsumption and (2) how consumers could be supported to more competently resist the lure of chocolate. We reviewed a series of studies showing that simple environmental modifications (nudges) can reduce chocolate overconsumption. We then proceeded by exploring how a temporary change could be consolidated, thereby enhancing consumers' competence to moderate chocolate consumption, even in the absence of supportive situational cues.

We propose that these two steps can be forged into an approach that we would like to introduce as behavioural engineering. Behavioural engineering is more than the sum of nudges and consolidation techniques. Putting the two steps together leads to the insight that nudges may vary in their suitability to lead to consolidation, and that consolidation techniques may vary with respect to their fit with nudging. We will first sketch some guidelines for the design of nudges from the point of view of consolidation, and then proceed with discussing how consolidation could be optimized in a nudging context.

Nudges are typically assessed in terms of their success in achieving the intended behavioural change *in the presence of the nudge*. We propose that nudges could also be assessed for their potential for subsequent consolidation. Our review of the consolidation research programme suggests that the experience of behavioural conflict during the temptation phase is a crucial ingredient for consolidation. This suggests that nudges that are very strong, and hence potentially very successful in the short run, may not be the best nudges in the long term. Strong nudges may reduce freedom of choice, and hence reduce the need to actively resist the temptation. For instance, putting the sweets in a vending machine in a remote section of the school may be very effective in reducing consumption (although the consumers can in principle still buy sweets), but may not trigger the behavioural conflict, and hence the changes in consumer preferences. Moderate nudges, on the other hand, may be less effective in stimulating the desired behaviour, yet, if they do, these behaviours may be more long lasting. For instance, rather than putting the vending machine in a remote section, the school may decide to add low-priced fruit to the vending machine. This would induce behavioural conflict for some consumers and some may choose fruit. We propose that the behavioural conflict may then lead to the consolidation of the choice for the fruit. An important challenge for future research is to determine what 'moderately strong' means exactly.

The consolidation techniques may also need fine-tuning depending on the type of nudge that is conceivable in a certain situation. In our review we focused on changes in preferences, but the consolidation of a behavioural change may also be achieved via praise or labelling. In a study with young children in a school setting, we offered children from 7 to 11 years of age the choice between chocolate sweets and grapes (Grubliauskiene et al. 2012). We added a little toy gift to the grapes to boost the children's choice for the grapes (this is a nudge). Then the teacher praised them when they chose the grape option. Three days later, the children came back to choose between sweets and grapes once more. This time, there was no extra toy involved in any of the options. Those who had been nudged to choose the grapes three days earlier and had been subsequently praised, became twice as likely to choose the grapes than those who had not been nudged or praised. In a different set of studies, we asked participants to consider buying a TV set. The ecological option was also the best in terms of quality and price. Most respondents chose this set, and the experimenter noted that they must be environmentally conscious consumers. In a later phase in the study, these participants displayed further green behaviour (e.g., they used paper more efficiently) (Cornelissen et al. 2007). We expect that this labelling technique may also work in the context of chocolate.

We acknowledge that much remains to be explored about the generalizability of both effects and their optimal match, despite the fact these effects are promising and remarkably robust across situations and populations. There may be important conditions for the behavioural engineering approach to work well, which have not yet been explored. The fact that telling respondents explicitly that they shouldn't eat seemingly backfires, illustrates the importance of such endeavours.

References

Bruyneel, S., S. Dewitte, K. D. Vohs, and L. Warlop. 2006. 'Repeated Choosing Increases Susceptibility to Affective Product Features'. *International Journal of Research in Marketing* 23 (2): pp. 215–25.

Cornelissen, G., S. Dewitte, L. Warlop, and V. Yserbyt. 2007. 'Whatever People Say I am That's What I am: Social Labeling as a Social Marketing Tool'. *International Journal of Research in Marketing* 24 (4): pp. 278–88.

De .Boer, C., D. de Ridder, E. de Vet, A. Grubliauskiene, and S. Dewitte. 2015. 'Towards a Behavioral Vaccine: Exposure to Accessible Temptation when Self-Regulation is Endorsed Enhances Future Resistance to Similar Temptations in Children'. *Applied Psychology: Health and Well-Being* 7(1): 63–84.

Duh, H., A. Grubliauskiene, and S. Dewitte. 2015. 'Pre-exposure to Food Temptation Reduces Subsequent Consumption: A Test of the Procedure with a South-African sample'. KU Leuven Working Paper.

Festjens, A., S. Bruyneel, and S. Dewitte. 2014. 'What a Feeling! Touching Sexually Laden Stimuli Makes Women Seek Rewards'. *Journal of Consumer Psychology* 24 (3): pp. 387–93.

Geyskens, K., S. Dewitte, M. Pandelaere, and L. Warlop. 2008. 'Tempt Me Just a Little Bit More: The Effect of Food Temptation Actionability on Goal Activation and Subsequent Consumption'. *Journal of Consumer Research* 35 (4): pp. 600–10.

Grubliauskiene, A. and S. Dewitte. 2014. 'Temptation in the Background: Non-Consummatory Exposure to Food Temptation Enhances Self-Regulation in Boys but Not in Girls'. *Frontiers in Psychology (Eating Behavior)* 5: pp. 788.

Grubliauskiene, A. and S. Dewitte. 2015. Triggering Restriction Goals during Exposure to Food Temptations Reduces their Subsequent Consumption in Adults and Children'. KU Leuven Working Paper.

Grubliauskiene, A., M. Verhoeven, and S. Dewitte. 2012. 'The Joint Effect of Tangible and Non-Tangible Rewards on Healthy Food Choices in Children'. *Appetite* 59 (2): pp. 403–8.

Hausman, D. M. and B. Welch. 2010. 'Debate: To Nudge or Not to Nudge'. *Journal of Political Philosophy* 18 (1): pp. 123–36.

Joye, Y. and S. Bruyneel. 2015. 'Gender Moderates the Influence of Part-Whole Organizations on Food Consumption'. KU Leuven Working Paper.

Kahneman, D. 2011. *Thinking, Fast and Slow*. New York: Farrar, Strauss & Giroux.

Kahneman, D. and A. Tversky. 1979. 'Prospect Theory: Analysis of Decision under Risk'. *Econometrica* 47 (2): pp. 263–91.

Kemps, E., M. Tiggemann, J. Orr, and J. Grear. 2014. 'Attentional Retraining Can Reduce Chocolate Consumption'. *Journal of Experimental Psychology—Applied* 20 (1): pp. 94–102.

Lee, A. Y. and A. A. Labroo. 2004. 'The Effect of Conceptual and Perceptual Fluency on Brand Evaluation'. *Journal of Marketing Research* 41 (2): pp. 151–65.

Loewenstein, G. F. 1996. 'Out of Control: Visceral Influences on Behavior'. *Organizational Behavior and Human Decision Processes* 65 (3): pp. 272–92.

Maas, J., D. D. T. De Ridder, E. W .M. De Vet, and J. B. F. De Wit. 2012. 'Do Distant Foods Decrease Intake? The Effect of Food Accessibility on Consumption'. *Psychology & Health* 27: pp. 59–73.

Mischel, W. and N. Baker. 1975. 'Cognitive Appraisals and Transformations in Delay Behavior'. *Journal of Personality and Social Psychology* 31 (2): pp. 254–61.

Roalf, D., N. Lowery, and B. I. Turetsky. 2006. 'Behavioral and Physiological Findings of Gender Differences in Global–Local Visual Processing'. *Brain and Cognition* 60 (1): pp. 32–42.

Stamos, A., S. Bruyneel, B. De Rock, L. Cherchye, and S. Dewitte. 2015. 'A Dual-Process Model of Economic Rationality: The Symmetric Effect of Hot and Cold Evaluations on Economic Decision Making'. KU Leuven Working Paper.

Thaler, R. H. and H. M. Shefrin. 1981. 'An Economic Theory of Self-Control'. *Journal of Political Economy* 89 (2): 392–406.

Thaler, R. H. and C. R. Sunstein. 2008. *Nudge: Improving Decisions about Health, Wealth, and Happiness*. New Haven, CT: Yale University Press.

Wansink, B. 2004. 'Environmental Factors that Increase the Food Intake and Consumption Value of Unknowing Consumers'. *Annual Review of Nutrition* 24: pp. 455–79.

Wansink, B. and P. Chandon. 2014. 'Slim by Design: Redirecting the Accidental Drivers of Mindless Overeating'. *Journal of Consumer Psychology* 24 (3): pp. 413–31.

Wertenbroch, K. 1998. 'Consumption Self-Control by Rationing Purchase Quantities of Virtue and Vice'. *Marketing Science* 17 (4): pp. 317–37.

Wooley, S. C. and O. W. Wooley. 1973. 'Salivation to the Sight and Thought of Food: A New Measure of Appetite'. *Psychosomatic Medicine* 35 (2): pp. 136–42.

9

Chocolate Brands and Preferences of Chinese Consumers

Di Mo, Scott Rozelle, and Linxiu Zhang

Chocolate is a relatively new food product to the consumers in China. Thirty years ago, almost no one in China had ever tasted chocolate. However, chocolate consumption has grown rapidly since the mid-1990s. In recent years the average annual growth rate was over 10 per cent. Per capita consumption is still low by international standards. Because of this and the rapidly growing economy and urbanization, the potential for growth in China is estimated to be huge. Experts believe China someday could consume up to 7 billion USD per year (*China Daily*, 2004). Such potential, of course, in part accounts for the fact that the top 20 world chocolate producers have all entered the China market (Scott-Thomas, 2011). Most of the chocolate (around 80 per cent) is produced by foreign companies, either in China or abroad. Foreign brands entered in the 1980s. In 2008 the largest chocolate producer in China, Mars, had a market share of around 40 per cent (Wang, 2008). Domestic players have been growing, although their market share is still relatively small. The largest domestic competitor, China National Cereals, Oils and Foodstuffs Corporation (COFCO), holds a market share of around 10 per cent. It is estimated that China now has around 250 chocolate companies with an annual production capacity of chocolate of 150,000 tons (Buffy, 2011).

In pursuit of China's potential chocolate bonanza, foreign companies have tried many different strategies. Foreign chocolate companies, like foreign companies in other sectors, have tried to build strong brands as a way to create an image of a company that produces authentic chocolate. The advertising and marketing strategies of many foreign chocolate firms have been to build brand images symbolizing wealth and good fortune (Ferrero), luxurious self-indulgence (Mars), or being cute and whimsical (Hershey). Most of these companies have been open about their foreign roots.

Some of these foreign chocolate brands have also tried to localize their taste and adapt to the Chinese culture (Wood and Grosvenor, 1997). For instance, Mars, Hershey, Cadbury, and Nestlé set up factories in China. They adapted their chocolate recipes as they began to believe that 'creamy' and 'nutty' are the favoured tastes of China's nascent chocolate fans. Following the path-breaking strategy of Ferrero in the 1980s,[1] chocolate companies have continued to push their product as a way to give unique gifts, using this as a cultural gateway. In doing so, foreign chocolate makers devote much in advertising and packaging to their efforts to promote chocolate as a gift that symbolizes love ánd friendship (Allen, 2010). Many of the earliest chocolate brands that used this strategy in the 1980s and 1990s still dominate China's market, despite the large number of local firms that emerged later.

During the past decade, global firms have sought to penetrate China's market in a different way: by directly exporting their chocolate products to China. During this time a large number of imported brands have entered China. Chocolate imports grew from $17.7 million in 1999 to nearly $50 million in 2003 (Freeman, 2005). If they so desire, consumers in China now have access to more than 70 foreign chocolate brands in supermarkets in the nation's large urban cities (*Chocolate News*, 2009). Consumers can purchase some of the world's most prestigious and popular brands. They can buy truffles from Belgium. They can purchase Côte d'Or milk chocolate. Imported brands have mostly been promoted as luxury food and are marketed to the top end of the China's consumer market (Freeman, 2005).

Importers are not alone in the battle for the hearts and wallets of China chocolate lovers. Local competitors have also joined the battle. Around 20 per cent of China's chocolate market is provided by domestic firms (*Shanghai Daily*, 2008). They, like their foreign competitors, have launched efforts to establish their brands among Chinese consumers. These brands often emphasize Chinese culture and tradition in advertising to invoke the patriotism of consumers (World Executive, 2004). It is believed that the growth of the market share of domestic brand can be partly attributed to Chinese consumers' support for domestic industries. However, partly due to their less-developed technology and less sophisticated marketing strategies, and partly due to the shorter history of production inside China, at least so far, domestic firms have been less competitive than the foreign ones in winning the China market (Allen, 2010). As a result, brands of domestic firms are mostly still underdeveloped. Advertising budgets are low. Surveys indicate that consumers believe that domestic firms use inferior ingredients (Buffy, 2011). In part because of this perception, Chinese chocolate firms (e.g., LeConte, a branded chocolate of COFCO, China's largest food company) price their product at only 75 to 80 per cent of the prices of their foreign competitors.

Although these chocolate brands have been battling it out in the Chinese chocolate market for decades, it is not clear how Chinese consumers respond to the various brands and how their perception actually affects their tasting experience. It is often hard to disentangle the impacts of branding and other characteristics of the food product (like chocolate) on consumer preferences. The current

---

[1] Ferrero, one of the world's largest chocolate firms, arrived in China in 1984, but chose not to target the traditional consumer market. Instead, it decided to focus on gift-giving. The firm designed packaging and advertising that catered to China's gift-giving culture (Allen, 2010). It succeeded. Today the Ferrero brand can be found throughout China.

study is the first to rigorously test the impact of (foreign) branding on consumer tasting experience in China's chocolate market, and separate it from the impacts of other features of the chocolate products.

The rest of the chapter is arranged as following. The section 'Influence of Brand Information on Consumer Preferences' provides insights from the economics and psychology literature on the consumer preference in branding. Then, we describe the research approach and present the results. We end with concluding remarks.

Influence of Brand Information on Consumer Preferences: Insights from the Literature

There is a large literature on how information about food products shapes the tasting experience of consumers (Deliza and MacFie, 1996). Consumer judgements can be influenced by information about a food product and/or its production (Caporale and Monteleone, 2004; Kihlberg et al., 2005). Among the various information cues, brands (or brand names) can influence consumer choice (Allison and Uhl, 1964; Aaker, 1992; Keller, 1993; de Chernatony and McDonald, 1998). Neuroscience research indicates that brand preferences recruit specific parts of the brains of potential buyers when they are making choices among different brands (Shiv et al., 2005; Lee, Broderick, and Chamberlain, 2007; Kenning and Plassmann, 2008). Brand names influence consumer choice by triggering a variety of associations, such as prior experiences with the brand and quality inferences (Erdem and Swait, 1998), and values and images that companies have tried to build through marketing and advertising strategies (Deliza and MacFie, 1996).

In developing and transitional economies, brands of new products that have arrived inside their borders from developed countries can be powerful sources of information. In particular, foreign brands are often associated with authenticity and high quality. When a product enters a new market where consumers have minimal prior experience with the type of product before its arrival, it is often difficult or impossible for consumers to make initial judgements about a product's legitimacy or quality (Carpenter and Nakamoto, 1989). In this case, foreign products lay claim to country-of-origin effects which may induce consumers to identify authenticity with foreign brands (Zhang, 1996). Indeed, Wong and Ahuvia (1998) found that many foreign products shape the expectations and desires for consumption of genuine products among consumers in East Asia.

Beyond authenticity, the information cues of foreign products also, in some cases, are associated with social and symbolic values. These values have been linked with concepts such as sophistication, modernity, novelty, and Western civilization (Zhou and Hui, 2003). Consumption of foreign products often becomes part of the path that individuals take towards a contemporary lifestyle. As the brand-associated values are widely accepted, consumers may prefer to buy foreign brands as this also enhances their self-image and makes them feel they are being cosmopolitan and modern (Friedman, 1990).

Despite the benefits that foreign products have in terms of shaping consumer preferences, there are challenges to their promotion in all countries, including China. One of the most well-known challenges is consumer patriotism. Pro-nationalist consumer preferences have been identified as influencing consumer choices between domestic brands and foreign brands (Han, 1988; Rawwas et al., 1996; Klein et al., 1998). Patriotism plays a significant role in consumer decision-making, especially when products are not necessities and when consumers perceive that the domestic industry is being threatened by imported products (Shimp and Sharma, 1987; Sharma, Shimp, and Shin, 1995). Facing patriotism, protectionism, and other challenges from local firms, multinational enterprises are sometimes forced/choose to cooperate with local firms instead of developing an independent brand (Arnold and Quelch, 1998).

Foreign companies, of course, recognize the partisanship of consumers in the domestic markets and often take measures to offset consumer patriotism. For example, foreign companies may have local branches or use local standards (for example, advertising content and packaging) to launch the production of certain products inside China (Batra, 1997; Yin, 1999). Belk (2000) has shown that McDonald's make conscious efforts to adapt their menu to local culinary types. They also choose facades and decor that reflect local sources of pride.

Experiment to Measure Chocolate Preferences

In this experiment, participants were randomly assigned to one of two conditions (Figure 9.1). In the blind condition, they tasted a series of chocolate samples without any information about the brands. In the non-blind condition, they

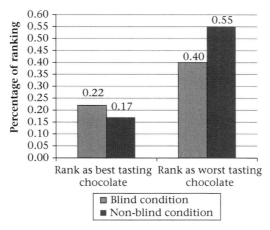

Figure 9.1 Percentage of participants that ranked Chinese domestic milk chocolate as the best-tasting or the worst-tasting chocolate in Experiment 1

were told the brands of the chocolate samples before they tasted them. A total of 234 participants were recruited and randomly assigned to one of the two conditions. Participants were randomly recruited at Renmin University and at the Olympic Forest Park in Beijing. We made sure that there was no interaction among participants.

Sample Chocolates

Chocolate samples were one of four 'different types' of chocolate: Chinese Domestic Milk Chocolate, Foreign-Branded Milk Chocolate/Produced in China, Imported Milk Chocolate, and Imported Truffles (one of the most sophisticated and expensive types of chocolate). These brands differ by the location of the producer's home firm (foreign or domestic), production location (foreign or domestic), and type (milk chocolate or truffle).

Three brands of milk chocolate and one brand of truffle were chosen from a supermarket in Beijing to represent the four different types of chocolates. They were selected from among the best-selling brands (according to interviews with the manager of the supermarket). In particular, we chose LeConte chocolate, produced by COFCO, to represent Chinese Domestic Milk Chocolate. We chose Dove Chocolate, produced by Mars, to represent Foreign Branded Milk Chocolate/Produced in China. We chose Belgian Côte d'Or to represent Imported Milk Chocolate. Belgian Truffles were chosen to represent Imported Truffles.

The three brands of milk chocolate all are known to have similar basic ingredients. According to the packaging, each type of milk chocolate contains cocoa powder, cocoa butter, sugar, and milk. However, the packaging also demonstrates that the ingredients vary slightly in amount. For example, the Chinese Domestic Milk Chocolate has a minimum of 25 per cent cocoa butter. In contrast, the Foreign-Branded Milk Chocolate/Produced in China has a minimum of 17 per cent cocoa butter. The Imported Milk Chocolate has a minimum of 18 per cent cocoa butter.

As real chocolate fans know, of course, the ingredients of Imported Truffles differ from those of milk chocolate. Specifically, because truffles contain more cream than milk chocolate, and they are dusted in cocoa powder, they have a different texture and are softer. Because of this, the taste is more exotic to Chinese consumers (as stated by many of the participants in the interviews after the experiment).

Different information was provided. In the 'blind condition', participants were not told about the chocolate brands that they tasted (or any other information). In the 'non-blind condition', before the tasting they were shown the chocolate brands and instructed about the nature of the chocolate—where it was made (inside China or outside of China); the country of firm that produced the chocolate (was it imported or not); and what type of chocolate it was (milk chocolate or truffles). The participants tasted sample chocolates and ranked the chocolates from the best tasting to the worst tasting.

The study includes two experiments. Experiment 1 included only the three milk chocolate brands: the Chinese Domestic Milk Chocolate, the Foreign-Branded Milk Chocolate/Produced in China, and the Imported Milk Chocolate. Experiment 2 added the Imported Truffles. Despite this difference, the experimental procedures were exactly the same.

Results

Experiment 1

The experiment shows that preference for chocolate is influenced by the information provided (Figure 9.1). Participants in the non-blind group, when participants received information about the chocolate brands, were 5 per cent less likely to rank the Chinese Domestic Milk Chocolate as the best-tasting chocolate than the blind group. Participants were 15 per cent less likely to rank the Chinese Domestic Milk Chocolate as the best- or second-best-tasting chocolate in the non-blind condition. In other words, the non-blind participants were 15 per cent more likely to rank the tastings of the Chinese Domestic Milk Chocolate as the chocolate that they favoured the least.

However, no significant difference was observed for the preference for Foreign Branded Milk Chocolate/Produced in China. The preferences are similar across the blind and non-blind conditions (Figure 9.2). Participants were 2 per cent more likely to rank the Foreign Branded Milk Chocolate/Produced in China as the best-tasting chocolate. At the same time, participants were 4 per cent less likely to rank the Foreign Branded Milk Chocolate/Produced in China as the worst-tasting chocolate in the non-blind condition than in the blind condition.

Interestingly, the Imported Milk Chocolate was ranked higher by participants that were in the non-blind condition than those in the blind condition (Figure 9.3). When participants received information about the brands (non-

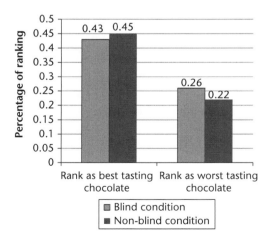

Figure 9.2 Percentage of participants that ranked foreign-branded milk chocolate/produced in China as the best-tasting or the worst-tasting chocolate in Experiment 1

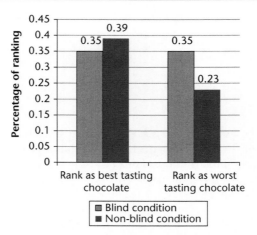

Figure 9.3 Percentage of participants that ranked imported milk chocolate as the best-tasting or the worst-tasting chocolate in Experiment 1

blind), they were 4 per cent more likely to rank the Imported Milk Chocolate as the best-tasting chocolate and 12 per cent less likely to rank it as the worst-tasting chocolate.

Experiment 2

In the second experiment, Imported Truffles were added. Participants demonstrated higher preference for the Imported Truffle when they were informed about the brands (Figure 9.4). The Imported Truffle was 14 per cent more likely to be ranked as the best-tasting chocolate and 14 per cent less likely to be ranked as the worst-tasting chocolate in the non-blind condition. Non-blind participants were 29 per cent more likely to rank Imported Truffle as the best- or the second-best-tasting chocolate among the four brands of chocolate than the blind participants.

To identify the source of change in preference, the rankings of brands in pairs between the blind participants and non-blind participants were compared. Four pairs of chocolate brands were compared: Chinese Domestic Milk Chocolate and Foreign Branded Milk Chocolate/Produced in China; Chinese Domestic Milk Chocolate and Imported Milk Chocolate; Foreign Branded Milk Chocolate/Produced and Imported Milk Chocolate; and Imported Milk Chocolate and Imported Truffles.

The results demonstrate a higher preference of Chinese consumers towards imported brands. The Imported Milk Chocolate was more likely to be preferred in the non-blind condition over both the Chinese Domestic Milk Chocolate and the Foreign Branded Milk Chocolate/Produced in China, by 11 per cent.

Interestingly, the biggest effect was for Truffles. Truffles are a special type of chocolate. Many Chinese consumers are not used to them. As a result, when moving from the blind (the condition in which most participants did not prefer

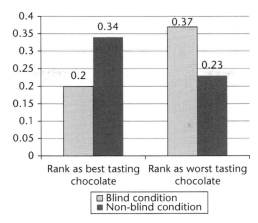

Figure 9.4 Percentage of participants that ranked imported truffles as the best-tasting or the worst-tasting chocolate in Experiment 2

Truffles) to the non-blind condition (in which the participants were told this was an Imported Truffle), participant preference for Truffles increased from 0.29 to 0.57. This is the largest shift that was observed. Between the imported brands, Truffles were also more preferred by 28 per cent over Milk Chocolate when participants received the brand information. As a more exotic and unknown type of chocolate, it seems likely that the signalling effects of Truffles (all types of associations with imported brands) were the strongest for Chinese consumers.

Conclusion

The results suggest that brand information does influence Chinese consumers' preferences for chocolate. More specifically, Chinese consumers have higher preferences for imported brands than the domestic brand or the foreign brand which is produced in China when they are informed about the brands. The reason for the higher preference for the imported brands is likely to be associated with the image of authenticity, high quality, or the social and symbolic value that Chinese consumers associate with the brands.

References

Aaker, D. A. 1992. *Building Strong Brands*. New York: The Free Press.

Allen, L. L. 2010. 'Chocolate Fortunes: The Battle for the Hearts, Mind and Wallets of Chinese Consumers'. *Thunderbird International Business Review* 52 (1): pp. 13–20.

Allison, R. and K. Uhl. 1964. 'Influence of Beer Brand Identification on Taste Perception'. *Journal of Marketing Research* 1: pp. 36–9.

Consumption

Arnold, D. J. and J. A. Quelch. 1998. 'New Strategies in Emerging Markets'. *Sloan Management Review* 40 (1): pp. 7–20.

Batra, R. 1997. 'Marketing Issues and Challenges in Transitional Economies'. *Journal of International Marketing* 5 (4): pp. 95–114.

Belk, R. W. 2000. 'Wolf Brands in Sheep's Clothing: Global Appropriation of the Local'. In *Brand New*, edited by J. Pavitt, pp. 68–9. Princeton, NJ: Princeton University Press.

Buffy, P. 2011. 'China's Chocolate Market Dominated by Foreign Brands'. Retrieved from: <http://www.article.directory4u.org/Article/China-s-Chocolate-Industry-Dominated-by-Foreign-Brands/354889> (accessed 15 September 2012).

Caporale, G. and E. Monteleone. 2004. 'Influence of Information about Manufacturing Process on Beer Acceptability'. *Food Quality and Preference* 15 (3): pp. 271–8.

Carpenter, G. S. and K. Nakamoto. 1989. 'Consumer Preference Formation and Pioneering Advantage'. *Journal of Marketing Research* 26 (3): pp. 285–98.

China Daily. 2004. 'Chocolate Strives for Standard'. Retrieved from: <http://www.chinadaily.com.cn/english/doc/2004-12/24/content_402994.htm> (accessed 15 September 2012).

Chocolate News. 2009. 'An Analysis on China's Chocolate Market' (in Chinese). Retrieved from: <http://www.qklnews.com/qkeliInfos/gnInfos/2009/0506/2380.html>.

De Chernatony, L. and M. H. McDonald. 1998. *Creating Powerful Brands*. Oxford: Butterworth Heinemann.

Deliza, R. and H. J. H. MacFie. 1996. 'The Generation of Sensory Expectation by External Cues and Its Effect on Sensory Perception and Hedonic Ratings: A Review'. *Journal of Sensory Studies* 11: pp. 103–28.

Erdem, T. and J. Swait. 1998. 'Brand Equity as a Signaling Phenomenon'. *Journal of Consumer Psychology* 7 (2): pp. 131–59.

Freeman, D. 2005. 'EU Chocolatiers Chase Chinese Market'. *Asia Times*. Retrieved from: <http://www.atimes.com/atimes/China/GG28Ad02.html> (accessed 15 September 2012).

Friedman, J. 1990. 'Being in the World: Globalization and Localization'. *Theory, Culture & Society* 7 (2): pp. 311–28.

Han, C. M. 1988. 'The Role of Consumer Patriotism in the Choice of Domestic versus Foreign Products'. *Journal of Advertising Research* 28: pp. 25–31.

Keller, K. L. 1993. 'Conceptualizing, Measuring, and Managing Customer-Based Brand Equity'. *Journal of Marketing* 57 (1): pp. 1–22.

Kenning, P. and H. Plassmann. 2008. 'How Neuroscience Can Inform Consumer Research'. *IEEE Transactions on Neural Systems and Rehabilitation Engineering in Press*.

Kihlberg, I., L. Johansson, O. Langsrud, and E. Risvik. 2005. 'Effects of Information on Liking of Bread'. *Food Quality and Preference* 16 (1): pp. 25–35.

Klein, G. J., R. Ettenson, and M. D. Morris. 1998. 'The Animosity Model of Foreign Product Purchase: An Empirical Test in the People's Republic of China'. *Journal of Marketing* 62 (1): pp. 89–100.

Lee, N., A. J. Broderick, and L. Chamberlain. 2007. 'What Is "Neuromarketing"? A Discussion and Agenda for Future Research'. *International Journal of Psychophysiology* 63 (2): pp. 199–204.

McClure, S. M., J. Li, D. Tomlin, K. S. Cypert, L. Montague, and P. R. Montague. 2004. 'Neural Correlates of Behavioral Preference for Culturally Familiar Drinks'. *Neuron* 44 (11): pp. 379–87.

Rawwas, M. Y. A., K. N. Rajendran, and G. A. Wührer. 1996. 'The Influence of Worldmindedness and Nationalism on Consumer Evaluation of Domestic and Foreign Products'. *International Marketing Review* 13 (2): pp. 20–38.

Scott-Thomas, C. 2011. 'Opportunities for Smaller Companies in Chinese Chocolate Market'. Retrieved from: <http://www.foodnavigator-asia.com/Markets/Opportunities-for-smaller-companies-in-Chinese-chocolate-market> (accessed 15 September 2012).

Shanghai Daily. 2008. 'China's Taste for Chocolate'. Retrieved from: <http://china.org.cn/business/2008-09/16/content_16461850.htm> (accessed 15 September 2012).

Sharma, S., Shimp T. A., and Shin J. 1995. 'Consumer Ethnocentrism: A Test of Antecedents and Moderators'. *Journal of the Academy of Marketing Science* 23 (1): pp. 26–37.

Shimp, T. and S. Sharma. 1987. 'Consumer Ethnocentrism: Construction and Validation of the CETSCALE'. *Journal of Marketing Research* 24: pp. 280–9.

Shiv, B., A. Bechara, I. Levin, J. W. Alba, J. R. Bettman, L. Dube, A. Isen, B. Mellers, A. Smidts, S. J. Grant, and A. P. McGraw. 2005. 'Decision Neuroscience'. *Marketing Letters* 16 (3/4): pp. 375–86.

Wang, B. 2008. 'A Note on the Strategies to Expand the Market Share of Chinese Chocolate Companies' (in Chinese). Retrieved from: <http://www.chinavalue.net/Finance/Article/2008-6-11/119686.html> (accessed 15 September 2012).

Wansink, B., S. Park, S. Sonka, and M. Morganosky. 2000. 'How Soy Labeling Influences Preference and Taste'. *International Food and Agribusiness Management Review* 3 (1): pp. 85–94.

Watson, J. L. 2000. 'China's Big Mac Attack'. *Foreign Affairs* 79 (3): pp. 120–34.

Wong, N. Y. and A. C. Ahuvia. 1998. 'Personal Taste and Family Face: Luxury Consumption in Confucian and Western Societies'. *Psychology and Marketing* 15 (5): pp. 423–41.

Wood, L. J. and S. Grosvenor. 1997. 'Chocolate in China: The Cadbury Experience'. *Australian Geographer* 28 (2): pp. 173–84.

World Executive. 2004. 'The Future of Chinese Domestic Chocolate Brands' (in Chinese). Retrieved from: <http://brand.icxo.com/htmlnews/2004/06/10/243930.htm> (accessed 15 September 2012).

Yin, J. 1999. 'International Advertising Strategies in China: A Worldwide Survey of Foreign Advertisers'. *Journal of Advertising Research* 39: pp. 25–35.

Zhang, Y. 1996. 'Chinese Consumers' Evaluation of Foreign Products: The Influence of Culture, Product Types and Product Presentation Format'. *European Journal of Marketing* 30 (12): pp. 50–68.

Zhou, L. and M. K. Hui. 2003. 'Symbolic Value of Foreign Products in the People's Republic of China'. *Journal of International Marketing*, Special Issue on Marketing in Transitional Economies 11 (2): pp. 36–58.

10

Consumers' Willingness to Pay for Fair Trade Chocolate

Pieter Vlaeminck, Jana Vandoren, and Liesbet Vranken

Introduction

The chocolate industry represents a multi-billion euros industry with important corporate social responsibility and sustainability issues (Bradu et al., 2013). The largest share of the main ingredient, cocoa, is produced in West African countries, accounting for 68 per cent of world production, followed by Asia (18 per cent) and South America (14 per cent) (Max Havelaar, 2012). The majority of cocoa producing countries are characterized by poor infrastructure and a low, or very low, gross domestic product (GDP) (ICCO, 2007). Most cocoa farmers face a considerable number of constraints: labour problems, including child labour, price volatility, low productivity, and shortfalls in both social and environmental sustainability have all been linked to the cocoa production sector in the past (Krain et al., 2011; Beyer, 2012; Bradu et al., 2013). Nevertheless, world cocoa production has risen at an average annual growth rate of 3.3 per cent from 2002 to 2012. Consumption peaked at a record level in 2010 of around 5.54 million tons, and forecasts estimate a growing demand due to rising GDP and population growth (ICCO, 2012).

The cocoa sector lately has been characterized by key sector players publically announcing ambitious targets for supplying certified cocoa, governments creating specific initiatives focusing on sustainable cocoa, and stakeholders such as non-governmental organizations (NGOs) and development organizations taking the initiative, with the common objective of fostering the sustainable production of cocoa (KPMG, 2012).

Fair Trade (FT) organizations aim to improve the livelihoods of excluded and disadvantaged producers by providing them with better trading conditions, and aim to increase the demand for FT products by raising awareness by campaigning (EFTA, 2001). For consumers, the FT label should serve as a guarantee that poor farmers receive a fair price. In addition, the label wants to improve environmental sustainability, community investments, and the working conditions of producers

(Loureiro and Lotade, 2005). On the consumer side of the chocolate market, sales of FT chocolate are rising, but actual market shares still represent only a small fraction in the total market (Bradu et al., 2013). A key question is why this demand has remained low. Do consumers not care about these ethical characteristics? Do they care about the characteristics but are there other barriers that impede an increase in the consumption of FT chocolate?

This chapter aims to address these questions. In particular, consumers' preferences for certified chocolate are assessed. Since FT is a credence attribute, consumers cannot infer ethical characteristics such as fair working conditions directly from consuming the product (Poelman et al., 2008). Accordingly, labelling schemes have been traditionally used as a mechanism to inform consumers about products with both public and private characteristics. However, lack of information and a label's inability to effectively convey information to consumers often reduces the effectiveness of the label and may thus hold back the consumption of ethically produced goods (Rousseau and Vranken, 2013; Vlaeminck et al., 2014). Therefore, we analyse whether the FT label is effective in conveying the ethical characteristics it stands for to consumers.

In this chapter we first provide insights from the literature on the willingness to pay (WTP) for FT products in general and then for FT chocolate in particular. Next, we provide insights from a survey and choice experiment (CE) that was conducted in Belgium in order to investigate: whether a FT label increases consumers' WTP, which underlying characteristics of FT are valued by consumers, and whether the low effectiveness of current labels can be explained because they do not adequately incorporate consumers' values towards FT.

Insights from the Literature

WTP for Fair Trade Products

Most studies on socially responsible products show that the majority of consumers are increasingly interested in the ethical characteristics of food products and are willing to pay a price premium for products that live up to certain ethical standards.

Based on a literature review study on FT consumption, Andorfer and Liebe (2012) conclude that there is clear empirical evidence of a positive WTP for such products. In a meta-analysis on the WTP for socially responsible products, Tully and Winer (2014) find that the mean percentage premium for socially responsible products (relating to environment, animals, and human) is 16.8 per cent, and that, on average, 60 per cent of respondents are willing to pay a positive premium. Besides, they find that the WTP for products where the socially responsible element benefits humans (e.g. labour practices) is greater compared to those that benefit the environment.

The majority of studies on WTP for FT products have focused on coffee, since it is the most popular and well-known FT product to date. These studies show that there is large variation in the price premium that some consumers are prepared to pay. The ethical premium ranges between €0.04/100g and €0.30/100g for FT coffee (Loureiro and Lotade, 2005; Hertel, Scruggs, and Heidkamp, 2009; Carlsson et al., 2010; Andorfer and Liebe, 2012), and the price premium for a FT label is higher than the price premium for organic labels (Loureiro and Lotade, 2005). De Pelsmacker and colleagues (2005) find that the average price premium consumers were prepared to pay for a FT label on coffee was €0.08/100g, but varied substantially from €0.25/100g for the 'FT lovers', who expressed a strong and clear preference for the FT label, to less than €0.03/100g for the 'taste and brand lovers', who only lay importance on the flavour or the brand and do not distinguish between other attributes.

Previous research on information and labels indicates that information provisioning can alter the demand for ethically produced food. Tagbata and Sirieix (2008) show that the WTP for FT labels increases when information is given regarding these labels. Also, Loureiro and Lotade (2005) find higher premiums for labelling programmes after consumers were previously informed about them. Trudel and Cotte (2009) confirm that consumers are willing to pay a premium and they also measured the effect of negative information (i.e. unethical behaviour of a firm). They find that the punishment/discount for unfair practices was nearly twice the impact of positive information. In addition, consumers perceive and reward all levels of ethical products similarly. Their WTP does not change for a product with ingredients that are all ethically produced compared to products for which only some ingredients are ethically produced. Finally, consumers' WTP for FT labels can increase if they are informed that a large share of consumers chooses the ethical alternative because they want to conform to this social norm or because they are concerned about their status (Carlsson et al., 2010).

So far, relatively few studies have measured the relationship between FT and consumers' WTP for chocolate. Rousu and Corrigan (2008) conducted an auction in a grocery store and found that participants are willing to pay a premium of €0.08/100g for FT chocolate. In addition, they found that, by providing reliable information, between 14 per cent and 18 per cent of participants switched to or from the FT chocolate bar. In another study, Tagbata and Sirieix (2008) use an experimental method with two organic and two FT chocolate products to value the environmental and social dimension. Results show that organic and FT labels increase consumers' WTP by €0.59/100g. In addition they identify three consumer clusters: (1) consumers that are insensitive to the label; (2) consumers that positively value the label; and (3) consumers where the label valuation depends on the product's taste. Lastly, Rousseau (2015) uses a CE and finds that respondents are willing to pay a premium of €2.04/100g for chocolate with a FT label.

The Attitude–Behaviour Gap

While consumers may be concerned about the ethical characteristics of food products, the reality shows that these general concerns are often not translated into actual behaviour when it comes to spending their own money (Padel and

Foster, 2005; Vermeir and Verbeke, 2006; Langen, 2011; Grunert et al., 2014). For Belgium specifically, a recent study in 2012 indicates that Belgian consumers are willing to pay a premium of 10–15 per cent for FT chocolate. Besides, 50 per cent of consumers reported having bought FT chocolate in their last shopping year and 96 per cent of the buyers reported being satisfied by their purchase (BTC, 2012). The market share of FT chocolate in Belgium, however, is estimated to be less than 1 per cent (Fairtrade International, 2012), demonstrating the existence of some sort of attitude/behaviour gap.

Previous literature identified several barriers towards the consumption of food with ethical characteristics, such as the relatively high price premium (e.g. De Pelsmacker et al., 2005), the real or perceived lack of availability (Vermeir and Verbeke, 2006), the lack of information (Rousseau and Vranken, 2013), low knowledge (e.g. McEachern and McClean, 2002), and a lack of trust in the label (e.g. Krystallis et al., 2008). The existence of an attitude/behaviour gap can, however, be attributed to other factors, not just purchase barriers.

In addition, methodological issues also play a role. Different valuation methods are used to assess consumers' preferences for FT products, ranging from surveys, CEs, lab experiments, and field experiments over retail scanner data (Andorfer and Liebe, 2012). These methods differ on the type of choices they measure, namely hypothetical or non-hypothetical choices, the environment where the choices are made, namely online, in a face-to-face interview, in the lab, or in the field, and whether data on revealed or stated buying behaviour is used. Besides, many studies focus on one product, one label, or one information message, while in reality consumers are faced with a multifactor decision world and constant trade-offs between price, brand, quantity, use-by-date, nutrition information, sensory quality, and healthiness (Grunert et al., 2014).

Several studies find a WTP that is higher than what consumers, in reality, want to pay, because methods differ in their capacity to predict actual behaviour. Social desirability bias and hypothetical bias are often put forward as key issues in the overstatement of WTP for FT labels (Cummings et al., 1995; Levitt and List, 2007). These issues relate to the propensity of people to portray themselves more positively than is shown by their behaviour in reality, and to the hypothetical or unfamiliar nature of stated preference methods and lab experiments.

Finally, a study from Rousu and Corrigan (2008) indicates that a welfare loss occurs when labels do not adequately inform consumers what they stand for. Label effectiveness is reduced when a label is not able to effectively convey the necessary information to consumers to allow them to make an informed choice. This may, consequently, hold back the consumption of ethically produced goods (Rousseau and Vranken, 2013; Vlaeminck et al., 2014). The section 'Insights from a Choice Experiment and Survey in Belgium' therefore covers the results of our experiment, which studied whether the current labels are effective in incorporating consumers' values towards the FT characteristics.

Insights from a Choice Experiment and Survey in Belgium

We conducted a survey and two CEs to provide additional insights into the effectiveness of FT labels. The difference between the two CEs lies in the way FT enters participants' choice sets. In the first CE, one of the chocolate bar attributes is a FT label. This forces participants to take the label explicitly into account in their multi-attribute trade-off. In the second CE we do not include the FT label as such, but use the main FT characteristics as attributes. This setup allows us to investigate whether a FT label increases consumers' WTP, which FT characteristics are valued by consumers, and whether current labels are effective in conveying the ethical characteristics of their products. The survey and CEs were conducted in Belgium. Belgians consume 6 kg of chocolate on average, per person per year, making chocolate a well-known and frequently bought product. Therefore, Belgium is a good country for this study.

Experimental Design and Data Collection

Since FT labels represent goods and services, such as fair employment conditions, that are not traded in markets, we employ a non-market valuation technique to estimate the value of these labels and their characteristics. A discrete CE is a stated preference elicitation method introduced by Louviere and Hensher (1982), especially suited to deal with multidimensional choices such as purchase decisions related to FT chocolate. A CE is a survey-based or experiment-based method for modelling preferences for goods,[1] where goods are described in terms of attributes (e.g. price) and the levels (e.g. different prices) that these attributes can take (Hanley et al., 2001). The underlying assumption is that utility is defined over the characteristics of goods rather than over goods themselves. People are presented with multiple choice sets with alternatives of a particular good, and are asked to choose their preferred alternative, in order to understand the trade-offs that respondents are willing to make among attributes. It is assumed that a consumer will choose the alternative that yields most personal utility. Because price is included as one of the attributes of the good, the WTP for each attribute can be indirectly recovered from people's choices. To ensure that results can be interpreted in standard welfare economic terms, a baseline alternative or 'no-choice' option is included. For details, we refer to Vlaeminck et al. (2014).

Next to the CEs, participants filled in a survey. The survey contained socio-demographic questions (gender, age, education, household constitution, etc.), questions measuring social and environmental attitudes (volunteering, travelled outside European Union (EU), member of environmental NGO, donations to charity, etc.), and questions relating to FT (prejudices, knowledge, trust, frequent buyer, belief, etc.).

---

[1] Choice experiments can be incentive compatible when they are based on binding experiments where participants have to make actual payments if they decide to buy the product under consideration.

Table 10.1 Attributes and attribute levels in the *CE with an FT label* and the *CE with FT characteristics*

CE with an FT Label		CE with FT Characteristics	
Attribute	Attribute Levels	Attribute	Attribute Levels
Quality	30% premium cocoa	Environmental standard	No standards
& taste	50% premium cocoa		EU standards
	70% premium cocoa		Organic standard
Label	No label	Price paid to producer	Bad
	FT label		Average
	Bio-FT label		Fair
Origin of cocoa	Ivory Coast	Level of community	Non-existent
	Indonesia	investment	Average
	Brazil		High
Price	€2	Working conditions	Unimportant
	€3	+ controls	Improved + infrequent controls
	€4		Improved + frequent controls
		Price	€1.5, €2, €2.5, €3, €3.5, €4

Participants completed two generic CEs. In the first CE, each respondent faced three different choice sets, each consisting of two alternative chocolate varieties (A and B) and the option not to buy any chocolate variety. The chocolate varieties were described using four attributes: quality and taste, label presence, origin of cocoa, and price (see Table 10.1 for the different levels that each attribute can take). Each respondent was asked which chocolate variety they would prefer to buy. As this CE explicitly includes the FT label as an attribute, we will refer to it as the *CE with an FT label* in the remainder of the chapter.

In the second CE, each respondent faced six different choice sets, each consisting of two alternative chocolate varieties (A and B) and the option not to buy any chocolate variety. The chocolate varieties were described using five attributes: environmental impact, price paid to producer, level of community investment, working conditions, and price (see Table 10.1 for the different levels for each attribute). Each respondent was asked which chocolate variety they preferred. They needed to assume the chocolate was of their preferred quality and taste and the cocoa came from developing countries so as to make their choices in a similar way to the first CE. As this second CE includes FT characteristics as attributes, we will refer to it as the *CE with FT characteristics* in the remainder of the chapter.

The CEs were conducted in a local supermarket in January 2013 with 144 participants. The average respondent was 42 years old. Thirty-eight per cent of the respondents were female and 72 per cent of our sample enjoyed education above secondary school level. A major share of respondents had a relatively high net household income of more than 3000 euros per month. Twenty per cent were members of a nature protection organization, 49 per cent had undertaken volunteer work at some time, and 73 per cent donated yearly to charity, giving us an indication of the pro-social values in our sample.

When asked whether they would purchase the conventional variant, or the FT variant if available, half of respondents stated they (almost) never purchase the FT option. Forty-two per cent regularly opted for FT and 5 per cent always purchased FT. In the group of FT buyers, 75 per cent stated they buy only between one and three different types of FT products. More than half of respondents rated FT products as worse on both price and availability. Only one fourth of respondents could identify the correct definition of FT. Seventy per cent of respondents believed that FT guarantees what it promises but only 50 per cent personally cared about the issues addressed. One fourth felt that FT did not fulfil all its promises but they still believed FT products to be better than conventional ones.

Results

The results of the *CE with an FT label* show that consumers attach importance to the ethical aspects linked to cocoa production. Both a FT label and a bio-FT label are preferred above no label being present on the chocolate. A bio-FT label is preferred to chocolate with just a FT label.

Second, there was a slight preference for cocoa coming from Brazil compared to the Ivory Coast, and no difference between Brazil and Indonesia. Belgian consumers probably link FT to South America, since FT organizations mostly showcase small producers from South American countries in their campaigns, making it the most familiar country. The fact that consumers do not differentiate much between the origins of the cocoa production should not come as a surprise since there is no a priori reason to believe an average consumer, without specific area or quality knowledge, would prefer cocoa from, for example, Africa over that from Asia.

Third, consumers have heterogeneous preferences for a bio-FT label and homogenous positive preferences for a FT label that stands alone (i.e. with no organic certification). This finding contrasts with past literature on ethical labels, where significant sample heterogeneity towards these ethical attributes is often found (e.g. Uchida et al., 2014).

In summary, consumers do value a FT label in their decision to buy chocolate but are rather indifferent to the cocoa origin. This suggests that consumers uniformly identify a FT label with products coming from developing countries, and they do not discriminate to which parts of the world their FT premium will be transferred. However, it is unclear which specific characteristics of FT drive this preference.

The results of the *CE with FT characteristics* as attributes indicate that all FT characteristics have a significantly positive impact on consumer preferences. Heterogeneity is present in the distribution of preferences towards these characteristics. Consumers prefer cocoa that is produced following certain environmental standards, such as the EU environmental standard and the organic standard. They dislike an unfair price paid to cocoa producers, although they are indifferent between an average and fair remuneration. Consumers prefer a high level of social community investment, such as capacity building and schools, compared to none or a low level. Lastly, consumers attach importance to the degree to which labour conditions are improved and to the level that these are controlled. In fact, when looking at the different FT characteristics assessed in this study, consumers attach the highest value to improved labour conditions, but only if these claims are frequently controlled. Hence, for FT organizations to be effective, they should run frequent controls and communicate this clearly.

Finally, we turn to the WTP estimates for the FT label and FT characteristics. Consumers are willing to pay a positive premium of €0.84/100g for a FT label on chocolate. Besides, we test whether consumers' WTP for the (bio-)FT label differs from the WTP for the labels' underlying characteristics. Since the FT definition is unclear to what extent, for example, fair labour conditions or community invest-ments are translated in reality, we created different bundles of FT characteristics to make our results more robust. In total, four different FT bundles were created, namely, *FT characteristics high*, *FT characteristics low*, *BioFT characteristics high*, and *BioFT characteristics low*. *FT characteristics high* is the FT bundle of interest since it broadly captures the definition that most FT organizations currently adopt and yields a high benefit for the producers: a fair price to producers, care for the environment (although organic is not the standard), a high level of community investment, and improved working conditions that are frequently controlled. *FT characteristics low* is the FT bundle that generates lower benefits: an average price to producers, care for the environment, an average level of community investment, and improved working conditions that are infrequently controlled. The two bio-FT bundles are similar to the FT bundles except that they take organic to be the environmental standard.

Figure 10.1 indicates that consumers value the bundle of FT characteristics significantly more than the FT label used on FT chocolate. We find the largest difference between the WTP for the FT label and the WTP for the bundle of FT characteristics with high benefits for producers (i.e. the bundle that captures the definition that most FT organizations currently adopt). This finding shows that FT labels do not completely incorporate and communicate the ethical characteristics of their products to consumers who value these characteristics.

As a reality check, we compared the estimated WTP for a FT label to the price premium that FT chocolate carries in today's supermarkets. We found that our estimated WTP of €0.84/100g corresponded closely to the price premium that consumers of FT chocolate nowadays pay in the supermarket (€0.81/200g). This suggests that the estimated values for the underlying FT characteristics are also truthfully revealed, and thus that the current labels are ineffective in conveying the underlying FT characteristics to consumers.

Critiques and Robustness

There is critique on CE research because several issues, such as priming, hypothet-ical bias, and social desirability bias, arise when researchers want to study con-sumers' ethical attitudes and behaviours (Lusk et al., 2011). Due to these issues, estimates can be distorted, which may result in inflated WTP estimates. To counter

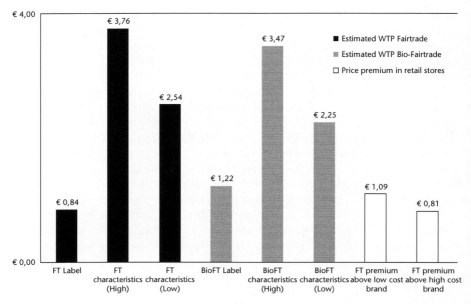

Figure 10.1 Consumers' estimated WTP for a (bio-)FT label and four bundles of FT characteristics (€/100g)

Note: *FT characteristics high (low)*: retribution of a fair (average) price to producers, care for the environment (but organic is not the standard), a high (average) level of community investment and improved working conditions that are frequently (infrequently) controlled. The two *BioFT* bundles are similar to the FT bundles except that they take organic as the environmental standard.

this, we introduced three treatments in our full experimental design in order to increase the robustness of our WTP estimations.

First, consumers were randomly allocated to a chocolate tasting treatment before answering the CE, since Tagbata and Sirieix (2008) find a negative inter-action between labels and taste in the valuation of chocolate. One group did not taste chocolate, another group did a blind tasting, and the last group tasted the chocolate and were given full information. Consumers' WTP of a FT label on chocolate did not differ between the three groups.

Second, people have the propensity to portray their behaviour more positively than in reality, and the hypothetical nature of an experimental environment can alter their behaviour (Cummings et al., 1995; Levitt and List, 2007). Several tech-niques exist to incentivize people to behave more realistically in experiments. In our study, 50 per cent of the participants received a reward to participate in the study, but they needed to buy one of the chocolate bars that they had chosen during the experiment. This mechanism forces them to reveal their true prefer-ences via a treat of a financial transaction and thus makes their choices incentive compatible.

The other half needed to read a cheap talk script explaining that people have the tendency to portray themselves more positively than in reality when answering questions in a survey. The cheap talk mechanism asks them to reveal their true preferences through creating awareness about their biases to inflate their WTP. Consumers' WTPs did not differ between the cheap talk and incentive compatible subsamples. Therefore, the supermarket environment combined with a cheap talk script can be economical ways to reduce hypothetical bias to an acceptable level.

Lastly, 50 per cent of participants got the survey questions regarding FT before making their choices and 50 per cent received the questions afterwards. Making consumers aware of FT before they made their choices could increase their WTP in a similar way that information campaigns can stimulate people to showcase a particular behaviour (de Magistris et al., 2013). However, the WTP of consumers who were primed by the FT survey questions did not differ from the non-primed subsample.

None of the three treatments significantly affects our estimates of consumers' WTP for a FT label on chocolate. We therefore conclude that our estimates are robust for both the label value and the values consumers attach to FT characteristics.

Conclusions

Why has the demand for FT remained low? Do consumers not care about these ethical characteristics? Do they care about the characteristics but are there other barriers that impede an increase in the consumption of FT chocolate? These are the questions that this chapter has tried to address. In this chapter we first provided insights from the literature on the WTP for FT products in general and then for FT chocolate in particular. There is clear empirical evidence that consumers are concerned about the ethical characteristics of food products. However, the reality shows that these general concerns are not always translated into actual behaviour when it comes to consumers' spending their own money.

Next, we provided insights from a survey and CE that was conducted in Belgium in order to investigate: whether a FT label increases consumers' WTP, which FT characteristics are valued by consumers, and whether current labels are effective in conveying the ethical characteristics of their products. Our study shows that consumers are willing to pay a price premium of €0.84/100g for chocolate with an FT label. Further, consumers highly value FT characteristics. They are particularly willing to pay a premium for chocolate made from cocoa that is produced under good labour conditions, when these conditions are frequently controlled.

Our analysis suggests that current labels do not adequately incorporate consumers' values towards FT practices, thereby limiting their effectiveness in current food markets. Linking the FT label closer to people's preferences and communicating clearly what the label stands for could, therefore, provide a major opportunity for FT organizations and other stakeholders to expand the FT market.

References

Andorfer, V. A. and U. Liebe. 2012. 'Research on Fair Trade consumption: a review'. *Journal of Business Ethics* 106 (4): pp. 415–35.

Beyer, D. 2012. 'Child labor in agriculture: some new developments to an ancient problem'. *Journal of Agromedicine* 17 (2): pp. 197–207.

Bradu, C., J. L. Orquin, and J. Thøgersen. 2013. 'The mediated influence of a traceability label on consumer's willingness to buy the labelled product'. *Journal of Business Ethics*: pp. 1–13.

BTC (Belgian Development Agency). 2012. Gedrag, attitudes en opinies van personen die in België wonen ten aanzien van producten uit eerlijke handel. Available at: <http://www.befair.be/sites/default/files/all-files/opinion-polls/Belgen%20en%20fair%20trade%202012.pdf> (accessed 12 October 2012).

Carlsson, F., J. H. Garcia, and A. Lofgren. 2010. 'Conformity and the demand for environmental goods'. *Environmental Resource Economics* 47: pp. 407–21.

Cummings, R. G., G. W. Harrison, and E. E. Rutström. 1995. 'Homegrown values and hypothetical surveys: Is the dichotomous choice approach incentive-compatible?' *American Economic Review* 85: pp. 260–6.

De Magistris, T., A. Gracia, and R. M. Nayga. 2013. 'On the use of honesty priming tasks to mitigate hypothetical bias in choice experiments'. *American Journal of Agricultural Economics* 95 (5): pp. 1136–54.

De Pelsmacker, P., L. Driesen, and G. Rayp. 2005. 'Do consumers care about ethics? Willingness to pay for fair-trade coffee'. *Journal of Consumer Affairs* 39: pp. 363–85.

EFTA (European Fair Trade Association). 2001. *Fair Trade in Europe: Facts and Figures on the Fair Trade Sector in 18 European Countries.* Available at: <http://www.european-fair-trade-association.org/efta/Doc/FT-E-2001.pdf> (accessed 7 January 2014).

Fairtrade International. 2012. *Challenge and Opportunity: Supplement to Annual Review 2010–11.* 2010 Financials and Global Sales Figures. Available at: <http://www.fairtrade.net/fileadmin/user_upload/content/2009/about_us/FLO_Annual-Financials-Sales_2010.pdf> (accessed 12 October 2012).

Grunert, K. G., S. Hieke, and J. Wills. 2014. 'Sustainability labels on food products: consumer motivation, understanding and use'. *Food Policy* 44: pp. 177–89.

Hanley, N., S. Mourato, and R. E. Wright. 2001. 'Choice modelling approaches: A superior alternative for environmental valuation?' *Journal of Economic Surveys* 15 (3): pp. 435–62.

Hertel, S., L. Scruggs, and C. P. Heidkamp. 2009. 'Human rights and public opinion: from attitudes to action'. *Political Science Quarterly* 143: pp. 443–59.

ICCO (International Cocoa Organization). 2007. *Sustainable Cocoa Economy: Comprehensive and Participatory Approach.* London: International Cocoa Organization.

ICCO (International Cocoa Organization). 2012. *The World Cocoa Economy: Past and Present.* Available at: <http://www.icco.org/about-us/international-cocoa-agreements/cat_view/30-related-documents/45-statistics-other-statistics.html> (accessed 22 January 2014).

KPMG. 2012. *Cocoa Certification.* Study on the costs, advantages and disadvantages of cocoa certification commissioned by the International Cocoa Organization (ICCO). <http://www.icco.org/about-us/international-cocoa-agreements/cat_view/30-related-documents/37-fair-trade-organic-cocoa.html> ((accessed 22 January 2014).

Krain, E., E. Miljard, E. Konan, and E. Servat. 2011. *Trade and Pro-Poor Growth: Introducing Rainforest Alliance Certification to Cocoa Production in Côte d'Ivoire.* Deutsche Gesellschaft für Internationale Zusammenarbeit (GIZ). Eschborn, Germany.

Krystallis, A., G. Maglaras, Mamalisc S. 2008. 'Motivations and cognitive structures of consumers in their purchasing of functional foods'. *Food Quality and Preference* 19 (6): pp. 525–38.

Langen, N. 2011. 'Are ethical consumption and charitable giving substitutes or not? Insights into consumers' coffee choice'. *Food Quality and Preference* 22 (5): pp. 412–21.

Levitt, S. D. and J. A. List. 2007. 'What do laboratory experiments measuring social preferences reveal about the real world?' *Journal of Economic Perspectives.* 21(2): pp. 153–74.

Loureiro, M. L. and J. Lotade. 2005. 'Do fair trade and eco-labels in coffee wake up the consumer conscience?' *Ecological Economics* 53 (1): pp. 129–38.

Louviere, J. J. and D. A. Hensher. 1982. *Design and Analysis of Simulated Choice or Allocation Experiments in Travel Choice Modeling.* Transportation research record (890). Transportation Research Board.

Lusk, J. L., J. Roosen, and J. F. Shogren. 2011. *The Oxford Handbook of the Economics of Food Consumption and Policy.* Oxford: Oxford University Press.

McEachern, M. G. and P. McClean. 2002. 'Organic purchasing motivations and attitudes: Are they ethical?' *International Journal of Consumer Studies* 26 (2): pp. 85–92.

Max Havelaar. 2012. *Cacao en Fairtrade. Fier op onze chocolade, zeker als het Fairtrade is.* Retrieved from: <http://fairtradebelgium.be/sites/default/files/brochure_cacao_nl-18web_fsc.pdf>.

Padel, S. and Foster, C. 2005. 'Exploring the gap between attitudes and behaviour: understanding why consumers buy or do not buy organic food'. *British Food Journal* 107 (8): pp. 606–25.

Poelman, A., J. Mojet, D. Lyon, and S. Sefa-Dedeh. 2008. 'The influence of information about organic production and fair trade on preferences for and perception of pineapple'. *Food Quality and Preference* 19 (1): pp. 114–21.

Rousseau, S. 2015. 'The role of organic and fair trade labels when choosing chocolate'. *Food Quality and Preferences* 44: pp. 92–100.

Rousseau, S. and L. Vranken. 2013. 'Green market expansion by reducing information asymmetries: evidence for labeled organic food products'. *Food Policy* 40: pp. 31–43.

Rousu, M. C. and J. R. Corrigan. 2008. 'Estimating the welfare loss to consumers when food labels do not adequately inform: an application to fair trade certification'. *Journal of Agricultural & Food Industrial Organization* 6 (1): article 3.

Tagbata, D. and S. Sirieix. 2008. 'Measuring consumer's willingness to pay for organic and Fair Trade products'. *International Journal of Consumer Studies* 32 (5): pp. 479–90.

Trudel, R. and J. Cotte. 2009. 'Does it pay to be good?' *MIT Sloane Management Review* 50: pp. 61–8.

Tully, S. M. and R. S. Winer. 2014. 'The role of the beneficiary in willingness to pay for socially responsible products: a meta-analysis'. *Journal of Retailing* 90 (2): pp. 255–74.

Uchida, H., Y. Onozaka, T. Morita, and S. Managi. 2014. 'Demand for ecolabeled seafood in the Japanese market: a conjoint analysis of the impact of information and interaction with other labels'. *Food Policy* 44: pp. 68–76.

Vermeir, I. and W. Verbeke. 2006. 'Sustainable food consumption: exploring the consumer "attitude–behavioral intention" gap'. *Journal of Agricultural and Environmental Ethics* 19 (2): p. 169.

Vlaeminck, P., J. Vandoren, and L. Vranken. 2014. 'Are labels delivering what they intend? Explicit value of fair-trade labels versus implicit value of fair trade characteristics'. Paper presented at the 2014 EAAE International Congress, 26–29 August, Ljubljana, Slovenia.

Part III
Governance and Industrial Organization

11

Sustaining Supplies in Smallholder-Dominated Value Chains

Corporate Governance of the Global Cocoa Sector

Niels Fold and Jeff Neilson

Introduction

In all countries where cocoa is grown, agricultural systems are dominated by smallholder farmers. At the other end of the supply chain, chocolate manufacturing is highly concentrated amongst a relatively small number of large multinational firms, and the intermediate processing stage of cocoa grinding is even more highly concentrated amongst major trading companies. The aim of this chapter is to illuminate the significant transformations in institutions and governance that are presently occurring along this cocoa–chocolate value chain. In particular, we believe we are witnessing a new level of corporate regulatory influence over the world's cocoa farmers that is largely unprecedented. This shift reflects the peculiarities of supply uncertainty in the global cocoa industry, but is also indicative of likely changes across other commodity sectors in an increasingly resource-constrained world economy. These emergent regulatory systems are often framed by a corporate discourse of 'sustainability', and especially the need to sustain supplies of cheap cocoa in the face of predicted growth in global chocolate consumption, especially in emerging markets such as China.

The global cocoa–chocolate value chain has a pronounced South-to-North orientation and is primarily based on smallholder production in Africa. The chapter deals with new forms of private regulation which have gradually replaced the former state marketing boards in West Africa, an institutional legacy from British and French colonial rule, and that have been introduced into a historically less state-driven institutional environment in Indonesia.

We will apply the concepts of 'institutions' and 'governance' borrowed from the field of global value chain (GVC) research to present insights into recent developments in the global cocoa–chocolate sector. The governance of GVCs is an important, and highly contested, theoretical concern within the GVC literature. In Gereffi's (1994) original formulation, a global commodity chain (GCC)—as it was then known—was seen to be coordinated, or governed, by key sets of lead firms in an increasingly buyer-driven fashion. Each value chain is comprised of an internal governance structure that describes the authority and power relationships within the chain, which are principally shaped by the actions and strategies of lead firms. While Gereffi (1994) had already acknowledged the important role of the state in shaping the governance structure of a chain, Gereffi (1995: 113) went on to refer explicitly to the external regulation of a GCC approach as the 'institutional framework that identifies how local, national, and international conditions and policies shape the globalization process at each stage in the chain'. This then established a fourfold framework for GVC analysis: (1) an input–output structure of how value is added along a production system; (2) the territoriality of where production nodes are located in space; (3) the governance of the chain by lead firms; and (4) the institutional environment in which the chain is embedded. In this sense, the GCC/GVC analytical framework encompassed external regulation through 'institutions' and internal regulation through 'governance'. In reality, however, these aspects of a value chain are mutually constituted to such an extent that such a distinction may be somewhat arbitrary (see, for example, Neilson and Pritchard, 2009).

Public regulation and the wider institutional framework have, for the most part, actually disappeared as an explicit (fourth) dimension in the succeeding development of the analytical approach. Various multilateral and national regulatory institutions are only taken into account in some of the empirical studies, for instance in Gereffi's own investigations of the apparel chain(s) originating in developing countries that end up in the US market (see Gereffi, 1994, 1999; Bair and Gereffi, 2001), and in Neilson and Pritchard's (2009) study of the South India tea and coffee sectors. Perhaps the implicit rationale is that it only makes sense to incorporate the institutional framework as a conditioning factor for GVC governance at the concrete level. Depending on the 'nature' of the product that constitutes the value chain, different sets of regulatory institutions are relevant: it is an empirical question how they interfere with chain governance dynamics. Moreover, these cases illustrate the opaque distinction between the external and internal regulation of GVC dynamics. Technical standards are mostly designed and monitored by public bodies in consultation with trade associations or dominant corporate actors, and ethical codes are created by various constituencies of corporations, non-governmental organizations (NGOs), trade unions, and/or public bodies. Whether these forms of institutional regulation have to be conceptualized as 'internalized external' regulation or 'externalized internal' regulation is hard to tell, as the case of the global cocoa sector suggests. A key element of the global cocoa industry, as presented in this chapter, is the emergence of such a hybrid internal–external regulatory system that is increasingly performing many of the functions once considered the exclusive domain of state-based actors.

The chapter is structured loosely around the fourfold analytical framework of Gereffi (1995). The chapter starts with a brief outline of the territoriality and input–output structure of the cocoa–chocolate chain, including an influential socio-ecological model of forest rents used to explain global cocoa production patterns. We argue, however, that this generalized model should be augmented with an incorporation of governance dynamics within the cocoa–chocolate GVC, which we then present in the section 'Governance in the Global Cocoa-Chocolate Value Chain'. The following section, 'A New Public–Private Hybrid Form of Value Chain Governance', presents what we interpret as a new public–private hybrid form of value chain governance across West Africa and Indonesia, where major players in the global cocoa–chocolate industry are becoming involved upstream in the chain to secure continuous and viable cocoa production at source. This trend has been reinforced by consumer awareness around labour conditions in African smallholder production, and indeed environmental and social concerns more broadly. These concerns have encouraged the introduction of various private sector interventions along the value chain under the banner of 'sustainability'. Finally, the chapter concludes with some brief reflections on the impact of these new forms of regulation on the livelihoods of the world's cocoa smallholders.

Structural and Territorial Patterns in the Global Cocoa–Chocolate Value Chain

At first glance, cocoa is the quintessential tropical commodity—produced in the global South, and both processed and consumed almost completely by the North as chocolate products in various forms. As will be discussed, however, this classic dichotomy has become complicated by recent industrial upgrading in the South through cocoa processing, and by increasing chocolate consumption across Asia and Latin America. Most cocoa is termed 'bulk' cocoa (generally derived from Forastero cocoa varietals), with about 5 per cent of global production based on 'fine and flavoured' cocoa (coming from other tree varieties and primarily used for high-quality dark chocolate). While cocoa grown in West Africa is fermented (a simple on-farm process requiring about five days), smallholder cocoa from Southeast Asia is generally unfermented and sold at a discount on global markets as a result. Most of the world's cocoa production (about 90 per cent) is carried out by smallholders, cultivating less than ten hectares and generally reliant on family and informal labour. Since the demise of cocoa cultivation in Malaysia in the 1990s, production in large-scale plantations has been largely limited to Latin America. World cocoa production is highly concentrated in a few countries (Table 11.1), especially the Ivory Coast, Ghana, and Indonesia, with Africa contributing approximately 72 per cent of total global production.

The downstream processing of cocoa is split into two distinct industrial processes: (1) the grinding of cocoa beans; and (2) the manufacturing of chocolate and other consumer products. After being cleaned and roasted, cocoa beans are ground into cocoa liquor. The cocoa liquor can be pressed into essentially two different products—cocoa butter and cocoa cake (the latter of which is ground into cocoa

Table 11.1 World cocoa production (four-year average, 2010–13)

Rank	Country	Volume (1,000 tonnes)	Share of global production (%)
1	Ivory Coast	1,421	36
2	Ghana	843	21
3	Indonesia	463	12
4	Nigeria	234	6
5	Cameroon	217	6
6	Brazil	192	5
7	Ecuador	170	4
	All Other Countries		11

Source: ICCO (2013).

powder). These are the basic intermediate cocoa products—or cocoa ingredients—that are traded internationally and utilized for the subsequent manufacturing of various consumer products. Chocolate is produced by mixing cocoa liquor with sugar (and possibly milk and other ingredients) and adding more cocoa butter in a process known as conching. The liquid chocolate can be used in the manufacturing of bars, filled goods, or as a coating on other types of confectionery goods. Cocoa powder is used in the manufacture of drinking chocolate or as a flavour in the food industry (biscuits, ice cream, cakes, etc.), whereas cocoa butter also has an important use in the cosmetic and pharmaceutical industries. These varied end-use consumer products for cocoa beans have an important influence on chain governance, by increasing the influence of cocoa grinders in the chain.

The International Cocoa Organization (ICCO) (2013) estimates that approximately 40 per cent of global production was processed by grinders located in origin countries in 2012/13 (an increase from 35 per cent in 2002/03); key countries are shown in Table 11.2. This reflects one of the most important recent trends affecting the value chain, as producing country governments attempt to value-add raw materials prior to export as a platform for resource-based industrialization. Many emerging middle-income countries, representing both producing and non-producing countries, have developed industrial capacity in cocoa processing. Malaysia, for example, is now a major international hub for cocoa grinding (Table 11.2). Although Malaysia is considered to be a producing country by the ICCO, in reality agricultural production of cocoa has totally collapsed in that country, with the grinding sector, for many years, using imported beans from Indonesia. Malaysian grinding is frequently, and erroneously, referred to as origin grinding, when its function in the value chain is essentially identical to that of the Netherlands, which imports raw beans and exports intermediate products. Singapore, Thailand, Brazil, and Mexico perform similar functions in the value chain, albeit on a smaller scale, with Brazil and Mexico only partially reliant on domestic production. Moreover, Brazil and Mexico can also be differentiated from Singapore and Malaysia because of their large domestic market for cocoa products, reflected in their much lower ratio of processed cocoa exports to grindings (Table 11.2). The most significant increase in grindings in recent years has occurred in Indonesia, increasing from 130,000 tonnes in 2009/10 to 270,000 tonnes

Table 11.2 Estimated cocoa grindings of major countries (2012/13 data)

Rank	Country	Grindings (1,000 tonnes)	Bean Production (1,000 tonnes)	Processed Cocoa Exports (% of grindings)
1	Netherlands	530	0	112
2	Ivory Coast	460	1,445	72
3	United States	412	0	22
4	Germany	400	0	43
5	Malaysia	293	7	86
6	Indonesia	255	420	77
7	Brazil	241	185	23
8	Ghana	225	835	68
12	Singapore	80	0	217
20	Mexico	42.5	25	16
29	Thailand	18	0.5	73

Source: ICCO (2013).

in 2012/13 (ICCO, 2013). Recent reports suggest that grinding capacity in Indonesia will reach 600,000 tonnes by the end of 2014, causing a major shift towards imported beans (Reuters, 2014). Reflecting the influence of state institutions on value chain structures, this industrial expansion in Indonesia followed the introduction of an export tax on raw cocoa beans in 2010, and has resulted in a dramatic collapse of raw bean exports (Neilson et al., 2014). Indonesia is thus following the path set earlier by Brazil and Malaysia, where cocoa beans effectively disappeared from international trade, from globally significant levels in the 1990s, due to the expansion of domestic cocoa grinding.

The dominant consumers of cocoa products are the European Union (EU) and the USA, with Japan and (more recently) Russia and Brazil emerging as important markets on a global scale (Table 11.3). Many of the world's leading chocolate manufacturers are based in these countries: Mondelēz International (USA), Mars (USA), Hershey (USA), Ferrero (Italy), and Nestlé (Switzerland). It is estimated that Europe and North America account for approximately 85 per cent of global production in the candy and chocolate manufacturing sector (IbisWorld, 2014). Chocolate consumption in Asia—outside of Japan—is still relatively low, but is expected to increase significantly over the next decade (particularly in China).

Important centres of cocoa bean production have shifted regularly over the past four centuries, from Mesoamerica to Venezuela and Brazil, and then to West Africa in the late nineteenth century, before expansion across Southeast Asia in the late twentieth century. The development and shifting patterns of global cocoa supply have been explained as a geographically dispersed series of expansion, stagnation, and internal erosion of 'cocoa frontiers' (Ruf, 1995). According to this understanding, global cocoa supply is not principally determined by prices, but by the existence of scarcely populated virgin forest areas that are relatively easy to clear and can be transformed into cocoa plantations. This enables the vital 'forest rent' to be captured in the initial phases of cocoa cultivation. The concept of 'forest rent' conceptualizes the important advantages provided by recently cleared land due to enhanced soil fertility and soil moisture, and reduced levels of pests, diseases, and weeds compared

Table 11.3 Apparent cocoa consumption* (2012/13 data)

Rank	Country	Consumption (1,000 tonnes)
1	United States	770
2	Germany	330
3	United Kingdom	223
4	France	218
5	Russia	205
6	Brazil	200
7	Japan	160
8	Spain	107
9	Canada	89
10	Italy	85
11	Australia	68
12	Poland	67
13	Mexico	65
14	Belgium	63
15	China	59

Note: *Grindings plus net imports of cocoa and of chocolate products in beans equivalent.
Source: ICCO (2013).

to mature cocoa plantings. It is the ability of producers in forest frontiers to operate at far lower costs than producers in mature areas that dictates the shifts between major supply centres. The exploitation of the 'forest rent' enables new areas to sustain and increase production in periods of falling prices while production in high-cost (mature) areas gradually stagnates or decreases. In the long term, this cycle explains the ebb and flow of production from one region to another.

It is clear that currently smallholders—in all their diversity—have a competitive edge compared to commercial plantations. Examples are many and include the dramatic decline since the 1980s of plantation production in Bahia, Brazil's most important cocoa region, and the subsequent production decline and removal of cocoa plantations in Malaysia during the 1990s. The scope for commercial plantations in these countries is limited by relatively high labour costs, high risks linked to pest and disease attacks (which are easily spread in vast mono-cropped areas), and modest economies of scale. Cocoa productivity is extremely sensitive to the allocation of farm labour, which therefore tends to increase the relative costs of monitoring labour in a plantation environment relative to smallholdings. Enhanced incentives for labour can therefore be obtained on farms cultivated directly by the owners, their families, and a few seasonal caretakers, where monitoring costs are substantially reduced. Arguably, the history of labour abuses—and indeed the practice of slavery—that have characterized historical cocoa production in Venezuela, Brazil, the Belgian Congo, and contemporary West Africa could be linked to the difficulties in effectively managing on-farm labour incentives, which are so critical for profitable cultivation. It is therefore questionable whether a significant price increase, such as the relatively high prices prevalent since around 2008, will constitute a sufficient incentive for capitalist agriculture to return into cocoa production.

Governance in the Global Cocoa–Chocolate Value Chain

It is significant that the 'atomistic' production structure constituted by small-holders in cocoa cultivation corresponds to a highly oligopolized structure in the rest of the GVC. The main loci for lead firms are in the two processing segments—cocoa grinding and chocolate manufacturing.

Due to increasing economies of scale and concentration in the processing industry, multinational grinders now tend to source their cocoa beans via subsidiaries in producing countries or process directly in these countries. Storage services are often outsourced and provided by specialized warehouse companies: a few of the specialized warehouses from the European 'cocoa-hub' in Amsterdam have established facilities in West Africa from where they service the inter-national grinders, which may locate their processing plants locally (in the Ivory Coast and Ghana) or in Europe and the USA. Hence, the previous 'functional role' of specialist traders has more or less disappeared, and international trading companies are no longer significant actors in the global cocoa–chocolate value chain. Many have been gradually transformed to become important grinders themselves. One of the last major cocoa trading companies was the UK-based Armajaro Trading, which had exploited the physical bean trade before it ran into heavy losses in 2012, and was taken over by Ecom Agroindustrial in 2013;[1] a company which commands grinding facilities in Holland, Mexico, and Malaysia.

Cocoa grinding worldwide is now highly concentrated in the hands of a few large multinational companies, with an estimated 60 per cent of processing conducted by just three companies: Cargill (USA); Barry Callebaut (Switzerland); and Archer Daniels Midland (ADM) (USA) (Euromonitor International, 2012. This trend towards consolidation is, moreover, accelerating: in 2013, Barry Callebaut took over the cocoa unit of Singapore-based Petra Foods, thereby adding substantial processing capacity in Southeast Asia to its portfolio and making the company the world's largest buyer of cocoa beans as part of its strategy to target emerging markets in Asia.[2] In late 2013, it was widely speculated that Cargill was finalizing plans to purchase ADM, which would have made it unambiguously the world's premier cocoa grinder,[3] but the deal was not finalized. Some grinders (such as Barry Callebaut and the US-based Blommer) specialize in basic cocoa products (variations of paste, powder, and butter, as well as some customized chocolate products), while others (ADM, Cargill) are versatile agro-food companies, where cocoa processing is just one line of business among other agro-processing activities. These latter versatile companies are able to transfer and adapt technical,

---

[1] <http://www.bloomberg.com/news/2013-11-11/armajaro-trading-agrees-to-merge-into-ecom-agroindustrial.html>.

[2] <http://www.bloomberg.com/news/2012-12-12/petra-foods-sells-cocoa-unit-to-barry-callebaut-for-950-million.html>.

[3] <http://www.confectionerynews.com/Commodities/Cargill-closes-in-on-ADM-Cocoa-reports>.

organizational, and managerial competences from one business line to another in a process known as inter-sectoral upgrading in value chain parlance. Important changes in logistics have occurred in the global chain in the last decade due to the introduction of high-volume bulk transportation by chartered ships and the 'flat' storage of beans in warehouses in importing countries. These practices are much more cost-efficient than previous systems of storage and liner transportation of beans in jute bags.

A similar, persistent consolidation process characterizes the other processing segment in the GVC—chocolate manufacturing. Some of the chocolate manufacturers are giant corporations in the global food industry, specializing in branding and marketing a number of different food products, including chocolate (Nestlé, Mondelēz), while others specialize in chocolate-based products and confectionaries (Mars, Hershey, and Ferrero). Most of the latter companies have also some in-house grinding capacity in order to maintain the ability to manufacture intermediate proprietary chocolate products. However, their activities are increasingly concentrated on the design of consumer products and the marketing of global brands. These companies need to be responsive to the shifting whims of the consumer market, which is characterized by the aging of 'traditional' chocolate consumers, increasing health consciousness, and a trend towards functional foods.

Even though some companies have activities spanning both processing segments (for example, Blommer, which still markets minor brands into local markets), the overall picture in the global cocoa–chocolate value chain is the relative absence of vertical integration. Actually, chocolate manufacturers have increasingly outsourced the production of intermediate cocoa ingredients (e.g. Nestlé and Petra), while grinders have sold off the chocolate manufacturing divisions of the companies they have acquired over the years. A relatively new phenomenon, however, is the trend towards backward integration of the dominant grinders into exporting operations, often in the form of direct control if not majority ownership of local exporting companies. In Indonesia, grinders actively engage in up-country purchasing operations, while in West Africa, fewer of the grinders have so far gone into domestic trading operations directly with producers. Here a hierarchy of local traders, some of which are being financed on a more or less daily basis by the grinders, carry out the sourcing activities. The trend among grinders towards integration or stricter control over upstream activities should be seen in relation to growing concerns among both grinders and manufacturers over both bean quality and volume of supplies. Both sets of powerful corporate actors—grinders and chocolate manufacturers—exert an influence over the value chain in what has been described by Fold (2002) as a characteristically bi-polar governance structure, and both have enacted corporate sustainability initiatives in recent years. However, as will be discussed in the section 'A New Public–Private Hybrid Form of Value Chain Governance', we are now observing chocolate manufacturers, whose higher degree of brand sensitivity is driving them to ensure defensive brand management, enforcing greater control throughout the entire chain.

A New Public–Private Hybrid Form of Value Chain Governance

The last few decades have witnessed a wholesale realignment of the institutional settings of the GVC for cocoa, away from state-based institutions towards a complex network of rules, standards, norms, and interventions instituted by various private sector and civil society actors. During the 1970s and 80s, the international cocoa trade was dominated by price regulation, quotas, and the maintenance of buffer stocks by the London-based ICCO, an intergovernmental organization under the auspices of the United Nations Conference on Trade and Development (UNCTAD). This era coincided with an influential role for nation-states in shaping the internal conditions for trade within the producing regions of West Africa. However, as a consequence of liberalization policies and the structural adjustment programmes of international banks, which started in the late 1980s (the economic clauses of the ICCO agreements were removed contemporaneously in 1988), the role of marketing boards and state-licensed companies in Africa was dramatically curtailed (Fold, 2002). While specific practices varied before the reforms, farmers generally sold cocoa at a fixed farm-gate price, which acted as the basis for predetermined margins for each participant in the value chain, ending with state-controlled export companies (which reaped either windfall profits or dramatic losses depending on fluctuations in world market prices). Importantly, liberalization was also associated with the relaxation of state-enforced quality controls in West Africa, thereby prompting a trend among major cocoa buyers during the 1990s towards integration or stricter control over their upstream activities (Fold, 2002, 2004). By 2000, Indonesia had emerged as an important alternative site for global cocoa production: here it was argued that cocoa expansion was actually facilitated through the 'hands-off' approach of the government (Akiyama and Nishio, 1997). Certainly, the state in Indonesia never assumed an interventionist approach to domestic cocoa marketing in the same way as had happened in West Africa, and the far larger and more diversified structure of the Indonesian economy reduced the degree of political dependence on the sector. The 1990s thus marked the first phase of a significant shift in the institutional settings of the value chain for cocoa towards greater deregulation.

Despite its current lack of market intervention, the ICCO has continued to constitute an important forum for intergovernmental discussions of issues related to the industry, and it is a credible source of industry data and statistics, conducting valuable research, and implementing a limited number of support programmes in cocoa-producing countries. The most recent International Cocoa Agreement of the ICCO (signed in 2010) emphasized two important 'breakthroughs': an institutional mandate for the development of a 'sustainable cocoa economy'; and the establishment of a private sector consultative board on the world cocoa economy (UNCTAD, 2011). These developments reflect broader trends in the emergent institutional settings of the value chain towards private sector governance. Furthermore, the founding of the World Cocoa Foundation (WCF) in 2000, quite separate from the ICCO and with headquarters in Washington DC, signalled another stage in this broader institutional shift.

As a membership-based organization representing more than a hundred cocoa and chocolate companies, most of whom are based in developed countries, the WCF has become increasingly active in programme and project delivery in cocoa-producing countries to an extent often surpassing the activities of the ICCO.

The next significant turning point in the evolution of private—and collective—global regulation along the cocoa value chain was the turmoil raised by press reports in 2000 and 2001 about the prevalence of child and slave labour on West African cocoa farms. This led directly to an amendment being passed in the United States Congress to introduce a 'slave-free' chocolate label in the USA, but which did not subsequently get voted on in the senate due to powerful pre-emptive lobbying by the industry. At the time, the industry was represented primarily by the Chocolate Manufacturers Association (CMA, which was subsumed within the National Confectioner's Association in 2008). The CMA instead negotiated a voluntary international agreement, known as the Harkin–Engel Protocol, in which chocolate companies—in partnership with national governments, international NGOs, and labour unions—committed to 'developing industry-wide standards of public certification that cocoa has been grown without any of the worst forms of child labor'. This agreement was globally significant in that it was a watershed in industry self-regulation, and epitomized the new institutional architecture of the value chain, which was fast assuming its currently pronounced public–private hybrid character.

The protocol was organizationally embodied within the International Cocoa Initiative (ICI), established under Swiss Law in 2002. In 2004, field activities to promote responsible cocoa labour practices were launched, initially covering 24 communities in the Ivory Coast and Ghana and tending to focus on the establishment and training of farmer groups, the improvement of cultivation practices, and the dissemination of technology for pest and disease management. These activities were embedded in an existing programme (The Sustainable Tree Crops Program—STCP) managed by the International Institute of Tropical Agriculture (IITA), a UK-based NGO, and appeared to dovetail primarily with broader concerns about supply sustainability and the need to expand production. The activities have now reached more than 800,000 people across 331 cocoa communities (ICI, 2013). A four-and-a-half-year research project, funded by the US Department of Labour to assess progress towards meeting obligations under the protocol found that 'important provisions of the Protocol have not yet been realized', including the key tenet of establishing credible standards of public certification (PCIDTT, 2011: 8).

The Harkin–Engel Protocol requirements appear to have been somewhat superseded by the rapid expansion of third-party certification systems in the sector. Indeed, the Payson Center for International Development and Technology Transfer (2011) suggested that the requirements of existing product certification programmes such as Rainforest Alliance, UTZ Certified, and the Fairtrade Labelling Organizations International (FLO) constitute vehicles through which the industry could meet its commitment to 'credible standards' under the protocol. Based on the volumes published by the certification agencies themselves, 534,614 metric tonnes (MT) of cocoa were UTZ Certified in 2012/13, along with 410,000 MT by

Rainforest Alliance, and 40,559 MT by FLO, which would collectively account for about 25 per cent of the annual crop estimated by the ICCO in 2012/13 (FLO, 2013; Rainforest Alliance, 2013; UTZ Certified, 2013). This is similar to the 20 per cent of global cocoa production estimated to be certified in a recent study commissioned by the International Finance Organization (IFC) (Molenaar et al., 2013). Furthermore, the rate of growth of the production volume covered by these programmes has been remarkable, with each of Rainforest Alliance and UTZ Certified more than doubling the volume certified each year since 2010. While the amount of certified cocoa produced appears to exceed the amount actually bought as such, many of the major manufacturers have announced public commitments to these third-party certification labels in recent years. In 2009, Mars committed to buying 100 per cent certified cocoa by 2020. Ferrero and Hershey followed soon after by becoming the second and third major manufacturers, respectively, to commit to 100 per cent certified cocoa by 2020 (although, by the end of 2013, Hershey had still only certified 10 per cent of its supply chain[4]).

Currently, in 2014, third-party certification programmes for sustainability are expanding at the same time as both chocolate manufacturers and international grinders are developing and implementing their own in-house 'sustainability' programmes in origin countries (Table 11.4). These programmes are not always directly linked to certification schemes, and so are not routinely audited externally. Instead, they frequently involve complex partnerships with local actors, NGOs, research institutes, governments, and development agencies, and appear to reflect an increasing corporate scepticism towards the effectiveness of certification alone to improve farmer welfare and increase agricultural productivity. Indeed, these programmes are increasingly implemented as support programmes for improved farm practices, and the adoption of superior technologies and planting materials, which, it should be noted, are not always embedded within existing certification schemes.

An increasingly accepted narrative within the industry, and indeed embraced by a number of rather sensationalist media reports,[5] is that the world is facing a looming chocolate crisis. There are certainly a number of serious constraints to long-term supply: the cocoa tree is susceptible to an unusually broad range of debilitating pests and disease problems; agricultural production has historically depended on expansion into forested areas that are ultimately finite and cannot be encroached indefinitely; and supply is concentrated in politically volatile West Africa, where cocoa has been used and abused by local governments as an important source of state revenue. New cocoa frontiers are difficult to identify, and the previous reliance on frontier expansion needs to be supplemented by conscious

---

[4] <http://www.confectionerynews.com/Manufacturers/Hershey-10-certified-cocoa-by-2013>.
[5] <http://www.forbes.com/sites/dougbandow/2013/10/14/rising-prices-signal-a-devastating-global-chocolate-crisis-should-government-act-to-save-us/>, <http://www.telegraph.co.uk/finance/commodities/8948444/Cocoa-shortage-leading-to-crisis-for-chocoholics.html>, <http://www.theguardian.com/sustainable-business/fairtrade-partner-zone/chocolate-cocoa-production-risk>, <http://www.independent.co.uk/life-style/food-and-drink/features/chocolate-worth-its-weight-in-gold-2127874.html>.

Table 11.4 In-house sustainability programmes in the cocoa sector

Lead Firm	Value Chain Function	Home Country	Sustainability Programme
Cargill	Grinder	USA	Cocoa Promise
Barry Callebaut	Grinder	Switzerland	Cocoa Horizons
Olam	Grinder	Singapore	Growcocoa programme
Blommer	Grinder	USA	Sustainable Origins
ADM	Grinder	USA	The Cocoa Livelihoods Programme/ Socially and Environmentally Responsible Agriculture Practices (SERAP)
Nestlé	Chocolate manufacturer	Switzerland	Cocoa Plan
Mondelēz	Chocolate manufacturer	USA	Cocoa Life
Hershey	Chocolate manufacturer	USA	Cocoa Link
Mars	Chocolate manufacturer	USA	Sustainable Cocoa Initiative
Ferrero	Chocolate manufacturer	Italy	Commits to Third-Party Certification

Source: Taken from the respective company websites.

efforts to reconquer degraded cocoa areas in order to maintain surplus supply. The rising costs of farm labour and the emergence of alternative livelihood options for farmers in Southeast Asia and Latin America has meant that these regions may not be obvious growth areas in the future. However, in a relatively free and open world market, supply shortages would presumably trigger price increases globally that would, at some point, increase the attractiveness of cocoa farming and thereby stimulate production increases. In this respect, it is indicative that cocoa prices have been elevated since 2006, and reached a 24-year high in the autumn of 2009 after 4 consecutive years where demand outstripped supply. Perhaps the supply crisis is a crisis of inexpensive cocoa for the major manufacturers as much as it is an absolute crisis in production. Either way, however, it is clearly prompting action on the ground in producing countries, and, for some corporate actors, Indonesia is viewed as a strategically important future source of supply.

In Indonesia, corporate-led sustainability programmes have resulted in the establishment of the Cocoa Sustainability Partnership (CSP), a membership-based organization that works cooperatively on common research priorities and in developing effective approaches towards agricultural extension. Lead firms in the sector, such as Mars, have strongly supported the CSP and also developed an extensive farm-level network, Cocoa Development Centres and Cocoa Village Clinics (Neilson and McKenzie, in press). Mondelēz has announced a new partnership with the Indonesian Coffee and Cocoa Research Institute (ICCRI), to work through suppliers such as Armajaro and Olam to 'promote sustainable Indonesian cocoa farming, improve cocoa bean quality and support the development of thriving Indonesian cocoa communities'.[6] Nestlé is similarly supporting cocoa farmers in West Sulawesi through the PISAgro Indonesian Sustainable Agriculture Partnership, through what they present as a 'new vision for world agriculture'

---

[6] <http://ir.mondelezinternational.com/releasedetail.cfm?releaseid=793508>.

based on greater corporate involvement in farm communities.[7] We should be clear that this does not reflect a global land grab in the cocoa sector, as the multinationals are content to encourage and facilitate the competitive advantage of cocoa smallholdings. However, it does suggest the development of a globally coordinated corporate provision of agricultural extension that is largely unprecedented. In the Indonesian case, this is emerging in a context whereby the state (usually considered an important provider of agricultural extension as a public good) lacks the capacity and willingness to provide technical support to cocoa farmers. Interestingly, the Indonesian state has shown a recent willingness to intervene in the sector to either promote resource-based industrialization (through the 2010 export tax), through a recently mandated system of regulated domestic trade (Permentan, 2014) or through the largely unsuccessful attempt to rejuvenate cocoa production through the highly political National Cocoa Movement (GERNAS) programme. This programme was mired in bureaucratic ineptness and may have actually had negative impacts on production levels through the distribution of substandard planting material (Gusli et al., 2012).

The institutional creativity of various industry stakeholders (including NGOs, states, and development agencies) in the cocoa–chocolate industry, apparently orchestrated by the dominant companies in the value chain, is a remarkable feature and represents a salient example of a new form of global private governance. A key issue for future research on global private (and hybrid) regulation in the global cocoa–chocolate value chain is to understand the nature, role, and relative strength of the NGOs and other development actors that are involved. The variations among NGOs are extremely wide and increasingly include spin-offs of trade associations and networks of business interests in addition to the traditional humanitarian and religious organizations. More knowledge on the constituencies, strategies, and influence of participating NGOs is warranted by the fact that they seem to be crucial for the establishment of links between global industry actors and development agencies. Another feature of many of the sustainability programmes presented in Table 11.4 is their tendency to evolve into 'partnerships' (Bitzer et al., 2012), which, in the process, frequently enables the mobilization of financial support from international development agencies. Partnerships between development agencies and the private sector are increasingly framed as value chains for development, whereby enabling smallholder integration with lead firms offers opportunities for upgrading and livelihood improvements (Neilson, 2014). Such partnerships do appear to offer genuine opportunities for livelihood improvements at the farm level through facilitating knowledge transfer, credit facilitation, and improved market prices (for an overview on possible developmental outcomes of these approaches, refer to reviews by Henriksen et al., 2010, and Humphrey and Navas-Alemán, 2010). However, these partnerships also respond directly to the growing supply chain concerns of chocolate manufacturers and their long-term corporate profitability. Industry-wide concerns over cocoa supply

---

[7] <http://pisagro.org/about/>.

appear to have reinforced what would otherwise be the inexplicably high degree of cooperation between lead firms that are otherwise engaged in cut-throat competition for market share (see, for example, Brenner, 1999). Indeed, the industry has a history of effective cooperation on issues of mutual interest, such as nutritional issues, cocoa butter substitutes, and labour abuses.

Conclusions

Recent developments in the cocoa–chocolate GVC indicate the emergence of a new set of institutional settings and governance regimes that embody an amalgam of traditional state-led regulatory functions interwoven with an increasingly dominant collection of lead firms exerting influence over smallholder production systems at the farm level. The processing industry has a common interest in maintaining a growing and continuous flow of inexpensive cocoa beans from the producer countries. Large contract manufacturers of cocoa-based ingredients and the branded manufacturers of chocolate products therefore have increasingly been involved in the organization of cocoa production on a world scale. The mechanisms for this mode of governance include various certification schemes, corporate sustainability programmes, the ICI, and the WCF. While presenting, on the one hand, increased investment in productivity improvements and farmer livelihoods that could improve the lives of cocoa-growing communities, global private regulation of these rural spaces also carries with it significant risks. Corporate interests will not always align with the interests of these rural communities, and dependence on lead firms for technology development and social facilities exposes these communities to higher risks should a new cocoa frontier be created and lead firms decide to focus their sourcing operation elsewhere.

The fundamental structural changes and supply barriers in the global cocoa–chocolate chain inform the nature of new forms of emergent private regulation. Despite being incorporated in rhetoric full of development buzzwords such as 'sustainability' and 'triple bottom-line accounting', and 'shared prosperity', the new initiatives are more than mere image cultivation. Maintenance of smallholder involvement is absolutely vital in order to secure stable and abundant supplies of inexpensive cocoa for the global industry. Therefore, we seem to be witnessing remarkable cooperation amongst the major cocoa companies and business associations in order to 'fill up what has been hollowed out', that is, to revive cocoa production among smallholders in (over)mature cocoa areas in West Africa and Indonesia. The organizational structure is still somewhat opaque and best conceptualized as being in a nascent phase.

The private regulation of the global cocoa–chocolate value chain has to be considered within the context of the ongoing erosion of two forms of public regulation. Firstly, various types of state regulation—mostly in the form of marketing boards in West Africa—have been dismantled as part of Structural Adjustment Programmes (SAPs). Irrespective of the lack of efficiency within many such agencies, former task and functions such as extension services, input supplies, pest and disease management, and quality control have now disappeared, and only a few private companies have replaced the state institutions. In Indonesia, agricultural extension services, particularly for 'estate crops' such as cocoa, have been dismantled in the midst of bureaucratic restructuring and political decentralization, and are assuming a much lower priority to broader strategic support for industrialization. Secondly, global public regulative institutions are also declining in importance. On the international scale, the Seventh International Cocoa Agreement was agreed upon in 2010 by a number of cocoa exporting and importing countries. Compared to previous international agreements, this new agreement explicitly recognized the growing importance of private sector governance in the sector through sustainability initiatives and the consultative board. The influence of corporate motivations is also apparent in the ICCO's Abidjan Cocoa Declaration, signed by member countries, which requires members to prepare national development plans, based on local public–private partnerships that work towards the 'sustainability of production'(ICCO, 2014b).[8]

Whereas the quality issue somehow divided the big companies in the industry, a major common concern is the prospect of a supply shortage in the medium term. No new comprehensive cocoa frontiers are immediately evident and mature cocoa areas are threatened by the aging of farmers, plant diseases, and civil strife. Hence, the global industry is being challenged to organize a concerted effort in order to consolidate and possibly increase production from existing cocoa areas. The materialization of these efforts was triggered by a growing awareness among consumers, NGOs, and politicians about working conditions—particularly 'the worst forms' of child labour. The combined effect of these ethical and commercial concerns has been the gradual evolution of a new set of private regulatory mechanisms and institutional development with a potential for global implementation. These mechanisms address both working conditions and productivity improvement by the establishment of community-based training and awareness-raising campaigns, are mediated by a network of northern and local NGOs and are funded by both public donors and some of the big global players in the industry. State institutions are on the sidelines, relegated to carry out periodic review exercises on the progress in working conditions and welfare improvements of the involved communities—the results of which are being monitored and certified by northern NGOs. Or, in some cases, the state is being actively enrolled by the cocoa industry in an attempt to improve supply (e.g. Indonesia's GERNAS programme).

Looking ahead, the crucial question appears to be how this shift from public to private governance will affect smallholder cocoa farmers, at the community, household, and individual level. So far, these new institutional forms have only been tested in a limited number of pilot communities. However, the second phase, in which the number of communities and households is set to increase

---

[8] And, somewhat paradoxically it could be argued, to promote sustainable consumption, defined as 'promoting cocoa consumption in traditional/mature markets and in emerging markets, as well as in origin (producer) countries'.

substantially, has recently started. As the new regulatory set-up is still in its inception phase it is too early for definite conclusions, but some preliminary reflections on the socio-political consequences are appropriate (see also Fold 2008).Whether the new forms of private regulation result in improved livelihoods for the farming households they incorporate in isolated 'privileged spaces' is an open question that has to be examined in concrete cases. Better availability of services must be juxtaposed with potential social differentiation due to differences in the ability to cope with intensified commoditization, which could be linked to the dispossession of indigenous communities of their land and increasing proletarianization (Li, 2002). Similarly, households and communities, outside these privileged spaces of corporate value chain engagement, would be effectively excluded from the cocoa–chocolate GVC, and so would be dependent on ordinary public service provisions. The increasing dependence on lead firms for the provisioning of social services, including in some cases health and education, could exacerbate local inequalities and create pockets of impoverishment if the capacity of state provision is significantly weakened as a result of these processes. Global private governance and the mobilization of state and development resources towards supply security regulation, rather than social service provision, could result in new patterns of uneven rural development across the developing world.

References

Akiyama, T. and A. Nishio. 1997. 'Sulawesi's cocoa boom: lessons of smallholder dynamism and a hands-off policy'. *Bulletin of Indonesian Economic Studies* 33 (2): pp. 97–121.

Bair, J. and G. Gereffi. 2001. 'Local clusters in global chains: the causes and consequences of export dynamism in Torreon's blue jeans industry'. *World Development* 29 (11): pp. 1885–903.

Bitzer, V., P. Glasbergen, and P. Leroy. 2012. 'Partnerships of a feather flock together? An analysis of the emergence of networks of partnerships in the global cocoa sector'. *Global Networks* 12 (3): pp. 355–74.

Brenner, J.G. 1999. *The Emperors of Chocolate: Inside the Secret World of Hershey and Mars*. New York: Broadway Books.

Euromonitor. 2012. *Cocoa Ingredients: Difficult Times for these Prized Ingredients*, Euromonitor, London.

FLO (Fairtrade International Organization). 2013. *Unlocking the Power Annual Report 2012–13*, Fairtrade International. Available at: http://www.fairtrade.net/fileadmin/user_upload/content/2009/resources/2012-13_AnnualReport_FairtradeIntl_web.pdf (accessed 6 July 2015).

Fold, N. 2002. 'Lead firms and competition in "bi-polar" commodity chains: grinders and branders in the global cocoa–chocolate industry'. *Journal of Agrarian Change* 2 (2): pp. 228–47.

Fold, N. 2004. 'Spilling the beans on a tough nut: liberalization and local supply system changes in Ghana's cocoa and shea chains'. In *Geographies of Commodity Chains*, edited by A. Hughes and S. Reimer, London: Routledge: pp. 63–80.

Fold, N. 2008. 'Transnational sourcing practices in Ghana's perennial crop sectors'. *Journal of Agrarian Change* 8 (1): pp. 94–122.

Gereffi, G. 1994. 'The organization of buyer-driven global commodity chains: how U.S. retailers shape overseas production networks'. In *Commodity Chains and Global Capitalism*, edited by G. Gereffi and M. Korzeniewicz, London: Praeger: pp. 95–122.

Gereffi, G. 1995. 'Global production systems and third world development'. In *Global Change, Regional Response: The New International Context of Development*, edited by B. Stallings, Cambridge: Cambridge University Press: pp. 100–42.

Gereffi, G. 1999. 'International trade and industrial upgrading in the apparel commodity chain.' *Journal of International Economics* 48: pp. 37–70.

Gusli, S., Samsuar, Useng, D., Darmawan, and L. Sarisi. 2012. *Field Performance of Cocoa Trees produced by Somatic Embryogenesis, Sulawesi*. Makassar: Pusat Penelitian dan Sumberdaya Alam Universitaas Hasanuddin.

Henriksen, L. F., L. Riisgaard, S. Ponte, F. Hartwich, and P. Kormawa. 2010. *Agrofood Value Chain Interventions in Asia: A Review and Analysis of Case Studies*. Vienna: UNIDO.

Humphrey, J. and L. Navas-Alemán. 2010. 'Value chains, donor interventions and poverty reduction: a review of donor practice', IDS Research Report 63, Sussex: Institute for Development Studies.

IbisWorld. 2014. *Global Candy and Chocolate Manufacturing: Market Research Report*. Available at: <http://www.ibisworld.com/industry/global/global-candy-chocolate-manufacturing.html> (accessed 23 January 2014).

ICCO (International Cocoa Organization). 2013. *Quarterly Bulletin of Cocoa Statistics. Volume XXXIX No. 4. Cocoa Year 2012/13*. London: International Cocoa Organization.

ICCO (International Cocoa Organization). 2014b. *The Abidjan Cocoa Declaration is a Legally Nonbinding Expression of Support for the World Cocoa Conference 2012*, Abidjan, 23 November 2012, London: International Cocoa Organization. Available at: <http://www.icco.org/about-us/international-cocoa-agreements/cat_view/57-world-cocoa-conference-2012-abidjan.html> (accessed 11 April 2014).

ICI (International Cocoa Initiative). 2013. *International Cocoa Initiative Annual Report 2012*. Geneva: International Cocoa Initiative. Available at: <http://issuu.com/cocoainitiative/docs/ici-2012-annual-report-issuu> (accessed 6 July 2015).

Li, T. M. 2002. 'Local histories, global markets: cocoa and class in upland Sulawesi'. *Development and Change*, 33 (3): pp. 415–37.

Molenaar, J. W., J. J. Kessler, M. El Fassi, J. Dallinger, E. Blackmore, B. Vorley, J. Gorter, L. Simons, S. Buchel, B. Vollaard, and L. Heilbron. 2013. *Building a Roadmap to Sustainability in Agro-Commodity Production*, Commissioned by the International Finance Organization (IFC). Available at: <http://www.aidenvironment.org/publications> (accessed 26 March 2014).

Neilson, J. 2014. 'Value chains, neoliberalism and development practice: the Indonesian experience'. *Review of International Political Economy* 21 (1): pp. 38–69.

Neilson, J. and F. McKenzie. In press. 'Sustainable solutions in the Indonesian cocoa sector: farmer-driven innovation and business-oriented outreach programs'. In *Innovations in Linking Sustainable Agricultural Practices with Markets*, Rome: Food and Agricultural Organization of the United Nations.

Neilson, J. and B. Pritchard. 2009. *Value Chain Struggles: Institutions and Governance in the Plantation Districts of South India*. Oxford: Blackwell.

Neilson, J., K. Fauziah, and A. Meekin. 2014. 'Effects of an export tax on the farm-gate price of Indonesian cocoa beans'. In *Proceedings of the Malaysian International Cocoa Conference, 7–8 October 2013*, Kota Kinabalu: Malaysian Cocoa Board: pp. 295–300.

PCIDTT (Payson Center for International Development and Technology Transfer). 2011. *Oversight of Public and Private Initiatives to Eliminate the Worst Forms of Child Labor in the*

Cocoa Sector in Côte d'Ivoire and Ghana, 31 March, Payson Center for International Development and Technology Transfer, Tulane University. Available at: <http://www.childlabor-payson.org> (accessed 26 March 2014).

Permentan. 2014. *Minister of Agriculture Regulation No. 67/Permentan/OT.140/5/2014 of the Republic of Indonesia on Quality and Marketing Requirements for Cocoa Beans.* Jakarta: Ministry of Agriculture of the Republic of Indonesia.

Rainforest Alliance. 2013. *Rainforest Alliance Annual Report, Special Focus: Climate Change.* Available at: <http://www.rainforest-alliance.org> (accessed 26 March 2014).

Reuters. 2014. Indonesia's cocoa grinding capacity to soar as output lags—industry groups, Jakarta, 3 April. Available at http://af.reuters.com/article/commoditiesNews/idAFL4N0MV2IT20140403 (accessed 6 July 2015).

Ruf, F. 1995. 'From "forest rent" to "tree capital": basic "laws" of cocoa supply'. In *Cocoa Cycles: The Economics of Cocoa Supply*, edited by F. Ruf and P. S. Siswoputranto, Cambridge: Woodhead: pp. 1–53.

UNCTAD (United Nations Conference on Trade and Development). 2011. International Cocoa Agreement, 2010, TD/COCOA.10/5. Geneva: UNCTAD.

UTZ Certified. 2013. *10 Years in Coffee, Cocoa and Tea: From Good to Better*, UTZ Certified Annual Report 2012. Available at: <http://www.utzcertified.org> (accessed 26 March 2014).

12

Beyond Fair Trade

Why are Mainstream Chocolate Companies Pursuing Social and Economic Sustainability in Cocoa Sourcing?

Stephanie Barrientos

Introduction

Fairtrade began to expand within the mainstream of chocolate retailing in the UK in the 2000s, when supermarkets began selling 'own brand' Fairtrade chocolate.[1] However, a number of large chocolate confectionary companies are now looking beyond Fairtrade, and adopting wider strategies to promote social and economic sustainability in their cocoa–chocolate value chains. Brands including Cadbury/Mondelēz, Nestlé, and Mars, as well as some cocoa processors, have established initiatives to support cocoa farmers and their communities in cocoa-producing countries. In addition, many companies are adopting certification, including Fairtrade, Rainforest Alliance and/or UTZ, for some of their main product ranges. The Netherlands and Germany have made serious commitments to expanding the future sale of certified cocoa. This chapter examines to what extent these moves are driven by deep commercial concerns over the future social and economic sustainability of cocoa sourcing within a changing cocoa–chocolate value chain?

Consumer concern over the livelihoods of cocoa farmers and their communities has long been stimulated by civil society campaigns and advocacy, leading to the expansion of initiatives such as Fairtrade in Europe and North America. Cocoa demand has recently been fuelled by rapid growth, albeit from a low base, in chocolate consumption in the global South, especially Asia. Challenges to cocoa supply has arisen in a context of an increasingly concentrated chocolate–cocoa

---

[1] An earlier version of this chapter was presented to the International Fairtrade Symposium, Liverpool Hope University (April 2012).

value chain, combined with a fragmented production base, that saw a secular decline in price during the 1990s and low levels of productivity or investment. The majority of cocoa farmers are smallholders who endure high levels of poverty and poor social infrastructure, and many younger farmers are leaving the sector in search of alternative occupations. The result has been a threat to the future resilience of cocoa supply. Company concern over the socioeconomic sustainability in their value chains was heightened in 2011 by a prediction by the cocoa trading company Armajaro that demand for cocoa is likely to outstrip supply by 2020 if no action is taken. Companies have themselves had to step into the role of addressing socioeconomic sustainability within their cocoa value chains with the rise of numerous initiatives since the late 2000s. Whether these are sufficient to address deeply embedded social issues within cocoa-producing countries is questionable. As an experienced agricultural development analyst commented: 'Companies are now running around Africa like NGOs, but they don't really know what to do' (personal communication).

This chapter draws mainly on research carried out on the sourcing of cocoa by Cadbury from Ghana. This research threw light on the fragility of a value chain where cocoa productivity is low and younger farmers are leaving cocoa farming to pursue their aspirations elsewhere, undermining the future socioeconomic sustainability of cocoa production. It also draws on complementary research in the Dominican Republic and India, as well as stakeholder interviews with industry and civil society personnel, held between 2010 and 2012.[2] The chapter explores the role of Cadbury's Cocoa Partnership (subsequently Cocoa Life) in developing community-level initiatives to address issues facing cocoa farmers. It considers this as part of a broader array of strategies (including certification) which many companies, trade bodies, multilateral organizations, and civil society actors are now pursuing in order to support the future of cocoa production.

The chapter is organized as follows: the next section, 'Changing Global Context of Cocoa–Chocolate Sourcing', examines the changing profile of the cocoa–chocolate sector over recent decades in relation to producers, the cocoa–chocolate value chain, and consumers. This provides the context in which the risks to supply resilience has arisen. Then, the chapter examines how the issue of social and economic sustainability has emerged as the cocoa–chocolate sector has been transformed. It looks at how civil society campaigns around poor socioeconomic conditions of producers, including child labour, have drawn companies out of their 'commercial box' to collaborate in addressing social issues at the core of cocoa

[2] This chapter is based on independent research carried out between 2005 and 2011, funded by Cadbury, on the social and economic sustainability of cocoa production in Ghana and India. In this chapter I do not go into the specific research methodology and findings of those studies which are published elsewhere (see Barrientos and Asenso-Okyere et al. 2008 and Berlan, Singh and Barrientos 2013). Here, I examine the wider implications of the research in terms of corporate engagement in the social and economic sustainability of cocoa production. I am grateful to my research collaborators in the UK, Ghana, and India for their important contributions to the country studies. I take sole responsibility for the analysis presented in this chapter. The views presented here in no way represent those of Cadbury/Kraft (or Mondelēz), whose funding was for independent research studies to be made publicly available.

sourcing. It considers responses by mainstream chocolate companies involving: (1) sustainability initiatives with different civil society and governments and (2) certification initiatives including Fairtrade, Rainforest Alliance, and UTZ. The concluding remarks asks whether more structural shifts are needed, both within value chains, but also through wider rethinking of development strategies in a global commercial context.

Changing Global Context of Cocoa–Chocolate Sourcing

It is important to situate current challenges facing cocoa production in the context of significant changes in the global cocoa and chocolate sectors over the past 20 years. This has involved the cocoa sector, which is predominantly characterized by small-scale family farming at the production level, shifting from state-led export models to 'bi-polar' global value chains as the channels through which cocoa is sold internationally. In this section we examine this shift, with a particular focus on Ghana, which has been both affected by, and, to some extent, bucked, this trend. It is argued that the processes undergone in the cocoa–chocolate value chain have led to disjuncture between a concentrated chocolate market and a fragmented cocoa producer base. This provides an underpinning to the current challenges facing cocoa production and concern by mainstream companies with regard to the socioeconomic sustainability of cocoa sourcing.

Cocoa farming is largely carried out by small-scale producers, who are responsible for an estimated 90 per cent of world production (WCF 2012). The majority of cocoa sourcing is from West Africa, with Cote d'Ivoire and Ghana responsible for 60 per cent of global exports as the first and second largest exporters respectively (ICCO 2012). West African cocoa production is characterized by small-scale family-based cocoa farming (1 to 2 hectares or even less being common), with over 2 million estimated small-scale cocoa producers. New supplier countries have expanded production, particularly in Asia, increasing the supply of cocoa to the world market.

From the 1950s to 1980s, the predominant model of support for cocoa farmers was through state-dominated export marketing boards or caisses (Daviron and Gibbon 2002; Fold 2002; Losch 2002). The marketing boards used to set farmer prices had monopoly control over cocoa purchases, provided the sole export channel, and were responsible for overseeing exports. The international cocoa market was largely characterized by arm's-length trading through commodity markets (London and New York), either through spot or forward contracts. Whilst there were many problems with marketing boards, they provided an important pillar of support to small-scale producers and ensured the quality of the cocoa exported.

During the 1980s, this system was transformed through agricultural liberalization and dismantling of the marketing boards in most producing countries under the structural adjustment programmes pursued by the International Monetary Fund (IMF) and the World Bank. Ghana was the only large cocoa producer to resist this process. It partially liberalized the sector through the introduction of private buyers at a local level who had to be registered as licensed buying companies (LBCs). But it kept its cocoa marketing board COCOBOD, which oversaw the LBCs, set the minimum producer price to be paid for cocoa each year, and continued to act as the sole export channel, ensuring the quality of cocoa exported. The outcome of the strategy of liberalization in most countries was to expose small-scale producers directly to the international market, and even in Ghana COCOBOD could only provide a partial buffer against the vagaries of price volatility and global trends (Barrientos, et al. 2008; Barrientos and Asenso-Okyere 2009; Hütz-Adams and Fountain 2012).

With the demise of marketing boards farmer prices in most countries have been set by international markets. The period after the mid-1980s, saw a downward trend in world prices, reaching a trough in the late 1990s. Although there was a partial recovery after 2000/01, in real terms average world market prices for cocoa were 13 per cent lower in 2005/06 than in 1993/94 (ICCO 2007a). Cocoa prices overall have risen since the mid-2000s, but prices have been volatile year on year with changes in market conditions (Hütz-Adams and Fountain 2012; ICCO 2012). In Ghana, COCOBOD partially protects farmers from annual seasonal price volatility, and ensures a price higher than the prevailing international average as a result of a premium paid for the quality of Ghanaian beans. But prices have still been subject to annual variations and international trends.

But despite recent price rises, the sector faces significant challenges in generating sufficient growth in the supply of cocoa in face of rising demand. Since liberalization, many countries have experienced a decline of quality (due to poor agricultural practices and producers short-cutting drying and fermentation) and low productivity in small-scale farming. Two explanations have been put forward for the decline in prices during the 1985–2005 period: (1) oversupply fuelled by liberalization and the entry of new producing countries (particularly in Asia); (2) increasing concentration of ownership and control at the downstream end of the chain counterposed with decreasing concentration and increased liberalization at the upstream growing end. We will now examine the latter as the other dimension of the changing profile of the cocoa–chocolate value chain.

Changing Global Cocoa–Chocolate Value Chain

There has been significant restructuring of the cocoa–chocolate value chain since the early 1980s. Global value chain analysis helps to track the linkages between commercial actors and firms at every segment of the chain, where lead firms play a key role in coordinating and governing supply (Kaplinsky and Morris 2002). Concentration in the cocoa–chocolate value chain has taken place both amongst the large cocoa processors as well as amongst chocolate manufacturers. As a result, the chain is described as encompassing a bi-polar governance structure because of the dual governance roles of dominant processor and manufacturer companies (Fold 2002, 2005). Here we will briefly examine value chain restructuring as a context for assessing emerging socioeconomic challenges faced in relation to cocoa sourcing from a fragmented farmer base.

Following liberalization, the number of specialized cocoa traders involved in trading on forward and spot markets declined rapidly, and, simultaneously, consolidation took place in the cocoa-processing industry (Barrientos, et al. 2008; Oxfam 2009). Processors (otherwise known as grinders) increased their upstream integration in many cocoa-producing countries, particularly where liberalization had opened up entry through the abolition of state marketing boards. At the same time there has been a trend among manufacturers to increase the outsourcing of processing to specialized processors (Fold 2002, 2005). Consolidation in the cocoa-processing industry led to three companies, Archer Daniels Midland (ADM), Cargill, and Barry Callebaut, holding over 40 per cent of market share (UNCTAD 2008). Developments in value chain logistics (bulk transportation, information technology, and communications), allowed companies to reduce the size of cocoa stock they held, and buy more directly from farmers (Kaplinsky 2004; ICCO 2012).

Concentration also occurred on the manufacturing side of the industry. By 2005, the top ten manufactures accounted for 43 per cent of world sales of chocolate confectionary (ICCO 2007b). It was estimated that six companies controlled 57.4 per cent of the world chocolate–confectionery market by 2008 (Oxfam 2009). Since then, industry concentration has continued, including the 2010 acquisition of Cadbury by Kraft Foods (later restructured to come under Mondelēz International). As shown in Table 12.1, in 2013 Mars was the largest global confectionary company by net sales, followed by Mondelēz and Nestlé.

The combination of fragmentation of cocoa producers and concentration amongst processors and manufacturers has contributed to shifts in value capture along the cocoa–chocolate value chain. Increases in consumer prices have not been passed onto producers, and the share of final chocolate price going to producers has declined (Morisset 1998; Kaplinsky 2004). The World Bank (2008) estimates that developing country claims on value added in the cocoa sector declined from around 60 per cent in 1970–72 to around 28 per cent in 1998–2000 (World Bank 2008). Data for the breakdown of value between commercial actors across the total cocoa–chocolate value chain is difficult to obtain. One estimate puts the indicative cocoa producer share of the cost of a bar of milk chocolate at 4 per cent, with other ingredients accounting for 6 per cent (Gilbert 2007). This is compared to the processor/manufacturer share of 51 per cent,

Table 12.1 Top five confectionary companies by net sales 2013

Company	Net Sales 2013 (US$ millions)
Mars Inc. (USA)	17,640
Mondelēz International (USA)	14,862
Nestlé SA (Switzerland)	11,760
Meiji Holdings Co. Ltd (Japan)	11,742*
Ferrero Group (Italy)	10,900

Source: Candy Industry, January 2014, cited by ICCO. Available at <http://www.icco.org/about-cocoa/chocolate-industry.html> (accessed April 2014).

Note: *Including production of non-confectionary items.

advertising 6.5 per cent, and retail share of 28 per cent, with transport and shipping costs accounting for the difference. Oxfam (2009) estimate that the share of cocoa in the final price of an average bar of chocolate is approximately 3.5 per cent to 6.5 per cent depending on the cocoa content (Oxfam 2009).

At the same time as restructuring within the cocoa–chocolate value chain, important changes have been taking place at the consumer end. Consumption of chocolate is traditionally highest in developed countries with high consumer incomes. It is estimated that chocolate consumption grew by 1.2 per cent annual average between 2002 and 2010 in the 19 developed countries for which data is available (ICCO 2012). However, the largest growth in chocolate consumption is currently coming from the rapid expansion of emerging markets in the global South. Much of this growth is being generated by countries in Africa, the Middle East, Latin America, and particularly in China and India, albeit from a low base. Data for these countries is more difficult to obtain, but, as an example, whilst India has a low per capita consumption of chocolate of 300 grams per capita, its estimated growth in consumption is forecast at 8–10 per cent per annum over the coming years (Datamonitor 2007; Berlan, Singh, and Barrientos 2013). It is predicted that, overall, the Asian market will account for 20 per cent of the market share by 2016 (ICCO 2012). Reasons for this growth include rising incomes, changing consumer trends, and the expansion of cool chain distribution networks able to keep chocolate at a low temperature. Whilst consumers in the South are not necessarily as quality sensitive as the North, this could change as social networking exposes them to global consumer trends.

The profile of consumer markets have also been rapidly changing and are now more differentiated. Whilst many consumers focus on low price, there is growing sensitivity to factors such as chocolate quality as well as social and environmental processes of production for which some are prepared to pay a premium. Three market segments are emerging: (1) high-volume low-value bulk chocolate; (2) mainstream quality chocolate; and (3) high-quality 'niche' chocolate (including single origin, fine flavour, Fairtrade, sustainability certified, and organic). Growth in the high-quality niche end of the market has been high in the global North, albeit from a low base. In the UK it was driven from the early 2000s by Fairtrade certification of supermarket own-brand chocolate (Barrientos and Smith 2007). There was a tenfold growth in UK retail sales of Fairtrade chocolate–confectionery from £32 million in 2008 to £343 million in 2010, when chocolate manufacturers introduced Fairtrade certification (Fairtrade 2011). Manufacturers and processors within the cocoa–chocolate value chain are having to be increasingly responsive to trends in this differentiated consumer market.

Rising Concern over the Socioeconomic Sustainability of Cocoa

Growing consumer awareness of the social origins of chocolate has increased pressure on chocolate manufacturers to address issues of the socioeconomic sustainability of their value chains—particularly at farmer level. Different factors have contributed to these pressures. An early trigger was media exposure in 2000 of the use of child labour (including the worst forms of child labour and trafficking of children) in cocoa farming,[3] particularly in West Africa.[4] There are debates over the causes of child labour in family-based farming, which have traditionally drawn all family members into production. Civil society organizations highlight poverty driven by low producer prices at farm level, rising labour costs, and lack of educational facilities due to constraints on state spending as factors compounding this issue (Anti-Slavery 2004).

Media exposure of the use of child labour in West African cocoa prompted the Harkin–Engel Protocol in the USA (Tulane 2007, 2009, 2011). This was introduced with the threat of legislation to force the labelling of bars of chocolate in the USA as being slave-free. The chocolate industry has since engaged in significant initiatives to address the issue. These include the International Cocoa Initiative (ICI), which provides the basis for cooperation between key companies in the global chocolate industry, concerned politicians, and key civil society actors engaged in combating the worst forms of child labour and forced labour in the growing and processing of cocoa (see <http://www.cocoainitiative.org>). Other industry bodies, such as the World Cocoa Foundation (WCF), have also pursued social strategies in the cocoa sector in order to address child labour. Within Ghana, the Ministry of Manpower, Youth and Employment developed a National Plan for the Elimination of Child Labour and played a key role setting up a collaborative programme with COCOBOD and the chocolate industry addressing labour issues. In 2010 the chocolate industry, together with government officials in the USA, Cote d'Ivoire, and Ghana issued a Joint Declaration and Framework of Actions to implement the Harkin–Engel Protocol, which aimed to reduce the worst forms of child labour by 70 per cent by 2020 (Hütz-Adams and Fountain 2012). An important outcome of these initiatives has been increasing engagement by companies in issues at the base of their value chains, and realization that issues of social development, however remote, can affect them commercially. But many chocolate companies further realized that the root causes were deeply embedded, with serious implications for the future of cocoa sourcing.

In sum, the process of liberalization in the cocoa sector did not lead to the predominance of a 'free' market across the whole cocoa–chocolate value chain. At production level, liberalization and dismantling of marketing boards exposed small-scale farmers directly to a more open global market. Cocoa producers faced a long-term decline in price accompanied by falling productivity and quality. But at an international level, the cocoa–chocolate sector went through a significant process of restructuring, with a decline in international traders and increasing concentration amongst cocoa processors and chocolate manufacturers. This meant fragmented small-scale farmers operating in a quasi 'free market' faced a

---

[3] The definition of child labour is derived from the United Nations Convention on the Rights of the Child and ILO Conventions 138 and 182 (see Berlan 2009).

[4] These issues have received considerable coverage in the TV and the print media in the UK and the USA since 2000 (see Berlan 2009 for a review of some of this coverage). Media exposés of child labour and trafficked labour have continued with a BBC Panorama Programme in the UK highlighting it again in 2010.

more oligopolistic group of processing and manufacturing companies operating in a bi-polar chocolate value chain. However, consumer markets have become more differentiated, with consumers in the growing quality segments increasingly aware of the socioeconomic origins of the chocolate they buy.

This led to a disjuncture between declining productivity and quality of cocoa production combined with rising demand for quality chocolate. The combination of rising demand, alongside challenges facing cocoa producers, led to increasing concerns as to whether the growth of supply would be sufficient to meet growing consumer demand. This concern intensified in 2011 when Armajaro, a major cocoa trader, estimated that, according to current trends, cocoa demand would outstrip supply with a deficit of approximately 0.8 million tons by 2020 (Armajaro 2011; Fairtrade 2011; LMC 2011).[5] This projection, whilst possibly overpessimistic, sent shock waves through the cocoa-processing and chocolate confectionary industries.

Strategies to Promote Social Sustainability and Fairtrade Cocoa

One of the first companies to address deeper concerns over the socioeconomic sustainability of cocoa sourcing was Cadbury (now under Mondelēz International). Cadbury has sourced cocoa from Ghana for over 100 years. It has a long-standing commercial relationship with the country and, reflecting its Quaker origins, has long provided social support through philanthropic and corporate social responsibility activities. The company thus had a strong interest in ensuring the future sustainability of supply (Croft and Cole 2011).

Cadbury is positioned within the mainstream-quality chocolate segment of the consumer market for chocolate confectionary. It differentiates itself from other mainstream brands through the specific flavour and quality of its chocolate. Cadbury buys nearly two thirds of its total cocoa from Ghana, which is used in all of its UK products.[6] Ghanaian cocoa has a quality premium over other supply sources, so thus provides an essential cocoa source for maintaining the quality of Cadbury products (Barrientos et al. 2008). Cadbury commissioned research on the socioeconomic sustainability of the cocoa value chain in Ghana in 2005.[7] An important aspect of the study was to examine both the commercial and social aspects of production in order to assess the prospects for the future of cocoa farming and communities (Croft and Cole 2011).

---

[5] A more nuanced but still pessimistic analysis of trends in cocoa supply and demand was provided to the World Cocoa Foundation by LMC International (LMC 2011). A less pessimistic view was expressed by the ICCO (2012).

[6] *Financial Times*, 10 March 2009.

[7] For the full report see: Barrientos, et al. (2008). Cadbury took the view from the outset that the research should be independent and made publically available because: (1) the issues were of concern to the whole chocolate confectionary industry and (2) a single company, even as large as Cadbury, was unable to address the issues alone. As independent research, the views presented here are those of the author, and do not represent the views of Cadbury, Kraft, or Mondelēz.

The cocoa sector in Ghana has an estimated 720,000 farmers and is characterized by small-scale family farming. The Cadbury study found that levels of productivity on cocoa farms was 40 per cent of potential output and productivity was lower amongst older farmers (the average age of farmers was 51 years). With little scope for expansion on virgin lands, future supply depended on raising productivity in the sector.[8] Although COCOBOD and the Ministry of Agriculture had invested in programmes to enhance production, the study found many challenges. These included low incomes, often below the poverty line, poor access to farm-level services, and lack of farmer information or awareness. Hazardous work, and some child labour, remained a problem on poor family farms which were unable to afford rising labour costs.[9] There was a lack of social services (including education and health) as well as infrastructure (including water, electricity, transport, and access to finance) in the cocoa regions. An important finding was that many youth were leaving cocoa farming, which they viewed as an occupation of last resort and low esteem. Many sought a better life in the urban sector, in occupations perceived as more modern, with higher earning potential (Barrientos, et al. 2008).

Challenges to the long-term sustainability of Ghanaian cocoa thus had economic and social dimensions, and both were found to be significant. Other reports have also confirmed similar trends in Ghana and other countries (Oxfam 2009; Fairtrade 2011; Ryan 2011; Hütz-Adams and Fountain 2012). Whilst rising prices may help to stimulate supply, there are important constraints on market forces operating at farm level. Firstly, an ageing smallholder farmer population is less innovative or responsive to price movements or less able to expand production or increase productivity sufficiently. Secondly, it takes five years from planting a cocoa tree to it reaching its full potential, indicating significant time lags. Thirdly, there is a move out of cocoa production (and agriculture more generally) by many younger farmers, for whom alternative opportunities have greater appeal. Fourthly, cocoa is often deemed a male crop, but further investigation of the Ghana research found that women actually play an important if unrecognized role in cocoa production (Barrientos 2014). If the challenges are deeply embedded in the social and economic fabric of the sourcing countries, market or production-led responses alone are unlikely to be sufficient.

From the perspective of Cadbury, it was clear from the study that the challenges of socioeconomic sustainability at the local level posed a potential threat to future supply. To help address the social and economic challenges identified by the research, Cadbury launched the Cocoa Partnership in 2008 to support cocoa farming in its main sourcing countries (Ghana, India, Indonesia, and the Caribbean). It took the decision to invest £45 million to support the work of the Cocoa Partnership. This

---

[8] The study was undertaken in six communities across three regions: Ashanti, Western South, and Eastern Regions. The case study was based on a survey of 217 farmers, focus group discussions (45 owner-operators and caretaker operators, 12 youth, and 12 women), 24 life histories, and key informant interviews with actors in each community.

[9] Following media exposures on child labour in West African cocoa, the ICI was formed to address the problems. Its members include the civil society organizations and key chocolate manufacturers. See: <http://www.cocoainitiative.org/>.

was an alliance with different stakeholders including United Nations Development Programme (UNDP), Anti-Slavery International, and Care International. Local alliances were also formed within each country, which in Ghana included COCOBOD and local non-governmental organizations (NGOs).

The approach adopted by Cadbury was to seek solutions through dialogue at community level, in order to be sensitive to the future needs of farmers themselves. The aim of the Cocoa Partnership was to work in alliance with local NGOs and government bodies, to identify initiatives, and develop farmer- and community-focused action plans. This facilitated the creation of a bottom-up and top-down agenda, without which Cadbury believed solutions are less sustainable. Initial support was provided to 100 villages/communities in Ghana, with a further roll-out to other countries, including the Dominican Republic and India. According to David Croft, then Cadbury's Director of Conformance and Sustainability: 'Cadbury is just as dependent on their cocoa farmers as they are on Cadbury' (personal communication). The aims of the Cocoa Partnership were to enhance business strategy and opportunities for farmers, promote sustainable livelihoods, and support community-centred development (Croft and Cole 2011). Following its takeover of Cadbury in 2011, Kraft Foods continued to support the Cocoa Partnership. In 2012, following company restructuring, Cadbury came under Mondelēz, which further extended its sustainability goals and scope through the launch of Cocoa Life. This is a US$400 million initiative that aims to support over 200,000 cocoa farmers and 1 million people in their communities internationally over the period 2012–22.[10]

Other companies also followed, helping to tackle key issues facing cocoa farmers, their families, and communities in order to create a better future for cocoa farming. Their aim is to help improve the livelihoods of farmers and their communities, as well as enhance the sustainability and quality of cocoa grown for generations to come.[11] Mars launched its iMPACT and Vision for Change programmes, with pilots launched in 2007 striving to 'make cocoa a vibrant industry from farm to factory'.[12] Nestlé launched their Cocoa Plan in 2009.[13] In addition, a wide number of cross-industry and multi-stakeholder initiatives were launched. The Bill and Melinda Gates Foundation initiated a large programme working with partners Deutsche Gesellschaft für Technische Zusammenarbeit GmbH (GTZ), WCF, and private sector companies (including Kraft, Hershey, and Mars), with $48 million in grants to help small cocoa and cashew farmers in sub-Saharan Africa increase their incomes in order to lift themselves out of hunger and poverty.[14] The

---

[10] See press release 'Mondelēz International to Invest $400 Million to Help One Million People in Cocoa Farming Communities' (23 November 2012). <http://www.mondelezinternational.com/Newsroom/Multimedia-Releases/Mondelez-International-to-Invest-400-Million-to-Help-One-Million-People-in-Cocoa-Farming-Communities>. Accessed April 2014.

[11] See Javier Blas, 'Falling Cocoa Yields in Ivory Coast', *Financial Times*, 28 May 2010.

[12] See <http://www.mars.com/global/brands/cocoa-sustainability/mars-and-cocoa-sustainability.aspx>.

[13] See <http://www.nestlecocoaplan.com/>.

[14] See <http://www.gatesfoundation.org/press-releases/Pages/african-cocoa-and-cashew-farmers-090218.aspx>.

WCF also launched the Cocoa Livelihoods Programme and, in the Netherlands, the Dutch Sustainable Trade Initiative (IDH) made cocoa one of its target crops. Many of these sustainability programmes focus more on support to increase yields and productivity through farmer training and enhancement of good agricultural practices than on social indicators (Hütz-Adams and Fountain 2012), indicating a divergence between a more technocratic approach and the more community-based approach pioneered by Cadbury's Cocoa Partnership. With so many different initiatives there is a risk of overlap, replication, and lack of coordination, especially if they are all chasing the same low-hanging fruit.

Certification is a parallel track which a number of companies and governments are also following in pursuit of sustainability. They are using different certification strategies and bodies (mainly Fairtrade, UTZ, and Rainforest Alliance). Cadbury pursued this route in 2009, announcing conversion of its Cadbury Dairy Milk (CDM) bars and drinking chocolate in the UK to Fairtrade, then extended this to the whole of its Green & Black's range (Croft and Cole 2011). Cadbury Fairtrade products are now sold in many other countries (including Ireland, Australia, New Zealand, Canada, Japan, South Africa, and Kenya). Nestlé and Mars also converted parts of their product ranges to Fairtrade (including KitKat in 2010, and Maltesers in 2011). Jointly, Cadbury/Kraft, Nestlé, and Mars contributed to an eightfold-plus increase in Fairtrade cocoa products sold in the UK, from £25.6 million in 2008 to £320.9 million in 2012, with UK sales of Fairtrade chocolate rising from 1 per cent to 12 per cent of total UK chocolate sales over the same years (Fairtrade 2012).

It is estimated that certification of total cocoa production has doubled from 3 per cent in 2009 to over 6 per cent in 2010, although less than this is actually sold as certified chocolate and double certification can take place (KPMG 2012). Whilst Fairtrade accounted for the largest share of certified cocoa (39 per cent) in 2010, this is changing with rapid growth of the other schemes. The Dutch scheme UTZ is experiencing the fastest growth, with its volume of certified cocoa (214,000 tons) overtaking that of Fairtrade (150,000 tons) in 2011 (KPMG 2012). This is, in part, accounted for by the Dutch government making a commitment in 2010, together with private companies and civil society organizations, to attain 100 per cent certified sustainable cocoa consumption in the Netherlands by 2025 (a similar but less stringent commitment was subsequently made by the German government). Mars and Ferrero have also committed to selling 100 per cent certified sustainable cocoa by 2020, and the UK supermarket Sainsbury aims to sell 100 per cent Fairtrade chocolate by 2020.

It can be seen, therefore, that a two-pronged strategy is emerging amongst companies, industry actors, governments, and civil society organizations along the cocoa–chocolate value chain. On one hand, a range of sustainability and farmer support initiatives are being pursued. On the other hand, there has been a strong move towards greater certification. However, underlying these strategies we can also discern different approaches. Some of the sustainability initiatives (such as the Cocoa Partnership/Cocoa Life) have a stronger community orientation, with a focus on addressing the social challenges facing cocoa farmers and their households. Other initiatives have a stronger productivity orientation, focusing on enhancing farmer yields. Likewise, the different certification schemes encompass differing approaches. Fairtrade is the oldest certification scheme, with its roots in social movements: it aims to address unfair trading relations, buffer price volatility by setting a minimum price, and invest in social upgrading through payment of a social premium. UTZ Certification and Rainforest Alliance have a stronger market orientation, with a greater emphasis on farmer training and support with the goal of enhancing yields and productivity (Barrientos and Dolan 2006; Raynolds and Wilkinson 2007; KPMG 2012). Certification generates benefits, but also challenges for cocoa farmers, and evidence on the impact is patchy. Certification in other advanced manufacturing sectors, such as apparel and electronics, has proved less effective than many companies had hoped (Locke 2013). This raises questions as to whether the cocoa–chocolate industry is being over optimistic in pursuing a similar compliance route.

The last three years have thus seen a rapid move by a number of large-scale chocolate confectionery companies to invest in social and economic sustainability at the base of their value chain networks. A number of factors have played a role. Civil society and media campaigns, and successful expansion of Fairtrade and other certified products, have been an important stimulus.[15] Projections of rapid future growth in markets within the South, and concerns over demand outpacing supply have also played a role. But if these were the only factors, companies could rely on the forces of supply and demand raising cocoa prices and output, and certification satisfying the niche end of the consumer market. However, the drivers appear to be deeper. Companies are realizing that the socioeconomic embeddedness of their sourcing base in poor and ageing farmer communities with low productivity within the South make them increasingly vulnerable commercially. Projections regarding future cocoa supply and demand is a serious challenge, but is linked to wider processes of socioeconomic change in cocoa-producing countries, which market forces alone are unlikely to address.

Concluding Remarks

This chapter has examined a complex process of change taking place in the cocoa–chocolate sector, and the challenges it poses to mainstream chocolate companies. It has considered these changes from two aspects: the commercial dynamics of a bi-polar value chain increasingly dominated by a few large processors and manufacturers sourcing from a fragmented supply base; and the socially embedded nature of that commercial activity in producer and consumer contexts, which

---

[15] These include the Oxfam Behind the Brands campaign which ranked leading food companies in relation to gender equity within their value chains (see <https://www.behindthebrands.org/>), prompting leading chocolate companies to more openly pursue gender equity strategies. For an examination of the gender dimension of cocoa production see Barrientos (2013).

are facing serious challenges to their future social and economic sustainability. Here we reflect on some wider development implications of the two.

Firstly, commercial value chains, rather than traditional arm's-length markets, are playing a critical role in shaping contemporary global development (for better or worse). Lead companies are more concentrated and integrated into the producer and consumer markets in which they operate. Consumer markets have become more differentiated, with middle income consumers becoming more aware of quality and the social origins of their purchases. The view that this is only a feature of Northern consumers should not be taken for granted. In an era of global social networking and information and communications technology (ICTs), there is an emerging awareness amongst Southern consumers. Cadbury would not have launched Fairtrade brands in South Africa and Kenya were this not the case. But, for too long, companies, and often governments, have assumed that commercial success could be built on an infinite supply of cheap raw materials from developing countries. This has resulted in a disjuncture between consumer-oriented value chains, and their producer base. In the cocoa market, the cracks are showing and could become chasms if no change takes place. Whilst there are tensions between commercial and social pressures, we are (hopefully) seeing the beginning of a re-visioning of socioeconomic sustainability in cocoa production.

Secondly, there is a realization that companies alone are unable to address the issues. Cadbury took an early view that it could only influence change in cocoa communities by working from the bottom up in alliance with local and international civil society organizations. Many other companies are working in various alliances with international development agencies and local organizations. But whether this is enough is questionable. The International Cocoa Organization (ICCO) in 2011 estimates that there are currently 60 initiatives to support cocoa farmers worldwide. It is concerned that whilst this will boost production, it will also fan volatility in the market. But deeper development issues are involved, such as endemic rural poverty, traditional land tenure systems, child labour, gender inequality (women often play an unrecognized role in family-based cocoa farming), and structural inequities within a cocoa–chocolate value chain where farmers have long reaped little reward for back-breaking work. Civil society organizations (Oxfam 2009; Fairtrade 2011) are calling for renewed public–private alliances, and reforming an international trade regime so that the rights and well-being of farmers and workers are more systematically promoted. In the long term, farmers need to see a future in cocoa farming if the cocoa–chocolate value chain is to be viable.

Thirdly, underpinning these changes is the shift of chocolate confectionery consumption South, with the rate of growth globally predicted at 2–3 per cent per annum, but in developing countries at 6–8 per cent (albeit from a low base). This is a dramatic change for a product based traditionally on raw material production in the South and consumption of the manufactured good in the North. But this is a reflection of a wider development shift that has been occurring through rapid economic growth in Asia, Africa, and Latin America, compared with economic stagnation and crisis in Europe and North America. The challenge chocolate companies face is double-edged—it is the growth of new income opportunities in the South that is both creating new demand for their products *and* luring younger more productive farmers and workers away from producing its key ingredient. Long-term strategies pursued by companies are therefore entwined with a wider development process involving a broad range of development actors and processes. It is in this context that business is waking up to and engaging with the challenges of development.

References

Anti-Slavery. 2004. *The Cocoa Industry in West Africa: A History of Exploitation*. London: Anti-Slavery International.

Barrientos, S. 2014. 'Gendered Global Production Networks: Analysis of Cocoa-Chocolate Sourcing.' *Regional Studies* 48 (5): pp. 791–803.

Barrientos, S. and K. Asenso-Okyere. 2009. 'Cocoa Value Chain: Challenges Facing Ghana in a Changing Global Confectionary Market.' *Journal Fur Entwicklungspolitik (Austrian Journal of Development Studies)* 25 (2): pp. 88–107.

Barrientos, S. and C. Dolan, eds. 2006. *Ethical Sourcing in the Global Food System*. London: Earthscan.

Barrientos, S. and S. Smith. 2007. 'Mainstreaming Fair Trade in Global Value Chains: Own Brand Sourcing of Fruit and Cocoa in UK Supermarkets'. In *Fair Trade: The Challenges of Transforming Globalization*, edited by L. Raynolds, D. Murray, and J. Wilkinson. London: Routledge.

Barrientos, S., K. et al. 2008. 'Mapping Sustainable Production in Ghanaian Cocoa'. Available at: <http://www.bwpi.manchester.ac.uk/medialibrary/research/ResearchProgrammes/businessfordevelopment/mappping_sustainable_production_in_ghanaian_cocoa.pdf>. Cadbury, London.

Berlan, A. (2009) 'Child Labour and Cocoa: Whose Voices Prevail?' *International Journal of Sociology and Social Policy* 29 (3/4): pp. 141–51.

Berlan, A., S. Singh, and S. Barrientos. 2013. *Social and Economic Sustainability in the Cocoa Value Chain in India: Research Overview*. Manchester: University of Manchester Press.

Croft, D. and A. Cole. 2011. 'A Glass and a Half Full: How Cadbury Embraced Fairtrade'. In *The Fairtrade Revolution*, edited by J. Bowes, pp. 107–24. London: Pluto Press.

Datamonitor. 2007. *Confectionary in India to 2010*. Available at: <http://www.MarketResearch.com>. Accessed August 2010.

Daviron, B. and P. Gibbon. 2002. 'Global Commodity Chains and African Export Crop Agriculture'. *Journal of Agrarian Change* 2 (2): pp. 136–61.

Fairtrade. 2011. *Fairtrade and Cocoa: Commodity Briefing*. London: Fairtrade Foundation.

Fairtrade. 2012. *Tracking Fairtrade Cocoa*. London: Fairtrade Foundation. Available at: <http://www.fairtrade.org.uk/press_office/press_releases_and_statements/archive_2012/archive_2012/october_2012/tracking_fairtrade_cocoa.aspx>. Accessed April 2014.

Fold, N. 2002. 'Lead Firms and Competition in Bi-polar Commodity Chains: Grinders and Branders in the Global Cocoa–Chocolate Industry'. *Journal of Agrarian Change* 2 (2): pp. 228–47.

Fold, N. 2005. 'Global Cocoa Sourcing Patterns'. In *Cross Continental Food Chains*, edited by N. Fold and B. Pritchard. London: Routledge.

Gilbert, C. 2007. 'Value Chain Analysis and Market Power in Commodity Processing with Application to the Cocoa and Coffee Sectors'. Rome: Revised paper to FAO Workshop (2006) on Governance, Coordination and Distribution along Commodity Value Chains.

Hütz-Adams, F. and A. C. Fountain. 2012. *Cocoa Barometer.* Multistakeholder Report. Available at: <http://www.cocoabarometer.org/Cocoa_Barometer/>. Accessed April 2014.

ICCO (International Cocoa Organization). 2007a. *Assessment of the Movement of Global Supply and Demand.* MC/9/2. Market Committee, ninth meeting. Kuala Lumpa: International Cocoa Organization.

ICCO (International Cocoa Organization). 2007b. *Cocoa Resources in Consuming Countries.* MC/10/06. Market Committee, tenth meeting. London: International Cocoa Organization.

ICCO (International Cocoa Organization). 2012. *The World Cocoa Economy: Past and Present.* EX/146/7. London: International Cocoa Organization.

Kaplinsky, R. 2004. *Competitions Policy and the Global Coffee and Cocoa Value Chains.* Geneva: United Nations Conference for Trade and Development.

Kaplinsky, R. and M. Morris. 2002. *A Handbook for Value Chain Research.* International Development Research Centre (IDRC)/Institute of Development Studies (IDS). Available at: <http://www.ids.ac.uk/globalvaluechains/tools/index.html>.

KPMG. 2012. *Cocoa Certification.* Study on the costs, advantages and disadvantages of cocoa certification commissioned by the International Cocoa Organization (ICCO). London: KPMG.

LMC. 2011. *Cocoa Sustainability.* Report to World Cocoa Foundation. Oxford: LMC International. Available at: <http://www.worldcocoafoundation.org/learn-about-cocoa/documents/LMC-WCFCocoaSustainabilityReport_2010-11.pdf>. Accessed June 2012.

Locke, R. 2013. *The Promise and Limits of Private Power: Promoting Labor Standards in a Global Economy.* New York: Cambridge University Press.

Losch, B. 2002. 'Global Restructuring and Liberalization: Côte d'Ivoire and the End of the International Cocoa Market?' *Journal of Agrarian Change* 2 (2): pp. 206–27.

Morisset, J. 1998. 'Unfair Trade? The Increasing Gap between World and Domestic Prices in Commodity Markets during the Past 25 Years'. *World Bank Economic Review* 12 (3).

Oxfam. 2009. *Towards a Sustainable Cocoa Chain: Power and Possibilities within the Cocoa and Chocolate Sector.* Oxford: Oxfam Research Report.

P. T. Armajaro. 2011. 'Cocoa Production in 2020'. Presentation to World Cocoa Foundation. Available at: <http://www.worldcocoafoundation.org/who-we-are/partnership-meetings/documents/PThornton-Armajaro.pdf>. Accessed June 2012.

Raynolds, L. and J. Wilkinson. 2007. 'Fair Trade in the Agriculture and Food Sector: Analytical Dimensions'. In *Fair Trade: The Challenges of Transforming Globalization*, edited by L. Raynolds, D. Murray, and J. Wilkinson, pp. 33–48. London: Routledge.

Ryan, O. 2011. *Chocolate Nations: Living and Dying for Cocoa in West Africa.* London: Zed Press.

Tulane. 2007. *First Annual Report: Oversight of Public and Private Initiatives to Eliminate the Worst Forms of Child Labour in the Cocoa Sector in Cote d'Ivoire and Ghana.* Tulane University: Payson Centre for International Development and Technology Transfer.

Tulane. 2009. *Third Annual Report: Oversight of Public and Private Initiatives to Eliminate the Worst Forms of Child Labor in the Cocoa Sector in Côte d'Ivoire and Ghana.* Tulane University: Payson Centre for International Development and Technology Transfer.

Tulane. 2011. *Final Report: Oversight of Public and Private Initiatives to Eliminate the Worst Forms of Child Labor in the Cocoa Sector in Cote d'Ivoire and Ghana.* Tulane University: Payson Center for International Development and Technology Transfer.

UNCTAD (United Nations Conference on Trade and Development). 2008. *Cocoa Study: Industry Structures and Competition.* Geneva: United Nations Conference on Trade and Development.

WCF (World Cocoa Foundation). 2012. *Cocoa Market Update.* Washington, DC: World Cocoa Foundation.

World Bank. 2008. *World Development Report.* Washington, DC: Agriculture for Development.

13

Policy Reform and Supply Chain Governance

Insights from Ghana, Côte d'Ivoire, and Ecuador

Sietze Vellema, Anna Laven, Giel Ton, and Sander Muilerman

Introduction

Major companies trading cocoa from tropical countries or companies processing cocoa and manufacturing chocolate have become increasingly concerned about a sustainable and secure access to cocoa beans. Combinations of old cocoa trees, aging farmers, declining soil fertility, and the spread of plant diseases, pose real threats to the viability of cocoa trade and the chocolate industry. Leading export and chocolate manufacturing companies in the sector explore different strategies to address these problems, for example introducing contracts with farmers' groups to arrange the transfer of inputs and know-how, building linkages with public agencies in producing countries to disseminate new trees, or implementing sustainability standards in alliance with international non-governmental organizations (NGOs) to provide incentives for increasing productivity and quality. The implementation of global sustainability standards, for example with Utz Certified or Rainforest Alliance, is accompanied by certification and auditing procedures and by various modes of training and organizing an increasing percentage of cocoa farmers. In 2014, a dozen of major cocoa and chocolate companies committed to a 'one industry' programme CocoaAction, facilitated by World Cocoa Foundation (WCF), and aligned with the origin governments' goals (Côte d'Ivoire and Ghana) and programmes managed by their national institutions. This signals a wider interest in public–private partnerships that goes beyond the collaboration between lead firms and NGOs in certification schemes. Hence, government bodies and public policy are also becoming part of arrangements underlying concerted action around shared knowledge and pooled resources to implement sector strategies addressing declining productivity levels that threaten continuity in the cocoa and chocolate industry.

In this context of evolving interactions between companies, NGOs, and governments, this chapter investigates histories of public regulation in cocoa producing countries. Here, the future of commodity-based sectors and economies has been shaped by public policy, which directs, for example, expenditures in research and development (R&D), extension services, and regulations of input market, buying practices, and export. Some countries have mechanisms to fix and stabilize prices, and some countries developed institutional arrangements in the value chain to target specific qualities with higher than average prices on the world market. Direct government involvement in supply management and price stabilization has decreased, partly due to the choices fundamental to the structural adjustments policies of the World Bank, the lending policies of the International Monetary Fund (IMF), and the trade policies negotiated in the World Trade Organization (WTO). The intergovernmental International Cocoa Agreement, which was designed to create a certain level of stabilization and rule setting in commodity markets, moved away from direct interventions in the markets to finding other measures. Nevertheless, in major producing countries, public organizations, such as marketing boards, and various forms of regulation still shape dynamics in cocoa chains, and, consequently, the conditions for enhancing sustainability, although public interference with market realities may be more limited in scope.

The chapter examines how policy reforms in producing countries and supply chain governance connect and may alter the economic playing field for sustainability in the cocoa sector. It will neither define nor measure sustainability in cocoa.[1] The chapter adopts a comparative framework to describe the evolution of public–private interaction in economic governance in the cocoa sector development. The case studies, based on primary data (Ghana and Côte d'Ivoire), secondary sources, and literature review, examine the involvement of national governments in managing and governing the economic realities in cocoa in two major West African producing countries, Ghana and Côte d'Ivoire, crucial for the mainstream market of chocolate, and one Latin American country, producing a specific quality cocoa, Ecuador. These case studies, reported more extensively in Ton and colleagues (2008), label several periods in each country's cocoa sector history according to the dominant 'mode of governance'. This builds on the framework of Griffiths and Zammuto (2005), which identifies how economic governance depends on the nature and degree of state involvement (Evans 1995; Whitley 1999) and the balancing of purely arm's-length market exchange or vertical integration of upstream activities by a handful of international cocoa processing firms (Daviron and Gibbon 2002; Losch 2002; Abbott et al. 2005).

---

[1] The sustainability impacts of standards and certification receives much attention in policy-oriented research (for a rich example see COSA 2013) and among practitioners (ISEAL Alliance 2013, 2014). This separate body of literature seeks ways to report on the net effects on, for example, incomes, or productivity of institutional interventions such as standards. The methodological difficulty to attribute effects to such interventions is discussed in evaluation literature (Ton et al. 2014) and motivates an interest to look more deeply into the institutional conditions under which global standards or policy frameworks make a difference in specific contexts (Vellema et al. 2013). The cross-context analysis in this chapter contributes to this interest.

The wider interest of this chapter is to explore whether and how both private and public endeavours connect in developmental and transformative endeavours. This shifts attention from a strong focus on private and voluntary forms of economic governance, in particular standards, to an interest in how the observed strategic vulnerability of commodity chains (Gereffi and Lee 2012; Gereffi 2013) results in new forms of institutional blending of private and public economic governance at global and national levels (Vellema and van Wijk 2014). Consequently, the outlook for a sustainable cocoa economy strongly depends on the possibilities to find a fit between supply chain governance and the specific political and economic histories that shaped rules and regulation in countries where the global commodity chains touch down (Helmsing and Vellema 2011).

Côte d'Ivoire

Cote d'Ivoire is the leading supplier of cocoa beans to the world market (OECD 2006: 237). In the 1990s, the country produced almost 50 per cent of internationally traded cocoa (Losch 2002: 206). In the following decade the institutional environment and sector policies that facilitated this changed profoundly (Table 13.1).

Period 1 1960–1990: Institutional Stability: State Governance

A mixture of private and public efforts drove cocoa production and export in Cote d'Ivoire, which was accompanied by an interlinked system of foreign investments, immigration, and land colonization (Toungara 2001; Woods 2003). The African cocoa growers united in 1944 in the trade union of African cocoa farmers, led by Félix Houphouët-Boigny; he later became the first elected and long-standing president of the country (1960–93). Production, collection, storage, conditioning, and shipping was in private hands. At the level of domestic marketing—called *traite*—coordination between agents (farmers, farm-gate buyers, wholesalers (called *traitants*), and exporters) rested on commercial channels based on long-standing

Table 13.1 Policy reforms and governance in the cocoa sector in Cote d'Ivoire

Period	Policy Reform	Governance
1) 1960–90	Creating stabilizing institutions	State governance
2) 1990–2000	Dismantling public regulation and expanding operations of larger buyers	Market governance
3) 2000–07	Linking levies and taxation in cocoa to military or political interventions	Predatory state governance
4) 2007–present	Regrouping cocoa-specialized public officials and increasing transparency and representation	Emerging partnerships blending market and state governance

'gentlemen's agreements' and a system of redeemable cash loans (*mandates*) granted by exporters using bank credit. Collection, storage, and export firms were dominantly foreign. Lebanese buying agents and transporters dominated collection and storage while French firms controlled the international marketing and shipping (Hecht 1983: 34).

The publicly managed stabilization system, created by the French colonial authorities, allowed private exporters to remain in business under the centralized management of the marketing board, called the Caisse de stabilization, abbreviated to Caisse or Caisstab, which regulated trading through a system of buying quotas, and fixed cocoa prices annually for each stage of the marketing chain. According to the principle of the Caisse de stabilization, private exporters were the owners of the cocoa. They managed product quality under final control of the Caisse de stabilization, which gave authorization for export. The public marketing board had the task to license private buying agents and export firms, setting producer prices, rates of remuneration, and commissions for traders; and giving final approval to sales contracts with overseas buyers of cocoa and of coffee (Hecht 1983). The country also used a stabilization system that offered producers a guaranteed price and outlet that did not take into account the quality of the product upstream in the chain (Losch 2002: 208). At the end of the 1970s, however, the Caisstab induced so-called 'direct' sales, in which it negotiated contracts itself and demanded private exporters implement them.

This system of strong vertical coordination was an arena full of political pressures. It led to the appearance of fictitious exporters, who benefited from political protection and so were able to generate profits in the market or to sell their quotas to exporters actually managing the trade of cocoa. Through export taxes, the marketing board gained 38 per cent of the export earnings from cocoa (Hecht 1983: 30). Some was reinvested in the cocoa sector, for instance to set up grinding companies. Yet the greater part went to a small elite, mainly within the government and industry in Côte d'Ivoire (Hecht 1983: 31–42).

The interventions in the cocoa sector in this period exemplify the conditions of state-driven vertical coordination. Although there was both private ownership (grinding companies, exporters, farmers) and cooperation between the public and private, the state played a central role. The Ivorian government directly influenced all economic actors involved. The tasks and responsibilities of the Caisse generated state control over the market and a certain degree of certainty for farmers, and, combined with the Ivorian land policy, this stimulated growth of cocoa production.

This level of institutional stability eroded towards the end of the 1980s. The first International Cocoa Agreement (concluded in 1972) united producer and consumer countries and installed a pricing system and an international buffer stock. After international price booms from 1977 to 1979, prices fell and those united under the agreement could do very little in response. Côte d'Ivoire left the agreement. Cote d'Ivoire tried to revive the Cocoa Producers' Alliance, founded in 1962, and the country attempted some unilateral actions, deluded by its position as the leading world supplier of cocoa. Actions were to pull out cocoa beans from the market, increase its grinding capacity and inaugurate the practice of block trading (Losch 2002: 211). Prominent in this struggle for improving price levels has been the historic cocoa strike. Between July 1987 and October 1989, the government of Côte d'Ivoire blocked all export. To keep its position in the international market, the country tried to organize warehouses in Europe. This endeavour failed because buyers in the market did not wait until Ivorian beans were again released and instead looked for other sources. The domestic consequences of these actions were disastrous: the cocoa blockade led to the implosion of the guaranteed prices system, non-payment to producers, and a bankrupt economy. Due to the virtual bankruptcy of all institutions that had been involved in paying higher-than-world-market prices, the banking system could not give advance loans to the farmers any more. The institutions that embodied the system of vertical coordination collapsed, and left many chain actors unprepared for doing business in uncontrolled markets.

Period 2 1990–2000: Liberalization in Progress

From 1990 on, a privatization and liberalization programme, negotiated between the International Monetary Fund (IMF) and the government of Côte d'Ivoire (IMF/GoCdI 2002a), was put in place. The state withdrew from production activities and service provision. In 1999, the key player in the old system, the Caisse de Stabilization, was dismantled. As administered prices disappeared from 1999 onwards, prices for cocoa became volatile and more vulnerable to changes in market prices. Quality showed a downward trend over the years 1997–2000 (Losch 2002). Instead of the Caisse, new institutions were created in the sector. In 2000, the Coffee and Cocoa Regulation Authority (Autorité de Régulation du Café et du Cacao—ARCC) organized, with World Bank support, agencies that would regulate quality, manage coffee and cocoa exchange and price risks, arrange export credits, and finance producer-sponsored rural development initiatives (World Bank 2003).

The implementation of these instruments directed at liberalization of the market coincided with a trend of concentration of downstream cocoa chain actors. Grinding parties and chocolate producing companies concentrated into a handful of multinationals. A small group of international grinders tried to capture primary production. By 2000, 85 per cent of all Ivorian exports were in the hands of foreign firms. Simultaneously, different attempts were made to control buying networks. One was the organization of a central purchasing pool by seven small exporters, which ensured product collection. The collecting company worked with traditional intermediaries as well as with cooperative organizations. In another initiative, producers groups associated and set up a system for the provision of technical support and equipment and a system of cash loans based on guaranteed payment at the official price. A third attempt was vertical integration by traders to overcome producer liquidity constraints (Losch 2002: 211–12). Another effect of liberalization and deregulation was that small local exporters were no longer able to obtain finance without the guarantees of the stabilization system. Exporting firms competed by securing the loyalty of their middlemen rather than of producers, as well as on liquidity (without guarantees) and their capacity to adjust rapidly to price movements (Losch 2002: 211–12).

Market forces became the overall governance mechanism. Decisions on the supply and processing of cocoa beans became 'internal' decisions made along the supply chain. Taking control of the supply chain has become the task of the few big grinders dominating international markets. The Ivorian government tried to keep some control on export revenues. The installation of several new institutions, based on World Bank suggestions, was funded by raising taxes and export levies. Yet, after a decade of liberalization, taxes on cocoa, the bulwark of the Ivorian economy, still composed nearly 40 per cent of the export price in the beginning of the 2000s (IMF/GoCdI 2002b).

Period 3 2000–07: Political Instability

The period since 2000 is characterized by a high level of political instability, triggered by a military coup in 1999, followed by an army rebellion in September 2002, and postponement of several presidential elections in 2005, 2006, and 2007. The ongoing conflict between the northern and southern part of Côte d'Ivoire crippled the role of the state in general. Most of the country's cocoa was produced in the southern forested areas controlled by the government. An estimated 10 per cent of the country's cocoa was grown in the rebel-controlled zone in the north. The conflict led to a cocoa blockade, which prevented the transit of northern cocoa towards the main export port in the south. The rebels controlling the north secured revenues from the cocoa trade by exporting beans via Ghana, Burkina Faso, and Togo. However, despite geographical separation and political instability, Côte d'Ivoire still accounted for 40 per cent of the world's production of cocoa in 2006.

The national government, and especially president Laurent Gbagbo, who came to power in 2001, succeeded in retaining control of the national cocoa and financial institutions. The tax pressure on cocoa remained high, partly due to the collapse of some sectors of the economy and the closure of many small and medium-sized companies, which meant that the government depended primarily on the tax levies on cocoa (OECD 2006). Taxes were also used to fund counter-insurgency actions. Civil society organizations, in particular Global Witness (2007), raised concerns about how financial flows in cocoa fuelled the ongoing conflict in the country. The Ivorian government reinstated some sort of minimum producer price and tried to regulate competition to limit market concentration. Gradually, a complex intertwining of private and government governance of the strategic and economically vital sector began to emerge, although, simultaneously, financial transparency of the institutions controlling the cocoa sector was reduced (Gilbert 2009; Ruf 2009).

Period 4 2007–Present: Policy Reform and Emerging Public–Private Partnerships

In more recent years, the continuation of cocoa production in Côte d'Ivoire increasingly became a concern of leading companies in the international trade and chocolate industry. In 2008, President Gbagbo announced the formation of the provisional Comité de Gestion de la Filière Café Cacao (CGFCC) (Grossman-Green and Bayer 2009), which maintained direct linkages with international buyers. By the end of 2011, all previous cocoa institutions, erected since 1999, were assembled under the umbrella of the Comité Café Cacao (CCC), with links to the Comité National des Sages (CNS). Also, global lead companies in the chocolate industry recognized the relevance of some level of bureaucratic autonomy and coordination among private players (Morgan 2010) to ensure a consistent supply of cocoa beans and to give strategic direction to R&D and technical support for the sector. The Fond Interprofessionnel pour la Recherche et le Conseil Agricoles (FIRCA), set up in 2002/03, but active only in 2007 (Stads and Doumbia 2010; Stads 2011) began to play a role in this. FIRCA brought together producers, processors, traders, and exporters (Byerlee 2011) to co-design the agenda for research and extension services and to act as a financing bodyFIRCA continued to collect funds in different government-controlled channels of input provision, while for other crops national sector-led savings mechanisms were put in place.

The political crisis and re-emerging violent conflict in 2010 and 2011 put pressure on this emerging cooperation in the cocoa sector. Despite the societal and political turbulence in the country, cocoa-based groups of government officials of the previous state agencies survived and the government recently made an effort to regroup them. Hence, bureaucratic and technocratic elements remained intact and gained more influence over quality control, the regulation of buyer margins, and the use of public funds for the sector itself. Moreover, the strategic importance of Côte d'Ivoire for the international trade in cocoa encouraged international trading and chocolate manufacturing companies to seek linkages with the government and to engage in public–private partnerships in a joint endeavour to address sustainability problems and to frame a national sector plan. Various private-led initiatives linked companies and farmers. Simultaneously, connectivity between public and private actions increased, which reshaped the governance of support to the sector as well as of technical dimensions of international trade, such as quality control, stock keeping, and compliance with a variety of standards.

Ghana

Ghana is the world's second largest producer of cocoa, and the commodity is still an important source of rural incomes and foreign exchange earnings. About three quarters of output is produced by some 700,000 small-scale farms. Cocoa is Ghana's dominant cash crop and single most important export product, equivalent to more than one third of Ghana's merchandise exports. The government and

Table 13.2 Policy reforms and governance in the cocoa sector in Ghana

Period	Policy Reform	Governance
1) 1940–80	Installing state control in input and output markets	State governance
2) 1980–2000	Reconsolidating role of state in local production and international trade by gradual reforms	State governance
3) 2000–present	Including new actors in buying and exporting, with consistent state	State governance blended with market governance

private extension providers stimulated an intensification of cocoa production (Ruf 2007). The Ghanaian government has always been actively involved with the development of the cocoa sector (Laven 2011). Also, with the introduction of structural adjustment programmes (SAPs) in the late 1980s, the Ghanaian state remained a pro-active and dominant actor in the cocoa sector. A history of gradual reforms (Table 13.2) reveals new actors entering the sector and taking over some of the previous state responsibilities, or starting to work together in partnerships.

Period 1 1940–80: Shift to State-Led Cocoa Sector

During the colonial period, the cocoa sector initially operated under a free market system. European companies controlled both local buying and exporting, with Cadbury as the leading British cocoa manufacturer. Public interventions took place through the involvement of the (colonial) Department of Agriculture, which encouraged the establishment of cooperative enterprises in Ghana's cocoa industry. In 1940, the West African Cocoa Control Board was established, and replaced by the wider West African Produce Control Board (WAPCB) in 1942. In 1947, the Cocoa Marketing Board (COCOBOD) was installed and it was decided that the British Ministry of Food was to be the only seller of the Ghanaian cocoa, using the COCOBOD channel. The existing (mainly expatriate) cocoa buying companies were appointed agents of the WAPCB and they continued to have responsibility for buying (Anin 2003). Companies such as Cadbury accepted marketing boards as a reality in the colonial cocoa commodity chain (Beckman 1976: 43). Public interventions took place through the involvement of the (colonial) Department of Agriculture, which encouraged the establishment of cooperative enterprises in Ghana's cocoa industry. Organizing farmers into cooperatives was seen as a way to ensure the production of good-quality cocoa for export. Many European traders were hostile to the promotion of cooperatives with government backing, because they worried that this would eventually eliminate them from the cocoa trade (DoC 1990: 9–16).

In 1961, four years after the country's independence, the Farmers' Council capitalized on the colonial heritage of public market regulation, took over cocoa trade, and became the monopoly buyer of cocoa. By doing so, it put an end to the direct involvement of foreign buyers in cocoa marketing. In the same year, the Cocoa Marketing Company (CMC) Ghana was set up as a commission agent of

COCOBOD. CMC Ghana became responsible for registering buyers, administering cocoa sales, and appointing local (Ghanaian) buying agents to facilitate foreign buyers' operations in Accra (Amoah 1998: 78–104).

The Ghanaian government established the pan-territorial fixed price policy, which guaranteed farmers a reliable, albeit low, price, and assured the public marketing company of a consistent cocoa supply (Ministry of Finance Ghana 1999: 82). This guaranteed price was substantially lower than the world market price, due to high taxes and marketing costs. The government compensated farmers by providing them with subsidies on inputs and services. The government undertook several attempts to channel rural credit to farmers and introduced a control system ensuring the export of good-quality cocoa, for which it received a premium on the world market. For a long time the only cocoa beans still consistently separated by national origin for grinding purposes were those from Ghana (Gibbon and Ponte 2005: 135–6). The state also invested in processing capacity, furthering state-led chain integration. In 1963, two cocoa processing factories were built, both owned by COCOBOD (Ministry of Finance Ghana 1999: 71–2). The state governance continued after a short disruption between 1966 and 1977. When, in 1966, the Nkrumah government was overthrown by a military coup, the Farmers' Council was dissolved and banned (Beckman 1976: 11–17).

During the following decade, characterized by political instability and mismanagement, cocoa prices for the Ghanaian cocoa farmer fell and cocoa production was halved. Competition among local buyers was reintroduced, but this did not last long due to problems with delayed payments. A single buying system was reintroduced and, from 1977 onward, the Produce Buying Company (PBC), a subsidiary of COCOBOD, was in control of internal marketing. In this period, different subsidiaries of COCOBOD provided support and services to the farmers. The Cocoa Services Division (CSD) had the monopoly on the procurement and distribution of inputs (Amezah 2003). The Cocoa Research Institute Ghana (CRIG) was the national centre of excellence for the study and cultivation of cocoa.

Period 2 1980–2000: Gradual Reforms

This period of state governance was challenged in the early 1980s. Economic and political crises formed the context for Lieutenant Rawlings to come to power in a coup in 1981. A drought in 1983 led to food shortages and declining production in cocoa, which made the government decide to invest significant public resources in agriculture. In the Economic Recovery Programme (ERP) launched in 1984, this translated into a strong focus on export crops and triggered institutional reforms in the cocoa sector already initiated in 1979 (Fold 2002). In the following years, the Ghanaian government opted for gradual reforms to reduce costs of inefficient marketing and pricing systems (Akiyama et al. 2001). The introduction of gradual reforms stimulated a recovery of the sector, visible in the increase in cocoa production, which was 'almost entirely due to the traditional method of expanding output by means of additional land' (Teal and Vigneri 2004: 8–12). Internal marketing, input distribution, and extension services were privatized. State-controlled processing activities were reorganized, as a way of expanding the country's low processing base.

In the early 1980s, a drastic reduction in COCOBOD's staff level took place, from approximately 120,000 in the early 1980s to 5,500 in 2006 (IMF 2009). Many former employees of COCOBOD found alternative employment in the cocoa sector, as private consultants, providers of extension services, and/or as buyers of cocoa.

The liberalization of internal marketing started in 1992 with the introduction of private licensed buying companies (LBCs) as competitors to the state-owned monopoly in buying cocoa from farmers. During 1996–97, 16 LBCs obtained the permission to buy cocoa alongside PBC, and 4 received provisional licences (Ministry of Finance Ghana 1999: 45). The number of buyers fluctuated, as did their active involvement in buying cocoa. The majority of LBCs were Ghanaian, only two were foreign-owned. One LBC was farmer-owned and set up with the support of international NGOs. PBC remained the largest buyer. CSD's monopoly on the procurement and distribution of generally free or heavily subsidized inputs ended (Haque 2004). In 1995, the Ghana Cocoa, Coffee, and Sheanut Farmers Association (GCCSFA) took over this responsibility.

COCOBOD continued to control external marketing, coordinate internal marketing, and check the final quality of cocoa beans. Producer bonuses were introduced to compensate producers if the producer price was lower than world market price. This involvement of the government created conditions which enabled the country to deliver consistent supplies of large volumes of relatively good-quality cocoa. Through a system of forward sales, COCOBOD managed to pre-finance the cocoa while price stabilization remained intact (Ministry of Finance Ghana 1999; Laven 2007a). Extension services shifted from services provided by the CSD (exclusively for cocoa farmers) to unified extension services provided by the Ministry of Food and Agriculture (MoFA) as the CSD was considered to be too costly. Unified extension was, however, a poor solution, with many farmers being underserved (Laven 2010).

Period 3 2000–present: Shifts from Within

In response to the reforms and the reduced role of COCOBOD and its subsidiaries, other actors and partnerships entered the cocoa sector, ready to fill the vacuum left by the (partly) retreating public sector. PBC is still the major buying company, although its buyers' share is declining. Recently, PBC itself was partly privatized and its shares were traded on the stock market, with COCOBOD being the company's major shareholder. Currently, the world's largest cocoa processing companies, Barry Callebaut, Cargill, and Archer Daniels Midland (ADM), have outsourced part of their processing facilities to Ghana. Although international traders moved 'closer' to the farmers this did not result in direct contractual relations between buyers and cocoa farmers.

Following liberalization of the internal marketing of cocoa, the government announced that qualified LBCs would be allowed to export part of their cocoa purchases, with effect from October 2000. This was never put into place, which frustrated, in particular, international buyers who set up local businesses and also some of the larger LBCs. LBCs did not openly complain about COCOBOD's practices, however. After all, the relationship between LBCs and COCOBOD remains a hierarchical one, as the former depend on the board for their licence to operate.

As a result of the gradual pace of the reforms, LBCs got locked into a system with few incentives for high performance, and little financial scope for establishing strong relations with farmers. From a set margin of the FOB price ('free on board' price) LBCs paid purchasing clerks (PCs), who buy cocoa at the community level on commission basis, thus encouraging them to buy as much cocoa as possible from the farmers in their communities. It is likely that the introduction of competition among local buyers based on volume (instead of prices or quality) reduced the incentive for LBCs and PCs to be strict about quality control, and it induced PCs to cheat farmers with wrongly adjusted scales used for weighing cocoa. In 2005, COCOBOD declared all bags of cocoa with more than 25 per cent 'purple beans' to be substandard, and paid local buyers only half of the producer price. This constrained LBCs' financial performance and seriously affected livelihood of farmers; not being able to sell (or store) their cocoa, they lost their main source of income (Laven 2007b).

More recently, private actors and NGOs expanded their activities in Ghana, increasingly in partnership. For example, a shift from public extension to extension services provided by a public–private partnership (Cocoa Extension Public–Private Partnership Ghana) implied more involvement by public, private, and NGO actors, all using the same extension manual. This was strongly driven by the risk of supplier failure due to low productivity levels and an aging farmer population. The partnerships recognized the contribution of extension to reach higher productivity in a most efficient way. The interventions were also driven by the increasing demand for certified cocoa, which induced the physical segregation of certified cocoa from conventional cocoa. This gave international buyers the option to determine the exact source of the cocoa they bought through COCOBOD, thus creating direct relations with local buyers and/or farmer groups. This change in the value chain provided room for stronger vertical collaboration and integration and gave an impulse for farmers to organize (a requirement for certification).

COCOBOD continued to intervene in the sector, using partly the same instruments as in the period between 1980 and the year 2000. Competition on price is still not possible in Ghana. The government recently loosened its control over the supply chain by allowing certified cocoa to be kept separately from bulk cocoa. Increasing competition among private buyers for certified cocoa has been the result. In their sourcing strategies, like COCOBOD, the private sector focuses on control of supply. Cocoa producers are increasingly locked into 'sustainable' value chains in which they have still little decision-making power and little information (Laven and Boomsma 2012).

Ecuador

The case of Ecuador contrasts with the developments in Côte d'Ivoire and Ghana. In these two latter countries, cocoa is of utmost strategic importance and they are the major suppliers to international buyers and markets. Ecuador is a major player not because of its volume of cocoa, but because of the quality of the beans. The market share of fine flavour cocoa fell dramatically over the last century, due to new processing technology, bulk cocoa beans proving to be as good, or even preferred, by some chocolate manufacturers. However, especially in Europe, the demand for specialty cocoa is growing and easily capable of absorbing production increases. International demand for fine flavour cocoa outweighs supplies, which creates a very attractive niche for cocoa chain development. The WCF estimates that Ecuador exports approximately 65 per cent of the global supply of fine flavour cocoa (WCF 2013). The quality of Ecuadorian cocoa has been a product of nature, without much additional policies, until the end of the twentieth century, when quality policies have been introduced to ensure its distinctiveness in comparison with other varieties in the market (Table 13.3).

Period 1 1900–25: Cocoa Boom and Private Banking

Ecuador was a major producer of cocoa until the early twentieth century. At the turn of the century, it provided 20–25 per cent of world production. High cocoa prices, coupled with abundant supplies of cheap labour and an infrastructure of rivers connecting production areas with global export markets, gave rise to a booming business controlled by a powerful oligarchy, made up of large producers, exporters, importers, and bankers (De Janvry 1981; Henderson 1997). The Ecuadorian cocoa boom concentrated state power and created a class of very rich families, who enjoyed a luxurious lifestyle (Larrea and North 1997). Though cocoa exports provided the main source of currency for imports of consumer goods and fiscal income of the state, little of this was invested in productive infrastructure or domestic manufacturing.

In this first period, there was very intense personal intertwining between cocoa associated private interests and the Ecuadorian state, and particularly relations between the private Banco Comercial y Agricola (BCA) and the Association of

Table 13.3 Policy reforms and governance in the cocoa sector in Ecuador

Period	Policy Reform	Governance
1) 1900–25	Supporting elites and banks to avoid collapse due to commodity prices and plant diseases	Hierarchical combination of state governance and market power
2) 1925–98	Embedding cocoa in national industrial and economic policy	Market governance
3) 2000–present	Creating strategic alliances to defend a niche market position	Market governance, with targeted state governance

Agriculturalists, which controlled most of the cocoa production, trade, and exports. During this period, the fiscal needs of the state have been negotiated in sync with the private interest of the oligarchy. Direct links between private family interests and the government manifested itself in the so-called *banquete de estado* (the state's banquet) in Guayaquíl, linked to two Guayaquíl banks, the Banco de Ecuador and the BCA, which funded the steadily mounting internal public debt (Henderson 1997: 179). BCA controlled virtually all aspects related with cocoa exports.

This strong link with the cocoa sector became a major problem for BCA after the First World War when commodity prices fell and cocoa plant diseases spread. Faced with the prospect of a major banking collapse (Cabrera 2005), and no doubt pressed by the BCA congressional bloc, the government rescued the bank. The financial problems of a private bank and its cocoa plantation owners were solved by shifting the burden to other sectors, which created an inflationary process that affected the entire economy. In 1925, a coup d'état attacked this intimate 'steering' of state policies in the interest of a class of very rich private families.

Period 2 1925–98: From Rent Seeking to Export Promotion

The 1925 *coup d'état* managed to break the financial–political oligarchy. They dismantled the BCA and re-engineered the monetary institutions to prevent a similar banking crisis (Drake 1989). However, the dependence of the Ecuadorian state on agro-export taxes made it dependant on the political power of the plantation owners in the lowlands.

All this changed during the 1960s and 1970s when oil became Ecuador's most important export product, replacing the agro-export sector as the major source of fiscal income. The upward spiral in oil prices during the 1970s and the boost to public sector revenues derived from oil exports freed the Ecuadorian government from persistent balance of payments deficits and from a strong reliance on taxation of export agriculture to fund public expenditures. Oil trade enabled the state to embark upon an ambitious programme of industrial development, infrastructure construction, and social investment (Corkill 1985). Also, the size of the state bureaucracy increased sharply. Ecuador registered one of the highest average annual growth rates in public sector employment in the developing world (in excess of 10 per cent for 1976–80), with the capital city benefiting disproportionately (Corkill 1985).

This oil 'bonanza' created the conditions for structural deficits in public finance. Revenues from oil exploitation made Ecuador a preferred client of international lenders. At the turn of the century this resulted in it being one of the most indebted countries in Latin America. The scarcity of hard currency and the balancing of the fiscal deficit were coped with by money creation and the associated devaluation of the local currency. Depreciation of the local currency made domestic costs relatively cheap and resulted in high revenues from exports. This favoured the cocoa sector and partially offset the negative impact of falling cocoa prices during the 1980 and 1990s.

The Ecuadorian cocoa economy collapsed in the 1995–98 period. The specialty cocoa markets found a major producer in Indonesia, and in this competitive field the volume of Ecuadorian cocoa supplied to the internal markets stagnated to the pre-1995 level. Moreover, vertical integration in the cocoa chain was significantly reduced, particularly because smallholders replaced the plantations as the prime production sector. The state tried to break with the oligarchy and the oligarchy itself diversified its activities, especially by shifting to banana plantations. In the public domain, cocoa sector policy became integrated with wider macro-economic policies of export promotion and import substitution that generated conditions for the development of local processing facilities. Consequently, the influence of state policies in the cocoa chain decreased.

Period 3 1998–2007: The 'Dollarized Economy' and Competitiveness

Political turmoil resulted in several short-lived presidencies. In 2000, a new president took office and turned Ecuador into a dollarized economy: the US dollar became the official national currency. This dollarization dramatically changed the possibilities for the Ecuadorian government to use the devaluation of the currency as means to offset production inefficiencies and falling prices. The 'dollarization' of the economy forced companies to be more efficient in order to compete in the international market.

The emphasis of the government's agricultural policy shifted to an increased facilitation of supply chain partnerships and supply chain development efforts. The role of the state was limited and focused on the creation of 'strategic alliances' between chain actors. The state played a pivotal role in generating the national organizations and consultative councils through which this corporate governance was effectively institutionalized. The government expected that coordinated action between private and public actors would enable the marketing of Ecuador as a national brand for special quality cocoa.

This enabling policy became manifest in the regulation of quality in the cocoa chain that led to a specific policy to steer the impacts of the introduction and marketing of a new cocoa variety: CCN51. National cocoa trees ('Arriba') that produce the fine flavour cocoa appreciated in the world market are low yielding and are mostly restricted to small and medium-sized farms. CCN51 by contrast is a relatively new, high-yielding variety, and is mostly produced on large-scale plantations. Ecuador's local cocoa processing and chocolate manufacturing industries preferred CCN51 because it has high cocoa butter fat content and suffers no mould problems. However, most cocoa exporters were in favour of the fine flavour cocoa and its associated premiums. Exporters' profitability relied heavily on this price differential (around 15 per cent). A public agency actively supported the value chain of fine flavour cocoa to recover/defend the special position of Ecuador cocoa on the world market. A major result of this chain coordination is the decree of July 2005 that defines fine flavour cocoa as that harvested from the 'Arriba' variety, which has to be marketed separately from the new CCN51 variety. The national cocoa sector strategy focused on further positioning Ecuador's fine flavour cocoa in the national and international markets.

Conclusions

In all three countries we see that, at a certain point in time, a transition has been made from an institutional governance system with strong state involvement in price setting and international trade to a system where transactions are more market based. Everywhere, cocoa liberalization reforms increasingly confronted producers and traders with risks within value chain transactions. This increased 'instability' in the cocoa value chain has been mediated in the three case studies with the unfolding of new or adjusted institutional arrangements between private chain partners and the state. The extent to which the state maintains a leading role in the current situation differs, and is a result of the entangled sector and country-specific histories.

In Côte d'Ivoire, the government retained some influence, despite the political turmoil. Certain groups within the state stayed intact as a kind of technocratic bureaucracy that recently initiated new institutional arrangements to enhance price predictability, to ensure quality control, and to arrange some stability in the market. Service provisioning by the state is weak, but now new spaces for coordinated public and private initiatives are seeming to emerge, which encourages lead companies and some NGOs to align with technical and administrative capacities within the state.

The Ghanaian government maintained state control on internal prices, which materializes in the yearly review of cocoa prices, margins, and bonus systems. Mainly because more direct relations between international and local suppliers has recently become an option, this has not run into conflict with incentives for buying companies to invest in cocoa production or with private strategies primarily responding to the international demand to comply with sustainability standards.

In Ecuador, the government mainly sees its role as facilitating chain alliances, which can enforce the special position of Ecuador's quality cocoa in the world market. Quality regulations and public–private partnerships play an important role in vitalizing this 'high-price niche market' strategy, and sustaining the country's position as a conserver of cocoa varieties potentially relevant for the chocolate industry.

The chapter suggests that policy and strategy targeting sustainability in the complex and layered cocoa chain may be more effective when they connect to existing governance structures and policy measures instead of replacing them with an entirely new and disarticulated organizational architecture, with a drastically changed division of labour between public and private sectors. Complementary to the strong interest in private and voluntary forms of governance, in particular global standards and certification schemes, this chapter draws attention to the existence, and it suggests a revaluation, of sector-specific public policies.

The chapter warns against adopting a 'best for all' policy recommendation; for example, either a fully privatized and deregulated sector governed by voluntary standards or complete public control over the cocoa economy. The challenge lies in finding balanced and effective institutional arrangements of private sector strategies with existing responsive sector policies grounded in evolving bureaucratic and professional involvement with specific cocoa sector problems and dynamics.

This implies the need for transparent public–private configurations to facilitate coordination around the cocoa supply chain. Such an interest relates to an emerging research agenda (Evans 1995; Bierschenk 2010; Bierschenk and de Sardan 2014) that aims to gain insights into newly unfolding or adjusted institutional arrangements between cocoa value chain operators and effective public policy instruments. These may set the conditions for coordinated strategies in response to threats to the cocoa value chain, and for both the private and public sector to take up transformative roles in making the cocoa sector and chocolate industry increasingly prepared for the future.

References

Abbott, P., M. Wilcox, and W. A. Muir. 2005. *Corporate Social Responsibility in International Cocoa Trade*. West Lafayette, IN: Purdue University.

Akiyama, T., J. Baffes, D. Larson, and P. Varangis. 2001. *Commodity Market Reforms: Lessons of Two Decades*. Washington, DC: International Bank for Reconstruction and Development/World Bank.

Amezah, K. A. 2003. *Draft: The Impact of Reforms (Privatization of Cocoa Purchases and CSD/Mofa Merger) on Cocoa Extension Delivery*. Accra: Ministry of Food and Agriculture, Directorate of Agric Extension Services.

Amoah, J. 1998. *Marketing of Ghana Cocoa, 1885–1992*, Cocoa Outline Series 2. Accra: Jemre Enterprises.

Anin, T. E. 2003. *An Economic Blueprint for Ghana*. Woeli Publishing Services.

Beckman, B. 1976. *Organising the Farmers: Cocoa Politics and National Development in Ghana*. Uppsala: Scandinavian Institute of African Studies.

Bierschenk, T. 2010. *States at Work in West Africa: Sedimentation, Fragmentation and Normative Double-Binds*. Mainz: Institut für Ethnologie und Afrikastudien, Johannes-Gutenberg-Universität.

Bierschenk, T. and J.-P. O. de Sardan. 2014. *States at Work: Dynamics of African Bureaucracies*. Leiden: Brill.

Byerlee, D. 2011. *Producer Funding of R&D in Africa: An Underutilized Opportunity to Boost Commercial Agriculture*. ASTI/IFPRI–FARA Conference on Agricultural R&D in Africa, December 5–7, 2011, Accra, Ghana. Conference working paper 4. Washington, DC: International Food Policy Research Institute (IFPRI) and Forum for Agricultural Research in Africa (FARA). Available at: <http://ebrary.ifpri.org/cdm/ref/collection/p15738coll2/id/127028> (accessed 10 July 2015).

Cabrera, A. 2005. *Informe sobre el Cacao Arriba de Ecuador*. Geneva: Bio Trade Facilitation Programme, UNCTAD.

Corkill, D. 1985. 'Democratic politics in Ecuador, 1979–1984'. *Bulletin of Latin American Research* 4: pp. 63–74.

COSA (Committee on Sustainability Assessment). 2013. *The COSA Measuring Sustainability Report: Coffee and Cocoa in 12 Countries*. Philadelphia: The Committee on Sustainability Assessment.

Daviron, B. and P. Gibbon. 2002. 'Global commodity chains and African export agriculture'. *Journal of Agrarian Change* 2 (2): pp. 137–61.

De Janvry, A. 1981. *The Agrarian Question and Reformism in Latin America*. Baltimore: Johns Hopkins University Press.

DoC (Department of Cooperatives). 1990. *History of Ghana Cooperatives 1928–1985*. Accra: Department of Cooperatives.

Drake, P. W. 1989. *The Money Doctor in the Andes: The Kemmerer Missions, 1923–1933*. Durham: Duke University Press.

Evans, P. B. 1995. *Embedded Autonomy: States and Industrial Transformation*. Cambridge: Cambridge University Press.

Fold, N. 2002. 'Lead firms and competition in "bi-polar" commodity chains: grinders and branders in the global cocoa–chocolate industry'. *Journal of Agrarian Change* 2 (2): pp. 228–47.

Gereffi, G. 2013. 'Global value chains in a post-Washington Consensus world'. *Review of International Political Economy* 21: pp. 1–29.

Gereffi, G. and J. Lee. 2012. 'Why the world suddenly cares about global supply chains'. *Journal of Supply Chain Management* 48 (3): pp. 24–32.

Gibbon, P. and S. Ponte. 2005. *Trading Down: Africa, Value Chains, and the Global Economy*. Philadelphia: Temple University Press.

Gilbert, C. L. 2009 'Cocoa market liberalization in retrospect'. *Review of Business and Economics* 54 (3): pp. 294–312.

GlobalWitness. 2007. *Hot Chocolate: How Cocoa Fuelled the Conflict in Côte d'Ivoire: A Report by Global Witness, June 2007*. Washington, DC: Global Witness Publishing Inc. Available at: <http://www.globalwitness.org/sites/default/files/pdfs/cotedivoire.pdf> (accessed 25 April 2008).

Griffiths, A. and R. F. Zammuto. 2005. 'Institutional governance systems and variations in national competitive advantage: an integrative framework'. *Academy of Management Review* 30 (4): pp. 823–42.

Grossman Greene, S. and C. Bayer (2009) A Brief History of Cocoa in Ghana and Côte d'Ivoire. Tulane University, Payson Center for International Development. New Orleans. Available at: <http://npeclc.gov.gh/Downloads/A%20Brief%20History%20of%20Cocoa%20in%20Ghana%20and%20C%C3%B4te%20d%E2%80%99Ivoire.pdf> (accessed 5 July 2014).

Haque, I. U. 2004. *Commodities under Neoliberalism: The Case of Cocoa*. New York and Geneva: UNCTAD.

Hecht, R. M. 1983. 'The Ivory Coast economic "miracle": what benefits for peasant farmers?' *Journal of Modern African Studies* 21 (1): pp. 25–53.

Helmsing, A. H. J. and S. Vellema. 2011. 'Governance, inclusion and embedding'. In *Value Chains, Social Inclusion and Economic Development: Contrasting Theories and Realities*, edited by A. H. J. Helmsing and S. Vellema, pp. 1–19. London and New York: Routledge.

Henderson, P. 1997. 'Cocoa, finance and the state in Ecuador, 1895–1925'. *Bulletin of Latin American Research* 16 (2): pp. 169–86.

IMF (International Monetary Fund). 2009. *Impact of the Global Financial Crisis on Sub-Saharan Africa*. Washington, DC: International Monetary/Fund, African Department. Available at: <https://www.imf.org/external/pubs/ft/books/2009/afrglobfin/ssaglobalfin.pdf> (accessed 12 October 2011).

IMF/GoCdI (International Monetary Fund/Government of Côte d'Ivoire). 2002a. *Côte d'Ivoire: Letter of Intent, Memorandum of Economic and Financial Policies, and Technical Memorandum of Understanding*. Washington, DC/Abidjan: IMF. Available at: <https://www.imf.org/external/np/loi/2002/civ/01/index.htm> (accessed 25 April 2008).

IMF/GoCdI (International Monetary Fund/). 2002b. *Côte d'Ivoire: Interim Poverty Reduction Strategy Paper*. Abidjan: IMF. Available at: <https://www.imf.org/external/np/prsp/2002/civ/01/013102.pdf> (accessed 25 April 2008).

ISEAL Alliance (International Social and Environmental Accreditation and Labelling Alliance). 2013. *Demonstrating and Improving Poverty Impacts: ISEAL Common Core Indicators*. London: ISEAL Alliance.

ISEAL Alliance (International Social and Environmental Accreditation and Labelling Alliance). 2014. *Code of Good Practice for Assessing the Impacts of Social and Environmental Standards Systems: Revision 2.0*. London: ISEAL Alliance.

Larrea, C. and L. L. North. 1997. 'Ecuador: adjustment policy impacts on truncated development and democratisation'. *Third World Quarterly* 18: pp. 913–34.

Laven, A. 2007a. *Marketing Reforms in Ghana's Cocoa Sector: Partial Reforms, Partial Benefits?* Background Note. London: Overseas Development Institute. Available at: <http://www.odi.org.uk/resources/download/420.pdf> (accessed 25 April 2008).

Laven, A. 2007b. 'Who is interested in good quality cocoa from Ghana?'. In *Tropical Food Chains, Governance Regimes for Quality Management*, edited by R. Ruben, M. v. Boekel, A. v. Tilburg, and J. Trienekes, pp. 189–211. Wageningen: Wageningen Academic.

Laven, A. 2010. *The Risks of Inclusion: Shifts in Governance Processes and Upgrading Opportunities for Cocoa Farmers in Ghana*. Amsterdam: KIT.

Laven, A. 2011. 'The Ghanaian state and inclusive upgrading in the global cocoa chain'. In *Value Chains, Social Inclusion, and Economic Development: Contrasting Theories and Realities*, edited by A. H. J. Helmsing and S. Vellema, pp. 121–47. London and New York: Routledge.

Laven, A. and M. Boomsma. 2012. *Incentives for Sustainable Cocoa Production in Ghana: Moving from Maximizing Outputs to Optimizing Performance*. Amsterdam: Royal Tropical Institute.

Losch, B. 2002 'Global restructuring and liberalization: Côte d'Ivoire and the end of the international cocoa market?' *Journal of Agrarian Change* 2 (2): pp. 206–27.

Ministry of Finance Ghana. 1999. *Ghana Cocoa Sector Development Strategy*. Accra: Ministry of Finance Ghana.

Morgan, J. 2010. *Thoughts on our Work in Cote d'Ivoire*. Available at: <http://cocoasustainability.com/2011/04/thoughts-on-our-work-in-cote-divoire/> (accessed 30 June 2014).

OECD (Organisation for Economic Co-operation and Development). 2006. *African Economic Outlook 2005–2006, Côte d'Ivoire*. Paris: OECD. Available at: <http://www.oecd.org/dev/36739479.pdf> (accessed 25 April 2008).

Ruf, F. 2007. *The Cocoa Sector: Expansion, or Green and Double Green Revolutions*. Background Note. London: Overseas Development Institute.

Ruf, F. 2009. 'Libéralisation, cycles politiques et cycles du cacao: le décalage historique Côte-d'Ivoire-Ghana'. *Cahiers agricultures* 18 (4): pp. 343–9.

Stads, G.-J. 2011. *Benchmarking Agricultural Research Investment and Capacity Indicators in West and Central Africa*. Washington, DC, and Abidjan: International Food Policy Research Institute and the West and Central African Council for Agricultural Research and Development.

Stads, G. J. and S. Doumbia. 2010. *Côte d'Ivoire: Les tendances à long-terme des investissements et de la capacité de la R&D agricole*. Washington, DC, and Abidjan: International Food Policy Research Institute and National Agricultural Research Institute.

Teal, F. and M. Vigneri. 2004. *Production Changes in Ghana Cocoa Farming Households under Market Reforms*. Oxford: Centre for the Study of African Economies.

Ton, G., S. Vellema, and L. Ge. 2014. 'The triviality of measuring ultimate outcomes: acknowledging the span of direct influence'. *IDS Bulletin*, 45 (6): pp. 37–48.

Ton, G., G. Hagelaar, A. Laven, and S. Vellema. 2008. *Chain Governance, Sector Policies and Economic Sustainability in Cocoa: A Comparative Analysis of Ghana, Côte d'Ivoire, and Ecuador.* Market, Chains and Sustainable Development Strategy and Policy paper, no.7. Wageningen: Wageningen University and Research centre. Available at: <http://www.kit.nl/sed/wp-content/uploads/publications/1502_Cocoa%20sector.pdf> (accessed 30 June 2014).

Toungara, J. 2001. 'Ethnicity and political crisis in Côte d'Ivoire'. *Journal of Democracy* 12 (3): pp. 63–72.

Vellema, S. and J. van Wijk. 2014. 'Partnerships intervening in global food chains: the emergence of co-creation in standard-setting and certification'. *Journal of Cleaner Production.* DOI: 10.1016/j.jclepro.2014.03.090.

Vellema, S., G. Ton, N. de Roo, and J. van Wijk. 2013 'Value chains, partnerships and development: using case studies to refine programme theories'. *Evaluation* 19 (3): pp. 304–20.

WCF (World Cocoa Foundation). 2013. 'Ecuador: WCF, LINDT & SPRÜNGLI, and USDA-ARS support fine-flavor cocoa research'. *WCF Newsletter March and April 2013.* <http://worldcocoafoundation.org/wcf-newsletter-march-april-2013/> (accessed 1 September 2014).

Whitley, R. 1999. *Divergent Capitalisms: The Social Structuring and Change of Business Systems.* Oxford: Oxford University Press.

Woods, D. 2003. 'The tragedy of the cocoa pod: rent-seeking, land and ethnic conflict in Ivory Coast'. *Journal of Modern African Studies* 41 (4): pp. 641–55.

World Bank. 2003. *Ivory Coast: Strengthening Public Expenditure Management and Controls Public Expenditure Review (Report No. 27141-IVC).* Washington, DC: World Bank. Available at: <https://openknowledge.worldbank.org/bitstream/handle/10986/14670/271410IVC.txt?sequence=2> (accessed 6 May 2008).

14

Chocolate Brands' Communication of CSR in Germany

Nina Langen and Monika Hartmann

Introduction

Ethical branding can provide a critical point of differentiation for companies, especially in highly saturated markets such as the European food markets. Furthermore, it has the potential to influence a number of stakeholder-related outcomes, such as their loyalty to the company and their perception of the firm. In fact, research suggests high and increasing levels of stakeholder interest in corporate social responsibility (CSR) (see Hartmann 2011 for an overview).[1] A crucial point for the consideration of a firm's ethical performance is the provision of adequate information to stakeholders when deciding, for example, on purchases, investments, or employment opportunities (Wood 2010). Thus, the communication of a firm's responsible conduct to its internal (e.g. employees) as well as external stakeholders (e.g. consumers) in a credible way is essential for a company to reap the full benefits of its CSR activities.

Enterprises can choose from a large variety of instruments to design their CSR communication. According to stakeholder theory, CSR communication should address different stakeholders and apply forms and channels of communication that match the individual needs of stakeholder groups. The consumer is one key stakeholder for food manufacturing companies. Other central stakeholders are employees, suppliers, retailers, the community, and non-governmental organizations (NGOs).

---

[1] According to ISO 26000 (ISO 2010), a newly introduced guideline defines social responsibility of organizations as the responsibility of an organization for the impacts of its decisions and activities on society and the environment, through transparent and ethical behaviour that contributes to sustainable development, including health and welfare of society, takes into account expectations of stakeholders, is in compliance with applicable law and consistent with international norms of behaviour, and is integrated throughout and practised in an organization's relationships.

In this chapter we first categorize the means of communication companies use to signal their CSR involvement with respect to addressees (different stakeholders), the character of communication (controllability, credibility, and visibility), and third party involvement. Second, we analyse the extent and types of CSR communication in the German chocolate sector via labels on products and via information provided on firms' websites.

The German chocolate sector has been selected because of its economic importance, and the existence of central CSR-related issues. Chocolate is one of the most favoured luxury foods in Germany, with 11.6 kg per capita consumption in 2010 (ICCO 2012).

In 2014, chocolate products with a value of 5.3 billion euros were produced in Germany, representing 43 per cent of the production value in the German confectionary industry (BDSI 2015a, b).[2]

Germany imports 13 per cent of the world's cocoa production and is thus the second biggest importer of cocoa after the USA (21 per cent) (ICCO 2012). Ninety per cent of the cocoa imported for the chocolate production in Germany originates from Western Africa. The Côte d'Ivoire is the world's most important cocoa producing country and, with 59.5 per cent of all cocoa imports in 2014, the primary source for Germany's cocoa imports (BDSI 2015c).

Accordingly, the working and living situation of the cocoa producers in the Côte d'Ivoire is from the German perspective of relevance. An investigation reveals that, on the one hand, cocoa is the most important cash crop, nourishing around 6 million people; most of them small-scale farmers with 1 to 3 hectares of land. On the other hand, property rights in cocoa production are unsettled, arising from the cocoa production drain away, and partly finance the war between government and insurgents in the region (see Hütz-Adams 2010). Furthermore, the small-scale cocoa producers lack general information with respect to the highly volatile market prices and are often greatly dependent on middlemen to sell their products. More importantly, child labour and child trafficking play a considerable role in cocoa production in the Côte d'Ivoire (e.g. Payson Center 2011). Just focusing on these last two issues—the absence of a fair pricing scheme for the small-scale farmers and the presence of child labour—reveals that basic international arrangements, such as the Universal Declaration of Human Rights (UN 2012), the standards set by the International Labour Organization (ILO) including the conventions on child labour (see ILO Convention No. 182 and No. 138; ILO 2012) do not hold in the Côte d'Ivoire (Hütz-Adams 2010). Chocolate manufacturing companies are seen to have responsibility for these issues as their business practices considerably influence producers' livelihoods. Therefore, CSR activities by chocolate firms are important, and the respective communication well suited to address this study's objectives.

---

[2] The ten largest (according to the sales volume) chocolate manufactures in Germany are Kraft Foods Inc., Nestlé, Ferrero, Lindt & Sprüngli, Franz Zentis GmbH und Co. KG, Stollwerck AG, Alfred Ritter GmbH und Co. KG, Hachez, Tchibo, and Erich Hamann (Uni Bremen n.d.).

This contribution is structured as follows. The next section, 'CSR Activities in the Chocolate Sector', provides background information regarding the status quo of CSR activities of chocolate producers. Afterwards, we discuss options for firms to communicate their responsible conduct, and also discuss the advantages and disadvantages of specific schemes. Then, we present the results of our study on CSR communication in the German chocolate sector, and conclude the chapter.

CSR Activities in the Chocolate Sector

Consumers who become aware of the abusive labour practices, human trafficking, and child slavery in the cocoa industry can become a critical mass if they start to spread this information and encourage others to also boycott firms who are not able to guarantee 'free of' chocolate (see e.g. the articles posted in the *Huffington Post* in the last few years (Robbins 2010; Gregory 2013)). Petitions signed by consumers are the result (e.g. around 30,000 signatures for the 'Raise the Bar, Hershey! Campaign' in 2011, over 5,000 signings in 2012 (Global Exchange 2011; ILRF et al. 2012)).

First Steps to End Child Labour

The public discussion about the social conditions in cocoa production and the responsibility of chocolate producers in this context started in the year 2000 with a TV report in the UK that revealed the true state of child labour and child trafficking in cocoa farming (Hütz-Adams 2010; Payson Center 2011). In response to this discussion, and to pre-empt a planned US law which was intended to make the cocoa processing companies responsible for the production circumstances in the producing countries, chocolate producing firms initiated a voluntary protocol—the Harkin–Engel Protocol—also called the cocoa protocol (Hütz-Adams 2010; CMA 2011). Signatories of the Harkin–Engel Protocol commit themselves to combat the worst forms of child labour. Due to Hütz-Adams (2010), the protocol falls short of a comprehensive approach to improve the labour conditions within cocoa production. From the perspective of the Payson Center (2011), the protocol is too ambitious and far-reaching, and thus an achievement of the declared goals could not have been expected. Both studies agree that the measures initiated though the Harkin–Engel Protocol have not, so far, been able to eliminate the worst forms of child labour. As a consequence, the success of the Harkin–Engel Protocol is considered to be rather marginal (Hütz-Adams 2010; Payson Center 2011). Parallel to the implementation of the Harkin–Engel Protocol, some companies individually initiated projects to improve the working conditions of cocoa farmers in their value chain (Hütz-Adams 2010).

The German Picture

A survey conducted by Hütz-Adams (2010) with 15 cocoa processing companies in Germany indicates that the kind and extent of chocolate manufacturers' efforts differ considerably. In general, firms are aware of the serious deficits in the field of labour rights, especially with respect to child labour in the Côte d'Ivoire and some other cocoa exporting countries. But, companies consider the governments in the respective countries to be primarily responsible for any improvement. Several firms refer to individual projects they support, but information regarding the success of the projects, for example, numbers of farmers benefiting from the project, is lacking. Certification of cocoa within programmes such as Fair Trade, Rainforest Alliance, and UTZ Certified is, in general, considered by chocolate manufacturers to be an effective strategy to advance producers' livelihood via minimum prices (e.g. in the case of Fair Trade) or to improve environmental or social conditions in cocoa production (e.g. in the case of Rainforest Alliance and UTZ Certified).[3]

To sum up, firms in the chocolate industry are increasingly confronted by stakeholders' expectations to not only behave responsibly with respect to internal firm behaviour but to cope with social and environmental responsibilities along their entire value chain, including the situation in the producing countries. Thus, chocolate companies risk public criticism. To neutralize potential threats or exploit the opportunities due to public concerns regarding production and processing, a comprehensive approach is needed. Addressing those CSR-related issues relevant for internal and external stakeholders (e.g. child labour and non-sustainable wages for producers) is of considerable importance (Piacentini et al. 2000; Heikkurinen and Forsman-Hugg 2011).

Communication of CSR

Conceptual Issues

For stakeholders, it is difficult to evaluate a firm's 'true' social and ecological performance as responsible conduct of firms is, in most cases, not observable. As a consequence, information asymmetry becomes an issue. This holds especially true for external stakeholders such as consumers. Enterprises can lower the level of information asymmetry by signalling their superior social and ecological performance, thereby complementing information on, for example, financial issues so far provided to investors, or on products, quality, and prices directed at consumers (Schoenheit et al. 2007). This, however, has its own challenges. Insights from the economics of information reveal that deception is most likely, while, at the same time, most harmful, in the case of credence attributes (e.g. Rubin 2000). CSR is a credence attribute characterized by a high level of complexity. The verification of the truthfulness of CSR-related information is difficult or actually impossible (e.g. for consumers) due to considerable or prohibitively high information costs. This leaves ample room for fraud. Due to the information asymmetry, 'signalling' responsible conduct is perceived as biased. Stakeholders assume that firms stress

---

[3] For prospects and constraints of these certifications see Hütz-Adams (2010: 65ff.).

positive achievements in their CSR communication while neglecting negative ones. In addition, consumers might wonder whether those who advertise their CSR activities most prominently are those most involved in social and ecological activities, or rather greenwashing their behaviour. Thus, CSR communication needs exactly what it wants to achieve: trust (Schoenheit et al. 2007; see also Hartmann 2011).

Despite those problems, 'CSR signalling' has gained considerable relevance over the last decade, with enterprises having a large variety of instruments for their CSR communication. Information regarding the ethical and ecological initiatives of a company can be distributed by advertisements on product packaging or in-store banners, via standards, reports, print media, the TV, radio, the Internet (e.g. via their website), or word-of-mouth marketing (Du et al. 2010). Different communication means can complement one another as the information distributed refers to different elements of the overall CSR concept. Some information provided by firms relates more to a single (selected) product(s) of the firm (e.g. product labels) while others present the firm's overall involvement regarding CSR (e.g. CSR reports). In addition, firms' communication differs in terms of third party involvement, with the latter increasingly used to strengthen credibility (Fliess et al. 2007; Schoenheit et al. 2007) and overcome the challenges discussed. In the following, those communication schemes with considerable relevance for companies in the food sector will be discussed and analysed with respect to their addressees (e.g. consumers), the character of communication, and their third party involvement.

Point of Sale Communication

In the food retail sector, in-store advertisements such as banners, posters, leaflets, or flyers are of considerable relevance (Jones et al. 2007; Schoenheit et al. 2007). Food retailers, in addition, increasingly include eco- and social labelled products in their assortment, as these signal to consumers that they pay attention to social and environmental issues in their product portfolio (Schoenheit et al. 2007). Labels that are used in this respect in the chocolate sector, with Europewide, in several cases worldwide, relevance, are, for example, those of the Fairtrade Labelling Organizations International and of the Rainforest Alliance, as well as the EU organic logo.[4] They refer to the production and/or trading process of the respective product and/or the environmental quality of the product,[5] but do not provide a statement regarding the entire CSR achievements of the respective company (Fliess et al. 2007; Schoenheit et al. 2007). In addition, one also can observe that food enterprises increasingly advertise their products with logos that refer to their individual CSR involvement. Product logos regarding cause-related marketing

---

[4] See <http://www.fairtrade.net/; rainforest-alliance.org/; ec.europa.eu/agriculture/organic/eu-policy/logo_en>.
[5] While eco-labels can relate to product- as well as to non-product-related production and process methods, social labels communicate information on non-product-related production and process methods only (Fliess et al. 2007: 22).

(CrM)[6] campaigns belong to this group and are also of relevance in the chocolate sector (see next section 'Standards and Codes of Conduct'). The clear advantage of this communication tool is that it allows firm-specific CSR involvement to be directly communicated to one important stakeholder group: consumers. CrM has gained increasing popularity over the last decade and seems to be of especial relevance in the food sector (Langen et al. 2010).

Standards and Codes of Conduct

The existing plethora of CSR-related labelling schemes on the food market implies that there is a danger of confusing consumers and leaving room for fraud, thereby eroding the labels' overall credibility (Fliess et al. 2007). Thus, while the strength of labelling schemes is their visibility and simplicity, their weakness is their credibility if they are not backed up by a third party certified standard.[7] CSR-related global and national labels such as Fair Trade are, in general, backed up by third party certified standards, while this is often not the case for firm-specific labels. The credibility of labels varies with the competence and independence of the institution that grants them, the transparency of the criteria, the control of their compliance, and the extent to which stakeholders are knowledgeable about these issues (Fliess et al. 2007; Schoenheit et al. 2007).

CSR-oriented standards ease not only communication to consumers via labels or emblems but are also of increasing relevance in business to business (B2B) relationships. Examples for B2B standards directed at elements of CSR and relevant at a global level are the standard of the International Organization for Standardization (ISO) with respect to the environment (ISO 14000) or CSR (ISO 26000), both going well beyond the chocolate and even the food sector.[8]

Enterprises, in addition, can signal their responsible behaviour by signing codes of conduct (CoC). There exist a large number of CoC that are applied by businesses with the aim to anchor ecological, social, and/or ethical principles into their business strategies. Some of these CoC are developed by single enterprises, with Unilever and Walmart being prominent examples (Schoenheit et al. 2007; Voss and Wilke 2008),[9] while others have arisen out of business associations (e.g. BSCI CoC) or of alliances of companies, trade unions, and voluntary organizations

---

[6] CrM is a marketing tool where the product purchase leads to a target-oriented donation regarding a designated cause promoted on the product by label. It allows the company to take up responsibility for a self-defined good issue, and it is also used to make a company's social or environmental commitment visible. Thus, CrM enables consumers to contribute, with their purchase, to a good cause.

[7] In fact, the central purpose of these standards is to communicate credible information on product and process characteristics, thereby easing coordination between actors in food chains across space and time (Hartmann 2011).

[8] See <http://www.iso.org/iso/home/standards/management-standards/iso14000.htm> and <http://www.iso.org/iso/home/standards/iso26000.htm>.

[9] See <http://www.walmartstores.com/media/cdnpull/statementofethics/pdf/U.S_SOE.pdf>; <http://www.unilever.com/aboutus/purposeandprinciples/ourprinciples/default.aspx>.

Table 14.1 Business participation in the United Nations Global Compact (2015)

Sector	All	Food Producers	Beverage Producers	Food and Drug Retailers
Number of Firms				
Registered firms	8320	379	132	30
Firms with active participation[*]	6371	300	109	23
Share of Active Firms in All Registered Firms				
Share of	77%	79%	83%	77%

Note: *Companies' status is dependent on the preparation of a CoP report. Firms with the status 'active participation' have provided their annual CoP report.

Source: United Global Conduct <http://www.unglobalcompact.org/participants/search>.

(e.g. Ethical Trading Initiative (ETI)).[10] Several CoC have been introduced over the last decades with a specific focus on the agri-food sector, such as the International Code of Conduct on the Distribution and Use of Pesticides, or even on a single product area, such as the Code of Conduct for Cocoa initiated by UTZ.[11] Many CoC not only request their members to comply and disseminate the respective information internally, but also to communicate and transfer their involvement into the supply chain by requesting their suppliers to take responsible conduct seriously. The latter also holds for the UN Global Compact,[12] the world largest voluntary initiative in the area of CSR, in which central UN declarations that relate to the areas of human rights, labour standards, the environment, and corruption were condensed into ten standards for responsible business conduct (Williams 2004; Moon and Vogel 2008; United Nations Global Compact 2013). Signatory firms are expected to meet those standards and are requested to prepare an annual communication on progress (CoP) report, to secure transparency and disclosure, which are seen critical for the success of the initiative. Of the 8320 companies registered in January 2015 in the UN Compact, 6371 had an active CoP status (see Table 14.1).[13] Of the registered firms, 379 are from the food, 132 from the beverage, and 30 from the food and drug retail sector. Of those, 300, 109, and 23, respectively have an active status. Only three of the world's ten largest confectionary companies that manufacture some form of chocolate are members of the UN Global Compact (United Nations Global Compact 2015).[14] Despite the success

---

[10] See <http://www.bsci-intl.org/>; <http://www.ethicaltrade.org/sites/default/files/resources/ETI%20Base%20Code%20-%20English_0.pdf>; see also Dlott et al. (2006).

[11] See <http://www.fao.org/agriculture/crops/core-themes/theme/pests/pm/code/en/>; <http://www.utzcertified-trainingcenter.com/home/images/stories/library_files/EN_UTZ_Cocoa_Module_2014.pdf>.

[12] <http://www.unglobalcompact.org/>.

[13] A company's status is dependent on the preparation of a CoP report. If the annual report is not provided on time it moves from the status 'communicating' or 'active' to 'non-communicating' or 'non-active'. If the deadline for submitting the CoP has passed by over 12 months, firms are expelled from the Global Compact participant list (see <http://www.unglobalcompact.org/>).

[14] Top ten confectionary companies that manufacture some form of chocolate measured by net confectionery sales value in 2014 (<http://www.icco.org/about-cocoa/chocolate-industry.html>).

of the UN Global Compact, this and many other CoC initiatives have not gone without criticism, as they often lack performance standards and verification procedures and thus leave room for opportunistic behaviour (Williams 2004). CoC are oriented as obligatory rules for employees of an enterprise but can also be transferred to partners in the supply chain. They are primarily relevant at the internal level of a company and serve, to a lesser extent, as a communication tool in the direction of, for example, consumers or the media.

CSR Report

As a response to the increasing information request of stakeholders, enterprises publish their ecological and social activities, and the respected objectives, successes, and, in some cases, also failures in special sustainability or CSR reports.[15] Reporting has grown steadily over the last two decades. At the beginning of the 1990s corporate non-financial reports (environmental, sustainability, and community reports), as well as annual reports with significant relevant sections on those issues,[16] played barely any role. In contrast, for the year 2013 a total of 3818 respective reports have been published.[17] From the 3818 companies reporting on CSR in 2013, 216 enterprises are food and beverage companies (see Table 14.2). Of the ten largest confectionary companies mentioned, four published a CSR report.[18]

To overcome a lack of accountability companies have increasingly followed sustainability reporting guidance and third party assurance schemes over the last few years (Du et al. 2010). Regarding the former, the Global Reporting Initiative (GRI) is by far the most widely used.[19] In 2013, about 70 per cent of all companies (62 per cent of all food companies) that worldwide provided for a CSR report followed the GRI guidelines (see Table 14.2). The GRI aims to enhance the quality, rigour, and comparability of disclosure on economic, environmental, and social performance (Freeman et al. 2010). The guidelines provide comprehensive reporting principles as well as structured report content incorporating indicators for the three performance dimensions (Owen and O'Dwyer 2008) and offer-specific

---

[15] CSR reporting by food companies is still voluntary in most countries, though some governments have implemented or are in the process of introducing, at least for some parts of their corporate sectors, binding measures or legislation on CSR disclosure. It should be also noted that disclosure on air, water, and land pollution is mandatory in all OECD and numerous non-OECD countries (Fliess et al. 2007: 28; Schoenheit et al. 2007: 26; GRI 2014).

[16] From the integrative view of CSR it would make sense for financial as well as non-financial matters to be communicated in one integrated report. Though, so far CRS reporting has overwhelmingly taken place in separate reports the share of integrated reports rose from 13% in 2010 to 21% in 2014 (reports published in the respective years) indicating that there is a trend towards a greater relevance of integrated reporting (own calculations based on information from the GRI Sustainable Disclosure Database <http://database.globalreporting.org/>, accessed 15 January 2015).

[17] Social disclosure, however, is, according to Owen and O'Dwyer (2008), far from being a recent phenomenon (for a brief historical overview see Owen and O'Dwyer 2008).

[18] See <http://www.icco.org/about-cocoa/chocolate-industry.html> and <http://www.unglobalcompact.org/participants/search>.

[19] In May 2013, GRI released the fourth generation of its guidelines.

Table 14.2 2013 CSR reports differentiated by sector and assurance level

Sector	Total Reports	Reports according to GRI Guidelines				
		All	Without External Assurance		With External Assurance	
	No. Firms (1)	No. Firms (2)	No. Firms (3)	% of all 4 = (3)/(2)	No. Firms (5)	% of all 6 = (5)/(2)
All Sectors	3818	2679	1567	58%	1112	42%
Food and Beverage Products	216	134	82	61%	52	39%

Source: Sustainable Disclosure database: <http://database.globalreporting.org/>.

supplements for some sectors. For example, for the food sector GRI launched a Food Processing Sector Supplement in 2010. This aims to facilitate effective reporting for food processing and covers areas specific for food sector companies such as food safety, animal welfare, and affordable food products (GRI 2014). The uptake of the GRI framework has steadily increased since its introduction in 2001. To further increase credibility, CSR reports can be supported by an external assurance. As Table 14.2 reveals, a considerable share of those (food) companies applying the GRI guidelines make use of this option. The main addressees of CSR reports are actual or potential shareholders, consumer pressure groups, media, policymakers, and, to a somewhat lesser extent, employees; the reports are generally not primarily directed at individual consumers (Jones et al. 2007; Schoenheit et al. 2007).

Communication of CSR via Media

The ecological, social, and ethical behaviour of firms is also communicated via traditional media (TV, radio, print media), which, in general, has two purposes: on the one hand, the channels are used as an advertisement tool by firms to disseminate information about their CSR conduct; on the other hand, they act as a critical observer informing about positive CSR conduct (e.g. awards such as the Rainforest Alliance Sustainable Standard-Setter Award, which honours companies with a responsible record; in 2012 the Blommer Chocolate Company obtained this award)[20] or uncovering unsustainable behaviour of firms and distributing this knowledge to the public (e.g. making reference to firms in documentary films on child labour such as *Chocolate: The Bitter Truth*; see also Schäfer et al. 2006). In general, more 'bad' news, information about, for example, food scandals and misconduct of food companies, is distributed than good news. Media information on CSR is oriented at an interested public, and although individuals are rather addressed as citizens and not in their function as consumers, such information might impact purchase decision-making (Schoenheit et al. 2007).

---

[20] See <http://www.rainforest-alliance.org/newsroom/press-releases/gala-honorees12>.

Though traditional media still plays an important role in influencing public opinion with respect to companies, its power is declining due to the Internet. Companies' CSR online communication is the norm in large food enterprises, especially in Europe (see Lang et al. 2006).[21] Blogs, green web sites, and Twitter have created an explosion of information sources regarding CSR. Though positive in many respects due to the infinitive quantity of information, its quality is hard to evaluate by stakeholders. Social media opens the possibility for companies to enter into a dialogue, especially with engaged and critical audiences, via CSR platforms and blogs about emerging issues before they become a crisis. Thereby, risk can be mitigated and reputation enhanced. Another advantage of new media is that it enables firms to pursue their own agenda setting, thereby avoiding the gatekeeper function of journalists. Main determinants to launch CSR communication successfully via social media are authenticity, transparency, and patience (Du et al. 2010; Fieseler et al. 2010). But social media does not only serve the needs of companies. It also allows stakeholders to share information, thereby connecting a huge community of 'Watchdogs' and 'Ambassadors' that report and thereby inform each other about the positive endeavours of (food) companies in the areas of environment and social issues (e.g. child labour) as well as perceived misconduct (Du et al. 2010; Fieseler et al. 2010).

While, for medium and large enterprises, CSR reports and advertising campaigns become state-of-the-art, micro and small enterprises tend not to communicate their CSR endeavours and, if so, do so in a localized and unsystematic manner (e.g. Murillo and Lozano 2006; Nielsen and Thomson 2009). Informal communication by managers and employees, word of mouth, or manager/owner civic engagement in the local community are often the main channels by which stakeholders are informed about micro- and small-sized companies efforts with regard to CSR (Lee et al. 2008; Walther et al. 2010).

The exposition given reveals that a large number of communication channels which allow (food) companies to disseminate information about their CSR involvement exist. The means differ with respect to the addressee, the ability to control and plan CSR communication by the company, and the credibility as it is perceived by stakeholders, with, in general, a trade-off between the latter two. The less controllable the source of the information is by the company the more trustworthy it is seen by its stakeholders (Nielsen and Thomson 2009; Du et al. 2010). Credibility of communication, however, is also influenced by factors such as stakeholders' perception of a company's authenticity, commitment, and motives with respect to its CSR endeavours. Regarding the latter, studies show that the communication of extrinsic, firm-serving motives besides intrinsic motives in the CSR message can enhance credibility and reduce scepticism (Du et al. 2010). Table 14.3 collates the findings and provides an overview of the different communication means and their characteristics.

---

[21] However, Lee et al. (2009) show for the USA that, of the top 100 US retailers, only 58% mentioned CSR principles on their websites.

Table 14.3 Characterization of CSR communication

Communication Means	Third party Involved	Controllability by the Company	Addressee	Public Visibility	Credibility
Cause-related Marketing	yes (NGOs)	medium	consumer	very high	low to high[1,2]
Advertisement					
Package	no	high	consumer	very high	low to medium[1]
In Store	no	high	consumer	high	low to medium[1]
Media and Internet	no	high	all stake-holders	high	low to medium[1]
B2C CSR Labels					
Not certified	no	high	consumer	high	low to medium[1]
Third party certified	yes	low	consumer	high	medium to high[1,3]
B2B Standards	yes	low	customer, supplier	very low	high[3]
CSR Reports					
plain	no	high	shareholders, activists, media	low	low to medium[1]
GRI	no	medium	shareholders, activists, media	low	low to high[1]
GRI + TPA	yes	low to medium	shareholders, activists, media	low	medium to high[1,3]
Code of Conducts	yes	low	employees, supply chain partners	very low	low to medium[1,4]
Traditional Media	yes	low to medium	interested public	high	low to medium[1,5]
Social Media	yes	low to medium	activists, media, company, consumer	low to medium	low to medium[1,5]

Note: Variation in credibility due to: (1) firm's reputation; (2) NGO reputation, transparency, cause-brand fit; (3) standard (assurance) agency's reputation; (4) the requests linked to the CoC and their control; (5) reputation of media outlet/channel.

Source: Own compilation based on Schoenheit et al. (2007); Jones et al. (2007); Du et al. (2010); Fieseler et al. (2007); Williams (2004); Kienzle and Rennhak (2009); Langen et al. (2010); European Commission (2009); Edelman (2011); GfK et al. (2009).

CSR Communication in the German Chocolate Sector

To assess the extent to which German chocolate manufacturers communicate their social and environmental engagement to stakeholders, two types of firms' CSR communications have been selected and analysed: (1) the communication on chocolate product packages; and (2) the communication on chocolate manufacturing and retail websites. As discussed, communication via labels is assumed to be primarily directed at consumers. It is examined at the point of sale (POS). Information given on websites potentially addresses several stakeholder groups such as retailers, investors, NGOs, employees, and consumers. Since the space available on a product package is limited, it is expected that information presented on the websites provides more detailed and a broader range of CSR information in comparison to that available at the POS.

CSR Communication via Label

To know which manufacturers offer chocolate bars in the German market, a complete inventory count of chocolate bars was conducted in the discounters Aldi and Lidl, the full-range food providers Edeka, Rewe, and Real, the food and department store Kaufhof, and the organic food shops Basic and Bergfeld's in Bonn in December 2011. With this selection we account for the plurality of private brands on the one hand and manufacturers' brands on the other. The retailers Rewe, Real, Edeka, and Lidl offer private and manufacturer chocolate brands. Aldi primarily concentrates on private brands while Kaufhof, Basic, and Bergfeld's almost exclusively sell manufacturer brands. In the eight retail stores, 1001 chocolate bars of 52 different brands were identified and analysed (see Table 14.4). Many chocolate bars of one brand are sold in different flavours. Not counting those bars that only differ by flavour (e.g. milk chocolate versus hazelnut chocolate) still leaves 293 different bars of chocolate brands. The size of packages varied from 420 g multi-packages to single 20 g bars.

Of the 293 chocolate bars, about 20 per cent (57 packages) carry a CSR-related label. We consider all labels that refer to the social and/or ecological production of the chocolate or of the enterprise as a CSR label. Thus, labels that refer to the organic production of the products are also seen as CSR labels. At this point it should be noted that, in a smaller 2010 inventory (carried out before the study) in the two stores Aldi and Edeka, we could not detect any chocolate bar with a CSR-related label. While, in 2011, Aldi still did not offer any chocolate bars with CSR labels, this does not hold for Edeka, which in the meantime sells four different chocolate bars with CSR labels. As we consider 'bio' to be a CSR label, all products of the organic supermarkets Basic and Bergfeld's carry a CSR label. However, almost 50 per cent of the chocolate bars in those two organic stores have, in addition, a second and even a third CSR-related label (e.g. the international Fair Trade label).

Table 14.4 Number of chocolate bars sold in the market with and without CSR labels

	Number of Chocolate Bars Sold				Number of Chocolate Bars with CSR Labels Sold			
	Considering Different Flavours		Not Considering Different Flavours		Considering Different Flavours		Not Considering Different Flavours	
	Total	Own brand	Total	Own brand	Total	Own brand	Total	Own brand
Discounter								
Aldi	14	13	10	9	0	0	0	0
Lidl	81	46	32	16	8	8	4	4
Full product range supermarkets								
Edeka	171	3	71	1	4	0	4	0
Rewe	122	22	37	7	9	3	4	1
Real	220	25	56	9	12	0	5	0
Kaufhof	242	0	48	0	3	0	1	0
Organic stores								
Basic	99	0	28	0	99	0	28	0
Bergfelds	52	0	11	0	52	0	11	0
Total over all stores	1001	109	293	42	187	11	57	5

Source: Own market survey conducted in December 2011.

When only considering products sold in the conventional retail stores, 18 products were identified with a CSR-related label. Table 14.4 reveals that Lidl, Rewe, and Edeka each offered four CSR-labelled chocolates, Real offered five, Kaufhof one, and, as mentioned, Aldi none. In percentage term it is Lidl which has the highest share in CSR-labelled chocolate (13 per cent), followed by Rewe (11 per cent), Real (9 per cent), Kaufhof (2 per cent), and Aldi (0 per cent).

On-product CSR communication mostly consists of social and ecological third party certified labels referring to the production process of the cocoa. Three chocolate bars hold an organic label, two a Fair Trade label, eight a Rainforest Alliance label, and four an UTZ Certified label. Four products were detected with other labels, such as CrM, indicating that, with the purchase of this chocolate bar, 6 m^2 of rainforest will be saved. Three products were detected with more than one label (e.g. UTZ and CrM in the case of Balisto yoghurt berries mix sold in the retail store Real).

Prices differ considerably between the analysed chocolate bars, with a range from 0.35 euros to 4.19 euros. The average unweighted price for 100 g chocolate per retail store being lowest in the two discount stores and highest in the organic stores (see Table 14.5). In addition, Table 14.5 displays the fact that chocolate bars with a CSR label are, on average, more expensive than those without such a label. Surprisingly, this does not hold for Lidl. Here, however, it should be noticed that all chocolate bars with a CSR label sold in Lidl are private brands. Table 14.5 also

Table 14.5 Unweighted average price (€) of chocolate bars sold in the market with and without CSR labels

	Unweighted average Price in €/100 g[a]			Difference of unweighted average Price with and without Label
	Total	Without CSR Label	With CSR Label	
Discounter				
Aldi	0.71	0.71	./.	./.
Lidl	0.85	0.87	0.72	−0.15
Full product range supermarkets				
Edeka	1.19	1.16	1.40	0.24
Rewe	0.93	0.83	1.50	0.67
Real	1.29	1.18	1.93	0.75
Kaufhof	2.37	2.37	2.49	0.12
Organic stores				
Basic	2.81	./.	2.81	./.
Bergfelds	2.18	./.	2.18	./.
Total over all stores[b]	1.54	1.19	1.86	0.67

Note: [a] Unweighted average over all products in the store without considering different flavours. [b] Unweighted average over all stores.

Source: Own market survey conducted in December 2011.

indicates that the difference in unweighted average prices between retail stores is much more pronounced than the difference between chocolate bars with and without a CSR label.

Table 14.6 displays the fact that Kraft Foods, Chocolat Schönenberger AG, Bremer HACHEZ Chocolade GmbH & Co. KG, and Mars GmbH are the only manufacturers offering chocolate with a CSR-related label. At the same time, the discounter Lidl, as well as the supermarket Rewe, provide certified chocolate under their private brand. While Lidl started to sell Fair Trade chocolate in 2006 under their private brand 'Fairglobe', Lidl's engagement under the term 'Auf dem Weg nach Morgen' is newer, as it was introduced in September 2011 (*CSR News* 2012a). Similar to this, Balisto began to sell UTZ Certified chocolate in July 2011 (*CSR News* 2012b). All products sold in the organic supermarkets have an organic label and thus, according to our definition, a CSR label. Furthermore, Rapunzel, Zotter, Naturata, Gepa, Schönenberger (Swiss Choco Roc), and Rio Napo provide additional CSR information (e.g. regarding Fair Trade) on their products.

CSR Communication on Websites

Online CSR communication was investigated in January 2012, via content analysis, separately for retail brands, organic/Fair Trade manufacturer brands, and non-organic/non-Fair Trade manufacturer brands.

Table 14.6 Chocolate bars with CSR labels in conventional retail stores

Brand	Manufacturer	Organic	Fair Trade	UTZ Certified	Rainforest Alliance	Other Label	POS
Bellarom	Lidl				X		Lidl
Fairglobe	Lidl		X				Lidl
Fin Carré	Lidl			X		Auf dem Weg nach Morgen	Lidl
Rewe Bio	Rewe	X	X				Rewe
Marabou	Kraft Foods				X		Rewe Real Edeka
Daim	Kraft Foods				X		Rewe
Côte d'Or (Sensations)	Kraft Foods				X		KaufhofEdeka
Hachez (Wild Cocoa de Amazonas 45% Cocoa)	Bremer HACHEZ Chocolade GmbH & Co. KG					Mit dem Kauf dieser Tafel retten Sie 6m² Regenwald[a]	Real
Hachez (Wild Cocoa de Amazonas 70% Cocoa)	Bremer HACHEZ Chocolade GmbH & Co. KG					wild gewachsener Cacao—Zertifiziert durch Regenwaldinstitut e.V.	Real
Sarotti Bio	Sarotti	X					Real
Ritter Sport Bio	Alfred Ritter GmbH & Co KG	X					Real Edeka
Balisto Joghurt-Beeren-Mix	Mars GmbH			X			Edeka

Note: [a] This is a CrM product.

Source: Own market survey conducted in December 2011.

Retail Brands' Online CSR Communication

The analysis for the six retail brands found in the 2011 inventory reveals that retailers provide information on their websites about their CSR activities to a different extent, but all exclusively in German. Lidl's and Rewe's CSR communications are the most detailed. They address 'the good' they do for society, employees, and the environment, as well as with respect to the products offered in their stores. As discussed, only Lidl, Rewe, and dennree (an organic retail brand available at basic) sell CSR-labelled chocolate and inform online about the meaning of the labels applied on the products. The information is provided in a rather formal manner and thus seems to be primarily directed at NGOs or employees, rather than addressed to consumers. The communication picks up the classical CSR topics one after another. The CSR topics addressed are environmental issues, albeit restricted to Germany, and social issues (employees and suppliers). While all six retail brands report their engagement for environmental issues, Edeka is the only one which does not communicate about its commitment to its employees. Aldi Süd, Lidl, and dennree, in addition, address their obligation to secure fair conditions for their suppliers. Figures enabling readers to judge the quality and extent of the companies' CSR engagement are not provided by any of the retail brands. Besides, none of the retailer refers to the specific challenges related to the production of cocoa.

Organic/Fair Trade Manufacturers' Brands' Online Communication

The ten organic/Fair Trade brands analysed communicate their engagement with society, the environment, employees, and supply chain partners in a different way to the retail brands. The content analysis leads to the conclusion that the addressee of the information is the customer. The information is, in contrast to that of the retail brands, provided in a less formal manner. The structure of the internet sites does not follow the classical CSR topics, fewer pictures are used, and the statements are less elaborated in the sense that it seems as if the companies do not have a special CSR manager for external communication. The languages in which the information is offered are not only German but, in the case of Gepa, also Spanish and English. English homepages are also provided by Natudis, Pronatec, Rosengarten, and Vivani.

Organic production and Fair Trade are explained on the Internet when respective labelled products are offered by the company and a link to the firms is accessible in case of further questions, for example, at Rosengarten. Gepa, especially, explains comprehensively the idea and rules of Fair Trade, and compares it with other certification schemes, such as organic production. It is remarkable that the organic/Fair Trade brands emphasize their engagement with the local environment but also the global environment. In addition, fair communication and handling with regard to suppliers is addressed by seven of the ten organic/Fair Trade firms. Gepa, Naturata, Rapunzel, and Zotter provide background information on the specific challenges related to the production of cocoa.

Besides, the organic firms differ from the conventional brands insofar as they have their long-term (in the case of Rapunzel) or innovative (in the case of Gepa) labelling concepts. For example, Rapunzel established in the early 1990s the so-called HAND IN HAND Programme, which connects Fair Trade and organic production. The respective label can be found on 87 of the Rapunzel products. The success of this programme is reported online: the projects supported are described and arising from the sales of HAND IN HAND products, the means by which the projects are funded are published. The only conventional firm following a somewhat similar path is Lidl. Lidl launched a firm-own label called 'Auf dem Weg nach Morgen'. They use this label on all products that contribute to social or ecological improvements in different fields. It is thought of as an umbrella label, and is actually accompanied by third party certification labels such as the UTZ Certified label.

Non-Organic/Non-Fair Trade Manufacturers' Brands' Online Communication

The content as well as the extent of CSR online communication of the 10 organic/ Fair Trade manufacturers' brands differ considerably from the 31 non-organic/non-Fair Trade manufacturers' brands' of our inventory. With respect to the languages in which the online information is provided, we can distinguish brands such as Milka, Ritter Sport, and Zentis, which make the information available in several languages besides German. The other extreme are brands such as Marabou, whose homepage is only in Swedish. Another characteristic of some manufacturer brands is that their CSR information is clearly addressing the consumer using interactive games, music, and films as well as photos. Companies that use this kind of more hands-on communication include Balisto, Côte d'Or, Hachez, Marabou, Milka, and Schogetten. Only few brands such as Balisto, Hachez, Milka, Ritter Sport, and Valrhona provide detailed information regarding cocoa production issues. The internet sites of Aero, Alpia, Feadora, Johan Lafer Confiserie Collection, Lohmann, and Piasten Schokolade do not provide any information on social or environmental issues related to business activities. But, there are some manufacturers' brands which not only state their engagement with the environment and social issues but also provide insights regarding their relationship with suppliers (Lindt and Sprüngli, Mars, Nestlé, Ritter Sport, Valrhona, and Zentis). Only Milka provides figures demonstrating the benefits of a project supported by them. Hachez describes their 'wild cocoa de Amazonas' charity promotion on their website.

Interestingly, neither product price nor enterprise size seems to determine the level and extent of CSR communication. Several of those brands that do not or barely communicate any CSR activities on their websites belong into the high price segment (e.g. Johann Lafer Confiserie Collection), while, for others, prices are at the lower end (e.g. Alpia from Stollwerck GmbH). Though information on total turnover per enterprise was not available for all manufacturers it seems that also size is not a crucial determinant to explain the considerable difference in CSR communication.

Conclusion

Responsible firm conduct can provide a critical point of differentiation if production-related social and environmental issues gain stakeholder attention and companies effectively communicate their CSR involvement to stakeholders. Chocolate companies face a situation in which the social conditions of chocolate production have been criticized by NGOs and intensively discussed in the media since the year 2000. This chapter provides an overview of the different means firms can use to communicate their CSR, and assesses the extent to which companies use two of those CSR communication strategies to inform their stakeholders in the chocolate sector: labels and websites.

The investigation reveals that about 20 per cent of the chocolate packages analysed provide CSR-related information. On-product CSR communication mainly consists of social and ecological third party certified labels referring to the production process of cocoa. There exists a considerable gap with respect to on-product CSR communication of chocolate bars sold in conventional retail stores compared to organic stores. This holds even if organic labels are not considered. While about 50 per cent of all chocolate bars sold in the organic stores provide, besides an organic label, additional CSR information (e.g. Fair Trade), this share is, in most cases, less than 10 per cent in conventional retail stores and even 0 per cent in the discounter Aldi.

Investigating the relationship between price and CSR label leads to two interesting results: (1) chocolate bars with a CSR label are, on average, considerably more expensive than those without such a label. This holds for all retail stores but Lidl. (2) However, the difference in unweighted average prices between retail stores is much more pronounced than the difference between chocolate bars with and without a CSR label.

As expected, CSR communication on websites is much more extensive than on product packages. Manufacturers selling their products in the two organic stores analysed in the study particularly communicate their responsible conduct on their websites on average in a very comprehensive way. Nevertheless, there are some conventional manufacturers, such as Mars GmbH with the brand Balisto (own website), that also provide detailed information on their CSR activities. Surprisingly, the discounter Lidl not only differentiates itself from other retailers (discounters and conventional ones) with its highest share of chocolate products carrying CSR labels, but the discounter communicates its CSR involvement on its website in a very comprehensive manner.

The results presented in this chapter make it obvious how diverse and heterogeneous CSR is communicated in the German chocolate sector. Areas for future research include the analysis of the determinants of chocolate firms' different efforts with respect to CSR and CSR communication. In addition, the relevance of CSR communication for stakeholders' perception and decisions and the determinants that influence the effectiveness of CSR communication are important areas which need further investigation (e.g. do customers consider CSR information on chocolate bars in their purchase decisions? Do consumers trust CSR information and what factors influence the perception and consideration of this information?). Furthermore, the question of whether consumers get confused when more than one CSR-related label is displayed on a product has not been analysed in this study but might be an interesting topic for future research.

References

BDSI (Bundesverband der Deutschen Süßwarenindustrie e.V.). 2015a. Die deutsche Süßwarenindustrie in Zahlen. Assessed 9 July 2015. <http://www.bdsi.de/fileadmin/re daktion/_processed_/csm_Infografik_Fakten2014_kompakt_b8a085e9b2.jpg>.

BDSI (Bundesverband der Deutschen Süßwarenindustrie e.V.). 2015b. *Produktion von Schokolade und Schokoladewaren, 2014*. Accessed 9 July 2015. < http://www.bdsi.de/fileadmin/redaktion/_processed_/csm_Produktion_Schoko_2014_e4b5c48178.jpg>.

BDSI (Bundesverband der Deutschen Süßwarenindustrie e.V.). 2015c. *Rohkakaolieferländer Deutschlands*. Accessed 9 July 2015. <http://www.bdsi.de/fileadmin/redaktion/_pro cessed_/csm_Rohkakaolieferl%C3%A4nder_2014_996b900d74.jpg>.

CMA (Chocolate Manufacturers Association). 2011. *The Harkin–Engel Protocol*. Accessed 10 July 2015. <http://www.cocoainitiative.org/en/documents-manager/english/54-harkin-engel-protocol >.

CorporateRegister. 2010. Accessed 20 January 2012.http://www.corporateregister.com/.

CSR News. 2012a. *Nachhaltige Schokolade: Lidl 'auf dem Weg nach Morgen'*. Accessed 20 January 2012. <http://csr-news.net/main/2011/09/20/nachhaltige-schokolade-lidl-auf-dem-weg-nach-morgen/>.

CSR News. 2012b. *Balisto: die nachhaltige Kakao-Offensive*. Accessed 20 January 2012. < ttp://csr-news.net/main/2011/07/21/balisto/>.

Dlott, J., D. Gunders, and A. Arnold. 2006. *Sustainability Trends in the Agrifood Sector*, Sure Harvest Briefing Paper, Soquel, California.

Du, S., C. B. Bhattacharya, and S. Sankar. 2010. 'Maximizing business returns to corporate social responsibility (CSR): the role of CSR communication'. *International Journal of Management Reviews* 12: pp. 8–19.

Edelman. 2011. *2011 Edelman Trust Barometer Findings: Annual Global Opinion Leaders Study*. Frankfurt: Edelman GmbH.

European Commission. 2009. *European Attitudes towards the Issue of Sustainable Consumption and Production: Analytical Report*. Brussels: Flash Eurobarometer 256.

Fieseler, C., M. Fleck, and M. Meckel. 2010. 'Corporate social responsibility in the blogosphere'. *Journal of Business Ethics* 91: pp. 599–614.

Fliess, B., H. J. Lee, O. L. Dubreuil, and O. R. Agatiello. 2007. *CSR and Trade: Informing Consumers about Social and Environmental Conditions of Globalised Production*, OECD Trade Policy Working Paper 47. Paris: OECD.

Freeman, R. E., J. S. Harrison, A. C. Wicks, B. L. Parmara, and S. De Colle (eds.). 2010. *Stakeholder Theory: The State of the Art*. Cambridge: Cambridge University Press.

GfK Panel Services Deutschland, Roland Berger Strategy Consultants GmbH, and BVE (Bundesvereinigung der Deutschen Ernährungsindustrie e.V) (Ed.). 2009. *Consumers' Choice 09: Corporate Responsibility in the Food Industry*. Nürnberg.

Global Exchange. 2011. *Thousands of Consumers Demand Hershey Stop Buying Child Labor Cocoa before Halloween*. Accessed 17 July 2014. <http://www.globalexchange.org/news/thousands-consumers-demand-hershey-stop-buying-child-labor-cocoa-halloween>.

Gregory, A. 2013. 'Chocolate and child slavery: say no to human trafficking this holiday season'. *Huffington Post*, 31 October. Accessed 17 July 2014. <http://www.huffingtonpost .com/amanda-gregory/chocolate-and-child-slave_b_4181089.html>.

GRI (Global Reporting Initiative). 2014. *Food Processing*. Accessed 12 June 2014. <https:// www.globalreporting.org/standards/sector-guidance/sector-guidance/food-processing/Pages/ default.aspx>.

GRI (Global Reporting Initiative). 2015. Sustainable Disclosure Database. Accessed 15 January 2015. <http://database.globalreporting.org/>.

Hartmann, M. 2011. 'Corporate social responsibility in the food sector'. *European Review of Agricultural Economics* 38 (3): pp. 297–324.

Heikkurinen, P. and S. Forsman-Hugg. 2011. 'Strategic corporate responsibility in the food chain'. *Corporate Social Responsibility and Environmental Management* 18 (5): pp. 306–16.

Hütz-Adams, F. 2010. 'Menschenrechte im Anbau von Kakao. Eine Bestandsaufnahme der Initiativen der Kakao- und Schokoladenindustrie'. In *INEF Forschungsreihe Menschenrechte, Unternehmensverantwortung und Nachhaltige Entwicklung 2010 (8)*, pp. 1–91. Duisburg: Institute for Development and Peace, University of Duisburg-Essen. Accessed 17 July 2014. <http://www.humanrights-business.org/files/menschenrechte_im_anbau_von_kakao_huetz-adams.pdf>.

ICCO (International Cocoa Organization). 2012. *The World Cocoa Economy: Past and Present*. Accessed 5 May 2014. <http://www.icco.org/about-us/international-cocoa-agreements/ cat_view/30-related-documents/45-statistics-other-statistics.html>.

ILO (International Labour Organization). 2012. *ILO Conventions on Child Labour*. Accessed 20 January 2012. <http://www.ilo.org/ipec/facts/ILOconventionsonchildlabour/lang–en/ index.htm>.

ILRF (International Labor Rights Forum), Green America, and Global Exchange. 2012. *Raise the Bar Coalition to Hershey and Cadbury: Get Child Slave Labor Out of our Easter Baskets*. Accessed 17 July 2014. <http://www.laborrights.org/releases/raise-bar-coalition-hershey-and-cadbury-get-child-slave-labor-out-our-easter-baskets>.

ISO (International Organization for Standardization) (Ed.). 2010. *Guidance on Social Responsibility* (ISO 26000:2010). Berlin.

Jones, P., D. Comfort, and D. Hillier. 2007. 'Marketing and corporate social responsibility within food stores'. *British Food Journal* 109: pp. 582–93.

Kienzle, S. and C. Rennhak. 2009. 'Cause-related marketing'. *Reutlingen Working Papers on Marketing & Management* 4: pp. 1–30.

Lang, T., G. Rayner, and E. Kaelin. 2006. *The Food Industry, Diet, Physical Activity and Health: A Review of Reported Commitments and Practice of 25 of the World's Largest Food Companies*. London: Centre for Food Policy.

Langen, N., C. Grebitus, and M. Hartmann. 2010. 'Is there need for more transparency and efficiency in cause-related marketing?' *International Journal on Food System Dynamics* 1 (4): pp. 366–81.

Lee, T., M. Ho, C. Wu, and S. Kao. 2008. 'Relationships between employees' perception of corporate social responsibility, personality, job satisfaction, and organizational commitment'. *Proceedings of the International Conference on Business and Information*. Kuala Lumpur, Malaysia.

Lee, M.-Y., A. Fairhurst, and S. Wesley. 2009. 'Corporate Social Responsibility: A Review of the Top 100 US Retailers'. *Corporate Reputation Review* 12: pp. 140–58.

Moon, J. and D. Vogel. 2008. 'Corporate social responsibility, government, and civil society'. In *The Oxford Handbook of Corporate Social Responsibility*, edited by A. Crane, A. McWilliams, D. Matten, J. Moon, and D. S. Siegel, pp. 303–26. Oxford: Oxford University Press.

Murillo, D. and J. M. Lozano. 2006. 'SMEs and CSR: an approach to CSR in their own words'. *Journal of Business Ethics* 67: pp. 227–40.

Nielsen, A. E. and C. Thomson. 2009. 'Investigating CSR communication in SMEs: a case study among Danish middle managers'. *Business Ethics: A European Review* 18: pp. 83–93.

Owen, D. L. and B. O'Dwyer. 2008. 'Corporate social responsibility: the reporting and assurance dimension'. In *The Oxford Handbook of Corporate Social Responsibility*, edited by A. Crane, A. McWilliams, D. Matten, J. Moon and D. S. Siegel, pp. 384–413. Oxford: Oxford University Press.

Payson Center for International Development and Technology Transfer Tulane University. 2011. *Oversight of Public and Private Initiatives to Eliminate the Worst Forms of Child Labor in the Cocoa Sector in Côte d'Ivoire and Ghana*. Accessed 20 January 2012. <http://www.childlabor-payson.org/Tulane%20Final%20Report.pdf>.

Piacentini, M. L. MacFadyen, and D. Eadie. 2000. 'Corporate social responsibility in food retailing'. *International Journal of Retail and Distribution Management* 28: pp. 459–69.

Robbins, J. 2010. 'Is there child slavery in your chocolate?' *Huffington Post*, 10 October. Accessed 17 July 2014. <http://www.huffingtonpost.com/john-robbins/is-there-child-slavery-in_b_737737.html>.

Rubin, P. H. 2000. 'Information regulation (including regulation of advertising)'. In *Encyclopedia of Law and Economics: The Regulation of Contracts*, vol. 3, edited by B. Boudewijn and G. De Geest, pp. 271–95. Northampton: Edward Elgar.

Schäfer, H., J. Beer, J. Zenker, and P. Fernandes. 2006. *A Survey of Internationally Established Rating Systems that Measure Corporate Responsibility*. Gütersloh: Bertelsmann Foundation.

Schoenheit, I., M. Bruns, and M. Grünewald. 2007. *Corporate Social Responsibility als Verbraucherinformation*, Arbeitspapier 17/2007. Hanover: IMUG.

UN (United Nations). 2012. *The Universal Declaration of Human Rights*. Accessed 20 January 2012. <http://www.un.org/en/documents/udhr/>.

Uni Bremen. n.d. *Die Top 10 auf dem deutschen Schokoladenmarkt*. Accessed 20 January 2012. <http://www.swa.uni-bremen.de/materialen/P_Schokoladenmarkt.pdf>.

United Nations Global Compact. 2013. *Global Corporate Sustainability Report 2013*. New York: United Nations.

United Nations Global Compact. 2015. What is UN Global Compact? Our participants. Accessed 14 January 2015. <https://www.unglobalcompact.org/what-is-gc/participants/>.

Voss, E. and P. Wilke. 2008. *Codes of Conduct and International Framework Agreements: New Forms of Governance at Company Level. Case Study: Unilever. European Foundation for the Improvement of Living and Working Conditions*. Ireland: Eurofound.

Walther, M., M. Schenkel, and M. Schüssler. 2010. 'Corporate social responsibility als strategische Herausforderung für den Mittelstand'. *Wertschöpfungsmanagement im Mittelstand. Tagungsband des Forums der deutschen Mittelstandsforschung*: pp. 87–102.

Williams, F. O. 2004. 'The UN global compact: the challenge and the promise'. *Business Ethics Quarterly* 14: pp. 755–74.

Wood, D. J. 2010. 'Measuring corporate social performance: a review'. *International Journal of Management Reviews* 12 (1): pp. 50–84.

15

Chocolate Regulations

Giulia Meloni and Johan Swinnen

Introduction

Chocolate and cocoa have been and are the subject of many regulations. These regulations have taken many forms and had different objectives. One objective was to increase the budget of governments. This played an important role in the cocoa trade in the sixteenth through to the eighteenth century and, more recently, in the post-colonial cocoa policies in West Africa.

Another objective was to protect consumers against frauds and health risks by imposing standards for the manufacturing (and the composition) of chocolate. Yet another objective is to prevent undesirable aspects of the cocoa production. This relates, among others, to the use of slave labour in cocoa production in the colonial periods, and to the use of child labour in more recent times.

In this chapter, we review various regulations that have been imposed in the cocoa–chocolate chain. While chocolate and cocoa have been subject to regulations and standards as long as cocoa has been cultivated and used,[1] within the limits of this chapter, we concentrate on the regulations and standards imposed since the growth of cocoa trade and chocolate consumption (i.e., the seventeenth century and later).

The chapter is organized as follows. The first section, 'Taxation and Monopolies to Raise Government Revenues', analyses regulations to tax cocoa trade and chocolate production, both in Europe in the sixteenth to nineteenth centuries and in post-colonial Africa. Afterwards we analyse regulation of the chocolate ingredients, starting with how the Catholic Church first defined chocolate, and then discussing how scientific inventions of the eighteenth and nineteenth centuries allowed better testing of the (cheaper and sometimes unhealthy) chocolate ingredients, leading to public outrage and safety and quality regulations—which

---

[1] For example, the Aztecs ruled that only the elite and warriors were allowed to consume cocoa drinks. Priests could use cocoa for religious services but were not allowed to consume it (see Chapter 2, this volume).

in some countries took the form of legal definitions of 'chocolate'. In the section 'The European Chocolate War', we explain how differences in these regulations created problems in the process of European integration, and how, after a 25-year 'chocolate war', a compromise European Union (EU) chocolate regulation induced regulatory adjustments in other countries. Finally, the section 'Recent Developments in Chocolate Regulation' reviews recent (and ongoing) discussions on chocolate regulation in the EU, linking 'quality' to the location of the production of chocolate and cocoa, looking at the growth of private ethical and sustainability standards related to cocoa sourcing, and drawing conclusions.

Taxation and Monopolies to Raise Government Revenues

That the natives of the province, now disposing a Company for this purpose, have to send two ships filled with fruits [cacao] of these kingdoms (. . .) to Caracas each year, armed with forty to fifty three cannons, mounted, and well crewed for battle (. . .) and they have to continue their journey to Spain.[2]
Real Cédula de Fundación de la Real Compañía Guipuzcoana de Caracas, 1728

The price of cocoa beans reflected the actions of governments as much as the skills of farmers and natural conditions.

William Gervase Clarence-Smith, *Cocoa and Chocolate 1765–1914*, 2000

Europe before World War I

When demand grew in Europe, in the seventeenth century, chocolate was increasingly perceived as a potential source of government income (as tea, coffee, and sugar). Governments in Europe regulated cocoa and chocolate with the aim of raising tax revenue. This was done in several ways: by taxing the cocoa trade or by selling production monopoly rights (to individuals, guilds, or private companies).

TRADE REGULATIONS AND TARIFFS
From the sixteenth century onwards, the King of Spain regulated cocoa production and trade. Cocoa beans were shipped from the Spanish colonies to the home country (Spain)[3] and the cocoa trade was heavily taxed to raise revenues for the Spanish Crown.[4] As cocoa and trade production became more profitable,

---

[2] Translation by the authors. 'Que los naturales de la provincia, disponiendo Compañía formal a este fin, han de enviar a Caracas dos navíos de Registro cada año, de cuarenta a cincuenta cañones, montados, y bien tripulados en guerra, cargando en ellos frutos [cacao] de estos reinos, y otros géneros (. . .) y tuvieren que proseguir el viaje a España.'

[3] Interestingly, not everybody initially realized the potential value of cocoa beans or chocolate. Early accounts narrate how, in the sixteenth century, English pirates were burning ships full of cocoa beans while thinking they were either useless or sheep dung. It was only much later that they discovered the 'secret' of the cocoa beans (Coe and Coe, 2013, p. 161).

[4] Large estates were structured through two institutions: the *encomienda* and the *hacienda*. The *encomiendas*, introduced during the conquest period, were governmental institutions, granting the

large export-oriented cocoa plantations expanded from Central America (mainly Guatemala and El Salvador) to South America (mainly Venezuela and Ecuador). Cocoa was transported from the production centres (such as Maracaibo in Venezuela) to Veracruz (a major port city in the Gulf of Mexico), from there it was shipped to Spain or to other export markets (such as Mexico). Despite the theoretical monopoly of Spain, the Dutch and the British were also trading cocoa and exporting it to Europe. Spain was therefore losing revenues from the profitable cocoa trade (Bergman, 1969; Castellote Herrero, 1981; Grivetti and Shapiro, 2009).

Spain decided to tighten its trade control by imposing restrictive regulations on trade.[5] All the cocoa produced by the colonies had to be sent to Spain in Spanish ships. Imposing high tariffs could not solve the problem of contraband cocoa trade. To this aim Spain established monopoly companies for cocoa trade that could also combat contraband (through army patrols and coastguard vessels). For instance, in Venezuela (where cocoa was the leading product and export), the Real Compañía Guipuzcoana de Caracas (the Caracas Company), established in 1728, had the exclusivity of the trade between Venezuela and Spain (Seville) and limited 'illegal' (and highly profitable) cocoa trade with other important export markets (Hussey, 1934; Arcila Farías, 1950; Gárate Ojanguren, 1990).[6]

Clarence-Smith's (2000) comprehensive review of trade and tariffs in the seventeenth to nineteenth century documents large differences in import tariffs on cocoa trade in Spain and other countries. He concludes that, despite increasing liberalism in the global economy, the cocoa bean trade was regulated and taxed until the middle of the nineteenth century. The Spanish Empire liberalized regulations on trade in the 1760s–1790s period: chartered companies (such as the Caracas Company) were abolished and import tariffs were reduced, leading to an increase in chocolate consumption. This trend reversed in 1796 when Spain declared war on Britain.

In general, conflicts in Europe, such as the Napoleonic Wars, which lasted until 1815, led to higher taxes for cocoa producers and traders. In the early post-war period, European countries kept import tariffs high in order to raise revenue to recover from the wars' expenses. Many governments favoured cocoa farms in their own colonies. For example, Spain's cocoa import tariffs for Spanish ships were half of the tariffs for foreign ships. The same was true for Britain later in the nineteenth century. As Figure 15.1 illustrates, Britain liberalized cocoa trade by reducing tariffs both on 'colonial cocoa' and 'foreign cocoa' during the first half of the nineteenth century. Most other countries reduced cocoa tariffs later, but by the 1860s virtually

conquerors Indians for labour and the right to collect the king's tribute. Later, by the mid-sixteenth century, *encomiendas* were replaced by *haciendas*. The *haciendas* were private institutions, acquired by purchase or by grant from the Spanish Crown to the settlers as a reward for services rendered (Lockhart, 1969; Keith, 1971).

[5] The Portuguese Crown also regulated trade and production. In 1679, King Pedro II issued a royal edict that encouraged all Brazilian landowners 'to plant cacao trees on their property' (Walker, 2007, p.87).

[6] In less than 25 years, between 1730 and 1754, exports to Spain doubled to 3,800 tonnes (MacLeod, 2000, p. 637).

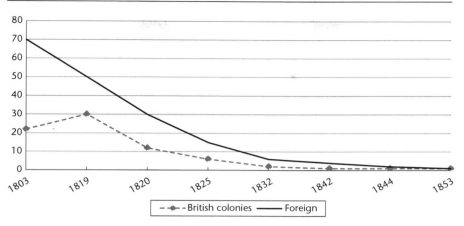

Figure 15.1 British import duties on cocoa beans for consumption, 1803–53 (British pence per pound, not deflated)
Source: Clarence-Smith (2000, p. 47).

all trade obstacles had been removed and free trade in cocoa prevailed. The removal of cocoa tariffs contributed to the decline of chocolate prices and 'the great chocolate boom of the late 19th century' (see Chapters 2 and 3, this volume).

However, free trade in cocoa did not last. Clarence-Smith (2000) documents how many countries had significantly raised imports tariffs again by the beginning of the twentieth century but with large differences among countries. Several small European countries (such as Belgium, the Netherlands, and Switzerland) kept import tariffs on cocoa low to stimulate their domestic cocoa grinding and cocoa manufacturing industries. Many larger countries, such as Germany, France, and Spain, had again high import tariffs on cocoa to finance their war expenditures.

MONOPOLIES IN CHOCOLATE PRODUCTION

Governments also tried to collect revenue by granting rights on the production and sale of chocolate. As chocolate spread to France in the seventeenth century,[7] the French King Louis XIV granted monopoly rights (letters patent) for chocolate production and sale in France in exchange for a significant sum of money. The amounts charged were so large that not all the holders could repay the loans they made to purchase the monopoly rights.[8]

---

[7] Chocolate was introduced in France in 1615 when Anne of Austria (daughter of King Philip III of Spain) married Louis XIII. Maria Theresa of Spain (daughter of King Philip IV), the first wife of King Louis XIV, also had a true passion of drinking chocolate and brought her own maid (named la Molina) from Spain to exclusively make chocolate for the Queen (Choquart, 1867). Franklin (1893, p. 166) states that: 'la nouvelle reine aimait tellement le chocolat au point de ne pouvoir s'en passer' ['the new queen loved chocolate so much to be unable to live without it'—translation by the authors].

[8] The system of the letters patent was widespread in others countries (as in England or in Italy) and for other goods (including salt or glasses). For instance, in 1449, King Henry VI of England granted John of Utynam a twenty-year privilege to produce coloured glass (Klitzke, 1959).

The first sale of chocolate monopoly rights was in 1659, when King Louis XIV granted David Chaliou the exclusive rights of manufacturing and selling 'a certain composition which is named the chocolate' in the entire kingdom for 29 years. Since chocolate was 'very healthy' and Chaliou wanted 'to share its composition with the public', the King grant him permission 'to make, sell and retail in all cities and other places of this kingdom (. . .) the said chocolate (. . .) for the period of twenty-nine consecutive years'. Moreover, the rights were exclusive as the King also prohibited 'all persons of any quality and condition they shall be to interfere to make, sell and retail the said chocolate' (Franklin, 1893, pp. 164–6).[9]

When Chaliou's monopoly ended, the monopoly rights to produce and sell chocolate was given to the Maîtres Limonadiers—a powerful guild in Paris established in 1676. The Limonadiers were the only ones who could sell exotic foods (such as coffee, tea, and chocolate). Their monopoly rights were temporarily interrupted in 1692 when the monopoly rights to sell chocolate ('le privilège de faire vendre et débiter seul (. . .) les chocolats') were sold to an individual, François Damame. However, Damame could not repay the debt that he contracted to purchase the privilege.[10] In 1693 (one year later) the Crown restored the trade monopoly to the Limonadiers. This system lasted until 1791 when many regulations and guilds (therefore also the Limonadiers) were abolished by the French Revolution (Franklin, 1893; Gordon, 2009a, p. 573; Spary, 2013).

Africa in Recent Times

Cocoa was a major source of government revenue for several developing countries after their independence. For this reason, state regulation of cocoa production, marketing, and exports was very strong in Africa in the 1960s and 1970s. State bodies controlled all aspects of the cocoa marketing chain by setting producer prices, buyer margins, and export taxes, often through monopolistic marketing boards. The revenues of these marketing boards were directed to a stabilization fund. The official objective was to achieve price stabilization (i.e., protecting farmers from volatile world prices), assuring cocoa quality and providing services for farmers. However, the taxes imposed on the cocoa exports were a very

---

[9] Translation by the authors: 'd'une certaine composition qui se nomme le chocolat, dont l'usage estant très sain, il désireroit en faire part au publicq (. . .). A ces causes (. . .) nous luy avons permis et permettons de faire, faire vendre et débiter, dans toutes les villes et autres lieux de ce royaume que bon luy semblera, ledit chocolat (. . .). Et ce, pendant l'espace de vingt-neuf ans entiers et consécutifs, durant lequel temps faisons très expresses inhibitions et deffenses à toutes personnes de quelque qualité et condition qu'elles soient de s'immiscer à faire faire, ny vendre ou débiter ledit chocolat, soubs quelque prétexte ou nouveau nom que ce soit' (Franklin, 1893, pp. 164–6).

[10] In 1692, François Damame is also granted by Louis XIV the exclusive privilege of selling tea in France. Interestingly, the tea business proved to be more successful as the company still exists as Dammann Frères, with a presence in 62 countries (Dammann Frères, 2015).

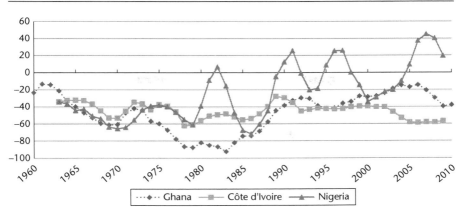

Figure 15.2 Cocoa nominal rate of assistance (%), 1960–2010 (three-year moving average)

Source: Anderson and Nelgen (2013).

important source of government income (Fold, 2001; Gilbert, 2009). Figure 15.2 illustrates how the taxation of cocoa farmers increased dramatically between 1960 and 1980, by using the nominal rate of assistance (NRA) to cocoa farmers (from the World Bank's data project coordinated by Kym Anderson). For example, in Ghana the cocoa NRA declined from around -10 per cent in 1960 to -90 per cent in 1980, implying a 90 per cent tax on cocoa production through government regulation of prices and trade.

In many African countries, a wave of market liberalizations in the 1980s and 1990s changed the market structure of cocoa production and reduced the taxation of cocoa farmers (see Chapters 11, 12, 13, 14, this volume). The liberalization process was driven by a number of factors. The state-controlled bodies were suffering from low world market prices and increased competition in the 1980s. Indonesia and Malaysia were two rising world producers with free market conditions that were increasing production successfully. Historically low commodity prices resulted in a struggle by the controlling and regulatory institutions in many African countries to maintain producer prices that were viable, and many stabilization agencies headed towards insolvency. Another factor was the structural adjustment programmes imposed by the World Bank and the International Monetary Fund (IMF) as conditions for further loans. These programmes required the reform of the state controls and reductions of farmers' taxation (Gilbert, 2009).

The liberalizations of these systems started in the 1980s and reduced the taxation of farmers. For example, in Ghana, the NRA for cocoa increased from less than -80 per cent in the early 1980s to around -15 per cent in the mid-2000s. Interestingly, as in the nineteenth century, these liberalizations of the cocoa trade preceded a major growth in global cocoa trade and chocolate consumption (see Chapter 2, this volume).

Defining Chocolate: The Catholic Debate

Liquidum non frangit jejunum.[11]

While most of the early regulations in the countries that imported cocoa and consumed chocolate were focused on raising government revenues, later regulations focused on defining the composition of chocolate and cocoa drinks, either to protect consumers or to protect domestic industries. The definition of 'chocolate' had both health and economic consequences. Interestingly, it also had religious consequences.

The first fight over the definition of 'chocolate' was within the Catholic Church. After the Spanish conquest of America, chocolate was imported to Europe and consumed as a beverage. In the sixteenth and seventeenth centuries in Catholic countries such as Spain, France, or Italy, the issue of whether or not it was permitted to drink chocolate during Christian fasting periods, for example, during the hours before the Holy Communion and during the forty days of Lent, arose. Christian fasting implied that flesh is 'mortified', therefore more 'nourishing' substances couldn't be taken. If chocolate was a drink, it did not break the fast, but if it was a food, then it could not be consumed during Christian fasting periods (Coe and Coe, 2013).

Catholic scholars debated the issue. Juan de Cárdenas (1591/1913) and Nicephoro Sebasto Melisseno (1665) argued that chocolate could not be consumed during the fast because of the addition of butter. Antonio de Escobar y Mendoza (1626), Antonio de León Pinelo (1636), and Tomás Hurtado (1645) had a different opinion. According to them, it depended if (and how much) nourishing substances were added to the chocolate. If mixed with water it became a drink and was thus permitted (as was wine), but if mixed with other substances (as milk, eggs, and dry bread) it became a food and, therefore, was forbidden. Cardinal Francesco Maria Brancaccio (1664) also argued that if the water component prevailed over the cocoa component, then chocolate did not break the fast (Grivetti, 2009; Balzaretti, 2014).

The religious orders were also divided on the issue. The Jesuits (who traded chocolate) argued that chocolate did not break the fast, while Dominicans argued the opposite. Several popes were asked to settle the dispute as leaders of the Catholic Church. According to Coe and Coe (2013), Popes Gregory XIII, Clement VII, Paul V, Pius V, Urban VIII, Clement XI, and Benedict XIV all agreed in private that chocolate did not break the fast. However, there was never an official Papal statement to end the debate.

The debate continued for over two centuries. Since there was no official decision from the Catholic authorities, the common practice became the rule. For instance, a 1848 document of the Archdiocese of Baltimore in north America, stated that: 'General usage has made it lawful to drink in the morning some warm liquid; as

[11] Translation by the authors. 'Liquids do not break the fast' (quote attributed to various Catholic authors).

tea, coffee, or thin chocolate, made with water, to which a few drops of milk may be added, serving rather to color the liquids, than to make them substantial food' (Grivetti and Shapiro, 2009, p. 764).

Hence, although nutritious, chocolate (as wine) was considered a drink and therefore did not break the fast. But it was allowed only once a day during fasting, and with maximum amounts of cocoa (from 30 to 60 grams) and sugar (from 15 to 45 grams) to be added to a cup of water (with a cup of water roughly equal to 250 ml). A food scale determined whether a sin had been committed or not. 'Liquidum non frangit jejunum' (Balzaretti, 2014, p. 28).[12]

The Industrial Revolution: Mass Production and Quality Control

> Do not use dishonest standards when measuring length, weight or quantity.
> Use honest scales and honest weights (. . .).
>
> Bible, Leviticus 19:35–6

> Those that mix maize in the chocolate do it perniciously,
> for they engender melancholy humours.[13]
>
> Colmenero de Ledesma, *Curioso Tratado de la Naturaleza y Calidad del Chocolate*, 1631

Even if the laws of Moses, written before the first millennium BCE, required honesty in business ('honest scales and honest weights'), food adulterations and frauds have existed as long as trade have existed. The addition of water in wine or in milk to increase the volume content has been documented throughout history and across the globe. Chocolate was no exception. Replacing the 'natural' ingredients of chocolate (such as cocoa powder or cocoa butter) and substituting them with cheaper products reduced costs and increased profits. Adulteration was already mentioned in the 1700s.[14] Navier (1772, p. 128) reports that: 'bad chocolates sold at a lower price (. . .) included cocoa shells, lots of sweet almonds, often a little beef marrow; (. . .) all linked together by means of some cooked flour and a little sugar'.[15]

During the nineteenth century, many countries introduced laws to regulate the safety and quality of chocolate, and food in general. That century witnessed a transformation of the concept of chocolate and its market. Chocolate was

---

[12] Translation by the authors. 'Liquids do not break the fast.'

[13] Translation by the authors. 'Los que mezclan maiz en el chocolate hazen perniciosarmente porque engédra humor melancólico.'

[14] Translation by the authors. 'Nous n'avons rien dit de ces mauvais chocolat que l'on débite à vil prix. (. . .) on y met tout au plus des épluchures de cacao, beaucoup d'amandes douces, souvent un peu de moelle de bœuf (. . .) le tout lié ensemble par le moyen de quelques farines cuites et un peu de sucre.'

[15] The fact that a large amount of cocoa shells alters taste was already common knowledge in the seventeenth century. Colmenero de Ledesma (1631, p. 23) wrote in his famous Curious Treatise of the Nature and Quality of Chocolate that: ' if you peel the cacao, and take it out of its shell, the drink will be more delicious' ['y si le quita la cáscara al cacao, es más regalado'].

transformed from a hot drink for the upper class to a solid food (chocolate bars) for the mass population.[16] The masses could 'now afford to buy white bread, red meat (instead of lard) and . . . chocolate' (Thouvenot, 1983, p. 52). It resulted in what Clarence-Smith (2000, p. 27) calls an: 'explosive growth of a mass market for chocolate'. Imports of cocoa for consumption increased fivefold in France (from 2,000 in 1850 to 10,000 tonnes in 1880) and fourfold in Britain (from 1,000 in 1850 to 4,000 tonnes in 1880). France became the world's largest cocoa importer (Clarence-Smith, 2000, p. 53).

There were several reasons for the increased demand. They included falling prices with reduced tariffs (with the adoption of free trade) and lower transportation costs, increasing income (with the Industrial Revolution) and technological developments. Technological innovations in chocolate production led to different types of chocolate, more consistent quality, and decreased costs. From the late eighteenth century onwards, steam-powered mixers allowed the large-scale manufacture of chocolate. In 1828, the Dutch producer Van Houten discovered a manufacturing process that allowed for a more digestible (lower fat content) cocoa. In the 1847, the British chocolate company Fry & Sons prepared the first chocolate bars (solid chocolate for eating) by mixing cocoa powder, sugar, and cocoa butter (instead of water). In 1867, the Swiss chemist Henri Nestlé developed powdered milk and, in 1879, the Swiss chocolate producer Daniel Peter used powdered milk to produce the first milk chocolate bars (Cidell and Alberts, 2006). These technological innovations and scale economies also led to the emergence of large chocolate companies, selling chocolate at cheaper prices. In the nineteenth century, companies such as Cadbury or Fry & Sons (Britain) and Meunier (France) grew rapidly in size (Gordon, 2009b).

The popularization of chocolate led to more concerns about the quality. Many chocolate producers substituted cocoa products with cheaper ingredients. Some ingredients could be identified by the consumer. For instance, when 'animal adulterants' (butter or lard) were added as a substitute for cocoa butter, the chocolate 'did not melt in the mouth' and had a 'cheesy' taste. Yet, many substitutive ingredients (mixed with chocolate) were difficult to detect by sight or taste (Brindle and Olson, 2009).

However, the Industrial Revolution changed this. It not only changed the production of chocolate—and its availability to the general population—but also quality controls. It resulted in important progress in the fight against adulterations

---

[16] In Britain, as in France, chocolate was at first adopted by the influential and wealthy upper class. Chocolate was introduced through the precursors of modern clubs (coffeehouses and chocolate houses) and the approval of the scientific community on its health benefits. Chocolate was consumed as a hot drink in the coffeehouses and chocolate houses where politicians and influential intellectuals gathered. One of the most famous chocolate houses in London was The Cocoa Tree. It was, at first, the headquarters of the Jacobite Party and then the centre of the literati, including members such as the poet Lord Byron. Chocolate was also adopted by the scientific community that claimed its health benefits, e.g., chocolate 'strengthened the heart and stomach, reduced gas and could be taken in moderation as a cure against coughs' (Head, 1903; Gordon, 2009b, p. 73).

due to new developments in chemistry and physics. Methods of detection (chemical analysis and the development of the microscope) made it easier to determine the presence of adulterations.

Using these techniques to analyse samples of food, the scientific community (pharmacists, chemists, and physicians) discovered that adulteration was practised on a large scale. These discoveries brought science to the forefront of a public health debate, and numerous books, articles, and pamphlets were published to alert the consumers. Mitchell (1848), Normandy (1850), and Hassall (1855) listed the following adulterants that were found with the new techniques in chocolate in the nineteenth century: animal fat (lard or tallow), starches (flour or potato starch), cocoa beans with their shells, sugar, cocoa beans oil, and mineral substances (brick dust, ochres, red lead, vermillion, sulphate of lime, or chalk). Most of these lowered the quality of the chocolate, and some were even dangerous for consumers. Mitchell (1848) wrote that higher quality chocolates were mixed with considerable quantities of starch and that 'the inferior chocolates' were adulterated with 'highly injurious' substances (such as the preparations of lead).

These discoveries (and the scientific evidence) led to public scandals and government regulations on chocolate in many countries.

Chocolate Safety and Quality Regulations

> There is death in the pot.
>
> Fredrick Accum, *A Treatise on Adulterations of Food, and Culinary Poisons*, 1820[17]

Many countries introduced regulations to ensure the quality and safety of food in the second half of the nineteenth century and the beginning of the twentieth century. Most countries also introduced specific standards and regulations for chocolate. In some cases, quality regulations for chocolate were, first, private standards, introduced by industry associations, or proposed by scientists and used in industry, and even courts.

Table 15.1 summarizes the first regulations and the time they were introduced for ten countries. In the rest of this section, we first discuss the introduction of the regulations in France and in Britain, which took quite different regulatory paths. In the last section, 'Other Countries', we briefly review regulations in other countries. We refer to Meloni and Swinnen (2015) for a more detailed review.

---

[17] In 1820, the chemist Fredrick Accum published A Treatise on Adulterations of Food, and Culinary Poisons where he exposed the dangers of food adulteration. On the cover of the book there was a banner bearing a skull and crossbones and, underneath, the biblical quotation: 'There is death in the pot'.

Table 15.1 Legal cocoa and chocolate compositions and the inclusion of vegetable fats

	Chocolate Regulations	Standards*	Compositional Standards	Addition of 'Other Fats' than cocoa butter
Austro-Hungarian Empire	1897	Private	Sugar (50–60%) Cocoa mass (40–50%) Cocoa butter (18–22%) Ash (3.5%) (max.) Crude fibre (3%) (max.) Starch (10.5%) (max.)	No
Belgium	1894	Public	Cocoa solids (35%) (min.) Cocoa butter (20%) (min.) Alkali (3%) (max.)	Yes if indicated in the label
France	1910	Public	Cocoa solids (35%) (min.) Cocoa butter (18%) (min.) Cocoa shells (5%) (max.)	No
Germany	1879	Private	Mineral substances (0%) Acorn flour (0%) Chicory (0%) Beet flour (0%) Animal fats (0%)	No
Germany	1933	Public	Sugar (60%) (max.) Cocoa solids (33%) (min.) Cocoa butter (21%) (min.) Cocoa shells (2%) (max.)	No
Italy	1931	Public	Sugar (65%) (max.) Cocoa butter (16%) (min.)	No—allowed if labelled 'surrogato' (and not 'chocolate')
UK**	1976	Public	Cocoa solids (35%) (min.) Cocoa butter (18%) (min.) Non-fat cocoa (14%) (min.)	Yes—up to 5%
USA	1903	Private	Cocoa fat (45%) (min.) Ash (3%) (max.) Crude fibre (3.5%) (max.) Starch (9%) (max.)	No
USA	1955	Public	Cocoa solids (35%) (min.) Cacao fat (50–58%) Cocoa shells (1.75%) (max.) Alkali (3%) (max.)	No—only allowed in 'chocolate and vegetable fat coatings'
Romania	1895	Public	Cocoa butter (22%) (min.) Potassium (2%) (max.) Cocoa shells (15%) (max.)	No
Spain	1908	Public	Sugar (60%) (max.) Cocoa shells (4%) (max.)	No—allowed if labelled 'Mezcla Autorizada' (and not 'chocolate')
Switzerland	1890s	Private	Sugar (70%) (max.) Fat and sugar (80–85%) Cocoa butter (10–20%) Non-fat cacao (15–20%) Ash (3.5–8%) Alkali (3%) (max.)	No

Switzerland	1905	Public	Sugar (68%) (max.)	No
			Starch (0%)	
			Meal (0%)	
			Foreign fat (0%)	
			Mineral substances (0%)	
			Colouring matter (0%)	
			Fat economisers (0%)	
			Cacao shell (0%)	

*Many countries introduced specific standards and regulations for chocolate in the late nineteenth century and the first half of the twentieth century. In some cases, quality regulations for chocolate were first private standards, introduced by industry associations, or proposed by scientists and used in industry, and even courts.

**Before 1976, the UK forbade the selling of adulterated food 'injurious to health', e.g., there was not an official composition of chocolate in UK but a general food safety law applying to all foodstuffs and prohibiting certain ingredients 'injurious to health'.

Note: Chocolate regulations also define other types of chocolates (such as milk chocolate and white chocolate). This table only focuses on the cocoa and the 'dark/bittersweet chocolate' definitions.

Source: Meloni and Swinnen (2015).

France

Food safety regulations in France date back at least to the thirteenth century. Laws were enacted forbidding the adulteration of beer, wine, bread, and butter. The guilds were the entities controlling the quality of food, which included enforcement of these regulations.

However, guilds were dismantled during the French Revolution. Food control was taken over by the state or local authorities (Hart, 1952; Combaldieu, 1974). New regulations confirmed that fraud and adulteration in food were criminal actions. The French Criminal Code of 1810 stated that cheating in selling food by using fraudulent measures and selling food damaging the health of consumers were crimes and punishable with up to two years of prison and payment of fines.[18]

Despite these regulations, the first half of the nineteenth century witnessed an intense public debate on health and food quality. The debate was triggered by new technologies that allowed better testing of food. The French scientific community was very involved in this public health debate. Doctors, pharmacists, chemists, and physicians were discovering large-scale food adulterations through new methods of analysis and they published the results (La Berge, 1992). In the 1850s, the pharmacist and chemist Alphonse Chevallier wrote numerous publications on the adulteration of foodstuffs and the methods for their identification. Specifically, Chevallier argued that chocolate had been subject to numerous falsifications: 'by wheat flour, rice, lentils, peas, beans, corn; by starch or potato starch; by olive oil, sweet almonds; by egg yolks, tallow veal or mutton, natterjack storax,

---

[18] 'Quiconque aura vendu ou débité des boissons falsifiées, contenant des mixtions nuisibles à la santé, sera puni d'un emprisonnement de six jours à deux ans, et d'une amende de seize francs à cinq cents francs' (Code pénal, 1810, Article 318). '(. . .) quiconque, par usage de faux poids ou de fausses mesures, aura trompé sur la quantité des choses vendues, sera puni de l'emprisonnement pendant trois mois au moins, un an au plus, et d'une amende qui ne pourra excéder le quart des restitutions et dommages et intérêts, ni être au-dessous de cinquante francs' (Code pénal, 1810, Article 423).

balsam of Peru, balsam of Tolu, benzoin, envelopes of dried and powdered cocoa, toasted almonds, tragacanth gum, gum arabic, dextrin, cinnabar, red oxide of mercury, the red lead, the ochreous red earth'[19] (Chevallier, 1850, p. 198).

These scientific demonstrations of adulterations of chocolate and other foods, and the public reactions following it, forced the French government to intervene. A law on frauds in food was introduced in 1851 and on frauds in beverages in 1855 (Loi, 1851; Stanziani, 2012).

However, despite the public outcry, the 1850s laws mainly regulated fraud in terms of false quantity indicators (on the weight or measure) rather than quality aspects. Article 1 of the 1851 law stated that persons will be punished that: 'have cheated or attempted to cheat on the quantity of goods delivered (. . .) by the use of false weights and false measures, or inaccurate instruments for weighing or measuring (. . .) or by fraudulently increasing the weight or volume of the good'.[20] These laws did little to protect consumer health from unhealthy ingredients—or to guarantee the quality of the food products. In fact, it took another 60 years for the French government to introduce regulations that restricted and determined the ingredients that could be used in the production of chocolate.

The 1910 Regulation on Chocolate

A law on frauds in chocolate was implemented in 1910, inspired by the general food law and the wine law which were introduced a few years earlier. The 1910 law on chocolate determined what 'quality' of chocolate meant. 'Quality' referred to the composition of cocoa mass, cocoa butter, and chocolate (Décret, 1910, Articles 16, 19, and 20). The main objective was to achieve a 'qualité saine, loyale et marchande' (a sound and fair merchantable quality). The law specified that 'chocolate' was to be obtained from the 'blend of sugar and cocoa mass, (. . .) with or without added cocoa butter so that 100 grams of the product contain (. . .) at least 35 grams of cocoa mass containing at least 18 grams of cocoa butter'.[21] The law listed cocoa butter as the key 'fat ingredient', but allowed the use of vegetable lecithin (up to 0.2 per cent) used as an emulsifier, for example, to keep the cocoa

---

[19] Translation by the authors. 'Le chocolat a été l'objet de nombreuses falsifications par les farines de blé, de riz, de lentilles, de pois, de fèves, de maïs; par l'amidon ou la fécule de pommes de terre; par l'huile d'olives, d'amandes douces; les jaunes d'œufs, le suif de veau ou de mouton, le storax calamite, le baume du Pérou, le baume de Tolu, le benjoin, les enveloppes de cacao séchées et réduites en *poudre*, les amandes grillées, la gomme adragante, la gomme arabique, la dextrine, le cinabre, l'oxyde rouge de mercure, le minium, les terres rouges ocreuses' (Chevallier, 1850, p. 198).

[20] Translation by the authors. 'Seront punis (. . .) ceux qui auront trompé ou tenté de tromper, sur la quantité des choses livrées (. . .) soit par l'usage de faux poids ou de fausses mesures, ou d'instruments inexacts servant au pesage ou mesurage (. . .) soit à augmenter frauduleusement le poids ou le volume de la marchandise (. . .)' (Loi, 1851, p. 130).

[21] Translation by the authors. 'La dénomination "chocolat" est réservée au produit de qualité loyale, saine et marchande, obtenu par le mélange de sucre et de pâte de cacao, ayant ou non fait l'objet d'un dégraissage partiel, additionné ou non de beurre de cacao en proportion telle que 100 grammes du produit contiennent, sous réserve des dispositions particulières relatives au chocolat au lait et au chocolat aux noisettes, au minimum 35 grammes de pâte de cacao renfermant au moins 18 grammes de beurre de cacao' (Décret, 1910, Article 20).

Table 15.2 Composition of chocolate defined by law (%) (min.)

		France (1910)	EU (1973)	EU (2000)*	Codex (1981)	Codex (2003)*
Chocolate	Total cocoa solids (dry)	35	35	35	35	35
	Cocoa butter	18	18	18	18	18
	Dry non-fat cocoa solids		14	14	14	14
Milk	Total cocoa solids (dry)	25	25	25	25	25
Chocolate	Dry non-fat cocoa solids		2.5	2.5	2.5	2.5
	Total milk solids (dry)	16	14	14	14	12–14
	Milk fat		3.5	3.5	3.5	2.5–3.5
	Total fat (cocoa butter and milk fat)	26	25	25	25	
	Sugars		55		55	

*Vegetable fats other than cocoa butter (as CBEs) may be used up to a maximum of 5% of the finished product.

Note: 'Total solids' is the sum of 'dry non-fat solids' and 'fats'.

Source: Author's calculations based on Décret, 1910; Directive 2000/36/EC; CFR, 1993; and Codex, 2003.

and cocoa butter from separating (Décret, 1910, Article 23).[22] Chocolate (and its quality) was now defined by law in France.

The 1910 law was amended several times (in 1925, 1939, and 1952), but the 1910 legal definition remained in place. After accession to the European Economic Community (EEC), the 1910 law was replaced by the Council Directive of 24 July 1973 (transposed into the French law in 1976) which had very similar regulations (see further), as is summarized in Table 15.2.

Britain

> 'Absolutely Pure, Therefore Best.'[23]
> Cadbury

As in France, the Industrial Revolution and the scientific discoveries that arose from this transformed the food and health debate. During the first half of the nineteenth century, the scrutiny on adulterations of food and drink became more intense as the British scientific community alerted the public and the government about the dangers of food adulteration. The turning point in food regulation was a series of articles published from 1851 to 1854 by the physician Arthur Hill Hassall in the medical journal *The Lancet*. Hassall not only showed extensive adulteration

---

[22] 'It is not considered an adulteration (. . .) the addition of vegetable lecithin to chocolates and chocolate coatings, and the amount of added phosphoaminolipids not to exceed 2 grams per 1,000 grams of the product.' [Translation by the authors. 'Ne sont pas considérés comme des falsifications (. . .) L'addition de lécithine végétale aux chocolats et aux couvertures de chocolat, la quantité des phosphoaminolipides ainsi ajoutée ne devant pas dépasser 2 grammes pour 1.000 grammes du produit'] (Décret, 1910, Article 23).

[23] During the second half of the nineteenth century, marketing campaigns linked cocoa with health benefits and demands for 'purity' (e.g., non–adulterated cocoa, free from starches). In 1866, the British chocolate company Cadbury developed a new product called 'Cocoa Essence', which was advertised as 'Absolutely Pure, Therefore Best'.

of common foods, but also published the names and addresses of merchants selling such foods.

Chocolate was an important item in Hassall's study. He found that 48 out of 56 chocolate samples he investigated (thus 90 per cent) were adulterated with the addition of cheaper products (replacing up to 50 per cent of the cocoa powder) such as sugar or starches (e.g., wheat, potato flour, or sago meal) (Hassall, 1855).[24] These cheaper ingredients were used to decrease costs and to increase the mass of chocolate. Some were not necessarily unhealthy, although they could make chocolate more difficult to digest, but other ingredients (such as red oxide of iron) were poisonous.

The public were shocked to hear that poisonous ingredients were being used in sweets and chocolates.[25] As in France, this resulted in a public scandal and forced the British Parliament to intervene. In 1855, a Select Committee of the House of Commons was appointed to investigate the matter and concluded that adulteration was extensive and that public health was endangered. The Committee reported that: 'Without entering into voluminous details of the evidence taken, your Committee would enumerate the leading articles which have been proved to be more or less commonly adulterated. These are: (...) cocoa with arrowroot, potato-flour, sugar, chicory and some ferruginous red earths' (Herbert, 1884, p. 12). A witness during the investigation on cocoa gave his recipe for cocoa: cocoa, lump (sugar), white (starch), and red (red oxide of iron) for colour—with only 30 per cent of cocoa (Hart, 1952).

In 1860, the British government responded to public pressure by issuing a general food safety law that was applied to all food articles: the Act for Preventing the Adulteration of Articles of Food or Drink. Adulteration was now a crime and a pecuniary sanction (five pounds) was applied to those knowingly selling adulterated foods. Local authorities in England, Scotland, and Ireland could appoint public analysts, who tested and ensured the safety of food (Glen, 1872; Rowlinson, 1982).

However, the law was barely enforced as the appointment of public analysts was voluntary.[26] Pressure to improve the legislation was exerted from various sides. The investigations of *The Lancet* continued and found adulterations of many food samples—including cocoa. Consumer guides such as as *Enquire Within Upon Everything* criticized the fact that '[the Acts of Parliament] have merely exposed the defect, frightened everybody, and produced no practical result'.[27] Moreover, a new

---

[24] Other adulterants were used for increasing chocolate's bulk and weight: Maranta, East India, and Tacca or Tahiti arrowroot; Tous-les-Mois (Canna Coccinea starch— a substitute for arrow-root); wheat, Indian corn, sago, potato, and tapioca; sugar, and chicory (Hassall, 1855).

[25] Hassall (1855, p. 615) described how poisonous ingredients were used in confectionary for painting a sugar dog: 'for the ears and nose, the usual non-metallic pigment; for the chief part of the back, a ferruginous brown earth, most likely burnt-umber; and for the stand on which the dog is represented as reclining, arsenite of copper or emerald green, in quantities so considerable as to be absolutely poisonous'.

[26] Only 2 counties out of 52 appointed public analysts (Dublin and Gloucestershire) (Rowlinson, 1982).

[27] To fill this gap, the consumer's guide gave homemade receipts to avoid adulterations. For instance, for bread, the first advice that is given in the book is to avoid buying the food article all together: 'Grind your own wheat, make your own yeast, and bake your own bread. The advantages

(and influential) pressure group was founded in 1871: the Anti-Adulteration Association, which started its own journal (the Anti-Adulteration Review), performed analyses, and lobbied for mandatory public analysts (Philp, 1871; Rowlinson, 1982; Burrows, 2009).

These pressures were successful, as an amendment to the Act was passed in 1872 and a new Sale of Food and Drugs Act was issued in 1875. The 1875 law increased the sanctions (20 and 50 pounds) for selling adulterated articles to 'the prejudice of the purchaser' that were not of 'the nature, substance, and quality of the article demanded' and were 'injurious to health'.[28] It also made the appointment of public analysts compulsory for local authorities.[29] Finally, the 1875 law obliged producers to list the ingredients in foods on the label,[30] and a pecuniary sanction was applied for false labelling (Rowlinson, 1982; Burnett, 1999; Scheuplein, 1999; Oddy, 2007).[31] These general laws applied to all food articles, including cocoa and chocolate.[32]

In summary, in contrast to France, where only fraud relating to quantities was tackled, the British government reacted to the new scientific evidence by introducing food safety and quality regulations protecting consumers' interests by forbidding the sale of adulterated food 'injurious to health', by requiring the labelling of the ingredients in food products and by introducing compulsory chemical-technical investigations and controls—by the public analysts. This also implied that, since flour, other starches, sugar, or (non-cocoa) vegetable oils were not poisonous ingredients '*injurious to health*', they were accepted legal additions but needed to be listed in the label.

The 1875 law effectively protected British chocolate consumers against the unhealthy practices of manufactures.[33] Therefore, when the UK joined the EEC

---

will be immense' (Philp, 1871, p. 349). For chocolate, starches could be detected if cocoa thickened in hot water.

[28] 'No person shall sell to the prejudice of the purchaser any article of food, or any drug which is not of the nature, substance, and quality of the article demanded under a penalty not exceeding twenty pounds' (Article 6, Law 1875). 'No person shall mix, colour, stain, or powder (. . .) any article of food with any ingredient or material, so as to render the article injurious to health (. . .) and no person shall sell such article under a penalty not exceeding fifty pounds' (Article 3, Law 1875).

[29] All the counties and boroughs in Britain appointed 'one or more persons possessing competent knowledge, skill, and experience, as analysts of all articles of food—and drugs sold' (Article 10, Law 1875).

[30] 'Provided that no person shall be guilty of any such offence (. . .) if at the time of delivering such article or drug he shall supply to the person receiving the same [article] a notice, by a label distinctly and legibly written or printed on or with the article or drug, to the effect that the same is mixed' (Article 8, Law 1875).

[31] 'And every person who shall wilfully give a label with any article sold by him which shall falsely describe the article sold, shall be guilty of an offence under this Act, and be liable to a penalty not exceeding twenty pounds' (Article 27, Law 1875).

[32] The adulteration of intoxicating liquors was regulated by the Licensing Act (1872), which listed the 'Deleterious Ingredients' considered to be adulterations: Cocculus indicus, chloride of sodium (otherwise common salt), copperas, opium, Indian hemp, strychnine, tobacco, darnel seed, extract of logwood, salts of zinc or lead, alum, and any extract or compound of any of the above ingredients.

[33] The law did induce different reactions from the leading chocolate manufactures, and thereby had a major impact on the British chocolate industry (see Meloni and Swinnen, 2015).

in 1973, there were no official regulations in the UK governing the composition of chocolate (e.g., the law did not define the minimum or maximum ingredient requirements).[34] Chocolate was subject only to the articles of the 1875 Act (and its successive amendments). EEC accession implied the requirement to transpose the Council Directive of 24 July 1973 into UK law (in 1976). However, as the UK chocolate companies used a greater amount of vegetable fats than was allowed in Belgium, France, Italy, Luxembourg, the Netherlands, and West Germany, this led to a major conflict (see section 'The European Chocolate War').

Other Countries

Table 15.1 summarizes the different regulatory approaches (and more details can be found in Meloni and Swinnen, 2015).[35] Several other countries followed the 'French approach' and defined chocolate by establishing a legal composition of its ingredients (e.g., the 'recipe' approach), as the amount of cocoa solids and milk solids that must be present or the inclusion/exclusion of certain additional ingredients. This was the case for Belgium (1894), Romania (1895), and Spain (1908), whose public regulations closely resembled the French and were introduced around the same time, that is, the late nineteenth and early twentieth century.

Other countries (initially) followed the 'British approach', and did not define the minimum (or maximum) ingredient requirements, but prohibited the use of ingredients *'injurious to health'*. This was the case, for example, in the USA and Canada in the nineteenth and the first half of the twentieth century.

Interestingly, in several countries there were periods where British-style general food laws (public regulations) were combined with private standards often proposed by scientists and often used by industry organizations. In most cases, these private standards later became the basis for public regulations.

---

[34] The only regulation introduced in Britain in the first half of the twentieth century concerned the manufacture and sale of cocoa powder—not of 'chocolate'. In 1918, the Cocoa Powder Order legally limited the amount of cocoa shells allowed in cocoa powder. The 1918 law established two 'quality' levels. The highest 'quality' level, 'Grade A cocoa powder' should not contain more than 2% of shell and was packed in cartons. The lowest 'quality' level, 'Grade B cocoa powder' did not contain more than 5% of shell and was packed in barrels or cases. Because of fears of cocoa shortages due to World War I, the British government also imposed maximum prices on cocoa: 3 shillings and 6 pence per pound for 'Grade A cocoa powder' and 2 shillings and 6 pence per pound for 'Grade A cocoa powder' (Knapp, 1920, p. 179; Fitzgerald, 1995, p. 135).

[35] The battle for a common definition of 'chocolate' would also be enacted at the international level. In 1908 and 1909, two International Congresses for the Repression of Fraud were organized, one in Geneva and one in Paris, by the Society of the White Cross of Geneva, to set international food standards and common regulations for the repression of fraud (*The Lancet*, 1909; Guillem-Llobat, 2014). During the congresses, the discussions on cocoa and its definition centred on whether alkali could be added to cocoa, and it was agreed that 2 per cent of alkali should be allowed (Douglas, 1909). Furthermore, in 1911, an International Congress of Chocolate and Cocoa Manufacturers was held in Bern, establishing international standards for chocolate and cocoa: 'Chocolate is a mixture of cacao mass and sugar, with or without the addition of cacao butter. (...) The amount of cacao mass and cacao butter contained in chocolates and chocolate powders should be at least 32 per cent of the whole' (Zipperer and Schaeffer, 1915, p. 285).

For example, in Germany, a general food safety law was enacted in 1879, containing penal enactments for food adulterations (Spiekermann, 2011). For the next 50 years, chocolate production was based on the combination of this general law and on a private standard used in the chocolate industry. The production rules for chocolate of the Association of German Chocolate Manufacturers excluded: 'all mineral substances, acorn flour, chicory, beet flour, and animal fats; [it] permits instead the use of all dyestuffs allowed by the police up to 2%' (Spiekermann, 2011, p. 24). The private standard also considered 'the addition of foreign fat to chocolate, cacao mass or cacao butter' an adulteration (Zipperer and Schaeffer, 1915, p. 302). Chocolate producers could use a 'guarantee label' of the Association on their packages if they followed these voluntary standards.

It was not until 1933 (under Nazi rule) that a government regulation defined chocolate by law: 'Chocolate is obtained from at least 40% of cocoa mass or from a mixture of cocoa mass and cocoa butter and from no more than 60% of sugar. The cocoa butter content is at least 21%. If cocoa butter is used, the content of cocoa mass is at least 33%' (Verordnung über Kakao und KakaoerzeugnisseS, 1933; in Fincke, 1965, p. 510). The addition of any fats other than cocoa butter was considered an adulteration.[36] The addition of milk fat to produce milk chocolate or the addition of coconuts to chocolate was allowed if clearly labelled, for example, as a 'coconut chocolate'.

The chocolate regulations under the Austro-Hungarian Empire were similar to the early German approach. An 1896 general food law was introduced to legally ban adulteration. In parallel to the general food law, food standards were defined by the Association of Food Chemists and Analysts and collected under the Codex Alimentarius Austriacus (1897–1911). In the Codex, chocolate was defined as: 'the cacao material evenly and regularly worked up with cane sugar (refined, ordinary or coarse)'—with good chocolate consisting of '40 to 50 per cent of cacao mass and 50 to 60 per cent of sugar'.[37] Moreover, the addition of fats other than cocoa butter was prohibited as 'the fat shall be pure cacao butter' (Zipperer and Schaeffer, 1915, p. 299). The Codex was not legally binding but became 'a kind of minimal standard broadly accepted, but still not obligatory' (Spiekermann, 2011, p. 18; Davies, 1970).[38]

Similarly, in Switzerland, the Association of Analytic Chemists first introduced a definition of chocolate and other food products in the late nineteenth century in *The Swiss Book of Nutritious Stuffs and Articles of Sustenance*, a list of private standards for foodstuffs where cocoa and chocolate were defined.[39] This work served as a

[36] As an example, the 1933 Law explicitly stated that: 'A chocolate where the cocoa butter to one part is replaced by e.g., peanut fat, would be hereafter considered adulterated.'

[37] See Zipperer and Schaeffer (1915, pp. 298–301) for the complete text of the Codex related to chocolate.

[38] The Codex influenced large parts of Europe and, in the 1960s, the international Codex Alimentarius, with the objective of harmonizing international food standards (see section 'Spillover Effects of the 2000 EU CBE Regulation on Other Countries').

[39] 'Chocolate is the description of a mixture of cacao and sugar which comes into commerce either molded or in powder form. The percentage of sugar amounts to between 40 and 70%. Admixture of other substances than cacao, sugar and the usual spices must be regarded as

guide for the definition of chocolate established by the Swiss 1905 Food Act (Zipperer and Schaeffer, 1915, p. 294).

In the USA, the Federal Food and Drugs Act was introduced in 1906. The law prohibited 'the manufacture, sale, or transportation of adulterated or misbranded or poisonous or deleterious foods, drugs, medicines, and liquors, and for regulating traffic therein, and for other purposes', and stated that confectionary was to be considered as 'adulterated' if 'it contain terra alba, barytes talc, chrome yellow, or other mineral substance or poisonous color or flavor, or other ingredient deleterious or detrimental to health, or any vinous, malt or spirituous liquor or compound or narcotic drug' (FFDA, 1906; Hutt and Hutt, 1984).

'Standards of Purity' for food products, including chocolate, were adopted as a guide for the officials of the US Department of Agriculture in enforcing the 1906 Food and Drugs Act. The Secretary of Agriculture commissioned the Association of Official Agricultural Chemists to establish such standards. These standards defined chocolate as: 'the solid or plastic mass obtained by grinding cocoa nibs without the removal of fat or other constituents except the germ' (US Department of Agriculture, 1903).

It took the FDA until 1955 to define public standards for chocolate. These (renamed) 'Standards of Identity' provided the definition that: 'Bittersweet chocolate (...) contains not less than 35 percent by weight of chocolate liquor' and were legally enforceable (Forte, 1966, p. 357; FDA, 1965, 2009.

Canada's regulations were similar to those of the USA. Canada introduced its first federal food law in 1875, the Inland Revenue Act (IRA), prohibiting the adulteration of food and drink. As in the USA, from 1894 to 1919, many specific standards (the so-called 'Standards of Quality') were defined by law (Lauer, 1993; Buckingham, 2002).

However, no specific (compositional) standards for cocoa or chocolate were in force in Canada. In 1920, a new Food and Drug Act closely followed the United States 1906 Pure Food and Drug Act (Ostry, 2006). That changed in 1949, when Canada introduced a legal definition of chocolate. 'Chocolate' was defined as: 'the mass obtained by grinding cacao nibs, and shall contain not less than 50 per cent of cacao butter, and on the dry, fat-free basis not more than a) 7 per cent of crude fiber, b) 8 per cent of total ash and, c) 0.4 per cent of ash insoluble hydrochloric acid' (Canada Gazette, 1949).

---

adulterations. (...) The following are to be considered as adulterations: 1. Admixtures of cacao or other shells, and sawdust. 2. Admixtures of foreign starch, meals, castania and resin. 3. Admixtures of mineral substances like ocre, clay and sand. 4. The substitution of cheaper fats, such as beef and pork dripping almond, poppy seed, cocoanut and vaseline oils. (...) Chocolate: although at the present time there are no limits fixed for cacao and sugar, it may nevertheless be safely assumed that the fat and sugar together may not exceed 80 to 85%, and that the rest shall be pure non-fatty cacao material, in the proportion of from 15–20%. The ash in a good chocolate does not exceed 3.5%. (...) the amount of added alkali is not to exceed 3%. In no case shall the ash content be more than 8%' (Zipperer and Schaeffer, 1915, pp. 294–5).

The European Chocolate War

The difference in chocolate regulations between European countries in the early twentieth century caused a conflict with European integration in the second half of the twentieth century.[40] The conflict centred on how much milk was allowed in 'milk chocolate' and whether cocoa butter equivalents (CBEs) were allowed in 'chocolate'. CBEs are vegetable fats (such as palm oil, mango kernel, etc.) with similar physico-chemical characteristics to cocoa butter, making them fully compatible with cocoa butter fat.[41]

The economic integration in the EEC required the integration of national chocolate regulations into one EU chocolate policy. The six founding members (Belgium, France, Italy, Luxembourg, the Netherlands, and West Germany) had similar pre-EEC chocolate policies. They had the same legal definition of chocolate (and its composition and manufacturing processes). As a result, the 1963 proposal for a Chocolate Directive submitted by the European Commission to the Council was very similar to the French 1910 law: 'In the manufacture of these products Member States shall allow the use only of cocoa beans of sound merchantable quality' (article 3, European Commission, 1963). The final 1973 European regulation defined chocolate as 'the product obtained from cocoa nib, cocoa mass, cocoa powder or fat-reduced cocoa powder and sucrose with or without added cocoa butter, having (. . .) a minimum total dry cocoa solids content of 35%—at least 14% of dry non-fat cocoa solids and 18% of cocoa butter (. . .)' (Council Directive of 24 July 1973). The percentages were very close to the percentages given by the 1910 French chocolate law. Moreover, the use of vegetable fats other than cocoa butter (such as CBEs) was prohibited.

In 1973 three countries (Denmark, Ireland, and the UK) joined the EEC. The national laws in these three countries allowed chocolates with a different composition. One difference was that their regulations allowed chocolate production with CBEs. Another difference was how much milk could be used in 'milk chocolate'. In the EEC-6, the minimum percentage of milk used in milk chocolate was 14 per cent, whereas the British and the Irish allowed a higher percentage of milk (up to 20 per cent).

---

[40] This part draws strongly on the excellent analysis of Cidell and Alberts (2006) and Alberts and Cidell (2006).

[41] CBEs are used to decrease costs (cocoa butter is five times more expensive) but also to expand the shelf life of chocolates (they maintain a shiny surface and do not melt easily in hot climates) and to increase the product range (as new products can be created) (Fold, 2000). CBEs were developed during the 1950s and adopted in chocolate production in many countries in the 1970s, as a consequence of the increase in cocoa prices. CBEs were used especially in Eastern European countries (in particular in Russia), in the UK, and in Japan (Campbell, 2004; Wardell and Fold, 2013). For example, Japan has different standards for 'chocolate' and 'quasi-chocolate'. The 'quasi-chocolate' is made of a minimum of 15% of cocoa solids and 3% of cocoa butter (much less than the average chocolate compositions of 35% and 18% in the EU) (see Table 15.2). This type of chocolate also allows for 18% of CBEs, much more than is permitted in the EU (5%) (Sohn, 2009; Talbot, 2014).

Much was at stake for the chocolate companies. British chocolate companies asked that their traditional recipes would be recognized as 'chocolate' in the entire EEC. They insisted on allowing for different percentages of ingredients in chocolate, with more milk, less cocoa, and the possibility of using vegetable fats that were not cocoa butter. However, the companies in the six founding members produced a chocolate with less milk and a higher cocoa percentage, and they only used cocoa butter (and not vegetable fats). So they wanted to keep the existing EEC rules. The Chocolate War began.

The arguments of the six founding members against the introduction of fat other than cocoa butter were to 'maintain craftsmanship',[42] to 'prevent fraud', and to 'preserve quality chocolate' (by guaranteeing the original recipe, and protecting the consumers) (Cidell and Alberts, 2006, p. 1004; Alberts and Cidell, 2006).[43] However, the existing EEC regulations were obviously also protecting chocolate producers in these countries from competition from large British chocolate companies.[44] Hence the question 'what is chocolate?' was not only related to the 'quality' of the product but also to who got access to the EEC chocolate market.

The Two Chocolates Policy

The European Council initially refrained from making a decision by claiming that 'the economic and technical data currently available are not sufficient to enable a final position to be adopted' and postponed its decision (initially for three years). Therefore, member states could transpose the 1973 Directive into national law, either 'authorizing or prohibition the addition of vegetable fats other than cocoa butter to the chocolate products' (Council Directive of 24 July 1973). The result was a 'Two Chocolates Policy' where the countries using CBEs (Denmark, Ireland, and the UK) obtained exemptions from the European Directive on Chocolate. They could use CBEs in their chocolate products but could not sell it as 'chocolate' in the countries where CBEs were outlawed—thereby effectively banning British chocolate from the continent. A similar policy of exemption for local consumption was enacted for milk chocolate (European Parliament, 1997a; Cidell and Alberts, 2006).

---

[42] Between 1962 and 1973, France introduced a series of laws focusing on artisanship (Terrio, 2000, p. 191).

[43] Fold (2000) also points to the fear of 'controllability and labelling' of chocolate containing CBEs. Since CBEs' chemical properties are very similar to the cocoa butter ones, it was very difficult to distinguish between the two and to determine the exact amount of CBEs that had been added to the product. Therefore, fraudulent producers could have added more CBEs than legally allowed. Now analytical controls are capable of determining with exactitude (with a level of uncertainty of about 1 to 1.5%) the CBE present in the chocolate.

[44] Another argument against the use of CBEs was the negative effect on non-EEC countries which produced and exported cocoa to the EEC. As a report of the European Parliament stated: 'While certain fats to replace cocoa butter originate in the same countries, their profits from exporting vegetable fats would obviously be less than from cocoa. The Community measures being contemplated would therefore probably be detrimental to those countries, which depend on revenue from commodity *exports*' (Nordmann, 1985, p. 16).

Table 15.3 EEC/EU members' position on the use of CBEs in chocolate*

	Not Allowing CBEs	Allowing CBEs
1957	Belgium, France, Italy, Luxembourg, the Netherlands, and West Germany	
1973		Denmark, Ireland, and the UK
1981	Greece	
1986	Spain	Portugal
1995		Austria, Finland, and Sweden

*The countries allowed CBEs for up to 5% of the total weight of a chocolate product, except Finland, which allowed 10% (European Parliament, 1997b).

Lobbying by the six founding members was successful in keeping British chocolate from their market in the 1970s and the 1980s. In January 1984, the European Commission put a proposal to the Council for one harmonized Chocolate Directive that would have permitted limited use of CBEs. After about six months, the European Commission withdrew the proposal after pressure from the EEC-6 producers and the European Parliament, 'who feared that such legislation would have a disastrous effect on demand for cocoa and on prices' (European Parliament, 1997b).

However, when other countries joined the EEC (such as Greece in 1981, Portugal and Spain in 1986, Austria, Finland, and Sweden in 1995), the political equilibrium changed as the pro-CBEs camp became stronger (see Table 15.3). Before accession, Austria, Finland, Sweden, and Portugal were allowing the use of CBEs whereas Spain and Greece were not. This meant that, by 1995, a total of seven countries were using CBEs (and obtained exemptions from the European legislation) and eight countries were manufacturing chocolate only with cocoa butter— almost a tie (Fold, 2000; Cidell and Alberts, 2006).

In 1996, the European Commission put a proposal to the European Parliament and the Council for one harmonized Chocolate Directive authorizing the use of CBEs in chocolate. In 1997 a compromise was reached between the two positions. It was decided that the addition of CBEs (up to a maximum of 5 per cent) was allowed in all member states, and that up to 20 per cent of milk was allowed in milk chocolate, provided that the addition was clearly mentioned on the labels. Therefore, the companies that were using CBEs or a higher percentage of milk could sell the chocolates in all EU countries as 'chocolate' (and not 'chocolate substitute') if they labelled the chocolate as 'containing CBEs' or 'milk chocolate with high milk content' near the list of ingredients (European Commission, 1996).

The outcome was a compromise. Companies using CBEs could name their chocolate as 'chocolate'; while the companies not using CBEs won their battle on the labelling (it required a description of the ingredients) and on the percentage and type of fats used (only natural vegetable fats were allowed, and up to a maximum of 5 per cent—banning synthetic fats).[45] With this compromise, the

[45] Only six vegetable fats were allowed (e.g., palm oil, illipe, sal, shea, kokum gurgi and mango kernel) (LMC International, 2006).

European Commission created a real common market for chocolate, harmonized the Chocolate Directive, and eliminated the various exceptions (Bailer and Schneider, 2006).

The 1997 compromise officially ended the 'Chocolate War' and British chocolate companies could sell their 'chocolate' in the rest of the EU, 25 years after the UK joined the EEC/EU. However, a few battles were still to be fought. First, an intense debate followed on what exactly had to be written on the label. Under British pressure, the labelling was changed in 2000, with the term 'family milk chocolate'—strongly resembling the 'chocolate familiar' labelling of the 1920s Spanish chocolate (Directive 2000/36/EC; Cidell and Alberts, 2006). Second, some countries (Italy and Spain) continued to insist on selling British chocolate as 'chocolate substitute' (and not under the name 'chocolate') because they were contained CBEs. In 2001, Spain and Italy were sued by the European Commission and, in January 2003, the European Court of Justice found both countries guilty and claimed that 'the Spanish and Italian rules are disproportionate and infringe the principle of the free movement of goods'. The Chocolate Directive was finally transposed into national laws by August 2003 (Court of Justice, 2003).

Spillover Effects of the 2000 EU CBE Regulation on Other Countries

The EU was not the first to relax its CBEs regulation. Since 1995, chocolate in Switzerland may contain up to 5 per cent of vegetable fats.[46] However, CHOCO-SUISSE (the Association of Swiss Chocolate Producers) states that Swiss chocolate makers have not taken advantage of this possibility yet (Chocosuisse, 2015). Similarly, there appears to have been little change in the EU despite new legislation, as 'very few EU-15 chocolate manufacturers have incorporated CBEs into their recipes' (LMC International, 2006, 2014).

However, the 2000 EU Chocolate Directive has impacted chocolate regulations on CBEs in other countries. For example, countries like Australia and New Zealand did not allow the use of CBEs in chocolate before 2000. These two countries changed their compositional requirements for chocolate immediately after the EU Chocolate Directive.[47] Since 1991, Australia and New Zealand have had a single regime on food standards (the Australia New Zealand Food Standards Code— ANZFA) that applies in both countries (Richardson and Porter, 2009). As part of a major review of the ANZFA in the early 2000s, a new definition of 'chocolate' (closely following the EU definition) was enacted. In 2001, they allowed CBEs in

---

[46] 'Fats or vegetable oils other than cocoa butter may be added to the chocolate by a maximum of 5% by weight of the finished product.' [Translation by the authors. 'Des graisses ou des huiles végétales autres que le beurre de cacao peuvent être ajoutées aux chocolats (…) dans une proportion maximale de 5% masse du produit fini.'] (FDHA, 1995, Article 351).

[47] Food safety laws in Australia and New Zealand were first introduced in the mid-nineteenth century as a response to food adulteration and to the influence of the British 1860 general food safety law (Lewis, 2003, p. 138).

chocolate production up to a maximum of 5 per cent (ANZFA, 2001; Talbot, 2014, p. 188).

In 2003, Brazil also changed its legislation to allow the use of CBEs in chocolate. This was due to the 'improved functionality', as CBEs give the chocolate a higher melting point so that chocolates do not melt easily in hot climates (LMC International, 2006).

Interestingly, the international Codex Alimentarius Commission (CAC) also changed its standards and definition of chocolate[48]—allowing for the use of vegetable fats in 2003. The 1981 original Codex Alimentarius defined the standard for chocolate and did not allow the use of vegetable fats, reflecting the standard in many European countries and the USA.[49] The standard was revised in 2003 and now allows the use of up to 5 per cent vegetable fat in chocolate,[50] bringing the international agreed standards into line with EU legislation.

Another country that will probably reverse the regulation prohibiting CBEs is India. India defined standards for chocolate in 1958.[51] The standard was revised in 1971 and in 1992. The regulation currently in force in India states that: 'The chocolates shall not contain any vegetable fat other than cocoa butter' (Bureau of Indian Standards, 1992; see Chapter 21, this volume). The Indian government has recently drafted a new standard for chocolate, allowing Indian firms to use up to 5 per cent of CBEs to make chocolates. The 2014 document states that 'The addition of vegetable fats other than cocoa butter shall not exceed 5% of the finished product' (Bureau of Indian Standards, 2014). The document still needs the recommendation of the Stimulant Foods Sectional Committee and the approval of the Food and Agriculture Division Council.

After the EU change, in the countries where vegetable fats other than cocoa butter are still prohibited, such as the USA, a legislative debate emerged on whether they should also introduce them or not. The US regulation does not allow the use of CBEs, it only allows its use in 'chocolate and vegetable fat

---

[48] The World Health Organization (WHO) and the UN Food and Agriculture Organization (FAO) established the CAC in 1963 with the objective of harmonizing international food standards. These standards are established through international negotiations and called the Codex Alimentarius ('Food Code' in Latin). These standards are not legally binding (they are no sanctions for non-compliance), but they represent models for national legislation (Davies, 1970; Zylberman, 2004).

[49] During the 1970s, the problem of cocoa substitutes also emerged in the Cocoa Agreement. Article 52 of the International Cocoa Agreement of 1972 stated that: 'Members recognize that the use of substitutes may prejudice the expansion of cocoa consumption. In this regard they agree to establish regulations on cocoa products and chocolate or to adapt existing regulations, if necessary, so that the said regulations shall prohibit materials of non-cocoa origin from being used in place of cocoa to mislead the consumer' (ICCA, 1972, Article 52). However, the Article also stated that 'members shall take fully into account the recommendations and decisions of competent international bodies such as (...) the Codex Committee'.

[50] 'The addition of vegetable fats other than cocoa butter shall not exceed 5% of the finished product' (Codex, 2003).

[51] Before independence in 1947, Indian provinces had food laws which were based largely on the British 1870s Food Law (Sattigeri and Appaiah, 2009, p. 12).

coatings', and it is unlikely to follow the EU soon.[52] In 2005, the Food and Drug Administration (FDA) and the Food Safety and Inspection Service (FSIS) started a procedure to modernize their standards on food (the so-called 'Standards of Identity'). The Grocery Manufacturers Association (GMA) requested a series of changes in standards. One such demand was by the Chocolate Manufacturers Association (whose members include some large chocolate companies as Hershey Company and Nestlé Chocolate & Confections) that were asking to 'use a vegetable fat in place of another vegetable fat named in the standard (e.g., cacao fat)' and sell the ensuing product as 'chocolate' (GMA, 2006). However, in 2007, as a response to growing concerns and newspapers' alarmist titles (as 'Hands Off My Chocolate, FDA!' or 'Chocoholics Unite!'), the FDA stated that: 'Cacao fat, as one of the signature characteristics of the product, will remain a principal component of standardized chocolate' (FDA, 2007).

Recent Developments in Chocolate Regulation

These are several recent developments in chocolate regulations and standards. Some of the main recent regulatory initiatives can be classified into two groups: first, the emergence and spread of private standards on sustainability and corporate social responsibility (CSR) in cocoa–chocolate value chains and, second, public regulations in the EU on the origin and geography of chocolate and its ingredients.

CSR and Private Sustainability Standards

In recent years there has been a rapid growth of the importance of private standards in chocolate value chains. What started out as a fringe activity by non-governmental organizations (NGOs) (such as Fair Trade chocolate) has now been taken over by the major brands, who have developed strategies to promote social and economic sustainability in their value chains and have adopted certification for their sourcing, including by Fair Trade, Rainforest Alliance, and Utz. Several chapters in this book discuss and analyse these private standards and their effects (especially Chapters 11, 12, 13, and 14). We refer to these chapters for more elaborate discussions of these issues.

Here, we just point at the historical precursors to these recent (mostly private) initiatives. In particular, recent attempts to protect children and prohibit child labour can be linked to earlier initiatives to improve the situation of labour used in cocoa production.

Since the growth of cocoa trade in the fifteenth century, there has been debate on the use of forced labour in cocoa production. Initially, this concerned the native Central American population. However, as many native workers died due to exploitation and imported diseases, labour shortages on cocoa plantations

---

[52] Legislation in Canada is similar to the USA and also does not allow CBEs in chocolate production (Gnirss, 2008).

induced the import of African slave labour (Clarence-Smith, 2000; MacLeod, 2000; Walker, 2007).

At first, Africans were traded with the approval of European religious author-ities.[53] However, as reports on slavery increased, Pope Paul III published a bull ('Sublimis Deus') in 1537, prohibiting the enslavement of the native population in Latin America; however, there was no mention of slave labour from Africa. The discussion lasted several centuries. Other popes would condemn slavery, but some kind of 'forced labour' by the native population was still possible if the Spaniards Christianized them (Maxwell, 1975).[54] Although slavery was legally abolished by the end of the nineteenth century,[55] major scandals around enslaved labour in cocoa production continued.[56]

More recently, there has been concern about the use of child labour in cocoa production. International Cocoa Agreements have tried, over the years, to set standards on child and forced labour practices in the cocoa sector (ILO/SIMPOC, 2002; Nkamleu and Kielland, 2006). The first International Labor Organization (ILO) Convention regulating child labour was in 1919. A minimum age for employment was fixed at 14. In 2002, ILO's IPEC (International Programme on the Elimination of Child Labour) established an International Cocoa Initiative (ICI): Working Towards Responsible Labor Standards in Cocoa Growing, aimed at 'eliminating child and forced labour practices in cocoa cultivation and processing' (ILO, 2005, p. 2; Rishikesh, 2008).

International Cocoa Agreements also tried to set labour standards and 'fair labor conditions' from 1975 onwards (Kofi, 1976). The 1975 Cocoa Agreement (article 64) stated that: 'Members declare that, in order to raise the levels of living of populations and provide full employment, they will endeavour to maintain fair labour standards and working conditions in the various branches of cocoa pro-duction in the countries concerned, consistent with their stage of development, as regards both agricultural and industrial workers employed therein' (ICCA, 1975).

---

[53] In 1454, Pope Nicholas V formally supported the Portuguese slave trade in Africa (Maxwell, 1975, p. 53).

[54] Pope Paul III, Pope Urban VIII, and Pope Benedict XIV distinguished between 'just' and 'unjust' enslavement and slave-trading depending on whether the native population accepted being baptized or not. 'Just' enslavement (the native population resisted conversion) was accepted, whereas 'unjust' enslavement (the native population accepted being baptized) was condemned. In 1839, Pope Gregory XVI condemned slave labour from Africa as 'unchristian and morally unlawful', but still distinguished between 'just' and 'unjust' enslavement. In 1888, Pope Leo XIII with his encyclical letter *Rerum Novarum*, finally condemned both types of enslavement, as human labour is 'personal since the active force inherent in the person cannot be the property of anyone other than the person who exerts it' (Maxwell, 1975, pp. 74 and 120).

[55] Slavery was abolished in Chile in 1823, in Spain in 1837, in the Dominican Republic in 1844, in Ecuador in 1851, and in Argentina in 1853, in Venezuela in 1854, in the USA in 1865, and in Brazil in 1888 (Maxwell, 1975, p. 105; Curran, 2003, p. 76). Legal slavery lasted three and a half centuries, with Brazil importing between 3.5 and 5 million African slaves—about 40% of the slave trade (Walker, 2007).

[56] For example, in 1908 Cadbury was accused of using slave labour in São Tomé, Africa (*The Standard*, 1908).

The impact of both the ILO and the Cocoa Agreements on labour conditions in cocoa production has been limited, which has triggered the emergence and spread of the private standards in recent years.

Towards Origin-Based EU Chocolate 'Quality' Regulations?

Cidell and Alberts (2006) provide an excellent discussion of the relationship between chocolate quality and location. They explain that, for chocolate, unlike, for example, wine, the association between quality and location is not so much the location of the basic ingredient but the location of the manufacturing of the final product (e.g., 'Swiss chocolate'). Two recent (proposed) regulations in the EU may influence this relationship. The first one attempts to provide a regulatory link between quality and location; the second extends this link to the origin of the main ingredients.

GEOGRAPHICAL PROTECTION FOR EU CHOCOLATE?

The link of product 'quality' with geographical locations of production started first as part of the European Common Wine Policy in 1962 (e.g., Appellation 'Bordeaux' or 'Champagne'), and has later been extended to other products, such as cheese and olive oil.[57] In 1992, the EU introduced the concept of 'geographical indications' (GIs) with two subcategories (so-called 'quality schemes'): 'protected designation of origin' (PDO), which requires that all the stages of production take place in the same defined geographical area, and 'protected geographical indication' (PGI). The list of agri-food products that could claim GI protection included beer, bread, cheese, confectionery, biscuits, and so on, but not chocolate (Council Regulations (EEC) No. 2081/92 and No. 2082/92).

Instead, 'Chocolate and other food preparations containing cocoa' could apply for another (lower) level of protection, the 'Certificate of Specific Character' (later called 'Traditional Speciality Guaranteed' or TSG). For a TSG there does not need to be a link with the origin of the product (a geographical area) but products must have a 'traditional character', for example, they must be produced according to a certain production method, but this may take place anywhere (as 'Mozzarella' cheese or 'Kriek' beer). In 2006, the GI regulation was extended to more products (mustard paste and pasta) but chocolate could still not claim GI status, only TSG (Council Regulation (EC) No. 509/2006 and No. 510/2006). However, at the time of writing, there is still no 'chocolate' registered as a TSG (DOOR, 2015).

In 2012, a new change to the GI rules further widened the eligibility scope for food products, and now includes 'chocolate and derived products'.[58] Since, for a PDO geographical protection, all the production steps must take place in the defined geographical area, a PDO scheme for chocolate is not possible as the raw

---

[57] Meloni and Swinnen (2013 and 2014) analyse the political economy mechanism that created existing wine regulations.

[58] Regulation (EU) No. 1151/2012 states that the 'inclusion in the current scheme of only certain types of chocolate as confectionery products is an anomaly that should be corrected'.

materials (cocoa beans) are not produced in the EU.[59] However, it is now possible for chocolate producers or processors to apply for a PGI (for discussion on PGI for 'Belgian chocolate' see Chapter 5, this volume).

TOWARDS A COMPULSORY ORIGIN LABELLING?

Another recent (and ongoing) discussion on chocolate involves the indication of the country of origin of the ingredients on the labelling, the so-called country of origin labelling (COOL) requirements. In 2011, the EU adopted a new regulation on food labelling, which includes, among others, mandatory nutrition information on processed foods and mandatory origin labelling of some foods, and ingredients that constitute over 50 per cent of a food.[60]

Milk chocolates are not affected by the new COOL requirements (as they contain about 25 per cent of cocoa) but dark chocolates could enter into the regulatory framework as they often contain more than 50 per cent of cocoa. The chocolate producers will then have to specify the country of origin of the cocoa beans used in the blending, for example, Ivory Coast, Ghana, Nigeria, and so on.[61]

The European Cocoa Association (ECA) is calling for an exemption for cocoa (as Switzerland has already done), arguing that the new (proposed) COOL regulation could harm the cocoa sector since the required investments to separate sourcing and processing would be costly and could force chocolate producers to abandon the practice of cocoa bean blending (Nieburg, 2013).

Conclusion

In this chapter, we reviewed various regulations that have been imposed in the cocoa–chocolate chain over time and across countries. We have concentrated on the regulations and standards imposed since the growth of cocoa trade and chocolate consumption (i.e., the seventeenth century and later). A first set of regulations were introduced to tax cocoa trade and chocolate production, both in Europe in the sixteenth to nineteenth centuries and in post-colonial Africa. A second set of regulations focused mostly on quality and safety to protect consumers against frauds and health risks by imposing standards on the manufacturing (and the composition) of chocolate. Scientific inventions of the eighteenth and nineteenth centuries allowed better testing of the (cheaper and sometimes unhealthy) chocolate ingredients. The publications of these new tests documented major frauds and led to public outrage and political initiatives to introduce safety regulations,

---

[59] There are exceptions to this rule (e.g., live animals, meat, and milk). Even though the raw materials (live animals, meat, and milk) come from an area different from the defined geographical area, the final product can still apply for a PDO (Regulation (EU) No. 1151/2012).

[60] European Commission, 2014; EU Regulation 1169/2011.

[61] Some chocolate manufacturers (such as Barry Callebaut) already use the 'Country Origin' chocolates as a marketing campaign, e.g., chocolates that are made from the cocoa beans harvested in one specific country (Barry Callebaut, 2007).

for example, to define which specific ingredients were not allowed in chocolate. In some countries, this led to a legal definition of 'chocolate'. Differences in regulations caused problems in the process of European integration as EU members conflicted when creating a single EU chocolate policy. Recent discussions on chocolate regulation in the EU are about linking 'quality' to the location of the production of chocolate and cocoa. However, the most important recent innovations in regulations are not public rules but private standards, which are increasingly widespread. They are also the subject of several other chapters in this book (especially Chapters 11, 12, 13, and 14).

References

Accum, F. 1820. *A Treatise on Adulterations of Food, and Culinary Poisons: Exhibiting the Fraudulent Sophistications of Bread, Beer, Wine, Spiritous Liquors, Tea, Coffee, Cream, Confectionery, Vinegar, Mustard, Pepper, Cheese, Olive Oil, Pickles, and Other Articles Employed in Domestic Economy*. Philadelphia: Abraham Small. Available at: <http://www.gutenberg.org/files/19031/19031-h/19031-h.htm> (accessed 18 February 2015).

Alberts, H. C. and J. L. Cidell. 2006. 'Chocolate Consumption, Manufacturing and Quality in Western Europe and the United States'. *Geography* 91 (3): pp. 218–26.

Anderson, K. and S. Nelgen. 2013. 'Updated National and Global Estimates of Distortions to Agricultural Incentives, 1955 to 2011', World Bank, Washington DC, June. Available at: <http://www.worldbank.org/agdistortions> (accessed 11 March 2015).

ANZFA (Australia and New Zealand Food Authority). 2001. *Food Standards Code*, vol. 2, incorporating amendments up to and including Amendment 58. Available at: <http://www.foodstandards.gov.au/code/Pages/default.aspx> (accessed 6 January 2015).

Arcila Farías, E. 1950. *Comercio entre Venezuela y México en los Siglos XVII y XVIII*. Mexico City: El Colegio de México.

Bailer, S. and G. Schneider. 2006. 'Nash versus Schelling? The Importance of Constraints in Legislative Bargaining'. In *The European Union Decides: Testing Theories of European Decision-making*, edited by R. Thomson, F. Stokman, C. H. Achen, and T. König, pp. 135–77. Cambridge: Cambridge University Press.

Balzaretti, C. 2014. *La Cioccolata Cattolica. Storia di una Disputa tra Teologia e Medicina*. Bologna: Edizioni Dehoniane.

Barry Callebaut. 2007. 'Barry Callebaut Offers Largest Selection of Origin Chocolates'. Available at: <https://www.barry-callebaut.com/news/2007/12/barry-callebaut-offers-largest-selection-origin-chocolates> (accessed 7 April 2015).

Bergman, J. L. 1969. 'The Distribution of Cacao Cultivation in Pre-Columbian America'. *Annals of the Association of American Geographers* 59: pp. 85–96.

Brancaccio, F. M. 1664. *De Chocolatis Potu Diatribe*. Rome: Zachariam Dominicum Acsamitek Kronenfeld.

Brindle, L. P. and B. F. Olson. 2009. 'Adulteration: The Dark World of "Dirty" Chocolate'. In *Chocolate: History, Culture, and Heritage*, edited by L. E. Grivetti and H.-Y. Shapiro, pp. 625–34. New York: John Wiley.

Buckingham, D. 2002. 'The Legislative Environment for Canada's Food. Labelling Laws: A Case Study from the "New World"'. Report—International Development Research Centre: IDRC. Available at <https://idl-bnc.idrc.ca/dspace/bitstream/10625/28442/1/120051.pdf> (accessed 23 April 2015).

Bureau of Indian Standards. 1992. 'Indian Standard Chocolates Specification, IS: 1163–1992'. Bureau of Indian Standards, New Delhi, India. Available at: <https://law.resource.org/pub/in/bis/S06/is.1163.1992.pdf> (accessed 10 December 2015).

Bureau of Indian Standards. 2014. 'Indian Standard Chocolates Specification (Third Revision of IS 1163), FAD 6 (2696) C Draft'. Bureau of Indian Standards, New Delhi, India. Available at: <http://www.bis.org.in/sf/fad/FAD%206(2696-2698)C_03112014.pdf> (accessed 20 December 2014).

Burnett, J. 1999. *Liquid Pleasures: A Social History of Drinks in Modern Britain*. London and New York: Routledge.

Burrows, J. D. 2009. 'Palette of Our Palates: A Brief History of Food Coloring and Its Regulation'. *Comprehensive Reviews in Food Science and Food Safety* 8 (4): pp. 394–408.

Campbell, I. 2004. 'An Exotic Tale'. *Nioto S.A.: Nouvelle Industrie des Oléagineux du Togo*, 3 August. Available at: <http://www.nioto-togo.com/spip.php?article28> (accessed 2 November 2014).

Canada Gazette. 1949. The Canada Gazette Part II (1947–1997), volume 83, number 15, Table of Statutory Orders and Regulations, 10 August, p. 67. Available at: <http://www.collectionscanada.gc.ca/databases/canada-gazette> (accessed 26 February 2015).

Cárdenas, Juan de. 1591/1913. *Primera Parte de los Problemas y Secretos Marauillosos de las Indias*. México: Museo Nacional de Arqueología, Historia y Etnología de México. Available at: <https://archive.org/details/primerapartedelo00cr> (accessed 2 October 2014).

Castellote Herrero, E. 1981. 'El Chocolate: Historia de su Elaboración en la Provincia de Guadalajara'. *Wad-al-Hayara: Revista de estudios de Guadalajara* 8: pp. 385–414.

CFR (Code of Federal Regulations). 1993. Food and Drug Administration (FDA), Code of Federal Regulations, Title 21: *Food and Drugs. Part 163—Cacao Products*. Available at: <http://www.ecfr.gov/cgi-bin/text-idx?SID=32f2918856ffe4025ff7f8952deb83d9&node=pt21.2.163&rgn=div5> (accessed 4 August 2014).

Chevallier, A. 1850. *Dictionnaire des Altérations et Falsifications des Substances Alimentaires, Médicamenteuses et Commerciales: Avec l'Indication des Moyens de les Reconnaître*, vol. 1. Paris: Béchet jeune. Available at: <http://gallica.bnf.fr/ark:/12148/bpt6k6517142j> (accessed 20 July 2014).

Chocosuisse. 2015. 'How Free is the Swiss Chocolate Industry with Regard to Manufacturing?' Chocosuisse. Available at: <http://www.chocosuisse.ch/web/chocosuisse/en/documentation/faq.html> (accessed 14 March 2015).

Choquart, C. 1867. *Chocolaterie Impériale. Aux Consommateurs de Chocolat et de Thé, Histoire de ces Deux Aliments*. Paris: Imprimerie de Walder. Available at: <http://gallica.bnf.fr/ark:/12148/bpt6k850499k> (accessed 10 September 2014).

Cidell, J. L. and H. C. Alberts. 2006. 'Constructing Quality: The Multi-National Histories of Chocolate'. *Geoforum* 37 (6): pp. 999–1007.

Clarence-Smith, W. 2000. *Cocoa and Chocolate 1765–1914*. London: Routledge.

Code pénal. 1810. 'Édition originale en version intégrale, publiée sous le titre: Code des Délits et des Peines'. Available at: <http://ledroitcriminel.free.fr/la_legislation_criminelle/anciens_textes/code_penal_de_1810.htm> (accessed 19 June 2014).

Codex. 2003. 'Standard for Chocolate and Chocolate Products'. Codex Alimentarius Commission. CODEX STAN 87-1981, Rev.1–2003. Available at: <http://www.codexalimentarius.org/input/download/standards/67/CXS_087e.pdf> (accessed 20 October 2014).

Coe, S. and M. Coe. 2013. *The True History of Chocolate*. 3rd edn. London: Thames & Hudson.

Colmenero de Ledesma, A. 1631. *Curioso Tratado de la Naturaleza y Calidad del Chocolate*. Madrid, Spain: Francisco Martinez. Available at: <http://bdh.bne.es/bnesearch/detalle/bdh0000090098> (accessed 6 August 2014).

Combaldieu, R. 1974. 'La Fraude en Matière Alimentaire'. *Revue Internationale de Droit Comparé* 26 (3): pp. 515–27.

Council Directive of 24 July 1973 on the approximation of the laws of the Member States relating to cocoa and chocolate products intended for human consumption (73/241/EEC). *Official Journal of the European Communities* No. L 228 of 16 August 1973.

Council Regulation (EEC) No. 2081/92 of 14 July 1992 on the protection of geographical indications and designations of origin for agricultural products and foodstuffs. *Official Journal of the European Communities* No. L 208/1 of 24 July 1992.

Council Regulation (EEC) No. 2082/92 of 14 July 1992 on certificates of specific character for agricultural products and foodstuffs. *Official Journal* No. L 208 of 24 July 1992.

Council Regulation (EC) No. 509/2006 of 20 March 2006 Council Regulation (EC) No. 510/ 2006 of 20 March 2006 on the protection of geographical indications and designations of origin for agricultural products and foodstuffs. Official Journal of the European Union No. L 93/1 of 31 March 2006.

Council Regulation (EC) No. 510/2006 of 20 March 2006 on the protection of geographical indications and designations of origin for agricultural products and foodstuffs. *Official Journal of the European Union* No. L 93/12 of 31 March 2006.

Court of Justice. 2003. 'Spain and Italy are Found to Have Wrongly Prohibited the Marketing under the Name "Chocolate" of Products containing Vegetable Fats other than Cocoa Butter'. Judgments of the Court of Justice in Cases C-12/00 and C-14/00, Commission v Spain and Italy. Press Release No. 03/03, 16 January. Available at: <http://curia.europa.eu/ en/actu/communiques/cp03/aff/cp0303en.htm> (accessed 20 January 2015).

Curran, C. E. 2003. *Change in Official Catholic Moral Teachings*. New Jersey: Paulist Press.

Dammann Frères. 2015. 'History'. Dammann Frères, Paris 1692. Available at: <http://www. dammann.fr/content/7-history> (accessed 9 March 2015).

Davies, J. H. V. 1970. 'The Codex Alimentarius'. *Journal of the Association of Public Analysts* 8: pp. 53–67.

Décret. 1910. 'Décret du 19 décembre 1910 relatif aux Fraudes et Falsifications en ce qui concerne les Produits de la Sucrerie, de la Confiserie et de la Chocolaterie. Titre IV: Cacaos et chocolats'. Available at: <http://www.legifrance.gouv.fr/affichTexte.do;jsessionid= 44CFB23BA60825A089970506D74CB220.tpdjo05v_3?cidTexte= JORFTEXT000000665620&dateTexte=20140729> (accessed 3 March 2015).

Directive 2000/36/EC of the European Parliament and of the Council of 23 June 2000 relating to cocoa and chocolate products intended for human consumption (2000/36/EC*). Official Journal of the European Communities* No. L 197/19 of 3 August 2000.

DOOR (Database of Origin and Registration). 2015. The Database of Origin and Registration (DOOR). European Commission, Agriculture and Rural Development, online database. Available at: <http://ec.europa.eu/agriculture/quality/door/list.html>. (accessed 20 February 2015).

Douglas, L. M. 1909. 'International Congress on Pure Foods and Alimentary Substances'. *Nature: A Weekly Illustrated Journal of Science*, edited by N. Lockyer, 82: pp. 25–6. Available at: <https://archive.org/details/nature8219091910lock> (accessed 8 September 2014).

Escobar y Mendoza, A. de. 1626. *Summula Casuum conscientiæ*. Pamplona: J. de Oteiza.

European Commission. 1963. 'Proposal for a Council Directive relating to the Approximation of the Regulations of Member States concerning Cocoa and Chocolate', Submitted by the Commission to the Council on 23 July. Available at: <http://aei.pitt.edu/6869/> (accessed 1 September 2014).

European Commission. 1996. 'Proposal for a European Parliament and Council Directive Relating to Cocoa and Chocolate Products Intended for Human Consumption COM(95)

722 final'. *Official Journal of the European Communities* No. C 231/1 of 9 August. Available at: <http://eur-lex.europa.eu/legal-content/en/ALL/?uri=OJ:C:1996:231:TOC> (accessed 5 February 2015).

European Commission. 2014. 'New EU Law on Food Information to Consumers'. European Commission, DG Health and Consumers. Available at: <http://ec.europa.eu/food/food/labellingnutrition/foodlabelling/proposed_legislation_en.htm> (accessed 26 January 2015).

European Parliament. 1997a. 'Chocolate, Cocoa versus Vegetable Fats'. European Parliament Background Information. Brussels, 15 October. Available at: <http://www.europarl.europa.eu/press/sdp/backg/en/1997/b971015.htm> (accessed 3 April 2014).

European Parliament. 1997b. 'Proposal for a Directive relating to Cocoa and Chocolate Products: Consequences for Exporting and Importing Countries'. Research and Documentation Papers, External Economic Relations Series, Working Paper W-14, 1–1997. Available at <http://aei.pitt.edu/5983/> (accessed 20 March 2014).

FDA (Food and Drug Administration). 1965. 'The Code of Federal Regulations of the United States of America'. Title 21—Food and Drugs. Parts 1 to 129. Washington: US Government Printing Office.

FDA (Food and Drug Administration). 2007. 'FDA's Standards for High Quality Foods'. Food and Drug Administration, 18 June 2007. Available at: <http://www.fda.gov/forconsumers/consumerupdates/ucm094559.htm> (accessed 13 March 2015).

FDA (Food and Drug Administration). 2009. 'Food Standards under the 1938 Food, Drug, and Cosmetic Act: Bread and Jam'. Food and Drug Administration. Available at: <http://www.fda.gov/AboutFDA/WhatWeDo/History/ProductRegulation/ucm132892.htm#ref48> (accessed 16 December 2014).

FDHA (Federal Department of Home Affairs). 1995. 'Ordonnance sur les Denrées Alimentaires (ODAl) SR 817.02 du 1er mars 1995 Article 351'. Federal Department of Home Affairs. Available at: <http://www.admin.ch/opc/fr/classified-compilation/81.html> (accessed 5 October 2014).

FFDA (Federal Food and Drugs Act). 1906. 'Federal Food and Drugs Act of 1906 (The "Wiley Act"). Public Law 59-384, 34 Stat. 768'. Available at: <http://www.fda.gov/RegulatoryInformation/Legislation/ucm148690.htm> (accessed 19 January 2015).

Fincke, H. 1965. *Handbuch der Kakaoerzeugnisse*. Berlin, Heidelberg, and New York: Springer-Verlag.

Fitzgerald, R. 1995. *Rowntree and the Marketing Revolution, 1862–1969*. Cambridge: Cambridge University Press.

Fold, N. 2000. 'A Matter of Good Taste? Quality and the Construction of Standards for Chocolate Products in the European Union'. *Cahiers d'Économie et Sociologie Rurales* 55/56: pp. 91–110.

Fold, N. 2001. 'Restructuring of the European Chocolate Industry and Its Impact on Cocoa Production in West Africa'. *Journal of Economic Geography* 1 (3): pp. 405–20.

Forte, W. E. 1966. 'The Food and Drug Administration and the Economic Adulteration of Foods'. *Indiana Law Journal* 41 (3), Article 2. Available at: <http://www.repository.law.indiana.edu/ilj/vol41/iss3/2> (accessed 17 August 2014).

Franklin, A. 1893. *La Vie Privée d'autrefois: Arts et Métiers, Modes, Moeurs, Usages des Parisiens, du XIIE au XVIIIE siècle/D'après des Documents Originaux ou Inédits. Le Café, Le Thé et Le Chocolat*. Paris: Librairie Plon. Available at: <http://gallica.bnf.fr/ark:/12148/bpt6k204416b> (accessed 3 March 2015).

Gárate Ojanguren, M. 1990. *La Real Compañía Guipuzcoana de Caracas*. San Sebastián: Sociedad Guipuzcoana de Ediciones y Publicaciones.

Gilbert, C. L. 2009. 'Cocoa Market Liberalization in Retrospect'. *Review of Business and Economics* 54: pp. 294–312.

Glen, W. C. 1872. *Law Relating to Public Health and Local Government.* London: Butterworth's. Available at: <https://archive.org/details/lawrelatingtopu01glengoog> (accessed 1 October 2014).

GMA (Grocery Manufacturers Association). 2006. 'Petition to Request the Commissioner of Food and Drugs to Issue Regulations of General Applicability to Modernize the Food Standards'. Grocery Manufacturers Association. Available at: <http://www.fda.gov/ohrms/dockets/dockets/07p0085/07p-0085.htm> (accessed 15 January 2015).

Gnirss, G. 2008. 'A History of Food Law in Canada'. *Regulatory Affairs*, 38.

Gordon, B. M. 2009a. 'Chocolate in France: Evolution of a Luxury Product'. In *Chocolate: History, Culture, and Heritage*, edited by L. E. Grivetti and H.-Y. Shapiro, pp. 569–82. New York: John Wiley.

Gordon, B. M. 2009b. 'Commerce, Colonies, and Cacao: Chocolate in England from Introduction to Industrialization'. In *Chocolate: History, Culture, and Heritage*, edited by L. E. Grivetti and H.-Y. Shapiro, pp. 583–94. New York: John Wiley.

Grivetti, L. E. 2009. 'From Bean to Beverage: Historical Chocolate Recipes'. In *Chocolate: History, Culture, and Heritage*, edited by L. E. Grivetti and H.-Y. Shapiro, pp. 99–114. New York: John Wiley.

Grivetti, L. E. and H.-Y. Shapiro. 2009. 'Chocolate Futures: Promising Areas for Further Research'. In *Chocolate: History, Culture, and Heritage*, edited by L. E. Grivetti and H.-Y. Shapiro, pp. 743–73. New York: John Wiley.

Guillem-Llobat, X. 2014. 'The Search for International Food Safety Regulation: From the Commission Internationale pour la répression des falsifications to the Société universelle de la Croix Blanche (1879–1909)'. *Social History of Medicine* 27 (3): pp. 419–39.

Hart, F. L. 1952. 'A History of the Adulteration of Food before 1906'. *Food Drug Cosmetic Law Journal* 7 (1): pp. 5–22.

Hassall, B. H. 1855. *Food and its Adulterations: Comprising the Reports of the Analytical Sanitary Commission of "The Lancet" for the Years 1851 to 1854.* London: Longman. Available at: <https://archive.org/details/fooditsadulterat00hassrich> (accessed 16 November 2014).

Head, B. 1903. *The Food of the Gods: A Popular Account of Cocoa.* London: R. B. Johnson Available at: <http://www.gutenberg.org/files/16035/16035-h/16035-h.htm> (accessed 12 February 2015).

Herbert, T. 1884. *The Law on Adulteration: Being the Sale of Food and Drugs Acts, 1875 and 1879.* London: Knight & Co. Available at: <https://archive.org/details/lawonadulterati00herbgoog> (accessed 20 July 2014).

Hurtado, T. 1645. *Chocolate y Tabaco Ayuno Eclesiastico y Natural: si este le Quebrante el Chocolate: y el Tabaco al Natural, para la Sagrada Comunion. Por Francisco Garcia, Impressor del Reyno. A Costa de Manuel Lopez.* Madrid: Mercador de Libros. Available at: <http://bvpb.mcu.es/es/consulta/registro.cmd?id=417721> (accessed 20 December 2014).

Hussey, R. D. 1934. *The Caracas Company, 1728–1784: A Study in the History of Spanish Monopolistic Trade.* Cambridge, MA: Harvard University Press.

Hutt, P. B. and P. B. Hutt. 1984. 'A History of Government Regulation of Adulteration and Misbranding of Food'. *Food, Drug, and Cosmetic Law Journal* 39: pp. 2–73.

ICCA (International Congress and Convention Association). 1972. 'International Cocoa Agreement (ICA) (with annexes): Concluded at Geneva on 21 October 1972'. United Nations—Treaty Series. Available at: <https://treaties.un.org/doc/Publication/UNTS/Volume%20882/volume-882-I-12652-English.pdf> (accessed 23 June 2014).

ICCA (International Congress and Convention Association). 1975. 'International Cocoa Agreement, 1975 (with annexes): Concluded at Geneva on 20 October 1975'. United Nations—Treaty Series. Available at: <https://treaties.un.org/pages/ViewDetails.aspx?src=TREATY&mtdsg_no=XIX-14&chapter=19&lang=en> (accessed 4 May 2014).

ILO (International Labour Organization). 2005. 'Combating Child Labour in Cocoa Growing'. Geneva: International Labor Office. Available at: <http://www.ilo.org/public//english/stand ards/ipec/themes/cocoa/download/2005_02_cl_cocoa.pdf> (accessed 8 July 2015).

ILO/SIMPOC (International Labour Organization/Statistical Information and Monitoring Programme on Child Labour). 2002. 'Every Child Counts: New Global Estimates on Child Labor'. Geneva: International Labor Office.

Keith, R. G. 1971. 'Encomienda, Hacienda and Corregimiento in Spanish America: A Structural Analysis'. *Hispanic American Historical Review* 51 (3): pp. 431–46.

Klitzke, R. A. 1959. 'Historical Background of the English Patent Law'. *Journal of the Patent Office Society* 41 (9): pp. 615–50.

Knapp, A. 1920. *Cocoa and Chocolate: Their History from Plantation to Consumer*. London: Chapman & Hall.

Kofi, T. A. 1976. 'The International Cocoa Agreements'. In *Cocoa Production: Economic and Botanical Perspectives*, edited by J. Simmons, pp. 82–99. New York: Praeger.

La Berge, A. F. 1992. *Mission and Method: The Early Nineteenth-Century French Public Health Movement*. New York: Cambridge University Press.

The Lancet. 1909. 'The Second International Congress for the Repression of Fraud'. *The Lancet* 174 (4497): p. 1385.

Lauer, B. H. 1993. 'The Rage for Cheapness: Food Adulteration in the United Canadas and in the Dominion 1850–1920'. Master's thesis, Carleton University, Ottawa.

Law. 1875. 'Sale of Food and Drugs Act 1875'. Chapter 63. Available at <http://www.legisla tion.gov.uk/en/ukpga/1875/63/contents/enacted> (accessed 17 February 2015).

Lewis, M. J. 2003. *The People's Health: Public Health in Australia, 1788–1950*. United States: Greenwood Press.

Licensing Act. 1872. 'An Act for Regulating the Sale of Intoxicating Liquors'. Chapter 94. Available at: <http://www.legislation.gov.uk/ukpga/Vict/35-36/94/introduction/enacted> (accessed 2 March 2015).

LMC International. 2006. 'Evaluation of the Impact of Directive 2000/36/EC on the Econ-omies of those Countries Producing Cocoa and Vegetable Fats Other than Cocoa Butter'. Final report prepared for the European Commission, DG Agriculture, and Rural Develop-ment. Available at: <http://ec.europa.eu/agriculture/eval/reports/chocolate/fullrep_en.pdf> (accessed 18 March 2014).

LMC International. 2014. 'World Cocoa and CBE markets'. Presentation to Global Shea 2014 by Robert Simmons, LMC International, Oxford. Available at: <http://www.globalshea. com/uploads/files/shea_2014_conference_presentations_file_b/simmons-_shea_2014nl_ 228.pdf> (accessed 5 January 2015).

Lockhart, J. 1969. 'Encomienda and Hacienda: The Evolution of the Great Estate in the Spanish Indies'. *Hispanic American Historical Review* 49 (3): pp. 411–29.

Loi. 1851. 'Loi des 10, 19 et 27 mars 1851 tendant à la répression plus efficace de certaines fraudes dans la vente des marchandises'. In *Bulletin officiel du Ministère de l'intérieur*, edited by Ministère de l'intérieur, pp. 130–2. Paris: Dupont. Available at: <http://gallica.bnf.fr/ ark:/12148/bpt6k5517111s.image> (accessed 6 December 2014).

MacLeod, M. J. 2000. 'Cacao'. In *The Cambridge World History of Food*, vol. 1, edited by K. F. Kiple and K. C. Ornelas, pp. 635–40. Cambridge: Cambridge University Press.

Maxwell, J. F. 1975. *Slavery and the Catholic Church: The History of Catholic Teaching Concerning the Moral Legitimacy of the Institution of Slavery*. London: Barry Rose Publishers.

Meloni, G. and J. Swinnen. 2013. 'The Political Economy of European Wine Regulations'. *Journal of Wine Economics* 8 (3): pp. 244–84.

Meloni, G. and J. Swinnen. 2014. 'The Rise and Fall of the World's Largest Wine Exporter: And Its Institutional Legacy'. *Journal of Wine Economics* 9 (1): pp. 3–33.

Meloni, G. and J. Swinnen. 2015. 'The Origin of Modern Food Safety and Quality Standards'. mimeo.

Mitchell, J. 1848. *Treatise on the Falsification of Food, and the Chemical Means Employed to Detect Them*. London: Hippolyte Bailliere.

Navier, P.-T. 1772. *Observations sur le Cacao et sur le Chocolat, où l'on Examine les Avantages et les Inconvéniens qui Peuvent Résulter de l'Usage de ces Substances Nourricières: le tout Fondé sur l'Expérience et sur les Recherches Analytiques de l'Amande du Cacao; Suivies de Réflexions sur le Système de M. de Lamure, touchant le Battement des Artères*. Paris: P.-Fr. Didot jeune. Available at: <http://gallica.bnf.fr/ark:/12148/bpt6k936661h> (accessed 22 September 2014).

Nieburg, O. 2013. 'Calls to Exempt Cocoa from Voluntary and Mandatory Origin Labeling'. *Confectionerynews*, 9 December. Available at: <http://www.confectionerynews.com/Tech nology/Ingredients/Calls-to-exempt-cocoa-from-voluntary-and-mandatory-origin-labeling> (accessed 24 November 2014).

Nkamleu, G. B. and A. Kielland. 2006. 'Modeling Farmers' Decisions on Child Labor and Schooling in the Cocoa Sector: A Multinomial Logit Analysis in Côte d'Ivoire'. *Agricultural Economics* 35: pp. 319–33.

Nordmann, J. T. 1985. 'Report Drawn Up by the Committee on the Environment, Public Health and Consumer Protection on the Proposal from the Commission of the European Communities to the Council (COM(83) 787 final- Doc. 1-1363/83) for a Directive on the Approximation of the Laws of the Member States relating to Cocoa and Chocolate Products Intended for Human Consumption'. Working Documents 1985–86, Document A 2-101/85, 30 September. Available at: <http://aei.pitt.edu/48982/> (accessed 12 February 2015).

Normandy, A. 1850. *The Commercial Handbook of Chemical Analysis*. London: G. Knight.

Oddy, D. J. 2007. 'Food Quality in London and the Rise of the Public Analyst, 1870–1939'. In *Food and the City in Europe since 1800*, edited by P. J. Atkins, P. Lummel, and D. J. Oddy, pp. 91–103. Aldershot: Ashgate.

Ostry, A. S. 2006. *Nutrition Policy in Canada, 1870–1939*. Vancouver: University of British Columbia Press.

Philp, R. K. 1871. *Enquire Within Upon Everything: To Which is Added, Enquire Within Upon Fancy Needlework*. London: Houlston & Sons.

Pinelo, A. L. de. 1636. *Question Moral. Si el Chocolate Quebranta el Ayuno Eclesiastico. Tratase de otras bebidas j confecciones, que se usan en varias provincias*. Madrid: González. Available at: <https://books.google.be/books?id=MWRKAAAAcAAJ&source=gbs_navlinks_s> (accessed 9 March 2015).

Regulation (EU) No. 1169/2011 of the European Parliament and of the Council of 25 October 2011 on the provision of food information to consumers. *Official Journal of the European Union* No. L 304/18 of 22 November 2011.

Regulation (EU) No. 1151/2012 of the European Parliament and of the Council of 21 November 2012 on quality schemes for agricultural products and foodstuffs. *Official Journal of the European Union* No. L 343/1 of 14 December 2012.

Richardson, K. C. and W. R. Porter. 2009. 'Australia and New Zealand'. In *Ensuring Global Food Safety: Exploring Global Harmonization*, edited by C. E. Boisrobert, A. Stjepanovic, S. Oh, and H. Lelieveld, pp. 26–32. New York: Elsevier.

Rico Linage, R. 1983. *Las Reales Compañías de Comercio con América. Los Órganos de Gobierno*. Seville: Editorial CSIC–CSIC Press.

Rishikesh, D. 2008. 'The Worst Forms of Child Labour: A Guide to ILO Convention 182 and Recommendation 190'. In *Child Labour in a Globalized World: A Legal Analysis of ILO Action*, edited by G. Nesi, L. Nogler, and M. Pertile, pp. 83–99. Aldershot: Ashgate.

Rowlinson, P. J. 1982. 'Food Adulteration: Its Control in 19th Century Britain'. *Interdisciplinary Science Reviews* 7 (1): pp. 63–72.

Sattigeri, V. D. and K. M. Appaiah. 2009. 'India'. In *Ensuring Global Food Safety: Exploring Global Harmonization*, edited by C. E. Boisrobert, A. Stjepanovic, S. Oh, and H. Lelieveld, pp. 12–15. New York: Elsevier.

Scheuplein, J. R. 1999. 'History of Food Regulation'. In *International Food Safety Handbook*, edited by K. van der Heijden, M. Younes, L. Fishbein and S. Miller , pp. 647–60. New York: Marcel Dekker.

Sebasto Melisseno, N. 1665. *De Chocolatis Potione: Resolutio Moralis*. Neapolis: Typis Hieronymi Fasuli. Available at: <http://catalog.hathitrust.org/Record/009309783> (accessed 20 September 2014).

Sohn, M.-G. 2009. 'Northeast Asia'. In *Ensuring Global Food Safety: Exploring Global Harmonization*, edited by C. E. Boisrobert, A. Stjepanovic, S. Oh, and H. Lelieveld, pp. 53–7. New York: Elsevier.

Spary, E. C. 2013. *Eating the Enlightenment: Food and the Sciences in Paris, 1670–1760*. Chicago: University of Chicago Press.

Spiekermann, U. 2011. 'Redefining Food: The Standardization of Products and Production in Europe and the United States, 1880–1914'. *History and Technology: An International Journal* 27 (1): pp. 11–36.

The Standard. 1908. 'We Learn with Profound Interest' [Editorial], *The Standard*, 26 September. Reprinted in L. J. Satre, *Chocolate on Trial: Slavery, Politics and the Ethics of Business*. Athens, OH: Ohio University Press, 2005, pp. 227–9.

Stanziani, A. 2012. *Rules of Exchange: French Capitalism in Comparative Perspective, Eighteenth to Early Twentieth Centuries*. Cambridge: Cambridge University Press.

Talbot, G. 2014. 'Fats for Chocolate and Sugar Confectionery'. In *Fats in Food Technology*, 2nd ed., edited by K. K. Rajah, pp. 169–211. London: John Wiley & Sons, Ltd.

Terrio, S. J. 2000. *Crafting the Culture and History of French Chocolate*. Berkeley: University of California Press.

Thouvenot, C. 1983. 'La Qualité Alimentaire d'Autrefois'. *Économie rurale* 154 (154): pp. 49–53.

US Department of Agriculture. 1903. 'Standards of Purity for Food Products'. Circular No. 10. Washington, DC: U.S. Dept. of Agriculture, Office of the Secretary. Available at: <https://archive.org/details/standardsofpurit10unit> (accessed 5 March 2015).

Walker, T. 2007. 'Slave Labor and Chocolate in Brazil: The Culture of Cacao Plantations in Amazonia and Bahia (17th–19th Centuries)'. *Food and Foodways* 15: pp. 75–106.

Wardell, A. and N. Fold. 2013. 'Globalisations in a Nutshell: Historical Perspectives on Changing Governance of the Shea Commodity Chain in Northern Ghana'. *International Journal of Commons* 7 (2): pp. 367–405.

Zipperer, P. and H. Schaeffer. 1915. *The Manufacture of Chocolate and other Cacao Preparations*. Berlin: M. Krayn; New York: Spon & Chamberlain. Available at: <https://archive.org/details/manufactureofcho00zipp> (accessed 11 January 2015).

Zylberman, P. 2004. 'Making Food Safety an Issue: Internationalized Food Politics and French Public Health from the 1870s to the Present'. *Medical History* 48 (1): pp. 1–28.

Part IV
Markets and Prices

16

The Dynamics of the World Cocoa Price

Christopher L. Gilbert

Introduction

The cocoa market is characterized by long but irregular cycles. In this chapter, my objective is to document and explain these cycles using relatively simple econometric tools. Two themes dominate. The first is the importance of investment (planting) decisions. The second is the importance of demand-side (consumption) shocks. I argue that it is the interaction of these two factors which gives rise to the long price cycles that have characterized the cocoa industry.

The standard view of price variability in commodity markets is that the persistence of price shocks arise through the storage process, and, in particular, as the consequence of the non-negativity constraint on stocks. I argue here that price cycles in cocoa, and probably also in other tree crop commodities, are generated by investment (planting) rather than stockholding decisions. These planting decisions are conditioned on the price history at the time of the investment. Cocoa trees remain productive for around four decades and hence decisions taken many years ago influence current production and hence current prices. In statistical terms, cocoa prices exhibit long memory.

The accepted view in agricultural economics is that supply is highly variable and demand is fairly stable. The consequence is that supply-side (harvest) shocks are more important than demand shocks as drivers of price movements. This is true of cocoa but only up to a point. On an annual basis, supply-side shocks are much larger than demand-side shocks and hence are the more important driver of short-term price volatility. I argue, however, that the effects of demand-side shocks are more persistent than those of supply-side shocks. A good or a bad harvest in any one year has little implication for harvests in the following years. Price effects are dissipated fairly quickly as the stock build-up or run-down is reversed. By contrast, shocks to consumption appear to be highly persistent, with any rise or fall in consumption demand in one year carried forward to successive years. The price impact of these demand shocks does not dissipate until production responds to the higher or lower prices, bringing the market back into balance. Because investment lags are long, this adjustment process takes considerable time. So although demand shocks are typically smaller than supply shocks, they have a comparably large long-term impact.

Long cycles can only be analysed using long datasets. The most important contribution of this chapter is to put together data on cocoa production, consumption (grindings), stocks, and price on a consistent basis over as long a period as possible. I construct US dollar cocoa prices back to 1850, production data back to 1929, and consumption and stock data back to 1946. These data are all from published sources, but many of the earlier data are not easily available on the internet and have hence been forgotten.

The structure of the chapter is as follows. I define what I mean by the world cocoa price in the next section, 'The World Cocoa Price', and then proceed to document the history of world cocoa prices back to 1850. Details of the sources and calculations are given in the Appendix. Afterwards, I outline an econometric model of the world cocoa market, the technical details of which are set out in Gilbert (2015) Then, I use the model to explore cocoa market dynamics and examine the history of cocoa prices in the light of the preceding analysis. Finally, I ask whether current cocoa market prices are consistent with sectoral sustainability and report the result of a simple forecasting exercise. Lastly, I provide brief conclusions.

The World Cocoa Price

Cocoa is a relatively homogeneous commodity. It comes in a single botanical form, albeit with variants, and, controlling for quality, differences across origins are small. Quality premia can be important but the bulk of cocoa entering world commerce is 'Fair Average Quality' (FAQ)[1] and it is this that is priced on the two major cocoa futures markets—NYSE-LIFFE in London and ICE in New York.[2] Furthermore, although there have been changes in grading criteria over time, cocoa beans are traded in much the same form and manner now as a century ago. It therefore makes sense to talk about a single-world cocoa price and to regard this price as defined consistently over time.

The standard reference points for cocoa prices in the financial markets are the London NYSE-LIFFE and the New York ICE cocoa futures markets. However, these markets quote prices for only five delivery dates per year. Both ICE and NYSE-LIFFE trade contracts for delivery in March, May, July, September, and December of each year, with delivery specified as the day following the final trading day of the contract, which is 11 business days immediately prior to the last business day of

[1] FAQ cocoa can contain up to 10% defective beans—Dand (1999, p. 224).

[2] NYSE-LIFEE prices at par lots containing no more than 5% 'slaty' (poorly fermented and hence grey-purple in colour) beans and 5% defective beans. ICE prices at par depending on origin. Many origins whose cocoa is deliverable at par on NYSE-LIFFE will receive a premium over the ICE price, which is therefore typically slightly lower than the corresponding NYSE-LIFFE price.

the delivery month. Interpreted literally, therefore, the exchange futures prices on any date other than a contract expiration date are market expectations of cash prices on those five delivery dates.

Only a relatively small proportion of international cocoa transactions result in delivery to or from exchange warehouses. The vast majority of commercial transactions are negotiated between the buyers and sellers basis one of the two major exchange prices. These contracts will denominate the quantity deliverable, the futures contract against which the delivery will be priced, for example the March 2015 contract, and a (negotiated) premium or discount relative to the futures price. The pricing basis may be specified as the contract settlement price on the delivery date (not known at the time of contracting) or an average of the settlement prices around that date, or it may allow the purchaser the option of fixing the price against the futures settlement price prior to delivery. The consequence is that different cocoa processors will end up paying somewhat different prices for cocoa of the same quality depending on their trading expertise and when they choose to take delivery.

Cocoa futures prices should, therefore be seen as reference prices and not as transaction prices. This is true of all futures-traded commodities. Many buyers and sellers may also lock into prices during the period intervening between contracting and delivery by hedging their positions on one of the futures markets or by undertaking an equivalent transaction through an intermediary. Realized transactions prices will, therefore, reflect the circumstances of that delivery, the identity of the parties concerned, and the success of any hedging programme undertaken. Although on any day there is a single set of reference prices—the exchange futures quotations—these will result in a range of realized transactions prices.

The London and New York futures markets price cocoa for delivery in northern European and East Coast US ports respectively. Spatial arbitrage will keep these prices fairly close. In order to produce a single, common, reference price, starting in 1960, the International Cocoa Organization (ICCO) has calculated a daily indicator price for cocoa beans. Currently, this price is calculated as the average of the quotations for cocoa beans of the nearest three active future trading months on NYSE-LIFFE and ICE futures markets at 16:50 London time, the time of the NYSE-LIFFE cocoa market close, and 12:00 noon New York time. Although the ICCO calculates the price in SDRs, it is generally quoted in terms of the US dollar equivalent.

It is important to distinguish between fob ('free on board') prices at origin and cif ('cost, insurance and freight') prices in importing countries. Although there is a single-world reference price for coffee in import markets, farmers in different exporting countries obtain very different prices. This relates in part to differences in transportation and other costs, which drive a wedge between the fob prices paid by exporters at the port of embarkation and the cif price paid at the delivery point, and in part to differences in taxes (or subsidies) and levies in the producing country, which drive a further wedge between the producer price at the farm gate and the fob price at the port. So although we can talk of a world cocoa price, this is a price on wholesale markets in the major importing countries, not the price received by farmers.

I have reconstructed cif US dollar cocoa prices on a broadly consistent basis back to 1850—see Appendix for details. In order to discuss the evolution of price over time, I deflate the nominal series to obtain real prices. Any so-called real price is, in effect, a relative price in relation to a specified basket of good. There are three commonly used types of deflator:

- developed country export unit values (the comparator basket comprises developed country exports),
- consumer prices (the comparator basket comprises retail consumer goods), and
- producer prices (the comparator basket comprises producer goods on the wholesale market).

While year-to-year price movements will vary little in relation to this choice, long-term price trends may be very different. The use of export prices is appropriate in considering terms-of-trade issues, but in that case one would wish to look at the entire basket of goods exported by a specific cocoa-producing country. Consumer prices are appropriate for retail goods, such as chocolate, but less so for raw materials. Furthermore, since purchasing power parity (PPP) fails to hold with any precision, conversion into local currency units and deflation by consumer prices will give results which differ across countries, undermining the notion of a world price. Instead, producer prices will show much less variation across countries. I deflate by the US producer price index (all items, 2005 = 100) and then rescale to convert prices into 2013 values. The resulting real price is then the relativity between cocoa prices and the basket of all producer prices. This choice finesses the Prebisch–Singer controversy (Singer, 1950; Prebisch, 1962), since any trend in real cocoa prices measured in this way would simply represent a differential rate of technical progress in cocoa production and marketing relative to the generality of products.

The resulting real price series is charted in Figure 16.1. One way to analyse a long time series is to decompose it into trend and cycle components. By way of illustration, I use the Koopman and colleagues' (2009) STAMP procedure to analyse the real cocoa price series into a smooth trend,[3] plus three cycles. The cycles have periods of 27.9, 8.9, and 4.7 years—see Gilbert (2015) for details. The long cycle is dominant. If only two cycles are estimated, the long cycle remains almost unchanged with the same periodicity, but the two shorter cycles are replaced by a cycle of length 7.2 years. The implication is that variation of the cocoa price about trend is dominated by long-term price movements. In order to understand why this is the case, we need to examine cocoa consumption and production.

The Cocoa Market Model

I use a four-equation model of aggregate cocoa production and consumption, stocks, and price. The stock equation is an identity—the change in stocks in any year is equal to the difference between production and grindings. This leaves three

---

[3] A smooth trend is a deterministic trend with a time-varying slope.

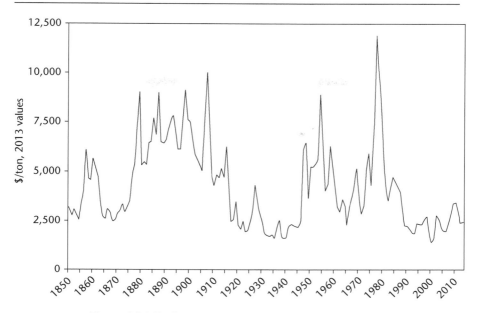

Figure 16.1 Real cocoa prices (2013 values), 1850–2013

equations to be estimated. By aggregating, all information about the geographical distribution of production and grindings is lost. The geographical distribution of production across origins is important, but a model which could account for the evolution of production in each origin would be a great deal more complicated than the model reported here, and would distract attention from the price dynamics focus of the current chapter.

I have crop-year (October to September) data on cocoa production from 1929/30 and on grindings and closing stocks from 1946/47. The data and sources are discussed in an Appendix. In this section, I give a brief description of the model. Full details may be found in Gilbert (2015).

Stationarity is a central concept in modern time series econometrics. If a series is stationary, it will revert over time to a constant mean. Trend stationarity generalizes this concept—a trend stationary series reverts over time to a deterministic trend. Stationarity is crucial in understanding the impact of shocks—if a series is stationary, shock impacts will dissipate as the series reverts back to its mean or trend. If, instead, the series is non-stationary, shocks will not fully dissipate and will have a permanent component.

Stationarity may be tested using the Augmented Dickey–Fuller (ADF) test. A sufficiently large negative value for the ADF(p) statistic rejects the null hypothesis of stationarity. The test requires serial independence of the residuals from the regression from which the statistic derives, a property which is ensured by a sufficiently long lag length p. However, a high value for p compromises the power of the test so the choice should be as low as is consistent with lack of serial correlation. I follow standard practice in choosing this parameter to minimize the Akaike Information Criterion (AIC).

Table 16.1 reports ADF tests. All the variables in the model are non-stationary but have stationary differences, that is, they are all integrated of order 1. However, the difference between the logarithms of production and consumption is stationary. Turning to variability (row 4), the standard deviation of the log changes of production (9.8 per cent) is more than twice that of grindings (4.5 per cent), confirming that shocks originate primarily on the supply side.

The results reported in Table 16.1 define the modelling context. Stationarity of the difference between the logs of production and consumption imply that these two variables are co-integrated and share a common trend. Over the long term, grindings and production necessarily move together, since otherwise stocks would either go to zero or become arbitrarily high. In technical terms, this implies that the two variables must be co-integrated, that is, although they are non-stationary a linear combination of the two, here the difference, is stationary. The price mechanism ensures that this will be the case.

Because grindings are non-stationary, it is not possible to identify a stable demand function. The demand function shifts in a random manner over time (but generally with a drift to the right). These shifts are due almost by definition to changes in consumer tastes for chocolate and other cocoa products. It is possible that advertising contributes to these shifts but, in the absence of data on advertising expenditure, this remains a conjecture. This does not prevent estimation of price and income responses, but these remain short term. The estimated relationship relates changes in grindings to changes in world GDP, and prices in the current year and over the previous four crop years.

Table 16.1 Descriptive statistics

	Stationarity		Volatility	Sample
	Levels	Differences		
ln(*grindings*)	ADF(0)	ADF(1)	4.5%	1953/54
	−0.47	−6.88**		2012/13
ln(*production*)	ADF(2)	ADF(1)	9.8%	1936/37
	0.22	−8.27**		2012/13
ln(*production*)−ln(*grindings*)	ADF(4)	ADF(4)	8.6%	1953/54
	−3.80**	−6.01**		2012/13
ln*GDP*	ADF(3)	ADF(2)	3.5%	1927
	−0.47	−5.90**		2013
Stocks	ADF(1)	ADF(0)	16.1%	1953/54
	−2.79	−6.51**		2012/13
ln(*price*)	ADF(2)	ASDF(1)	25.3%	1923
	−2.09	−9.17**		2013

Note: ADF lag lengths selected using the AIC. Stocks are in terms of months of normal consumption. Prices and GDP are on a calendar and not a crop-year basis. Volatilities are log standard deviations except for stocks (standard deviation divided by sample mean).
* significant at 5%, ** significant at 1%.

Table 16.2 Estimated price elasticities

	Grindings	Production
Short run	−0.088	−0.078
Long run	−0.029	−0.285

Note: Consumption: short term is 0–1 years, long term is 1–4 years. Production: short term is 2–3 years, long term is 4–48 years.
Source: Gilbert (2015).

Cocoa production is seen as primarily driven by the stock of trees of different ages which remain productive and by their yields. This implies a type of vintage production function. Lacking historical data on plantings, I hypothesize that potential cocoa production capacity depends on a lag distribution of prices over the previous 48 years where the lag weights reflect estimated yields of trees of different ages. The capacity equation also includes a linear time trend. Farmers can choose to vary their time and other inputs into the cocoa production process. Production differs from capacity production both because of harvest shocks and in response to recent price changes.

Table 16.2 summarizes the estimated price elasticities of production and grindings. Short-run adjustments appear to be equally divided between production and consumption responses, while, in the long run, the burden of adjustment falls almost entirely on cocoa production. In the short run, a poor harvest or a jump in the demand for cocoa result in a rise in price and a squeeze on stocks. The price rise results in increases in production and reductions in consumption of the same order of magnitude. However, the responsiveness of cocoa consumption to price is lower in the long run than the short run. This pushes the burden of adjustment to persistent excess supply or demand onto the producers. Leaving aside weather shocks, the cocoa crop is determined by the number of trees and their age distribution. Adjustment is slow since, with extensive production, smallholders will ignore their cocoa rather than grub up trees in periods of low prices, while, in high price periods, new plantings will only impact production once the young trees become productive.

In line with the standard competitive storage model, the cocoa price is seen as determined by availability, equal to current production plus the carryover (closing stock) from the previous crop year. This modelling approach works well for cocoa, although I modify the relationship to allow for shifts of the demand curve resulting from recent demand shocks and price changes. The model is based on the fact that the farmer's production decisions are all made prior to revelation of the current year's price, implying that, in any given crop year, consumers and stockholders are obliged to undertake the entirety of any adjustment. The price must be such that either the available cocoa is consumed or put into storage for the following year. At this point, it does not matter whether a particular bag of cocoa arises from the current or a previous harvest. Furthermore, the relationship between price and availability will be non-linear, since at low levels of availability, and hence high prices, only working stocks will still be held and these cannot easily be further reduced. The model fits price as a quadratic function of availability to capture this non-linearity.

Cocoa Price Dynamics

I use the model described to examine the dynamics of the world cocoa price. Although the model departs in a number of respects from the Vector AutoRegression (VAR) structure, I calculate impulse response functions (IRFs) in the same way as is standard in VARs. This involves giving a shock to each variable and tracing the time path of the items of interest (production, grindings, stocks, and price) relative to the base unshocked case. Because the model is non-linear the resulting response profiles will vary according to the level of availability. The results reported in what follows start from the position at the end of the 2012/13 crop year, when cocoa availability was close to its average level over the model estimation sample.

There are four sets of shocks to be considered—shocks to production (harvest shocks), to grindings ('taste' shocks), to price (idiosyncratic factors affecting price in particular years), and to world gross domestic product (GDP). Stocks are formed as an identity and therefore do not provide an independent source of variation. The shocks are all of one standard deviation of the residuals of the relevant equation over the common sample crop years 1949/50–2012/13 (calendar years 1950–2013 for price and GDP). They are imposed in year 1 (2013/14). In each case, I report simulations of the model for 50 years forward.

Figure 16.2 charts the IRFs for a one standard deviation shock (3.6 per cent) to the grindings equation. The price (heavy solid line, right axis) is seen as rising by 18 per cent in the following year and by a further 5 per cent in the second year. This price impact dissipates by the sixth year, but this six-year period of high prices stimulates new plantings which increase the crop (lighter solid line, left axis) over the following two decades by around 1 per cent of its non-shocked value. The price averages 2.4 per cent lower over the 14-year period from years 14 to 27 (defined as relative to the initial shock). These lower prices reduce plantings so the price cycle continues into the future. Extension of the simulation out to 150 years (not charted) shows a slowly decaying low amplitude cycle with a periodicity of around 24 years.

The world GDP IRF, charted in Figure 16.3, is very similar (note the change in scale on the vertical axes). The one standard deviation shock amounts to 1.7 per cent, so the initial magnitude is one half of that of a grindings shock. However, the GDP shows slightly greater persistence in its impacts because of the autoregression in the GDP equation (a positive shock this year tends to be associated with a positive shock next year). The maximum price impact, which occurs in year 3, is of the order of 13.2 per cent.

The crop impulse response functions are somewhat different—see Figure 16.4. The crop shock is administered as a production shortfall. The one standard

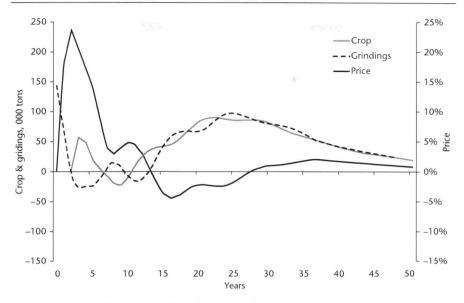

Figure 16.2 Grindings impulse response function

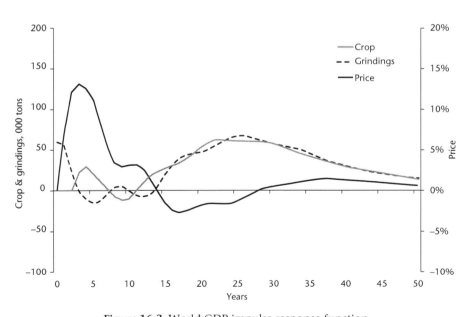

Figure 16.3 World GDP impulse response function

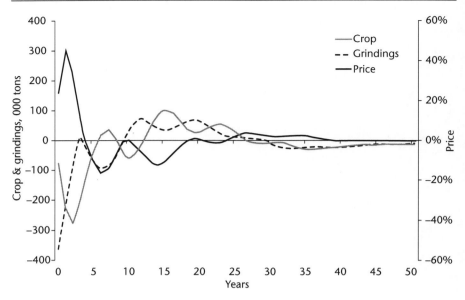

Figure 16.4 Crop impulse response function

deviation crop shock amounts to a 9 per cent fall in production. This reduces availability and raises the price by 23.6 per cent in the same year. The price impact peaks at 44.7 per cent in the following year as the consequence of the reduced level of stocks. This is twice the maximum impact of a one standard deviation shock to grindings. However, the impact dissipates completely by year 4, more quickly than the impact of the grindings shock. As in the case of the grindings shock, there is a second round of impacts as the lower price encourages higher consumption in the following years, resulting in a price rebound.

Price shocks show even lower persistence—see Figure 16.5. The one standard deviation shock amounts to 16.9 per cent resulting in an immediate 1 per cent fall in grindings. However, the price rise is immediately reversed, with the price 9 per cent lower than the base case in year 3 as the consequence of the decline in consumption. This rapid oscillation of prices leaves investment (new plantings) largely unaffected with the consequence that the cyclical movements quickly become negligibly small.

The cocoa harvest is the single largest source of variability in the cocoa supply and demand balance, followed by changes in tastes and by changes in purchasing power (as measured by GDP). All three types of shock generate long-lasting price fluctuations, but the two demand-side shock categories result in the greatest price persistence. Cyclicality arises because farmers' planting decisions (or decisions not to replant) have a delayed but long-lasting impact. Because trees take time (around four years) to bear fruit, it is impossible for farmers to rapidly adjust production to changing prices but, once planted, trees will remain productive for four decades even if demand turns downward.

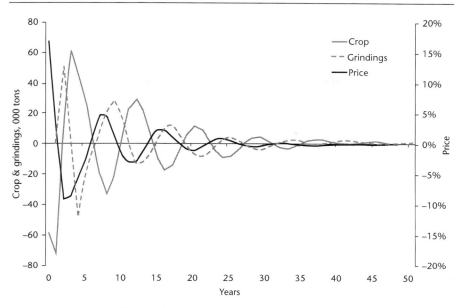

Figure 16.5 Price impulse response function

A rise of fall in cocoa demand this year will typically carry forward into future years as a consequence of the non-stationarity of cocoa grindings and GDP. Harvest shocks are not persistent—a poor harvest this year has no implication for future years. A poor harvest generates a large price impact in the shock year and the two following years as destocking makes up the initial shortfall and then recovers to normal levels, but thereafter the market returns to normal, disturbed only by the new plantings generated by the temporally high prices. The overall result is that, although smaller than supply shocks, demand shocks generate price impacts which are of comparable magnitude and longer duration.

The fourth source of shocks is shocks to the price itself. In terms of magnitude, these appear even larger than harvest shocks. However, this is misleading since these price shocks encompass all the factors omitted from the econometric model. A more detailed modelling exercise might succeed in attributing much of this variation to these omitted factors. What remains true is that these 'price' shocks appear to have very little persistence. We might see these shocks as noise overlaying the movements in market fundamentals.

Cocoa Price Cycles

The account I have given in this and the previous section, 'Cocoa Price Dynamics', indicates that, while year-to-year movements in the cocoa price are driven primarily by harvest shocks, shifts in consumption are as important in accounting for medium-term price movements. Furthermore, the evolution of grindings over

Table 16.3 Cocoa cycles, 1927–2013

Peak and Trough Years		Average Growth Rates		Difference	Average Price Change
		Grindings	Production		
1927–39	P → T	–	−3.0%	–	6.8%
1939–54	T → P	1.7%	0.5%	1.2%	11.3%
1954–65	P → T	5.4%	6.0%	−0.5%	−12.3%
1965–77	T → P	0.8%	−0.9%	1.7%	13.7%
1977–2002	P → T	3.2%	3.6%	−0.4%	−9.4%
2002–13	T → P	2.5%	1.9%	0.6%	4.5%

Note: The table reports average growth rates for production and grindings over periods defined by successive peaks (P) and troughs (T) in the real cocoa price. For production and grindings, the years are crop years ending in the stated year. The grindings growth rate listed for 1939–54 is for crop years 1946/47 to 1953/54, since I lack reliable data prior to 1946/47. Grindings data are unavailable for the period 1926/27–1938/39. The production growth rate listed for 1927–39 is for 1929/30–1938/39. The year 2013 is the final one in my sample and is not a peak year.

time appear to be due more to changes in consumer tastes than to changes in income or to cocoa prices. Cocoa production, which is price responsive over the long term, adjusts to the new levels of consumption. The consequence is that levels of rapid consumption growth are associated with higher prices, while periods of low consumption growth are associated with low prices.

A simple but crude way to see this is to identify the cycles defined by peaks and troughs in the real cocoa price. Table 16.3 reports this analysis for the period from the late 1920s, for which I have production and grindings data. Using the data charted in Figure 16.1, I identify three cyclical peaks in 1927, 1954, and 1977, and three troughs 1939, 1965, and 2002.[4] Periodicity appears to be around 25 years, in line with the cycles generated by the grindings and world GDP impulse response functions—see Figures 16.2 and 16.3. In the three trough-to-peak (T → P) cycles, growth in grindings exceeds growth in production as production struggles to keep pace with increased demand. The reverse is the case for the two P → T cycles for which data on grindings are available. The correlation between the excess of grindings growth over production growth and the average price change (the final two columns in Table 16.3) is 0.988.

In what follows I look in greater detail at the five most recent decades using ICCO data on production disaggregated by producing country (origin), which are only available from crop year 1960/61. Figure 16.6 charts production levels for the three most important producers over the period from 1960/61. The full data are given in Table 16.A3.

Over the five crop years 1960/61 to 1964/65, Ghana was responsible for an average of 49.4 per cent of African cocoa production and 36.7 per cent of world production. Ghanaian production peaked at 566,000 tons in crop year 1964/65, and then declined more or less steadily to only 159,000 tons in crop year 1983/84

---

[4] The long (71-year) cycle identified by the STAMP procedure and discussed in the 'World Cocoa Price' section gives exactly the same peaks and troughs, with the exception that the trough I have identified in 1939 is moved back to 1935 and a peak is called in 2011.

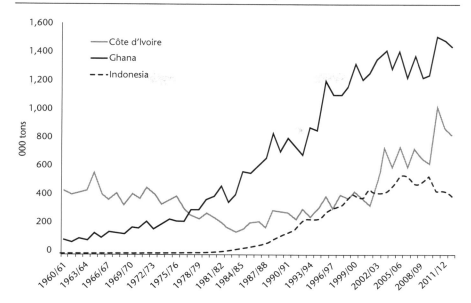

Figure 16.6 Cocoa production for three leading producers, 1960/61 to 2012/13

as a consequence of excessive taxation of the sector. This decline in production on the part of the major producer was sufficient to ensure that production growth lagged growth in grindings over the period to 1977. The 1965–77 T → P rise in prices therefore seems attributable to supply shocks (although political more than meteorological) originating in Ghana.

The subsequent 1977–2002 P → T price rise also appears to have its origin primarily on the supply side. Ivorian cocoa production grew from a low base to overtake Ghana, resulting in Côte d'Ivoire becoming the leading cocoa producer in the crop year 1977/78. Ivorian production increased by a factor of 4 over the 24-year period 1977/78 to 2001/02, from 304,000 tons to 1,265,000 tons. Over the same period, Indonesian cocoa production increased from just 4,000 tons in 1977/78 to 455,000 tons in 2001/02, the year in which it was temporarily the second largest producer. Ghanaian production was also recovering by the end of this period as a consequence of cocoa sector reforms and a higher pass-through from fob to farm-gate prices—see Gilbert (2009). Taken together, these developments ensured production growth exceeded growth in grindings over this later period.

The period since 2001/02 has seen a stabilization of production in Côte d'Ivoire and Indonesia against the background of continued recovery in Ghana. Overall production growth rates have slowed while consumption growth has accelerated. Factors which might account for this faster consumption growth include faster GDP growth up to 2008, increased access to chocolate and other cocoa products in Eastern Europe following the ending of communism, and increased taste for chocolate in the rapidly growing Asian economies. These recent price movements therefore appear largely attributable to demand-side shifts.

I am unable to repeat this exercise prior to 1927 because of the lack of data on production and grindings. Figure 16.1 shows that cocoa prices were high and volatile between the late 1870s and the peak in 1907. A trough can be identified in 1868 and an earlier peak in 1857. The year 1923 was a trough year. Clarence-Smith (2000, pp. 27–31) defines the period 1880–1914 as 'the great chocolate boom'. He states, 'The explosive growth of a mass market for chocolate from the 1880s transformed world consumption more radically than at any other time in history.' Using his Appendix 2 figures on reported exports from cocoa-exporting territories, one finds that that these grew at an average annual rate of 4.85 per cent over the 25 years between 1880 and 1914, as compared with only 1.9 per cent over the 25 years between 1850 and 1874. This strongly suggests that the high prices over the period 1880–1910 were also the consequence of a rightward shift in the demand curve in conjunction with an upward sloping supply curve. It is tempting to believe that this high price period was brought to an end by a decline in demand forced by the First World War, but the price decline set in well before 1914. The year 1907 was the last to experience very elevated prices, and, by 1910, the price was only slightly more than half its 1907 level.

The pre-First World War cocoa consumption boom was largely a European phe-nomenon, although the USA also had an impact. European governments, in their capacity as administrators of their African colonial territories, saw rising chocolate consumption and high prices as an opportunity to supply domestic markets and provide stable incomes for African households. Prior to the 1890s, almost all cocoa exports had originated from Latin America and the Caribbean, with the Portuguese colonies of Angola and São Tomé and Príncipe forming the only exceptions. From 1890, however, African cocoa production grew rapidly, most dramatically in São Tomé and Príncipe and the (British) Gold Coast (Ghana), but also in (German) Cameroon, (Spanish) Equatorial Guinea, and (British) Nigeria.

Figure 16.7, which I have adapted from Figure A2.1 of Clarence-Smith (2000), shows African and total world reported cocoa exports from 1850–1914. It is appar-ent from this figure that there was a substantial rightward shift in the cocoa supply curve over the period from 1895. The average annual growth rate of non-African cocoa exports was 3.75 per cent over the two decades 1875–94 and 3.31 per cent over the two decades 1895–1914. These two averages do not differ significantly ($t_{19} = 1.14$). The corresponding averages for total world reported exports were 2.33 per cent and 5.61 per cent respectively. These two averages do differ significantly ($t_{19} = 7.97$). The fall in cocoa prices in the years immediately prior to the First World War was the result of the emergence of Africa as a major cocoa-producing continent.

Clarence-Smith (2000, pp. 123–4) states that it was the high 1907 price that stimulated a new wave of planting in Brazil and West Africa and that the resulting addition to production dragged down prices in the following decades. The start of the rapid increase in West African production had already started by 1907 and it seems more likely that these increases result from more than two decades of high prices of which 1907 was simply the culmination—see Figure 16.7. It was this West African expansion of cocoa production which led the long decline in real cocoa prices to the 1923 trough.

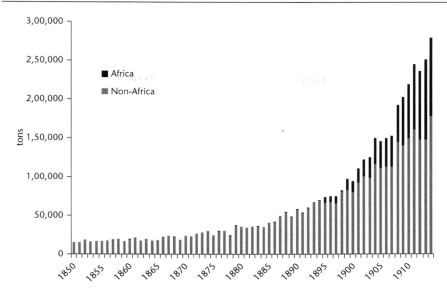

Figure 16.7 African and non-African cocoa exports, 1850–1914

This historical account complements the econometric analysis in attributing the major cocoa price cycles, in a fairly equal manner, between supply- and demand-side factors. The rise in prices from 1850 to 1879 resulted from a demand-side shift—the birth of the modern chocolate industry. Prices remained high but volatile until 1907. The subsequent fall in prices from 1908 to 1924 is attributable to a supply-side shift—the growth of West African cocoa production. The cocoa price then remained generally low until 1947, when cocoa demand again increased as part of the post-war recovery, remaining high (but again volatile) until 1961. The subsequent fall in prices to the 1964 trough may have been due to the expansion of Ghanaian production at a time when Ghana was already the most important producer. Equally, the subsequent rise to the 1977 peak was largely due to the decline in Ghanaian production under the Nkrumah government, while the fall from 1977 to 2002 can also be attributed to a supply-side development, in this case the expansion of Ivorian production. The more recent stabilization and modest price recovery can probably be located in demand-side developments.

The Future

I turn now from the distant past to the near future. A number of speakers at the 2014 ICCO World Cocoa Conference expressed the view that cocoa supply may be insufficient to meet growing demand over the coming decade. In particular, there was concern that many trees are becoming old, as are the farmers who tend them, and that insufficient new planting is taking place. It was suggested that recent and current cocoa prices are insufficient to ensure sustainability.

The ICCO cocoa price averaged $2,439 per ton in 2013. An economist is likely to argue that if cocoa production is insufficient to meet demand growth, prices will rise to the extent necessary to stimulate the required production increase. The complicating factor is that the long gestation lags between planting new trees and the mature harvest yields may imply that prices will rise by more than the amount required for long-term sustainability, with overinvestment the likely consequence.

At the time of writing (December 2014), the cocoa price has risen to $2,900 per ton (all prices are quoted in 2013 values). Experienced economists will always be wary of committing themselves to firm forecasts. Nevertheless, it is worth examining the implications of the model set out for cocoa prices over the coming years, taking fully into account the uncertainties associated with any forecasting exercise. The results of this exercise are charted in Figure 16.8. The forecasts are based on 100,000 simulations using bootstrapped errors drawn from the model residuals over the common sample 1949/50 (1950 for price and GDP) to 2012/13 (or 2013) in such a way as preserve the historical error correlation structure. Because the model is non-linear, the median forecast price is different from, and indeed noticeably lower than, the average forecast price. The median forecast path, charted as the solid line in Figure 16.8, may be interpreted as the most likely outcome. The figure also includes the price path corresponding to the 25 per cent and 75 per cent outcomes (broken lines) and 10 per cent and 90 per cent outcomes. The 25 per cent: 75 per cent band encompasses precisely half the forecast outcomes.

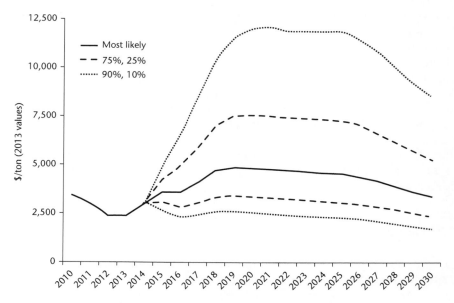

Figure 16.8 Projected cocoa prices, 2015–30

The forecast exercise shows that the cocoa price is indeed more likely to rise than to fall over the coming years. The model sees a 75 per cent probability of a price rise in 2015 with the median forecast of $3,601 per ton, 20 per cent higher than its value at the end of 2014. In the most likely case, the price is seen as rising fairly steadily towards $5,000/ton by the end of the decade. The median forecast for 2020 is $4,920 per ton but there is a 37 per cent probability of a price in excess of $6,000 per ton and a 22 per cent chance of a price in excess of $8,000 per ton. There is a 10 per cent probability that, in real terms, the 2020 price will exceed the all-time high level achieved in 1977. These higher prices will stimulate additional panting, with the result that prices will drift back towards current levels in the following decade.

Nevertheless, these price rises are far from certain and there is an 18 per cent probability of a 2020 price no higher than the 2014 level. Low prices will continue if tastes shift away from chocolate, if world economic growth disappoints, or if there are further generous harvests (the Ivorian crop rose by 20 per cent in crop year 2013/14 compared with 2012/13).

In summary, the rise in the cocoa price over 2014 seems likely to be sustained with a high probability of further increases in the coming years. These forecasts therefore broadly support the views expressed at the 2014 ICCO World Cocoa Conference that cocoa production is not sustainable at the level of prices prevailing at that time. However, there is no guarantee that price rises of this order will occur but, at the same time, there is a non-negligible probability that we will see exceptionally high prices by the end of the decade.

Concluding Remarks

The principal contribution of this chapter has been to put together comprehensive data on cocoa prices from the middle of the nineteenth century, and data on production, consumption, and stocks from around and slightly before the Second World War. The crop year is the natural unit for analysing agricultural markets, and short series of higher frequency data are no substitute for long series of annual data. These considerations are reinforced in tree crop commodities such as cocoa, since, once planted, trees remain productive for many decades. Decisions taken at the time that African cocoa-producing countries gained their independence are continuing to influence current cocoa production today.

I have used these data to construct a simple aggregate model of cocoa production consumption and prices. Cocoa trees remain productive for over 40 years, although yields decline after 13–15 years. I model production using a vintage approach, reflecting the differing yield levels of trees of different ages. This leads to a formulation in which production depends on a long distributed lag of past prices. The model shows production as reacting slowly but decisively to price changes and, as a consequence, possibly overreacting. The cocoa price is seen as being determined in line with the standard competitive storage model, which sees price as depending on availability, equal to the current harvest plus the stock carryover from the previous crop year. The relationship is non-linear, allowing the price to rise very sharply when availability becomes low. The model generates price cycles with a periodicity of around 25 years. Production decisions are therefore inherently very risky, but the long-term nature of these risks implies that standard insurance and hedging procedures will be largely impotent when dealing with this risk.

While the structure of the model is fairly standard, it generates results that differ from the consensus view in agricultural economics. This standard view is that, in agriculture, supply (harvest) shocks are more important than demand (consumption) shocks. This holds for cocoa in the short term, where supply shocks are larger than demand shocks and are responsible for a comparable share of year-to-year price volatility. But, although smaller, demand-side shocks are more persistent. This is because production reverts to trend (the harvest in any one year does not affect potential yield in the following years), whereas changes in taste for chocolate and cocoa products affect demand in future years as well as in the current year. The consequence is that production is constantly chasing taste- (or advertising-) induced changes in consumption.

This provides a framework within which the cocoa price history can be examined. The four decades from 1870 to 1910 saw rapid growth in the consumption of chocolate in Europe and the USA. Cocoa production, almost entirely limited to Latin America and one small Portuguese island colony in Africa, struggled to keep pace. High prices stimulated the growth in the West African colonial territories which, as independent states, have come to dominate cocoa exports. However, the resulting rapid growth in production resulted in 15 years of declining prices. The subsequent story revolved around the decline in production in Ghana, previously the world's leading producer, and the increase in production in Côte d'Ivoire, now the largest producer, and Indonesia.

Many in the cocoa industry are currently worried that cocoa production will fail to keep pace with the growing demand for chocolate and other cocoa products. A forecasting exercise using the estimated econometric model suggests that significant rise in the cocoa price towards \$4,000 per ton, and possibly much higher, by the end of the current decade. The price may rise by more than this, but there is also a smaller probability that prices will fall back to the lower levels of recent years.

Data Appendix

I have reconstructed an annual series for world cocoa prices, on a cif basis, extending back as far as possible. I use the word 'reconstruct' since cocoa traders and chocolate manufacturers will have known the prices they paid. However, records of these prices have not always been kept on a consistent basis and much of this information has been lost. Part of my objective in documenting the currently available information is to stimulate scholars to augment or contradict the series which I produce.

I have prices covering the 164-year period 1850–1913. The period breaks down into three subperiods:

- 1850–96: Hamburg was the principal European market for cocoa at that time and possibly the most important world market.
- 1897–1912: There is a relative lack of reliable cif cocoa price series over this 16-year period.
- 1913–2013: London and New York established themselves as the leading world cocoa markets. Prices are based on these markets.

Starting with the most recent (1913–2013) period, I use four different sources with the objective of obtaining a consistent annual price series extending from 1850 to 2013. This switching between sources results from the fact that different agencies have taken responsibility for compiling and disseminating cocoa prices at different times. Moving backwards in time, the sources are:

a) The ICCO price ($/ton)[5] as published by the ICCO in the *Quarterly Bulletin of Cocoa Statistics* (*QBCS*). I understand that the ICCO calculated these statistics starting in 1957. *QBCS* publishes the data from 1990 to 2013. The ICCO has provided me with a series extending back to 1975. Since the ICCO price is based on terminal market prices, it is on a cif basis.

b) The ICCO price ($/ton) as reported by the International Monetary Fund (IMF) in *International Financial Statistics* (*IFS*). These data cover 1948–2013. However, the data source prior to 1957 (the start of the ICCO series) appears to be different from that stated.[6]

c) Weymar (1968, Table 4A.7) gives monthly averages of main crop Accra beans in New York (c/lb) from 1946 to 1963. These should also be cif prices.

d) The Food and Agriculture Organization (FAO) (1955) reports annual averages of main crop Accra beans in New York (c/lb) for the period 1913 to 1954. These statistics are reproduced in Kofi (1974).

Figure 16.A1 graphs the four series.

Grilli and Yang (1988) is an additional source of price data. They give prices on an index number basis (1977–79 = 100) for 24 commodities covering the period 1900–86. The data source is given as Grilli and Yang (1987) but no known copy of this paper is extant. It is implicit in the Grilli and Yang discussion that prices are nominal and in US dollars, but it is unclear whether these prices are fob or cif. This uncertainty over the definition and source of these numbers makes it dangerous to employ them.

Since the ICCO price has become the most common reference price, I form a unified series by extrapolating this series back from 1975. I use the IMF's *IFS* series from 1964–74. The difference between the *IFS* and ICCO average prices for 1975 is less than 0.1 per cent, giving a smooth join. As noted, the *IFS* series appear unreliable prior to 1957. Weymar's price averages differ from the *IFS* series by

---

[5] Tons are metric tons (1,000 kg, 2,204.6 lbs) throughout.

[6] Evidence for this can be seen from the fact that the IFS quotes prices in c/lb and not $/ton from 1948–56. This discrepancy is not noted in the source.

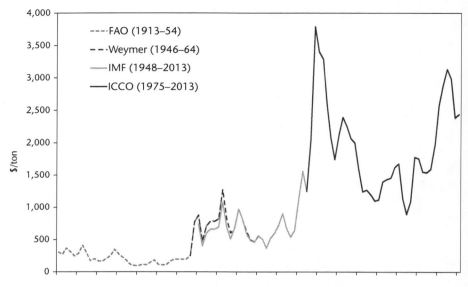

Figure 16.A1 Nominal US dollar cocoa prices, 1913–2013

over 6 per cent in 1960 and over 2 per cent in 1961. The two series differ substantially different over the period 1948–57. It is possible that the *IFS* is reporting the Grilli and Yang prices over this period. In the light of these problems and uncertainties with the *IFS* series, I use Weymar's prices up to 1963, the final year for which they are available. The period 1913–54 is straightforward. The figure given by FAO for 1954 coincides with Weymar's figure, again giving a smooth join.

I switch now to the initial period, 1850–96. Clarence-Smith (2000, p. 230, Figure A1.3) reports the average price of cocoa imports (unspecified origin) through Hamburg (marks/100 kilos) from 1850 to 1896, as reproduced from Mitchell (1992).[7] These will again be cif prices. I have converted these to $/ton using the pre-1914 exchange rate $1 = 4.198 marks. I use this series over the complete period 1850–96.

This leaves a gap over the period 1897–1912, during which there does not appear to be any reliable record of a cif price. William Gervase Clarence-Smith has also provided me with a series described as the highest price paid by Cadbury for São Tomé cocoa, yearly, from 1880 to 1911 (British shillings/cwt). I interpret these prices as being fob. I have converted them to $/ton at the pre-1914 exchange rate of £1 = $4.76.[8] The series correlates well with the Hamburg series over the common

---

[7] I am grateful to William Gervase Clarence-Smith for providing me with the original data. He states the source as *Der Gordian*, III, 3, 1898, 1108, 1189. *Der Gordian* was a German cocoa trade journal founded in 1895 (Clarence-Smith, 2000, p. 121).

[8] São Tomé and Príncipe became an important exporter of cocoa from the mid-nineteenth century and was the major African exporter until the end of the century—see Clarence-Smith (2000, pp. 236–9, Tables A2.5 and A2.6). There were 20 shillings in £1. One cwt is equal to 112 lbs.

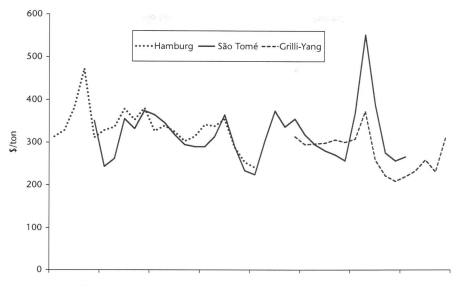

Figure 16.A2 Nominal US dollar cocoa prices, 1876–1915

period 1880–96, with the prices differing by less than $2/ton (½ per cent) in 1894. This suggests extrapolation of the Hamburg cif price forward, using the São Tomé fob price.

Figure 16.A2 charts the São Tomé and Hamburg prices together with the Grilli–Yang series converted to a $/ton basis using the *IFS* prices averaged for 1977–79 (the Grilli–Yang base years). The São Tomé series shows greater variability than the Hamburg and Grilli–Yang series. It appears anomalously low in 1881 and 1882 relative to the Hamburg series and anomalously high in 1907 relative to Grilli–Yang.

This still leaves a one year gap between the 1911 end of the São Tomé series and the 1913 start of the FAO series. I am obliged to use the Grilli–Yang series to bridge that gap. However, it makes little sense to insert a single price plucked from that series. The FAO price for 1913 ($306.44/ton) is 11.6 per cent higher than the 1911 São Tomé price ($267.03/ton). Over the same two-year period, the Grilli–Yang series shows a 14.8 per cent rise. I therefore apportion the 11.6 per cent gap in the ratio of the Grilli–Yang price rises in each of 1912 and 1913 to get a 1912 price of $275.05/ton.

This generates a complete US dollar price series from 1850–2013. The prices are listed in Table 16.A1. It may be possible to extend this price series back further. Clarence-Smith (2000, p. 229, Figure A1.2) reproduces prices for Caracas cocoa in Philadelphia over the period 1825–54 from the Commodity Research Bureau (1939). He also has prices for Caracas cocoa on the Amsterdam exchange over the period 1760–1804, with occasional prices thereafter to 1818 from Posthumus (1946).

hence there are 20 cwt in a long ton and 19.68 cwt in a (metric) ton. The citation is University of Birmingham Library, Cadbury Papers, file 304.

Table 16.A1 Cocoa prices, 1850–2013

	Hamburg	São Tomé	FAO	Grilli–Yang	Weymar	IFS	ICCO	Combined	US PPI	Real (2005 = 100)
1850	154.05							154.05	6.31	3156
1851	134.52							134.52	6.23	2789
1852	157.62							157.62	6.61	3082
1853	160.71							160.71	7.28	2851
1854	160.95							160.95	8.11	2565
1855	216.43							216.43	8.26	3386
1856	244.52							244.52	7.88	4008
1857	393.81							393.81	8.34	6105
1858	251.67							251.67	6.98	4657
1859	252.86							252.86	7.13	4580
1860	309.05							309.05	6.98	5719
1861	272.62							272.62	6.68	5271
1862	288.10							288.10	7.81	4767
1863	270.95							270.95	9.99	3506
1864	307.14							307.14	14.49	2739
1865	279.05							279.05	13.89	2596
1866	314.05							314.05	13.07	3106
1867	280.00							280.00	12.16	2974
1868	228.57							228.57	11.86	2489
1869	224.29							224.29	11.34	2556
1870	228.10							228.10	10.14	2908
1871	228.81							228.81	9.76	3029
1872	266.43							266.43	10.21	3371
1873	230.24							230.24	9.99	2979
1874	236.90							236.90	9.46	3236
1875	243.33							243.33	8.86	3549
1876	313.33							313.33	8.26	4902
1877	328.57							328.57	7.96	5334
1878	381.19							381.19	6.83	7208
1879	472.14							472.14	6.76	9028
1880	311.67	351.36						311.67	7.51	5363
1881	328.81	243.61						328.81	7.73	5494
1882	336.19	262.35						336.19	8.11	5357

Year						
1883	379.05	356.04		379.05	7.58	6458
1884	353.57	332.62		353.57	6.98	6542
1885	380.95	374.78		380.95	6.38	7713
1886	327.14	365.41		327.14	6.16	6865
1887	339.76	346.67		339.76	4.88	8995
1888	325.48	318.57		325.48	6.46	6513
1889	303.57	295.14		303.57	6.08	6449
1890	314.52	290.46		314.52	6.16	6601
1891	342.38	290.46		342.38	6.11	7237
1892	338.81	313.88		338.81	5.72	7655
1893	354.76	365.41		354.76	5.85	7835
1894	288.81	290.46		288.81	5.25	7111
1895	254.29	234.24		254.29	5.35	6146
1896	241.67	224.87		241.67	5.09	6130
1897		304.51		304.51	5.11	7707
1898		374.78		374.78	5.31	9114
1899		337.31		337.31	5.72	7621
1900		356.04	314.38	356.04	6.15	7485
1901		318.57	295.67	318.57	6.06	6794
1902		295.14	297.52	295.14	6.45	5910
1903		281.09	299.41	281.09	6.53	5562
1904		271.72	306.89	271.72	6.54	5368
1905		257.66	301.26	257.66	6.58	5056
1906		370.10	308.75	370.10	6.77	7063
1907		552.81	374.09	552.81	7.14	10,000
1908		388.84	260.11	388.84	6.89	7291
1909		276.40	222.67	276.40	7.41	4822
1910		257.66	209.60	257.66	7.71	4317
1911		267.03	220.82	267.03	7.11	4853
1912			233.89	275.05	7.57	4695
1913		306.44	260.11	306.44	7.65	5178
1914		273.37	232.04	273.37	7.46	4734
1915		368.17	312.49	368.17	7.61	6248
1916		313.05	265.71	313.05	9.37	4318
1917		246.92	209.60	246.92	12.87	2478

(continued)

Table 16.A1 Continued

	Hamburg	São Tomé	FAO	Grilli-Yang	Weymar	IFS	ICCO	Combined	US PPI	Real (2005 = 100)
1918			284.39	241.41				284.39	14.39	2555
1919			410.06	348.04				410.06	15.19	3489
1920			299.83	254.49				299.83	16.92	2290
1921			171.96	145.96				171.96	10.69	2078
1922			202.82	172.15				202.82	10.59	2474
1923			167.55	142.22				167.55	11.02	1964
1924			167.55	142.22				167.55	10.75	2014
1925			209.44	177.78				209.44	11.34	2387
1926			253.53	215.19				253.53	10.96	2990
1927			348.33	295.67				348.33	10.47	4300
1928			282.19	239.52				282.19	10.62	3435
1929			229.28	194.60				229.28	10.43	2842
1930			178.57	153.45				178.57	9.47	2437
1931			114.64	97.30				114.64	7.98	1856
1932			97.00	82.33				97.00	7.13	1757
1933			97.00	82.33				97.00	7.22	1736
1934			114.64	97.30				114.64	8.20	1807
1935			110.23	93.56				110.23	8.77	1624
1936			149.91	127.26				149.91	8.85	2188
1937			185.19	157.19				185.19	9.45	2533
1938			114.64	97.30				114.64	8.60	1723
1939			105.82	89.82				105.82	8.45	1618
1940			112.44	95.45				112.44	8.60	1690
1941			167.55	142.22				167.55	9.58	2261
1942			196.21	166.56				196.21	10.81	2346
1943			196.21	166.56				196.21	11.32	2240
1944			196.21	166.56				196.21	11.38	2228
1945			196.21	166.56				196.21	11.59	2187
1946			255.73	215.19	252.98			255.73	13.23	2498
1947			771.61	653.08	769.23			771.61	16.24	6138
1948			879.64	742.94	874.86	741.15		879.64	17.58	6465
1949			473.99	404.16	476.20	403.25		473.99	16.70	3667
1950			707.68	600.64	706.58	599.27		707.68	17.36	5267

Year								
1951	784.84	664.27	783.37	662.75		784.84	19.34	5244
1952	784.84	662.52	780.80	660.88		784.84	18.80	5394
1953	817.91	694.34	818.65	692.62		817.91	18.54	5700
1954	1274.26	1081.71	1274.26	1079.06		1274.26	18.58	8862
1955		701.68	826.73	700.08		826.73	18.64	5731
1956		510.79	602.59	509.66		602.59	19.24	4047
1957		572.67	674.06	676.63		674.06	19.81	4397
1958		828.94	977.01	975.73		977.01	20.07	6290
1959		684.90	806.34	805.42		806.34	20.11	5180
1960		531.42	625.19	589.02		625.19	20.13	4013
1961		423.04	496.77	485.03		496.77	20.06	3200
1962		392.97	462.97	458.87		462.97	20.11	2975
1963		473.38	558.32	552.29		558.32	20.06	3597
1964		437.72		503.83		503.83	20.10	3239
1965		323.75		365.31		365.31	20.50	2303
1966		456.60		517.63		517.63	21.17	3159
1967		544.70		598.11		598.11	21.22	3641
1968		643.64		720.87		720.87	21.75	4282
1969		855.16		903.25		903.25	22.61	5163
1970		640.15		673.93		673.93	23.42	3718
1971		501.35		538.59		538.59	24.20	2876
1972		604.49		642.61		642.61	25.27	3286
1973		1205.13		1130.82		1130.82	28.59	5111
1974		1835.84		1560.23		1560.23	33.97	5935
1975		1399.87		1245.90	1245.37	1245.37	37.11	4336
1976		2045.26		2045.76	2044.89	2044.89	38.84	6804
1977		3789.84		3791.12	3788.77	3788.77	41.22	11,878
1978		3405.62		3404.56	3402.26	3402.26	44.42	9897
1979		3293.39		3292.82	3291.96	3291.96	49.99	8509
1980		2601.15		2603.42	2602.73	2602.73	57.05	5895
1981		2077.07		2076.55	2076.54	2076.54	62.27	4309
1982		1734.10		1741.81	1741.79	1741.79	63.52	3544
1983		2117.63		2118.70	2118.69	2118.69	64.32	4257
1984		2451.16		2395.72	2395.71	2395.71	65.85	4701
1985		2295.58		2254.55	2254.54	2254.54	65.53	4446

(continued)

Table 16.A1 Continued

	Hamburg	São Tomé	FAO	Grilli–Yang	Weymar	IFS	ICCO	Combined	US PPI	Real (2005 = 100)
1986				2131.96		2068.31	2068.14	2068.14	63.64	4199
1987						1997.76	1996.22	1996.22	65.32	3949
1988						1583.75	1584.57	1584.57	67.94	3014
1989						1242.20	1241.12	1241.12	71.31	2249
1990						1268.00	1268.33	1268.33	73.85	2219
1991						1192.61	1195.21	1195.21	74.02	2087
1992						1099.42	1099.48	1099.48	74.45	1908
1993						1111.27	1117.24	1117.24	75.55	1911
1994						1395.68	1396.11	1396.11	76.52	2357
1995						1432.54	1433.31	1433.31	79.26	2337
1996						1455.25	1455.70	1455.70	81.12	2319
1997						1618.74	1618.75	1618.75	81.07	2580
1998						1676.00	1675.85	1675.85	79.06	2739
1999						1135.05	1140.10	1140.10	79.72	1848
2000						903.91	887.69	887.69	84.32	1360
2001						1088.38	1088.75	1088.75	85.26	1650
2002						1779.04	1778.07	1778.07	83.30	2758
2003						1753.07	1754.92	1754.92	87.75	2584
2004						1550.74	1548.48	1548.48	93.18	2147
2005						1544.66	1538.08	1538.08	100.00	1988
2006						1590.62	1590.67	1590.67	104.67	1964
2007						1958.11	1952.20	1952.20	109.69	2300
2008						2572.76	2580.78	2580.78	120.45	2769
2009						2895.02	2888.76	2888.76	109.85	3398
2010						3130.60	3133.00	3133.00	117.37	3449
2011						2978.49	2980.05	2980.05	127.73	3015
2012						2377.07	2391.87	2391.87	128.44	2406
2013						2439.09	2439.08	2439.08	129.22	2439

Note: A horizontal line indicated a break in the source—see text for discussion.

Source: Columns 1 and 2, Clarence-Smith (2000); column 3 FAO (1955) and Kofi (1974); column 4: Grilli and Yang (1988); column 5: Weymar (1968); column 6: ICCO, *QBCS* (various issues); columns 7 and 9: own calculation; column 8: US Census Bureau, *Historical Statistics of the United States*, updated using *IFS* CD-ROM.

Real prices are obtained by deflating by the US Producer Price Index (PPI, all items) obtained from US Census Bureau, Historical Statistics of the United States, BLS, E23 (rescaled).

The pre-1890 source is Table E52, which derives from Warren and Pearson (1933). For the period 1890–1948 the source is Table E23. Post-1948 data are obtained from IMF, *IFS* (CD-ROM).

Data on world cocoa production, consumption ('grindings'), and end crop-year stocks are made available by the ICCO (<http://www.icco.org>), and historical data on a crop-year (October–September) basis are provided in the *Quarterly Bulletin of Cocoa Statistics* (*QBCS*) Earlier figures were produced by cocoa broker Gill & Duffus, now part of ED&F Man, and, previous to that, by the League of Nations. I have data on a consistent basis from crop year 1946–47 to 2012–13. I extend the production series back to 1941–42 using information in FAO (1952, p. 104), and to 1929–30 using data for 1929–38 originally compiled for the International Institute of Agriculture and reproduced in Montgomery and Taylor (1947, p. 15). However, the wartime data appear subject to uncertainty and hence the pre-1946/47 data should be regarded as less reliable than those that follow.

Closing stocks are converted onto a 'months of normal consumption' basis by dividing by a smooth trend fitted to the grindings data using the STAMP software package (Koopmans et al, 2009). Division by the fitted trend is preferable to division by actual consumption, since that imports grindings shocks into the transformed stock series, complicating subsequent statistical analysis.

The production (crop) and consumption (grindings) figures are charted together in Figure 16.A3. The data are listed in Table 16.A2. Table 16.A3 summarizes ICCO production data for major producing countries from crop year 1960/61.

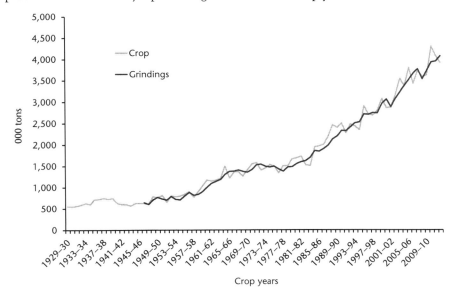

Figure 16.A3 Cocoa production and consumption, 1929–30 to 2012

Table 16.A2 Production, consumption (grindings), and closing stocks

Crop Year	Crop	Grindings		Closing Stock		Availability	
		Grindings	Trend	Actual	Months	Actual	Months
1929/30	553						
1930/31	545						
1931/32	563						
1932/33	587						
1933/34	624						
1934/35	602						
1935/36	716						
1936/37	722						
1937/38	746						
1938/39	725						
1939/40	741						
1940/41	627						
1941/42	601						
1942/43	600						
1943/44	566						
1944/45	619						
1945/46	627						
1946/47	624	639	631	178	3.39		
1947/48	603	600	656	158	2.89	781	14.30
1948/49	781	705	682	211	3.70	939	16.51
1949/50	765	765	705	179	3.05	976	16.59
1950/51	810	729	721	236	3.94	989	16.47
1951/52	655	702	731	158	2.59	891	14.64
1952/53	798	786	740	139	2.26	956	15.50
1953/54	781	719	748	177	2.84	920	14.76
1954/55	799	707	762	247	3.89	976	15.37
1955/56	841	798	784	261	4.00	1088	16.66
1956/57	899	881	811	245	3.63	1160	17.17
1957/58	773	816	841	166	2.37	1018	14.52
1958/59	905	837	880	205	2.80	1071	14.61
1959/60	1040	902	931	317	4.09	1245	16.04
1960/61	1172	1002	995	461	5.56	1489	17.97
1961/62	1149	1095	1065	504	5.68	1610	18.14
1962/63	1172	1140	1137	524	5.53	1676	17.69
1963/64	1210	1186	1207	536	5.33	1734	17.23
1964/65	1505	1305	1273	716	6.75	2041	19.24
1965/66	1221	1377	1327	548	4.96	1937	17.52
1966/67	1364	1381	1366	517	4.54	1912	16.80
1967/68	1371	1408	1392	466	4.02	1888	16.28
1968/69	1259	1377	1411	334	2.84	1725	14.67
1969/70	1417	1356	1429	380	3.19	1751	14.70
1970/71	1554	1418	1452	503	4.16	1934	15.99
1971/72	1580	1527	1473	544	4.43	2083	16.97
1972/73	1409	1544	1485	385	3.11	1953	15.78
1973/74	1452	1497	1485	325	2.63	1837	14.84
1974/75	1538	1477	1476	376	3.05	1863	15.14
1975/76	1499	1495	1464	369	3.03	1875	15.36
1976/77	1343	1429	1454	274	2.26	1712	14.13
1977/78	1504	1379	1454	388	3.20	1778	14.67
1978/79	1509	1478	1470	409	3.34	1897	15.49
1979/80	1671	1485	1499	584	4.68	2080	16.65
1980/81	1695	1558	1541	709	5.52	2279	17.75
1981/82	1732	1601	1591	831	6.26	2441	18.41

1982/83	1531	1628	1650	717	5.22	2362	17.17
1983/84	1512	1704	1717	515	3.60	2229	15.58
1984/85	1952	1864	1789	593	3.98	2467	16.55
1985/86	1974	1849	1862	705	4.55	2567	16.55
1986/87	2011	1910	1938	792	4.91	2716	16.82
1987/88	2197	1986	2020	988	5.87	2989	17.76
1988/89	2464	2133	2107	1302	7.41	3452	19.66
1989/90	2406	2202	2194	1489	8.15	3708	20.28
1990/91	2506	2331	2277	1647	8.68	3995	21.06
1991/92	2278	2325	2354	1584	8.07	3925	20.01
1992/93	2485	2415	2429	1637	8.09	4069	20.10
1993/94	2436	2511	2502	1545	7.41	4073	19.53
1994/95	2348	2532	2573	1346	6.28	3893	18.16
1995/96	2915	2719	2642	1522	6.91	4261	19.35
1996/97	2710	2711	2704	1502	6.67	4232	18.78
1997/98	2693	2752	2763	1424	6.19	4195	18.22
1998/99	2808	2744	2825	1469	6.24	4232	17.98
1999/00	3077	2960	2893	1564	6.49	4546	18.85
2000/01	2865	3065	2964	1344	5.44	4429	17.94
2001/02	2877	2886	3038	1315	5.19	4221	16.67
2002/03	3179	3077	3132	1395	5.34	4494	17.22
2003/04	3548	3237	3242	1682	6.23	4943	18.30
2004/05	3378	3382	3359	1644	5.87	5060	18.07
2005/06	3808	3522	3473	1892	6.54	5452	18.84
2006/07	3430	3675	3572	1613	5.42	5322	17.88
2007/08	3737	3775	3653	1538	5.05	5350	17.58
2008/09	3592	3537	3720	1557	5.02	5130	16.55
2009/10	3634	3737	3797	1418	4.48	5191	16.41
2010/11	4309	3938	3883	1746	5.40	5727	17.70
2011/12	4085	3957	3972	1833	5.54	5831	17.61
2012/13	3929	4083	4066	1640	4.84	5762	17.00

Note: Crop years are October–September. The grindings trend is a smooth trend estimated using the STAMP software (Koopmans et al., 2009). Availability is the current crop plus the previous year's closing stock. Stocks and availability are converted to a 'months of normal consumption' basis by dividing by the grindings trend. Sources: ICCO, *QBCS*, and FAO (1952).

Table 16.A3 Production in major cocoa-producing countries (000 tons)

	Cameroon	Cote d'Ivoire	Ghana	Nigeria	Africa	Brazil	Ecuador	America	Indonesia	Malaysia	Asia	World
1960/61	74	94	440	198	63	124	42	135	0	0	19	1189
1961/62	75	82	417	194	61	118	38	133	1	0	21	1140
1962/63	76	103	429	179	67	113	39	143	1	1		1176
1963/64	85	99	443	219	69	125	36	129	1	1	27	1234
1964/65	91	148	566	298	80	119	48	125	1	1	31	1508
1965/66	79	113	417	185	72	173	36	121	1	1	28	1226
1966/67	86	150	382	267	84	175	53	119	1	1	33	1351
1967/68	92	147	422	239	81	144	69	124	1	2	33	1354
1968/69	104	145	339	192	90	165	53	113	2	2	37	1242
1969/70	108	181	416	223	85	201	55	130	2	2	32	1435
1970/71	112	180	392	308	106	182	61	114	2	4	38	1499
1971/72	123	226	464	255	94	167	67	142	3	5	37	1583
1972/73	107	181	418	241	81	162	43	125	2	9	28	1397
1973/74	110	209	350	215	70	246	72	123	3	10	40	1448
1974/75	118	242	377	214	60	273	78	131	3	13	40	1549
1975/76	96	231	397	216	61	258	63	130	3	17	40	1512
1976/77	82	230	320	165	48	234	72	128	3	21	35	1338
1977/78	107	304	268	207	55	283	79	144	4	23	38	1512
1978/79	106	312	250	137	59	314	86	158	7	26	40	1495
1979/80	124	379	285	172	63	294	95	138	7	35	39	1631
1980/81	120	403	258	156	60	349	84	147	16	48	40	1681
1981/82	122	465	225	183	52	314	87	153	23	60	45	1729
1982/83	106	360	178	156	50	336	46	170	30	73	43	1548
1983/84	108	418	159	115	65	302	42	164	32	95	40	1540
1984/85	120	571	175	151	68	403	116	156	36	99	45	1940
1985/86	118	563	219	110	75	385	96	174	45	131	46	1962
1986/87	123	614	228	80	50	368	70	181	56	171	48	1989
1987/88	131	667	188	150	50	388	77	200	65	227	51	2194
1988/89	129	840	300	160	41	336	87	175	102	222	69	2461
1989/90	121	717	295	170	44	355	101	199	115	240	61	2418
1990/91	107	804	293	170	43	380	104	184	147	224	53	2509
1991/92	108	748	243	110	31	310	83	193	169	217	59	2271
1992/93	99	697	312	130	30	305	70	201	234	219	59	2356

Year												
1993/94	97	887	255	142	30	280	79	198	251	204	50	2473
1994/95	109	862	310	144	27	230	83	192	238	120	51	2366
1995/96	135	1200	404	158	32	231	103	198	285	115	53	2913
1996/97	126	1108	323	160	37	185	103	197	325	100	49	2712
1997/98	115	1113	409	165	39	170	30	203	331	65	50	2690
1998/99	124	1163	398	198	37	138	75	156	390	75	55	2808
1999/00	120	1325	440	165	35	125	95	168	410	60	60	3003
2000/01	133	1212	395	177	30	163	89	171	392	35	60	2858
2001/02	131	1265	341	185	31	124	81	173	455	25	57	2867
2002/03	160	1352	497	173	50	163	86	179	410	36	64	3169
2003/04	169	1407	737	180	60	163	117	182	430	34	62	3541
2004/05	188	1286	599	200	104	171	116	156	460	29	71	3381
2005/06	171	1408	740	200	129	162	114	174	560	34	76	3768
2006/07	169	1229	615	220	133	126	125	167	545	33	71	3433
2007/08	185	1382	729	230	167	171	118	178	485	31	75	3750
2008/09	227	1222	662	250	158	157	149	195	490	22	86	3617
2009/10	209	1242	632	235	168	161	150	204	550	15	68	3634
2010/11	229	1511	1025	240	220	200	161	198	440	7	79	4309
2011/12	207	1486	879	245	113	220	198	237	440	4	67	4095
2012/13	225	1449	835	235	89	185	192	245	410	3	74	3942

Source: ICCO, *QBCS* (various issues). Row sums may differ from the total on account of rounding.

References

Clarence-Smith, W. G. 2000. *Cocoa and Chocolate, 1765–1914*. London: Routledge.

Commodity Research Bureau. 1939. *Commodity Year Book*. New York: Commodity Research Bureau.

Dand, R. 1999. *The International Cocoa Trade*. Cambridge: Woodhead Publishing.

FAO (Food and Agriculture Organization). 1952. *The State of Food and Agriculture: Review and Outlook 1952*. Rome: FAO.

FAO (Food and Agriculture Organization). 1955. 'Cocoa'. *Commodity Series Bulletin* 25. Rome: FAO.

Gilbert, C. L. 2009. 'Cocoa market liberalization in retrospect'. *Review of Business and Economics* 54: pp. 294–312.

Gilbert, C. L. 2015. *Stockholding, Investment and Commodity Price Dynamics: The World Cocoa Market*. Available at: <https://sites.google.com/site/christopherlesliegilbert/publications/unpublished-manuscripts>.

Grilli, E. R. and M. C. Yang. 1987. *Long-Term Movements in Non-Fuel Commodity Prices*. Working Paper. Washington DC: International Economics Department, World Bank.

Grilli, E. R. and M. C. Yang. 1988. 'Primary commodity prices, manufactured good prices and the terms of trade of developing countries: what the long run shows'. *World Bank Economic Review* 2: pp. 1–47.

Kofi, T. A. 1974. 'Vertical price relationships in the international cocoa market and implications for Ghana's marketing policies'. In *Economics of Cocoa Production and Marketing*, edited by R. A. Kotey, C. Oklai, and B. E. Riurke. Legon: Institute of Statistical, Economic and Social Research, University of Ghana.

Koopman, S. J., A. C. Harvey, J. Doornik, and N. Shephard. 2009. *STAMP 8.2: Structural Time Series Analyser, Modeller and Predictor*. London: Timberlake.

Mitchell, B. R. 1992. *International Historical Statistics, Europe 1750–1988*. London: Macmillan.

Montgomery, E. G. and A. M. Taylor. 1947. *World Trade in Cocoa*, Industrial Series 71. Washington, DC: US Department of Commerce.

Posthumus, N. W. 1946. *Inquiry into the History of Prices in Holland*, vol. 1: *Wholesale Prices at the Exchange of Amsterdam 1585–1914; Rates of Exchange at Amsterdam, 1609–1914*. Leiden: E.J. Brill.

Prebisch, R. 1962. 'The economic development of Latin America and its principal problems'. *Economic Bulletin for Latin America* 7: pp. 1–22. Initially released (1952) as a separate document by the United Nations.

Singer, H. 1950. 'The distribution of gains between investing and borrowing countries'. *American Economic Review, Papers and Proceedings* 40: pp. 473–85.

Warren, G. F. and F. A. Pearson. 1933. *Prices*. New York: Wiley.

Weymar, F. H. 1968. *The Dynamics of the World Cocoa Market*. Cambridge, MA: The MIT Press.

17

Concentration and Price Transmission in the Cocoa–Chocolate Chain

Catherine Araujo Bonjean and Jean-François Brun

Introduction

The history of the chocolate industry is a succession of technological and product innovations, which have led to a rapid increase in the production and consumption of chocolate. The chocolate industry was born in the eighteenth century in Bristol, England, when the apothecary Charles Churchman and his son Walter developed the first water-powered machinery to grind cocoa beans.[1] In 1761, another apothecary, Joseph Fry, and John Vaughan, bought Churchman's shop and founded Fry, Vaughan & Co. Chocolate production truly entered the industrial era in 1795 when J. Fry's son began using Watt's steam engine to grind cocoa beans.[2] After J. Fry, Casparus and Coenraad van Houten revolutionized the grinding industry with the invention of the Dutching process in 1828. Later, in 1879, Rodolphe Lindt, the founder of a chocolate factory in Berne, Switzerland, invented the conching machine, which enabled production of a better-quality chocolate (the 'chocolat fondant').

In the meantime, the great-grandson of Joseph Fry innovated, and in 1847 produced a solid chocolate, obtained by mixing cocoa powder with cocoa butter and sugar. In 1875, Daniel Peter in Vevey, Switzerland, developed the recipe for milk chocolate. In 1900, Milton Hershey created a new market with the first chocolate-based confectionery bar. He was followed in 1923 by Frank Mars (creator of the Milky Way bar), and Peter Paul who created the Mounds bar in 1921. Chocolate would later be used for confectionery, pastry, ice creams, and so on.

The new technologies and products spread rapidly during the nineteenth century. The chocolate industry developed close to the large consumer centres, in Europe and the USA. At the beginning of the twentieth century, the major chocolate-producing countries were Switzerland, Spain, Germany, France, UK,

---

[1] The patent was filed in 1729.
[2] <http://www.gracesguide.co.uk/J._S._Fry_and_Sons>.

and the USA. A century later, the chocolate industry is still expanding in emerging markets in Asia, Brazil, and Russia.

The history of the chocolate industry is also a long process of industrial acquisitions, mergers, and restructuring, leading to a high degree of horizontal concentration at the main stages of the cocoa–chocolate chain. In that respect, the history of the company started by Joseph Fry is symbolic of the evolution of the chocolate industry from the eighteenth century to the present day. In 1919, the company established by Joseph Fry—then called J.S. Fry & Sons Limited—merged with John Cadbury's chocolate factory (founded in 1831 in Birmingham, UK), giving birth to the British Cocoa and Chocolate Company. The company changed its name in 1969 to become the Cadbury Group Ltd. After four decades of growth across the globe and acquisitions, the Cadbury group had become, by the end of the 2000s, the world's third-largest chocolate manufacturer. The story did not end there. In 2010, Cadbury plc was bought by the US agri-food business giant Kraft Foods, founded by the Kraft brothers in 1909 in Chicago.

History has repeated itself for most of the pioneers of the chocolate industry. For example, the Van Houten company, founded in 1815 in Amsterdam, the Netherlands, by Coenraad Johannes Van Houten, developed in Europe and in the USA before being bought in 1986 by Jacobs Suchard AG (Switzerland). Van Houten was then integrated into the Barry Callebaut Group, one of the three current leaders in cocoa processing. The Peter-Cailler & Cie company, founded in 1867 by Daniel Peter, acquired in 1904 the company founded by Amédée Kohler—the inventor of hazelnut chocolate—and merged in 1911 with the Maison Cailler de Broc. In 1929, Peter-Cailler Kohler, Chocolats Suisses S.A., merged with the Nestlé company, which was, in 2013, the third-largest chocolate manufacturer in the world.

Concentration in the chocolate industry accelerated at the end of the 1980s when two multinationals, Archers Daniels Midland (ADM) and Cargill, entered the cocoa industry. These large trading companies integrated upstream in the cocoa chain by buying export companies in producing countries. They also integrated downstream into the grinding of cocoa beans and manufacturing of industrial chocolate.[3] At the same time, the major chocolate manufacturers, such as Cadbury, Suchard, and Nestlé, which were involved in the entire cocoa transformation process, from cocoa grinding to the manufacture of the consumer product, outsourced the production of the semi-finished cocoa products.

At present, the chocolate chain is split into two segments. The upstream part of the chain is dominated by three trading companies which buy the cocoa directly from the growers' cooperative and have integrated into the early processing stage of cocoa and the production of industrial chocolate. Downstream, the sector is dominated by eight major food companies which have refocused on their core business, the manufacture of chocolate products.[4] On the supply side, cocoa marketing and pricing in Cote d'Ivoire, the main producer country, was liberalized

---

[3] Industrial chocolate is also referred to as couverture.
[4] See Table 17.A1 in the appendix for a more detailed presentation of the different stages of the cocoa–chocolate chain.

in 1999. The Ivorian authorities withdrew from the world cocoa market to the benefit of transnational corporations. On the consumer side, chocolate is often considered to be an affordable luxury whose consumption is recession-proof.[5] This is the case in France where consumers favour premium and dark chocolate and are ready to pay for quality. However, confronted by rising chocolate prices and recurrent threats of cocoa shortage consumers fear that the chocolate price might increase again.

The purpose of this chapter is to outline the recent changes in the structure and in the power relationships within the chocolate industry. These changes are illustrated by a price analysis at different stages of the cocoa–chocolate chain, which reaches from the Ivorian cocoa grower to the French consumer of tablets of chocolate. First, we focus on the relationships between the main producing country, Côte d'Ivoire, and the cocoa traders and processors. The declining share of the Ivorian producer in the world cocoa price shows that growers did not benefit from the liberalization process. Second, we consider the changes in the upstream segment of the cocoa industry. Comparison of the price of cocoa beans and semi-finished cocoa product shows a sharp increase in the gross margin of cocoa processors at the beginning of the 2000s. Third, we consider the structure of the chocolate market, and examine the power relationships within the chocolate chain through an econometric analysis of the price transmission mechanism from the cocoa bean to the tablet of chocolate.

Power Relationships in the Main Producing Country

After independence, the cocoa production increased quickly in Côte d'Ivoire despite low producer prices. At the end of the 1980s, the Ivorian public authorities controlled about 40 per cent of the world cocoa supply but were unable to significantly influence the world price. After the 1999 liberalization of cocoa marketing and pricing, a handful of private transnational companies took control of cocoa purchasing, grinding, and trading. The producer's share in the world cocoa price remained low and even decreased.

The Lessons of the Cocoa Wars

West Africa is the largest cocoa-producing region, accounting for more than 70 per cent of world supply and 77 per cent of exports in the 2012/13 crop year. Cocoa supply is concentrated in two countries: Cote d'Ivoire and Ghana. Côte d'Ivoire supplies about 36 per cent of the world's cocoa beans, and Ghana more than 20 per cent. Cameroon and Nigeria come in equal fourth place, with about 6 per cent of cocoa supply (Table 17.1).

Until the late 1990s, cocoa production in Côte d'Ivoire developed under the close control of the *Caisse de Stabilisation*, the state-owned marketing board.

---

[5] See Castroviejo (2009).

Table 17.1 Production of cocoa beans

	2010/11		2011/12*		2012/13**	
	(1000 t)	(%)	(1000 t)	(%)	(1000 t)	(%)
Africa	**3224**	**74.77**	**2919**	**71.54**	**2813**	**71.56**
Cameroon	229	5.31	207	5.07	225	5.72
Côte d'Ivoire	1511	35.04	1486	36.42	1445	36.76
Ghana	1025	23.77	879	21.54	835	21.24
Nigeria	240	5.57	235	5.76	225	5.72
Others	220	5.10	113	2.77	83	2.11
America	**561**	**13.01**	**650**	**15.93**	**618**	**15.72**
Brazil	200	4.64	220	5.39	185	4.71
Ecuador	161	3.73	193	4.73	192	4.88
Others	201	4.66	237	5.81	240	6.11
Asia & Oceania	**526**	**12.20**	**510**	**12.50**	**500**	**12.72**
Indonesia	440	10.20	440	10.78	420	10.68
Papua New Guinea	48	1.11	39	0.96	41	1.04
Others	39	0.90	32	0.78	39	0.99
World total	**4312**	**100**	**4080**	**100**	**3931**	**100**

Note: * estimates; ** forecasts. Totals may differ from sum of constituents due to rounding.
Source: ICCO QBCS 29 (4), Cocoa year 2012/13.

The domestic marketing of cocoa and international sales were handled by private companies but prices, from the farmer to the exporter, were set by the *Caisse de Stabilisation*. The *Caisse de Stabilisation* was also responsible for authorizing and controlling exports, quota allocation between exporters, and direct sales on foreign markets.

In 1987, facing low prices in world markets, the Cote d'Ivoire imposed an embargo on the export of cocoa beans and organized cocoa storage in European warehouses. This attempt to manipulate the world price, known as the 'cocoa war', lasted from July 1987 till October 1989, and was a failure. The withholding of cocoa had no noticeable impact on world prices, and the Ivorian authorities were forced to halve the price paid to growers. The cocoa war led the country into an economic and political crisis, which, ten years later, resulted in the dismantling of the *Caisse de Stabilisation* and the complete liberalization of the cocoa sector (Losch, 2000, 2001; Araujo Bonjean et al., 2001; Ruf, 2009).

This experience suggests that the Côte d'Ivoire, which at the time was supplying approximately 40 per cent of world's cocoa, did not have market power. One of the main reasons relates to the technical difficulty of protecting stocks of cocoa beans from humidity in this tropical country. To overcome this issue, President Houphouët-Boigny tried to develop grinding capacities in China and USA, with mixed success (Losch, 2000).

The second 'cocoa war' took place in early 2011 and shows how vulnerable the international market is to fluctuations in the Ivorian cocoa supply. When the outgoing president refused to leave office after the presidential election in November 2010, the newly elected president, Alassane Ouattara, ordered a halt to coffee and cocoa exports. This decision was backed by the European Union (EU), which prohibited European vessels from docking in the ports of San Pedro and Abidjan. The export ban resulted in a temporary rise in the cocoa price of approximately 20 per cent between November 2010 and March 2011. Earlier, the failed coup in September 2002 organized by rebel forces from Burkina Faso had resulted in the division of the country between north and south, and had been followed by a sharp rise in the world price of cocoa between March and October 2002 (Figure 17.1).

These 2002 and 2011 episodes of price increases were preceded by massive purchases of cocoa by the trading company Armajaro. These purchases of cocoa, equivalent to 7 per cent of the annual world production in July 2010 and 5 per cent in 2002, cleared out the market, contributed to the rise in prices, and led to suspicions of insider dealing (Agritrade, 2011).

Compared to the first 'cocoa war', the 2011 embargo on cocoa exports occurred in a demand-driven market characterized by rising cocoa prices, which may explain the higher sensitivity of the market to the threat of scarcity. Moreover, EU support may have rendered the embargo more credible and thus more effective. Since Cote d'Ivoire is the largest cocoa supplier and the second-largest cocoa grinder, the cocoa market remains vulnerable to political instability and to marketing and pricing policy in the country. The weakness of Ivorian institutions also favours collusive behaviour and attempts from privately informed operators to manipulate the market.

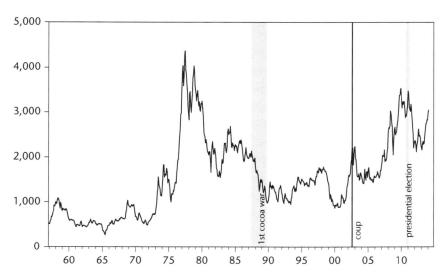

Figure 17.1 World price of cocoa beans and political events in the Côte d'Ivoire (US$/MT)
Note: Average of London and New York Stock Exchange prices.
Source: International Financial Statistics, IMF.

Taking Control of Cocoa Exports and Processing

The pre-announced end of the system of guaranteed prices and export regulation ushered in a period of uncertainty for private operators in the mid-1990s. For local traders, credit access became more costly as risk increased. For foreign buyers of cocoa beans, the liberalization generated a counterparty risk previously offset by the *Caisse de Stabilisation* (Araujo Bonjean et al., 2001). The development of joint ventures or alliances between local trading companies and international processors was an answer to these two kinds of risks. Such agreements allowed the domestic firms to access foreign capital at a lower cost and the foreign ones to secure cocoa sourcing via direct access to the raw material.

In 1995, Grace Cocoa (USA) developed a partnership with Sifca (Société Immobilière et Financière de la Côte Africaine), the major Ivorian cocoa export company. Cacao Barry (France) acquired shares in the SHAC (Société Havraise Africaine de Commerce), and ED&F Man (UK) took over Tropival (Société ivoirienne de produits tropicaux et aliments). In 1997, through its acquisition of Grace Cocoa, ADM became a shareholder of Union Ivoirienne de Traitement de Cacao (Unicao), a local cocoa trader and processor. In 2001, ADM bought shares in SIFCA,[6] and acquired Unicao (Losch, 2000, 2001).

The resulting concentration of trade was also the consequence of the development of bulk shipping of cocoa beans. This mode of shipping, used for cereals and adapted for cocoa by Cargill and ADM, generates important economies of scale, but requires large volumes of export. Shipping cocoa liquor in liquid rather than solid form is also a cost-saving mode that is expanding now. But only the large-scale traders and processors sourcing large volumes of cocoa beans or butter are able to benefit from these economies of scale (Fold, 2002; Ecobank, 2014).

The foreign exporters drove out the local independent exporters, whose market share felt from 43 per cent in 1997/98 to less than 30 per cent in 2010/11.[7] The concentration of the export sector increased significantly. In 1997/98, the top ten exporters purchased 60 per cent of all cocoa production (Losch, 2001). This share increased to over 80 per cent in 2010. During the 2010/11 marketing year, the three world's leading cocoa multinationals—Cargill, ADM, and Barry Callebaut—purchased over 40 per cent of the Ivorian cocoa production. In 2010/11 also, over 70 per cent of the Ivorian cocoa production was bought from growers' cooperatives or local intermediaries by foreign companies (Table 17.2).[8]

The new entrants in cocoa trading also invested in grinding capacities, while the historic operators, notably Barry Callebaut, consolidated their position in Côte d'Ivoire. The French chocolate manufacturer Cémoi and Cargill invested in new processing plants in 1996 and 1999 respectively. Barry Callebaut took full control

---

[6] Sifca was founded by Pierre Billon in 1964. In 1993 Sifca merged with Comafrique, giving birth to the Sifcom group (<http://www.groupesifca.com/>).

[7] See Araujo Bonjean et al. (2001).

[8] Information on market shares is fragmentary and should be considered with caution.

Table 17.2 Main cocoa purchasers in Côte d'Ivoire (%)

	2007/08*	2010/11**
Cargill (USA)	15.96	17.89
ADM Cocoa (USA)	9.03	13.66
Barry Callebaut (Switzerland)	7.72	11.84
SAF Cacao (Côte d'Ivoire)	12.54	5.93
Outspan Ivoire-Olam (Singapore)	6.75	7.01
CIPEXI-Continaf (the Netherlands)	4.68	
Tropival—ED&F Man (UK)	4.10	
Touton Négoce (France)	n/a	6.57
Cocaf Ivoire Noble (UK/Singapore)		5.12
Estève (Brazil)		5.11
Armajaro (UK)[1]		4.06
Total	60.78	77.19

Note: *Source: Oxfam (2008). **Source: Jeune Afrique <http://www.jeuneafrique.com/Article/ARTJAJA2650p060-063.xml0/>.
[1] In November 2013, Armajaro Holding Ltd sold its cocoa and coffee trading unit to Ecom Agroindustrial Corp. (Switzerland), a family-owned commodities trading house, the third-largest cocoa trader (Bloomberg, 11 November 2013).

of Saco (Société Africaine de Cacao) in 2000, and ADM took over Unicao in 2001.[9] In 2013, according to estimates, the grinding capacity in Côte d'Ivoire had reached 655,000 tons per year; five multinationals—Barry Callebaut, Cargill, ADM, Cémoi, and Olam—owned 86 per cent of this capacity (see Table 17.3).

The grinders benefited from fiscal incentives that were set after independence by the public authorities to promote the development of a local grinding industry. The government's aim was to increase the value of mid-crop cocoa beans, which are of lower quality, by processing them locally. Moreover, grinding is a crucially important operation since it allows the transformation from raw cocoa, a perishable product highly sensitive to humidity and mould, into an inert product, which is much easier to store.[10]

The first local grinding company (Saco) was established in 1964 by Cacao Barry (France). In 1975, Saco invested in a chocolate factory (Chocodi) with support from the government. Chocodi produces industrial chocolate for export and chocolate-based products for the domestic market (Losch, 2001). However, as industrial chocolate is difficult to transport, production needs to take place as close as possible to the consumer markets. Moreover, in order to obtain a high-quality chocolate, it is necessary to blend cocoa beans of different origins and qualities. For these reasons, and due to the low domestic consumption of chocolate, the profitability of Chocodi has been low.[11] The recent expansion of the Ivorian and regional markets may open up new perspectives.[12]

[9] Unicao owned a processing plant in Abidjan. It belonged to the Ivorian group Sifcom, with Grace Cocoa the main shareholder as of 1996.
[10] This first stage of the cocoa processing consists of roasting and grinding fermented cocoa beans to obtain cocoa mass, butter, and powder (see the appendix). Cocoa liquor is cooled and hardened before export. Liquor is remelted at the chocolate factory, incurring additional time and cost (Ecobank, 2014).
[11] In 2008 Barry Callebaut sold Chocodi to the group of Charles Kader Gooré (CKG Holding).
[12] Cémoi plans to expand chocolate production in Cote d'Ivoire to supply the West African market.

Table 17.3 Grinding capacity in Côte d'Ivoire

	2003/04	2012/13		Cumulative
	1000 MT*	1000 MT**	%	%
Barry Callebaut (Saco)	100	190	29.0	29.0
Cargill (Micao)	100	120	18.3	47.3
ADM (Unicao)	85	86	13.1	62.6
Cémoi	65	100	15.3	75.7
Olam		70	10.7	86.4
SAF Cacao (Choco Ivoire)		32	4.9	91.3
Sucso		24	3.7	95.1
Tafi		8	1.2	98.8
Total	350	655	100	100

Note: * Source: French Embassy, Mission Economique, March 2005. ** According to Ecobank (2014).

The Producers' Share Declines

It was expected that the liberalization of the cocoa marketing and pricing system would lead to a reduction in marketing costs and an increase in the farm-gate price. However, the farm-gate price relative to the world cocoa price did not increase after 1999. Compared to the 1985–98 period, the price ratio fell by about 10 per cent during the post-liberalization period 1999–2010 (see Figure 17.2 and Table 17.4).

Several factors may explain the low producer's share: a decline in the quality of beans, export tax, informal levies, or the administrative cost of the new regulatory structure set up by the government (Gilbert, 2009). Another reason may be the high concentration of buyers. While the supply of cocoa beans comes from a multitude of small farmers, generally grouped into poorly organized cooperatives, there are a few powerful cocoa buyers potentially forming a monopsony.

Of course, the degree of competition in the market and prices are not directly related to the number of firms. Competition may exist in a concentrated market if there are no barriers to entry or exit. Indeed, there was some evidence of price competition between cocoa buyers in the years immediately following the reforms. Firms competed to purchase cocoa in order to operate at full capacity, and competition has probably been exacerbated by the declining quality of cocoa beans. Moreover, the farm-gate price is only one element in the remuneration package of the producer, and the price level is not the sole criterion of competition. Competition between cocoa buyers also affects the services offered to producers, such as access to credit and to inputs, price risk insurance, and so on, that are more difficult to measure.

In 2011/12 the Ivorian authorities started new reforms in the cocoa sector that aimed at raising the purchasing power of cocoa growers. The government again set guaranteed minimum farm-gate prices, stricter control of bean quality, and a marketing mechanism based on forward sales through auctions. The new reforms also included the suppression of the tax incentive, which benefited local grinders (Agritrade, 2012; Ecobank, 2014).

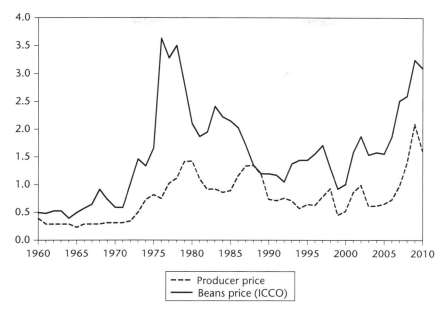

Figure 17.2 World cocoa price and producer price in Cote d'Ivoire (USD/kg)
Source: Caisse de Stabilisation and ICCO.

Table 17.4 Cocoa producer price in Côte d'Ivoire as a share of the world bean price

	1960–69	1970–79	1980–89	1990–99	2000–10	1985–98	1999–10
Mean	0.531	0.409	0.625	0.536	0.479	0.609	0.498
Std. Dev.	(0.142)	(0.121)	(0.232)	(0.122)	(0.087)	(0.209)	(0.103)

Paradoxically, these reforms aiming at protecting the farmers from unfair practices tend to strengthen the position of the large and well-established traders and grinders. This is the case of the tax policy reform that clearly discourages new entrants in cocoa grinding. Moreover, growing concern by consumers about social and environmental issues favours collusive behaviour, as it encourages alliances among buyers to meet environmental standards and to prevent the use of child labour.

The Upstream Segment of the Chocolate Industry

At the international level, the upstream segment of the cocoa–chocolate chain is dominated by three agribusiness giants. They expanded backward to gain control over cocoa sourcing, and forward, moving into the production of industrial chocolate.

The Three Leading Processors

The processing industry changed radically in the 1990s when the two agribusiness giants, Cargill and ADM, entered the cocoa sector. These two companies belong to the 'ABCD group',[13] the four transnationals that dominate agricultural commodities trade and processing. They diversified from grains into cocoa trading and processing in 1987 (Cargill) and 1997 (ADM). They quickly gained large market shares of world grinding through the acquisition of large European processors. At the same time, they invested massively in the main producing countries of West Africa and South America. As seen for Côte d'Ivoire, they acquired local export companies or purchased an equity stake and invested in new processing capacities. This strategy allowed them to gain control over all activities, from the purchase of the beans at the cooperative level to the production of industrial chocolate.[14] Faced with these two giants, Cacao Barry and Callebaut, two historic operators, merged in 1996 to become a leading cocoa-processing company.

In 2006/07,[15] the three companies controlled about 40 per cent of world cocoa grinding: Cargill processed 14 per cent of all cocoa beans, ADM 14 per cent, and Barry Callebaut 12 per cent. Petra Foods (Singapore) and Blommer (USA) also played a significant role, with, respectively, 7 per cent and 5 per cent of world grinding capacity.[16] In July 2013, Barry Callebaut bought the cocoa ingredients division from Petra Foods and so acquired factories in Indonesia, Malaysia, and Thailand. As of 2014, Barry Callebaut is the largest cocoa processor in the world, accounting for 25 per cent of world cocoa processing. According to estimates, Cargill, ADM, and Barry Callebaut control about 60 per cent of world grinding.[17]

Following a different strategy to ADM and Cargill, Barry Callebaut reached a higher degree of vertical integration by investing massively in the manufacturing of chocolate products for final consumption. However, the company started moving out of the consumer segment in 2007. Barry Callebaut sold Brach's Confections to the Farley's & Sathers Candy Company in 2007, and sold Stollwerck to the Baronie Group (Belgium) in 2011. As of 2014, Barry Callebaut has recentred on its core business, the production of industrial chocolate, and has developed long-term supply agreements with the Baronie Group,[18] and with other leading global confectionery companies, such as Nestlé, Hershey, and Mondelēz.

A new distribution of activities within the cocoa–chocolate chain is emerging. Upstream, cocoa traders/processors control all activities, from cocoa bean sourcing to the production of industrial chocolate. Downstream, the big chocolate

---

[13] The ABCD group includes four companies: ADM, Bunge Ltd, Cargill, and Louis Dreyfus Corp.

[14] See the different stages of the chocolate fabrication process in the appendix.

[15] The only year for which data are available.

[16] Source: Oxfam (2008) and Unctad (2008).

[17] *Financial Times*, the Commodities Note, 10 October 2013. <http://www.ft.com/intl/cms/s/0/f06f00fa-3184-11e3-817c-00144feab7de.html#axzz35dEG8NMD>.

[18] The transaction with the Baronie Group includes a long-term supply agreement for about 25,000 tons of chocolate annually (see Barry Callebaut website: <http://www.barry-callebaut.com/51?release=6998>).

Box 17.1 THE EMERGENCE OF THE THREE MAIN COCOA PROCESSORS

Cargill (USA) entered cocoa processing in 1980 by building a cocoa-processing plant in Ilhéus, Brazil. A few years later, in 1987, Cargill acquired the General Cocoa Co. (Netherlands), a leading cocoa processor, and so gained processing facilities in Europe, and took control of Gerkens Cacao Industrie B.V. and Fennema BV. Cargill consolidated its cocoa-processing segment in 2004 with the acquisition of Nestlé cocoa-processing facilities in York (UK) and Hamburg (Germany). Then Cargill invested downstream in the chocolate industry with the acquisition in 1992 of Wilbur Chocolate Co., a US chocolate manufacturer, and the acquisition of two makers of industrial chocolate: OCG Cacao (France) in 2003, and Schierstedter Schokoladenfabrik GmbH & Co. (Germany) in 2005. Cargill strengthened its position in the US industrial chocolate market when it bought Peter's Chocolate from Nestlé (USA) in 2003. In 2007, Toshoku, a Japanese company that trades cocoa beans and cocoa products, merged with Cargill to become Cargill Japan Limited.

ADM (USA) entered the cocoa and chocolate industry in 1997 with the acquisition of Grace Cocoa Company (USA), an important grinder and supplier of industrial cocoa, and formed ADM Cocoa. With Grace Cocoa, ADM took control of the Ambrosia, the deZaan, and the Merckens brands of cocoa and chocolate products, and became a leading industrial chocolate manufacturer in North America. In 1998, ADM Cocoa purchased the cocoa-processing business of ED&F Man Group plc, and became a world leader in cocoa grinding. In 2006, ADM acquired Classic Couverture Ltd, a chocolate manufacturer based in the UK. ADM consolidated its position in the European chocolate industry in 2009 with the acquisition of Schokinag-Schokolade-Industrie Herrmann GmbH & Co. KG, one of Europe's leading producers of chocolate and cocoa powder. More recently, ADM has opened a new cocoa and chocolate manufacturing plant in Hazleton, PA, USA.

The Barry Callebaut Group of Switzerland, subsidiary of Jacobs Holding AG, was created in 1996 by the merger of Callebaut (Belgium), a leading European manufacturer of industrial chocolate, with Cacao Barry (France), a leading cocoa trader and processor. Barry Callebaut consolidated its position in the industrial chocolate segment with the integration of Carma (Switzerland) in 1999. In 2002, Barry Callebaut entered the consumer products segment with the acquisition of the Stollwerck Group, a leading German chocolate manufacturer (founded in 1839) with factories in Eastern Europe and Russia.[19] In 2003, Barry Callebaut further expanded its consumer business with the acquisition of US-based Brach's Confections Holding, Inc. from KJ Jacobs AG, and the acquisition of Luijckx Beheer B.V., the Netherlands and Belgium chocolate manufacturer, in 2003.

manufacturers have withdrawn from the production of intermediary products and have focused on chocolate manufacturing, packaging, and marketing. However, further restructuring in the cocoa-processing sector is expected. In October 2013, ADM announced its intention to sell its cocoa and chocolate businesses to Cargill.[20] This merger, which raised anti-competition concerns, especially in

---

[19] Among the Stollwerck's portfolio of brands: Alpia, Alpenrose, Sarroti, and Jacques.
[20] The acquisition of the ADM cocoa and chocolate division would have given Cargill 35% of the world cocoa-processing market (against 25% for Barry Callebaut), and a dominant position in Europe as well as in the two main cocoa-producing countries, Côte d'Ivoire and Ghana.

Europe, did not occur. In April 2014, ADM decided to retain its cocoa-processing activity, but reiterated its intention to sell its chocolate business.[21]

Cocoa Processing Moves to Origin

With the entry of ADM and Cargill in the cocoa-processing business, the production of intermediate products, previously concentrated in Europe, shifted towards those cocoa-producing countries offering tax incentives (especially Ghana and Côte d'Ivoire). The semi-finished products made in producing countries are mostly exported and processed close to the main consumer markets of Europe, Asia, and America.

The EU remains the main region and the Netherlands the most important country for the processing of cocoa beans, with approximately 13 per cent of the global market in 2011 (Table 17.5). Since the beginning of the 2000s, the EU has been losing market share to Africa and Asia.[22] Côte d'Ivoire is becoming the biggest cocoa grinder in the world. The strategic choices made by the multinationals

Table 17.5 Grinding of cocoa beans by country 2009–12

	2009/10		2010/11*		2011/12**	
	1000 tons	%	1000 tons	%	1000 tons	%
Africa	**684.5**	**18.3**	**657.1**	**16.8**	**731.5**	**18.3**
Côte d'Ivoire	411.4	*11*	360.9	*9.2*	440	*11*
Ghana	212.2	*5.7*	229.7	*5.9*	235	*5.9*
Others	60.9	*1.6*	66.5	*1.7*	56.5	*1.4*
European Union	**1400.4**	**37.6**	**1477.7**	**37.7**	**1426.6**	**35.7**
France	145	*3.9*	150	*3.8*	153	*3.8*
Germany	361.1	*9.7*	438.5	*11.2*	455	*11.4*
Netherlands	525	*14.1*	537	*13.7*	515	*12.9*
Others	369.3	*9.9*	352.2	*9*	303.6	*7.6*
Americas	**814.7**	**21.8**	**859.9**	**21.9**	**851.9**	**21.3**
Brazil	226.1	*6.1*	239.1	*6.1*	240	*6*
USA	381.9	*10.2*	401.3	*10.2*	400	*10*
Others	206.7	*5.5*	219.5	*5.6*	211.9	*5.3*
Asia & Oceania	**707.7**	**19**	**794.6**	**20.2**	**812.6**	**20.4**
Indonesia	130	*3.5*	190	*4.8*	225	*5.6*
Malaysia	298.1	*8*	305.2	*7.8*	290	*7.3*
Others	279.6	*7.5*	299.4	*7.6*	297.6	*7.5*
World Total	**3730.7**	**100**	**3923.3**	**100**	**3993**	**100**
Grinding in Country of Origin	**1526.9**	**40.9**	**1597.8**	**40.7**	**1684.2**	**42.2**

Note: * estimates; ** forecasts. Totals may differ from sum of constituents due to rounding.
Source: ICCO *QBCS* 38 (1), Cocoa year 2011/12.

[21] Reuters <http://www.reuters.com/assets/print?aid=USL2N0N71DT20140415> and <http://uk.reuters.com/article/2013/10/02/uk-cargill-cocoa-adm-idUKBRE99102220131002>.
[22] Europe's share declined from 43% to 36% during the period 2002–11, Africa's share increased from 14% to 18%, while the share of Asia and Oceania rose from 16% to 20% (Icco, 2012).

explain the development of cocoa capacity grinding in West Africa. The increase of grinding in Malaysia and Indonesia is associated with the increase in incomes, and in the consumption of chocolate in Asia.

ADM, Cargill, and Barry Callebaut, the leading cocoa processors, operate in Europe (Netherlands, France, Germany, and the UK), but also in Asia, the Americas (Brazil), and in West Africa (Côte d'Ivoire, Cameroon, and Ghana).

The Price of Semi-Processed Products

According to Fold (2002), the extreme concentration of the upstream activities in the cocoa industry results from economies of scale and economies of scope in cocoa trading and processing.[23] The economies of scale—a reduction in the unit production cost associated with larger quantities—come from fixed costs which constitute a barrier to entry. The economies of scope arise from the joint production of a range of goods using the same technology. The diversification of activities allows the spreading of the fixed costs over a larger number of products and the reduction of the unit cost.

The extension of ADM and Cargill activities, from cereals to cocoa trading, can be seen as evidence of economies of scope in transport, infrastructure, and logistics. The existence of natural barriers to entry into cocoa processing (capital cost, R&D costs, etc.) is more debatable. For instance, the European Commission authorized the merger of Barry and Callebaut in 1996, considering that the market was open to potential new entrants. In contrast, the three leading processors may benefit from economies of agglomeration. The main factories of ADM, Cargill, and Barry Callebaut are located in the Netherlands close to those of the chocolate manufacturers, so transport and processing costs are reduced.[24]

Concentration in the cocoa-processing industry, as far as economies of scale, scope, and agglomeration can be exploited, is cost-efficient and may benefit consumers through lower prices. The relative transparency in the price setting of some of the intermediate products (cocoa butter and cocoa powder) tends to support the hypothesis of well-functioning markets. However, the price of couverture chocolate, the main output from the processing stage, is not known.

The price of cocoa butter and cocoa powder are set by multiplying cocoa futures in London or New York by a ratio.[25] The ratios and futures usually move in opposite directions. Traditionally, the butter ratio has been higher than the powder ratio, but the relationship between the cocoa butter ratio and the cocoa powder ratio fluctuates, reflecting changes in consumption patterns. For instance, the powder ratio rose from 0.5 to 2 during the period 2008–12, due to the increasing

---

[23] See also Unctad (2008).

[24] The geographic proximity of the cocoa processors with the chocolate manufacturers allows the cocoa butter in liquid form (in tanks) to be transported on a just-in-time basis. Transport over longer distances requires cooling the product before transport, then reheating before use by the chocolate manufacturer (Fold, 2001, 2002).

[25] Cocoa beans are traded on the NYSE Euronext and the Intercontinental Exchange (ICE).

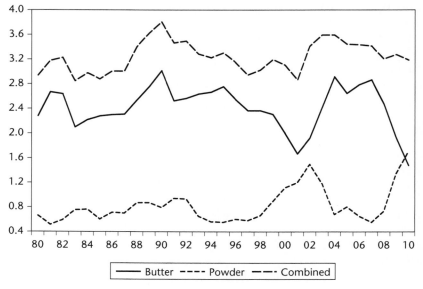

Figure 17.3 Cocoa ratios
Source: ICCO.

demand for powder in emerging countries, particularly in Asia. During the same period, the butter ratio fell from 3 to 1 (Icco, 2012) (see Figure 17.3).

The butter ratio varies according to the origin and the reputation of the grinder. For instance, in June 2014, the price of cocoa butter in Asia was 2.5 times the cocoa futures price in London. In the USA, it was around 2.7 times the ICE Futures U.S. cocoa contract, and in Europe it was around 2.6 times the London contract. The profitability of cocoa grinding depends on the 'combined cocoa ratio', which is given by the sum of the butter and powder ratios.[26] Large and well-known grinders can, to some extent, raise butter prices to compensate for reductions in powder prices in order to keep the combined ratio stable (see Table 17.6).[27]

As expected, the correlation between the butter ratio and the price of cocoa beans is negative (-0.41) over the 1980–2010 period. The correlation between the combined ratio and the price of beans is negative but weak (-0.342). This correlation was stronger in 1980–90 (–0.91) when world prices were low, and not significantly different from zero in 1990–2010 when cocoa prices reached a peak. This resulted in a sharp increase in the gross margins of the processors from 2002 to 2010 (Figure 17.4).[28] Because the data set is limited, it is not possible to know if this increase has been transitory or not.

---

[26] Combined cocoa ratio = (Price of cocoa butter + Price of cocoa powder)/Price of cocoa beans.
[27] Barry Callebaut website: https://www.barry-callebaut.com/about-us/faq.
[28] Calculated as the difference between the average price of butter and powder minus the price of beans.

Table 17.6 Correlation coefficients (1980–2010)

	Butter Ratio	Powder Ratio	Combined Ratio	Beans Price
Powder Ratio	−0.722	1		
	(−5.626)			
Combined Ratio	0.580	0.144	1	
	(3.833)	(0.786)		
Beans Price	−0.406	0.203	−0.342	1
	(−2.395)	(1.117)	(−1.961)	

Note: t-statistic in brackets.

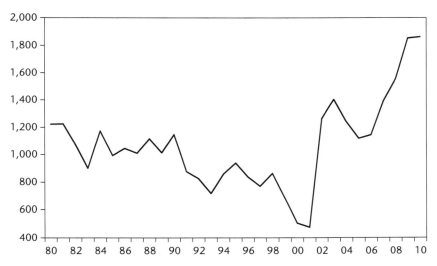

Figure 17.4 Processor gross margin (USD/MT)
Source: ICCO.

The Consumer Products Segment

The cocoa-processing sector is dominated by three firms, but their power is balanced by the power of chocolate manufacturers. The chocolate industry has become highly concentrated, which has led Fold (2002) to consider that the cocoa value chain is 'bipolar'. The mechanisms of the price pass-through from the world cocoa market to the chocolate retail market in France are symptomatic of non-competitive behaviour in the cocoa–chocolate chain.

The Top Ten Chocolate Manufacturers

Candy Industry magazine publishes an annual list of the hundred leading manufacturers of candy and chocolate products in the world. They are ranked according to net sales. The biggest five confectionery companies which manufacture some

Table 17.7 Top 10 global confectionery companies by net confectionery sales value in 2013

	Company	US$ Millions	Share in %	Cumulative Share %
1	Mars Inc. (USA)	17,640	13.3	13.3
2	Mondelēz International Inc. (USA)	14,862	11.2	24.4
3	Nestlé SA (Switzerland)	11,760	8.8	33.3
4	Meiji Holdings Co Ltd (Japan)	11,742*	8.8	42.1
5	Ferrero Group (Italy)	10,900	8.2	50.3
6	Hershey Foods Corp (USA)	7,043	5.3	55.6
7	Arcor (Argentina)	3,700	2.8	58.4
8	Lindt & Sprüngli AG (Switzerland)	3,149	2.4	60.7
9	Ezaki Glico Co Ltd (Japan)	3,018*	2.3	63.0
10	Yildiz Holding (Turkey)	2,500	1.9	64.9

Note: *Data include production of non-confectionery items.

Source: Candy Industry, January 2014. The total turnover of the hundred companies is estimated at $133 billion.

form of chocolate represented more than 50 per cent of the total confectionery sales value in 2013.[29] These companies are: the Americans Mars Inc. and Mondelēz International, the Swiss Nestlé, the Japanese Meiji, and the Italian Ferrero. Hershey (USA) and Lindt & Sprüngli (Switzerland) come respectively in sixth and eighth positions (Table 17.7).

The market structure has not significantly changed during the last five years. In 2008, six manufacturers, which were in the 2013 top ten, already dominated the world market for chocolate products: Mars (15 per cent), Nestlé (12.5 per cent), Kraft Foods (8.1 per cent), Cadbury Schweppes (7.2 per cent), Hershey (7.2 per cent), and Ferrero (7.2 per cent). With Lindt & Sprüngli (3.6 per cent), they controlled more than 60 per cent of the market for finished chocolate products.

Since 2008, two major events are worth noting: the acquisition of Cadbury by Kraft Foods in 2010, and the creation of Mondelēz International Inc. by Kraft Foods. In 2012, Kraft Foods separated its businesses into two public entities—Mondelēz International Inc., which handles the global snacks business, including confectionery and gum, and Kraft Foods Group Inc., which handles the North American grocery business.

The degree of concentration of the chocolate market can be much higher at the regional or national level. This is the case for Europe, and especially for the UK where Cadbury, Mars, and Nestlé controlled 75 per cent to 80 per cent of the chocolate confectionery market in 2008 (Unctad, 2008). In France, five manufacturers controlled about 70 per cent of the market in 2013: Ferrero (23.4 per cent), Mondelēz (18.3 per cent), Lindt & Sprüngli (15.2 per cent), Nestlé (12.8 per cent), and Mars (10.2 per cent).[30]

Except for Lindt & Sprüngli and Ferrero, whose core activity is the production of high-quality consumer chocolate, the other large-scale manufacturers have progressively withdrawn from the grinding sector. This is the case, for instance, for

[29] Confectionery splits into chocolate, gum, and sweets.

[30] LSA N° 2286. <http://www.lsa-conso.fr/le-chocolat-lutte-contre-la-depression,146966>.

Nestlé and Hershey, which both outsourced the production of semi-finished cocoa products and industrial chocolate to the large-scale cocoa processors.

The concentration in the manufacture of chocolate products is not as high as in cocoa processing, but market segmentation is much more important. While the semi-finished cocoa products are relatively homogeneous, the chocolate manufacturers try to increase their profits by differentiating their products. The brand is an essential element in product differentiation and market segmentation that leads to monopolistic competition.[31] Product innovation is another differentiation strategy which plays an extremely important role in the mature markets of the developed countries. In France, innovation accounts for most of the chocolate market growth.[32]

It should also be noted that the distribution sector in France is highly concentrated. Hypermarkets and supermarkets sell the quasi-totality (85 per cent) of the chocolate tablets consumed in France.[33] In the hypermarket and supermarket sector, concentration has also increased during the last decade.

The Retail Price of a Chocolate Tablet in France

Assessing the consequences for the consumer of the changes in the chocolate industry over recent decades is a difficult task. One of the reasons relates to the changing nature of the final goods due to a continuous process of product innovations, and investment in packaging and marketing. The price of the raw material, cocoa beans, only represents a small and decreasing part in the final product value.

Nevertheless, an original data series allows us to trace the changes in the retail price of a homogenous tablet of dark chocolate which has been sold on the French market since 1949. It is a 100g bar of dark chocolate with unchanged characteristics.[34] The tablet contains a minimum of 43 per cent of cocoa, equivalent to 38g of liquor and 5g of cocoa butter. The equivalent of a tablet of 100g of chocolate in cocoa beans is 54.7g.[35] In France tablets are the leading segment in chocolate confectionery, with a 33 per cent market share.[36] Tablet is the chocolate preferred by 97 per cent of French people.[37]

---

[31] The top five chocolate manufacturers own the most famous brands of chocolate products. For instance, Nestlé's portfolio of brands includes: Aero, Butterfinger, Cailler, Crunch, KitKat, Orion, Smarties, Toil House, Wonka. Mars's portfolio encompasses: M&M's, Snickers, Dove, Mars, Twix, Musketeers, Bounty, Maltesers, Celebrations, Balisto, Combos, Revels, Kudos, Tracker, Goodness Knows, Milky Way, Galaxy, American Heritage, Amicelli. Mondelēz International manages: Alpen Gold, Cadbury, Côte d'Or, Kent, Lacta, Marabou, Mikado, Milka, Poulain, Suchard, Toblerone. Ferrero: Ferrero Rocher, Raffaello, Mon Chéri, Nutella, Kinder.

[32] © 2014 William Reed Business Media SAS. <http://www.confectionerynews.com/ Manufacturers/Mondelez-to-innovate-in-premium-French-chocolate-market>.

[33] Source: Syndicat du Chocolat, May 2013.

[34] Source: INSEE, France.

[35] Grinding 100kg of cocoa beans yields approximately 80kg of cocoa liquor and 17kg of residues (husks, shells, skins). A total of 100kg of liquor yields approximately 47kg of butter and 53kg of powder (Kox, 2000).

[36] Market share of the different products in the French market: tablets (33%), toffees (19%), spreads (19%), bars (11%), cocoa powder (7%). Source: Syndicat du Chocolat, *Le Figaro*, October 2013.

[37] <http://www.retailmenot.fr/2013/10/etude-les-francais-et-le-chocolat/>.

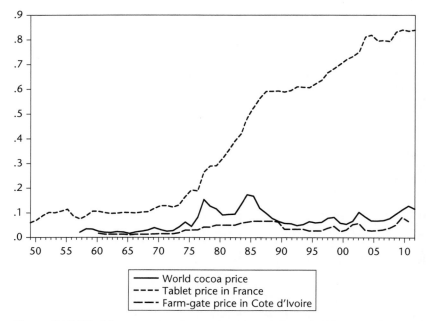

Figure 17.5 World cocoa price, farm-gate price, and retail tablet price (euros)

The share of the cocoa bean value in the tablet price fell from approximately 23 per cent in the period 1960–70, to 10 per cent in the period 2000–11;[38] most of the downfall took place in the 1980s. The Ivorian producer share in the tablet price also fell dramatically from approximately 12 per cent during the period 1960–70, to 5.6 per cent in the period 2000–11 (Figure 17.5).

An equivalent drop in the share received by cocoa producers was observed by Gilbert (2006) over the period 1976–85 when comparing the chocolate price in the UK market and the cocoa producer price in different origin countries. For the author, this was a consequence of the increase in the cost of other raw materials (sugar and milk), and processing, marketing, and distribution costs.

Araujo Bonjean and Brun (2008) considered an alternative explanation for the drop in producer share. They developed a game theory model in which the main cocoa producer, the Côte d'Ivoire, and the chocolate manufacturers compete for price leadership. The econometric estimates of a system of price equations showed a structural break in model parameters at the end of 1980s, which they took as evidence of a reversal in price leadership. The authors concluded that concentration in the chocolate industry during the 1980s resulted in a transfer of the price leadership from Côte d'Ivoire to the chocolate companies.

---

[38] The world price of cocoa beans is taken as the average of London and New York Stock Exchange prices. Source: International Financial Statistics of the IMF.

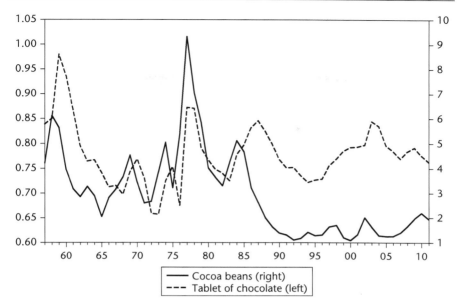

Figure 17.6 Real price of cocoa beans (euros/kg) and tablet (euros/100g)

Note: Prices are expressed in constant euros (100 = 1990). Deflator is the consumer price index (CPI) in France.

Source: INSEE and IMF.

Other elements supporting the market power hypothesis can be found when looking more closely at the relative evolution of the world price of cocoa beans and the retail price of the chocolate tablet in the French market (Figure 17.6). First, it can be seen that cocoa price fluctuations are passed on to the price of the chocolate bar with a delay of roughly one year. Second, positive shocks in the cocoa price appear to be fully transmitted to the retail chocolate price, particularly as observed during the 1970s. By contrast, cocoa price decreases are passed on to the chocolate price in a lesser way or are not transmitted at all. For instance, the cocoa price experienced a sharp fall during the second half of the 1980s which was not fully transmitted to the chocolate price. Moreover, from 1985 until the end of the 1990s, the cocoa price experienced a long phase of decline while, during the same period, the chocolate price did not change much.

These features of the price movements within the cocoa–chocolate chain suggest the existence of important lags and asymmetries in price transmission, with increases in the price of the raw material being more fully transmitted to the output price than equivalent decreases. Such phenomena have been observed in other sectors, particularly in the oil sector (see, for instance, Chen et al., 2005), and have given rise to a vast empirical literature. In this literature, asymmetry in the transmission of positive and negative shocks between the input and the output price is taken as evidence of imperfect competition in the processing/distribution chain. Asymmetry in the transmission of large and small shocks is imputed to adjustment costs referred to as 'menu costs' in the packaging and distribution stage of the marketing process (e.g. Peltzman, 2000; Meyer and von Cramon Taubadel, 2004). Fixed adjustment costs are expected to create a price band inside which the retail price does not adjust to fluctuations in the raw material price as the adjustment cost would exceed the benefit. For instance, the cost of reprinting price lists or catalogues may lead to late and asymmetric adjustment of prices. As a consequence, processors and/or distributors respond to 'small' input price fluctuations by increasing or reducing their margins. The output price will adjust only if the fluctuations in the input price exceed a critical level.

Looking for Asymmetry in the Transmission of the Cocoa to the Chocolate Price

Due to lack of data we cannot analyse the relationships between the price of the chocolate tablet and that of the semi-finished products (liquor, butter, and industrial chocolate). Thus, we examine the relationship between the world cocoa bean price and the price of the tablet of chocolate in France, considering implicitly the fact that cocoa processors, chocolate manufacturers, and distributors constitute a sole intermediary.[39]

The actual chocolate price Pc_t is allowed to deviate from its value justified by the cocoa price due to inertia in the adjustment process. The relationship between P^*c_t, the chocolate price that would correspond to the level of the cocoa price, and the bean price is given by:

$$Pc_t^* = \alpha_0 + \alpha_1 Pb_t + \mu_t$$

Pb_t is the cocoa bean price; P^*c_t is also called the justified value or target price; μ_t is a white noise.

The discrepancies between the justified value of chocolate price and its previous actual value are corrected according to:[40]

$$Pc_t - Pc_{t-1} = \lambda(Pc_t^* - Pc_{t-1}) \quad \text{with} \quad 0 \leq \lambda \leq 1$$

λ measures the speed of adjustment of the chocolate price. When $\lambda = 1$, adjustment is instantaneous; when $\lambda = 0$, there is no adjustment.

The short-run dynamic of the chocolate price is given by:

$$\Delta Pc_t = \lambda(Pc_{t-1} - \alpha_1 Pb_{t-1} - \alpha_0) + \lambda\alpha_1 \Delta Pb_t + e_t$$

The right term in parenthesis is referred to as the error correction term (*ect*). It measures the discrepancy between the previous chocolate price and its previous justified value.[41]

---

[39] See Araujo Bonjean and Brun (2014) for a detailed presentation of the econometric analysis and results.

[40] This is the well-known partial adjustment model; see, for instance, Hendry (1995).

[41] e_t is a stochastic process. Δ is the difference operator.

In case of symmetric adjustment, the adjustment speed (λ) is constant. In the asymmetric scenario, the adjustment speed varies according to the size and the sign of the error correction term. When the *ect* is large and positive (higher than τ_2), the chocolate price is above its value justified by the level of the cocoa bean price, and the speed of adjustment is expected to be low. Conversely, when the *ect* is large and negative (lower than τ_1), the chocolate price is below its justified value, and the speed of adjustment is expected to be large. When $\tau_1 \leq ect \leq \tau_2$ the discrepancy is small and no adjustment is expected to take place.

Araujo Bonjean and Brun (2014) estimated the adjustment speed on a sample of annual price series covering the period 1949–2011. According to the results, summarized in Figure 17.7, the historical booms in the cocoa price recorded in 1974, 1977, and 1984 were transmitted rapidly to the chocolate consumer (red periods). Between the 1977 and 1984 booms, the discrepancy between the chocolate price and the value corresponding to the level of the cocoa price remained at a relatively low level; as a consequence, prices did not adjust despite the 1980 fall in the cocoa price. The phase of sharp and prolonged reduction in world cocoa prices that started in 1986 resulted in a large price disequilibrium (the chocolate price being above its justified value), that was corrected only at the end of the 1980s (black period). Over the 1990–2000 period, the chocolate consumers were fully insulated from cocoa price fluctuations. The price disequilibrium was not large enough to trigger an adjustment of the retail chocolate price. In 2000–07, the chocolate price was well above its justified value and the low cocoa price drew

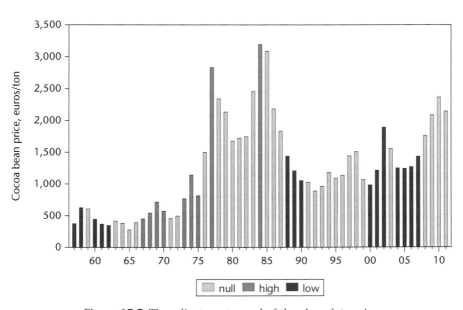

Figure 17.7 The adjustment speed of the chocolate price

down the chocolate price (black periods). The 2010 cocoa price recovery was not large enough to trigger correction in the chocolate price and was not passed on to consumers.

Further Comments and Conclusion

The analysis of the relationship between the cocoa and the retail chocolate price shows that they are unrelated over the greater part of the 1955–2011 period. The consumer price does not adjust to small positive or negative shocks in the price of cocoa beans. Moreover, the chocolate price adjusts faster to large increases in the price of the raw material than to large decreases. The consequence is that the price of chocolate quickly corrects any disequilibrium following an increase in the cocoa price, but reverts back more slowly to its justified value when the cocoa price declines.

The rigidity of the retail chocolate price may result from large adjustment costs signalling possible inefficiencies in the processing, manufacturing, and distribution of chocolate products. Cocoa price fluctuations may also be partly compensated by inverse variations in the cost of other inputs entering in the chocolate production process. Alternatively, price rigidity may reflect the price-smoothing strategy of chocolate manufacturers. Inventory management may allow firms to dampen cocoa price shocks and protect risk-adverse consumers against fluctuations in the price of the raw material. However, chocolate prices are more rigid downward than upward after an input shock, meaning that consumers bear the burden of an asymmetric price-smoothing strategy.

Another interpretation is that the asymmetry in transmission of large positive and negative shocks reflects non-competitive behaviour in the cocoa–chocolate chain. At least two main categories of intermediaries—cocoa processors and chocolate manufacturers—between the world cocoa market and the consumer, are in a position to exert market power. The first part of this chapter has shown that the chocolate industry underwent a radical transformation during the 1990s. The acquisition or the merger of the historical cocoa trading and processing leaders gave Cargill, ADM, and Barry Callebaut a dominant position in cocoa processing. They are also in leading positions for the manufacture of industrial chocolate. In the downstream segment of the chocolate chain, five multinational food companies dominate the chocolate sales in France. The bipolar structure of the chocolate industry suggests that cocoa processors are not in position to set prices, for semi-finished cocoa products and couverture, above the competitive market price. The chocolate manufacturers, engaged in a strategy of product differentiation, are more likely to set a non-competitive price for the chocolate tablet.

References

Agritrade. 2011. 'Executive Brief Update 2011: Cocoa sector', Executive briefs. Technical Centre for Agricultural and Rural Cooperation (CTA), July. <http://agritrade.cta.int/en/Agriculture/Commodities/Cocoa/Executive-Brief-Update-2011-Cocoa-sector>.

Agritrade. 2012. 'Côte d'Ivoire's cocoa sector reforms 2011–2012'. Special Report, Technical Centre for Agricultural and Rural Cooperation (CTA), December. <http://agritrade.cta.int/en/Agriculture/Commodities/Cocoa/Special-report-Cote-d-Ivoire-s-cocoa-sector-reforms-2011-2012>.

Araujo Bonjean, C. and J.-F. Brun. 2008. 'Pouvoir de marché dans la filière cacao: l'hypothèse de Prébish et Singer revisitée'. *Economie et Prévision* 186: pp. 133–44.

Araujo Bonjean, C. and J.-F. Brun. 2014. 'Chocolate price fluctuations may cause depression: an analysis of price pass-through in the cocoa chain'. *Etudes et Documents* 20, CERDI. <http://www.cerdi.org/back.php/production/show/id/1608/type_production_id/1>.

Araujo Bonjean, C., G. Chambas, and J.-L. Combes. 2001. 'Echecs de marchés et pauvreté: l'exemple de la filière cacao en Côte d'Ivoire'. *Oléagineux, Corps gras Lipides (OCL)* 8 (6): pp. 577–83.

Castroviejo, M. 2009. 'Is chocolate recession proof? European chocolate industry in 2009'. Report. Rabobank's Food & Agri Research and Advisory (FAR).

Chen, L. H., M. Finney, and K. S. Lai. 2005. 'A threshold cointegration analysis of asymmetric price transmission from crude oil to gasoline prices'. *Economic Letters* 89: pp. 233–9.

Ecobank. 2014. 'Côte d'Ivoire's cocoa grinders: at the crossroads'. *Middle Africa Insight Series, Soft Commodities, Cocoa*, 29 January.

Fold, N. 2001. 'Restructuring of the European chocolate industry and its impact on cocoa production in West Africa'. *Journal of Economic Geography* 1: pp. 405–20.

Fold, N. 2002. 'Lead firms and competition in 'bi-polar' commodity chains: grinders and branders in the global cocoa–chocolate industry'. *Journal of Agrarian Change* 2 (2): pp. 228–47.

Gilbert, C. L. 2006. 'Value chain analysis and market power in commodity processing with application to the cocoa and coffee sectors', *Discussion Papers*, Università degli Studi di Trento.

Gilbert, C. L. 2009. 'Cocoa market liberalization in retrospect'. *Review of Business and Economics* 3: pp. 294–312.

Hendry, D. F. 1995. *Dynamic Econometrics*. Oxford: Oxford University Press.

ICCO (International Cocoa Organization). 2012. 'The world cocoa economy: past and present'. Executive Committee, EX/146/7, 26 July.

Kox, H. L. M. 2000. 'The market for cocoa powder'. Background paper for 'Modelling and forecasting the market for cocoa and chocolate', prepared for the Netherlands Ministry of Foreign Affairs.

Losch, B. 2000. 'Coup de cacao en Côte d'Ivoire. Économie politique d'une crise structurelle'. *Critique internationale* 9: pp. 6–14.

Losch, B. 2001. 'La libéralisation de la filière cacaoyère ivoirienne et les recompositions du marché mondial du cacao: vers la fin des pays producteurs et du marché international?' *Oléagineux, Corps gras, Lipides* 8 (6): pp. 566–76.

Meyer, J. and S. von Cramon-Taubadel. 2004. 'Asymmetric price transmission: a survey'. *Journal of Agricultural Economics* 55 (3): pp. 581–611.

Oxfam. 2008. 'Towards a sustainable cocoa chain', Oxfam International Research Report. January. <https://www.oxfam.org/en/research/towards-sustainable-cocoa-chain>.

Peltzman, S. 2000. 'Prices rise faster than they fall'. *Journal of Political Economy* 108 (3): pp. 66–502.

Ruf, F. 2009. 'Libéralisation, cycles politiques et cycles du cacao: le décalage historique Côte-d'Ivoire-Ghana'. *Cahiers Agricultures* 18(4): pp. 342–9.

UNCTAD (United Nations Conference on Trade and Development). 2008. *Cocoa Study: Industry Structures and Competition*. New York and Geneva: United Nations.

Appendix

Table 17.A1 The cocoa–chocolate chain

	**Raw material** Cocoa pods Cocoa beans	Cocoa pods—the seeds of the cocoa tree—are opened up to separate the beans from the pods. The beans are cleaned, fermented, dried, sorted, and sold by farmers or cooperatives to intermediaries or are delivered to the grinder's plant.
	**Semi-finished cocoa products** Cocoa liquor Cocoa butter Cocoa powder	Beans are crushed. Then the nibs are roasted and ground into cocoa liquor (also referred to as cocoa mass or paste). The cocoa mass is pressed to separate the butter (liquid part) from the cake (solid part). The cake will be crushed then sifted to give the cocoa powder.
	Industrial chocolate Couverture	The cocoa butter is mixed with cocoa paste (defatted or not), sugar, and flavouring (vanilla) to make dark chocolate. To obtain milk chocolate, powdered milk is added to the blending. The blend is ground to obtain a fine paste. The paste is conched to give liquid chocolate referred to as couverture. Couverture can be delivered in liquid form in heated tanks or in solid form (in blocks, sticks, or nuggets) to be further processed. The couverture is sold to the companies that make chocolate products for consumers (*chocolatiers*). Chocolatiers are the large manufacturers of leading consumer brands or artisanal producers (confectioners, bakers, pastry chefs . . .). Couverture can be customized to fit the specific needs of the chocolate maker.
	**Final chocolate products** Chocolate bars, bonbons, truffles, etc.	Couverture is tempered before being used for the fabrication of chocolate products. It can be moulded to make bonbons, truffles, and chocolate bars, or used as coating in the manufacture of confectionery, biscuits, cakes, ice cream . . . The last stage of the chocolate value chain involves packaging, marketing, and retailing.

18

Belgian Chocolate Exports

Quality and Reputation versus Increased Competition

Filip Abraham, Zuzanna Studnicka, and Jan Van Hove

Introduction

Belgian chocolate is among the best in the world: Belgium invented the praline in 1912, Belgian chocolatiers win many international awards, and Belgium is internationally known as the capital of chocolate. As a result, Belgium is the largest chocolate exporter in the world, exporting over 1 billion euros every year (United Nations, 2014). One would expect that chocolate export relationships are relatively stable: if you taste Belgian chocolate once, you will love it forever. However, despite Belgian chocolate's strong international reputation, this Belgian crown jewel is facing increased international competition (see e.g. *BBC News Magazine*, 2012) which may reduce the stability or survival of Belgian chocolate export relationships. Apart from international competition, shifts in global preferences for specific chocolate products or exporting firms' strategies may also determine how long chocolate exports continue in specific products or to specific markets.

In this chapter we use detailed firm-level data to study the characteristics and performance of Belgian chocolate exporting firms. In particular, we focus on a recent phenomenon in the international trade literature, that is, the duration of exports. This indicator measures the stability of existing export relationships. Apart from studying the evidence and determinants of export survival, this chapter is the first study looking into the characteristics and export performance of Belgian chocolate exporting firms. Thanks to access to confidential firm-level data, we are able to study the number of chocolate exporters, the share of chocolate in their total exports, and the main destination markets for Belgian chocolates. Our insights also contribute to a better understanding of the determinants of export survival of high-quality, culture-related products in general (see also recent work by Crozet et al, 2012).

The duration of trade has previously been analysed for countries as well as firms. At the country level, the seminal work by Besedeš and Prusa (2006a, 2006b) uses detailed bilateral product-level trade data in order to examine to what extent product differentiation affects the duration of US import trade. They conclude that the median duration of the US imports is extremely short—about two years. This evidence has been confirmed by Besedeš (2008) and Hess and Persson (2012) for US imports, by Nitsch (2009) for German imports, by Brenton et al. (2010) for developing countries, by Fugazza and Molina (2011) for 96 countries, by Hess and Persson (2011) for European Union (EU) imports, and by Studnicka and Van Hove (2014) for EU exports. In general, firm-level findings confirm country-level evidence: several authors find that the median survival of firms' exports is very short—only about two years (e.g. Volpe-Martincus and Carballo, 2008; Godart et al., 2011; Békés and Muraközy, 2012; Görg et al., 2012; Cadot et al., 2013; Esteve-Pérez et al., 2013; Abraham et al., 2014).

We explore the richness of our firm-level data by calculating the export duration of Belgian chocolate exporters at different levels. Four dimensions can be distinguished: (1) firm duration, that is, how many years a chocolate firm continues to export; (2) firm-product duration, that is, how long a chocolate firm continues to export a particular chocolate product; (3) firm-destination duration, that is, how long a chocolate firm continues to export (any chocolate product) to a particular destination market; and finally (4) firm-product-destination duration, that is, how long a chocolate firm exports a particular chocolate product to a particular destination market. Our approach is unique in the literature and can be regarded as a combination of previous studies' levels of analysis.[1]

Apart from providing evidence on the duration of Belgian chocolate exports, this chapter also provides evidence on the factors driving export survival. Our results indicate that the chocolate export duration is very short, but slightly longer than the export duration of other products.

Following the literature, we study the impact of various factors potentially affecting chocolate export duration. These factors control for exporting firm characteristics, product characteristics, spell characteristics, as well as destination market characteristics. Our main results can be summarized as follows. Larger exporters and larger export flows survive longer. Geographical diversification has a positive impact on chocolate export duration, whereas product diversification has a negative impact. Moreover, Belgian chocolate exports last longer if directed to EU27 countries. Finally, international competition does not seem to hurt Belgian chocolate exporters. By contrast, more competition may signal a general appetite for chocolates in the market which helps Belgian chocolate exporters.

The remainder of this chapter is organized as follows. The next section, 'Data', describes our data. Then, we present the characteristics of Belgian chocolate exporters, and describe the main destination markets. Afterwards, we present the

---

[1] Among firm-level duration studies Volpe-Martincus and Carballo (2008) analyse trade survival at the firm level, Görg et al. (2012) at the firm-product level, Esteve-Pérez et al. (2013) at the firm-destination level.

calculation and evidence on trade duration and discuss the determinants of Belgian chocolate export survival. The final section concludes.

Data

We construct a unique data set using several data sets covering the period 1998–2010. Our principal source of data is a confidential data set provided by the National Bank of Belgium (NBB) (NBB, 2014) covering bilateral foreign trade flows by Belgian firms. These data include the value, volume, and units of exports at the combined nomenclature (CN) 8-digit level. Hence, these data allow us to study evolutions in firm-level trade patterns at detailed product levels, distinguishing between geographical destinations.

In general, in the CN classification, some product categories may change every year. However, as far as chocolate is concerned, its categories did not change during the studied period.[2]

We define as chocolate category all products belonging to the HS4 1806 code, that is, 'chocolate and other food preparation containing cocoa', as well as CN8 code 17049030, that is, 'white chocolate'.[3] Hence, in total we consider 22 different chocolate products. Our final data set includes 1403 Belgian chocolate exporting firms. In our analysis we will also compare the export duration of these chocolate exporters with the export duration of 80,153 Belgian non-chocolate exporters.

The rest of the data comes from various sources. Export destination characteristics are derived from the gravity data provided by Centre d'Études Prospectives et d'Informations Internationales (CEPII) (CEPII, 2014). Imports data come from the BACI (Gaulier and Zignago, 2010) data set. The BACI data is developed by CEPII using the United Nations (UN) Comtrade database. The data on gross domestic product (GDP) come from the World Development Indicators (World Bank, 2014) and the International Monetary Fund (IMF) World Economic Outlook (IMF, 2014).

Characteristics of Belgian Chocolate Exporters

Most studies using firm-level data emphasize several characteristics of firms involved in export activities. First of all, only a small fraction of firms exports and only a small fraction of this fraction account for the majority of aggregated trade in terms of the number of products exported and the value of exports (see e.g. Bernard and Jensen, 1999; Mayer et al., 2007). This means that a large proportion of firms export only one product to one destination.[4] These findings confirm the

---

[2] The fact that the CN classification is stable for chocolate products may already indicate a certain stability in chocolate exports too.

[3] See Table 18.A1 in Appendix 18.B for a detailed list of all CN8 codes.

[4] For France, according to Mayer and colleagues (2007), 30 per cent of firms export only one product to only one market, while 10 per cent of firms export more than ten products to more than ten markets.

theoretical predictions of Melitz (2003) that exporters are more productive than non-exporters. According to Mayer et al. (2007), exporting firms are 'superstars': they pay higher wages, they have higher value added and skill and capital intensities.

As far as Belgian firms are concerned, Abraham and Van Hove (2010) confirm the results of Mayer et al. (2007). They find that many Belgian exporters are single-variety firms,[5] and therefore export only one product to one destination. However, their number decreases, during the period 1998 and 2006 because of expanding product portfolios, indicating that Belgian firms become multi-variety firms. According to Muûls and Pisu (2009), Belgian importing firms have similar characteristics to exporting firms, since imports are also concentrated among a few, more productive firms. This means that the number of trading firms decreases with the number of export destinations or import origins. The same is true if one considers the number of products traded.

In addition, Bernard et al. (2012) find that more than three quarters of exported products, and more than one quarter of total exports by Belgian exporters, are goods that were produced by firms other than the exporting firm. Hence, exports are often taken care of by distributors or export-specialized firms.

We now check to what extent these general features hold for Belgian chocolate exporters. Table 18.1 presents some features of Belgian chocolate exporters. First, during the period 1998–2010, the average number of firms exporting at least one

Table 18.1 Characteristics of Belgian firms exporting chocolate

Year	No. of Firms	No. of Chocolate-Only Exporters	No. of Chocolate Products by Firm	Average No. of All Products by Firm	Average Ratio of Chocolate Exports to Total Exports
1998	427	72	2.7	60.8	0.4
1999	425	73	2.8	68.5	0.38
2000	446	78	2.9	66.1	0.4
2001	447	93	3	69.6	0.42
2002	460	75	3	76.8	0.38
2003	467	87	3	77.3	0.39
2004	469	81	3.1	80.1	0.37
2005	461	73	3.2	78.9	0.37
2006	407	99	3.1	79.1	0.44
2007	405	98	3.2	89.1	0.42
2008	480	95	3.1	79.3	0.4
2009	442	88	3.3	91.3	0.4
2010	466	91	3.3	90.7	0.4

Source: Own calculations based on NBB (2014).

---

[5] We define variety as the number of products exported multiplied by the number of destination markets.

chocolate product to at least one destination per year was 447. The average number of chocolate products exported by a firm was 3.1 and the highest number of chocolate products exported by a firm was 21 (out of maximum 22 different chocolate products). Although the number of chocolate products exported by Belgian firms was relatively small, this number represents a large share of the firms' total export value (on average 44 per cent of firms' total export values). Secondly, contrary to the overall evolution of Belgian exporters described in Abraham and Van Hove (2010), the number of single-variety exporters in the chocolate sector is quite stable and smaller than in the total population of Belgian firms (around 10 per cent of firms). An average firm exports all products to 13.8 destination markets, and chocolate to 5.8 destinations. This implies that a Belgian firm exports chocolate, on average, to over 60 per cent of its total destination markets.

From this analysis we can conclude that even if Belgian chocolate exporters do not export only chocolate products, chocolate generates almost 50 per cent of their value of exports and is exported to most of the destination markets they serve. Hence, one can say that Belgian chocolate exports are not characterized by substantial product differentiation. Moreover, the geographical diversification in exports is also limited compared to other Belgian exporters. Finally and interestingly, only a very small fraction of chocolate exporters exported only chocolate products. Most of them exported a wide range of products—77.6 on average, up to 4103 products. Hence, chocolate exports originate from firms producing and exporting a large variety of goods. Clearly, chocolate exporters are often involved in other economic activities, most often activities which are likely to be directly related to chocolate production, mainly in the food sector (25 per cent of the total variety and 68 per cent of total exports by firms on average), the machinery sector (12 per cent of the total variety and 25 per cent of total exports by firms on average), and the chemical sector (11 per cent of the total variety 41 per cent of exports by firms on average). The largest chocolate exporting firms tend to focus more exclusively on chocolate exports. Around 90 per cent of exports of the top five exporters consist of chocolate exports. Even the remaining part of their exports consists of products often related to chocolate, for example, machinery for the industrial preparation or manufacture of food or drinks. However, the largest chocolate-only exporting firms are usually ranked below the tenth position and they constitute around 20 per cent of chocolate exporters.

Export Destinations

As far as the destination markets are concerned, Figure 18.1 shows the value of exports by destination, while Figure 18.2 concentrates on the extra-European Union (EU) chocolate exports by destination. Figure 18.1 shows that the main importers of Belgian chocolate are: France, Germany, the Netherlands, the UK, Italy, and the USA, and that the ranking of the main export destinations is stable over time.

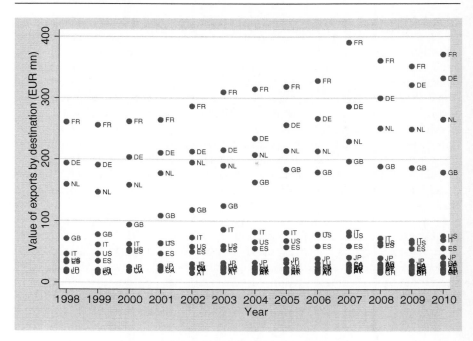

Figure 18.1 Value of exports by destination

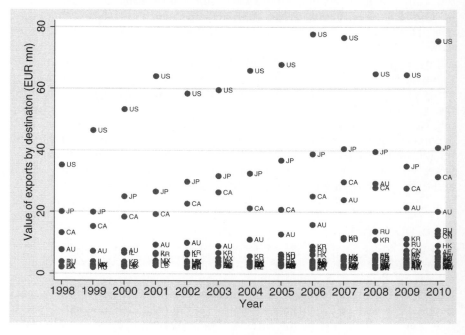

Figure 18.2 Value of exports by destination, excluding Europe

Most firms start exporting to rather close destinations. Thus, most of the time products are introduced in contiguous markets, that is, Luxembourg, France, Germany, and the Netherlands. However, firms also choose the USA, Canada, and Japan to introduce new products. In addition, in the last three years of our sample, we can see a growing importance of China and Russia as new destinations. This tendency, however, does not concern other emerging markets. To give a quantitative example: in 1999 only 12 firms exported chocolate products to China and 22 to Russia. In 2010, 65 firms exported to China and 55 to Russia. By way of comparison, the number of firms exporting to France and to the Netherlands decreased respectively from 167 in 1999 to 158 in 2010, and from 165 in 1999 to 153 in 2010.

Calculation and Evidence of Chocolate Export Duration

In this section we first present the methodology of calculating the duration of trade. In what follows we discuss the evidence on the duration of Belgian chocolate exports.

Calculation of Export Duration

We calculate the duration of trade as the number of years a particular trade relation was active. We do it at four different levels: firm level, firm-product level, firm-destination level and firm-product-destination level. At the firm level, the duration of trade refers to the time a firm was engaged in exporting activity. At the firm-product level, it refers to the time a firm was exporting a particular chocolate product. At the firm-destination level, the duration of trade can be defined as the time a firm was exporting to a particular destination. Finally, the last level, that is, the firm-product-destination level takes into account all possible dimensions and refers to the time a firm was exporting a particular chocolate product to a particular destination.

As we study a period of 13 years and control for left censoring, the maximal length of a trade relationship is 12.[6] Some trade relationships might be stopped and re-established after a break. However, the majority of them take place over a single time span (a so-called 'spell'). We take multiple spells into account by calculating the duration of each of them separately. Hence, the maximum number of spells is six for a relationship that stopped every other year and experienced six stops. Table 18.2 presents the number of spells for each of the four levels of analysis, with and without taking into account the problem of left-censored observations (respectively lower and upper part of the table). This table shows that the majority of chocolate export spells takes place only once. However, a substantial number of spells that are stopped are restarted later on.

---

[6] See Appendix 18.A for methodological details.

Table 18.2 Number of spells

	1998–2010		
	No. of spells	No. of single spells	No. of multiple spells
Firm	1019	731	288
Firm-product	5769	3795	1974
Firm-destination	21,044	12,518	8526
Firm-product-destination	27,636	17,515	10,121
	1999–2010		
	No. of spells	No. of single spells	No. of multiple spells
Firm	521	355	166
Firm-product	4248	2885	1363
Firm-destination	13,441	8411	5030
Firm-product-destination	21,323	14,298	7025

Source: Own calculations based on NBB (2014).

Evidence of Chocolate Export Duration

During the period 1998–2010, 447 firms on average exported chocolate each year. However, this does not imply that these were the same firms all the time. To the contrary, within the whole period, the total number of chocolate exporting firms was 1403. That means that each year new firms started while other firms stopped exporting chocolate. We first aim to study evidence of the duration of Belgian chocolate exports.[7]

Figure 18.3 presents the Kaplan–Meier estimators of the survival functions for firms exporting chocolate as well as other exporting firms, distinguishing between the four different levels mentioned.[8]

It shows that the fraction of surviving firms gets smaller period by period, but the conditional probability of failure decreases year by year. This finding indicates that longer trade relationships are more likely to continue.

From the figure it is obvious that most trade spells cease within the first two years at each of the four levels, especially at the firm-product and firm-destination levels. The decline is the fastest in the first year. After the first year, around 75 per cent of firms continue exporting. However, only 50 per cent of chocolate products and 60 per cent of destinations survive the first year. This means that establishing a trade relationship in a market might be easier than keeping this relationship active for more than just a few years. This finding suggests also that importers switch to other products or switch to other supplying firms, rather than stop importing chocolate from Belgian firms.

As far as the length of survival is concerned, it depends on the level of analysis and the needs to take into account multiple spells and left censoring. Table 18.3

---

[7] At the two levels including the product dimension, we compare chocolate products with other products, whereas at the two levels excluding the product dimension, we compare chocolate exporters with other exporters.

[8] See Appendix 18.A for more details.

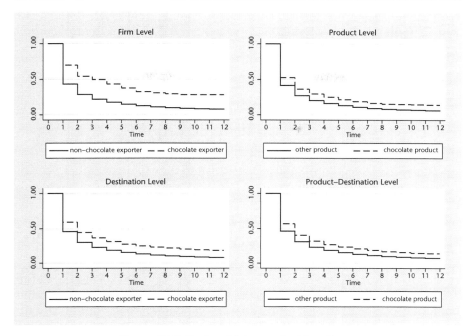

Figure 18.3 Kaplan–Meier survival functions

Table 18.3 Average length of trade spells

| | 1998–2010 | | | |
| | Single Spells | | Multiple Spells | |
	Chocolate	Non-chocolate	Chocolate	Non-chocolate
Firm	6.8	6.7	3.3	2.1
Firm-product	3.5	2.4	2.3	2.0
Firm-destination	4.7	3.1	2.8	2.3
Firm-product-destination	3.4	2.3	2.3	2.0

| | 1999–2010 | | | |
| | Single Spells | | Multiple Spells | |
	Chocolate	Non-chocolate	Chocolate	Non-chocolate
Firm	3.8	2.4	2.5	1.4
Firm-product	2.5	1.9	2.0	1.8
Firm-destination	2.9	2.2	1.8	2.0
Firm-product-destination	2.5	2.0	1.6	1.8

Source: Own calculations based on NBB (2014).

presents the averages of survival at each level, distinguishing between multiple and single spells for the periods 1998–2010 and 1999–2010. From this table we can conclude that (with the exception of multiple spells at the firm-destination and firm-product-destination levels for 1999–2010) chocolate exporters and chocolate products survive longer than other firms and products. This confirms our starting point that high-quality goods have a different duration pattern and that they are more stable than other export relationships.

Determinants of Chocolate Export Duration

In this section we study which factors drive the duration of Belgian chocolate exports. We estimate a complementary log-log model (cloglog)[9] for each of the four dimensions mentioned. Our explanatory variables can be divided into four groups, that is, firm characteristics, destination market characteristics, product characteristics, and spell characteristics.

As far as firm characteristics are concerned, we control for the initial size of exports by each firm (see e.g. Volpe-Martincus and Carballo, 2008; Esteve-Pérez et al., 2013), the initial number of products exported relative to the total possible number of CN8 lines by each firm (initial firm-product diversification),[10] and the initial number of destinations relative to the total number of possible destinations by each firm (initial firm-geographic diversification).

We do that because larger, multi-product, and more geographically diversified suppliers might be less sensitive to changing market conditions and entry costs. Moreover, according to Volpe-Martincus and Carballo (2008), small initial export size can be the consequence of limits from both the supply and the demand side, like imperfections in capital markets. We want to see which of these three characteristics are more important for firm survival. These variables are common to all four levels.

As far as destination market characteristics are concerned, we study the impact of various possible driving forces. First, we add traditional gravity model controls (see e.g. Chaney, 2008). The gravity model is a very popular tool for empirical trade analysis that explains bilateral trade flows by the size of the trading partners (proxied by GDPs), the distance between them (having a negative effect), and several other geographic features or policy aspects of any bilateral trade relationship. As these factors affect the value of trade between countries, they are also likely to affect the duration of these trade flows (see e.g. Besedeš and Prusa, 2006a, 2006b). More precisely, we include the GDP of the destination country, the distance (in km) between Brussels and the importer country's capital city, and various variables indicating contiguity (i.e. controlling for potential border effects), the existence of bilateral and multilateral trade agreements, EU membership of the destination market, and a common language between Belgium and its

---

[9] See Appendix 18.A for details.
[10] We use relative measures to take into account the fact that the number of possible products exported is much larger than the number of possible destinations.

trading partner (Dutch, French, German). We also control for the initial value of the export relationship in a destination to account for the initial level of confidence the trading partners originally had in the sustainability of this relationship (Brenton et al., 2010) and to check the finding by Besedeš (2008) that trade relations starting large last longer.

Secondly, apart from these gravity model factors, we control for the level of international competition Belgian chocolate exporters face on each market (see e.g. Mayer et al., 2014). We proxy this level by the value of chocolate imports from other countries (excluding Belgium). International competition may affect chocolate export duration in two ways. On the one hand, countries importing a large amount of chocolate may also import more chocolate from Belgium because of a strong preference for chocolate. On the other hand, if international competition is tougher, Belgian firms may find it more difficult to compete with other exporters.

Finally, we control for the relative number of products exported to this destination (product diversification by destination). The intuition behind this is that firms export fewer products to markets with high entry costs. If those products are complementary to each other, exporting a larger number of products may increase the survival of each individual product. If products are not complementary, however, similar to the prediction of Eckel and Neary (2010) and Mayer and colleagues (2014), a firm will focus on its core competence, and hence reduce its product scope.

Product characteristics are taken into account in the specifications, including the product dimension (see e.g. Görg et al., 2012). First, we test for the impact of higher quality on exports. Following the trade literature, we proxy the quality of exported chocolate by relative export unit values (RUV). This variable measures the export price of one unit of exported chocolate product relative to the average unit price of the same product across all firms in a given year. Higher export unit values are associated with higher quality, as higher quality products can be priced higher in the market. Secondly, we include the initial value of trade by product to see whether products with higher initial transaction values survive longer. Finally, we also include the relative number of destinations by product (geographic diversification by product) to control for the fixed costs of exporting a particular product to an additional destination.

As far as spell characteristics are concerned, we control for the length of the current spell, since there might be a negative length dependence (see e.g. Hess and Persson, 2011) between the probability of stopping a spell and its length, arising from factors such as sunk costs, learning by exporting, and so on. We present our results in Table 18.4.

Coefficients in both tables represent hazard ratios. These should be interpreted as follows: a coefficient greater (smaller) than one implies that the associated factor increases (lowers) the hazard rate and hence the factor has a negative (positive) effect on export duration, whereas a coefficient equal to one should be interpreted as the factor not affecting the hazard rate.

We obtained the following findings. First, in line with Volpe-Martincus and Carballo (2008) and Esteve-Pérez and colleagues (2013), size appears to matter for chocolate export duration. Firms with initially larger total exports survive longer.

Table 18.4 Estimations results

	(Firm-Level)	(Product-Level)	(Destination-Level)	(Product and Dest. Level)
Initial exports	0.8143***	0.9365***	0.9309***	1.0590***
	(0.0358)	(0.0151)	(0.0091)	(0.0108)
Initial firm-product diversification	1.1150*	0.8020***	1.2162***	1.1548***
	(0.0734)	(0.017)	(0.0141)	(0.0155)
Initial firm-geo. diversification	0.7632**	1.2914***	0.8090***	1.0879***
	(0.0956)	(0.0381)	(0.0182)	(0.0217)
Initial exports by product		0.9134***		0.9687***
		(0.0115)		(0.0104)
Geo. diversification by product		0.3367***		0.5689***
		(0.0183)		(0.0104)
Quality		1.0547		0.9926
		(0.0341)		(0.0161)
Initial exports by dest.			0.9257***	0.9042***
			(0.0074)	(0.0067)
Product diversification by dest.			0.5939***	0.7753***
			(0.0107)	(0.0124)
Chocolate imports			0.9193***	0.9302***
			(0.0151)	(0.0165)
Distance			1.0321	1.0103
			(0.0265)	(0.0200)
GDP dest.			0.9751*	0.9956
			(0.0131)	(0.0133)
EU27 dummy			0.9141*	0.7455***
			(0.0449)	(0.0306)
Contiguity dummy			1.5436***	1.0748
			(0.1231)	(0.055)
Common language dummy			0.8958***	0.9758
			(0.0380)	(0.0360)
WTO membership dummy			0.8975**	0.9843
			(0.0422)	(0.0491)
RTA membership dummy			0.9696	1.0663
			(0.0450)	(0.0442)
ln spell length	0.5297***	0.7437***	0.6182***	0.7062***
	(0.0694)	(0.0475)	(0.0184)	(0.0229)
Constant	1.667	0.0072***	0.1986***	0.1651***
	(1.8800)	(0.0032)	(0.0684)	(0.0385)
N	1703	9901	30,913	45,334
Number of groups	595	3484	12,817	15,938
Year FE	YES	YES	YES	YES

Note: Dependent variable: stopping a trade spell at time t. Coefficients: hazard ratios. Standard errors in parentheses. ***$p<0.01$, **$p<0.05$, *$p<0.1$. All variables other than dummy variables are in logs.

They continue exporting their chocolate products longer and they remain active on particular destination markets longer. However, they are actually more likely to stop exporting a particular chocolate product to a particular market, signalling that they follow more dynamic export strategies that may differ for the chocolate products compared to their other exports. It still holds that larger initial chocolate exports prolong the export relationship. However, the size of the effect is rather small—10 per cent higher initial exports of a chocolate product lowers the hazard rate by around 0.3 per cent.

Secondly, diversification matters too. On the one hand, chocolate firms are more likely to continue exporting if they are more geographically diversified. This holds in general as well as for each destination market. More geographical diversification in chocolate exports only has an additional positive effect on export survival: firms exporting chocolate products to more markets are more likely to continue exporting each of these varieties. Hence, this implies that geographical diversification, both in general and for chocolate products in particular, is a very good strategy to sustain existing chocolate export relations. On the other hand, apart from geographical diversification, product diversification also matters. Firms exporting a larger variety of products will export each of them for a longer time. However, general product differentiation at the firm level will reduce the export survival of chocolate products. Hence, our findings only partially confirm those of Volpe-Martincus and Carballo (2008), who conclude that geographical diversification matters more for survival than product diversification at the firm level.

Thirdly, quality does not seem to affect export survival. It has neither a positive nor a negative effect on Belgian chocolate exports. A possible explanation is that Belgian chocolates are perceived in foreign markets to be products of similar (high) quality. Hence, quality differences do not really affect the demand for Belgian chocolates.

Fourthly, several destination characteristics affect chocolate export duration too. Chocolate firms exporting more and/or a larger variety to a particular destination market, are more likely to continue exporting (a particular chocolate product) to that market. Exporting chocolate products to EU27 countries continues longer than exporting them to non-EU27 countries (the hazard rate is between 9 and 25 per cent lower for exports to the EU27). This could be explained by the proximity of the EU27 markets, as well as by the European internal market, which makes it easier and cheaper for Belgian chocolate exporters to export and continue exporting to these markets. The positive EU27 impact on chocolate export survival could be considered as a compensation for the short export survival on neighbouring markets (however, only at the product and destination level). Since new as well as smaller exporters tend to concentrate on neighbouring markets first, chocolate exports to these markets are also most volatile. Note that exports to more distant markets are not necessarily for a shorter period of time. Despite the robust finding in the literature that distance between trading partners affects export duration negatively due to higher trade costs, this does not hold for Belgian chocolate exporters. This could be interpreted, on the one hand, as a sign that Belgian chocolate exporters often manage to survive in more distant markets despite the higher trade costs that may be compensated by reputation and a continued appetite for Belgian chocolates on global markets. On the other hand, the lack of a positive distance effect signals that, although more distant markets are becoming more important destinations for Belgian chocolate exporters, those export relationships are not necessarily stable over time. Note that the size of the destination market and whether the importing country belongs to the World

Trade Organization (WTO) or to a trade agreement with the EU has no significant impact on chocolate export duration.

Finally and interestingly, facing higher competition on destination markets has a positive effect on Belgian chocolate export duration. This finding indicates that it is easier to survive in countries importing a lot of chocolate and signals a strong preference for chocolate in those markets. One may conclude that the survival of Belgian chocolate exports depends more on the competitive strengths with respect to other Belgian competitors than on competition caused by non-Belgian exporters in foreign markets.

Conclusion

In this chapter we analyse the characteristics and duration of Belgian chocolate exports using detailed firm-level data. We find that chocolate exporters are very diversified, exporting a large set of products, not necessarily restricted to chocolate products. Chocolate constitutes, however, the largest part of their export value. Although the number of chocolate exporting firms is rather stable over time, there is a large variation in their export survival. The average export survival time for a chocolate exporter is short, but slightly longer than for other Belgian firms and products. This confirms our starting point that high-quality goods have a different duration pattern and that they are more stable than other export relationships.

Surviving the first year is crucial for a firm, suggesting that export promotion policies promoting firm entry without taking into account their survival may not be efficient. Hence, more effort should be made in order to keep firms in a market.

This chapter points to firm heterogeneity and market and product specific entry cost as determinants of trade duration. In particular, a firm's initial export size, its geographical diversification in terms of all products or chocolate products, as well as the variety in its chocolate exports affect the survival positively. Belgian chocolate exports also last longer on EU27 markets. Offering a better quality product than other Belgian chocolate exports does not improve export survival. Finally, tougher competition in an export market does not harm Belgian chocolate exporters. That means that Belgian chocolate is not easily substitutable. Perhaps the best proof that Belgian chocolate is the best in the world.

References

Abraham, F. and J. Van Hove. 2010. 'Can Belgian firms cope with the Chinese dragon and Asian tigers? The export performance of multi-product firms on foreign markets'. Working Paper Research 204, National Bank of Belgium.

Abraham, F., Z. Studnicka, and J. Van Hove. 2014. 'Export survival and returning to exports'. Unpublished manuscript.

Arkolakis, C. 2010. 'Market penetration costs and the new consumers margin in international trade'. *Journal of Political Economy* 118 (6): p. 1151.

BBC News Magazine. 2012. 'Is Belgium still the capital of chocolate?', 31 December.

Békés, G. and B. Muraközy. 2012. 'Temporary trade and heterogeneous firms'. *Journal of International Economics* 87 (2): p. 232.

Bernard, A. B. and J. Jensen. 1999. 'Exceptional exporter performance: cause, effect, or both?' *Journal of International Economics* 47 (1): p. 1.

Bernard, A. B., E. J. Blanchard, I. V. Beveren, and H. Y. Vandenbussche. 2012. 'Carry-along trade'. NBER Working Papers 18246, National Bureau of Economic Research, Inc.

Besedĕs, T. 2008. 'A search cost perspective on formation and duration of trade'. *Review of International Economics* 16 (5): p. 835.

Besedĕs, T. and T. Prusa. 2006a. 'Ins, outs, and the duration of trade'. *Canadian Journal of Economics* 39 (1): p. 266.

Besedĕs, T. and T. Prusa. 2006b. 'Product differentiation and duration of US import trade'. *Journal of International Economics* 70 (2): p. 339.

Brenton, P., C. Saborowski, and E. Von Uexkull. 2010. 'What explains the low survival rate of developing country export flows?' *World Bank Economic Review* 24 (3): p. 474.

Cadot, O., L. Iacovone, M. D. Pierola, and F. Rauch 2013. 'Success and failure of African exporters'. *Journal of Development Economics* 101 (C): p. 284.

CEPII (Centre d'Études Prospectives et d'Informations Internationales). 2014. Data retrieved from CEPII database, 2014.

Chaney, T. 2008. 'Distorted gravity: the intensive and extensive margins of international trade'. *American Economic Review* 98 (4): p. 1707.

Crozet, M., K. Head, and T. Mayer. 2012. 'Quality sorting and trade: firm-level evidence for French wine'. *Review of Economic Studies* 79 (2): p. 609.

Eckel, C. and J. P. Neary. 2010. 'Multi-product firms and flexible manufacturing in the global economy'. *Review of Economic Studies* 77 (1): p. 188.

Esteve-Pérez, S., F. Requena-Silvente, and V. J. Pallard-Lopez. 2013. 'The duration of firm-destination export relationships: evidence from Spain, 1997–2006'. *Economic Inquiry* 51(1): p. 159.

Eurostat. 2014. Data retrieved from Eurostat: Ramon database, 2014. Available at : <http://ec.europa.eu/eurostat/ramon/index.cfm?TargetUrl=DSP_PUB_WELC>.

Fugazza, M. and A. C. Molina. 2011. 'On the determinants of exports survival'. UNCTAD Blue Series Papers 46, United Nations Conference on Trade and Development.

Gaulier, G. and S. Zignago. 2010. 'Baci: international trade database at the product-level. The 1994–2007 version'. Working Paper 2010-23, CEPII.

Godart, O., H. Görg, and A. Hanley. 2011. 'Surviving the crisis: foreign multinationals vs domestic firms in Ireland'. CEPR Discussion Paper 8596.

Görg, H., R. Kneller, and B. Muraközy. 2012. 'What makes a successful export? Evidence from firm-product-level data'. *Canadian Journal of Economics* 45 (4): p. 1332.

Hess, W. and M. Persson. 2011. 'Exploring the duration of EU imports'. *Review of World Economics (Weltwirtschaftliches Archiv)* 147 (4): p. 665.

Hess, W. and M. Persson. 2012. The duration of trade revisited. *Empirical Economics* 43 (3): p. 1083.

Hosmer, D., S. Lemeshow, and S. May. 2008. *'Applied Survival Analysis: Regression Modeling of Time to Event Data'.* New York: John Wiley. Available at: <http://eu.wiley.com/WileyCDA/WileyTitle/productCd-0471754994.html>.

IMF (International Monetary Fund). 2014. Data retrieved from IMF World Economic Outlook database, 2014. Available at: <https://www.imf.org/external/pubs/ft/weo/2014/02/weodata/index.aspx>.

Kaplan, E. and P. Meier. 1958. 'Nonparametric estimation from incomplete observations'. *Journal of the American Statistical Association* 53 (282): p. 457.

Mayer, T. and G. Ottaviano. 2007. *'The happy few: the internationalisation of European firms'.* Brussels: Bruegel, 2007.

Mayer, T., M. J. Melitz, and G. I. P. Ottaviano. 2014. 'Market size, competition, and the product mix of exporters'. *American Economic Review* 104 (2): p. 495.

Melitz, M. J. 2003. 'The impact of trade on intra-industry reallocations and aggregate industry productivity'. *Econometrica* 71 (6): p. 1695.

Muûls, M. and M. Pisu. 2009. 'Imports and exports at the level of the firm: evidence from Belgium'. *The World Economy* 32 (5): p. 692.

NBB (National Bank of Belgium). 2014. Data retrieved from the National Bank of Belgium, 2014.

Nitsch, V. 2009. 'Die another day: duration in German import trade'. *Review of World Economics (Weltwirtschaftliches Archiv)* 145 (1): p. 133.

Studnicka, Z. and J. Van Hove. 2014. 'Evidence and determinants of the duration of European exports'. Unpublished manuscript.

United Nations. 2014. Data retrieved from Comtrade database, 2014.

Volpe-Martincus, C. and J. Carballo. 2008. 'Survival of new exporters in developing countries: Does it matter how they diversify?' IDB Publications 9291, Inter-American Development Bank. Available at: <http://comtrade.un.org/>.

World Bank. 2014. Data retrieved from World Development Indicators database, 2014. Availaable at: <http://data.worldbank.org/data-catalog/world-development-indicators>.

Appendix 18.A

The survival analysis can be divided into two components: (1) the descriptive analysis and (2) the analysis of the determinants of survival.

In our descriptive analysis we calculate the number of export spells, estimate the survival functions, and calculate the average length of export survival.

One of the issues arising at this stage and in the subsequent analysis is the fact that we do not know if a given trade flow was active before 1998 (left censoring) and after 2010 (right censoring). Survival analysis solves the problem of right-censored observations (see e.g. Hosmer et al., 2008), but not of the left-censored ones. To deal with this issue, we calculate the number of spells as well as the averages of the duration of trade with and without left-censored observations, and exclude trade spells starting in 1998 from the analysis of the survival functions and the determinants of survival. In addition, it is important to note that the number of spells at the firm level is different from the number of chocolate exporters. This is related to the fact that we calculate the duration of trade as the number of years a firm was engaged in exports in general. Thus, a firm may have finished exporting chocolate before ending its exports. This firm at the end of the spell will not be classified as a chocolate exporter.

In the survival function analysis, we estimate the survival functions using the Kaplan–Meier (1958) product limit estimator for the period 1999–2010 (in order to control for left-censored observations). The Kaplan–Meier estimator is obtained, at any point of time, by multiplying a sequence of conditional survival probability estimators. Each conditional probability estimator is obtained from the observed number at risk n_k (number of spells still active at time k) and the observed number of failures d_k at this period.

$$s(j) = \Pi_{k=1}^{j} \frac{n_k - d_k}{n_k}$$

Finally, in the analysis of the determinants of export survival, since our survival data is recorded in grouped time intervals of one year (interval-censored data) and a typical spell length is short, we use a discrete-time rather than a continuous-time modelling framework. The main advantages of the former, in the duration of trade analysis, were recently discussed in Hess and Persson (2011, 2012). According to these authors, using discrete-time modelling in the duration of trade analysis solves several issues present in continuous-time models such as the Cox model. Hence, in our analysis we use a random effects complementary log-log (cloglog) model, which allows us to take into account unobserved heterogeneity and solves the issue of many tied duration times (more than one firm with the same survival time). Our random effects depend on the level of analysis. At the firm level we use firm random effects, at the firm-product level we use firm-product random effects, at the firm-destination level we use firm-destination random effects, and a combination of the three at the firm-product-destination level. In addition, we add year dummies to control for unobserved factors varying over time. The complementary log-log model, however, maintains the assumption of proportional hazards. Therefore, as a robustness check we use a probit model in which this assumption is no longer preserved. Since our results are almost identical, we do not report them in this study. They are, however, available upon request.

Appendix 18.B

Table 18.A1 List of chocolate products (CN8 classification)

CN8 Code	Description
17049030	White chocolate
Cocoa powder, containing added sugar or other sweetening matter	
18061015	Containing no sucrose or containing less than 5% by weight of sucrose (including invert sugar expressed as sucrose) or isoglucose expressed as sucrose
18061020	Containing 5% or more but less than 65% by weight of sucrose (including invert sugar expressed as sucrose) or isoglucose expressed as sucrose
18061030	Containing 65% or more but less than 80% by weight of sucrose (including invert sugar expressed as sucrose) or isoglucose expressed as sucrose
18061090	Containing 80% or more by weight of sucrose (including invert sugar expressed as sucrose) or isoglucose expressed as sucrose
Other preparations in blocks, slabs, or bars weighing more than 2 kg, or in liquid, paste, powder, granular, or other bulk form in containers or immediate packing, of a content exceeding 2 kg	
18062010	Containing 31% or more by weight of cocoa butter or containing a combined weight of 31% or more of cocoa butter and milk fat
18062030	Containing a combined weight of 25% or more, but less than 31% of cocoa butter and milk fat
18062050	Containing 18% or more by weight of cocoa butter
18062070	Chocolate milk crumb
18062080	Chocolate flavour coating
18062095	Other
Other, in blocks, slabs, or bars	
18063100	Filled
18063210	With added cereal, fruit, or nuts
18063290	Other
18069011	Cholates (including pralines), whether or not filled, containing alcohol
18069019	Cholates (including pralines), whether or not filled, other

(continued)

Table 18.A1 Continued

CN8 Code	Description
18069031	Cholates (including pralines), whether or not filled, other filled
18069039	Cholates (including pralines), whether or not filled, other not filled
18069050	Sugar confectionery and substitutes made from sugar substitution products, containing cocoa
18069060	Spreads containing cocoa
18069070	Preparations containing cocoa for making beverages
18069090	Other

Part V
New Chocolate Markets

19

The Burgeoning Chocolate Market in China

Fan Li and Di Mo

Introduction

Like most Asian diets, the Chinese diet includes few sweet products such as chocolate (Wood and Grosvenor, 1997; Allen, 2010). People in China traditionally preferred salty snacks (Wu and Cheung, 2002; Newman, 2004). Restaurants commonly served fruit or salty nuts (such as peanuts, walnuts, or sunflower seeds) as snacks. Almost no one in China (either the younger or older generation) had tasted chocolate before the opening up of the economy (Wood and Grosvenor, 1997; Allen, 2010). In fact, people had rarely heard about chocolate until then.

Chocolate first entered China in the 1980s (Wood and Grosvenor, 1997).[1] Ferrero Rocher was the global chocolate industry's first ambassador to China (Allen, 2010). Afterwards, however, the chocolate industry in China experienced a steady increase. From 1996 to 2005, per capita consumption of cocoa in China grew at about 6 per cent per year (ICCO, 2007). In 2003, 38 per cent of urban residents in China either purchased or consumed chocolate. This means that there were more than 26 million chocolate consumers (or, as the chocolate industry likes to call them, emerging chocolate lovers) in the urban areas (*China Daily*, 2004). The growth rate of China's chocolate market has accelerated between 2004 and 2010 by 10 to 15 per cent per year (Allen, 2010; Buffy, 2011). This growth rate is high internationally, more than five times the growth rate of the global chocolate market, which grew only around 2 to 3 per cent per year during the 2000s.

Growing chocolate consumption in 1990s and 2000s was accompanied by large amounts of investment into the chocolate industry (Wood and Grosvenor,

---

[1] The earliest records of chocolate in China date back to the seventeenth century, to the Qing Dynasty (Gordon, 2009). Although some documentaries by food historians state that chocolate actually had entered China by the seventeenth century, this was only within a small region and it was mostly experienced by higher officials at the time.

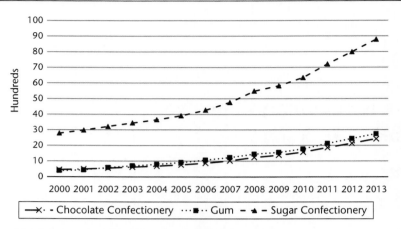

Figure 19.1 Market size of confectionery industry in China
Note: Market share is calculated by using retail value (retail selling price—RSP), and recalculated into USD by year-to-year exchange rates.
Source: Euromonitor International (2014).

1997). Foreign chocolate producers, mostly from European countries, increased their investment in China's chocolate industry, and gradually established their production facilities in China (Allen, 2001). Chocolate importers continued to diversify their import sources and products, leading domestic confectionery producers to contribute to the growth in production and variety of chocolate products in China (Figure 19.1). By the 2000s, consumers in urban China could, for the first time, access more than 70 foreign chocolate brands in supermarkets (*Chocolate News*, 2009).

China's chocolate market has great potential to grow in the future (Allen, 2001). On the demand side, household income continues to grow, which may contribute to higher purchasing power and a shifted preference towards quality chocolate. At the same time, the hidden force of globalization is transforming China's food culture (Wu and Cheung, 2002). Influenced by foreign culture, the Chinese, especially the younger generation, are embracing the once exotic snack food. On the supply side, various market players continue to cultivate the Chinese taste for chocolate. Foreign companies are leading the game. Ferrero attracts increasing amounts of Chinese consumers by incorporating China's gift-giving tradition into chocolate sales (Allen, 2010). Mars, the biggest chocolate producer in China, continues to innovate and diversity its chocolate products to both meet and affect consumer preferences. Chocolate importers from the UK, Belgium, Germany, Switzerland, and many other countries across the world are catching up by marketing the 'authenticity and tradition' of chocolates (Euromonitor International, 2013).

Although China's growing chocolate consumption presents rich opportunities, its underdeveloped supply chain raises great challenges to both foreign and domestic companies. There are weaknesses in many links of the chain, including obtaining raw materials, logistics, and retailing. Increased food safety concerns after the 2008 milk scandal, inefficient transportation due to inadequate cooling facilities and equipment, and fragmented retailing sectors are constraining the chocolate supply chain.

To better understand the evolution of the Chinese chocolate market and its future challenges, this chapter is organized as follows. In the following section, 'Conversion from Non-Chocolate Eaters to Chocolate Lovers', we discuss the driving factors of the consumption growth of China's chocolate products. Then, we investigate the weaknesses in the chocolate supply chain in China. The final section concludes.

Conversion from Non-Chocolate Eaters to Chocolate Lovers

It took Chinese consumers 40 years to embrace chocolate. Chocolate has a short history in China. In the initial development, most chocolate eaters were concentrated in the first-tier cities, such as Shanghai, Beijing, and Guangzhou. Chocolate slowly expanded into the second-tier and third-tier cities in the late 1990s. Nowadays, chocolate is readily accessible for 300 million of China's 1.3 billion people (Allen, 2010). The market has grown remarkably in the past, though it is still largely untapped at present (Euromonitor International, 2013). With a population of 1.3 billion, China is believed to have the largest potential market for any product in the world. Chocolate is no exception.

Low Per Capita Consumption with Great Potential to Grow

Compared with Western countries and developed countries in Asia, on a per capita basis the Chinese still consume a relatively small amount of chocolate (Scott-Thomas, 2011). Per capita chocolate consumption in China was only 120 grams in 2007 (Figure 19.2), while the average per capita consumption of the 15 European Union (EU) member nations in 2007 was 7.2 kilograms. For example, the Swiss ate 10.8 kilograms per person per year in 2007, and Ireland ate 11.8 kilograms, which was the highest in the world. Chinese consumers have a low chocolate consumption even when compared to other countries in East Asia, such as Japan and South Korea—the populations of which, on average, ate about 2 kilograms per capita (Figure 19.2; *Shanghai Daily*, 2008).

The low per capita consumption of chocolate does not seem to be due to the Chinese's dislike of sweets. The chocolate industry is on a much smaller scale, when compared with other confectionery products in China, than in other countries. Sugar confectionery is the biggest confectionery sector, and accounted for more than half of the confectionery sales in 2007. Gum followed in second place (Figure 19.3). In 2007, when the total confectionery sales were more than one thousand million US dollars (Euromonitor International, 2013), the chocolate confectionery sales were only 13 per cent of the total confectionery sales. This share of chocolate among confectionery products was low, even compared with other developing countries. For example, India had a chocolate market size of

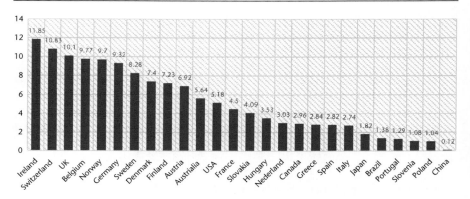

Figure 19.2 Per head chocolate confectionery consumption (kg) by country, 2007
Source: Association of Chocolate, Biscuit and Confectionery Industries of the European Union, retrieved from <http://www.caobisco.com>.

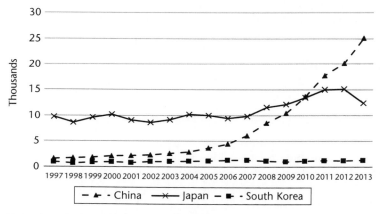

Figure 19.3 Chocolate confectionery sales in East Asia
Note: Sales are calculated into values in USD based on the year-to-year exchange rate.
Source: Euromonitor International (2014).

more than 35 per cent of the total confectionery in 2007. Mexico's chocolate market size was over 21 per cent, Argentina's 34 per cent, in 2007. When compared with other developed countries, the market statistics are even more striking. For example, Belgium's chocolate market accounted for almost 65 per cent of its total confectionery products in 2007, and France's chocolate market accounted for 69 per cent of all confectionary products in the same year (Euromonitor International, 2013).

Although the current consumption is low, the chocolate market in China has seen remarkable growth in recent years (*China News*, 2013). During the short history of chocolate consumption in China, the market has grown fast. The initial

Table 19.1 Confectionery sales and growth rate in China (US$ millions)

Year	Chocolate		Gum		Sugar Confectionery	
	Sales (US$ Millions)	Growth Rate (%)	Sales (US$ Millions)	Growth Rate (%)	Sales (US$ Millions)	Growth Rate (%)
2004	683.2	9.82%	797.1	13.42%	3656.4	6%
2005	762.2	11.56%	917.6	15.12%	3909.7	6.93%
2006	874.9	14.79%	1070	16.61%	4269.6	9.21%
2007	1023.9	17.03%	1234.8	15.40%	4759.4	11.47%
2008	1241.6	21.26%	1450.3	17.45%	5482.6	15.20%
2009	1383.8	11.45%	1556.5	7.32%	5818.9	6.13%
2010	1569.4	13.41%	1776.7	14.15%	6339.4	8.94%
2011	1863.9	18.77%	2127.4	19.74%	7211.7	13.76%
2012	2138.7	14.74%	2446.9	15.02%	7993.4	10.84%
2013	2422.6	13.27%	2750.4	12.40%	8784.6	9.90%

Source: Euromonitor International (2014).

growth after chocolate entered China in the 1980s was steady (Euromonitor International, 2013). The growth accelerated during 2000s. Before 2004, China's chocolate market was almost at the same level as that of South Korea. As we can see in Figure 19.3, it was a small market in 2000 (453 thousand million US dollars), which equals one eighth of Japan's chocolate market. The most significant growth has taken place between 2007 and 2013. After 2004, the chocolate sales in China increased at around 10 to 18 per cent per year. As a result, China surpassed Japan in 2010, and became the largest chocolate market in East Asia. In 2013, Chinese total chocolate sales reached 2.5 billion US dollars: twice the size of Japan's.

This fast growth of the chocolate market reflects the shift in preference towards chocolate rather than other sweets. In Table 19.1, we list the chocolate, gum, and sugar confectioneries' market size and year-to-year growth rate. We found that the annual growth of China's chocolate market was about 10 per cent after 2004, while the sugar confectionery sectors were growing much slower. The average annual growth rate of sugar confectionery was only about 5 per cent (Table 19.1).[2] In the year 2013, chocolate confectionery took almost 24 per cent of the total confectionery market share.

The growing trend of chocolate in China will almost certainly continue (Euromonitor International, 2013). The developed countries are now consuming 12 kilograms per capita per year. The Eastern Asian countries, which have similar diets to China, consume an average of 1.28 kilograms per capita. With only 0.12 kilograms of consumption per capita, China is believed to have great potential for future growth. The driving force of demand continues to affect the market today. In the following subsection, 'Factors that Contribute to the Growth of the Chocolate Market in China', we discuss the main driving factors of the market growth.

---

[2] The gum sector also experienced a fast growth period after 2004. According to a Euromonitor International report, this can mainly be attributed to health concerns and the invention of functional chewing gum (Euromonitor International, 2013).

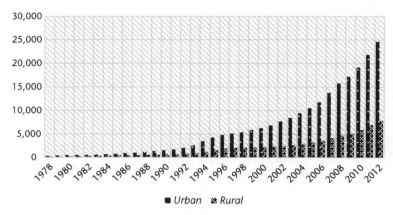

■ *Urban* ✱ *Rural*

Figure 19.4 Average per capita disposable income in urban and rural China
Note: Income is calculated in Chinese yuan.
Source: Chinese National Bureau of Statistics (2013).

Factors that Contribute to the Growth of the Chocolate Market in China

There are many factors that contribute to the growth of the chocolate market in China. In this chapter, we discuss four main drivers of market growth: purchasing power of consumers, urbanization, market players, and cultural factors.

GROWING PURCHASING POWER OF THE CHINESE CONSUMERS
Fast-growing household income is a strong driver of the growth of the chocolate market. In the urban areas, the per capita disposable income has been growing at around 13 per cent per year since 1978 (Figure 19.4). After 1996, the growth of urban income level further accelerated. The number of urban household earning more than 5,000 US dollars per year is estimated to grow annually by 24 per cent, creating tens of millions of new consumers for higher-value food (Wang et al., 2013). The rural economy has seen rapid growth as well. As people got richer, they had more demand for diverse food products. People from the upper and middle classes started to spend more on sweets and demand variety. Chocolate was an appealing product to meet such new demand. As the younger generation are born into families with stronger purchasing power, they are expected to drive the further growth of chocolate consumption.

URBANIZATION
China's urbanization contributed to better market access to chocolate (Wang et al., 2013). Urbanization has been progressing annually at 1.3 per cent from 2005 to 2011. In 2005, 43 per cent of the population was rural. In 2011, the urban population reached 50 per cent (Chinese National Bureau of Statistics, 2013). Continuous urbanization has enhanced the accessibility of chocolate for the Chinese consumer: the higher concentration of population in urban cities has

directly reduced the distribution costs for producers, while the increased number of supermarkets, chain stores, and other retailers has made it much easier for chocolate products to reach consumers.

MARKET PLAYERS' EFFORT IN SHAPING CONSUMER PREFERENCES

Experts believe that China could someday consume up to 7 billion US dollars' worth of chocolate per year (*China Daily*, 2004). The market potential has attracted both domestic and international producers. In competing for market share, domestic and foreign producers have contributed to shaping and developing the Chinese chocolate market.

In the 1980s, chocolate was totally new to Chinese. The opening-up policy of China has allowed foreign chocolate producers to enter the market. Since then, most of the chocolate sold in China (around 80 per cent in volume) has been produced by foreign companies, either in China or abroad. The top 20 world chocolate producers have all entered China's market (Scott-Thomas, 2011). Consumers in China can now purchase some of the world's most prestigious and popular brands, such as Ferrero Rocher from Italy, Guylian from Belgium, and Lindt from Switzerland. About 90 per cent of the market share goes to foreign producers (Table 19.2). The most popular chocolate brands in China, Galaxy and Dove, together take about 35 per cent of the chocolate market. Following Galaxy and Dove, Nestlé and Ferrero Rocher take 9.9 and 8.5 per cent respectively (Table 19.3).

Table 19.2 Market share of China's chocolate producers

Chocolate Producers	2008	2009	2010	2011	2012	2013
Mars Inc.	33.5	35.7	37.2	38.2	38.9	39.5
Ferrero Group	6.4	7.1	8.3	9.5	10.5	11.4
Nestlé SA	8.9	9.6	9.9	11.2	11	11.1
COFCO*	6.3	5.9	5.6	5.5	5.3	5.1
Mondelēz International Inc.	–	–	–	–	3.5	3.4
Hershey Co.	1.5	1.8	1.8	1.9	2	2.1
Fujian Yake Food Co. Ltd	1.6	1.7	1.8	1.8	1.8	1.7
Meiji Holdings Co. Ltd	–	1	1	1.2	1.2	1.3
Shanghai Golden Monkey Food Co.	3.8	3.7	3.2	2.7	1.9	1.3
Lotte Group	1.3	1.2	1.1	1	0.9	0.9
Chocoladefabriken Lindt & Sprüngli AG	–	0.2	0.2	0.2	0.2	0.2
Shanghai Bainuo Food Co. Ltd	0.3	0.3	0.2	0.2	0.2	0.1
Beijing Yi Li Food Co. Ltd	0.1	0.1	0.1	0.1	0.1	0.1
Kraft Foods Inc.	1.1	1.1	3.6	3.5	–	–
BVI Hsu-Fu-Chi Holdings Ltd	0.9	0.9	0.9	–	–	–
Cadbury plc	2.8	2.6	–	–	–	–
Meiji Seika Kaisha Ltd	1	–	–	–	–	–
Others	30.6	27.1	25	22.9	22.5	21.8
Total	100	100	100	100	100	100

Note: (1) China National Cereals, Oils and Foodstuffs Import and Export Corporation. (2) Calculated by using the RSP.
Source: Euromonitor International (2014).

Table 19.3 Market share of top 12 chocolate brands in China from 2008 to 2013

Chocolate Brands	Producers	2008	2009	2010	2011	2012	2013
Galaxy/Dove	Mars Inc.	29.1	31.3	32.8	33.7	34.1	34.6
Nestlé	Nestlé SA	7.4	8.5	8.9	9.5	9.8	9.9
Ferrero Rocher	Ferrero Group	4.5	5	5.8	6.8	7.6	8.5
Le Conté	COFCO	5.7	5.4	5.2	4.9	4.7	4.5
M&M's	Mars Inc.	2.7	2.6	2.5	2.7	2.9	3
Cadbury	Mondelēz International Inc.	–	–	–	–	2.4	2.4
Co Co	Fujian Yake Food Co. Ltd	1.6	1.7	1.8	1.8	1.8	1.7
Snickers	Mars Inc.	1.2	1.3	1.4	1.3	1.3	1.4
Meiji	Meiji Holdings Co. Ltd	–	1	1	1.2	1.2	1.3
Hsu-Fu-Chi	Nestlé SA	–	–	–	1	1.1	1.2
Golden Monkey	Shanghai Golden Monkey Food Co.	1.9	1.7	1.6	1.4	1.2	1
Hershey's	Hershey Co., The	0.6	0.7	0.7	0.8	0.9	1

Note: (1) China National Cereals, Oils and Foodstuffs Import and Export Corporation. (2) Calculated by using the RSP.
Source: Euromonitor International (2014).

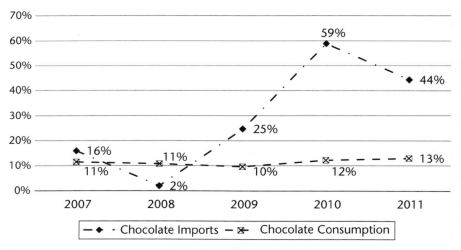

Figure 19.5 Growth rates of China's chocolate imports and total consumption
Source: (1) Import data are from UN Commodity Trade Statistics Database, <http://comtrade.un.org/db/>; Commodity Code: 1806 'Chocolate and Other Foods Contain Cocoa'. (2) The total consumption data come from Euromonitor International (2014).

Imported brands have mostly been promoted as a luxury food and are marketed to the top end of China's market (Freeman, 2005). Imported chocolate in China has been growing at an unprecedented pace (Figures 19.5, 19.6). Before China joined the World Trade Organization (WTO) in 2001, the amount of imported chocolate was relatively small (17.7 million US dollars in 1999). However, after 2001, the imported chocolate grew to reach nearly 50 million US dollars in 2003 (Freeman, 2005). During 2010 and 2011, the imports rose at 40 per cent per year (Euromonitor International, 2013).

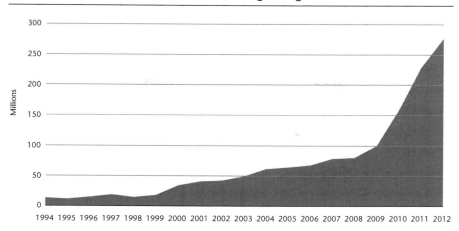

Figure 19.6 China's chocolate imports from 1995 to 2012

Note: Imports were calculated in value in USD. All of the trade data shown on the site is either in the SITC (standard international trade classification) or HS (harmonized system) four-digit level.

Source: The Observatory of Economic Complexity, retrieved from <http://atlas.media.mit.edu/>.

Domestic producers have also emerged. It is estimated that China already has around 250 chocolate companies with an annual production capacity of chocolate of 150 thousand tons (Buffy, 2011). Domestic players have been growing, although their market share is still relatively small. The largest domestic company, COFCO, holds about 5 per cent of the market share in 2013. Partly due to their less-developed technology (and less sophisticated marketing strategies), and partly due to the shorter history of production inside China, at least so far, domestic firms have been less competitive than foreign brands. Local chocolate makers are disadvantaged with regard to knowledge, technology, and investment. They mostly target the lower end of the market with low costs and profit margins (LI & FUNG Research Report, 2006).

Chocolate producers, domestic or foreign, have employed various strategies to boost chocolate consumption. First, some of the foreign chocolate brands have tried to localize their taste or adapt to Chinese culture, so that it is easier for China to accommodate the exotic food (Wood and Grosvenor, 1997). For instance, Mars, Hershey, Cadbury, and Nestlé set up factories in China. They adapted their chocolate recipes as they began to believe that 'creamy' and 'nutty' are the favoured tastes of China's nascent chocolate fans. Some companies marketed their products as a way to give unique gifts, using this as a cultural gateway. In doing so, foreign chocolate makers devote much time in advertising and packing in their efforts to promote chocolate as a gift that symbolizes love and friendship (Allen, 2010). Many of the earliest chocolate brands, which used this strategy in the 1980s and 1990s, still dominate China's market, despite the large number of local firms that emerged later.

Second, foreign brands have also advertised their products as high quality and representative of a Western lifestyle (Sin, Ho, and So, 2000). Consumers in China are heavily influenced by these advertisements and believe that products from overseas (or those produced by the overseas companies within China) are more authentic or of superior quality (Li, Fu, and Murray, 1997). Perceived social and symbolic values have been documented to increase the purchase of foreign products by Chinese consumers (Li, Li, and Kambele, 2012). The advertising and marketing strategies of many foreign chocolate firms have tried to build brand images symbolizing wealth and good fortune (Ferrero), luxuriousness and self-indulgence (Mars), and cuteness and whimsicality (Hershey). Most of these companies have been open about their foreign roots as a proof of high quality and reputation.

Third, other producers have tried educating Chinese consumers about the benefits of eating chocolate in an effort to increase sales. For example, chocolate, especially its ingredient cocoa, is advertised to reduce high blood pressure and boost health (Green, 2013). Others cite studies that show chocolate's ability to increase happiness and creativity levels (Savastano, 2012). These benefits of chocolate have convinced many consumers to eat chocolate or buy chocolate for their children.

CULTURAL TRANSFORMATION

Globalization has led to a dramatic convergence between Eastern and Western diet habits and lifestyles. Many Asian countries in economic and demographic transition have had similar patterns of transition in food consumption (Shetty, 2002; Pingali and Khwaja, 2004). For example, Asian countries that developed an appetite for sweets during the 1990s to 2000s consumed more sugar, from 14kg per capita in 1979 to 17kg in 2001 (Pingali, 2007). The per capita expenditure on sugar and confectionery in China increased from 6 per cent in 2001 to almost 26 per cent in 2013 (Figure 19.7). In China, the declining intake of cereals and coarse grains during the past two decades in both urban and rural populations was accompanied by a dramatic increase in the consumption of fat and protein (Ma et al., 2004; Mendez et al., 2004). The same trends occurred in the consumption of dairy and meat products, such as cheese, yogurt, and beef. The shifts in consumption were most apparent in younger generations, China's future consumers (Parraga, 1990; Mendez et al., 2004). Being more exposed to social media and global trends in consumption, the younger generation is expected to be able to transform China's chocolate culture of gift-giving into self-consumption.

Challenges to Future Growth: A Weak Supply Chain

Although the past and current growth of China's chocolate market seems to suggest a bright future, there are several challenges that are face both domestic and foreign producers. China has an underdeveloped supply chain of chocolate. Weaknesses exist in producing and obtaining the raw ingredients, the logistics services, and the distribution channels. Now we will discuss each of these weaknesses.

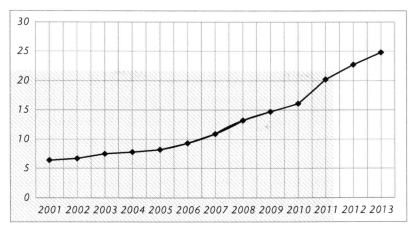

Figure 19.7 China's per capita expenditure on sugar and confectionery
Source: Euromonitor International (2014).

Food Safety Issues: Raw Ingredients

Milk chocolate was the favourite flavour among Chinese consumers, accounting for 38 per cent of sales of chocolate in 2007 (Euromonitor International, 2013). However, providing safe and high-quality milk chocolate is problematic for chocolate producers with production facilities in China.

China's biggest food scandal occurred in 2008 when it was discovered that milk suppliers (including traders and milk collection stations) were adding melamine, a colourless crystalline compound, to artificially boost the protein-readings of their milk (BBC, 2008; *Xinhua News*, 2008). Distrusting consumers dramatically reduced milk consumption, and dairy production fell substantially in early 2009 (Jia, et al., 2012). In the provinces which publish time series data on the number of dairy farmers, there was a sharp drop in the number of dairy households reported at the end of 2008. This crisis significantly influenced China's diary sector, and influenced the Chinese government to issue new food safety regulations, which are much tougher and more comprehensive (Wang et al., 2008; Ramzy, 2009). Although literature exists on the impact of the milk scandal on food safety regulations, less is known about its impact on chocolate.

First of all, the shortage of milk and the loss of confidence in domestic production after the crisis pushed most chocolate companies (both international and domestic companies) and other retailors to increase the imports of chocolate in the short run. The growth rate of chocolate imports after 2008 spiked and reached almost 60 per cent of all chocolate supply during 2009 and 2010. As the chocolate production recovered from the crisis, the import went down slowly to its pre-crisis level. The spike is unlikely to be due to the sudden demand growth, as there is no spike in chocolate total consumption. The growth rate of China's chocolate consumption remains at 10 to 12 per cent per year.

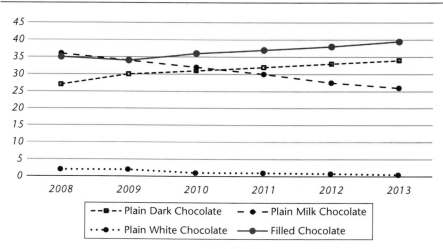

Figure 19.8 Per cent of retail of chocolate tablets by type
Note: Calculated in values (USD) by year-to-year exchange rate from 2008 to 2013.
Source: Euromonitor International (2014).

Secondly, the direct impact of the milk scandal can also be observed from the changes in customer preferences. After the crisis, there has been a shift away from milk chocolate to other types of chocolate products. Before the milk scandal, the percentage of sales of milk chocolate tablets was around 36 (Figure 19.8). It was higher than filled chocolate, significantly higher than dark chocolate, and significantly higher than white chocolate. Dark chocolate was below 30 per cent. However, the product structure changed dramatically after 2009. Both sales of plain dark chocolate tablets and filled chocolate tablets increased rapidly after 2008. In contrast, the sales of milk chocolate fell as much as the rise of dark or filled chocolate. Both the shortage of milk and safety concerns about milk and sugar may have led to the decreased consumption of milk chocolate.

The newly issued food safety regulations of 2009 have led to two different scenarios for domestic chocolate producers and international producers in China. To meet the new food safety regulations, domestic chocolate producers, who were mainly serving the lower-end markets, were forced to improve their producing and distributing environment, such improvements included: higher basic hygienic requirements for production and trading processes, better tracking of the sources of ingredients, clearer labelling, identification and instructions relevant to comply with the food safety regulations (Petry and Wu, 2009). All these measures significantly increased the cost of domestic small-scale chocolate production. From Table 19.2, we find that the market share of other producers (mainly small-scale chocolate producers) decreased dramatically after 2008. At the same time, both the international chocolate producers' (Figure 19.9) and domestic

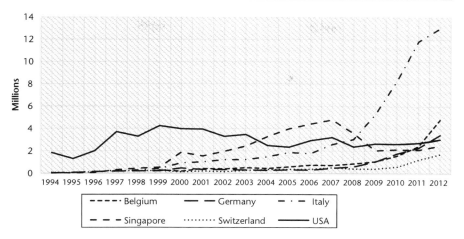

Figure 19.9 Main source countries importing chocolate to China
Note: Calculated by volume, Commodity Code: 1806 'Chocolate and Other Foods Contain Cocoa'.
Source: UN Commodity Trade Statistics Database, <http://comtrade.un.org/db/>.

large-scale producers' market shares are continually growing. The market has become more concentrated in the top ten companies.

With the continuous enforcement of this new food safety regulation and citizens' increasing awareness of food safety, China's chocolate market will keep concentrating on high-end premium chocolate. The international chocolate producers will be relatively more competitive than domestic producers. However, as long as food safety remains a concern in China, both domestic chocolate production and domestic companies are disadvantaged. Domestic production (both international companies and Chinese companies) faces the challenges of finding higher-quality raw ingredients, and having little trust from consumers. Domestic companies, with more disadvantages in production technologies and reputation, will find it even harder to compete with foreign companies or chocolate importers.

Underdeveloped Logistic Services

How the chocolate products are delivered to the final consumers is another challenge. With government support, China's logistic sector has grown by 12.3 per cent, reaching 158.4 trillion yuan in 2011 (Fung Business Report, 2013). The China Logistics Prosperity Index (LPI) shows that logistics enterprises have continued to increase investment to expand facilities and services.[3] However, the

---

[3] LPI was first launched in March 2013 by the China Federation of Logistics and Purchasing (CFLP). The index was compiled from survey responses by nationwide logistics enterprises regarding their logistics activities and inventory levels of the current month, along with their business expectations for the following three months.

expansion does not imply a higher quality of logistic services. In fact, China's logistic services are still underdeveloped (KPMG, 2011).

In order to preserve the chocolate before it reaches consumers, the chocolate industry relies heavily on a well-designed logistics network. Chocolate needs to be preserved in an environment of 5 to 18 degrees Celsius and 50 to 60 humidity degrees. Refrigeration is a basic need for storage and transportation.

There is an inadequacy of facilities and equipment in the logistic services and it is also inefficient in transportation. China's total cold storage capacity is about 7 million square metres, which is mainly used for the storage of meat and aquatic products (Wang et al., 2013). The country currently has only 30,000 refrigerated vehicles, which only accounts for 0.3 per cent of total cargo transportation. Only 2 per cent of China's rail carriages are equipped with refrigerators. The cold storage capacity in China covers only about 25 per cent of total output of chocolate, compared to 70 to 80 per cent in developed countries. The transportation system in China is also known to be inefficient and uncertain (Fung Business Report, 2013). The wholesale networks are fragmented. The lack of logistics services that meet the requirements of storing and transporting chocolate hinders the future growth of chocolate production, marketing, and retailing.

Fragmented Retail Markets

Over the past decade, the supermarket sector in China has grown rapidly from its initial establishment in a few metropolitan cities in 1990 to a 55 billion US dollar industry today. There were 53,000 supermarkets in 2002 and they covered more than 30 per cent of urban food retailing. Supermarkets have spread from large cities to secondary cities, and now to towns. They moved from areas of upper- and middle-income consumers to those of the urban poor, and from the rich eastern regions to the poor western regions of China (Hu et al., 2004). China has risen to become the world's seventh-largest retail market as of 2007, with a volume of 860 billion US dollars (Lu, 2010).

China's retail market is highly fragmented, with many small- and medium-sized retailers. Unlike the USA or Europe, which are dominated by big-box retailers, China was home to about 549,000 retail enterprises, with an average of 15 employees, in 2008 (Fung Business Report, 2013). Although the number of chain stores has been growing in recent years, cross-provincial retailers are still rare in China, in part due to market barriers (Lu, 2010).

As supermarkets are the major retailing facilities for chocolate confectionery in China, the scattered small- and medium-sized retailers may make it difficult to increase efficiency in product distribution. Almost 70 per cent of chocolate retailing happened in the supermarket or hypermarket in 2010s (Table 19.4). The fragmented supermarket sector in China makes it hard for chocolate producers to take advantage of the scale of economies in distribution.

Table 19.4 Market share by distribution channels of confectionery in China, 2010 and 2013

	2010(%)	2013 (%)
Stored-Based Retailing	94.3	91.2
- Grocery Retailers	87.9	84.3
☐ Supermarkets/Hypermarkets	68.1	68.5
☐ Convenience Stores	1.4	1.6
☐ Forecourt Retailers	1.1	1.4
☐ Traditional Grocery Retailers	17.3	12.8
- Non-Grocery Retailers	6.4	6.9
Non-Store Retailing (inc. Vending and Internet Retailing)	5.7	8.8
- Vending	5.3	4.4
- Internet Retailing	0.4	4.4
Total	100	100

Source: Euromonitor International (2014).

Conclusion

Rising household income, urbanization, and globalization have all contributed to the enormous increase of chocolate consumption in China in the past decade. However, per capita, chocolate consumption in China is still much lower than the world average. This suggests there is a large potential market of chocolate, as China continues to grow and converge with the rest of the world.

However, there are several challenges in the supply chain that may make it difficult for the producers to meet such a growing demand. The 2008 milk scandal is just one case that has illustrated China's poor quality control of food products and caused rising public concern regarding food safety. Underdeveloped logistic services for storing and transporting chocolate will be an obstacle for expanding either production or distribution. The fragmented retail market makes it hard for companies to reach wider regions without having to substantially increase the distribution costs.

The future competition of the chocolate market is likely to be intensive. The numbers of chocolate producers in China and chocolate importers are growing. Although domestic producers may be able to catch up with production technologies by learning and innovating themselves, they face more of a challenge with food safety and combating their reputation of low-quality chocolate production. Foreign companies, which have better technology and marketing, may have more disadvantages in adopting the local logistic services and distribution channels. Those who overcome these challenges may gain more margins in winning China's chocolate war.

References

Allen, L. L. 2010. 'Chocolate Fortunes: The Battle for the Hearts, Mind and Wallets of Chinese Consumers'. *Thunderbird International Business Review* 52 (1): pp. 13–20.

BBC. 2008. 'China to Punish Baby Milk Makers'. BBC, 12 September. Available at: <http://news.bbc.co.uk/2/hi/asia-pacific/7611732.stm> (accessed 1 April 2015).

Buffy, P. 2011. 'China's Chocolate Market Dominated by Foreign Brands'. Available at: <http://goarticles.com/article/China-s-Chocolate-Market-Dominated-by-Foreign-Brands/4745782/> (accessed 15 June 2015).

China Daily. 2004. 'Chocolate Strives for Standard'. *China Daily.* Available at: <http://www.chinadaily.com.cn/english/doc/2004-12/24/content_402994.htm> (accessed 1 April 2015).

Chinese National Bureau of Statistics. 2013. *China National Statistic Year Book 2013.* Available at: <http://www.stats.gov.cn/tjsj/ndsj/2014/indexeh.htm> (accessed 15 June 2015).

Chocolate News. 2009. 'An Analysis on China's Chocolate Market' (in Chinese). *Chocolate News.* Available at: <http://www.qklnews.com/qkeliInfos/gnInfos/2009/0506/2380.html> (accessed 12 February 2015).

Euromonitor International. 2013. 'Chocolate Confectionery in China'. Euromonitor International from trade associations, trade press, company research, trade interviews, trade sources. Available at: <http://www.euromonitor.com/> (accessed 15 February 2015).

Euromonitor International. 2014. *Market Size of Chocolate.* Available at: <http://www.euromonitor.com/> (accessed 15 February 2015).

Freeman, D. 2005. 'EU Chocolatiers Chase Chinese Market'. *Asia Times.* Available at: <http://www.atimes.com/atimes/China/GG28Ad02.html>.

Fung Business Report. 2013. 'Retail Market in China: Fung Business Intelligence Centre'. Available at: <http://www.funggroup.com/eng/knowledge/research/china_dis_issue114.pdf>.

Gordon, B. M. 2009. *Chinese Chocolate: Ambergris, Emperors, and Export Ware. Chocolate: History, Culture, and Heritage.* Edited by Grivetti and Shapiro. John Wiley & Sons, Inc., Hoboken, NJ, USA.

Green, A. P. 2013, 'Healthy Chocolate in 2013'. Online report. Available at: <http://www.adampaulgreen.com>.

Hu, D., T. Reardon, S. Rozelle, P. Timmer, and H. Wang. 2004. The emergence of supermarkets with Chinese characteristics: challenges and opportunities for China's agricultural development. *Development Policy Review* 22 (5): 557–86.

ICCO (International Cocoa Organization). 2007. 'Assessment of the Movements of Global Supply and Demand'. ICCO report by Market Committee at the ninth meeting in Kuala Lumpur, 14 March.

Jia, X., J. Huang, H. Luan, S. Rozelle, and J. Swinnen. 2012. 'China's Milk Scandal, Government Policy and Production Decisions of Dairy Farmers: The Case of Great Beijing'. *Food Policy* 37: pp. 390–400.

KPMG. 2011. 'China's 12th Five Year Plan: Transportation and Logistics'. KPMG International (China). Available at: <https://www.kpmg.com/CN/en/IssuesAndInsights/ArticlesPublications/Documents/China-12th-Five-Year-Plan-Transportation-Logistics-201104.pdf>.

LI & FUNG Research Report. 2006. 'Packaged Food Market in China: Part I, Confectionery'. Available at: <http://www.funggroup.com/eng/knowledge/research/industry_series4.pdf>.

Li, G., G. Li, and Z. Kambele. 2012. 'Luxury Fashion Brand Consumers in China: Perceived Value, Fashion Lifestyle, and Willingness to Pay'. *Journal of Business Research* 65: pp. 1516–22.

Li, Z., S. Fu, and L. Murray. 1997. 'Country and Product Images: The Perceptions of Consumers in the People's Republic of China'. *Journal of International Consumer Marketing* 10 (1/2): pp. 115–39.

Lu, S. 2010. 'Understanding China's Retail Market'. *China Business Review.* Retrieved from: <http://www.chinabusinessreview.com/understanding-chinas-retail-market/>.

Ma, H., A. Rae, J. Huang, and S. Rozelle. 2004. 'Chinese Animal Product Consumption in the 1990s'. *Australian Journal of Agricultural and Resource Economics* 48 (4): pp. 569–90.

Mendez, M., S. Du, and B. Popkin. 2004. 'Urbanization, Income and the Nutrition Transition in China: A Case Study'. In *Globalization of Food Systems in Developing Countries: Impact on Food Security and Nutrition*, edited by FAO. FAO-Food and Nutrition Paper 83. Rome: Food and Agriculture Organization.

Newman, J. M. 2004. *Food Culture in China*. CT, USA: Greenwood Press.

Parraga, I. 1990. 'Determinants of Food Consumption'. *Journal of the American Dietetic Association* 90 (5): pp. 661–4.

Petry, M. and B. Wu. 2009. 'Food Safety Law of the People's Republic of China, 2009'. GAIN Report, USDA Foreign Agricultural Service, Report Number: CH9019.

Pingali, P. 2007. 'Westernization of Asian diets and the transformation of food systems: implications for research and policy.' *Food Policy* 32, no. 3: pp. 281–98.

Pingali, P. and Y. Khwaja. 2004. 'Globalisation of Indian Diets and the Transformation of Food Supply Systems'. Inaugural Keynote Address to the 17th Annual Conference of the Indian Society of Agricultural Marketing, Hyderabad, 5–7 February.

Ramzy, A., 2009. Will China's new food-safety laws work? *TIME*. Available at: <http://www.time.com/time/world/article/0,8599,1882711,00.html> (accessed 3 March 2015).

Savastano, S. 2012. 'The Impact of Soft Traits and Cognitive Abilities on Life Outcomes: Subjective Wellbeing, Education Achievement, and Rational Choices: A Chocolate Tasting Experiment'. CEIS Working Paper No. 241.

Scott-Thomas, C. 2011. 'Opportunities for Smaller Companies in Chinese Chocolate Market'. Retrieved from: <http://www.foodnavigator-asia.com/Markets/Opportunities-for-smaller-companies-in-Chinese-chocolate-market>.

Shanghai Daily. 2008. 'China's Taste for Chocolate'. *Shanghai Daily*, 16 September. Available at: <http://china.org.cn/business/2008-09/16/content_16461850.htm>.

Shetty, P. S. 2002. 'Nutrition Transition in India'. *Public Health and Nutrition* 5 (1A): pp. 175–82.

Sin, L., S. C. Ho, and S. So. 2000. 'Research on Advertising in Mainland China: A Review and Assessment'. *Asia Pacific Journal of Marketing and Logistics* 12 (1): pp. 37–65.

Wang, Z., Y. Mao, and F. Gale. 2008. Chinese consumer demand for food safety attributes in milk products, *Food Policy* 33: pp. 27–36.

Wang, J., C. Tang, J. Li, S. Zhang, J. Shen, and R. Zhang. 2013. 'China Food Manufacturing Annual Report'. Global Agricultural Information Network (GAIN) Report. Available at: <http://gain.fas.usda.gov/Recent%20GAIN%20Publications/China%20Food%20Manufacturing%20Annual%20Report_Beijing%20ATO_China%20-%20Peoples%20Republic%20of_1-31-2013.pdf> (accessed 12 April 2015).

Wood, L. J. and S. Grosvenor. 1997. 'Chocolate in China: The Cadbury Experience'. *Australian Geographer* 28 (2): pp. 173–84.

Wu, D. Y. H. and S. C. H. Cheung. 2002. *The Globalization of Chinese Food*. Honolulu: University of Hawai'i Press.

Xinhua News. 2008. 'China Focus: Chinese Premier Calls on Sick Infants'. *Xinhua News*, 21 September. Retrieved from: <http://news.xinhuanet.com/english/2008-09/21/content_10088285.htm> (accessed 12 April 2015).

20

Hot Chocolate in the Cold

The Economics and Politics of Chocolate in the Former Soviet Union

Saule Burkitbayeva and Koen Deconinck

Introduction

The Russian chocolate market is considered one of the most promising emerging chocolate markets in the world. While the consumption of chocolate in Russia is still far below the levels observed in Western European countries, chocolate consumption has been rising in recent years. Despite the relatively low consumption levels, Russia's love for chocolate was already worth 8 billion dollars in 2012 (KPMG 2012).

This chapter tells the story of the emergence and development of the chocolate market in Russia. We start with the arrival of chocolate in Russia in the mid-nineteenth century, and track the fate of chocolate during the Soviet period from 1922 to 1991. Next, we discuss how the collapse of the USSR affected the Russian chocolate market during the early transition years (1991–2000) as well as in the more recent past (2000–2013). We devote a separate section, 'The Political Economy of Chocolate', to the link between chocolate and politics, focusing both on Soviet-era issues and on the 'chocolate war' between Russia and Ukraine in 2013, which was a prelude to the political crisis between the two countries. We conclude this chapter with an outlook for the future.

How Chocolate Came to Russia

Chocolate arrived in Europe in the middle of sixteenth century, quickly winning the hearts of the European elite and aristocracy (Ward 2009). However, it took another two centuries for chocolate to reach Russia, where it remained a luxury good until the end of the nineteenth century.

The exact circumstances of the introduction of chocolate to Russia remain a subject of much debate. Although some speculate that it was Peter the Great (1672–1725) who brought chocolate, along with coffee, to Russian society, most historians seem to agree that it was Catherine the Great (1729–1796) who made chocolate drinking a tradition at the royal palace (Kruchina 2002). This suggests that chocolate reached Russia in about the second half of the eighteenth century, or one hundred years after its introduction in Britain (Ward 2009).

One way of tracking the introduction of chocolate in Russia is by looking at references to it in literature (Karpukhina 2011). One of the earliest references is by the satirist Ivan Krylov, who mentions 'a cup of chocolate' in a 1789 piece. At any rate, chocolate was clearly well established in Russia by the nineteenth century. Characters of the most prominent Russian poets and writers such as Pushkin, Lermontov, or Goncharov, drink cocoa, eat bars of chocolates, or give chocolate as presents to their loved ones. Inspiration went both ways: in the 1880s a brand of chocolate was labeled 'Pushkin: The Chocolate of Russian Poetry' in honour of the celebrated poet Alexander Pushkin (1799–1837).

By the end of the nineteenth century, chocolate, first consumed solely by aristocrats, spread to the masses. Chocolate became a popular treat and a traditional present among ordinary Russians. Numerous chocolate and confectionary factories began to appear across the country in the second half of the nineteenth century (Maliutenkova 2004). Factories such as Einem, Siu, Borman, and Abrikosov were among the largest chocolate and confectionary producing factories in the country, competing for the prestigious title of Purveyor to the Court of His Imperial Majesty (Sheipak 2010). By 1917, there were approximately 150 chocolate producing establishments of various sizes around Moscow, Saint Petersburg, Kharkov, and Nizhniy Novgorod (Kruchina 2002). Data on consumption are not available. However, given that cocoa beans cannot be grown in Russia, statistics on cocoa bean imports can be used as an indicator of trends in chocolate consumption (with some caveats, as discussed in Chocolate during the USSR Period).[1] These statistics, shown in Figure 20.1, reveal the growing popularity of chocolate in pre-revolutionary Russia. Imports of cocoa beans grew from 1,740 tons in 1900 to 4,300 tons in 1916.[2] Before 1917, cocoa beans were imported from Germany, Great Britain, the Netherlands, and France. Thus, on the eve of the October Revolution of 1917, chocolate was well established in Russia.

---

[1] Imported cocoa beans were consumed domestically, with virtually no exports of cocoa beans or confectionary products based on cocoa until very recently.

[2] The official statistics reports of the Russian Empire were written in both Russian and French. Cocoa beans imports were measured in thousands *pood* (1 *pood* = 16.3 kg). All cocoa bean import numbers in this chapter have been converted from *pood* to tons.

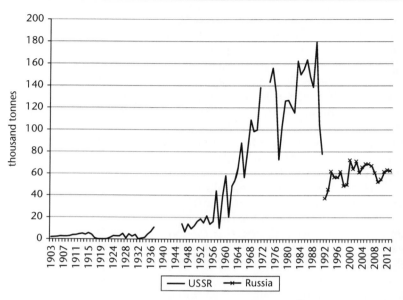

Figure 20.1 Imports of cocoa beans in the USSR and Russia, 1903–2012 (in thousand tons)

Source: Istmat (n.d.), FAOSTAT(n.d), TradeMap (n.d), and RBC (2001).

Chocolate during the USSR Period

The October Revolution in 1917 had a large impact on chocolate production in Russia. All private chocolate and confectionary factories were nationalized and renamed according to the new economic and political system.

During the turmoil of the early years, cocoa imports decreased. However, by 1927, cocoa bean imports reached 5,100 tons, surpassing for the first time the pre-revolutionary peak of 3,500 tons. The highest level of cocoa bean imports recorded before the outbreak of World War II was 11,000 tons in 1937. While no data is available for the 1938–45 period, this does not necessarily imply that there was no chocolate production during the war. Many existing confectionary factories were re-specialized for the production of warfare supplies, but a limited amount of chocolate production remained, and chocolate with an increased amount of caffeine and theobromine to stimulate the nervous system was included in soldiers' rations (Karpukhina 2011).

After World War II, the growth in cocoa imports appears to have been modest up until 1954. In that year, cocoa bean imports were 21,000 tons. In the following years, imports would grow strongly, albeit with large fluctuations. Cocoa bean imports reached a maximum of 179,000 tons in 1989, before collapsing during the turmoil of transition (discussed in the next section, 'Russian Chocolate in Transition'). This period, from the end of the 1950s to 1989, was characterized by rapid

Figure 20.2 Confectionary production in the USSR and Russia, 1928–2012 (in thousand tons)
Source: Istmat (n.d.) and GosKomStat (n.d.).

growth and development and can be considered the 'blooming period' of the Soviet chocolate industry and the Soviet confectionary industry more broadly (ICCO 2001). Factories were re-equipped and processing capacities were increased. Confectionary production (which often, though not always, involved cocoa) was backed by rigorous scientific analysis carried out by the Scientific Research Institute of the Confectionary Industries (SRICI) and factory laboratories.

Figure 20.2 shows the evolution of confectionary production in the USSR and Russia. From 1960 to 1989, production of confectionary products in the USSR almost tripled,[3] from 1.7 to 5 million tons of confectionary products annually. Given that exports were negligible, this implies a per capita consumption of confectionary products of 17.4 kilograms per person in 1989.

However, the strong growth in this period was accompanied by considerable turmoil during the second half of the 1970s, coinciding with a general economic crisis in the USSR (Bacon and Sandle 2002). The era of economic stagnation translated into plummeting imports of cocoa beans (see Figure 20.1). In 1977, cocoa bean imports fell by more than 50 per cent from the 1975 levels. As a result, chocolate production took a hit (Figure 20.3). From 1975 to 1980, chocolate production decreased from 96,000 to 70,000 tons. However, once the imports of cocoa beans returned to their previous levels, chocolate production also recovered, increasing to 102,000 tons in 1985. Chocolate production would remain around this level until 1989.

The economic stagnation of the 1970s implied that the increased and improved processing capacities in the confectionary industry would go underutilized. In

---

[3] Confectionary products in Soviet statistics included soft candies, hard candies, chocolate products, cakes and biscuits, cookies, pastries, and other sweets.

Figure 20.3 Production of chocolate in the USSR and Russia, 1932–2009 (in thousand tons)

Source: Istmat (n.d.) and GosKomStat (n.d.).

Table 20.1 Production of confectionary products by Soviet Republics 1940–87 (in thousand tons)

	1940	1971	1987	% of Total in 1987
USSR Total	790	2,890	4,632	100
Russia	501	1,616	2,475	53
Ukraine	192	623	992	21
Kazakhstan	4	123	236	5
Belarus	41	120	174	4
Uzbekistan	13	87	173	4
Azerbaijan	9	42	104	2
Other	30	279	478	10

response, the SRICI developed recipes that required less raw materials and/or their substitution by cheaper and lower quality inputs. The Russian confectionary industry started using such ingredients as apple powder, soy flour, and substitutes for cocoa butter (ICCO 2001). As a result, the drop in cocoa bean imports had no negative impact on the production of confectionary products (Figure 20.2). Over the 1965–1987 period, the production of confectionaries kept growing steadily at around 3 per cent rate annually.

Russia, Ukraine, Kazakhstan, and Belarus were the top confectionary producers in the Soviet Union. As shown in Table 20.1, more than half of Soviet confectionary production in 1987 took place in Russia. Together, Russia and Ukraine accounted for nearly three quarters of total confectionary production in Russia. After the collapse of the Soviet Union, Russia and Ukraine remained the largest confectionary producers among the countries of the former Soviet Union (FSU).

Russian Chocolate in Transition

The transition from a command economy to a market economy had its toll on all sectors of the economy in the FSU. The early 1990s were characterized by a sharp decline in production, driven by a dismantling of the existing economic ties and value chains (Rozelle and Swinnen 2004). Adjusting to the realities of a market economy was made even more difficult by the competition from foreign goods. For many countries in the FSU, including Russia, it would take until the early 2000s before incomes again reached the pre-transition levels.

The turmoil of transition also affected chocolate and confectionary production. While data for chocolate production is missing for the crucial 1991–94 period, the evolution of the market for confectionary illustrates the general trends during transition. Figure 20.4 shows domestic production and imports of confectionary between 1990 and 2010. Since exports were non-existent or negligible in the first decade, the sum of production and import data represents total domestic consumption of confectionary. The data presented in Figure 20.4 can thus be used to analyse the impact of transition on the consumption of confectionary, as well as the impact of transition on the competitiveness of Russian producers.

By and large, consumption of confectionary mimics the evolution of Russian incomes over the same period, showing a decline until 1998 and a recovery afterwards.

The evolution of production and imports reflect the changing fortunes of Russian confectionary producers during transition. The decline in production after 1991 was larger than the decline in consumption, indicating that Russian households not only decreased their consumption of confectionary but also increasingly switched to imported products at the expense of domestic confectionary. Over

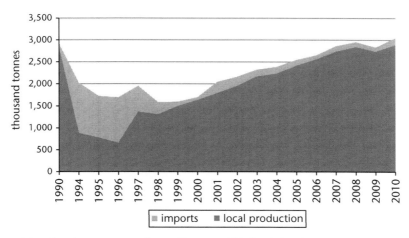

Figure 20.4 Confectionary market in Russia, 1990–2010 (in thousand tons)
Source: RBC (2001), ASKOND (2011), Skopinceva (2009), and GosKomStat (n.d.).

the 1994–96 period, more than half of the Russian confectionary market consisted of imports. After 1996, however, this situation changed rapidly. While total consumption levels remained depressed, local production picked up and the share of imports in the Russian confectionary market declined to 7 per cent in 1999. The strong growth was not limited to confectionary; as shown in Figure 20.3, chocolate production shows an equally strong revival during these years.

The dramatic reversal can be explained in large part by the inflow of foreign investment into the Russian chocolate and confectionary industry.[4] In the initial stages of transition, Russia imported Western confectionary. However, Western confectionary producers such as Mars, Cadbury, and Stollwerck quickly realized the potential of investing in local production for the Russian market. This process was accelerated by the ruble crisis of 1998. The economic crisis and consumers' changing tastes forced foreign multinationals to change their strategies. Foreign companies importing goods to the Russian market began to position themselves as local. They increased their local production by building new factories and buying existing ones locally. Foreign firms were now able to offer local consumers a familiar product. Branding and advertising used local-sounding names and images, thus making it easier for the Russian customer to relate to a product that nonetheless maintained Western quality levels (Lewis 2008). Since 1998, on average, the share of imports in the Russian confectionary market remained at around 11 per cent annually. During the first decade of transition, the Russian confectionary market thus went through an enormous transformation. The initial fall in local production and rise in imports was followed by a rapid expansion of local production and a corresponding decrease in imports.

Recent Trends (2000–13)

Production

After the remarkable turnaround during transition, Russian chocolate and confectionary production have both shown strong growth. As made clear in Figure 20.3, chocolate production increased from 50,000 tons in 1996 to almost 300,000 tons in 2009: a growth rate of 7.7 per cent.[5] Likewise, the production of confectionary (shown in Figure 20.2) tripled during these years, growing from less than 1 million tons in 1996 to more than 3 million tons today (2015).

---

[4] The Russian confectionary industry includes the production of chocolate, chocolate-containing products, sweets, cakes, biscuits, pastries, and crackers.

[5] The data shown in Figure 20.3 is only available up to 2009. Since then, the classification used in the official statistics has changed, and the data for chocolate and chocolate products now also includes other types of sweets, which makes recent data hard to compare to historical figures. For instance, whereas total chocolate production was almost 300,000 tons in 2009, the new series, including other types of sweets, gives a total of 1.4 million tons for 2010.

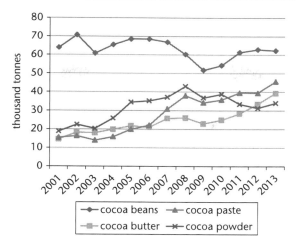

Figure 20.5 Imports of main cocoa materials in Russia, 2001–13 (in thousand tons)
Source: TradeMap (n.d.).

Raw Materials

Interestingly, the strong growth in chocolate production has led to increases in the imports of some, but not all, raw materials.

Whereas the imports of cocoa beans form a reliable indicator of chocolate production during the Soviet era, Figure 20.1 makes it clear that Russian imports of cocoa beans are nowhere near the numbers seen during the Soviet era, even when taking into account the fact that Russia only accounts for part of the Soviet total. By contrast, chocolate production (Figure 20.3) is markedly higher than in the Soviet era.

The solution to this paradox is that chocolate producers have increasingly switched to other types of raw materials. This can be seen from Figure 20.5, which shows the imports of main cocoa materials in Russia from 2001 to 2013. During this period of spectacular growth in chocolate production, total imports of cocoa beans remained constant, while there was moderate growth in the imports of cocoa butter and strong growth in the imports of cocoa paste and cocoa powder. Extrapolating these trends backwards in time, it appears plausible that the major transformation of the Russian chocolate industry during transition also involved a change in production techniques, moving away from raw cocoa beans to using more processed cocoa inputs.

In addition to this shift, Russian chocolate producers also appear to have reduced the cocoa content of their products over time, especially following the high prices for cocoa products in 2002–03 following the political unrest in Cote d'Ivoire (ICCO 2010). One strategy is to move towards so-called 'cocoa butter substitutes' (CBS) and 'equivalents' (CBE). EFKO Group, one of the largest oils and fats suppliers in Russia, has reported growing sales of CBS due to increasing prices of raw cocoa materials (EFKO 2013). CBS and CBE are imported and exported in small amounts in Russia, and also produced locally (Tochieva 2011). The lack of conclusive data on production, imports, and exports of CBS and CBE in Russia makes it hard to obtain a good overview of this phenomenon. Nevertheless, data for 2008–10 indicates an increasing trend for imports of both CBS and CBE. In 2010, imports of CBS and CBE were equal to 46,100 and 16,600 tons respectively (Tochieva 2011), which means that, in 2010, Russia imported more CBS than actual cocoa butter (25,000 tons).

Chocolate Trade

Russia is a net importer of chocolate, yet the gap between imports and exports is shrinking. Figure 20.6 shows the evolution of trade in chocolate over the 2001–13 period.

Imports of chocolate fluctuated around 140,000 tons in the 2001–10 period, with the exception of two large declines in 2006 and 2009. While the 2009 decline was clearly caused by the global recession, the 2006 decline was caused solely by a strong decrease in chocolate imports from Ukraine, which fell by 34 per cent. We return to this in the The Political Economy of Chocolate.

The imports of chocolate grew strongly from 2010 onwards. A part of the increase is due to the formation of a customs union with Kazakhstan and Belarus in 2010, which had a positive impact on imports of chocolate products. From 2010 to 2013, imports of chocolate from Belarus have doubled in volume; the volume of imports from Kazakhstan in 2013 (4,250 tons) were eight times larger than those reported in 2010 (506 tons). However, even after the strong

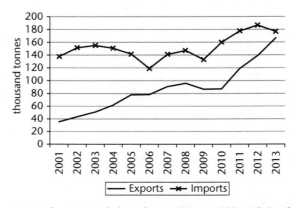

Figure 20.6 Imports and exports of chocolate in Russia, 2001–13 (in thousand tons)

Note: Data includes chocolate and other food preparations containing cocoa. Russia did not report its trade with Kazakhstan and Belarus for certain years; missing data was corrected using trade data for these countries.

Source: TradeMap (n.d.).

Table 20.2 Top ten origin country of Russian chocolate imports, 2013 (% of imports by volume)

		%
1	Ukraine	53
2	Germany	12
3	Italy	5
4	Poland	5
5	Netherlands	5
6	Belgium	4
7	Belarus	3
8	Kazakhstan	2
9	France	2
10	Switzerland	1

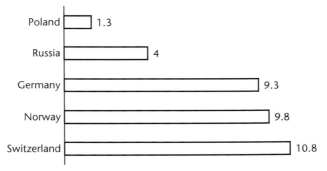

Figure 20.7 Russian chocolate confectionary market index volume and value, 1999–2013

Source: Euromonitor (n.d.).

growth, these two countries were jointly responsible for only 5 per cent of chocolate imports to Russia.[6]

Table 20.2 shows the top ten origin countries for chocolate imports into Russia in 2013. More than half of all Russian chocolate imports originated from Ukraine. The rest of the imports are divided among European countries and countries of the former USSR.

Russian chocolate exports show a remarkable growth. Total exports doubled between 2001 and 2010, and again between 2010 and 2013. There thus appears to be a clear acceleration of export growth after 2010. Part of the growth may again be due to the customs union with Kazakhstan and Belarus: exports of Russian chocolate to Kazakhstan and Belarus have also doubled from 2010 to 2013.

---

[6] Part of the increase may also be due to a change in classification in trade statistics following the adoption of the harmonized system (HS) of trade statistics. However, given the strong growth both before and after the introduction of the new classification in 2010, this factor probably plays only a minor role.

Table 20.3 Top ten destination country for Russian chocolate exports, 2013 (% of exports by volume)

		%
1	Kazakhstan	32
2	Ukraine	21
3	Belarus	9
4	Azerbaijan	8
5	Kyrgyzstan	5
6	Tajikistan	4
7	Mongolia	4
8	Georgia	3
9	Turkmenistan	3
10	Armenia	2

In contrast to the import side, exports to Kazakhstan and Belarus are a significant portion of total Russian exports, accounting for 41 per cent of total exports in 2013.

By contrast, it appears that Russia's accession to the World Trade Organization (WTO) in 2012 had no major impact on its exports of chocolate. The bulk of chocolate is still exported to the FSU countries where Russia faces no trade barriers. Table 20.3 shows the top ten destination countries for Russian chocolate in 2013. Most of the Russian chocolate was exported to the neighbouring FSU countries. Kazakhstan (35 per cent), Ukraine (20 per cent), Azerbaijan (8 per cent), and Belarus (6 per cent) are among the biggest importers of chocolate produced in Russia.

Market Value and Volume

Over the 2000–13, the chocolate confectionary market in Russia has been growing rapidly.[7] The evolution of Russian chocolate confectionary market in 1999–2013 in terms of indexed value and volume can be observed in Figure 20.8. In value terms, the chocolate confectionary market has been growing at 15 per cent per year, compared to a volume growth of 5 per cent per year (see Table 20.4). While Russian consumers' appetite for chocolate is thus increasing in general, they are at the same time moving towards more expensive types of chocolate. Russians are willing to buy new chocolate products and premium brands, whether imported or local. The popularity of high-quality handmade chocolate is growing. Retail sales of dark chocolate, considered the healthiest and lowest in calories, are increasing as well (Euromonitor 2013). The Russian chocolate market is thus witnessing a move towards higher-quality products.

---

[7] The Russian chocolate confectionary market constitutes retail selling values of real chocolate and chocolate compound containing substitute raw material ingredients such as cocoa butter extenders (Datamonitor 2001).

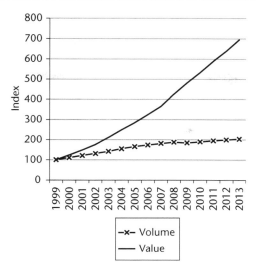

Figure 20.8 Chocolate consumption per capita in selected countries, 2011 (in kg per year)
Source: KPMG (2011).

Table 20.4 Russian chocolate confectionary market, 1999–2013

Year	Per Capita Consumption (kg)	Volume (thousand tons)	Value (millions US$)
1999	2.5	364	1,519
2000	2.8	403	1,872
2001	3.0	442	2,261
2002	3.3	478	2,675
2003	3.6	516	3,212
2004	3.9	563	3,790
2005	4.2	603	4,319
2006	4.4	631	4,924
2007	4.6	661	5,545
2008	4.8	683	6,464
2009	4.7	671	7,310
2010	4.8	689	8,100
2011	5.0	710	8,943
2012	5.1	726	9,719
2013	5.2	741	10,577
1999–2013 CAGR*	*7%*	*5%*	*15%*

* CAGR is the compound annual growth rate. Volume and value data from Euromonitor (n.d.). Per capita data from authors' own calculations using population statistics from GosKomStat and World Bank.

Competition

The Russian chocolate confectionary market is characterized by a significant share of foreign investment. In the late 1990s, the chocolate market was mostly dominated by foreign companies such as Mars, Nestlé, Stollwerck, and Cadbury. In 2001,

Table 20.5 Russian chocolate confectionary market shares in 2001 (% by total sales value)

Producer	% Share
Stollwerck	20.1
Nestlé	18.2
Mars	12.4
Cadbury	8.6
Red Oktober	8.8
Slad & Ko	8.5
Babayevskoe	8.4
Bolshevik	5
Rot Front	4
Other	6

Table 20.6 Russian chocolate confectionary market shares in 2013 (% of total sales value)

Producer	% Share
Uniconf	18.7
Mars	14.4
Nestlé	11.9
Mondelēz International Inc. (Kraft)	9.8
Ferrero Group	9.1
Orkla Group	4.2
KONTI Group	3.8
Slavyanka KO	3.3
Roshen Corp.	2.9
Other	21.9

Stollwerck, Nestlé, and Mars together accounted for more than 50 per cent of the chocolate confectionary market (see Table 20.5). Red Oktober and Babayevskoe were among the few local producers who were able to keep up with the foreign competition. Small local producers, fighting the consequences of the economic crisis in the beginning of 1990s and the aftermath of the 1998 crisis, started to consolidate (RBC 2001). For example, in 2002 three confectionary factories (Red Oktober, Rot Front, and Babayevskoe) combined into Uniconf. Nowadays, Uniconf is the largest confectionary holding in Eastern Europe, uniting 16 factories and 8 logistics centres. In general, most regional producers are now operating under large company names. The process of consolidation, merger, and acquisition in the Russian chocolate market is still ongoing (Euromonitor 2013).[8]

The main competitors in Russia's chocolate market are listed in Table 20.6. In 2013, the leading position belonged to Uniconf, which is Russian-owned. Foreign

[8] In addition to the consolidation process taking place inside Russia, there is also consolidation taking place at a global level. Thus, Kraft acquired Stollwerck in 2002 and merged with Cadbury in 2010.

companies such as Mars, Nestlé, Kraft, and Ferrero dominate the rest of the chocolate market, accounting for 45 per cent. As market leader, Uniconf appears quite active in terms of innovation. The company has introduced product lines aimed at health-conscious consumers, as well as kosher chocolate and chocolate without animal fat for religious consumers. The market is characterized by heavy promotion and advertising efforts by the main producers (Euromonitor 2013).

The Political Economy of Chocolate

Both during the Soviet era and more recently, the market for chocolate in Russia has been affected by geopolitical considerations. We first discuss how Cold War considerations affected Soviet imports of cocoa, and then discuss how the recent conflicts between Russia and Ukraine have affected the trade in chocolate.

In the context of the Cold War, Soviet imports of cocoa were inevitably linked to geopolitical considerations. Most of the cocoa bean imports in the USSR were from Africa, particularly Nigeria, Ghana, and Cameroon, in addition to imports from Brazil and Ecuador.

Between the 1960s and the 1980s, ties between the USSR and African countries grew, as can be seen from the growing number of treaties and agreements during this period, many of which dealt with trade relations. In exchange for cocoa beans, the USSR often sent weapons, machinery, or equipment.[9] For instance, Nigeria supplied cocoa beans to the Soviets in partial exchange for weapons (Porter 1986). Likewise, in 1962 the USSR signed a trade agreement with Cameroon to provide Soviet machinery and equipment, cement, fertilizers, and more in exchange for Cameroon's cocoa beans, timber, and other traditional export items (Ginsburgs and Slusser 1981).

Interestingly, Cote d'Ivoire (now the largest-volume cocoa producer in the world) played an insignificant role in Soviet cocoa imports. The USSR began importing cocoa beans from Cote d'Ivoire in 1959, but the trade was abruptly halted after only two years, in 1961 (Brzezinski 1963). The trade later resumed yet remained sporadic due to political reasons. One of the factors hampering Soviet–Ivorian relations was the close relation between the USSR and Guinea, which allegedly fuelled the opposition in Cote d'Ivoire (Meyer 1970). Diplomatic relations between the USSR and Cote d'Ivoire were renewed in 1967 and once again severed in 1969 after allegations of Soviet political interference within the country. Ties were restored only in 1986. Decisions about cocoa imports were thus closely linked to geopolitical considerations.

---

[9] The numbers involved in such treaties were quite significant. A treaty signed between the USSR and Ghana in 1965 arranged the delivery of 150,000 tons of cocoa between 1966 and 1967 alone (Ginsburgs and Slusser 1981), which would have worked out to more than half of total Soviet imports in that period. Another trade protocol between USSR and Ghana in 1966 provided for cocoa imports from Ghana to reach 120,000 tons by 1970. Since total Soviet imports never exceeded 180,000 tons, this is a considerable number. It is not clear to what extent the goals set in these treaties were actually met.

The link between politics and chocolate still exists today, as illustrated by the recent 'chocolate wars' between Russia and Ukraine. In October 2005, Russia introduced new import tariffs on certain products from Ukraine, including confectionaries. The effect on trade was dramatic: total Russian imports of Ukrainian chocolate fell by 34 per cent in 2006.[10] Given that Ukraine accounts for more than half of Russian chocolate imports (Table 20.2), this drop in imports shows up in the aggregate statistics on imports, as discussed in Chocolate Trade. The high import tariffs on Ukrainian imports were widely seen as Russian retaliation, as part of the 2005–06 conflict between Russia and Ukraine over gas deliveries (see Woehrel and Gelb 2007).

Although the gas conflict was eventually settled, relations between the two countries remained tense. While Ukraine was in negotiations with the European Union (EU) for closer economic and political cooperation in 2013, Russia was, at the same time, exerting pressure on Ukraine to join the customs union with Belarus and Kazakhstan.

In July 2013, Russia banned imports of products from Roshen, the biggest confectionary producer in Ukraine. Such embargos on foodstuffs from neighbouring countries are not uncommon in Russia, with some import bans over the last decade targeting Georgian and Moldovan wine and Lithuanian dairy. Rospotrebnadzor, Russia's consumer watchdog, often justified these bans (as well as the bans on Ukrainian chocolate) by concerns over the safety of the products. Russian government officials denied any underlying political motive for these trade restriction measures, although Moscow's import bans are often seen by the countries involved as 'arm-twisting' forms of political pressure.

The story of the Roshen chocolate ban provides an interesting view of the political economy of import bans in Russia. On the one hand, the official reason for the ban has been challenged. On the other hand, Roshen's owner is influential in Ukrainian politics and had been a vocal supporter of closer ties with the EU, to the detriment of relations with Russia.

As motivation for the import ban, Rospotrebnadzor referred to allegedly high levels of the toxic hydrocarbon benzopyrene in Roshen's chocolates.[11] Roshen denied that there was any risk for consumers.[12] In August 2013, Kazakhstan's sanitary authorities held their own investigation, which yielded no signs of benzopyrene, and Kazakhstan abstained from banning Roshen products.[13] Belarus initially blocked the transit and re-exports of Roshen products through its border to Russia and started its own inspection. However, it later announced that no safety

---

[10] The decree on introducing import tariffs on a number of products from Ukraine is published in *Rossiyskaya Gazeta* 2005, from 19 October, available at: <http://www.rg.ru/2005/10/19/poshliny-ukr-dok.html> (accessed 11 September 2015).

[11] <http://ria.ru/economy/20130729/952728663.html> (accessed 11 September 2015).

[12] <http://www.confectionerynews.com/Regulation-Safety/Roshen-in-the-dark-over-Russian-import-ban> (accessed 11 September 2015).

[13] <http://rus.ruvr.ru/news/2013_08_16/Kazahstan-otkazalsja-zapreshhat-konfeti-Roshen-3225/> (accessed 1 October 2013).

violations or toxic materials were found in Roshen products.[14] A number of other FSU countries, including Kyrgyzstan, Armenia, Tajikistan, and Moldavia, came to similar conclusions after conducting their own analyses. Thus, the official grounds for the import ban appear questionable.

Ukraine challenged Russia's ban in the WTO, drawing the attention to Russia's non-transparent actions. Ukraine claimed the ban to be discriminatory and in-compliant with the WTO's Agreement on the Application of Sanitary and Phyto-sanitary Measures (SPS) that set the rules for food safety and animal and plant health standards. In response, Russia justified the ban by referring to Roshen's non-compliance with Russia's technical regulations rather than SPS issues. In particular, Roshen's products violated the technical requirements for labelling, providing false information on protein fat and carbohydrate content.[15] As of 2015, the issue has not resolved.

On the other hand, Roshen is owned by Petro Poroshenko, an influential Ukrainian businessman and pro-EU politician, who is one of the wealthiest people in Ukraine according to *Forbes*.[16] Given Poroshenko's influence and pro-EU pos-ition, the attack on Roshen can be seen as an attempt to intimidate or pressure an important supporter of closer ties with the EU.

Poroshenko started his business career selling cocoa beans and acquired several confectionary companies during the 1990s, eventually consolidating these into Roshen. Nowadays, Roshen is one of the largest confectionary manufacturers both in and outside of Ukraine. The company was ranked 18th among the top confec-tionary companies in the world.[17] In 2013, it operated four Ukrainian factories, production sites in Russia and Lithuania, and two buttermilk plants.[18]

During the anti-government protests in Kiev, Poroshenko gave numerous pro-EU speeches throughout the entire period of protests. In addition, Poroshenko also owns Ukraine's most popular news channel, known for its pro-opposition content during the protests. These demonstrations, demanding closer integration with the EU, started immediately after Ukraine had withdrawn from negotiations to sign a free trade agreement with the EU at the end of November 2013. The protests eventually escalated in a major civil unrest known as Euromaidan, which resulted in the ousting of President Yanukovich in February 2014.

Given Poroshenko's political influence and his preference for closer ties with the EU, the import ban targeting Roshen can be seen as part of the wider conflict between Russia and Ukraine. In March 2014, the Russian government seized and shut down Roshen's Lipetsk confectionary factory in Russia.[19] The new Ukrainian government condemned the move as 'the logical continuation of a politically

---

[14] <https://www.kyivpost.com/content/ukraine/belarus-finds-no-problems-with-roshen-produce-330293.html> (accessed 11 September 2015).

[15] WTO 2014. Committee on Technical Barriers to Trade. Minutes of the meeting of 19–20 March (accessed 11 September 2015).

[16] <http://www.forbes.com/profile/petro-poroshenko/> (accessed 11 September 2015).

[17] <http://www.candyindustry.com/Top25candycompanies> (accessed 11 September 2015).

[18] <http://roshen.cn/en/about/general/> (accessed 11 September 2015).

[19] <http://www.bbc.com/news/business-26661220> (accessed 11 September 2015).

motivated campaign' which violates international law.[20] Later that month, Poroshenko, often referred to as a 'sponsor of Euromaidan', declared his candidacy for presidential elections of May 2014.[21] Poroshenko won the presidential elections and was sworn into the office in early June 2014.[22] One of his stated objectives is moving Ukraine's focus away from Moscow and towards the EU.[23]

Conclusion

In this chapter, we have traced the history of chocolate in Russia. While chocolate was only introduced in Russia at a relatively late stage compared to other European countries, its popularity (as measured by cocoa beans imports) was clearly growing by the eve of the 1917 Russian Revolution. In Soviet times, chocolate and related confectionary products experienced a strong growth between 1960 and 1989. However, the turmoil of transition inevitably affected the industry. In the first years of transition, domestic consumption declined but domestic production declined even more, signalling a shift by consumers towards imported Western confectionary. Around 1996, however, domestic production recovered strongly. While this was in large part due to the decision of foreign producers to produce locally, the market is currently dominated by a Russian-owned company (Uniconf). We have also highlighted the ways in which political motives affect the chocolate market in Russia, referring both to Soviet times and to the current (2015) conflict with Ukraine.

As documented in this chapter, the Russian chocolate market has witnessed strong growth in the past decade, driven by a growing appetite for chocolate. This trend is expected to continue in the future. According to KPMG, Russians consumed 4 kg of chocolate per capita in 2011. While this is a higher level than in some other former communist countries such as Poland, the figure is still below the levels seen in Western countries such as Germany and Norway, not to mention Switzerland (see Figure 20.8. This relatively low level of consumption suggests that the Russian market still has upward potential in pure volume terms, although growth could be hampered by the development of non-chocolate snack alternatives (KPMG 2011). Moreover, consumers are increasingly switching to more expensive chocolates, causing the market to grow even more strongly in value terms. Observers expect growth to come from new product development such as healthy snack alternatives or the introduction of new flavours and shapes (Euromonitor 2013). For these reasons, the Russian chocolate market is considered to be one of the most promising chocolate markets in the world.

[20] <http://www.kmu.gov.ua/control/en/publish/article?art_id=247121913&cat_id=244314975> (accessed 11 September 2015).

[21] <http://rus.postimees.ee/2744216/sponsor-majdana-petr-poroshenko-idet-v-prezidenty-ukrainy> (accessed 11 September 2015).

[22] <http://www.telegraph.co.uk/news/worldnews/europe/ukraine/10883243/Petro-Poroshenko-sworn-in-as-Ukraine-president.html> (accessed 11 September 2015).

[23] <http://www.telegraph.co.uk/news/worldnews/europe/ukraine/10731848/Petro-Poroshenko-the-billionaire-chocolate-baron-hoping-to-become-Ukraines-next-president.html> (accessed 11 September 2015).

References

Bacon, E. and M. Sandle. 2002. *Brezhnev Reconsidered*. London: Palgrave Macmillan.

Brzezinski, Z. 1963. *Africa and the Communist World*. Stanford, CA: Published for the Hoover Institution on War, Revolution, and Peace by Stanford University Press.

Datamonitor. 2001. Chocolate Confectionery Industry Profile: Russia. Reference Code: 153–38. Datamonitor Industry Market Research.

EFKO. 2013. As cited in Cocoa butter substitute use growing in Russia, says EFKO available at: <http://www.confectionerynews.com/Ingredients/Cocoa-butter-substitute-use-growing-in-Russia-says-EFKO>. Accessed 11 September 2015.

Euromonitor. 2013. Chocolate Confectionary in Russia. Passport. Available at: <http://go.euromonitor.com/Passport-Home>. Accessed 12 February 2014.

Euromonitor. n.d. Packaged Food, Chocolate Confectionary Statistics. Available at: <http://www.%20euromonitor.com>. Accessed 3 March 2014.

FAOSTAT. Food and Agriculture Organization of the United Nations Statistics. Available at: <http://www.faostat3.fao.org/home/E>. Accessed 11 September 2015.

Ginsburgs, G. and R. M. Slusser. 1981. 'A Calendar of Soviet Treaties, 1958–1973'. Alphen aan den Rijn, Netherlands: Sijthoff & Noordhoff International Publisers BV.

GosKomStat. n.d. Federalnaya Sluzhba Gosudarstvennoi Statistiki [Federal State Statistics Agency]. Available at: <http://www.gks.ru>. Accessed 2 February 2014.

ICCO (International Cocoa Organization). 2001. The generic promotion of cocoa consumption in the Russian Federation project. Feasability Study. International Cocoa Organization. Available at: <http://www.icco.org/about-us/international-cocoa-agreements/cat_view/50-projects.html>. Accessed 1 March 2014.

ICCO (International Cocoa Organization). 2010. 'The World Cocoa Economy: Past and Present'. International Cocoa Organization's 142nd Meeting, Bloomsbury House, London, 14–17 September.

Istmat. n.d. Stattistika Rosiiskoi Imperii, SSSR I Rosiiskoi Federacii Proekt 'Istoricheskie Materiali' [Statistics of Russian Empire, USSR and Russian Federation 'Historical Materials' Project]. Available at: <http://istmat.info/statistics>. Accessed 11 September 2015.

Karpukhina, V. 2011. 'Shokolad. Vkusnii celitel' i lekarstvo ot 3000 boleznei' ['Chocolate: Sweet Healer and Remedy for 3000 Diseases']. The ACT publishing house. Moscow: Russia.

Kruchina, E. 2002. *Цоколад* [*Chocolate*]. Moscow: Zhigulskogo.

KPMG. 2011. 'In Focus: Food and Beverage Markets in Russia'. KPMG International. Available at: <http://www.kpmg.de/docs/Food-and-beverage-survey-2011.pdf>. Accessed 11 September 2015.

KPMG. 2012. 'The Chocolate of Tomorrow'. KPMG International. Available at: <http://www.kpmg.de/docs/chocolate-of-tomorrow.pdf>. Accessed 2 January 2014.

Lewis, C. P. 2008. *How the East was Won: Impact of Multinational Companies in Eastern Europe and the Former Soviet Union*. London: Palgrave Macmillan.

Maliutenkova, S. M. 2004. *Tovarovedenie I ekspertiza konditerskih tovarov: Ucheb. Posobie dlya vuzov* [*Commodity and Confectionery Products Expertise: Educational Manual for Universities*]. Saint Petersburg: Piter Print.

Meyer, F. S. 1970. *The African Nettle: Dilemmas of an Emerging Continent*. Freeport, NY: Books for Libraries Press.

Nosenko, S. M. 2011. 'Rinok konditerskih izdelii Rossiiskoi Federacii. Formirovanie edinogo economicheskogo prostranstva'. ASKOND (Association of Confectionary Producers).

Russia, Belarus, Kazakhstan ['Confectionary Market of the Russian Federation: Shaping the Common Economy: Russia, Belarus, Kazakhstan]. Presented at 'Sugar Market of CIS Countries 2011: Realities and Prospects' Conference.

Porter, B. D. 1986. *The USSR in Third World Conflicts: Soviet Arms and Diplomacy in Local Wars 1945–1980*. Cambridge: Cambridge University Press.

RBC (RosBusinessConsulting). 2001. *Obzor otrasli: Conditerskaya promishlennost [Market Outlook: Confectionary Industry]*. Moscow: RBC.

Rozelle, S. and J. Swinnen. 2004. 'Success and Failure of Reforms: Insights from Transition Agriculture'. *Journal of Economic Literature* 43 (June): pp. 404–56.

Sheipak, A. A. 2010. *Istoriya nauki I techniki. Materiali I technologii. Chast pervaya [History of Science and Technology: Materials and Technologies: Part One]*. Moscow: Moscow State Industrial University.

Skopinceva, E. 2009. 'Krizisi na polzu rosiiskim sladkoezhkam' ['Sugar Addicts are Better Off in Crisis']. *Economy and Life* 20: online issue. Available at: <http://www.eg-online.ru/articicle/66920/>. Accessed 11 September 2015.

Tochieva, L. 2011. 'Na Pole Zamena! Obzor Rosiiskogo Rinka Zamenitelei I Ekvivalentov Kakao Masla' ['A Field Change! Overview of the Russian Market for Cocoa Butter Equivalents']. *Russian Food and Drinks Market Magazine* 5. Available at: <http://www.foodmarket.spb.ru/archive.php?year=2011&number=124&article=1607>.

TradeMap. n.d. Trade Statistics for International Business Development by International Trade Center. Available at: <http://www.trademap.org>. Accessed 11 September 2015.

Ward, G. W. R. 2009. 'Silver Chocolate Pots of Colonial Boston'. In *Chocolate: History, Culture, and Heritage*, edited by L. E. Grivetti, and H.-Y. Shapiro, pp. 143-156. Hoboken, NJ: John Wiley.

Woehrel, S. and B. Gelb. 2007. 'Russia's Cutoff of Natural Gas to Ukraine: Context and Implications'. In *Focus on Politics and Economics of Russia and Eastern Europe*, edited by U. L. Nichol, pp. 59–64. New York: Nova Science Publisher.

21

Too Hot to Handle

The Explosive Growth of Chocolate in India

Emma Janssen and Olivia Riera

Introduction

India is the fastest growing market for chocolates in the world. Over the past decades, its growth rate has been twice that of other fast-growing markets. In combinations with its huge population, the recent growth in chocolate consumption has been huge, as is the untapped market potential: consumption is still low in absolute terms and quite concentrated in urban areas. This makes the Indian chocolate market one of, if not the most promising emerging chocolate markets in the world.

The dramatic transformation of the Indian chocolate market is a combination of several factors: (1) the trade liberalization initiated in 1991 has resulted in many processed foods entering the Indian market and chocolates being available in the smallest stores' shelves; (2) the foreign direct investment (FDI) liberalization, which was initiated following the 1991 trade liberalization, has led to a surge in foreign investments in the retail and food processing industry; and (3) the rapid economic (income) growth has lifted millions of households out of poverty and given rise to an emerging middle class with new consumption patterns and preferences.

In this chapter, we first briefly present the history of chocolate in India that is closely linked to the British company Cadbury's initial efforts to develop chocolate in the British former colony. Next, we characterize and explain factors that have contributed to the recent boom in the chocolate consumer market. Last, we identify several specificities of the Indian market and describe how the sector adapts to its inherent opportunities and challenges. One interesting issue is the development of new types of chocolates to address Indian consumers' preferences, and of new production technologies to make chocolate less sensitive to India's warm climate.

A Brief History of Indian Chocolate to 2000

India is a relatively new player on the cocoa and chocolate market. Historically, black tea ruled for several decades in the British colony. Cocoa was initially introduced by the East India Company during the eighteenth and nineteenth centuries. The company maintained several gardens across the country to cultivate exotic crops (e.g. cinnamon). Several cocoa plants were dispersed over these gardens and, over the years, some of these plants produced a number of seedlings. Some Catholic missionaries also grew cocoa for their own use in the south-west (Clarence-Smith, 2003). At this point, cocoa production was more of an experiment than a commercial activity: the number of plants was very low and, as a result, so was total cocoa production in India. The drinking of chocolate was reserved for the elites and hence consumption remained very low until the end of the nineteenth century. It is because of Cadbury's efforts to introduce chocolate and cocoa after independence that the story of India's chocolate actually took off.

In 1948, Cadbury India Private Limited (a subsidiary of Cadbury) commenced its operation in India. Initially, the company imported and repacked finished chocolate products. These were consumed by the elite and were far too expensive for the masses. In 1949, the company opened up its first local factory. At that time, domestic production of cocoa beans was far too low to provide the industry with sufficient cocoa supplies. Therefore, in order to produce locally, the company had to buy the required beans on the world market. But Cadbury encountered many problems in sourcing from the world market, including fluctuating cocoa prices and high transport costs. This encouraged the firm to start commercializing cocoa cultivation in India.

In 1951, Cadbury carefully investigated and tested various varieties of beans in London and decided that locally produced cocoa of the Criollo variety was best suited for commercial production in the Indian context, and competitive, in terms of quality, with the beans produced in other parts of the world. The Indian government also became involved in the cocoa chain. They entrusted the responsibility for the commercialization of cocoa production to the Indian Council of Agricultural Research (ICAR), an autonomous organization operating under the Ministry of Agriculture. Encouraged by the successes of ICAR's experimental cocoa farms, the government sanctioned a scheme for the promotion of cocoa cultivation in the states of Kerala, Tamil Nadu, and Karnataka during the Third Five-Year Plan (1961–66).[1]

The combination of the government's efforts and Cadbury's investments in the 1960s made cocoa into a commercially viable cash crop. (Mondelēz International, 2014). The company provided seedlings, and offered several extension services and incentives to local farmers to promote cocoa. The latter was done in collaboration with the Ministry of Agriculture and Irrigation, the ICAR, and the concerned

---

[1] The planned economic development of India began in 1951 after independence. Since then, five-year plans setting out the centralized and integrated national economic programmes and objectives of the government have been established after each election.

agricultural departments of the state governments. Seed material was brought from Malaysia. Next, the company resorted to various mass media communication to spread the idea of cocoa cultivation.

In 1976 the Indian council for areca and spices was renamed Indian Arecanuts, Cocoa and Spices Development Council, and was charged with the further promotion of cocoa. It launched several schemes aiming at educating farmers on how to cultivate the crop (e.g. pest control and how to prune and trim the trees) and set up several demonstration farms. These combined efforts of the government and Cadbury ensured that cocoa production spread rapidly. The area under cocoa cultivation as well as the production increased exponentially, particularly in the southern state of Kerala.[2] However, although the state was involved in stimulating cocoa cultivation in India, little effort was put into developing infrastructure for processing and marketing cocoa during this period.

The symbiotic relationship between Cadbury and the Indian authorities was shaken in the early 1980s. The combination of a sharp fall in cocoa prices on the world market during the period 1978–80 (see Figure 21.1) and a labour strike in one of Cadbury's manufacturing plants prompted Cadbury to withdraw from cocoa purchasing and processing in India and to import cocoa beans from the world market. Cadbury claimed that the quality of local cocoa was inferior and that imports were needed to blend with Indian beans. The Indian government gave in to Cadbury's request and the stringent import restrictions for cocoa beans were relaxed (World Bank, 2006).

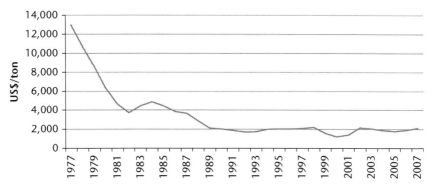

Figure 21.1 Average daily international cocoa prices US$, deflated to 2009 (1977–2007)

Source: Dand, 2010.

---

[2] The area under the crop increased from 6057 ha in 1977–78 to 24118 ha in 1980. Furthermore, in 1975–76, total cocoa production in India was about 100 tonnes, of which 75% was produced in Kerala. By 1977–78, total production had risen to 500 tonnes and Kerala's share to 80% (Kurian, 2010).

The vacuum Cadbury left was significant, even more so because local demand had been overestimated. The only way out seemed to export the surplus, but because world prices had reached rock bottom at that time, the surplus failed to be exported at profitable rates. However, this did not last long. With a declining domestic market, low world market prices, and increasing imports, many cocoa planters stopped production. The remaining cocoa farmers put pressure on the government to ban imports of cocoa beans. When the labour problems at Cadbury's factory were resolved, the company resumed its procuring and processing activities of Indian beans. At the same time, mounting pressure from local cocoa farmers forced the Indian government to restrict cocoa imports again.

In the following years, initiatives were taken to decrease dependence on Cadbury but without much success. The exception was the Central Arecanut Marketing and Processing Co-operative Society (CAMPCO) in Kerala. This cooperative was formed a decade earlier by areca nut growers. CAMPCO set up its first chocolate factory in 1986, supported by the Indian government. At that time it was the biggest chocolate factory in South-East Asia, outside of Japan, with a capacity to process 9,000 tonnes of cocoa beans per year. CAMPCO posed a challenge to Cadbury's market power. Over the years, the cooperative managed to develop a relatively small but stable position in the chocolate market, selling finished products, as well as industrial cocoa products such as cocoa powder and cocoa butter, in the domestic market as well as in the international market. At the same time, through aggressive advertising and brand development, Cadbury managed to maintain its dominant position. In fact, Cadbury became almost a synonym for chocolate (Mythili and Sowmiya, 2014).

Recent Developments

Today, Cadbury still has a large share of the Indian market but the sector has been transformed by three factors: (1) the opening of the Indian economy for foreign investors; (2) the liberalization of trade; and (3) strong income growth. International manufacturers are the main players in the Indian chocolate market (see Table 21.1). Cadbury India still dominates the market but its share has declined

Table 21.1 Company shares of chocolate confectionery (% of retail value)

Companies	2009	2013
Cadbury India	57.9	–
Mondelēz International	–	56.3
Nestlé India	30.1	21.3
Ferrero India	3.7	4.7
Gujarat Cooperative	3.2	1.2
Mars Confectionery	–	1.1
Lindt	0.1	0.2
Others	4.9	15.1

Source: Euromonitor International (2014).

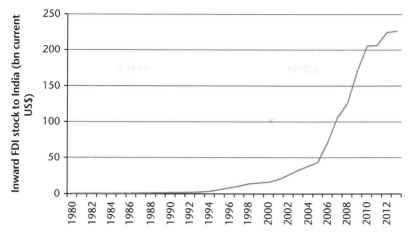

Figure 21.2 Inward FDI stock in India (billion US$) (1980–2013)
Source: UNCTADstat (2013).

slightly to 56.3 per cent in 2013. Nestlé India, the second-largest company, had a market share of 21.3 per cent in 2013. The two biggest companies have lost ground to newcomers such as Ferrero India. In recent years, their combined market share has declined from 88 per cent in 2009 to 77 per cent in 2013. The increasing competition among manufacturers is also reflected in the category 'others' (Table 21.1) which experienced a significant increase over the period 2009–13, from 4.6 per cent to 15 per cent. A crucial factor in the structure of the chocolate industry was the liberalization of India's FDI policy. In 2006, the government decided to allow FDI up to 51 per cent foreign ownership in several industries including the confectionery and retail sectors. In 2012, this was extended, subject to certain conditions, to 100 per cent in single-brand retail and to 51 per cent in multi-brand retail. As shown in Figure 21.2, the change in rules has given rise to a rapid inflow in FDI generally, but also in the chocolate industry in particular, with new players such as Lindt, Royce, or Leonidas entering the Indian market.

THE FOUR MAIN COMPANIES IN THE INDIAN CHOCOLATE MARKET

Cadbury India

As explained, Cadbury has been active in chocolate manufacturing in India since 1948. At that time, the company mainly imported and repacked final products. Today, it has six manufacturing facilities at Thane and Pune (Maharashtra), Bengaluru (Karnataka), Hyderabad (Andra Pradesh), Malanpur (Madhya Pradesh), and Baddi (Himachal Pradesh) (Mondelēz International, 2014). Its 'star products' include Cadbury Dairy Milk, 5 Star, Perk, Eclairs, Celebrations, Temptations, and Gems. Over the past decade, Cadbury's share has been dropping (Table 21.1) with increased FDI of (other) Western companies. On 21 April 2014, Cadbury India changed its name to Mondelēz India Foods Ltd. Today, Cadbury is still involved in cocoa cultivation.

(continued)

Continued

Nestlé India

Nestlé India is a subsidiary of Nestlé SA of Switzerland. The company started its activity in India in 1912. At that time, the company imported and sold finished Nestlé products as 'The Nestlé Anglo-Swiss Condensed Milk Company (Export) Ltd' (Euromonitor International, 2014). In 1961, Nestlé India's first manufacturing facility was set up in Moga, Punjab. Today, Nestlé has eight operational manufacturing facilities in India and, in November 2012, it opened its first local research and development centre.

Ferrero India

Ferrero India is a relatively new player in the Indian chocolate market. The company first entered India in 2004, when it set up a branch office in Chennai. At the time, India barely had a market for premium chocolates. However, Ferrero Rocher was an immediate success in India, especially for gifting during festive seasons (Mukherjee and Malviya, 2012). In 2011, Ferrero India set up a production plant in Maharashtra to manufacture Ferrero Rocher and other chocolates locally (Euromonitor International, 2014. Today, Ferrero has made India its hub and now exports half of its local production to other Asian countries (Shashidhar, 2014).

Gujarat Cooperative

The Gujarat Cooperative Milk Marketing Federation started as a dairy cooperative in 1946 and is today jointly owned by 3 million milk producers in the state of Gujarat. Milk still accounts for the bulk of its value sales but the company has diversified its product portfolio, which today includes milk-associated products such as ice cream, butter, yoghurt, and chocolates. The company markets almost all its product under the flagship brand Amul. It has well-established distribution resources for its products all over the country, and is one of the leaders in the Indian dairy and packaged food sectors. It is the largest Indian chocolate manufacturer despite the fact that chocolate accounts for less than 2 per cent of the company's turnover.

A Booming Consumer Market

Consumption Trend

While per capita chocolate consumption in India is still very low, India is currently the fastest growing chocolate market globally. Recent data presented in Figure 21.3 confirms that India's chocolate consumption growth has been tremendous and is projected to stay well above the other BRICS countries' (Brazil, Russia, India, China, and South Africa) consumption. In 2012, the average per capita consumption was around 300 grams in urban areas, compared to 1.2 kg in China, 3.4 kg in Brazil, 8 kg in the USA, and 13.2 kg in Germany (Figure 21.4a). Despite its very large population, India's chocolate consumption is also low in absolute numbers (Figure 21.4b). A total of 416,000 tonnes of chocolate were consumed in India in 2013, while 673,000 tonnes were consumed in Brazil, 1.1 million in Russia, and 1.6 in China. However, the potential for the market to grow is huge and chocolate is increasingly becoming popular among Indians, gradually replacing traditional sweets.

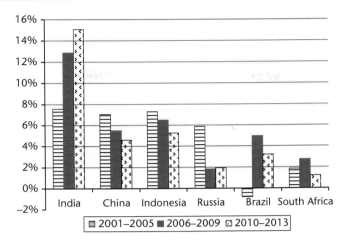

Figure 21.3 Average growth (year on year) of chocolate consumption in selected countries (2001–05, 2006–09, 2010–13)
Source: Euromonitor International (2014).

As can be seen in Figure 21.5, the chocolate confectionary market has been stable since 2000 and started to grow rapidly as of 2008. Consumption in volume has increased by 136 per cent over five years, from 55,000 tonnes in 2008 to 130,000 tonnes in 2013. Numbers are even more impressive when looking at the increase in value. More precisely, between 2008 and 2013, the value of sales of chocolate confectionery in India has increased by 267 per cent. On an annual basis, the market has been growing at 29 per cent per year in value terms between 2008 and 2013, compared to a volume growth of 18 per cent per year. While forecasts for the period 2014–18 predict a minor slowdown, with a yearly growth of 21 per cent in value and of 12 per cent in volume, the sector is expected to maintain its significant development.

This remarkable growth and enthusiastic forecasts can be explained by several factors. Until a few years ago, chocolate was unaffordable for many Indians and considered a premium in comparison to gum and sugar confectionery. This is less and less the case and can be attributed, to some extent, to tremendous growth in the country's middle- and upper-income classes in the last decade. Between 1993/94 and 2009/10, the income of the average household in urban India has grown by about a third, from US\$1.78 purchasing power parity (PPP) to US\$2.37 per capita per day. This has lifted millions of households out of poverty and given rise to an emerging middle class with new consumption patterns and preferences (Meyer and Birdsall, 2012).

In addition, major players in the market have found channels to manufacture and distribute their products at more affordable prices and chocolate is now considered to be mid-priced. Initially explicitly targeted towards children, manufacturers have also managed to expand their consumer base and reach out to the adult segment of the Indian population. Through strong and successful advertising strategies, the perception of chocolate has evolved from being

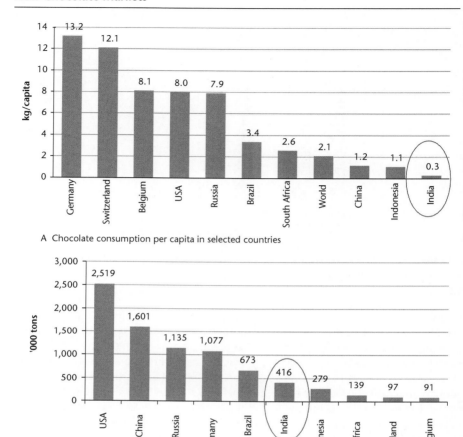

A Chocolate consumption per capita in selected countries

B Chocolate consumption

Figure 21.4 Chocolate consumption in selected countries (2013)
Source: Euromonitor International (2014).

'a surrogate of parental affection for children' to being portrayed as a 'catalyst for real and carefree joy' among all segments of the population (Kazemi and Esmaeili, 2010, p. 148).

Indians' preference for chocolate is also evolving towards better-quality and more expensive chocolate, especially in urban areas. This is mainly due to the entry of Ferrero on the Indian market in 2004, as it introduced the concept of premium chocolates. Consumers are increasingly upgrading to premium and luxury varieties of chocolates (Euromonitor International, 2014) and manufacturers have adapted their products to strengthen their position in the Indian premium chocolate market (Mukherjee and Malviya, 2012). Cadbury initially reacted by launching Dairy Milk Silk in 2009 as a high-quality alternative to the Ferrero

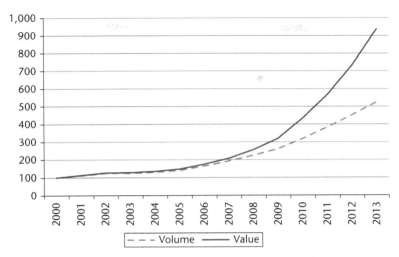

Figure 21.5 Chocolate confectionary market index volume and value (2000 = 100) (2000–13)

Source: Euromonitor International (2014).

products, and the company is now launching Toblerone in India.[3] Recently, Nestlé also has increased efforts to introduce premium brands from its international portfolio. One example is the introduction of Alpino in the Indian market, chocolates that have a shape resembling that of Ferrero Rocher.

As shown in Figure 21.6, consumers are in fact increasingly buying premium goods and downgrading at the same time. The mass category of chocolate sales saw its share increase from 21 per cent in 2010 to 31 per cent in 2012. Likewise, the premium chocolate market share has increased from 18 per cent to 26 per cent in the same time frame. Meanwhile, the popular or middle-segment market share decreased from 60 per cent in year 2010 to 43 per cent in 2012 (Agarwal, 2013).

Trade

Along with consumption, trade in chocolate and its raw materials has also changed greatly since 2000. Rapidly growing demand and trade liberalization have caused a dramatic increase in imports in recent years. India is a net importer of chocolate and other preparations containing cocoa. Figure 21.7 shows the evolution of trade in chocolate between 1999 and 2013. While India was a closed economy until the early 1990s, it has gradually been opening up to trade since then and several sectors have benefited considerably. Chocolate imports have multiplied by almost 30 times in value terms in 15 years, from US$2.7 million in

---

[3] Note that third-party importers have already been selling Toblerone independently for years.

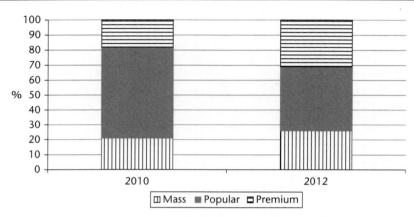

Figure 21.6 Contribution of distinct chocolate categories to total sales value (2000, 2012). Mass: <80% average price/kg of respective category Popular: 80–120% average price/kg of respective category Premium:>120% average price/kg of respective category
Source: Agarawal (2013).

1999 to US$76 million in 2013 (UNCTADstat, 2014). Asia and Europe are the two key regions exporting chocolate to India. The main exporting countries are Malaysia, Singapore, the Netherlands, Italy, and Turkey (in descending order).

However, it is not only imports that have increased, exports have also risen strongly. Exports of chocolate have rapidly grown in the last 15 years—and especially since 2011, from US$3 million in 1999 to US$65 million in 2013. This is due to the fact that manufacturers are increasing their processing capacity in India. Ferrero opened a factory in 2011 which has become its hub for Asian exports. In 2013, Cadbury announced it would build its largest manufacturing plant in the Asia-Pacific region in the state of Andra Pradesh to address not only the local demand but also neighbouring markets. More than 80 per cent of the chocolate exported was to Asian countries, with China, Saudi Arabia, and Sri Lanka being the largest beneficiaries. Africa (Algeria and Egypt) was the destination of 12 per cent of chocolate exports from India.

The development of processing and manufacturing facilities has also led to an increase in trade in raw materials (see Figures 21.8a and 21.8b). Cocoa raw materials includes cocoa powder, cocoa paste, cocoa butter, and cocoa beans. Cocoa beans are the raw material imported in biggest quantity and their share in the composition of raw materials has remained constant over time. They are crushed and transformed into cocoa butter, both for the national and international markets. The key trade partners from which beans are imported are Ghana, Indonesia, and the Dominican Republic. Imports of cocoa powder have also increased over the years. In 2012, more than 90 per cent of it was imported from Malaysia and Indonesia. As can be seen from Figure 21.8b, exports of raw materials are considerably smaller than imports. Notably, exports of cocoa butter produced in India, essentially from imported cocoa beans, have grown rapidly in recent years, mostly to Germany, the Netherlands, the USA, and Turkey.

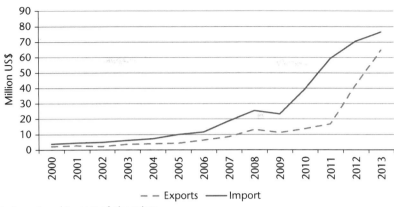

A Export and import of chocolate

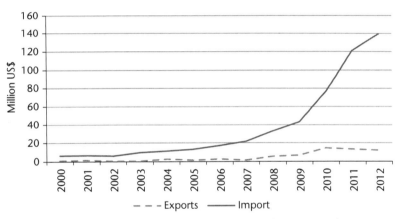

B Export and import of chocolate raw materials (Cocoa beans, cocoa butter, cocoa paste and cocoa powder)

Figure 21.7 Trade of chocolate in India (million US$) (2000–13)
Source: UNCTADstat (2013).

Cocoa Production

Cocoa production in India is concentrated in the southern states of Kerala, Tamil Nadu, Karnataka, and Andra Pradesh (Velayutham et al., 2013). Most of the famers cultivate cocoa beans by intercropping, often with cashew, areca, or coconut. While starting from very low levels, cocoa production in India has almost tripled in 14 years, rising from 5,200 tonnes in 1999 to 15,000 tonnes in 2013. According to the International Cocoa Organization (ICCO), India currently accounts for only 0.3 per cent of global cocoa production. The sector has experienced a positive trend in production but the area harvested has increased even further over the same period, leading to a significant decrease in cocoa yields, from 4,200 hg/ha in 1999 to 2,400 hg/ha in 2012 (Figure 21.9).

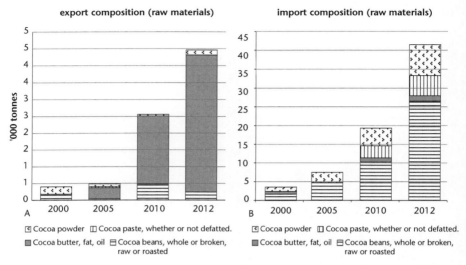

Figure 21.8 Trade composition of raw materials in India ('000 tonnes) (2000, 2005, 2010, 2012)
Source: UNCTADstat (2013).

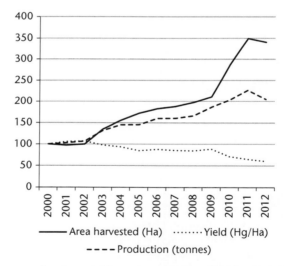

Figure 21.9 Cocoa production, yields, and area indices (2000 = 100) (2000–13)
Source: FAOSTAT (2014).

One reason for the sharp incline in area harvested could be that cocoa has increasingly won ground as the preferred intercrop in coconut plantations because of its yield-increasing effects (Devanathan, 2013). Another possible explanation could be that high international cocoa prices, rising domestic demand, high transportation cost from West Africa, and high Indian import duties have induced chocolate manufacturers to increasingly look for opportunities to source cocoa locally. One such initiative is Mondelēz's (Cadbury India's) 'cocoa life programme' launched in 2012, which is designed to 'transform the lives and livelihoods of cocoa farmers and their communities' (Mondelēz International, 2013). More precisely, the objective is to help farmers plant cocoa and intercrop it with coconut, providing them with seedlings and subsidized prices as well as free technical know-how (Mondelēz International, 2013). With 6.5 million cocoa seedlings being planted and 100,000 farmers being targeted in the states of Karnataka, Tamil Nadu, Kerala, and Andra Pradesh, the programme is quite ambitious. Since cocoa plants take on average three years to reach maturity, more recent data is needed to assess whether Cadbury's programme has been successful in sustainably increasing local production. In 2014, Mars announced it would follow Cadbury's lead and explore sourcing opportunities in India. These recent developments have led the Directorate of Cashew Nut and Cocoa Development (DCCD) Board to make optimistic predictions, according to which Indian cocoa production would double in 20 years: from 15,000 tonnes to 30,000 tonnes in 2025 (DCCD, 2013).

Tariffs and Regulations

While chocolate imports have grown tremendously over the last 15 years, companies and manufacturers engaged in trade still face several challenges that represent significant barriers to trade in agricultural goods and processed foods. First, companies have to cope with high import duties. The average 'ad valorem' duty on chocolate imports (chocolate products and all cocoa raw materials) imposed by India is about 30 per cent, while China's tariff is, on average, 11 per cent, Brazil's 14 per cent, Indonesia's 8.6 per cent, and Malaysia's 9.1 per cent (WTO, 2013). Under the leadership of Switzerland, the issue of tariff reduction on chocolate products is currently under discussion in the framework of the European Free Trade Agreement, which is under negotiation between India and Lichtenstein, Norway, Iceland, and Switzerland.

Second, stringent packaging and labelling norms are imposed on retailers by the Indian Food Safety and Standards Authority, a regulatory body under the Ministry of Health. Since a new Food Safety and Standards Act came into force in 2011, hundreds of tonnes of imported chocolates from Godiva, Lindt, and Mars, among others, have been held at Indian ports and airports. The dispute is about alleged non-compliance with India's specific labelling rules on nutritional information and product origin, and has led Lindt to threaten to leave the Indian market (F&B News, 2014).

Another issue currently at stake is the content of vegetable fat or oil in imported chocolates—India having stipulated that no vegetable fat was allowed, while the international Codex Alimentarius permits the usage of 5 per cent vegetable fat in chocolates' final products (FSSAI, 2011).[4] This has also resulted in several consignments of chocolates being blocked at customs.

Marketing and Specificities of the Indian Market

As mentioned, with its rapidly expanding consumer base and its sweet taste, India represents an extremely attractive market. Nonetheless, to be successful, companies operating there have to embrace the country's complexity and the particular needs of its diverse consumers. They face several opportunities and challenges in that respect.

India's Sweet Tooth

Companies will continue to make use of India's tradition of giving sweets and its culture of tea and biscuits. Eighty per cent of households consume biscuits on a daily basis, and cookies and snacks can be found at literally every corner, both in rural and urban areas. Chocolate snacking has made a significant breakthrough, as consumers are replacing or supplementing traditional snacks with chocolate (Barry Callebaut, 2012). While countlines are still the most popular, two particular products have gained importance: chocolate boxes and chocolates with toys. The former has become very popular for gift purposes, especially during celebrations such as Diwali (start of the Hindu New Year) and Holi (the spring harvest season). According to Mintel (2012), many Indian consumers consider chocolate assortment boxes to be premium, more hygienic, and longer-lasting than the traditional 'mithai' Indian sweets. Chocolate with toys, such as the famous Kinder from Ferrero, were non-existent before 2009, and have seen impressive success due to its low initial level and growing popularity among children. Leading companies have specifically launched new products to target the young consumer base in urban areas, and these have supported recent growth sales in the total volume of chocolate (see Figure 21.10) (Euromonitor International, 2014).

Increased Health Awareness

The chocolate boom can be attributed not only to Indians' sweet taste but also to the increasing awareness and the new demand for healthy food. Because chocolate confectionery can be associated with negative health consequences, retailers have adapted their products to attract consumers who are, in general, more and more

---

[4] At the time of writing (2015), the Indian government had drafted a new standard for chocolate allowing Indian firms to use up to 5% of vegetable fats other than cocoa butter to make chocolates. However, the document still needs the recommendation of the Stimulant Foods Sectional Committee and the approval of the Food and Agriculture Division Council (see Chapter 15, this volume, for further details).

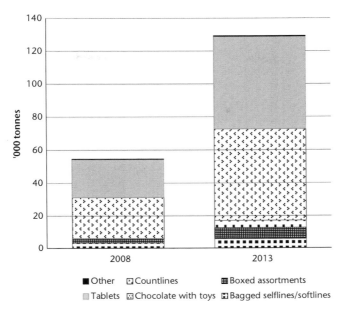

Figure 21.10 Sales of chocolate confectionery by category (2008, 2013)
Source: Euromonitor International (2014).

demanding and interested in healthy food, and, in particular, in sugar-free and diet chocolates. A good example of this marketing presenting chocolate as both healthy and indulgent is the 'Raisin and Nut Fine Dark Chocolate' released in 2010 by Cadbury. It was advertised as rich in antioxidants and was successful from the start (Lahouasnia, 2013).

As can be seen from Table 21.2, ordinary milk chocolate continues to dominate the market but dark chocolate, which is considered to be healthier, has strongly gained in popularity. Sales of ordinary dark tablets have experienced the highest increase in the last five years. In addition, to target some of the 65 million Indians that are estimated to suffer from diabetes (which represent 90 per cent of the adult population with diabetes in the South-East Asia region) (IDF, 2013), companies have also launched sugar-free chocolate bars. The fact that Mars has recently set up a completely new assembly line to manufacture and introduce vegetarian Snickers for the Indian market is another example of firms' adaptation to demands and specificities of Indian consumers (Euromonitor International, 2014).

Reaching Out to Rural Consumers

Around 60 per cent of the chocolate consumption is in urban markets where 31 per cent of the total population lives (Mukherji, 2012). This leaves a huge

Table 21.2 Sales of chocolate tablets by type (% of retail value breakdown)

	2008	2013
Plain Dark	1.5	6
Plain Milk	71	60
Plain White	6.5	3.5
Filled	21	30.5

Source: Euromonitor International, 2014.

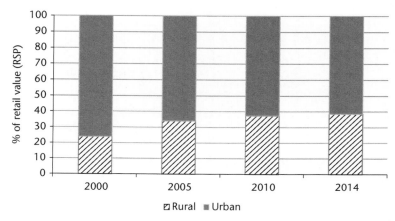

Figure 21.11 Sales of chocolate in urban and rural areas (2000, 2005, 2010, 2014)
Source: Euromonitor International, (2014).

expansion potential in rural areas, given the small rural penetration so far. Manufacturers realize that Indian chocolate is highly price-sensitive, that is, chocolate bars have to be cheap to win rural consumers. To reach out to them, gain volume, and widen the consumer base, companies have introduced smaller packs sold at affordable prices of Rs 2 or Rs 5 (US$0.04 to US$0.1). This affordable pricing of mass brands and small packs has led to a modest but steady growth of sales in rural areas (see Figure 21.11 for the evolution of the breakdown of sales between rural and urban areas) (Barry Callebaut, 2012).

A similar approach was used to launch premium brands in urban markets: smaller pack sizes to make it affordable for consumers to try out (Euromonitor International, 2014). A good indication of the importance of prices to reach out to new and poor consumers is the fact that more than half of Cadbury sales comes from products that cost less than Rs 5 (Merchant, 2003). According to Euromonitor International (Lahouasnia, 2013), almost 90 per cent of all chocolate confectionery in India is sold in 0–50 gram packs, compared to 65 per cent in North America and 49 per cent in Western Europe.

Distribution Channels

With more than 12 million retail outlets, India has one of the highest retailing densities in the world (Bhalla et al., 2007). According to Reardon and Minten (2011), the pace of modern retail growth in India was five times higher than gross domestic product (GDP) growth in the past years and among the fastest in the world. But food retailing still lies in the hands of the traditional sector. This is also the case for the distribution and sales of chocolates, where independent small grocers, such as the traditional 'kirana stores', which are widespread all over India, have been and are likely to remain dominant. Since such stores are located in local neighbourhoods, they are preferred by consumers, especially for impulse purchases. Nonetheless, as can be seen in Figure 21.12, sales through super and hypermarkets are likely to continue to rise, along with the country's economic development (Euromonitor International, 2014). According to Nielsen (2014), super and hypermarkets are increasingly being used by companies as laboratories to test product innovations.

While India's retail sector is experiencing notable transformations with the rapid growth of modern retail, companies still face several challenges due to underdeveloped logistic services and infrastructure (Trebbin, 2014). Significant gaps in road and telecommunications connectivity, lack of reliable electricity and water supplies, and limited distribution infrastructure such as cold storage and refrigerated transport make it difficult for companies to fulfil India's latent demand. With the optimal storage and transport temperature for chocolate lying between 10° and 18°C, and average temperatures in the centre and south of India averaging around 27°C, it is key to have a properly developed cold value chain. It is estimated that about 25,000 refrigerated vehicles were running in India in 2010, of which 80 per cent were used for fruits and vegetables. This is not only insufficient

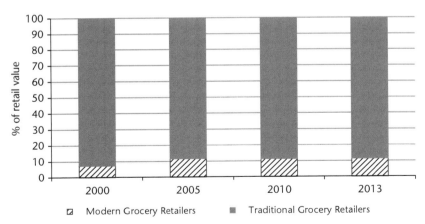

Figure 21.12 Sales of chocolate confectionery by modern and traditional retailers (2000, 2005, 2010, 2013)

Source: Euromonitor International (2014).

but all the more problematic because they are unevenly distributed across the country (Emerson, 2013).

Nestlé has experienced the lack of cold storage facilities the hard way. Because of poor anticipation and adaptation to the Indian context, its chocolates became liquid instantly when they first entered the Indian market. The company then developed a new liquid chocolate product, a mix between a bar and a drink (*The Economist*, 2003). In the same vein, manufacturers have had to revise their recipes to make chocolate better withstand heat. Using less milk fat to make chocolate more heat-resistant, and crystallizing sugar for longer periods to make it harder, are some of the techniques currently used by manufacturers to produce heat-resilient chocolate.

Interestingly, along the same line, in a plea to further tap the huge market potentials of warm climate countries such as India and Brazil and address the deficiencies of the supply chain to handle temperature fluctuations, Cadbury, and later Nestlé and Mars, have all filed patents for temperature-tolerant chocolate. Cadbury will soon commercialize chocolates produced with a different refining methodology, which do not melt even if exposed to temperatures of 40°C for more than three hours (while traditional chocolate softens at about 28°C and melts at 32°C–35°C). Nestlé has announced it had developed a methodology to produce chocolates where only the core of the product would melt under high temperatures, while the chocolate shell, with added humectant liquid, would remain solid and retain its shape and texture. Mars has developed a mix of chemical components (polyol and monosaccharide) that is added before the moulding to make chocolate more heat tolerant. Until the retail market becomes more integrated and the cold storage capacity is improved significantly, innovations to make chocolate more heat-resistant will be key for manufacturers to continue tapping India's huge chocolate market potential.

Conclusion

In this chapter, we have laid out the factors that have contributed to the extraordinary boom of India's chocolate market. Although the Indian chocolate love story is a recent one, chocolate consumption growth has been tremendous and is projected to stay well above the consumption pattern of other BRICS countries. These promising prospects are explained by India's sweet taste, continued rising household incomes, an untapped market potential, especially in rural areas, and an increasing preference for premium chocolates. Successful brands have managed to adapt to the specificities of the India market and propose a wide range of different products to address specific consumer tastes and preferences, such as small-sized packs, specific chocolate toys, healthy bars, premium chocolate, and boxes. Companies have also developed new production technologies to make chocolate better resilient to India's heat.

However, manufacturers still face several challenges. The opening up of the Indian economy has led to booms in the processing and retail sectors and considerably stimulated the chocolate market. At the same time, however, import tariffs remain high and FDI policies are still subject to strict requirements. Furthermore, imposed standards remain highly demanding. Finally, inadequate infrastructure and logistical services pose additional difficulties to the further development of the chocolate sector in India. The way companies will attempt to address these hurdles will determine the extent to which they manage to fulfil India's huge latent demand for chocolates.

References

Agarawal, S. 2013. 'The New Consumer'. Live Mint, 26 July. Accessed 22 August 2014 (<http://www.livemint.com/Industry/fJzcHZFSVFWWR6tmQfg7AP/The-new-consumer.html>).

Barry Callebaut. 2012. 'The Amazing World of Chocolate'. *Journal, 2011–12*: pp. 1–58.

Bhalla, V., A. Bhattacharya, A. Singhi, and S. Verma. 2007. 'Creating a Distribution Advantage in India'. The Boston Consulting Group (BCG), Go-to-Market Publications.

Clarence-Smith, W. G. 2003. *Cocoa and Chocolate, 1765–1914*. New York: Routledge.

Dand, R. 2010. *The International Cocoa Trade*. 3rd edn. Cambridge: Woodhead Publishing.

DCCD (Directorate of Cashew Nut and Cocoa Development). 2013. 'News and Events'. Accessed 6 August 2014 (<http://dccd.gov.in/news.htm>).

Devanathan, V. 2013. 'Cocoa Intercropping Picks Up in Coconut Plantations as Crop Yield Improves'. *The Times of India*, 17 June. Accessed 27 September 2014 (<http://timesofindia.indiatimes.com/city/madurai/Cocoa-intercropping-picks-up-in-coconut-plantations-as-crop-yield-improves/articleshow/20623650.cms>).

The Economist. 2003. 'The Big Candyman'. 30 October. Accessed 5 August 2014. (<http://www.economist.com/node/2184417>).

Emerson. 2013. 'Food Waste and Cold Storage Infrastructure Relationship in India, Developing Realistic Solutions'. The Emerson Climate Technologies Report: pp. 1–18. Accessed 10 August 2014 (<http://www.emerson.com/SiteCollectionDocuments/India%20Cold%20Storage%20Report%202013/Report_layout_Reduced.pdf>).

Euromonitor International. 2014. 'Chocolate Confectionery in India'. Passport. January. Accessed 1 August 2014 (<http://www.euromonitor.com/chocolate-confectionery-in-india/report>).

FAOSTAT. 2014. Statistical Database of the Food and Agriculture Organization of the United Nations Accessed 15 August 2014 (<http://faostat.fao.org>).

F&B News. 2014. 'Imported Foods Worth Rs 22,000 Crore Stuck'. Food & Beverages News, by Ashwani Maindola, 14 August 2014. Accessed 16 August 2014 (<http://www.fnbnews.com/article/detnews.asp?articleid=35931&sectionid=1>).

FSSAI (Food Safety and Standards Authority of India). 2011. 'Food Safety and Standards Regulations: Packaging and Labeling and Food Product Standards and Food Additives' (F.No. 2-15015/30/2010).

IDF (International Diabetes Federation). 2013. *IDF Diabetes Atlas*. 6th edn. Accessed 12 August 2014 (<http://www.idf.org/diabetesatlas>).

Kazemi, F. and M. Esmaeili. 2010. 'The Role of Media on Consumer Brand Choice: A Case Study of Chocolate Industry'. *International Journal of Business and Management* 5 (9): p. 147.

Kurian, M. 2010. 'Economics of Cocoa Cultivation in Kerala: A Case of Dependent Development'. Thesis, Mahatma Gandhi University Library.

Lahouasnia, L. 2013. 'Mars Proves that Good Things Come in Small Packages with Galaxy India Launch'. Euromonitor International, December.

Maindola, A. 2014. 'Imported Foods Worth Rs 22,000 Crore Stuck'. *Food & Beverages News*, 14 August. Accessed 16 August 2014 (<http://www.fnbnews.com/article/detnews.asp?articleid=35931&sectionid=1>).

Merchant, K. 2003. 'Love in a Warm Climate: India'. *The Financial Times*, 24 July. Accessed 4 August 2014 (<http://search.proquest.com/docview/249518157>).

Meyer, C. and N. Birdsall. 2012. 'New Estimates on India's Middle Class'. Center for Global Development, Technical Note, November.

Mintel. 2012. 'India's Craving for Chocolate Unwraps Business Opportunities for Manufacturers'. 7 November. Accessed 5 August 2014 (<http://www.mintel.com/press-centre/food-and-drink/indias-craving-for-chocolate-unwraps-business-opportunities-for-manufacturers>).

Mondelēz International. 2013. 'Investing in India's Cocoa Farming Communities'. Accessed 5 August 2014 (<http://www.mondelezinternational.com/Newsroom/Multimedia-Releases/Mondelez-International-to-Invest-400-Million-to-Help-One-Million-People-in-Cocoa-Farming-Communities>).

Mondelēz International. 2014. 'About Us: Our Business in India'. Accessed 5 August 2014 (<http://in.mondelezinternational.com/about-us/india-business>).

Mukherjee, W. and S. Malviya. 2012. 'Cadbury to Launch Kraft Foods' Toblerone in India, to Take on Ferrero Rocher'. *The Economic Times*, 11 June 2012. Accessed 1 August 2014 (<http://articles.economictimes.indiatimes.com/2012-06-11/news/32175169_1_cadbury-india-chocolate-brand-premium-chocolate>).

Mukherji, U. P. 2012. 'Chocolates Market Likely to Touch Rs 7,500 Crore by 2015: Assocham'. *The Times of India*, 9 October. Accessed 12 August 2014 (<http://timesofindia.indiatimes.com/business/india-business/Chocolates-market-likely-to-touch-Rs-7500-crore-by-2015-Assocham/articleshow/16738116.cms>).

Mythili, S. and G. Sowmiya. 2014. 'Consumer Behaviour and Brand Preference of Chocolate in Thanjavur District'. *International Journal of Engineering and Management Research* 3 (3): pp. 36–9.

Nielsen. 2014. 'Retail Revolution: Consumers'. 22 August. Accessed 30 August 2014 (<http://www.nielsen.com/in/en/insights/reports/2014/retail-revolution.html>).

Reardon, T. and B. Minten. 2011. 'Surprised by Supermarkets: Diffusion of Modern Food Retail in India'. *Journal of Agribusiness in Developing and Emerging Economies* 1 (2): pp. 134–61.

Shashidhar, A. 2014. 'How Italian Confectionery Giant Ferrero Created a Market for Premium Chocolate in India'. *Business Today*, 30 March. Accessed 2 August 2014 (<http://businesstoday.intoday.in/story/confectionary-firm-ferrero-in-india-premium-chocolate-market/1/204086.html>).

Trebbin, A. 2014. 'Linking Small Farmers to Modern Retail through Producer Organizations–Experiences with Producer Companies in India'. *Food Policy* 45: pp. 35–44.

UNCTADstat (United Nations Conference on Trade and Development). 2014. Website. <http://unctadstat.unctad.org/>.

Velayutham, T., K. Rajamani, N. Shoba, A. J. Joel, and N. Senthil. 2013. 'Variability Studies and Identification of High Yielding Plus Trees of Cocoa in Tamil Nadu'. *African Journal of Agricultural Research* 8 (26): pp. 3444–53.

World Bank. 2006. 'India–Bangladesh Bilateral Trade and Potential Free Trade Agreement: Chapter 3: India's Trade Policies'. *Bangladesh Development Series Paper No. 13*. Accessed 8 October, 2014 <http://siteresources.worldbank.org/INTBANGLADESH/Resources/Trade.pdf>.

WTO (World Trade Organization). 2013. 'Tariff Download Facility'. Accessed 16 August 2014 (<http://tariffdata.wto.org/Default.aspx>).

22

Back to the Roots

Growth in Cocoa and Chocolate Consumption in Africa

Seneshaw Tamru and Johan Swinnen

Introduction

Africa is the world's major supplier of cocoa beans, and has been for most of the twentieth century. Close to two-thirds of all cocoa beans produced in the world comes from Africa, with the Ivory Coast, Ghana, Nigeria, and Cameroon being the largest contributors to cocoa production (Chapter 2, this volume). In 2012, the Ivory Coast alone accounted for about 34 per cent of world cocoa production (FAOSTAT, 2014). Yet, despite Africa's dominant contribution to world cocoa production and supply, the continent has been mostly estranged from consuming chocolate until recently (Afoakwa, 2010). In fact, it has also been deprived of most value added in the value chain, since most cocoa beans were exported after harvest. This is now changing. Consumption of cocoa and chocolate in Africa has increased significantly over the past 15 years. This is due to two distinct factors. On the one hand, there has been a significant increase in cocoa grinding facilities in Africa, as many (often multinational) grinding and trading companies have invested in grinding facilities in cocoa-producing countries. The second is the increase in consumption of chocolate.

Chocolate has remained a highly luxurious commodity for the region. In 2014, per capita confectionery consumption in Middle East and Africa was only 0.7 kg,[1] which is the lowest of any region in the world. Africa's chocolate consumption was even below that of Asia (0.9 kg/capita), and much lower than in Australia (8.4 kg), North America (7.5 kg), or Western Europe (7.5 kg) (Euromonitor, 2014g).

In addition to the non-affordability due to low levels of income, chocolate consumption in Africa, particularly in tropical ambient regions, has been limited because most of the chocolate brands imported do melt at local 'room temperature'

---

[1] Including cocoa and chocolate confectioneries.

(25–30°C). This phenomenon has added to the lower demand for chocolate in these relatively high temperature zones (Ogunwolu and Jayeola, 2006; Stortz and Marangoni, 2011).[2] Other factors have contributed to the lower rate of chocolate consumption in the continent. Most of Africa's population, especially in Sub-Saharan Africa (SSA), live in rural areas, where roads are often difficult to traverse, with subsequently very high transportation costs and with a very low level of electricity and cooling facilities, including refrigeration (Mirko and Kearney, 2014).

However, Africa's chocolate consumption has increased significantly since 2000 (ICCO, 2012). Total world consumption of chocolate, as approximated by volume of chocolate retail sales, increased from 5.6 million tons to 7.2 million tons over the period 2000–13. In 2013, Africa's share in total chocolate consumption was 5 per cent of the world—more than 50 per cent higher than a decade ago, when it was only 3 per cent. The rapid economic growth in Africa is the major factor behind the rise in chocolate consumption in the continent. Africa is showing tremendous economic growth. It is the fastest growing continent, with most countries in the continent displaying significant economic growth, which is associated with better infrastructure and much more electrification (WESP, 2015). Furthermore, increasing urbanization and population growth, expansion of retail shops and supermarkets, and development in taste for packed foods influenced by modernization and globalization also contributed to the increase in chocolate consumption in Africa (Sundaram et al., 2011; ATKearney, 2014).

In this chapter we document the rise in cocoa and chocolate consumption and relate it to these factors. The chapter is organized as follows. The next section, 'Growth of Cocoa Consumption (Processing) in Africa', discusses the growth in cocoa processing and consumption in Africa. The following section, 'The Growth of Chocolate Consumption in Africa', looks at the growth of chocolate consumption in Africa and documents chocolate consumption within Africa by first considering the difference between North Africa and SSA, and later at the country level. We then compare Africa's chocolate consumption trend with the two fastest growing chocolate markets in the world: China and India. Next we discuss the potential major drivers behind the change in chocolate consumption in Africa, and we look at the major multinational chocolate confectionery companies operating in the continent. The last section concludes.

Growth of Cocoa Consumption (Processing) in Africa

Africa, and in particular West Africa, is the main producer of cocoa beans, as Figure 22.1 illustrates. Yet, Africa traditionally exported almost all its cocoa beans. Not only was there very little consumption of the final products (as chocolate) but even 'cocoa consumption' in the form of grinding and the production of

---

[2] Various attempts have been made to develop thermo-resistant chocolate, including enhancing the microstructure of the materials, adding a polymer, and increasing the melting point of the fat phase (Stortz and Marangoni, 2011).

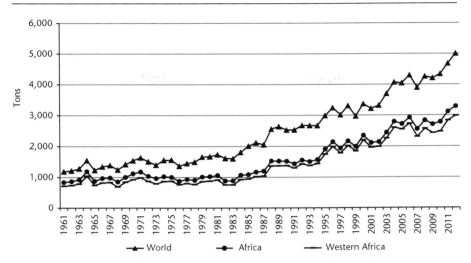

Figure 22.1 Trends in cocoa production (1961–2013)
Source: Based on FAOSTAT (2014).

intermediate products like cocoa butter, cocoa paste, and cocoa powder occurred mostly in Europe and America. Africa thus captured very little rents from the cocoa–chocolate value chain.

However, this scenario is changing. There is a strong positive trend in Africa's cocoa consumption as measured by cocoa grindings. Origin processing is expanding substantially as some of major cocoa-producing countries worldwide are reverting to cocoa processing themselves, both for local consumption and export. Subsequently, the share of origin processing has considerably increased over time, and has risen from 39 per cent in 1975 to 48 per cent in 2010 (Chapter 2, this volume). In line with this changing trend in origin cocoa processing, and supported by government policies that encourage the export of semi-finished products with higher value added rather than raw cocoa beans, Africa is increasing its cocoa processing sizably (Akiyama et al., 2003). Cocoa grinding in Africa increased by 51 per cent over the 2005–13 period: from 501,000 tons in 2005 to 755,000 tons in 2013. Cocoa processing in Europe increased by only 14 per cent, and in America by only 3 per cent, over the same period. In 2013, Africa grinds 19 per cent of the world total, up from 15 per cent in 2005 (Table 22.1).

This considerable shift in cocoa grindings from the developed world to poorer African cocoa-producing countries is linked to the substantial liberalization of the cocoa sector and the markets' subsequent larger role in price settings, trading, and production allocation. This, in turn, has induced major investments and takeovers by multinational cocoa traders and processors in African cocoa-producing countries. These companies have started to process more and more of the cocoa locally before exporting the cocoa (intermediate products); a move that is also supported by local policies (Raikes and Gibbon 2000; Fold, 2001; Chapter 2, this volume).

Table 22.1 Cocoa consumption (grinding) by region (2005–13)

Countries	2005		2009		2013*	
	'000 tones	% of total	'000 tones	% of total	'000 tones	% of total
Africa	501	14.9	622	17.6	755	18.6
Ivory Coast	364	10.9	419	11.9	460	11.4
Others	137	4.1	203	5.8	295	7.3
Americas	853	25.4	780	22.1	878	21.7
Asia and Oceania	622	18.5	655	18.5	845	20.9
Europe	1379	41.4	1475	41.8	1575	38.9
World total	3354	100.0	3531	100.0	4052	100.0
Origin	1262	37.6	1419	40.2	1743	43.0

Source: 2004/05–2006/07: Afoakwa (2010); 2007/08–2009/10: ICCO (2012); 2010/11–2012/13: ICCO (2014); *ICCO estimates.

The Growth of Chocolate Consumption in Africa

Overall Growth

Global demand for chocolate consumption is increasing in both developed and developing markets (KPMG, 2014). However, chocolate consumption, as measured by retail volume share, has increased more in Africa than in the other regions in the world. While global chocolate consumption since 2000 grew by 28 per cent, the growth in Africa—approximated by the growth rate in Middle East and North Africa region (MENA)—was 104 per cent. This is in sharp contrast with the growth in North America (11 per cent), and in Western Europe (10 per cent). As a result, the MENA region has increased its share of global chocolate consumption from 3 per cent in 2000 to 5 per cent in 2013. East Europe, Asia Pacific, and Latin America have also gained considerable shares over the period, while North America and Western Europe are losing shares (Figure 22.2).

Chocolate Consumption by African Sub-Regions and Countries

Analysis of changes in chocolate consumption in Africa by sub-regions is limited by data availability. Some data sources provide data for 'North Africa' others for 'Middle East and North Africa (MENA)'. Hence, we are limited to looking at the chocolate consumption trends of eight countries in the continent: four from each of the two sub-regions (North Africa: Algeria, Egypt, Morocco, and Tunisia; SSA: Cameroon, Kenya, Nigeria, and South Africa). However, in spite of the data limitation, given the spread location of the countries considered, they are probably representative for the respective sub-regions.

NORTH AFRICA

Chocolate consumption in North Africa increased substantially over the period 2000–13. Table 22.2 shows the growth in chocolate consumption in North Africa and SSA countries. Over the stated period, most of the North African countries

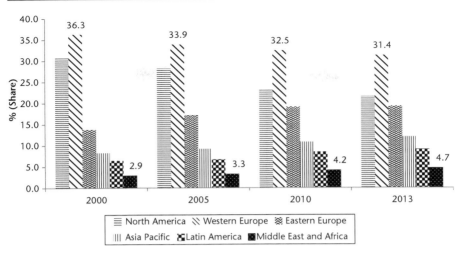

Figure 22.2 Share of chocolate confectioneries (of volume sales) by region (2000–13)
Source: Based on ICCO (2010, 2012) and Euromonitor (2014).

Table 22.2 Growth of chocolate consumption by region (2000–13)

Region	Volume of chocolate consumption ('000 tons)			Per capita chocolate consumption (kg/person)		
	2000	2013	Growth (%)	2000	2013	Growth (%)
North Africa	**44.3**	**126.4**	*185.3*	**0.42**	**0.96**	*129.4*
Algeria	8.0	40.2	*402.5*	0.25	1.03	*306.4*
Egypt	16.4	37.0	*125.6*	0.25	0.45	*82.2*
Morocco	7.6	19.4	*155.3*	0.26	0.59	*121.5*
Tunisia	8.7	19.5	*124.1*	0.91	1.78	*95.5*
SSA (excluding SA)	**2.9**	**9.5**	*223.1*	**0.03**	**0.06**	*85.5*
Cameroon	1.0	2.8	*180.0*	0.06	0.13	*100.8*
Kenya	1.2	2.1	*75.0*	0.04	0.05	*23.5*
Nigeria	0.4	3.5	*775.0*	0.00	0.02	*519.7*
South Africa (SA)	**35.9**	**45.5**	*26.7*	**0.80**	**0.85**	*6.3*
China	**62.0**	**193.0**	*211.3*	**0.05**	**0.14**	*189.5*
India	**24.0**	**129.0**	*437.5*	**0.02**	**0.10**	*347.9*

Source: Based on Euromonitor (2014) and UN DESA (2015).

increased their consumption. Chocolate consumption in Algeria,[3] Egypt, Morocco, and Tunisia grew by 403 per cent, 126 per cent, 155 per cent, and 124 per cent respectively. The consumption grew from 8,000 tons to 40,200 tons in Algeria; from 16,400 tons to 37,000 tons in Egypt; from 7,600 tons to 19,000 tons

---

[3] Between 2007 and 2012, Nigeria and Algeria were the two fastest growing chocolate markets in Africa and the third and ninth fastest in the world respectively. Over this period, chocolate consumption in Nigeria grew by 286 per cent and in Algeria by about 110 per cent (KPMG, 2014).

in Morocco; and from 8,700 tons to 19,500 tons in Tunisia chocolate markets over the 2000–13 period. The quick growth in Algeria and other markets is associated with the fast expanding modern retail sectors and a subsequent 'supermarket revolution' since the mid-2000s (Euromonitor, 2014a).

The average per capita chocolate consumption in North Africa was about 0.5 kg over the 2000–13 period. In 2013, Tunisia, with a consumption of over 1.78 kg/ person, consumed most chocolate per person in the region, while per capita chocolate consumption in Algeria, Morocco, and Egypt was 1.03 kg, 0.59 kg, and 0.45 kg respectively (see Table 22.2 and Figure 22.7).[4]

As expected, growth in chocolate consumption drives an increase in chocolate imports. Table 22.3 shows trend in chocolate imports in Africa. Over the 2000–11 period, chocolate imports in the continent grew by 390 per cent—that is, from 26,563 tons in 2000 to 130,116 tons in 2011. North Africa displayed the largest growth (1,306 per cent). Algeria's chocolate import grew from just 44 tons in 2000 to 32,358 tons in 2011, while Egypt's chocolate import also grew almost five times, from 2,186 tons in 2000 to 12,370 tons in 2011. Similarly, chocolate imports in Morocco and Tunisia grew by 298 per cent and 160 per cent respectively over the same period.

SSA

Countries in SSA also displayed a significant growth in chocolate consumption over the 2000–13 period. Table 22.2 and Figure 22.6 display the growth of chocolate consumption in the region. Chocolate consumption in Nigeria was almost zero up until 2005, but suddenly jumped between 2006 and 2013. The overall growth was 775 per cent—from 400 tons in 2000 to 3,500 tons in 2013. Chocolate consumption in Cameroon grew by 180 per cent (from 1,000 tons in 2000 to 2,800 tons in 2013) and in Kenya by 75 per cent (from 1,200 tons to 2,100 tons). In contrast, chocolate consumption in South Africa grew by only 27 per cent (from 35,900 tons in 2000 to 45,500 tons in 2013), but it obviously started from a higher level.

In 2013, with an average amount of only 0.2 kg/person, per capita chocolate consumption in SSA is considerably lower than that of North Africa. The exception is South Africa, with per capita chocolate consumption of about 0.9 kg. During the same year, per capita chocolate consumption in Cameroon is 0.13 kg, in Kenya 0.05 kg, and in Nigeria 0.02 kg (Table 22.2, Figure 22.7).

Countries in SSA also significantly increased their chocolate imports. Total imports in SSA grew by 165 per cent over the period 2000–11. Imports increased in Middle Africa by 422 per cent, in West Africa by 251 per cent, in Eastern Africa by 216 per cent, and in Southern Africa by 57 per cent. Looking in further detail at the country level, chocolate imports in Kenya increased by 300 per cent (from 326 tons in 2000 to 1,305 tons in 2011), in Cameroon by 271 per cent (from 368 tons

---

[4] The growth of per capita chocolate consumption between 2000 and 2013 for Algeria, Egypt, Morocco, and Tunisia was 306%, 82%, 122%, and 96% respectively (Table 22.2).

Table 22.3 Growth of chocolate imports (2000–11)

Region	Volume of chocolate imports (tons)		
	2000	2011	Growth (%)
Africa	**26,563**	**130,116**	*389.8*
North Africa	**5,225**	**73,458**	*1,305.9*
Algeria	44	32,358	*73,440.9*
Egypt	2,186	12,370	*465.9*
Morocco	1,523	6,061	*298.0*
Tunisia	781	2,028	*159.7*
SSA	**21,338**	**56,658**	*165.5*
East Africa	4,083	12,892	*215.7*
Middle Africa	2,521	13,165	*422.2*
Southern Africa	10,890	17,094	*57.0*
Western Africa	3,844	13,507	*251.4*
Cameroon	368	1,364	*270.7*
Kenya	326	1,305	*300.3*
Nigeria	1,000	2,440	*144.0*
South Africa	4,441	14,263	*221.2*
China	**39,843**	**84,931**	*113.2*
India	**1,730**	**14,452**	*735.4*

Source: Based on FAOSTAT (2014).

in 2000 to 1,364 tons in 2011), by 221 per cent in South Africa, and by 144 per cent in Nigeria (Table 22.3).

Comparison with Other Fast-Growing Markets: China and India

In this section, we compare chocolate consumption growth in Africa with the two fastest growing chocolate markets in the world: China and India. Table 22.2 displays the growth in chocolate consumption in North Africa, SSA, China, and India between 2000 and 2013. Over the stated period, chocolate confectionery in India increased the most: from 24,000 tons in 2000 to 129,000 tons in 2013—that is, a growth of 438 per cent. Chocolate consumption in China increased by 211 per cent: from 62,000 tons in 2000 to 193,000 tons in 2013. Chocolate consumption in North Africa grew by 185 per cent (from about 44,300 tons in 2000 to 126,400 tons in 2013), and in SSA by 'only' 40 per cent (from 43,351 tons in 2000 to 60,691 tons in 2013) (Table 22.2). But, as we have explained, this relatively slow growth in SSA was mostly due to slower growth in South Africa.

However, discounting for population size and looking at per capita chocolate consumption convey a different story. The last columns of Table 22.2 present per capita chocolate consumption (kg/person) over the period 2000–13 for the four regions. In 2013, North Africa, with an average 0.96 kg/person, consumed the largest amount of chocolate, compared to SSA, China, and India. With chocolate consumption of 0.26 kg/person in 2013, SSA also had larger per capita chocolate than China and India. In the same period, per capita chocolate consumption in China and India were only 0.14 kg/person and 0.10 kg/person respectively (see also Figure 22.5). However, the SSA consumption per capita is below the Chinese and Indian levels if one excludes South Africa.

Chocolate imports also considerably increased over the period 2000–11 in each of these countries. Between 2000 and 2011, North Africa registered the largest increase of chocolate imports compared to the other regions, with chocolate imports growing by 1,306 per cent. Chocolate imports in China and India grew by 113 per cent and 735 per cent, respectively, between 2000 and 2011, while imports grew by 165 per cent in SSA over the same period (Table 22.3).

In summary, chocolate consumption and imports in Africa grew at remarkable rate, with a growth even comparable with that of China and India—the two fastest growing chocolate markets. The next section, 'Drivers of Growth in Consumption', discusses possible factors behind this significant growth in chocolate consumption in Africa.

Drivers of Growth in Consumption

There are several factors which may explain the growth in chocolate consumption in Africa.[5] In this section, we look at potential major drivers behind the increasing trend in chocolate consumption in the continent. The rising economic growth, Western influence through quickly expanding cable TV ownership, and a subsequent shift in taste, growing urbanization, and fast expansion of modern retail, are presumed to be among the major factors for the increasing trend in chocolate consumption in Africa.

Economic Growth

The most obvious reason is economic growth. Almost all regions in Africa have registered remarkable gross domestic product (GDP) growth rates over 2000–2011 period. These regions showed tremendous improvement in their economy, with significantly higher growth rates than the world averages over that period. Figure 22.3 documents the growth of GDP in Africa from 2000 to 2013. SSA showed consistently significant economic growth between 2000 and 2013, with growth rates of 4 per cent or higher for all years except 2009, the year of the global financial crisis. The same holds for North Africa for the 2000–2010 period, but in recent years North Africa's economic development has been significantly affected by the conflicts in the region. Most of the countries in North Africa were considerably hit by the 'Arab uprising' during this period. The countries in SSA also seemed to have felt the effect of the 'uprising' (Khandelwal and Roitman, 2013). According to the United Nations Department of Economic and Social Affairs (UN DESA), economic growth is predicted to continue in Africa, at least in the near future.

It is well known that food consumption changes when households and countries become richer. In particular, there is typically a shift from staple foods to

---

[5] We focus mostly on the growth in chocolate consumption. Growth in cocoa processing is discussed in earlier Chapters: 1, 2, 12, and 13.

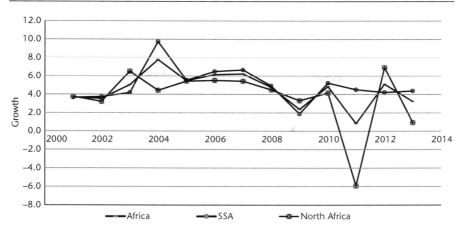

Figure 22.3 Growth of GDP by region (2000–13)
Source: Based on World Bank (2015) data.

other food products such as meat and dairy products, fruits and vegetables, and so on. A number of studies (e.g., Caballero and Popkin, 2002; Gerbens-Leenes et al., 2010) confirm a link between rising income and a consumption transition towards more affluent food consumption patterns, including consumption of chocolate (UNEP, 2012).

Figure 22.4 shows that there is a considerable correlation between economic growth and the growth in chocolate consumption at the regional level between 2000 and 2011. In North Africa, SSA, China, and India, the strong growth in chocolate consumption goes in tandem with the increasing GDP.

From Figure 22.4, it can be seen that chocolate consumption in North Africa grew by almost 140 per cent over the 2000–11 period, while the growth in income over the same period was 69 per cent. In comparison, chocolate confectionery in India increased by 292 per cent, with an increase of income of about 120 per cent. Chocolate consumption in China grew by about 175 per cent, which almost matched the growth rate in income of 196 per cent. In contrast, chocolate consumption in SSA grew by only 40 per cent over the period 2000–11, which is much lower than the 75 per cent growth in GDP over the same period. Interestingly, during the first half of the 2000–11 period, the growth of chocolate consumption in SSA stayed close to zero and hence did not follow the growth in GDP. Only after 2006 did chocolate consumption increase.

On the other hand, Figure 22.5 presents a relationship between per capita chocolate consumption (kg/person) and per capita income (USD/person) over the 2000–11 period for the four regions. Figure 22.5 shows that North Africa consumed by far the largest amount of chocolate per capita for a given level of per capita GDP. Its numbers are higher than those of SSA and much higher than those in China for the same income level. Interestingly, the difference between SSA and China is also significant.

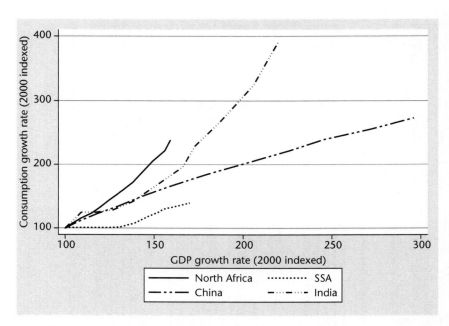

Figure 22.4 Correlation of growth of chocolate consumption and growth of GDP in Africa, China, and India (2000–11: 2000 = 100)
Source: Euromonitor (2014), World Bank (2015), UN DESA (2015).

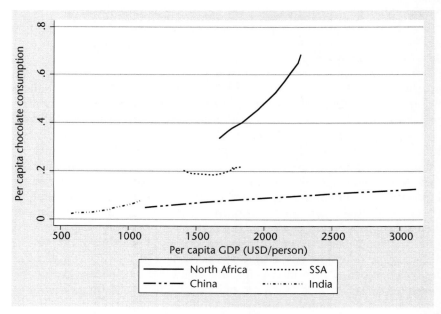

Figure 22.5 Per capita chocolate consumption (kg/person) and per capita GDP (USD/person) in Africa, China, and India (2000–11)
Source: Euromonitor (2014), World Bank(2015), UN DESA (2015).

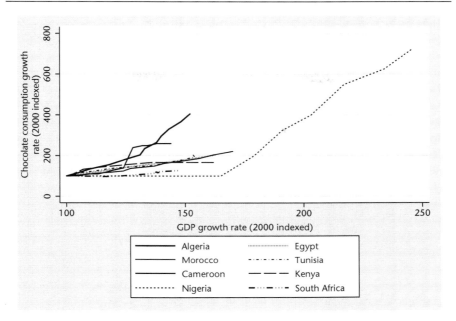

Figure 22.6 Correlation of growth of chocolate consumption and growth of GDP (2000–11: 2000 = 100) by country

Source: Euromonitor (2014), World Bank (2015), UN DESA (2015).

Figures 22.6 and 22.7 present similar correlations to Figures 22.4 and 22.5 but at the country level. Figure 22.6 shows how, in particular in Nigeria and South Africa, income growth did not translate into chocolate consumption growth (in Nigeria consumption growth only started after growth reached 160 per cent). Figure 22.7 illustrates how chocolate consumption grew particularly strongly and reached high levels, especially in Tunisia and Algeria.

Other Factors

SHIFT IN TASTE, AND GROWTH OF ADVERTISING AND COMMERCIAL MEDIA

The second possible explanation is related to the apparent shift in taste towards chocolate. Recently, chocolate consumption has gained enormous popularity among African consumers, with rising chocolate sales associated with Valentine's Day and other occasions (Euromonitor, 2013). The gradual shift in taste could be related to the fast expanding cable TVs in Africa—which allow more exposure to Western lifestyles.[6]

[6] Since early 2000, there has been advancement in the broadcasting industry in the continent, with a major emphasis on the digital television (Maxbauer, 2008). The advancement in the sector

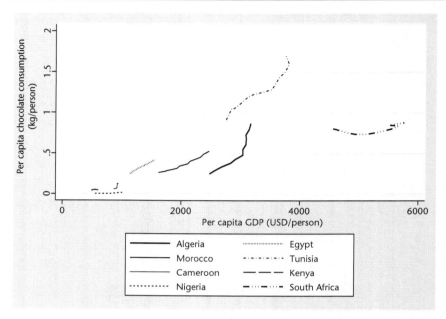

Figure 22.7 Per capita chocolate consumption (kg/person) and per capita GDP (USD/person) (2000–11) by country
Source: Euromonitor (2014), World Bank (2015), UN DESA (2015).

This phenomenon, coupled with growing number of expatriates and consequent modernization, is believed to have a profound effect on African society's lifestyle—especially with regard to the younger generation. These changes in lifestyle and subsequent shift in consumption habits are presumed to have also resulted in a higher demand for chocolate (ATKearney, 2014). Furthermore, the intensive advertising by chocolate confectionery companies in Africa, where they link chocolate to love and affection, has also contributed to the rise in chocolate sales (Euromonitor, 2014c, 2014e).

RELATIVE AFFORDABILITY
Another factor behind the rise in chocolate consumption in Africa could be the recent affordability of chocolates. In addition to the rising income levels, the import of cheaper variants of chocolates from Asia and supply of chocolates in smaller pack sizes helped considerably to attract price-sensitive consumers

also increased the variety of affordable cable TVs on offer as compared to the earlier providers—e.g., accessing Canal+ content or DStv programmes were only for the very few upper-income groups who could afford the complementary parabolic antenna requirements of the TV packages. However, the recent advancements in technology drastically changed the trend, with digital TVs—i.e., no antenna requirements—more providers and hence more competition, and a subsequent lower price—increasing their affordability (Engouang and Yun, 2013).

(Euromonitor, 2014f).[7] Local and regional manufacturers that offer more competitive prices by attracting the relatively low-income and price-sensitive consumers have also become increasingly important. The reduced prices and smaller packages have made chocolate more affordable and have contributed to the change in chocolate consumption trend in Africa. Accordingly, with more affordable prices, many consumers in African economies have recently shifted from sugar confectioneries to chocolate confectioneries (Byrne, 2011).

URBANIZATION

Yet another factor is related to the rapidly increasing urbanization in Africa. By providing convenience, enhanced opportunities, and greater access to commerce, urbanization is generally associated with important economic and social transformations (UN DESA, 2014). According to the recent world urbanization prospect of UN DESA, Africa is urbanizing faster than the other regions of the world and is projected to become 56 per cent urban by 2050 (UN DESA, 2014). Urbanization in Africa increased from 33 per cent in 1995 to 40 per cent in 2015. North Africa is the most urbanized sub-region, with about 52 per cent of its population living in urban areas during 2015. In SSA, the most rapidly urbanizing sub-region, urbanization rose from 29 per cent in 1995 to 38 per cent in 2015. This rapid expansion in urbanization is expected to continue and, by 2050, 63 per cent and 55 per cent of North Africa and SSA's population respectively are expected to live in urban areas (UN DESA, 2014). As has been widely documented (e.g., Henderson, 1974; Bairoch, 1988; Abdulai et al., 1999; Polese, 2005), consumption patterns change with urbanization—with cities generally offering a greater variety of goods and services by creating competitive environments and developing different lifestyles (Navamuel et al., 2014). Hence, the growing urbanization in Africa can be considered a major cause of the rising trend in chocolate consumption in Africa.

RETAIL EXPANSION

Africa's retail sector has been dominated by traditional ('informal') retail options, including small independent stores and small kiosks, with little involvement of such formal retail options as malls and shopping centres (Mirko and Kearney, 2014). However, analogous to the growing rate of urbanization and the ever-rising demand for goods and services, many African cities are experiencing a quick expansion of modern retail shops (Bruckner, 2012; OADBS, 2012). Recently, the formal retail options are taking larger shares, including significant evolution of hypermarkets in urban areas of bigger economies such as South Africa, while basic cooperative stores serve the rural areas where formal retail options are virtually non-existent (Ntloedibe, 2004). For example, in 2014, supermarkets and hypermarkets accounted for the distribution of more than 60 per cent of total chocolate retail value sales in Kenya (Euromonitor, 2013). This phenomenon gradually diminishes the role of traditional retail options and provides access and

[7] For example, Kraft Foods South Africa (Pty) Ltd has reduced the sizes of some of its brands from 100 g to 80 g.

convenience to different consumer goods. It is probably an important factor in increasing the demand for such 'Western-style' consumer goods as chocolate.

Multinational Chocolate Confectionery Companies in Africa

There are a number of local and multinational chocolate confectionery companies operating in North African and SSA countries. The importance of specific international chocolate confectionery companies varies quite strongly across the countries in the region (Table 22.4). Except for Algeria and Morocco, the main multinational companies had a market share of 50 per cent or more. They are particularly strong in Egypt (82 per cent, with 50 per cent for Cadbury alone), Nigeria (75 per cent), and South Africa (70 per cent, with 42 per cent for Kraft Foods) (Table 22.4).

In 2013, Ferrero had significant market shares in two of the five chocolate markets in which it was involved. It is the most important chocolate confectionery company in Cameroon and Algeria. It accounted for 26 per cent of chocolate retail values in Cameroon and 10.1 per cent in Algeria, making it the most active company in these two countries. It also had 3.8 per cent, 4.4 per cent, and 1.2 per cent retail value shares in Egypt, Nigeria, and South Africa's chocolate markets respectively.

In 2013, Kraft Foods is active in all but Egypt's chocolate markets. It especially had considerable presence in South Africa, where it was the most important chocolate confectionery, with 41.8 per cent retail value shares. Kraft Foods is also the second most important chocolate confectionery in Algeria, with a 8.3 per cent market share. It also accounted for 10.4 per cent of the chocolate market share in Nigeria. Though not dominant, it was also involved in Cameroon (6.6 per cent), Kenya (4.6 per cent), and Morocco (1.7 per cent).

Nestle is also present in all but the Moroccan chocolate markets. In 2013, it had 21.9 per cent in Nigeria, and 21.7 per cent in South Africa—making it the second most important chocolate confectionery company in each of the two markets. It

Table 22.4 Shares of international companies in African chocolate confectioneries (% value 2014)

% Retail Value Company Group	Share (%) of value						
	Algeria	Cameroon	Egypt	Kenya	Morocco	Nigeria	South Africa
Ferrero	10.1	25.5	3.8	–	–	4.4	1.2
Kraft Foods	8.3	6.6	–	4.6	1.7	10.4	41.8
Nestlé	6.3	6.8	6.1	8.1	–	21.9	21.7
Cadbury	5.2	–	50.1	32.9	–	26.3	–
Mars	5.1	10.5	–	–	26.2	11.6	2.5
Lindt	6.0	–	–	–	–	–	3.3
Master Foods	–	–	22.7	10.9	–	–	–
Others	59.0	50.6	17.6	43.4	72.1	25.4	29.5
Total	100.0	100.0	100.0	100.0	100.0	100.0	100.0

Source: Based (Euromonitor 2013, 2014g).

also had substantial shares in Algeria (6.3 per cent), Cameroon (6.8 per cent), Egypt (6.1 per cent), and Kenya (8.1 per cent).

Cadbury had dominant market shares in all three chocolate markets in which it was active: Egypt, Kenya, and Nigeria. In Egypt in particular, it had 50.1 per cent. Its retail value share in Kenya (32.9 per cent) and Nigeria (26.3 per cent) were also significantly higher than the other companies.

Mars had dominant market shares in Morocco, Nigeria, and Cameroon, where, in 2013, it accounted for 26.2 per cent, 11.6 per cent, and 10.5 per cent respectively, though it had smaller market shares in Algeria (5.1 per cent) and South Africa (2.5 per cent).

Master Foods is involved in Egypt and Kenya, where, in 2013, it was the second most important chocolate confectionery company, with a 22.7 per cent market share in Egypt and a 10.9 per cent market share in Kenya. In contrast, Lindt seemed less involved in chocolate confectionery in Africa, as evidenced by only a 6.0 per cent share in Algeria and a 3.3 per cent share in South Africa.

Conclusion

Despite consistently supplying more than two-thirds of world's total cocoa supply, Africa has been alienated from consuming cocoa products, especially chocolate. However, recently the trend has been changing, with growing demand for cocoa and chocolate. Increasingly, cocoa beans are no longer exported, as grinding is taking place in the cocoa-producing countries. On the other side of the value chain, chocolate consumption on the continent has also been rising rapidly over the last few years. The growth rate of chocolate consumption in both North Africa and SSA is comparable with that of China and India, and is even higher per capita wise than the latter two countries.

This sizable growth rate of chocolate consumption in the continent—albeit from a lower base—can be attributed to five major factors. First, Africa has become the fastest growing continent over the last decade. Most of the countries in the continent displayed significant economic growth. This rise in income is believed to be a primary factor behind the rise in chocolate consumption in the continent. Second, by offering a greater variety of goods and services, creating a competitive environment, and developing different lifestyles, increasing urbanization could be another factor behind the rise in chocolate consumption trend in Africa. Third, by mainly providing access and convenience to different consumer goods, the expansion of retail shops is also believed to be among the major factors leading to increases in the demand for such 'Western-style' consumer goods as chocolate. Fourth, the rapidly expanding relatively affordable cable TVs, by introducing Africa's population to the 'Western lifestyle', and the intensive advertisement of chocolate confectionery companies—linking chocolate consumption with modernization—may have also contributed to a shift in consumption patterns of a large part of Africa's population—towards such 'westernized' consumption patterns as chocolate. Fifth, the affordability of chocolate, due to the recent large imports of cheap chocolate variants (e.g., from Asia) and smaller package size, have also attracted the price-sensitive portions of society—this could thus be among the major factor leading to the rise in chocolate consumption in the continent.

The African confectionery sector is dominated by international companies. The importance of these multinational companies varies across countries. Their market share is particularly large in Egypt, Nigeria, and South Africa, and much lower in Morocco and Algeria.

As growth is predicted to continue in the coming years on the African continent, one should expect these trends of growth in cocoa and chocolate consumption to continue, and, thus, the share of Africa in the cocoa–chocolate value chain to increase.

References

Abdulai, A., D. Jain, and A. Sharma. 1999. 'Household food demand analysis in India'. *Journal of Agricultural Economics* 50: pp. 316–27.

Afoakwa, O. E. 2010. *Chocolate Science and Technology*. Chichester: John Wiley.

Akiyama, T., J. B. Donald, F. Larson, and P. Varangis. 2003. 'Commodity market reform in Africa: some recent experiences'. *Economic Systems* 27: pp. 83–115.

A.T. Kearney. 2014. 'Seizing Africa's Retail Opportunities'. *African Retail Development Index*. A.T. Kearney, Inc. Korea. Website: <https://www.atkearney.com/documents/10192/4371960/Seizing+Africas+Retail+Opportunities.pdf/730ba912-da69-4e09-9b5d-69b063a3f139>.

Bairoch, P. 1988. *Cities and Development: From the Dawn of History to the Present*. Chicago: University of Chicago Press.

Bruckner, M. 2012. 'Economic growth, size of the agricultural sector, and urbanization in Africa'. *Journal of Urban Economics* 71 (1): pp. 26–36.

Byrne, J. 2011. 'South African Market Sweet; Sales up 19 per cent, notes Leatherhead'. *Confectionery news*. Confectionery news.com. Website: <http://www.confectionerynews.com/Markets/South-African-market-sweet-sales-up-19-per-cent-notes-Leatherhead>.

Caballero, B. and B. M. Popkin. 2002. *The Nutrition Transition: Diet and Disease in the Developing World*. London: Academic Press.

The Economist. 2011. 'Africa's impressive growth', 6 January. <http://www.economist.com/blogs/dailychart/2011/01/daily_chart>.

Engouang, T. D. and L. Yun. 2013. 'Africa on the way to global wireless digital television'. *International Journal of Soft Computing and Engineering*. 3 (3). ISSN: 2231-2307.

Euromonitor. 2013. Chocolate Confectionary in Cameroon. Euromonitor International Passport. December 2013. London.

Euromonitor. 2014a. Chocolate Confectionary in Algeria. Euromonitor International Passport. November 2014. London.

Euromonitor. 2014b. Chocolate Confectionary in Egypt. Euromonitor International Passport. March 2014. London.

Euromonitor. 2014c. Chocolate Confectionary in Kenya. Euromonitor International Passport. October 2014. London.

Euromonitor. 2014d. Chocolate Confectionary in Morocco. Euromonitor International Passport. October 2014. London.

Euromonitor. 2014e. Chocolate Confectionary in Nigeria. Euromonitor International Passport. November 2014. London.

Euromonitor. 2014f. Chocolate Confectionary in South Africa. Euromonitor International Passport. September 2014. London. UK.

Euromonitor. 2014g. Global Confectionery Overview: Key Categories, Countries and Trends to 2019. Euromonitor International Passport. July 2014. London. UK.

FAOSTAT (Food and Agriculture Organization of the United Nations). 2014. Website. <http://faostat.fao.org>. Accessed December 2014.

Fold, N. 2001. 'Restructuring of the European chocolate industry and its impact on cocoa production in West Africa'. *Journal of Economic Geography* 1: pp. 405–20.

Gerbens-Leenes, P. W., S. Nonhebel, and M. S. Krol. 2010. 'Food consumption patterns and economic growth: increasing affluence and the use of natural resources'. *Appetite* 55 (3): pp. 597–603.

Henderson, J. V. 1974. 'The sizes and types of cities'. *American Economic Review* 64: pp. 640–56.

ICCO (International Cocoa Organization). 2010. The World Cocoa Economy: Past and Present. July 2010. EX/142/6. Website: <http://www.icco.org/about-us/international-cocoa-agreements/cat_view/1-annual-report.html>.

ICCO (International Cocoa Organization). 2012. The World Cocoa Economy: Past and Present. July 2012. EX/146/7. Website : <http://www.icco.org/about-us/international-cocoa-agreements/cat_view/1-annual-report.html>.

ICCO (International Cocoa Organization). 2014. Annual Report. London, UK. Website: <http://www.icco.org>.

Khandelwal, P. and A. Roitman. 2013. 'The economics of political transitions: implications for the Arab Spring'. IMF Working Paper 13 (69).

KPMG. 2014. 'A taste of the future'. The trends that could transform the chocolate industry. Consumer Markets Report-June 2014. KPMG International Cooperative ("KPMG International"). Haymarket Network Ltd. kpmg.com.

Maxbauer, A. 2008. 'Emerging DTV markets: Africa'. *IMS Research*. Report-2008 Edition. England. www.imsresearch.com.

Mirko, W. and A. T. Kearney. 2014. 'Retail: Sub-Saharan Africa's next big frontier'. *New African* 540: pp. 66–9.

Navamuel, E. L., F. R. Morollón, and D. Paredes. 2014. 'City size and household food consumption: demand elasticities in Spain'. *Applied Economics* 46 (14): pp. 1624–41.

Ntloedibe, M. N. 2004. 'The South African market is booming'. *AgExporter* 16 (4): p. 12.

OADBS (Oxford Analytical Daily Brief Service). 2012. 'AFRICA: retail sector expands on city-by-city basis'. *Oxford Analytica Ltd.* <http://search.proquest.com/docview/917919033?accountid=17215>. Accessed December 2014.

Ogunwolu, S. O. and C. O. Jayeola. 2006. 'Development of non-conventional thermo-resistant chocolate for the tropics'. *British Food Journal* 108 (6): pp. 451–5.

Polèse, M. 2005. 'Cities and national economic growth: a reappraisal'. *Urban Studies* 42: pp. 1429–51.

Raikes, P. and P. Gibbon. 2000. 'Globalisation and African export crop agriculture'. *Journal of Peasant Studies* 27 (2): pp. 50–93.

Stortz, T. A. and A. G. Marangoni. 2011. 'Heat resistant chocolate'. *Trends in Food Science & Technology* 22 (5): pp. 201–14.

Sundaram, J. K., O. Schwank, and R. V. Arnim. 2011. 'Globalization and development in Sub-Saharan Africa'. United Nations/Department of Economic and Social Affairs Working Paper No. 102.

UN DESA (United Nations: Department of Economic and Social Affairs). 2014. Population Division. <http://www.un.org/en/development/desa/population/>. Accessed January 2015.

UNEP (United Nations Environment Programme). 2012. 'The critical role of global food consumption patterns in achieving sustainable food systems and food for all'. A UNEP Discussion Paper. Website: <http://www.unep.org>. Accessed: February 2015.

WESP (World Economic Situation and Prospect). 2015. World Economic Situation and Prospects: Mid-2015 Update. <http://www.un.org/en/development/desa/policy/wesp/>. Accessed January 2015.

World Bank. 2015. Website. <http://data.worldbank.org/country/united-states>. Accessed January 2015.

Index

Page references to Figures or Tables will be in *italics*

Printed and bound by CPI Group (UK) Ltd, Croydon, CR0 4YY